THE CAMBRIDGE HANDBOOK OF TECHNICAL STANDARDIZATION LAW

Technical standards like USB, Wi-Fi, and Bluetooth are ubiquitous in the modern networked economy. They allow products made and sold by different vendors to interoperate with little to no consumer effort and enable new market entrants to innovate on top of established technology platforms. This groundbreaking volume, edited by Jorge L. Contreras, assesses and analyzes legal aspects of technical standards and standardization beyond those covered in its companion volume (patents, competition, and antitrust). Bringing together leading international experts, it focuses on key areas of technical standardization law including administrative, trade, copyright, trademark, and certification law. This comprehensive, detailed examination sheds new light on the standards that shape the global technology marketplace and will serve as an indispensable tool for scholars, practitioners, judges, and policymakers everywhere.

JORGE L. CONTRERAS is a Professor of Law at the University of Utah S.J. Quinney College of Law and an internationally recognized authority on the law of technical standard-setting. His work has been cited by scholars, courts, and regulatory agencies throughout the United States, Europe, and Asia, and he has published more than 100 scholarly articles and chapters. He has twice received first prize in the Standards Engineering Society's scholarly paper competition, and in 2018 was awarded the Standards Education Award by the Institute of Electrical and Electronics Engineers (IEEE) Standards Association.

The Cambridge Handbook of Technical Standardization Law

Further Intersections of Public and Private Law

Edited by

JORGE L. CONTRERAS

University of Utah

CAMBRIDGE
UNIVERSITY PRESS

University Printing House, Cambridge CB2 8BS, United Kingdom

One Liberty Plaza, 20th Floor, New York, NY 10006, USA

477 Williamstown Road, Port Melbourne, VIC 3207, Australia

314–321, 3rd Floor, Plot 3, Splendor Forum, Jasola District Centre, New Delhi – 110025, India

79 Anson Road, #06-04/06, Singapore 079906

Cambridge University Press is part of the University of Cambridge.

It furthers the University's mission by disseminating knowledge in the pursuit of education, learning, and research at the highest international levels of excellence.

www.cambridge.org
Information on this title: www.cambridge.org/9781107129719
DOI: 10.1017/9781316416785

© Cambridge University Press 2019

This publication is in copyright. Subject to statutory exception and to the provisions of relevant collective licensing agreements, no reproduction of any part may take place without the written permission of Cambridge University Press.

First published 2019

Printed in the United Kingdom by TJ International Ltd, Padstow Cornwall

A catalogue record for this publication is available from the British Library.

ISBN 978-1-107-12971-9 Hardback

Cambridge University Press has no responsibility for the persistence or accuracy of URLs for external or third-party internet websites referred to in this publication and does not guarantee that any content on such websites is, or will remain, accurate or appropriate.

Contents

List of Figures	*page* vii
List of Tables	viii
List of Contributors	ix
Preface Benedict Kingsbury	xv
Acknowledgements	xix

	Introduction Jorge L. Contreras	1
	PART I STANDARDIZATION AND THE STATE	5
1	International Trade Law and Technical Standardization Panagiotis Delimatsis	7
2	Government Use of Standards in the United States and Abroad Emily S. Bremer	28
	PART II STANDARDIZATION, HEALTH, SAFETY AND LIABILITY	43
3	Technical Standards in Health and Safety Regulation: Risk Regimes, the New Administrative Law, and Food Safety Governance Timothy D. Lytton	45
4	Tort Liability for Standards Development in the United States and European Union Paul Verbruggen	60
	PART III COPYRIGHT AND STANDARDS	89
5	Questioning Copyright in Standards Pamela Samuelson and Kathryn Hashimoto	91

6	Integrating Technical Standards into Federal Regulations: Incorporation by Reference Daniel J. Sheffner	108
7	Public Law, European Constitutionalism and Copyright in Standards Björn Lundqvist	124
8	Termination of Copyright Transfers and Technical Standards Jorge L. Contreras and Andrew T. Hernacki	143
	PART IV STANDARDS AND SOFTWARE	157
9	Open Standards Jay P. Kesan	159
10	Standardization, Open Source and Innovation: Sketching the Effect of IPR Policies Martin Husovec	177
11	OSS and SDO: Symbiotic Functions in the Innovation Equation David J. Kappos	198
	PART V TRADEMARKS, CERTIFICATION AND STANDARDS	203
12	Trademarks, Certification Marks and Technical Standards Jorge L. Contreras	205
13	The Unregulated Certification Mark(et) Jeanne C. Fromer	231
14	The Certification Paradox Jonathan M. Barnett	252
References		269
Index		299

Figures

8.1	Scenario 1: Work-made-for-hire for grantee (no termination)	*page* 152
8.2	Scenario 2: Work-made-for-hire for grantee (no termination)	152
12.1	Standards and trademarks	218
12.2	Arbitrary standard-names and designs	222
12.3	The Wi-Fi Certified logo	228

Tables

12.1	Distinctiveness of standard-names	*page* 221
12.2	Standard-mark types of registration	223
14.1	Selected certification "failures"	256
14.2	Selected certification markets	258
14.3	Organizational choices of certification entities in financial services markets	266

Contributors

Jonathan M. Barnett, J.D. (Yale), B.A., M.A. (University of Pennsylvania), M.Phil. (Cambridge University), is a professor at the University of Southern California, Gould School of Law. Barnett specializes in antitrust, intellectual property, contracts, and corporate law. Barnett has published in the *Harvard Law Review, Journal of Legal Studies, Jurimetrics, Review of Law & Economics, Yale Law Journal*, and other scholarly journals. Prior to academia, Barnett practiced corporate law as a senior associate at Cleary Gottlieb Steen & Hamilton LLP in New York, specializing in private equity and mergers and acquisitions transactions.

Emily S. Bremer, J.D. (New York University), is an Associate Professor of Law at the University of Notre Dame. Before moving to academia, Professor Bremer served as the Research Chief of the Administrative Conference of the United States (ACUS), a U.S. federal administrative agency that studies administrative process and makes recommendations for improvements to the Congress, President, other agencies, and the Judicial Conference. She joined ACUS as an Attorney Advisor after working as an Associate in the Telecommunications and Appellate Litigation practice of Wiley Rein LLP. Professor Bremer also served as a law clerk to Hon. Andrew J. Kleinfeld of the United States Court of Appeals for the Ninth Circuit. She was ACUS's in-house researcher for Recommendation 2011–5, *Incorporation by Reference*, which addresses a variety of issues that U.S. federal agencies must address when using standards in regulation. Recommendation 2011–5 was subsequently adopted by the U.S. Office of Management and Budget, the U.S. Office of the Federal Register, and various U.S. federal agencies. Professor Bremer has continued to write extensively about government use of standards in the United States and abroad.

Jorge L. Contreras, J.D. (Harvard), B.S.E.E., B.A. (Rice University), is a Professor of Law at the University of Utah S.J. Quinney College of Law. He has written and spoken extensively on the institutional structures and policy of intellectual property, technical standardization, and scientific research. Professor Contreras serves as Co-Chair of the ABA Section of Science & Technology Law's Interdisciplinary Division, and a member of the American National Standards Institute (ANSI) IPR Policy Committee. He previously served as a member of the U.S. National Academy of Science's (NAS) Committee on IP Management in Standard-Setting Processes, which produced the 2013 report *Intellectual Property Challenges for Standard-Setting in the Global Economy*. In addition to the companion volume of this series, Professor Contreras has edited, *inter alia*, the *Technical Standards Patent Policy Manual* (2007), *Patent Pledges: Global*

Perspectives On Patent Law's Private Ordering Frontier (with Meredith Jacob, 2017), and *Patent Remedies and Complex Products: Toward a Global Consensus* (with C. Bradford Biddle, Brian J. Love and Norman Siebrasse, 2019). He has also published more than one hundred scholarly articles, reports, white papers, and book chapters in a range of publications including *Science, Nature, Standards Engineering, Georgetown Law Journal, University of Illinois Law Review, Washington Law Review, North Carolina Law Review, Antitrust Law Journal, Harvard Journal of Law and Technology*, and *Berkeley Technology Law Journal*. He is the founding editor of SSRN's *Law, Policy and Economics of Technical Standards* e-journal, and was the winner of the Standards Engineering Society's (SES) 2011 and 2015 scholarly paper competitions. In 2018, Professor Contreras was awarded the IEEE's Standards Education Award "for outstanding contributions to understanding the interaction of standardization systems with intellectual property rights, and educating students, policy makers and the public regarding these issues." Before entering academia, Professor Contreras was a partner at the international law firm Wilmer Cutler Pickering Hale and Dorr LLP, where he practiced international corporate and intellectual property transactional law in Boston, London, and Washington, DC.

Panagiotis Delimatsis, Ph.D. (University of Neuchâtel), LL.M. (Institute of European Studies, University of Saarland), LL.B. (Democritus University of Thrace Law School), is Professor of European and International Trade Law at Tilburg University. Since 2011, he has served as Director of the Tilburg Law and Economics Center (TILEC), an interdisciplinary Center of Excellence of some 40 researchers, the biggest of its kind in Europe, studying the governance of economic activity. He leads the "Institutions and Governance" research cluster within the TILEC Research Programme 2018–2023 and TILEC's work on standardization, competition, and innovation. In the academic year 2015–2016, Professor Delimatsis was a visiting Scholar at Harvard Law School and a Fellow with the Program on International Financial Systems, on research leave from Tilburg University. In 2016, Professor Delimatsis was awarded an ERC Consolidator Grant (2 million Euros), the most prestigious mid-level personal grant at the EU level, for his research project on the resilience of non-State regulatory bodies and the role of the law. His research focuses on the comparative regulation of services industries, issues of transnational governance, and the regulation of international trade. Currently, he is interested in the institutional and substantive aspects of standardization, financial regulation and energy, using interdisciplinary methods. His work has appeared in top refereed international and European journals. He is the author of *International Trade in Services and Domestic Regulations – Necessity, Transparency, and Regulatory Diversity* (International Economic Law Series). He also co-edited two collective volumes, the first on *The Prospects of International Trade Regulation* (2011) and the second on *Financial Services at the Crossroads – Implications for Supervision, Institutional Design and Trade*. More recently, he edited a comprehensive book on *The Law, Economics and Politics of International Standardization*, published in 2015 and a *Research Handbook on Climate Change and Trade*, published in 2016.

Jeanne C. Fromer, J.D. (Harvard), S.M. (Massachusetts Institute of Technology), is a Professor of Law at New York University School of Law and Faculty Co-Director of the Engelberg Center on Innovation Law & Policy. Professor Fromer is currently an Adviser for the American Law Institute's Restatement of the Law, Copyright. In 2011, Professor Fromer was awarded the American Law Institute's inaugural Young Scholars Medal for her scholarship in intellectual property. Before coming to NYU, Professor Fromer served as a law clerk to Justice David H. Souter of the U.S. Supreme Court and to Judge Robert D. Sack of the U.S. Court of Appeals for the Second Circuit. She also worked at Hale and Dorr LLP (now WilmerHale) in the area of intellectual property law. Professor Fromer was a visiting professor at Harvard Law School, and she also previously taught at Fordham Law School. Recent publications on trademark law have appeared in the *Harvard Law Review* and *Stanford Law Review*.

Kathryn Hashimoto, J.D. (University of San Francisco), is a Copyright Research Fellow at the Berkeley Center for Law & Technology, University of California, Berkeley, School of Law.

Andrew T. Hernacki, J.D. (American University), is an associate in the Commercial Litigation Group of Venable LLP in Washington, DC. He focuses on complex civil litigation and has experience across a broad spectrum of issues, ranging from antitrust, commercial, and contract litigation to trademark disputes, business tort cases, partnership disputes, and general business issues. He also represents clients in a variety of government investigation and law enforcement actions, including those initiated by the Federal Trade Commission (FTC) and Consumer Financial Protection Bureau (CFPB).

Martin Husovec, Ph.D. (Max Planck Institute for Innovation and Competition and Ludwig Maximilian University), is an Assistant Professor at Tilburg University, the Netherlands, appointed jointly by Tilburg Institute for Law, Technology and Society (TILT) and Tilburg Law and Economics Center (TILEC), and an Affiliated Scholar at Center for Internet and Society (CIS) of Stanford Law School. His scholarship focuses on innovation and digital liberties, in particular, regulation of intellectual property and freedom of expression. Dr. Husovec's doctoral work related to injunctions against intermediaries (published with Cambridge University Press, 2017). He was a visiting researcher at Stanford Law School (2014), Japanese Institute for Intellectual Property (2015), and the European University Institute (2018). He is also a visiting professor at the Central European University (CEU). Tilburg Law and Economics Center (TILEC) benefits from financial support by Qualcomm, Inc. Professor Husovec is also a volunteer member of the legal team of the Free Software Foundation Europe (FSFE).

David J. Kappos, J.D. (University of California, Berkeley), is a partner at Cravath, Swaine & Moore LLP. Prior to joining Cravath, Mr. Kappos served as Under Secretary of Commerce and Director of the United States Patent and Trademark Office from August 2009 to January 2013 and served as IBM's Vice President and Assistant General Counsel for Intellectual Property from 2003 to 2009. Mr. Kappos is widely recognized as one of the world's foremost leaders in the field of intellectual property, including intellectual property management and strategy, the development of global intellectual property norms, laws, and practices as well as commercialization and enforcement of innovation-based assets. Mr. Kappos has received numerous accolades for his contributions to the field of intellectual property, including the 2014 Global Agenda Council Vision Award for the Intellectual Property Council's pro bono initiative from the World Economic Forum, the 2014 Jefferson Medal from the New Jersey Intellectual Property Law Association (NJIPLA), the 2013 Board of Director's Excellence Award from the American Intellectual Property Law Association (AIPLA), the 2013 Champion of Intellectual Property Award from the District of Columbia Bar Association and the 2013 North America Government Leadership Award from Semiconductor Equipment and Materials International (SEMI). He was named one of the "Top 25 Icons of IP" by *Law360*, one of the "50 Most Influential People in Intellectual Property" by *Managing IP*, one of the "Top 50 Intellectual Property Trailblazers & Pioneers" and one of the "100 Most Influential Lawyers in America" by *The National Law*

Journal, "Intellectual Property Professional of the Year" by the Intellectual Property Owners Association and inducted into the Intellectual Property Hall of Fame by *Intellectual Asset Management Magazine* in 2012, among others. He is also a frequent speaker and has authored many published articles on various intellectual property, innovation, and leadership topics.

Jay P. Kesan, J.D. (Georgetown), Ph.D. (University of Texas), is a Professor and H. Ross & Helen Workman Research Scholar at the University of Illinois at Urbana-Champaign. At Illinois, he is appointed in the College of Law, the Department of Electrical & Computer Engineering, the Information Trust Institute, the Coordinated Science Laboratory, and the College of Business. He served as one of the inaugural Thomas A. Edison Distinguished Scholars at the U.S. Patent and Trademark Office (USPTO). He has been actively involved in virtually every aspect of patent litigation as counsel, technical expert, legal expert, Special Master, and appellate counsel. Professor Kesan received his J.D. *summa cum laude* from Georgetown University. After graduation, he clerked for Judge Patrick E. Higginbotham of the United States Court of Appeals for the Fifth Circuit. Prior to attending law school, Professor Kesan worked as a research scientist at the IBM T.J. Watson Research Center in New York. He is a registered patent attorney and practiced at the former firm of Pennie & Edmonds LLP in the areas of patent litigation and patent prosecution. He has published numerous scientific papers, and he has obtained several patents in the United States and abroad.

Benedict Kingsbury, LL.B. (University of Canterbury, New Zealand), M.Phil. (Oxford), D.Phil. (Oxford), is Vice Dean and Murry and Ida Becker Professor of Law at New York University School of Law. He has served as Director of the Institute for International Law and Justice since its founding in 2002, and in 2018 was appointed as the faculty director of the Law School's newly-inaugurated Guarini Institute for Global Legal Studies. Projects he has co-directed at the IILJ include the Program in the History and Theory of International Law (with Professor Rob Howse and Global Professor Martti Koskenniemi); the Global Administrative Law Project (with Professor Richard B. Stewart); and the research project on Indicators and Global Governance by Information (with Professors Kevin Davis and Sally Engle Merry). His major current projects focus on large-scale global ordering such as TPP and the Belt & Road Initiative (Megareg); physical, digital, and informational infrastructure (Infrareg, with Sally Merry); and global data/tech law. From 2013 to 2018 he was joint Editor in Chief (with Jose Alvarez) of the *American Journal of International Law*, a premier journal in the field, and helped create the online *AJIL Unbound*. He is one of the editors (with Andrew Hurrell and Dick Stewart) of the Oxford University Press Law and Global Governance book series. His research projects on global governance issues have been supported by the National Science Foundation, Carnegie Corporation of New York, the Bill & Melinda Gates Foundation, and the Rockefeller Foundation.

Björn Lundqvist, Ph.D., M.Res. (European University Institute), LL.M. (University of Michigan), LL.M., LL.B. (Uppsala University), is Associate Professor of Law at the Law Department, Stockholm University. He is the Director of the European Economic LL.M. programme and Head of the EU Law Research Group. Professor Lundqvist's research focuses on Innovation, Competition, Property, and Law. He has published two monographs, *R&D collaborations under the Competition Rules of the European Union and The Antitrust Laws of the United States* and *Standardization under EU Competition Rules & US Antitrust Laws: The Rise and Limits of Self-Regulation*. Professor Lundqvist publishes in highly rated academic journals; some recent publications include: "Standardization for the Digital

Economy: The Issue of Interoperability and Access Under Competition Law" (*The Antitrust Bulletin*, 2017), and "European Harmonized Standards as 'Part of EU Law': The Implications of the *James Elliott* Case for Copyright Protection and, Possibly, for EU Competition Law" (*Legal Issues of Economic Integration*, 2017). Professor Lundqvist is also active on SSRN and his recent paper "Big Data, Open Data, Privacy Regulations, Intellectual Property and Competition Law in an Internet of Things World" was the fourth most downloaded Antitrust paper on SSRN in 2017. He has worked as an attorney-at-law for leading business law firms in Europe for several years, most recently as Head of EU Competition Law in Stockholm for the Law Firm Roschier.

Timothy D. Lytton, J.D. (Yale), is Distinguished University Professor and Professor of Law at Georgia State University. He currently serves as Associate Dean for Research and Faculty Development of the College of Law and is a faculty member in the Center for Law, Health & Society. His research examines health and safety regulation, with a particular focus on the interaction of public law, private standards, and civil litigation. He has published numerous books and articles examining gun violence, clergy sexual abuse, climate change, and food safety. His most recent book, *Outbreak: Foodborne Illness and the Evolving Food Safety System* (2019), analyzes the interplay of government regulation, industry supply chain management, and tort liability in risk regulation. His previous book, *Kosher: Private Regulation in the Age of Industrial Food* (2013), traces the development of kosher certification as a model of successful private governance in the food industry. He teaches administrative law, legislation, torts, and products liability.

Pamela Samuelson, J.D. (Yale), is the Richard M. Sherman Distinguished Professor of Law and Information at the University of California, Berkeley, and co-director of the Berkeley Center for Law and Technology. Professor Samuelson is recognized as a pioneer in digital copyright law, intellectual property, cyberlaw, and information policy. She serves on the board of directors of the Electronic Frontier Foundation (since 2000) and on advisory boards for the Electronic Privacy Information Center, Public Knowledge, and the Berkeley Center for New Media. She is a co-founder and executive officer of Authors Alliance, a not-for-profit organization for authors in the digital age. Professor Samuelson is a fellow of the Association for Computing Machinery (ACM), a contributing editor of *Communications of the ACM*, a past fellow of the John D. and Catherine T. MacArthur Foundation, an honorary professor at the University of Amsterdam, and received the Woman of Vision Award for Social Impact in 2005 from the Anita Borg Institute. In 2013 she was elected to the American Academy of Arts & Sciences.

Daniel J. Sheffner, J.D. (Saint Louis University), is a legislative attorney in the American Law Division of the Congressional Research Service, a component of the Library of Congress. He was previously an attorney advisor with the Administrative Conference of the United States.

Paul Verbruggen, Ph.D. (EUI, Florence), is Associate Professor of Private Law at Tilburg University. He writes on the design and operation of regulatory regimes (both public and private), focusing on questions of legitimacy, accountability and enforcement. His research interests concern comparative private law, EU law, regulatory policy and risk regulation. Dr. Verbruggen has held visiting positions in Oxford and London (LSE) and is a NWO-Veni grant laureate (2017–2020). His work on standardization concerns the broad field of product safety and has appeared in the *Annals of the American Academy of Political and Social Science, European Law Review,* and *Regulation & Governance*. He is the author of the monograph *Enforcing Transnational Private Regulation: A Comparative Analysis of Advertising and Food Safety* (2014) and (co-) editor of the collections *Hybridization of Food Governance: Trends, Types and Results* (2017) and *Regulating Private Regulation: Understanding the Role of Private Law* (2019).

Preface

Technical standardization policy has been animated for more than a century by pursuit of efficiencies from interoperability, and also in recent decades by active facilitation of economic and innovation gains achievable through competitive markets benefiting from network effects. Science and technology studies (STS) or Foucaldian power-knowledge frameworks diversify this perspective, animating inquiry into ways in which standards enact power allocations, distinguish as well as unify, exclude as well as normalize. National security priorities and geopolitical considerations add additional layers, as do state industrial or protectionist policies. Whether and how to take account of wider societal interests and state interests affected by standards and standardization processes, and what allocative mechanisms or compensatory remedies should accompany the distributional effects and externalities (positive and negative) of standards, are public policy questions that manifest themselves also in public law, but in the fragmentary and uneven ways traced in this lucid and thoughtfully constructed book.

Whereas the companion volume examines intersections of political economy and law in the relations of technical standards to patents and the relations of standards and patents to antitrust or competition law, the present volume traverses other topics of technical standardization law with private–public implications that, if for the most part less litigated, are nonetheless fundamental. By "law" the contributors tend to mean formal law (state/national law, or intergovernmental law), in contrast to social norms or other forms of normative ordering with law-like features. The term "regulation" may be deployed to encompass this wider range of normative orderings. While the organizing frame of the book is technical standardization and formal law, the specificity of this frame in fact enables the book to shed much light on relations between standardization and regulation more broadly.

The contrast routinely drawn between formal (state) law and technical standardization owes much to U.S. styles of capitalism and regulation, including the federal government policy which since 1980 has explicitly been to favor private standard-setting and to prioritize use of private standards in government regulation and procurement. Characteristic of U.S. technical standardization practiced by private standards development organizations (SDOs) are the general principles that such standardization should be voluntary, open, balanced, transparent, and consensus-based. Such principles may be incorporated into the constitutive or membership rules of the SDO, or the social norms shared by its participants inter se. Much of their de facto superintendence and enforcement, however, comes from state action, ranging from legislative delegation or ratification, to administrative actions and import controls, to government procurement rules and consumer protection, to decisions of courts in collateral litigation or on tort liability of SDOs. The deployability of this suite of state measures in relation to foreign or transnational SDOs and their standards depends on the technology and on the state's position in the global market. Small and less technology-capable states often have little or no impact on private SDOs, and many prefer standard-setting by or under the auspices of bodies with governmental participation such as the International Telecommunications Union (ITU) or the Codex Alimentarius. In transnational contexts, some meta-regulation of SDOs-as-regulators is supplied by bodies such as ISEAL, the International Organization for Standardization (ISO), and the World Trade Organization (WTO). These meta-regulators are themselves in turn regulated, including through global administrative law and some state controls. This entire zone of regulation and meta-regulation generates numerous research questions on inter-institutional relations, the legal management of hierarchies and their intersections with networks, the resolution of conflicts among different entities and interpretive competence for different standards, the place of conflicts of laws (private international law) doctrines and techniques in this regulatory zone, and legal puzzles concerning the maintenance or desuetude of older standards which retain their formal status but may have been partially eclipsed by newer instruments or practices.

These issues with regard to regulation and meta-regulation are instantiations of a broader topic: to what extent is work on legal aspects of technical standardization informative for other areas of standardization? Technical standardization and the administrative law of regulated economic sectors share the general characteristic that they blend sector-specific practices and norms on the one hand, with cross-cutting principles and institutions distinctive to the whole field on the other; and in each case the blend is in some measure embedded in wider structures of constitutional law, international law, and global political economy. Much of the modern legal material animating the companion volume relates to telecommunications, information technology, and digital economy industries. For the issues addressed in this volume, the cross-cutting features are to the fore, the sectors currently or prospectively implicated are more diverse, and the range of articulated interests is wider.

Health and safety regulation, and the specifics of food safety governance, each examined in this volume, have distinctive standardization and supervisory practices in which public interests have a formalized salience but mixed success in continuous struggles with large economic interests. These practices grapple with pervasive problems of regulatory capture and asymmetric information, but also with immense global capabilities gradients and preference divergences, and with newer regulatory problems such as combinations of individually benign standards-compliant products inadvertently co-producing dangerous risks.

At a more distant remove from the locus of technical standardization are the practices of environmental, social, and governance (ESG) standardization. The multi-stakeholder institutional forms for standards production and certification as exemplified by the private Forest Stewardship Council (FSC) or the hybrid private–public Extractive Industries Transparency Initiative (EITI), contrast in various dimensions with major information technology technical standardization bodies such as the Internet Engineering Task Force (IETF) or the IEEE. But even these wide chasms are bridged by some cross-cutting issues on which this book provides much informative material. The following are four examples.

The business models of different SDOs depend on finding means to raise revenue. Some claim copyright in their standards or trademarks in their distinctive names, and seek income from licensing fees; others privilege members of the SDO in access to or use of these standards or trademarks, in part as recompense to (or inducement of) members for their support of standards development. Chapters in this book highlight numerous challenges to these strategies, including longstanding rule-of-law objections to commercial controls on free access to those standards which have status in formal law.

Open standards and open-source culture in software development provide an important counter-point to single-company or platform standard-setting and to SDO standardization amidst thickets of patents and contract-chains. The open standards ecosystems necessarily employ some regulatory forms with regulatory effects, which in turn are touched by formal law. The standpoints brought to the study of these in this volume provide useful insights for open-standards as complements to or substitutes for traditional standardization in areas beyond software.

Certification of compliance with standards can be undertaken by SDOs, by standards users directly (self-certification), or by third-party organizations that may or may not be specifically accredited for this function. As the relevant chapters in this volume show, the law of certification, certification marks and labeling, certification intermediaries, and accreditation is piecemeal and likely in need of some elaboration and reform, particularly in transnational contexts.

Standardization, and the formalization of standardization process, can be undertaken with an eye to averting the prospect of formal legal regulation, or to influencing the approach taken by regulators or by courts in litigation.

In concluding, an observation on the shifting extent and configuration of the space of technical standardization may be made. The present volume, with its more eclectic range of topics, concentrates geographically on the United States and Europe. The companion volume, however, in its study of FRAND licensing and other issues concerning standards-essential patents, includes chapters on China, the EU, India, Japan, and the United States, as well as South Korea. While the shaping of practice on technical standardization in the contemporary global economy has been much influenced by North Atlantic industries and regulatory ideologies, together with Japanese participation, the rising scope of other Asian advanced-tech economies and the re-equilibration of global politico-military and soft power are prompting changes in participation in existing SDOs as well as the growing influence of a more diverse set of standardizers and approaches to standardization. Struggles over standard-setting for, and deployment of, 5G wireless communications technology were an early marker of the judders involved in this global re-balancing. Searches for new pathways in this more contentious environment include cross-operable devices capable of running on different platforms, such as politically facilitated agreement on commercial mobile communications devices enabling the user to move between any of the four main governmental Global Navigation Satellite Systems (GPS, Glonass, Galileo, Beidou). The coexistence of deep globalization with intensified nationalism and perturbations in existing orders poses heightened challenges to hitherto dominant models and institutions of technical standardization. As the chapters in this book demonstrate, law in this field is always engaged with maintenance and innovation. Both can be expected to take on a new valence under unsettled conditions of global re-ordering.

Benedict Kingsbury

Acknowledgements

This book would not have been possible without the hard work and dedication of many individuals, including each of the authors who contributed to this collective work. I am especially grateful for the tremendous efforts of Luke Hanks at the University of Utah. Support for the production of this book came from the University of Utah S.J. Quinney College of Law and the Albert and Elaine Borchard Fund for Faculty Excellence. I would also like to express thanks to Matt Gallaway and the editorial staff at Cambridge University Press.

Much of the relevance and timeliness of this book can be attributed to the deep engagement of its authors in the issues and controversies surrounding technical standardization and the law. As such, many of us have been directly involved in counseling, litigation, and transactions affecting the cases, agencies, and organizations discussed in this book, including as attorneys, experts, arbitrators, and employees. Personally, I served for two decades as legal counsel to the Internet Engineering Task Force, a major international standards-development organization, I have represented numerous firms in their dealings with other standards bodies, I have formed and represented several standards-development consortia, I have appeared as an expert witness in standards-related litigation on behalf of both patent holders and product manufacturers, I have served as an arbitrator in a large FRAND-related dispute, and my academic research has been supported by grants from both public and private sources. The details of these relationships, as well as similar relationships enjoyed by many of the chapter authors in this volume, are disclosed in greater detail in the relevant papers, articles, and chapters, the biographical sketches contained in this volume, and our personal and institutional websites. Nevertheless, the reader is assured that all views expressed herein are of the individual authors, writing as respected experts in their fields, and do not reflect the views or opinions of any employer, client, or funder.

The Editor

Introduction

Jorge L. Contreras

As noted in the Introduction to the companion volume, technical interoperability standards are ubiquitous in the modern networked economy. They enable products made and sold by different vendors to interact with little to no consumer intervention. They allow new market entrants, small and large, to innovate on top of established technology platforms, bringing technological advances to all corners of the globe. They expand consumer choice, eliminate duplicative development efforts, and accelerate product and feature design. Standards have enabled connected systems for more than a century, beginning with railroad tracks and telegraph lines and today forming essential elements of the modern communications, computing, manufacturing, healthcare, and transportation industries. And in the near future, technologies such as automated vehicles, power distribution, artificial intelligence, and the Internet of Things will be made possible through the use of standardized technologies.

Given their importance to the global technology marketplace, it is not surprising that technical standards and standardization have become increasing topics of legal regulation, policy debate, and litigation. Yet despite this attention, the scholarly analysis of standards and standardization has been fractured. The development of standards, primarily by industry associations and governmental bodies, has been analyzed through the lenses of industrial organization, game theory, and neoclassical microeconomics. The complex relationships among standards developers and the actions that they take in the marketplace have been scrutinized under antitrust and competition laws. Standards themselves are often protected by intellectual property rights such as patents and copyrights, which have been the subject of extensive analysis. And the role of standards in governmental rules and regulations have likewise attracted significant attention in the fields of administrative law, public health, and political science.

This volume, like its companion volume, addresses the legal aspects of technical standards and standardization. The companion volume described the role of technical standards in the modern global marketplace and the institutional infrastructure under which technical standards are developed, the analysis of standards development organizations (SDOs) under competition and antitrust laws around the world, and the impact on these systems of patents that are essential to the implementation of technical standards. In this volume, a distinguished group of international scholars address a range of legal, technical and economic issues that arise with respect to standardization at the intersection of public and private law. That is, how the largely private activity of standardization is overseen, regulated, and constrained by a range of legal frameworks including international trade law, administrative law, tort law, copyright, trademark, and certification. This volume is unique in its coverage of topics across different realms of public and private law, both in the United States and Europe and offers the reader an unprecedented survey of the legal landscape affecting standardization today.

Part I addresses the direct influence that public law mechanisms have over standardization. In Chapter 1, Panagiotis Delimatsis explores current issues involving standardization and the WTO Agreement on Technical Barriers to Trade (TBT), particularly the influence that WTO rules have had on the internal rules of SDOs. He argues that, given its potent dispute resolution mechanisms, the WTO can, and should, become a more powerful driver of change within international standard-setting. In Chapter 2, Emily Bremer focuses on governmental use of standards in the United States and Europe, critically analyzing the similarities and differences in the legal and policy frameworks employed by each.

Part II turns to the legal constraints on standardization motivated by health and safety considerations. In Chapter 3, Timothy Lytton addresses health and safety regulation using, as a detailed case study, the U.S. regime for food safety regulation. And in Chapter 4, Paul Verbruggen explores health and safety issues from the perspective of private tort liability in both the United States and Europe.

Part III addresses some of the many copyright issues raised by technical standardization. In Chapter 5, Pamela Samuelson and Kathryn Hashimoto question the very notion of copyright in standards, arguing that standards may be unprotectable as utilitarian or informational systems and under the *scenes a faire* and merger doctrines. They also consider the impact of incorporating standards into law on an SDO's copyright in a standards document, an issue that has resulted in significant controversy in recent years. In Chapter 6, Daniel Sheffner offers an in-depth analysis of the effect of a government's incorporation of standards into law or regulation, and what such incorporation means for public access to the content of incorporated standards and to the copyrights held by standards developers. And in Chapter 7, Björn Lundqvist addresses the incorporation and access issues from a European perspective, focusing on the effect of the EU's "New Approach" to standardization. Finally, in Chapter 8, Andrew Hernacki and I examine the effect on standards documents of statutes permitting the creator of a copyrighted work to terminate assignments and licenses of that work – a statutory scheme that was implemented to protect neophyte artists, musicians and authors, but which could arguably be invoked in the very different world of technical standards.

Part IV explores the legal landscape surrounding standards that are implemented in software. In Chapter 9, Jay Kesan focuses on the complex status of "open standards," which play a large role in governmental procurement and purchasing programs for software and other information assets. In Chapter 10, Martin Husovec explores the ecosystems underlying the development of technical standards and open source software, arguing that perceived differences between these seemingly incompatible methodologies for developing technological solutions are not as different as one might expect. In Chapter 11, David Kappos also discusses the use of open source software in technical standards, particularly the compatibility of open source licensing with SDO requirements that patents be licensed on "fair, reasonable and nondiscriminatory" (FRAND) terms (itself a topic extensively covered in the companion volume).

Part V turns to the law relating to the labeling and branding of technical standards and the certification of standardized products. In Chapter 12, I discuss the role that trademarks, service marks and certification marks play with respect to technical standards. The final two chapters then turn to the understudied question of product certification and offer proposals for the improvement of certification systems for standardized products based on the experience of other industries. In Chapter 13, Jeanne Fromer discusses the wide latitude that owners of certification marks have to certify, or refuse to certify, certain products, and recommends that more robust procedural regulation be applied to certification standard-making and decision-making, with a particular focus on the case of the Swiss Made certification for watches. And in Chapter 14, Jonathan Barnett examines the role of certification intermediaries, particularly in view of the prominent failures of certification in the financial services and other sectors. He concludes that even though certification intermediaries may periodically fail, such failures are inherent to well-functioning markets for certification services, and certifier performance may best be enhanced not through legal penalties, but through regulatory action that influences certifiers' organizational choices.

As with the companion volume, it is hoped that this comprehensive examination of legal issues affecting standardization will serve as a useful tool for scholars, practitioners, judges, and policy makers as they wrestle with these complex issues, and that the diverse perspectives offered by the contributors to this volume will give rise to new understanding, theory and resolution as standards continue to shape the global technology marketplace.

PART I

Standardization and the State

1

International Trade Law and Technical Standardization

*Panagiotis Delimatsis**

A.	Deciphering the Nature of International Standardization	9
	1. Informal, Voluntary and Yet Influential as Ever	9
	2. Certain Traits of SSOs	10
B.	The Treatment of International Standards Under the TBT Agreement	13
	1. Referencing International Standards in the TBT Preamble	13
	2. The Substantive Scope of TBT: The Distinction Between a Technical Regulation and a Standard	14
	3. TBT Basics Revisited: Blurring the Distinction Between Technical Regulations and Standards	15
	4. The TBT Code of Good Practice Relating to Standards	17
	5. Unfolding the Conundrum of 'Relevant International Standards'	19
	6. Recognized International Standardization Bodies	22
	7. The TBT Committee Decision	24

Increased international standardization by the private sector results from an ever-increasing demand of consumers for better and safer products, technological advances, the expansion of global trade and the ever-increasing focus on social and sustainability issues.[1] International standards affect our everyday life in multiple ways. Standards bring about and solidify technological evolution, innovation and diffusion of knowledge. In that respect, they have an important impact on consumer wellbeing. They play a decisive role as to whether the business and market environment will be conducive to increased innovation and trade. They form an important condition for doing business and affect access to markets, determining the profitability, growth and ultimately the survival of entrepreneurs and economic operators alike. Hence, standards have a crucial *trade facilitation function*.

---

* This chapter builds heavily on a previous version that appeared in Delimatsis (2015). Several colleagues have influenced my thinking on standardization-related issues, including Alessandra Arcuri, Axel Marx, Petros Mavroidis, Jens Prüfer, Charles Sabel, Harm Schepel, Florian Schütt and Jan Wouters. For its research on competition, standardization and innovation, TILEC has received funding from Qualcomm Inc., which is gratefully acknowledged. The research on which this article is based was conducted in accordance with the rules set out in the Royal Dutch Academy of Sciences (KNAW) Declaration of Scientific Independence. Any remaining errors or misconceptions are the author's alone.

[1] Egan 2001.

Yet, standards can also be adopted with a view to restricting access to a given market, thereby neutralizing any trade concessions made in other fora, including the World Trade Organization (WTO) or preferential trade agreements (PTAs). When standards are very diverse and are applied in a thoughtless manner, trade is negatively affected and economies of scale become more difficult to attain. For small entrepreneurs in particular, the costs of compliance with this heterogeneous set of standards may be prohibitive, de facto precluding any possibility for gaining access to foreign markets.[2]

As standards can potentially constitute impactful 'behind-the-border' (so-called non-tariff) technical barriers that nullify trade concessions and distort the expectations of traders, the WTO takes a clear stance in favour of the creation of and adherence to international standards. Already the preamble of the WTO Agreement on Technical Barriers to Trade (TBT) commences with an orthodox assumption, that is, that international standards improve efficiency of production and facilitate the conduct of international trade.[3]

However, the WTO has no capacity or expertise that would allow it to set technical standards. In addition, the Committee on Technical Barriers to Trade (hereinafter, the TBT Committee) does not develop nor adopt standards itself. Rather, as exemplified already by its preamble, the TBT exerts a high level of deference towards technical rationality as expressed through international standard-setting activities *outside* the WTO. Indeed, standards developed within international standard-setting organizations (SSOs) acquire a prominent role within the WTO through the very text of the TBT. The latter not only requires that WTO Members use 'relevant international standards' but also presumes compliance with the TBT when such standards are used as a basis for domestic technical regulations.

Is this regulatory outsourcing justified? The answer is not so trivial, in particular when one considers the consequences of such outsourcing. Arguably, it essentially suggests that certain non-WTO rules still are WTO-compatible as long as they are relevant to the product at issue in a WTO dispute; and this regardless of the process that led to their adoption (which process, by the way, is totally out of the control of the WTO). Quite astonishingly, the TBT entails such delegation of regulatory power[4] without any inquiry as to the actual processes used throughout the development of international technical standards. This is even more surprising if one considers that such delegation of international standard-setting activities relates to private actors active in the creation of standards.

This constellation brings to the forefront the importance of procedural guarantees within international SSOs, notably with regard to representation of varying interests and opportunities for participation offered to all WTO Members. However, our knowledge about the mechanics of international standard-setting is relatively limited at best and a black box in certain cases.

The vantage point of this chapter is that such deferential approach adopted by the WTO is untenable. Attributing to international standards developed elsewhere automatic legal force in the WTO may clash with contemporary demands for more transparency and due process within global governance institutions, more generally, and openness in international standard-setting, in particular.[5] It can also give the wrong signals to international SSOs which have become the global standard-setters in certain categories of products and services. The key argument of the chapter is that the WTO can play an instrumental role in improving standard-setting processes

---

[2] Messerlin 2001.
[3] Swann et al. 1996, 1297–1313.
[4] For a similar observation under the SPS, see Büthe (2008, 219).
[5] *Cf.* Von Bogdandy 2012, 315.

within international SSOs, because its very foundational treaty (and the TBT in particular through the presumption of WTO compatibility we mentioned earlier) makes it a prominent promoter of such standards and indeed a high-level diffusion mechanism. The chapter argues that, due to its powerful dispute resolution system, the WTO can become a potential drive for change in transnational standard-setting. Section B describes the nature of international standards, tilting between public and private, in a grey area of law, whereas Section C analyses the position of international standards and the bodies that create them from a positive and normative viewpoint. Section D concludes.

A. DECIPHERING THE NATURE OF INTERNATIONAL STANDARDIZATION

1. *Informal, Voluntary and Yet Influential as Ever*

Standard-setting resembles law-making, as standards, like laws, are the outcome of discussion, bargaining, deliberation and compromise among non-state actors.[6] However, standards established by international SSOs such as the ISO are not law per se, but rather serve a clear regulatory function prescribing rules for others to follow.[7] An important distinction, again, is that, whereas domestic standardization can encompass both binding and voluntary technical specifications and standards, international standardization, as noted previously, typically involves standards with which compliance is voluntary. Once international standards are adopted, it is a country's prerogative to adopt these standards in the form of domestic technical regulations (compliance with which is mandatory), or as standards (compliance with which is optional). Depending on the domestic constitutional structures, such standards may be adopted through the relevant national standard-setting bodies or public regulatory agencies. A third option for a country is to maintain or adopt its own standards or allow for some leeway to domestic companies to decide as to whether they would like to comply voluntarily with the international standards at stake.[8]

Standards, no matter how well-crafted, can interfere with market access. This is mainly because standards reflect domestic preferences and values, which may diverge, thereby inflating compliance costs and values for companies.[9] It is then compliance costs which corroborate the case for the development of international standards. Indeed, if developed internationally, then substantial gains can be made through the diminution of such costs and by addressing network externalities and information asymmetries. Thus, taking into account pure efficiency considerations, the locus of standardization is to be found outside national borders.[10]

With the emergence of global supply chains, the importance of international standards increases, suggesting that compatibility standards of high quality can yield substantial network effects that can make such standards self-enforcing.[11] However, the reduction of compliance costs may be only a long-term effect, as, in the short run, the effect of international standards may vary in that compliance costs will rise for some firms, as the new standard used may be more sophisticated. At the same time, an international standard, the theory suggests, would lead to the diminution of consumer costs due to better information and the possibility to compare prices.[12]

---

[6] *Cf.* Kingsbury et al. 2005, 15.
[7] *See also* Black 2009, 246.
[8] *See* Nakagawa 2011, 109.
[9] Staiger & Sykes 2011, 149.
[10] Büthe & Mattli 2003, 1.
[11] WEF 2012.
[12] *See* WTO 2012c, 136.

Standards constitute a form of codified technical knowledge that enables the development of products and processes. Standards regularize and constrain behaviour (regulative function); lend a taken-for-granted quality to certain technologies and *modi operandi* (cognitive function); and favour cooperative strategies over adversarial ones (normative function).[13] In the absence of standards, technological progress would lack an important instrument for benchmarking and capitalizing on advances in the field of technology. In addition, first-mover advantages in standardization are substantial incentives for firms to innovate.[14] In that sense, standards are essential enabling components of any functioning market and a decisive instrument for economic growth.[15] For instance, studies in France, Germany or the UK have shown that the impact of standards on growth can range between 0.3 and 0.9 of national GDP.[16]

Contextually, international standardization is part of the undisputed rise in transnational law-making, as SSOs become more private actor-driven. Such transnational regimes have often evolved in a vacuum, avoiding any frontal confrontation with State law. In the case of standard-setting at the international level, whereas there are private-driven SSOs, in practice state-driven actors such as regulators or government-sponsored bodies may develop partnerships – be it formal or informal – with private actors to generate what can be termed 'informal law'. It is not only the informal character of the actors, but informality extends to the output of SSOs as well: Whereas domestic standardization can encompass both binding and voluntary technical standards and specifications, international standardization typically involves standards with which compliance is *voluntary*.

2. Certain Traits of SSOs

As there are manifold technological approaches, an SSO offers a forum where competitors and competing vested interests can learn from each other as to the best available technologies but also resolve conflicts and coordination problems. In practice, SSOs serve as an important information- and knowledge-sharing forum with mutual learning occurring among participants; crucial laboratories for the preparation of standards based on a chosen or dominant technology and certification checkpoints of those standards at the post-development stage; and, finally, as instrumental regulators on the use of those standards, for instance, when it comes to the licensing of the standardized technology.[17]

Generally, international SSOs choose consensus as the decision-making mode *par excellence*, which the ISO defines as 'general agreement, characterized by the absence of *sustained opposition* to *substantial issues* by *any important part of the concerned interests* and by a process that involves seeking to take into account the views of all parties concerned and to reconcile any conflicting arguments' (emphasis added). However, it is made clear that consensus need not imply unanimity.[18] In other SSOs of private nature, a stricter view with respect to the meaning of consensus may be adopted also to increase the legitimacy of processes.

---

[13] Lane 1997, 197.
[14] Again, and more generally, if we consider standardization as infrastructure, it can promote but also hamper innovation. *See also* Acemoglu et al. 2012, 570.
[15] Blind & Jungmittag 2008, 51.
[16] *See* European Commission 2016a, 4.
[17] *See* Lerner & Tirole 2015, 547–548.
[18] *See* ISO/IEC Dir 1, clause 2.5.6. This definition is generally accepted as reflecting the understanding of what consensus entails in standard-setting bodies. *See also* EU Regulation 1025/2012, Annex II, para. 3(b).

Although unanimity is not often required, most international organizations aim at consensus building and have those mechanisms in place in their constitutions and secondary law. Consensus however can cause delays, whereby competitors argue for their preferred solution or simply hold out until one side concedes or withdraws to the benefit of the other.[19] Endorsement of a given standard at the end of the process can generate substantial rents which make the effort quite worthwhile,[20] but also confirms the value of (and, in the end, legitimizes) the standard-setter as a stabilizing factor in its capacity as a coordinating authority.

In addition, it was shown that, in areas of rapid technological change and innovation and thus important rents being at stake (distributional conflicts), the standard-setting process may be slower in a consensus-based standard-setting body, but delays will be efficient when the underlying technology improves with the time. Thus, and quite importantly, at the end of the lengthy process higher quality outcomes will be produced.[21] This means that, contrary to conventional belief, and somehow counter-intuitively, striving for consensus may have a very limited impact on the technical and scientific excellence of a given standard. However, when vested interests are strong, relaxing the way consensus is required or identifying a neutral participant to break deadlock (i.e. binding arbitration) may be preferable to increase the effectiveness of a given standard.[22]

Due to the importance of standardization for businesses, substantial financial resources are invested in standardization fora.[23] Indeed, an active participation in standardization activities is necessary to boost innovation, notably in case of highly competitive markets, but is also quite expensive. The increase of standards-related patent disputes, the emergence of industry-sponsored consortia, but also actions against allegedly anticompetitive practices within SSOs is indicative of the importance of standardization and the stakes at play, notably in high-tech areas.[24]

In practice, not only competition among *firms* to innovate and standardize but also competition among *standard-setting groups* to attract such firms constitutes a typical feature of private standard-setting. Standard-setting groups compete on offering the most attractive institutional setting for the development and update of standards. What will many times determine the choice of forum (i.e. standard-setting body) is whether for a given firm the possibility to dictate a standard carries more weight in its standards-related behaviour than the reputation of a given standard-setting body, that is, whether reputation costs are lower than the benefits of dictating the standard in a second-best standard-setting scheme. This choice will essentially depend on the size of the market and the attractiveness of the technology.[25] The role of possibilities within a given SSO for addressing and resolving disagreements and potential conflicts, for instance, flexible rules relating to participation or expedited mechanisms for solving disputes, may be equally crucial for the survival and continuous relevance of a particular SSO.[26]

---

[19] Farrell and Saloner first described this tactic as a 'war of attrition', suggesting that it may lead to the technically best solution, but with a significant delay. See Farrell & Saloner 1988, 235.
[20] Rysman & Simcoe 2008, 1920.
[21] Simcoe 2012, 305.
[22] See Farrell & Simcoe 2012.
[23] See id. at 236–38; see also the observation of the Advocate-General Campos Sanchez-Bordona in the recent *Elliott* case before the CJEU that '[i]ndustry assumes the greater share of the costs of standardization'. *James Elliot Construction Ltd.* (CJEU 2016, ¶ 58).
[24] See Vol. 1; *see also* Larouche & Van Overwalle 2015.
[25] Chiao et al. 2007.
[26] Delimatsis & Kanevskaia 2018.

As noted earlier, the stakes are quite high in standard-setting procedures and thus participants are self-interested agents who aim to extract the maximum rents. In this process, rents can be extracted, for example, when a particular technology is considered standard-essential or when a given legislation adopted by public bodies refers to a standard created within an SSO as a benchmark for compliance with law. One can easily identify a certain pattern in standardization activities and the incentives to participate therein. Even though standards are adopted mainly through soft-law processes by non-state actors, these actors aspire to capitalize on their success and see the initially non-binding norms they champion transformed into hard law to gain rents from first-mover advantages through expedited enforcement.

This constellation and modus operandi does not necessarily imply that inferior technologies will prevail thanks to strategic behaviour. On the contrary, more often than not, strategic behaviour and market power will still not bear fruit unless it is backed up by important technological strength. This result is typically due to the dynamic process that characterizes standardization and substantial investments on research and development (R&D). The standardization-related procedures may also often have the necessary safeguards or remedies in place to avoid blatant negligence against the best available technology.[27] This would suggest that procedures within SSOs should be continuously reviewed to ensure that distortions of this type are duly addressed and avoided. Thus, standard-setting bodies are important coordination devices.

The stakeholders involved in international standardization are of hybrid nature and, like self-regulators, have a conflict of interest inherent in their functions: they are there to serve the interests of their constituents but also the national interest.[28] In many cases, domestic industries are so deeply convinced of the superiority of their standards that they believe they promote the public interest – along with their own – when they strive for the application of standards which actually reflect characteristics of their own standards. At this level, industry representatives and SSBs participating in the international standard-setting process become the missionaries who convey a strikingly paradoxical message of globalization: as we move towards closer integration and interdependence at a global level,[29] societies may prove to be less prepared to abandon long-established practices and important values that have shaped their lives for decades or even centuries. The result is that when they discuss and negotiate in a globalized context, they tend to defend fiercely or to attempt to impose their domestic preferences and values.

This probably explains why creating globalized standards or achieving harmonization of technical regulations is a utopian ideal in the short run.[30] Thus, the formula '1+1+1', that is, 'one standard, one test and one conformity assessment procedure accepted everywhere' is not realistic. Without the necessary procedural guarantees in place, the beneficial effects of standardization can be undermined if standardization cannot resist market power nor has the institutional sensitivity and accommodating structures to take into account the views of smaller market players or important societal values.[31] Thus, several international SSOs have taken steps to ensure effective participation, including the ability to attend meetings through electronic means; the disclosure of all minutes of the meetings; the possibility for partnerships with more advanced participants and the like.

---

[27] For certain problematic features of the remedies system within the ISO, see Delimatsis (2018).
[28] See, e.g., U.S. Trade Agreements Act of 1979 (providing that the representation of U.S. interests before any private international standards organization shall be carried out by the organization member, defined as 'the private person who holds membership in a private international standards organization'). See also Schepel 2011, 404.
[29] Lazer 2001.
[30] Sykes 1999.
[31] Abbott & Snidal 2001; see also European Commission 2011a, 11ff.

B. THE TREATMENT OF INTERNATIONAL STANDARDS UNDER THE TBT AGREEMENT

The impressive reduction of tariffs since the inception of the General Agreement on Tariffs and Trade (GATT) in the late 1940s and the outright prohibition of the use of quantitative restrictions that the GATT requires has a led to the use by WTO Members of 'behind-the-border', domestic instruments to protect their industries.[32] These non-tariff barriers (NTBs) have ultimately emerged as persistent trade barriers.[33] To make things worse from a market access standpoint, rules, specifications, standards and other documents with some normative content created by non-state actors regularly impinge on economic action. Thus, delegation of regulatory power to private actors and the rise of private government and transnational networks are not unproblematic from an international law viewpoint, as these activities may fall outside the scope of traditional inter-state rules.[34]

The GATT is a negative integration contract. It is essentially based on one obligation which is imposed on the WTO Membership: every domestic policy that impacts on trade has to be applied in a non-discriminatory manner, thereby ensuring equality of opportunities between domestic and foreign products, but also among foreign products only. On the other hand, policies affecting trade are to be unilaterally prescribed at a national level and thus there is no predefined set of policies by which all WTO Members must abide. This means, inter alia, that the GATT does not imply any compulsory adherence to international standards.

However, with the adoption of the TBT in the mid-90s and the establishment of the WTO, the WTO drafters decided to go beyond non-discrimination to promote regulatory efficiency domestically in areas such as technical or food safety regulations.[35] As we will see below, this shift of focus inevitably included voluntary international standards as expressions of international technical consensus developed in international SSOs such as the ISO or the Codex Alimentarius. With this change in the multilateral trading system, the processes used within international SSOs, neglected by many up to that point in time, came to the forefront, leading to ensuing transformations of their modus operandi.[36]

1. Referencing International Standards in the TBT Preamble

The TBT substantiates Members' attempt to effectively deal with NTBs and harness badly designed and badly applied technical regulations, specifications, standards and procedures domestically. However, it also acknowledges Members' prerogative to autonomously pursue public policy objectives such as those relating to the protection of the environment or consumers, provided that the non-discrimination principle is observed.[37] Early on in its preamble, the TBT points to the importance of harmonization of compatibility standards by acknowledging the role of international standards as trade facilitators and technology transfer vectors. In other words, the TBT encourages the development of such harmonized standards at the international

---

[32] Kono 2006 (showing that democratic regimes have asymmetrical influence over the various types of protection, i.e. while leading to lower tariffs, they lead to higher NTBs).
[33] Wilson 2002.
[34] See, e.g., Donnelly 2007.
[35] See Marceau & Trachtman 2002; Howse & Langille 2012.
[36] For instance, Motaal (2004) unequivocally describes the transformation that international SSOs, which prepare, draft and adopt SPS standards, have undergone since 1994 due to the entry into force of the *SPS Agreement* at the conclusion of the Uruguay Round.
[37] See also WTO 2015, para. 213.

level. The TBT explicitly refers to international standardization as a highly relevant process for addressing technical barriers to trade, thereby endorsing by reference the importance of the work of several decades done within international SSOs to advance technological progress. The fact that the TBT, contrary to the SPS, does not explicitly refer to particular international SSOs does not alter this observation.

Thus, both the TBT and the SPS make a rather considerate choice in favour of international standards. If one is to strike a reasonable balance between concealed protectionism and the well-meant pursuit of legitimate objectives by a benign government, benchmarks (or proxies) are needed. Under the GATT, the necessity test of the general exceptions provision enshrined in Article XX GATT exerts this role,[38] allowing to identify measures that exceed what is necessary to achieve the degree of contribution that a given measure makes to the pursuit of a legitimate objective.[39] A necessity test as a proxy in the case of the TBT and the SPS would be necessary (and indeed such a test is to be found in both agreements), but it is not sufficient for a treaty that aims at *positive* integration through harmonization. Additional common denominators or heuristic devices are needed. Due to their unambiguous technical expertise, international SSOs and the instruments they create, i.e. international standards, are deemed appropriate for this role.

At the same time, and perhaps contrary to the mainstream literature about TBT,[40] there is no *carte blanche* for international standard-setting processes enshrined in the TBT preamble. Rather the approach is much more critical when one looks carefully at the preamble. Indeed, the TBT preamble, after hailing the importance of harmonizing international standards and conformity assessment systems, refers to Members' desire to ensure that technical regulations and standards do not create unnecessary trade barriers. Arguably, this relates not only to domestic measures but also to international standards. This interpretation is reasonable due to the use of the word 'however' in the fifth recital of the TBT preamble. It is only plausible to suggest here that 'however' refers to what preceded under the third and fourth recitals, which exclusively refer to *international* instruments.

2. The Substantive Scope of TBT: The Distinction Between a Technical Regulation and a Standard

Rationae materiae, the TBT distinguishes between technical regulations and standards. More specifically, it covers mandatory technical regulations and voluntary product standards (such as those relating to size, quality, composition, or labelling) as well as conformity assessment procedures. Despite the reference to ISO/IEC Guide 2:1991, which was subsequently revised within ISO, the TBT offers definitions for the three main categories of measures coming under the TBT ambit in Annex 1 of the agreement. For our purposes, we will focus on the first two categories. Thus, a technical regulation is defined as a:

> [d]ocument which lays down product characteristics or their related processes and production methods, *including the applicable administrative provisions*, with which *compliance is mandatory*. It may also include or deal exclusively with terminology, symbols, packaging, marking or labelling requirements as they apply to a product, process or production method. (emphasis added)

---

[38] *See* Delimatsis 2011.
[39] *Cf.* WTO 2015, para. 319.
[40] *See, e.g.*, Appleton 2005.

Furthermore, it defines a standard as a:[41]

> [d]ocument *approved by a recognized body,* that provides, for common and repeated use, rules, guidelines or characteristics for products or related processes and production methods, with which *compliance is not mandatory*. It may also include or deal exclusively with terminology, symbols, packaging, marking or labelling requirements as they apply to a product, process or production method. (emphasis added)

The two definitions overlap already in their very wording. More strikingly, the second sentence in both definitions is identical. Importantly, both definitions make clear that they cover labelling requirements and production and process methods (PPMs). After the Appellate Body decision in *EC – Sardines,* the traditional view that allowed drawing the line between the two categories of products was whether non-compliance with a given measure in fact prohibits access to a given market (technical regulation) or whether access to a given market was possible irrespective of compliance with a given specification (standards).[42]

The Appellate Body examined the constitutive elements of a technical regulation under the TBT in *EC – Asbestos* and *EC – Sardines,* and, more recently, in *EC – Seal Products.* First, it found that a technical regulation may lay down one or more *binding* product characteristics in a *positive* or *negative* form, i.e. it may require that a product possesses (or not) particular characteristics. Thus, the document at stake must have a certain normative content.[43] According to the Appellate Body, this includes any objectively definable features, qualities, attributes, or other distinguishable marks of a product. Those product characteristics may be intrinsic or they may be related to the product such as the means of identification, the presentation and the appearance of a product.[44] Additionally, it should be applicable to an identifiable product or group of products. Finally, compliance is mandatory, suggesting that non-compliance would allow an enforcement mechanism to sanction a particular producer.[45]

In *EC – Sardines,* the Appellate Body found that compliance with the relevant EC Regulation was mandatory because the legislative instrument used was binding and directly applicable in all EU Member States. In view of the many similarities among the definition of technical regulation and that of a standard, two appear to be the main differences between the two types of measures: the first is that, whereas the technical regulation is adopted by a governmental body and thus is a State measure, a standard is typically issued by private or semi-private standardizing bodies, that is, bodies with standardization activities. A standard can later become a technical regulation if adopted or used as a basis for a legislative act by the State. The second difference is that, unlike a technical regulation, compliance with a standard is voluntary.

3. TBT Basics Revisited: Blurring the Distinction Between Technical Regulations and Standards

The actual contours of the definition of a technical regulation and its relationship with the definition of a standard under the TBT was more recently discussed in the controversial *US – Tuna II* dispute relating to a dolphin-safe labelling scheme for tuna products.[46] Under the measure

---

[41] For the negotiating history of this definition, see TBT Committee (1995).
[42] *Cf.* Van den Bossche 2008. As discussed below, the Appellate Body decoupled the two in *US – Tuna II*. See WTO 2015, para. 196.
[43] WTO 2014, para. 5.10.
[44] WTO 2001, para. 67.
[45] *See* WTO 2001, para. 76; WTO 2002a, para. 176.
[46] *See also* Mavroidis 2013.

at issue, tuna products sold in the United States could be labelled 'dolphin-safe' only if certain requirements were met, in particular with respect to the way tuna was harvested. Crucially, for tuna to be imported, no 'dolphin-safe' label was required.

The Panel first and the Appellate Body at the last instance found that the measure at issue was a technical regulation within the meaning of Annex 1.1 TBT. Both considered that whether the measure at issue was imposing conditions on the access to the 'dolphin-safe' label rather than the U.S. market as a whole was important and indeed decisive in this respect. A critical element in this case appears to have been that the U.S. measure covered the 'entire field' of what 'dolphin-safe' meant in relation to tuna products in the United States.[47] In the Appellate Body's words:[48]

> In effect, the measure at issue establishes a single definition of 'dolphin-safe' and treats any statement on a tuna product regarding 'dolphin-safety' that does not meet the conditions of the measure as a deceptive practice or act.

After observing that the measure at issue consisted of U.S. federal legislative and regulatory acts and that included administrative provisions, the Appellate Body found that the 'dolphin-safe' labelling requirement was a technical regulation for the purposes of the TBT.

Arguably, the analyses of the Panel and the Appellate Body are not convincing[49] and make much of Annex 1.2 TBT superfluous by blurring the distinction between mandatory and voluntary compliance. More fundamentally, it deprives Annex 1.2 TBT of its *effet utile*, rendering it redundant. Systemically, it may have significant repercussions for various sustainability-related labelling schemes, organized and applied by both governmental or hybrid and private standardizing bodies. This is particularly so in cases where: (i) no governmental scheme is present in the market and (ii) some connection with the government or administrative guidance can be proven, thereby linking the standardization body with the State. If none of the two happens, then only a very marginal set of rules could come within the definition of a standard under Annex 1.2 TBT, taking into account the similarity of the second sentence of Annex 1.1 and 1.2 TBT.[50]

It is submitted that both the Panel and the Appellate Body failed to give meaning to the fact that the U.S. measure was not concerned with setting characteristics for a product to be regarded as tuna. Rather, the measure at issue set the traits of *dolphin-safe* tuna products. Tuna products, no matter how they were harvested, could still enter the U.S. market. Both the Panel and the Appellate Body invoked *EC – Sardines* to corroborate their findings. However, they both seemed to neglect a fundamental difference between the two cases: the EC regulation allowed only one particular species of sardines to be marketed as preserved sardines within the EU. Thus, it was clear that no other sardines could enter the market with the label 'preserved sardines'. Nevertheless, in *US – Tuna II*, traders were free to access the tuna market without any labels relating to their 'dolphin safety'. Note, in stark contrast, that in *EC – Sardines*, Peruvian sardines could not enter the EU market. In the facts of *US – Tuna II*, though, tuna products could still be marketed and sold as ordinary tuna even if they do not comply with the 'dolphin-safe' labelling requirements.[51] Thus, the WTO judiciary conflated the requirements for access to the *label*

---

[47] See WTO 2015, para. 193.
[48] *Id.* at para. 195.
[49] Note that one of the panelists in the panel stage filed a separate opinion on this particular matter. See WTO 2011b, para. 7.146ff.
[50] Taking *US – Tuna II* as an example, if the same dolphin-safe scheme was promulgated by a private standardizing body, then the scheme would have been classified most likely as a standard and not a technical regulation. However, is it only the governmental involvement that determines whether we apply Annex 1.1 or 1.2 TBT? The focus on compliance and exclusion of the market for a given product seems to be safer a criterion.
[51] *See also* the EU arguments in WTO 2015, para. 155; and the panelist's dissenting opinion in WTO 2011b, para. 7.164.

with the requirements for access to the *market*. In *US – Tuna II*, it was at the discretion of the producer to comply or not with the requirements of the label. However, in *EC – Sardines*, that was definitely not the case.

To show the problematic character of this interpretation, one can juxtapose it to the U.S. measure that was at stake in the COOL dispute. In this case, the measure at issue imposed an obligation on retailers selling specific meat products in the U.S. downstream market to label those products depending on their country of origin.[52] In this case, such products could not get to the final point of sale without such label. If the *US – Tuna II* interpretation holds, then the COOL measure and the 'dolphin-safe' label would be labelling systems producing the same effects. However, they clearly do not, as in the case of country of origin labelling for meat, the meat product would not be allowed to reach consumers unless such label is affixed to the product. This result does not appear to hold a strict scrutiny of consistency. The *EC – Seal Products* Appellate Body Report only comes to corroborate the argument made here. In this case, the Appellate Body underscored that the EU relevant legislation prescribes rules relating to the *placing* on the EU market of seal products in a *binding* fashion.[53]

For the sake of comparison, long-established case law in the EU would suggest that a measure of this type would most likely survive the scrutiny of the Court of Justice of the European Union (CJEU). Indeed, not much can be said against the legality of the labelling scheme at issue when juxtaposed to the *Keck* formula: the U.S. measure applies to all relevant traders operating in the market and affects in the same manner, both in law and in fact, the selling of domestic products and of those from other Members.[54]

From a systemic point of view, the WTO judiciary brought under the definition of technical regulation of the TBT non-incorporated PPMs, that is, PPMs that are not observable on the product itself. This may be a welcome development, as the WTO judiciary would like to keep thorough judicial review of such measures for itself. From a legal point of view, it confounds the different categories of TBT measures and, arguably in a broader sense, the balance among the WTO agreements. Indeed, in that case, a more apposite and case-law consistent interpretation of the facts should have led the WTO judiciary to find that the TBT was not applicable and thus roll back to the application of Article III:4 GATT. However, one problematic feature of this option was that the Appellate Body would be unable to complete the analysis because the Panel exercised judicial economy with respect to the Mexican claims under the GATT, after finding that the TBT is *lex specialis* and after making findings under the latter agreement.

4. The TBT Code of Good Practice Relating to Standards

The structure of the TBT reveals a hierarchical relationship between the two types of instruments we discussed earlier. Whereas the obligations for technical regulations are in the main body of the TBT, the obligations regarding the development, adoption and application of standards are to be found in Annex 3 incorporating a Code of Good Practice (hereinafter 'the Code'). This is in stark contrast with the previous, plurilateral Standards Code adopted in the Tokyo Round where rules for technical regulations and standards belonged to the main body of the agreement without differentiation between the two categories of measures. On substance, this does not make the provisions relating to standards any less binding, as the Annex is an integral

---

[52] *See* WTO 2012a, para. 239.
[53] WTO 2014, para. 5.22.
[54] *See Keck and Mithouard* (CJEU 1993), para. 16.

part of the TBT by virtue of Article 15.5 TBT. More importantly, the obligations under the Code relating to standards and Article 2 regarding technical regulations are for all practical purposes the same, thereby minimizing the importance of locating the obligations for the two main TBT instruments in two different places.

Having said this, it appears that the Code is not incorporated in the TBT but in a separate annex because the Code includes obligations that are mainly addressed to self-regulated and -governed national standard-setting bodies, whereby many of those bodies, as noted earlier, are private bodies composed of industry representatives. For this reason, the TBT foresees the possibility for the Code to be accepted by standardizing bodies, be it governmental or non-governmental; central, regional or local – established in the territory of any WTO Member. Indeed, the Code is open for acceptance and the ISO/IEC Information Centre keeps track of such acceptances.[55] As of February 2016, 174 standard-setting bodies from 128 WTO Members accepted the Code; among them there are 96 central government bodies, 67 non-governmental bodies, three statutory bodies, two parastatal bodies, three non-governmental regional bodies (the three European standard-setters, i.e. CEN, CENELEC and ETSI), one central hybrid body, one central governmental/local body and one autonomous body.[56] While the acceptance of the Code generates important signalling effects, Article 4 TBT provides that Members' obligations relating to compliance of domestic standard-setting bodies with the Code remain intact regardless of whether a domestic standard-setting body has accepted the Code.

Even if this serves consistency, some interpretive challenges remain. For instance, paragraph D of the Code requires that standardizing bodies accord equal treatment to foreign products when compared to other foreign or domestic products. Nevertheless, this obligation seems to be without content, for such bodies do not deal with products directly. Taking into account the work that typically SSOs deal with, it appears illogical to require from SSOs the type of non-discrimination that the TBT and WTO law in general requires from States. Rather, one would expect the Code to focus on fair and non-discriminatory access to standardization activities, participation, transparency, necessity and the like. For the sake of comparison and as an example of how non-discrimination could be phrased adequately, Article 5.5 of ISO/IEC Guide 59 of 1994 provides that standards shall neither be written nor adopted so as to discriminate among products on the basis of the place of origin.[57] Another example of this kind is to be found in Article 5.5.3 of the ISEAL Alliance Code of Good Practice which requires that membership criteria and application procedures in standard-setting organizations be transparent and non-discriminatory.[58]

While not explicitly referring to the relationship between the TBT and ISO, the former has numerous references to the ISO, more particularly ISO/IEC Guide 2: 1991. The TBT provides that whenever terms that are included in this Guide are also mentioned in the TBT, then the meaning that these terms have according to the Guide becomes the authoritative one.[59] Thus, the ISO/IEC Guide 2:1991 constitutes important context for dispute settlement purposes by virtue of the Vienna Convention on the Law of Treaties (VCLT), directing the judiciary to have recourse to a non-WTO document to clarify certain TBT terms.[60] Together with Article

---

[55] See Memorandum of Understanding on 'WTO Standards Information Service Operated by ISO'. Every standardization body that accepted the Code is obliged to prepare a biannual work programme in which it provides information about the standards under preparation and the standards that it adopted in the preceding period.
[56] See TBT Committee 2016.
[57] See TBT Committee 1993.
[58] See ISEAL Alliance 2010.
[59] See WTO 1995, Annex 1, introductory paragraph.
[60] Similar to the Harmonised System's explanatory notes. See, e.g., WTO 2008a, paras. 149ff.

1.1 TBT, they substantiate the attempt of the TBT drafters to position the agreement within the broader standardization community and to relate it to the existing international standard-setting processes in a positive manner. In addition, the Code reproduces principles and rules known from the ISO without however explicitly referring to it. For instance, paragraph G of the Code provides that national standard-setting bodies shall strive to be represented in international SSOs through one delegation to ensure coherence (national delegation principle).

5. Unfolding the Conundrum of 'Relevant International Standards'

The idea of favouring global convergence of technical regulations permeates the TBT.[61] Article 2.4 requires that *relevant international standards* or *relevant parts* thereof (when they exist or are about to be adopted) be used as *a basis for* domestic technical regulations unless they are ineffective or inappropriate means for meeting the public policy objectives pursued. No grandfathering was allowed at the moment of adopting the agreement. In *EC – Sardines*, the Appellate Body confirmed that this obligation applies not only to technical regulations that were adopted after the entry into force of the WTO agreement, but also to technical regulations that already existed before the entry into force of the TBT but continued to produce effects.[62]

Standards would be subject to a similar obligation. This means that a series of international standards that were adopted before the mid-90s and typically applied on a voluntary basis suddenly become mandatory reference points for domestic technical regulations. Thus, interest in international standard-setting activities as a gateway to influence the normative contents of the benchmarks potentially used in future WTO adjudication was also revived as a result.

In *EC – Sardines*, the concept 'as a basis for' was interpreted to mean that an international standard is used in this way when it is the principal constituent or fundamental principle for the purpose of enacting the technical regulation at stake, thereby revealing a very strong and close relationship between the two.[63] If only parts of a given international standard are used, then those that are relevant shall be used as a basis for the technical regulation at issue. At a minimum, the international standard and the regulation cannot contradict each other.

Finally, it bears noting that it is for the complaining party to prove that the international standard at issue is effective (capable of accomplishing the legitimate objective pursued) and appropriate (suitable for the fulfilment of the objective pursued) for the achievement of the objective pursued. In this analysis it would be for the judiciary to examine and determine the legitimacy of the objectives of the measure. Effectiveness focuses on the *results* of the means used, whereas appropriateness focused on the *nature* of the means used.[64] Adjudicating bodies may be more willing to deny such qualities to international standards, for instance, when perceptions and expectations of consumers are not satisfied by it[65] or when the technical regulation at issue sets higher standards (e.g. more detailed and accurate information) for consumer protection.[66]

---

[61] Other than standards, this is also obvious in the case of conformity asseessment procedures. See, e.g., WTO 1995, Article 9.
[62] WTO 2002a, para. 205.
[63] Id., paras. 244–45.
[64] Id., para. 285.
[65] Id., para. 289.
[66] See WTO 2011a, para. 7.734. This excerpt actually is one of the most striking ones in this Panel report. The Panel seems to examine indirectly, but still quite critically, the substantive content of the relevant international standard, leaving the window for the circumvention of international standards (a Codex standard in this case) wide open. In addition, the Panel appears to disregard the fact that one of the purposes of the Codex standard was indeed to protect

Pursuant to Article 2.5 TBT, a technical regulation is presumed to comply with the TBT and more specifically Article 2.2, if it is in accordance with *relevant international standards* and provided that is prepared, adopted or applied to protect national security; prevent deceptive practices; protect human and animal health or safety; or the environment. The rationale behind this 'safe haven' is that voluntary international standards ostensibly incorporate international preferences and unambiguous technical superiority. Furthermore, Article 2.9 provides for additional notification requirements in case relevant international standards are not used.

Thus, other than requiring Members to use relevant international standards in a positive manner and creating a rebuttable presumption of consistency as an extra 'carrot', the TBT imposes additional, burdensome conditions that Members need to comply with in case of neglecting international standards. In other words, in those areas where international standards exist, which, as noted earlier, are mainly of voluntary nature, they become the reference point and de facto mandatory normative technical material to be used by WTO Members. As a result, a mass of documents of at best uncertain legal normativity are transformed into international obligations equivalent to treaty text.[67]

Article 2 TBT mentions various times the term 'relevant international standard' but lacks any provision that would offer a definition. This is in stark contrast to the importance of this exercise.[68] We mentioned earlier the TBT definition of a standard. The ISO/IEC Guide 2:2004, on the other hand, defines a standard as a

> document, established by *consensus* and approved by a *recognized* body, that provides for common and repeated use, rules, guidelines or characteristics for activities or their results, aimed at the achievement of the optimum degree of order in a given context.
>
> Note: Standards should be based on the consolidated results of science technology and experience, and aimed at the promotion of optimum community benefits.[69] (emphasis added)

Furthermore, and quite tautologically, the Guide defines as international a standard that is adopted by an international standardizing/standards organization and made available to the public.[70] Later on, the ISO/IEC Guide defines an international standardizing organization as the organization (that is, the body that is based in the membership of other bodies or individuals and has an *established constitution and its own administration*) whose membership is open to the relevant national body from every country.[71] This seems to suggest that an international standard is not any different from a national standard in terms of *content*. Common and repeated use as well as fitness for purpose are important traits for both of them. What rather makes it distinct is the *nature* of the body preparing and adopting it, i.e. the *international* standardizing organization.[72]

---

consumers from unduly confusing and detailed information. Thus, both the international standard and the domestic labelling scheme pursued the same legitimate objective. Why then opt for the domestic standard when the actual objective of the TBT is convergence and harmonization through the use of *international* standards? Interestingly, it would seem to suggest that the international standard may not have been 'relevant' in the first place. Unfortunately, the Panel's findings in this respect were not appealed.

[67] *See also* Howse 2006, above n. 28, pg. 383.
[68] *Cf.* WTO 2015, para. 348.
[69] *See* ISO/IEC 2004, Art. 3.2.
[70] Echoed in the EU Regulation 1025/2012, Art. 2(1)(a). Both documents avoid the question as to whether such documents should be made available to the public for free. The latter would go against the SSOs' current business model whereby standards are documents for sale to interested parties and economic operators.
[71] *See* ISO/IEC 2004, Art. 4.3.2., in conjunction with Art. 4.2.
[72] Compare the distinction between international, European and national standard in the EU Regulation 1025/2012, Article 2(1) (a), (b) and (d).

These definitions are important and relevant for the purposes of TBT interpretation, because the introductory paragraph of Annex 1 TBT provides that terms used in it that remain undefined in the TBT should have the same meaning as in the ISO/IEC Guide 2:1991.[73] Thus, in reconstructing the definition of a relevant *international* standard for TBT purposes, one would need to take elements from both the TBT definitions and the ISO/IEC Guide's definitions.[74]

While not offering an explicit definition of what constitutes an international standard, the TBT definition of standard in Annex 1.2 TBT also deviates from the ISO definition in that it also considers as standards for TBT purposes those documents that are not based on consensus. This is a considerate deviation,[75] as the explanatory note in Annex 1.2 TBT is clear on the TBT drafters' awareness of the fact that international standards are typically based on consensus.

Thus, in *EC – Sardines*, the Panel first and the Appellate Body later rejected the EU's argument that only standards adopted by consensus can be regarded as relevant for purposes of Article 2.4 TBT. The EU, in this case, suggested that a standard such as the Codex Stan 94 which is accepted by only 18 countries, of which only four accepted it fully, cannot be regarded as an international standard.[76] Interestingly, in order to answer the EU's claim regarding the relevance of the Codex Alimentarius standard, i.e. an *international* standard, the Appellate Body had recourse to the generic definition of standard enshrined in the last two sentences of the explanatory note of Annex 1.2 TBT. This is an ambiguous interpretive technique to construct a definition by using elements from another definition and can be problematic: arguably, this has been the case here as well.

A careful reading of the explanatory note allows two different interpretations which seem to be equally plausible. The Panel and Appellate Body in *EC – Sardines* found that the word 'also' in the last sentence makes clear that the word 'document' in the same sentence can only refer to international standards. However, a reading leading to the opposite outcome is equally possible: the explanatory note serves the role of *concretizing* the generic term of standard enclosed in Annex 1.2 TBT and not international standards.

The note refers to the two general traits of standards: their voluntary character and the method of adopting them (consensus). However, even if the one before the last sentence refers to the international standardization community, this does not change the fact that the Note is there to give flesh to the *generic* definition of standards for TBT purposes. In this respect, it is no coincidence that the Appellate Body was quite reluctant in *US – Tuna II* to revisit the analysis in *EC – Sardines*.[77]

The interpretation suggested here would have an important repercussion: if the last two sentences of the explanatory note are to be read independently, then international standards *not* adopted by consensus would not benefit from the presumption of Article 2.5 TBT. Not only would such an interpretation be in consistency with the letter and spirit of the agreement; it would also, quite importantly, be an interpretation that fully respects and takes into account the peculiarities of the international standardization world.

---

[73] Note that the relevant definitions of the ISO/IEC Guide 2 : 1991 have remained identical in the ISO/IEC Guide 2: 2004.
[74] Recall that the TBT definition of standard prevails over the ISO one as per WTO (1995, Annex 1.2).
[75] *Cf.* WTO 2002b, para. 225.
[76] *See id.* at para. 4.33.
[77] *Cf.* WTO 2015, para. 353.

6. Recognized International Standardization Bodies

Even so, interpretive challenges remain. For instance, which bodies are 'recognized standardization bodies'? Which among them constitute the 'international standardization community'? The TBT refers to 'relevant international standardizing bodies' in the Code with particular ease, as if it was clearly defined and identified.[78]

Contrary to the TBT, the SPS explicitly recognizes the international SSOs that should be deemed as relevant points of reference: the Codex Alimentarius Commission, the International Office of Epizootics (OIE); and the International Plant Protection Convention.[79] Even if the list is not exhaustive, it covers the most important international SSOs in the area of sanitary and phytosanitary issues. Importantly, all these bodies are intergovernmental organizations.

The TBT, in turn, does not have a similar provision, although one could plausibly argue that at least the ISO and IEC should be the first bodies to be regarded as having recognized activities in the area of technical standardization. A fundamental difference between the two areas of standardization is that technical standardization is in principle of private nature, organized within associations of bodies rather than intergovernmental organizations, as we explained earlier. Thus, any explicit reference to or incorporation of normative work done in an essentially private body would lie uncomfortably within an otherwise State-to-State international contract.[80]

The peculiar nature of technical standardization is also implicitly acknowledged in the TBT definition of standard. A TBT standard is typically adopted by a body, be it international, regional or central government one. In turn, the ISO/IEC Guide defines a body as a legal or administrative entity that has specific tasks and composition.[81]

Obviously, the many references to the ISO would seem to suggest that this non-governmental federation of national standards bodies belongs to the international standardization community and thus its standards are international. The same would most likely apply to IEC. Yet, other international standard-setting bodies exist as well. The Annex 1.4 TBT, consistent with the WTO legacy, defines international bodies in an open-ended manner; international are those bodies or systems whose membership is open to the relevant bodies of all Members. This is largely in line with the ISO/IEC Guide definition of an international standardizing organization. Thus a regional body which is open to only some of the Members would not fall within this definition.

---

[78] WTO 1995, Annex 3, parass G and H.
[79] WTO 1994c, Annex A.3.
[80] In *dicta*, the Appellate Body in WTO (2015) noted that, by not expressly referring to particular international SSOs, the TBT aims to encourage the development of international standards by bodies that were not already engaged in standardizing activities in the time of the entry into force of the TBT. This statement has a twofold meaning: first, it makes clear the Appellate Body's willingness to be open to assessing the capacity of new international SSOs to create relevant international standards within the meaning of WTO (1995, Art. 2.4) and thus benefit from the presumption of TBT consistency, which arguably would increase their legitimacy within the international standardization community and the multilateral trading system. Second, the Apppellate Body reminds us that such a recognition has a price, as it may be dependant on the standardizing body at issue showing that it meets the high due process criteria of the TBT Committee Decision (see *infra*). This is a responsibility *shared* by international SSOs and WTO Members participating therein. In acknowledging some 'bite' to an otherwise best-endeavour TBT provision relating to special and differential treatment (S&DT), the Appellate Body clarifies its intention in the future to make WTO Members accountable for their sincere efforts to ensure that international SSOs are organized and operated in a manner that ensures representative participation, taking the particularities of the developing countries into account. See WTO 2015, para. 379 and n. 745.
[81] See also WTO 2011b, para. 7.679. To show the diversity of bodies that can come under this definition, the ISO/IEC Guide provides that a body can be, for instance, an organization, an authority, a company or even a foundation. Thus, organizations can also be bodies, but the definition of organization under the ISO/IEC Guide is narrow. See ISO/IEC 2004, Art. 4.2. This however is not always straightforward. For instance, in *US – Tuna II*, the Appellate Body seems to have misread this. See WTO 2015, para. 356.

If, however, membership to this body is not a priori excluded vis-à-vis a particular Member or its relevant standardizing body, then under certain circumstances its standards may still be regarded as international standards for TBT purposes.

For this to happen, the body would need to be a recognized one. This is reminiscent of Article 4.3 of the ISO/IEC Guide 2:2004 which defines as standardizing those bodies that have 'recognized activities' in standardization.[82] However, the Guide does not specify what recognized activities in standardization would mean and who should recognize such activities – and the same goes for the TBT. At the same time, the Guide does specify that standardization is the activity of establishing provisions for common and repeated use, aimed at the achievement of the optimum degree of order in a given context, more particularly the activity of preparing and implementing standards. It also makes clear that a recognized body in this area can be a body that, among other rules, also promulgates standards (standardizing body), but also a body whose main function is, pursuant to its statutes, the preparation, approval or adoption of standards that are publicly available (standards body).[83] The former category is broader and it is probably no coincidence that the Code uses this broad term to also cover bodies that incidentally develop standards.

However, with respect to 'recognition', neither the Guide nor the TBT establish a quantitative benchmark. For instance, can a Member invoke as a defence against a standard that, for instance, its relevant body did not participate in the standardization activities of a given body or that, even if it participated, it objected or voted against that standard? Taking into account that consensus does not imply unanimity in the international standardization community, a critical mass of negative votes would be needed to raise doubts against the international character of a standard adopted within this setting.

In *US – Tuna II*, the Appellate Body dealt with the meaning of 'recognition'. It first found that recognition implies that Members know, or at least expect that the international body at stake is active in standardization. Furthermore, recognition would be an issue to examine on a case-by-case basis, examining evidence of recognition by Members and/or standardizing bodies at the regional, national or sub-national level. Thus, the Appellate Body avoided establishing a general test which would imply a *de minimis* rule for recognition, other than noting that 'the larger the number of countries that participate in the development of a standard, the more likely it can be said that the respective body's activities in standardization are "recognized"'.[84]

Thus, it was made clear that recognition by WTO Members, rather than the standardization community (its 'peers') would cover a broad part of the scope of recognition within the meaning of Annex 1.2 TBT. However, bodies having developed a single standard would not come outside the scope of the TBT, simply due to the fact that they do not have extensive standardization activities. Elements such as wide participation of WTO Members in the development of the standard; wide recognition of the validity and legality of the single standard; or adherence to the TBT Committee Decision of 2000 on principles for the development of international standards (the 'TBT Committee Decision')[85] would reveal a body with recognized activities in standardization.[86]

---

[82] In *US – Tuna II*, the Appellate Body found that the ISO definition of a standardizing body should assist in the interpretation of the TBT term 'recognized body'. See WTO 2015.
[83] ISO/IEC 2004, Arts. 4.3 and 4.4.
[84] WTO 2015, para. 390.
[85] See TBT Committee 2000, para. 20 and Annex 4.
[86] See WTO 2015, para. 394.

In this respect, an important argument was brought forward by Canada: Canada suggested that a recognition of activities of an international standardizing body cannot be assessed independently of the TBT Committee Decision of 2000 on principles for the development of international standards (the 'TBT Committee Decision').[87] Put differently, an international standardizing body is 'recognized' if it develops standards or engages in standardizing activities in accordance with certain recognized principles such as those developed in the TBT Committee Decision. The Appellate Body correctly agreed that evidence about adherence to the TBT Committee Decision would be relevant for determining whether the body at issue has recognized activities.[88] It is to the TBT Committee Decision that we now turn.

7. The TBT Committee Decision

Article 2.4 TBT appears to endorse international standards and international SSOs without any meaningful qualifications or conditions. It essentially transforms voluntary standards into de facto mandatory norms. This raises concerns regarding the way that such international standards are set and whether they indeed reveal international preferences and absolute technical superiority. Practice suggests that various standards fail to achieve this. In several instances, international standards were adopted with a narrow majority of the absolute number of votes and despite conflicting scientific opinions.

Take for instance the case of *EC – Sardines*, as noted previously, where a small minority of Codex Members adopted the relevant Codex standard (18 out over 150 at the time). The same goes in the case of *EC – Hormones*. The GMO standard is of course an SPS standard, but it is indicative of the concerns that international standardization may raise: the relevant Codex standard was adopted with a very narrow majority of 33 votes to 29 with 7 abstentions. Indeed the TBT Agreement, as interpreted by the WTO adjudicating bodies, endorses standards adopted by international SSBs without examining their representativeness, comprehensiveness, or process of adoption. Can standards of this type be accepted as 'international' without running counter to any conceivable notion of fairness?

In 2000, the TBT Committee, which is responsible for the implementation of the TBT, adopted a decision during the TBT Second Triennial Review incorporating six principles and procedures that should be observed during the development of international standards. It was generally felt more input from a wider set of interests was needed in the international standardization community. According to the dominant view, bodies operating with open, impartial and transparent procedures that afforded a fair opportunity for consensus among interested parties in all WTO Members would most likely prepare effective and relevant standards.[89] Clearly the TBT Committee Decision constituted a broader observation by WTO Members that rules and procedures within international SSOs needed to improve and strengthen. Clearly, it was an external call for reform of the international standardization community practices.[90]

The principles identified in the TBT Committee decision are: transparency; openness; impartiality and consensus; effectiveness and relevance; coherence; and addressing the concerns of developing countries. In *EC – Sardines*, the EU alleged that the Codex

---

[87] See TBT Committee 2000, para. 20 and Annex 4.
[88] See WTO 2015, para. 376.
[89] See TBT Committee 2001, p. 12.
[90] Cf. WTO 2015, para. 371 and n. 736.

Alimentarius standard at issue was not a 'relevant international standard' because it was not adopted by consensus and thus was inconsistent with the principle of relevance laid down in this Decision. The Panel disagreed and stated that this Decision was not binding, but merely a 'policy statement of preference', confirming the WTO adjudicators' unwillingness to examine with a critical eye the standards development process. The findings remained unappealed for several years.

However, in the recent *US – Tuna II* decision, the Appellate Body found that the TBT Committee Decision constitutes a 'subsequent agreement' within the meaning of Article 31(3)(a) VCLT and thus should be read together with the TBT when interpreting standards-related TBT provisions.[91] The Appellate Body was led to this conclusion based on various elements such as the fact that it was adopted by consensus; it bears specifically upon the interpretation and application of a TBT provision; and Members' expressed intention to: (a) develop a better understanding of international standards within the TBT; (b) ensure the effective application of the TBT; and (c) clarify and strengthen the concept of international standards.[92]

Indeed, agreements subsequent to the conclusion of a previous agreement aiming to specify how existing rules or obligations are to be applied (rather than to create new or extend existing obligations) can fall under Article 31(3)(a) VCLT, constituting a further authentic element of interpretation to be taken into account along with context.[93] However, considering the TBT Committee Decision as 'subsequent agreement' barely squares with the *EC – Sardines* previous finding that the last sentence of the Explanatory Note in Annex 1.2 TBT also relates to international standards. Quite crucially, if consensus should not be required for a standard to be regarded as a 'relevant *international* standard', then the TBT Committee Decision, by requiring consensus, amounts to an *amendment* of the TBT text.[94]

After juxtaposing the Committee Decision principles to the standard that the Panel found to be a 'relevant international standard' within the meaning of the TBT, the Appellate Body reversed the Panel's finding because the standard-setting body at issue was not open to at least all Members, as participation was possible by invitation only. In a clear message towards international SSOs, the Appellate Body found that standardization bodies must be open and

---

[91] VCLT 1969, Art. 31 (*General rule of interpretation*) provides:
1. A treaty shall be interpreted in good faith in accordance with the ordinary meaning to be given to the terms of the treaty in their context and in the light of its object and purpose.
2. The context for the purpose of the interpretation of a treaty shall comprise, in addition to the text, including its preamble and annexes:
    (a) any agreement relating to the treaty which was made between all the parties in connection with the conclusion of the treaty;
    (b) any instrument which was made by one or more parties in connection with the conclusion of the treaty and accepted by the other parties as an instrument related to the treaty.
3. There shall be taken into account, together with the context:
    (a) *any subsequent agreement between the parties regarding the interpretation of the treaty or the application of its provisions*; (emphasis added)

[92] WTO 2015, paras 371–72.
[93] *Cf.* WTO 2008b, para. 391; and WTO 2012b, para. 265.
[94] Interestingly, this goes against the letter and spirit of the WTO treaty. We find contextual support in WTO (1994b, Article IX.2) prohibiting the abuse of the provision relating to authoritative interpretation to undermine the amendment provisions in WTO (1994b, Article X). *Cf.* WTO 2008b, para. 383. By the same token, Decisions by WTO organs (such as the TBT Committee) cannot be used to circumvent the amendment provisions of the WTO. We believe that this is yet another indication that decoupling the last two sentences of the Explanatory Note so that its last sentence only refers to domestic and regional standard is the only reasonable interpretation of this provision.

transparent at every stage of standards development, thereby demonstrating the potential 'bite' of the WTO as an *ex post* arbiter of the legitimacy of standards.[95]

Tuna II should be assessed within its specific context: it was confined to a discussion of practices and institutional structures of a *regional* standardizing body, whereas it discussed shortly only one out of the six principles identified in the TBT Committee Decision. Even so, *Tuna II* marks a shift from previous rulings where international standards were endorsed without examining under which procedural and substantive safeguards international SSOs had elaborated them. It demonstrates the WTO's incipient determination to delve into the very essence of the international standardization processes.

Nevertheless, it is argued that the principles set out in the TBT Committee decision are not sufficiently inclusive. From a normative point of view, for a standard to be regarded as a genuinely international standard, additional, but at the same time more concrete criteria may need to be developed to reflect concerns about adequate levels of participation, transparency, coherence and relevance. In this respect, a new and more comprehensive conceptual framework could be developed to assess the international character of international standards.[96] This new framework could be inspired from more recent work on good regulatory practices (including transparency, participation, deliberation, impact assessment and periodic review), development and sustainability. At the same time, however, any additional requirements or interference with the technical standardization world, notably when safety concerns may not be that apparent, would have to be fair and balanced so that dynamic efficiency gains and innovation incentives continue to be in place to make sure that fair and non-discriminatory returns exist which allow for the innovation spiral to continue apace.

CONCLUSION

With its presumption of consistency when relevant international standards are used as a basis for domestic regulations, the TBT shows undue deference to the international standardization regimes. WTO cases where standards were used to defeat national regulatory autonomy have led to serious questions about the legitimacy of these regimes and their standards. By initially applying narrowly the TBT and the ensuing TBT Committee Decision, the WTO adjudicating bodies have legitimized certain standards which do not reflect a critical mass of international preferences and thus should not be used as reference points or benchmarks because of certain deficiencies identified in the process of their adoption.

In what preceded, we showed that the erosion of State consent in international law and the transfer of power to technocrats can sometimes lead to absurd results which are in dire need of being mapped and addressed. International standard-setting is emblematic of such challenges. Anecdotal evidence suggests that international standard-setters often behave as a de facto intractable club, excluding voices which increasingly seek to be heard in such fora. There are examples demonstrating the political imbalances that create distortions and elitist standards. However, demands for more openness and representativeness that come from emerging economies and other developing countries suggest that the current formation of regulatory-making in this arena reflects anachronistic international geopolitics and can no longer hold. Power is now more equally distributed among the nations of the world. Such redistribution has to be reflected

---

[95] *See* WTO 2015, para. 382.
[96] *See also* '"Relevant International Standards" and "Recognized Standardization Bodies" under the TBT Agreement' in Delimatsis 2015.

within international organizations as well, notably those that may have substantial effects on the economic emancipation and welfare of a given country. At the same time, investment in R&D and innovation is a prerequisite if less advanced players want to benefit from reformed standard-setting processes. To be sure, important IP-related issues would need to be part of the equation that strives to bring more equality in the ecology of international technical standardization.

US – Tuna II can herald a new era of more transparent and open international standard-setting. The jurisprudential shift towards more critical thinking about the activities of the international standardization community certainly affects international SSOs such as the International Organization for Standardization (ISO) or the Codex Alimentarius Commission (CAC), which are interested in remaining relevant for the trade regulation regime. Additionally, their reputation may suffer if their standard-setting practices are found to lack legitimacy.

More empirical research is needed to develop analytical tools and heuristic devices which would objectively assess the mechanics of international standard-setting and, if needed, make the case for institutional reform within international SSOs with a view to increasing deliberation, representativeness, openness, transparency, due process and accountability without jeopardizing economic progress and technological innovation. This possibility is not merely theoretical: arguably, the interpretation of the *COOL* Panel as to when a standard constitutes an effective and appropriate means for achieving a legitimate objective may indeed go in that direction – a lock, stock and barrel interpretation of the message conveyed by the Appellate Body in *US – Tuna II*.

2

Government Use of Standards in the United States and Abroad

*Emily S. Bremer**

A.	Government Use of Standards in the United States	29
	1. The U.S. Standardization System	29
	2. U.S. Standards Law and Policy	32
B.	Government Use of Standards in the European Union	35
	1. The European Standardization System	35
	2. EU Standards Law and Policy	37

Worldwide, the vast majority of standards are developed by private or nongovernmental standards development organizations. These standards are used by many different people and entities across all sectors of industry, ensuring smooth functioning of the economy, facilitating technological advancement, and protecting public health and safety. Standards are also frequently used by local, state, and national governments, usually in accord with established legal and policy frameworks. These frameworks frequently contemplate some degree of governmental participation in the standards development process and also enable government agencies and officials to use the resulting standards to support both procurement and regulatory activities. In procurement, the standards allow governments to describe with specificity the materials and products they need to purchase. In regulation, governments use standards to serve a more varied array of purposes, including protecting public health and safety by giving voluntary standards the force of law, integrating public regulatory requirements with private standards regimes, specifying the technical details of regulatory requirements, and helping government officials to evaluate regulatory compliance and enforce the law.

This chapter explores the legal and policy frameworks that the U.S. federal government and the EU institutions have established to facilitate government use of standards. Although the private standardization systems in the United States and Europe have much in common, they are also different in key respects that reflect each polity's unique history and political reality. These differences affect the structure and operation of the legal and policy frameworks that each government has established to guide and control its use of standards. Understanding each government's standards framework thus requires an understanding of the underlying standardization system that the policy has been designed to accommodate. This chapter accordingly

---

* This chapter draws liberally from Bremer (2016).

explores each polity's standardization system before explaining the basic contours of its legal and policy framework for government use of standards.

A. GOVERNMENT USE OF STANDARDS IN THE UNITED STATES

1. *The U.S. Standardization System*

In the United States, standards are developed through a nongovernmental standardization system that is predominately private, highly decentralized, and market-based. This system is large, diverse, and productive. Standards are typically developed by non-profit organizations, including pure standards development organizations (e.g., ASTM International), trade associations (e.g., the American Petroleum Institute (API)), and professional societies (e.g., the American Society of Mechanical Engineers (ASME)), as well as (increasingly) by non-traditional standards development bodies, such as consortia (e.g., the World Wide Web Consortium (W3C)).[1] These organizations convene and administer the work of "technical committees," through which standards are developed according to established procedures. Each technical committee generally has a subject-matter based jurisdiction and is composed of volunteers who work in or with the affected industry and who possess the technical expertise necessary to contribute to standards development. For example, ASTM International's Committee F 37 "addresses issues related to design, performance, quality acceptance tests, and safety monitoring for light sport aircraft." Twice a year, the approximately 175 members of this committee convene and attend two to three days of technical meetings, during which the standards are developed.[2] The committee is divided into seven subcommittees and has jurisdiction over a portfolio of more than 36 standards, including F2564-14 Standard Specification for Design and Performance of a Light Sport Glider[3] and F2316-12(2014) Standard Specification for Airframe Emergency Parachutes.[4]

Although available estimates vary, the U.S. standardization system is enormous by any measure. Baron and Spulber, who do not confine their attention to the U.S. standardization system, have estimated that there are approximately 1,000 standards organizations, which create tens of thousands of standards every year.[5] The American National Standards Institute (ANSI), which focuses more particularly on domestic U.S. standards development activities, has estimated that there are more than 600 standards development organizations and approximately 100,000 active standards in use throughout the United States.[6] Standards development activity is not equitably distributed across the many standards development organizations, however, as some organizations are significantly more active than others. Reflecting this reality, ANSI has estimated that the 20 largest U.S. standards development organizations are responsible for producing about 90 percent of all technical standards in the United States.[7]

The determination of which standards should be developed or maintained is highly decentralized in the U.S. standards system.[8] These decisions are made independently by the individual standards development organizations, as are determinations about the timing of standards development and updating. Most standards are updated approximately every two to

---

[1] For an extensive discussion of the standardization "ecosystem" see companion volume, Chapter 2.
[2] ASTM 2018b.
[3] ASTM 2018e.
[4] ASTM 2018f.
[5] Baron & Spulber 2018, 2.
[6] ANSI 2018f.
[7] ANSI 2018b.
[8] Bremer 2013a, 183–99.

five years, depending on market forces, technological evolution, and the ever-changing needs of industry. Although most standards development organizations set a schedule for reviewing and revising their standards, they typically update the standards as frequently as is necessary to respond to changing circumstances. In the U.S. system, there is no state, local, or federal government entity or other centralized coordinator that has the authority to command a standards development organization to develop or maintain a particular standard. As further explained below, when a federal agency needs a technical standard to flesh out regulatory requirements, it ordinarily selects among available standards that have already been privately developed. In rare instances, a federal agency may ask a standards development organization it works with regularly to create a new standard or revise an old standard to address an issue that has been revealed to the agency through its program and enforcement activities. More broadly, "where no suitable voluntary consensus standards exist, an agency may … solicit interest from qualified standards development organizations for development of a standard."[9] Regardless of the reasons, agency requests for a standards development organization to develop a specific standard are just that: requests. They are not mandatory. They are also the exception, not the norm.

Nor does the U.S. standardization system have any centralized coordinator outside government that has the authority to direct the activities of the many individual U.S. standards development organizations. The American National Standards Institute (ANSI), a non-profit organization created in 1918 through public–private collaboration,[10] does have an important role as the "administrator and coordinator" of the U.S. standards development system. But this role does not entail centralized control of the standards development process. Rather, ANSI administrates and coordinates the U.S. standards system by sharing information and accrediting the procedures of standards development organizations based on their conformity to ANSI's *Essential Requirements* for the development of voluntary consensus standards.[11] ANSI does not control or direct the activities of U.S. standards developers and is not responsible for determining what standards should be created or maintained.

Although U.S. federal agencies may participate in private standards development activities, they do so on the same footing as other, private sector participants. Indeed, U.S. law generally encourages agencies to participate in the work of relevant technical committees, while also imposing safeguards to prevent agencies from exerting too much influence over the standards development process. Like private businesses and entities, agencies participate in standards development by assigning individual employees with the appropriate technical expertise to participate in a technical committee's work. In some cases, an agency may be legally required to so participate.[12] For example, the Federal Emergency Management Agency (FEMA) is statutorily required to "support the development, promulgation, and updating … of national voluntary consensus standards for the performance, use, and validation of equipment used by … emergency response providers."[13] And the Department of Energy is required to participate in and support the development of certain efficiency-promoting building standards.[14] Even in the absence of a mandate, U.S. law authorizes agencies to pay the costs for their own employees to participate in appropriate standards development activities. Federal law and policy caution that

[9] Bremer 2013a, 155; OMB 2016, 20 (¶ 5(d)).
[10] For a discussion of the historical development of ANSI, see companion volume, Chapter 9.
[11] ANSI 2018a.
[12] 15 U.S.C. §§ 1193(g) & (h), 1262(f), (g), & (h), 2054(a)(4).
[13] 6 U.S.C. § 747.
[14] 42 U.S.C. § 16194.

"agency representatives should avoid the practice or the appearance of undue influence relating to their participation in standards bodies and activities."[15]

Administration of the U.S. standardization system is privately, not publicly, financed. Individual standards development organizations are responsible for funding their own standards development activities and generally do not receive financial support from the government.[16] The organizations typically obtain the necessary funding using one or more of three basic approaches. First, the organizations assert copyright in the standards they produce, and many rely on the revenue generated by the sale of their standards to fund the standards development process.[17] The resulting barrier to free online public access to the standards that are later used by government in legally binding regulations has caused much controversy in the United States.[18] The second approach is to fund standards development activities using revenue obtained through the collection of organizational membership fees. This approach is perhaps most common among the trade organizations and professional societies that (among other things) develop standards.[19] Third (and less prominently), some organizations receive charitable contributions that can help to cover the costs of standards development. For example, the Internet Engineering Task Force (IETF) is the principal worldwide developer of standards and protocols for the Internet. IETF is currently operated as an organized activity of the Internet Society (ISOC), a non-profit corporation that solicits charitable contributions for various purposes, including to support IETF activity. Each of these approaches has pros and cons, and the standards development organizations often use them in combination.

Just as the costs of administering the standards development process are borne privately, so too are the costs of participating in the technical committees' work. As noted above, standards development organizations provide logistical support to their technical committees, which are composed of individual experts who work in or with the relevant industry and volunteer their time to participate in standards development. These individuals, or their employers, also pay any costs associated with their participation (e.g., travel costs, membership fees). These costs can be significant. One case study concluded that, over a 12-month period ending in May 2003, the direct cost of participant travel for ASTM's F37 Committee totaled $194,098, while the value of the time volunteers contributed to the committee's activities was $834,880. These costs were in addition to the $124,744 in administrative costs covered by ASTM International.[20] Overall, the work of this one technical committee required a total of $1,153,722 in costs paid by private persons and entities. Although the U.S. federal government does not fund or subsidize private participation in standards development, some standards development organizations voluntarily provide subsidies or other cost-reducing measures to facilitate the participation of representatives of interests that face funding limitations.[21] This promotes a balance of interests in the standards development process by enabling the participation of those representing interests that might not otherwise have a voice in the process (e.g., consumer advocates).

Standards developed by U.S. standards development organizations are voluntary, although they may subsequently acquire some degree of persuasive or even coercive effect. The standards are voluntary in that members of private industry can choose whether or not to conform to the

---

[15] OMB 2016, 28.
[16] Büthe & Mattli 2011, 155; Breitenberg 2009, 29.
[17] Bremer 2013a, 155.
[18] *See* Chapters 5 and 6; Bremer 2013a; Bremer 2015; Mendelson 2014; Strauss 2013.
[19] Bremer 2015, 309–13.
[20] ASTM 2018a.
[21] Bremer 2013a; Olshefsky & Hugo 2003.

standards. Market forces, contractual relationships, and common law usage of the standards may restrict this choice as a practical matter, providing compelling reasons for members of industry to use the standards.[22] And in some cases, local, state, and federal government entities give formal legal effect to the standards by adopting them as law or incorporating them by reference into rules or regulations. This distinction between adoption qua law and the incorporation by reference of extrinsic standards can have profound consequences for the continuing degree of copyright protection afforded to the code or standard so used by government.[23] From the perspective of private industry, however, the principal consequence is to make conformity to the standards mandatory. At the federal level, U.S. agency use of standards to support regulatory activities is frequently accomplished via the standards' "incorporation by reference" into legally binding regulations. This and other federal government uses of standards are governed by federal standards law and policy, to which the next section turns.

2. U.S. Standards Law and Policy

U.S. federal standards law and policy provide a framework for government use of standards that is designed to accommodate and fit with the private, decentralized, and market-based nature of the U.S. standardization system. The framework first emerged in the late 1970s and today is embodied in the National Technology Transfer and Advancement Act of 1995 (NTTAA) and Office of Management and Budget (OMB) Circular A-119.[24] The NTTAA generally requires agencies to use privately developed voluntary consensus standards "to carry out policy objectives or activities"[25] unless doing so "is inconsistent with applicable law or otherwise impractical."[26] As the statutory language suggests, this requirement extends to all agency activities, including both procurement and regulation. If an agency decides to create its own, "government-unique" standard instead of using an available private standard, it must report and explain its decision to the National Institute of Standards and Technology (NIST), a non-regulatory component agency of the Department of Commerce[27] that has substantial responsibility for facilitating the implementation of federal standards law and policy.[28] Among other things, NIST is responsible for preparing an annual report on U.S. government standards activities, including agency decisions to create government-unique standards. It transmits this annual report to Congress through the OMB.[29] If there is no voluntary consensus standard available to serve an agency's need, however, the agency may develop its own standard without triggering the reporting requirement. Thus, for example, the Environmental Protection Agency (EPA) is one of the largest developers of standards used in federal regulations, but it rarely reports its standards development activity because there usually is not a private standard available that meets the agency's needs.[30]

U.S. standards policy does not regulate the internal operations of standards development organizations, but it indirectly influences the standards development process by extending the requirement for agencies to use available private standards only to those standards that have

---

[22] Bremer 2015, 308–09.
[23] *Veeck* (5th Cir. 2002).
[24] NTTAA 1996, § 12(d); OMB 2016; ACUS 1979; Hamilton 1978, 1379–86.
[25] NTTAA 1996, § 12(d)(1).
[26] NTTAA 1996, § 12(d)(3).
[27] 15 U.S.C. § 1511(3).
[28] Bremer 2013a, 188–90.
[29] NTTAA 1996, § 12(d)(3); OMB 2016, ¶¶ 9, 10, 11.
[30] NIST 2018.

been developed through a voluntary consensus process.[31] The framework defines voluntary consensus standards[32] as those which have been developed through: (i) an open process; (ii) in which the participants represent a balance of interests; (iii) due process is respected; (iv) an appeals process is provided; and (v) the resulting standards reflect a consensus among the participants.[33] In this context "consensus" means "general agreement, but not necessarily unanimity," achieved "using fair, impartial, open, and transparent processes" that ensure "comments and objections are considered."[34] Individual agencies are responsible for determining whether the process used to develop a particular standard meets these requirements. This responsibility may be more easily discharged if the standard in question is an American National Standard, a designation indicating that ANSI has accredited the standard developer's process as conforming to ANSI's *Essential Requirements* of voluntary consensus standards.[35] Although the NTTAA and Circular A-119 establish a preference for agencies to use voluntary consensus standards,[36] process is not the sole determinant of whether a standard can or will be used in regulation. NIST advises agencies to select a standard for government use based on both procedural considerations and the standard's substantive "fit for purpose." Agencies are permitted to use private standards that are not voluntary consensus standards if those standards offer a greater fit for purpose.

The principal way agencies use private standards to support regulatory activities is by giving the standards legal force by incorporating them by reference in federal regulations.[37] In all cases, the federal agency has the authority and responsibility to determine the regulatory requirements. An incorporated standard "may provide detail, but a regulation should, by itself, make the basic concept of the rule understandable without the need for the reader to refer to the incorporated material."[38] Although regulatory incorporation by reference is common, it affects only a very small percentage of all private standards.[39] A previous case study of standards incorporated by reference in federal pipeline regulations is illustrative. Most of the standards used in those regulations (73 percent) were created by just three organizations: API, ASTM International, and ASME International.[40] Yet the standards represented only a small fraction – 3.7 percent, one-tenth of 1 percent, and 2 percent – of the respective standards development organization's overall standards portfolio.[41]

A provision of the Freedom of Information Act (FOIA) provides the legal definition of regulatory "incorporation by reference." Under FOIA, agencies are required to publish certain kinds of materials, including legally binding regulations, in the *Federal Register*, a daily publication created to serve as a central repository of federal executive and administrative pronouncements.[42] Publication is intended to provide constructive notice to regulated parties.[43] Legally binding regulations are first published in the *Federal Register* and subsequently appear in the *Code of Federal Regulations*, a special edition of the *Federal Register* that is intended to

---

[31] NTTAA 1996, § 12(d)(1); OMB 2016, ¶¶ 2(d), 2(e).
[32] OMB 2016, ¶ 2(d), 5(b).
[33] OMB 2016, ¶¶ 2(e)(i)–(v).
[34] OMB 2016, ¶ 2(e)(v).
[35] ANSI 2018a.
[36] OMB 2016, ¶ 5(b).
[37] Bremer 2013a, 145–53.
[38] ACUS 2011, 2259 (¶ 15).
[39] Bremer 2015, 306.
[40] *Id.* at 306–07.
[41] *Id.* at 307.
[42] Griswold 1934; Note 1966.
[43] 5 USC. § 552(a); *Fed. Crop. Ins. Corp. v. Merrill*, 332 U.S. 380, 385 (1947).

provide a compact, practical, and orderly codification of agency pronouncements of general applicability and legal effect.[44] If an agency does not fulfill the publication requirement, it will be prevented from enforcing the non-published material against any person or entity that did not have actual notice of the material in question.[45] For purposes of this non-publication sanction, however, material incorporated by reference in the *Federal Register* is "deemed published" if it is "reasonably available to the class of persons affected" and the Director of the Office of the Federal Register (OFR) has approved the incorporation.[46] OFR regulations and guidance establish the procedures and requirements agencies must follow to secure approval to incorporate by reference.[47]

In addition to these publication requirements, agencies must observe "notice-and-comment" procedures when adopting legally binding or "legislative" rules,[48] and these requirements also have unique implications for the regulatory use of standards. In brief, the Administrative Procedure Act (APA) requires agencies to publish a notice of proposed rulemaking and offer a period during which the public can submit comments on the proposal before finalizing the regulations by publishing a final rule.[49] OMB Circular A-119 and OFR's incorporation by reference regulations prohibit "dynamic incorporations," which direct regulated parties to conform to the "current" or "most recent" edition of a standard. Thus, agencies must identify the specific version of the standard they are incorporating by reference in a regulation.[50] When a new version of an incorporated standard becomes available, an agency must typically conduct another notice-and-comment rulemaking in order to update the regulatory reference.[51] These requirements make it challenging for agencies to keep regulations up to date as new versions of incorporated standards become available. But the requirements also promote clarity and ensure that agencies retain primary responsibility for determining whether, to what extent, and in what circumstances a particular private standard is appropriate for regulatory use.

U.S. agencies also use private standards in other ways that do not involve giving the standards formal legal effect. In procurement, agencies often use private standards as a way of precisely identifying the qualities of the goods or services they are seeking or have contracted to purchase. In the regulatory context, agencies use standards in a variety of ways. In some cases, an agency may identify a private standard as a regulatory safe harbor, such that conformity with the identified standard may earn regulated parties a presumption of regulatory compliance, but alternative approaches to demonstrating compliance are also permitted. Although conformity to standards so used is not formally mandatory, courts have identified regulatory safe harbors as necessarily legislative in character, a classification that triggers the APA's procedural and publication requirements.[52] In other cases, agencies may use standards in voluntary programs, as the Department of Energy and the EPA do in the Energy Star Program.[53] Finally, agencies sometimes use standards passively when they choose not to regulate based on a determination that

---

[44] 5 C.F.R. §§ 8.1(a), 8.2.
[45] 5 USC. § 552(a)(1); *Appalachian Power Co.* (4th Cir. 1977, p. 457).
[46] 5 USC. § 552(a)(1).
[47] 5 C.F.R. pt. 51; OFR 2017.
[48] 5 U.S.C. § 553.
[49] 5 U.S.C. § 553.
[50] 1 C.F.R. § 51.1(f); OFR 2017; Bremer 2013a, 184–86.
[51] Bremer 2013a, 137, 184.
[52] *Cohen* (D.C. Cir. 2009, p. 9); *Ctr. for Auto Safety* (D.C. Cir. 2006, pp. 809–10); *Nat'l Ass'n of Home Builders* (D.C. Cir. 2005, p. 15); *Gen. Elec. Co.* (D.C. Cir. 2002, p. 383); Bremer 2016, 365.
[53] 42 U.S.C. § 6294a. Energy Star is a voluntary governmental certification program that is jointly administered by the EPA and the Department of Energy and is designed to encourage energy efficiency. ENERGY STAR 2018.

there is sufficient conformity throughout the marketplace to a private standard that adequately protects the public interest or safety.[54] The framework for government use of standards that is embodied in the NTTAA and OMB Circular A-119 applies to all of these various U.S. federal agency activities.

B. GOVERNMENT USE OF STANDARDS IN THE EUROPEAN UNION

1. *The European Standardization System*

There is much in common between the U.S. and European standardization systems. As in the United States, standards in Europe are typically developed through the work of technical committees that are administered by the standards development organizations and composed of unpaid volunteers drawn from industry. Each committee typically has jurisdiction over a specific subject area, with the composition of the committees reflecting the organization of private sector industry. In addition, standards development in European nations is intended to be market-driven and responsive to evolving technologies and the ever-changing needs of industry. As the European Commission has explained, "[i]t is essential that the European standardization system should respond readily and appropriately to differing market needs in different sectors."[55] Finally, as in the United States, the standards developed through the European standardization system are voluntary.[56] At the national level, a government may make a previously developed standard mandatory by referencing it in regulation,[57] although standards given such effect have long been regulated by European Community restrictions designed to promote the free movement of goods and to protect competition.[58]

The principal distinguishing characteristic of the European standardization system is a much closer relationship between government and the standards development organizations. Historically, each national government has recognized a single, national standards body that is responsible for standardization across all economic sectors. In addition, some nations have recognized a national electrotechnical standards body. These organizations "predate the formal establishment of national standards institutions,"[59] and have thus been able to retain a separate identity and operational independence from the general national standards bodies.[60] The mechanisms used to create or identify the national standards development organizations vary across Europe. At one extreme are those nations, such as Portugal and Greece, in which the national standards body is a department within the government.[61] The more common approach, however, has been for each national government to officially recognize a single, nongovernmental organization as the exclusive developer of that nation's technical standards. This recognition may be conveyed via a contractual relationship between the State and the institution (as in Germany or the United Kingdom) or through public regulation (as in France, Italy, and Spain).[62] For example, the British government has officially recognized the British Standards

---

[54] 15 U.S.C. §§ 2056(b)(1), 2058(b).
[55] European Commission 2003, 9.
[56] *Knooble* (2012 Neth.); Delaney & van de Zande 200, 3, 11; Nicolas 1994, 16–17, 90.
[57] European Commission 1992, 7–8.
[58] Schepel & Falke 2000, 55.
[59] Nicolas 1994, 26.
[60] Schepel & Falke 2000, 61–62.
[61] Schepel & Falke 2000, 69, 70.
[62] Nicolas 1994, 25; Schepel & Falke 2000, 71–81.

Institute (BSI) as *the* developer of its national standards, a position that was initially solidified through Royal Charters granted in the 1920s.[63]

The ultimate consequence of the European approach is that, "[i]n stark contrast to the American system, standardization in European countries is hierarchical, coordinated, and regulated."[64] Most European nations have only one or two official standards development organizations. This is far different from the U.S. standardization system, in which decentralization and private control have promoted the proliferation of hundreds of standards development organizations. Another implication of the hierarchical, coordinated structure created by the sole recognition of national standards bodies is that the standards that emerge from the system, although voluntary, are generally considered to be "national standards" without any subsequent action or endorsement by government authorities. In essence, that endorsement has already been provided on the front end, with the government's official recognition of *the* national standards organization.

The nation-centric, institutionally based character of the European standardization system is further entrenched by the fact that national standardization organizations are ordinarily responsible for representing the interests of the nation's stakeholders in regional and international standards development processes. Indeed, international standardization is patterned off the European model.[65] Thus, for example, the members of the International Organization for Standardization (ISO) "are the foremost standards organizations in their countries and there is only one member per country. Individuals or companies cannot become ISO members."[66] When U.S. interests participate in ISO, they must conform to this model. As a result, ANSI represents U.S. stakeholders in ISO, despite that it is neither a traditional standards development organization nor a national standards organization in the European sense.[67]

National governments in Europe also typically provide significant financial support for private standards development activities. This includes public funding for the standards development process, although the national standards organizations also derive funding from other, non-public sources, such as membership fees, industry donations, and revenue generated through the sale of standards and other services.[68] In addition to providing subsidies directly to their standards organizations, public authorities in European nations often provide financial assistance to small businesses and noncommercial interests (e.g., consumer groups) to ensure their participation in the work of the technical committees.[69] This helps to promote a balance of interests in the standards development process and thereby contributes to the legitimacy of the resulting standards.

In exchange for providing public financing, national governments also regulate the internal operations of their national standards bodies. Thus, for example, the national standards organizations are usually subject to rules requiring the participation of representatives of a broad array of interests, including "public authorities and ministerial departments," in the technical committees.[70] In addition, the national standards organizations must generally "comply with comprehensive rules on public enquiry and publication."[71] For example, although the technical

---

[63] Büthe & Mattli 2011, 153.
[64] Büthe & Mattli 2011, 151.
[65] Nicolas 1994, 24.
[66] ISO 2018a (emphasis removed).
[67] ANSI 2018e.
[68] Schepel & Falke 2000, 89–90.
[69] Büthe & Mattli 2011, 154–55.
[70] Schepel & Falke 2000, 64.
[71] Büthe & Mattli 2011, 154.

committees are responsible for drafting the standards, those drafts generally must be circulated for public comment prior to the standards' adoption. As with the formal recognition of the national standards bodies, the various regulations governing the national standards bodies' operations and the standards development process may be found either in contracts between the State and the organization or in public regulations.

2. EU Standards Law and Policy

The EU's legal framework for government use of standards reflects and embraces the hierarchical, coordinated, and institution-focused nature of the European standardization system. Under EU law, the core of which is Regulation No. 1025/2012 of the European Parliament and of the Council, the only standards eligible for government use in procurement or regulation are "European standards," which are institutionally defined.[72] That is, "European standards" are standards adopted by one of the three officially recognized European standards development organizations: the Comité Européen de Normalisation (European Committee for Standardization or CEN), the Comité Européen de Normalisation Electrotechnique (European Committee for Electrotechnical Standardization or CENELEC), and the European Telecommunications Standards Institute (ETSI).[73] This approach reflects that which has long dominated at the national level, including by reflecting the traditional division between general and electrotechnical standardization. Regulation No. 1025/2012 delegates to the Commission the authority to "update the list of European standardisation organizations set out in Annex I to take into account changes in their name or structure," but not to recognize additional standards organizations.[74]

The institutional focus of the EU framework is also evident in the regulation's definitions of "international standards" and "national standards." "International standards" are those developed by certain recognized organizations headquartered in Geneva: ISO, the International Electrotechnical Commission (IEC), and the International Telecommunication Union (ITU).[75] Finally, the law defines "national standard" as "a standard adopted by a national standardisation body" that has been officially recognized as such by the appropriate national government.[76] Each member state is required to notify the Commission of the identity of its national standardization body, and the Commission publishes the resulting list of recognized standardization bodies.[77] EU law charges these organizations with the responsibility of facilitating access to standards and the standards development process for the stakeholders from their nation, including small and medium enterprises (SMEs).[78]

The development of the standards that are used to support EU legislation is substantially government-driven. The EU institutions have concluded that "[t]he viability of the cooperation between the Commission and the European standardisation system depends on careful planning of further [Commission] requests for the development of standards."[79] Indeed, "[t]he

---

[72] European Commission 2012, art. 1. A modest exception is made for information and communications technology (ICT) standards, when those standards are used in procurement and "primarily to enable interoperability." *Id.* art. 13(1), annex II.
[73] European Commission 2012, art. 2(1)(b), art. 2(8) & annex I.
[74] European Commission 2012, art. 20(a).
[75] European Commission 2012, p. 12, art. 2(1)(a) & art. 2(9).
[76] European Commission 2012, art. 2(1)(d) & art. 2(10).
[77] European Commission 2012, art. 2(10) & art. 27; *see also* European Commission 2017.
[78] European Commission 2012, art. 6.
[79] European Commission 2012, p. 27.

Commission plays a key role in planning and initiating standardization," including by issuing standardization requests and identifying voluntary standards that may be used to support EU legislation.[80] When EU primary legislation requires the use of a standard, the Commission typically issues a request to one or more of the three European standardization organizations to draft an appropriate standard by a specified deadline.[81] Until Regulation 1025/2012 was adopted in 2012, the Commission's standards requests were called "mandates."[82] Although the terminology has changed, the process has remained substantially the same, and the old terminology continues to be used in some contexts.

Beyond the initiation of standardization, EU standards law and policy preserves a substantial role for government in determining the content and operation of European standards, while simultaneously promoting market-based standards. Regulation 1025/2012 provides that standards "shall be market-driven, take into account the public interest as well as the policy objectives clearly stated in the Commission's request and based on consensus."[83] Meanwhile, the Commission's request and the legislation according to which that request has been issued establish the "essential requirements" that the content of the standard must satisfy. After the standard has been developed, the European standardization organization and the Commission determine whether the standard meets the relevant essential requirements.[84] If it does, the Commission references the standard in the *Official Journal of the European Union*.[85] Once referenced, the standard becomes a "harmonised standard," which is defined as "a European standard adopted on the basis of a request made by the Commission for the application of Union harmonisation legislation."[86]

Public financing is ordinarily provided to the European standardization organization that accepts a standardization request from the EU Commission.[87] Although the law provides that financing "may" be provided, in practice, such financing is almost always provided, and European standardization organizations have been known to condition their acceptance of a request on the availability of the necessary funding. According to the Commission, the overall amount of public financing provided to the European standardization system has remained stable at approximately €20 million annually.[88] The EU's framework also provides for public financing of a wide variety of European standardization activities. This is accomplished through direct grants to European standardization organizations for preparatory, ancillary, and core standards development work, as well as through public financing for other stakeholder representatives to participate in standards development.[89] This helps to promote the participation of potentially underrepresented interests, such as SMEs.

EU standards law and policy also directly regulates the internal operations of European standards development organizations, from agenda-setting to standards development procedures to reporting requirements. With respect to agenda-setting, each European and national standardization organization is required to publish an annual "work programme" that provides information about all the standards it plans to develop or amend in the coming year.[90] This requirement

---

[80] European Commission 2018.
[81] European Commission 2012, art. 10(1).
[82] European Commission 2012; European Commission 2018.
[83] European Commission 2012, art. 10(1).
[84] European Commission 2012, art. 10(5).
[85] European Commission 2012, art. 10(6).
[86] European Commission 2012, art. 1(c).
[87] European Commission 2012, art.15(1)(a).
[88] European Commission 2018.
[89] European Commission 2012, art. 15, 16, & 17.
[90] European Commission 2012, art. 3(1)–(3).

extends beyond the standardization activities undertaken in response to Commission requests and applies to national as well as European standardization organizations. In addition, "[t]he Commission shall adopt an annual Union work programme for European standardisation which shall identify strategic priorities for European standardisation, taking into account Union long-term strategies for growth."[91] This program must also identify what standards the Commission intends to request during the covered period. In developing standards, the European standardization organizations are required to observe procedures that are designed to ensure openness, transparency, and the participation of a balance of interests.[92] Finally, the European standardization organizations are subject to annual reporting requirements.[93]

One of the key differences between the U.S. and EU standards policies is that when the EU Commission references a standard, it does not thereby give the standard formal legal effect. Rather, referenced standards *always* remain voluntary. Indeed, EU standards policy defines all "standards," including "harmonised standards," as technical specifications "with which compliance is not compulsory."[94] This point is especially important in the EU context because it protects the single market and reduces potential conflict between standardization and EU competition law. The voluntary nature of European standards means that regulated parties are free – as a formal, legal matter – to demonstrate compliance with the essential requirements of EU legislation by conforming to a standard other than that which is referenced. Regulated parties are permitted to develop their own alternative standards or may use an appropriate standard that has been developed by someone else. In all cases, however, regulated parties remain responsible for complying with the law's essential requirements and for demonstrating that conformity to the alternative standard ensures regulatory compliance.

In practice, however, the voluntary nature of referenced standards may be largely theoretical. Although European standards are technically voluntary, they often are de facto mandatory, in part because it is extremely difficult for a regulated party to demonstrate regulatory compliance by conforming to an alternative standard. Developing or identifying an adequate alternative standard and demonstrating that standard's equivalence to the referenced standard is costly. It is also very risky – there is no way for an innovative regulated party to be certain that its alternative standard will be acceptable to EU officials in the event of an enforcement action.[95] In addition, although regulated parties are formally permitted to conform to a non-referenced standard to demonstrate compliance with regulatory requirements, EU law embraces a "standstill principle" that requires the withdrawal of most other standards that might serve as viable alternatives.[96] When a European standard is issued, national standardization bodies are required to withdraw any standards they have previously adopted on the same subject matter. The same principle applies to EU legislation, restraining member states from enacting laws contrary to a newly issued EU directive during the time between the directive's enactment and its effective date.[97] The standstill principle is imposed by both the EU standards framework and the European standardization organizations' own rules.[98] It bears emphasizing that the standstill principle is *not* concerned with the essential requirements of the relevant EU legislation. Any standard in

---

[91] European Commission 2012, art. 8(1).
[92] European Commission 2012, art. 4, 5, 6, & 7.
[93] European Commission 2012, art. 24(1).
[94] European Commission 2012, art. 2(1).
[95] Büthe & Mattli 2011, 17; Majone 2000, 596.
[96] European Commission 2012, 14.
[97] *Inter-Environnement Wallonie*, C-129/96 (EU/Belgium).
[98] European Commission 2012, art. 3(6).

conflict with the newly adopted European standard must be withdrawn, regardless of whether it conflicts or fully accords with the law's essential requirements. Also, the national standards bodies are urged to use an abundance of caution in evaluating whether a standard must be retracted under the rule, likely resulting in the removal of standards that are not in any actual conflict with the newly adopted European standard or the essential requirements of the overarching EU legislation.[99] Observance of the standstill principle may thus have the effect of reducing the availability to regulated parties of alternative voluntary standards that may be fit for regulatory purpose. It also reinforces the hierarchical and coordinated nature of the European standardization system. As CEN and CENLEC have explained it, the European standardization system is "unique in the world" because "[a]fter the publication of a European Standard, each national standards body or committee is obliged to withdraw any national standard which conflicts with the new European Standard. Hence, one European Standard becomes the national standard in all the 33 member countries of CEN and/or CENELEC."[100]

CONCLUSION

There are a number of apparent similarities in how the United States and EU approach standardization and government use of standards in procurement and regulation. On both sides of the Atlantic:

- Standards are developed by private standards development organizations, which administer the work of technical committees. The jurisdiction of the various technical committees is designed to reflect the organization of private sector industry. Members of the technical committee are experts drawn from industry who volunteer their time to participate in the standards development process.
- The standards development process is designed to be market-driven and responsive to evolving technical, industrial, and commercial needs.
- The resulting standards are voluntary.
- The government has a well-established legal framework addressing government participation in private standards development and government use of the resulting standards.
- The legal framework generally requires government to use privately developed standards to meet governmental standardization needs.
- The government prefers that standards be developed using a voluntary consensus process that is designed to be fair and transparent and to ensure the participation of a broad and diverse array of interests in the standards development process.
- Standards used in regulation are "referenced" or "incorporated by reference."
- Standards are copyrighted and typically must be purchased from the standards developer for a fee.

Despite these similarities, the American and European approaches to standardization and the government's use of standards are fundamentally different in ways that reflect each government's unique history, political values, and legal commitments. In Europe, national governments established close relationships with private standards development organizations, resulting in a standardization system that, while nongovernmental, is coordinated, hierarchical, and directly regulated. EU standards law and policy embraces and replicates this model.

[99] Bremer 2016, 353.
[100] CEN/CENELEC 2018a.

The U.S. government, in contrast, historically took a more indirect and informal approach to collaborating with private standards development organizations, resulting in a nongovernmental standardization system that is highly decentralized, nonhierarchical, and market-driven. U.S. standards law and policy are designed to accommodate and promote this very different approach to standardization.

These fundamental differences between the U.S. and EU approaches to standardization and the government use of standards result in a variety of discrete distinctions between each government's framework. Some of these differences are more striking and significant than others:

- In the United States, "essential requirements" refers to ANSI's due process requirements for American National Standards. In the European Union, this term refers to the core legislative requirements that a privately developed standard must be designed to meet.
- The United States takes a process-based approach to defining the standards that may or should be used by government, while the EU takes a more rigid, institution-based approach.
  - U.S. federal agencies may use any standard that is "fit for purpose," although they are strongly encouraged to use "voluntary consensus standards." "Voluntary consensus standards" are defined as standards that have been created using a process that meets basic due process requirements, regardless of the identity of the standards development organization.
  - The EU government may only use "European standards," which are defined as standards created by one of three recognized organizations.
  - The process-institution distinction carries over into the governments' respective definitions of "international standards." The United States defines "international standards" as standards created through a process that includes representatives of interests from many different nations and used internationally.[101] The EU defines "international standards" as those created by one of three recognized international standardization bodies headquartered in Geneva.[102]
- The U.S. federal government regulates the standards development process only indirectly, through its strong preference for federal agencies to use voluntary consensus standards. The EU directly regulates the internal operations of the European standardization organizations, including by requiring them to use voluntary consensus procedures.
- U.S. federal agencies generally use available standards that individual standards development organizations have previously decided to develop in order to meet private sector needs. The EU Commission initiates the development of referenced standards by issuing requests for a European standardization organization to create a new standard that will meet the essential requirements of EU legislation.
- In the United States, federal agencies have final authority and responsibility for determining whether a standard is fit for purpose and should be used. In the EU, the European standardization organizations and the Commission appear to share, at least in some measure, the responsibility for determining whether a standard meets the law's essential requirements. The Commission may only use standards created by a recognized European standardization organization and does not have the authority to recognize additional standards development organizations.

---

[101] ANSI 2018f.
[102] European Commission 2012, art. 2(1)(a).

- The U.S. standards development process, including the participation of private sector entities and interests, is privately financed. The EU publicly finances the development of European standards, including by funding the participation of representatives of certain private stakeholders.
- U.S. federal agencies sometimes (but not always) use standards in regulation by giving the standards the force of law through regulatory incorporation by reference. In the EU, referenced standards always remain formally voluntary.

Understanding the similarities and differences between the U.S. and European approaches to standards development and the government's use of standards therefore requires careful attention to detail, history, and context. These efforts are worthwhile, not only for the general cause of international understanding and exchange, but also to facilitate trade, regulatory harmonization, and technological exchange across the Atlantic.

PART II

Standardization, Health, Safety and Liability

3

Technical Standards in Health and Safety Regulation: Risk Regimes, the New Administrative Law, and Food Safety Governance

Timothy D. Lytton

A.	Industry Guidelines and Agency Guidance	46
B.	Marketing Agreements and Government Regulations	50
C.	The Role of Private Standards and Conformity Assessment in Risk Regimes	54
D.	Concerns about the Legitimacy of Private Governance	56
E.	The Administrative Law of Private Governance	57

Technical standards developed by nongovernment entities are an integral part of health and safety regulation. These "private" standards – produced by industry associations and standards development organizations – frequently inform health and safety guidance and rules issued by government agencies.[1] In some industries, private health and safety standards are more rigorous than government regulations. Private standards may also be the only source of health and safety norms in the absence of government regulation. In addition, private standards govern an array of consulting, auditing, testing, and certification services, which play an essential role in monitoring and incentivizing standards conformity and regulatory compliance related to health and safety.

A growing appreciation for the role of private standards in health and safety regulation has led scholars to question the descriptive accuracy of the traditional distinction within regulatory theory between private ordering and public regulation and to replace it with the concept of risk regimes.[2] Discussions of regulatory policy often entail disagreement between advocates of less government intervention in industrial affairs and proponents of greater government involvement in, for example, protecting the environment, managing the economy, and advancing public health. However, the dichotomy underlying these terms of debate – the implicit choice between unregulated markets and government mandates – obscures the interaction and interdependence of private industry and public authority in developing regulatory standards, monitoring compliance, and disciplining those who fail to conform.[3] As one scholar explains,

---

[1] I use the term "private" standards in this chapter as a shorthand for technical standards that derive from procedures conducted by nongovernment entities. However, as the analysis below will make clear, government representatives may participate extensively in the development of "private" standards. Scholars increasingly describe such government involvement in private standard-setting as a "hybrid" form of governance. I discuss hybridization in food safety governance below. For a detailed analysis of this concept, see, e.g. Verbruggen & Havinga 2017.

[2] Hood 2001; Freeman 2000, 857; *see also* Levi-Faur 2011, 13–14; Scott 2012, 61, 67.

[3] This dichotomy also obscures the role of government regulation in making markets possible. *See* Schepel 2013a, 192–195; *see also* Salter 1988, 179.

"social steering is becoming more and more a property of the interaction of organizations, networks, and associations involving both public and private actors, rather than a product of government control of and intervention in society."[4] Thus, concludes a second scholar, "contemporary governance might be best described as a regime of 'mixed administration' in which private actors and government share regulatory roles."[5] The concept of a risk regime denotes the infrastructure of private and public entities engaged in regulatory governance.

The role of private standards in governance is not unique to health and safety regulation, nor is awareness of it new. Social theorists dating back to the nineteenth century have appreciated that economic and social regulation have never really been the exclusive domain of government authorities and that private entities perform regulatory functions.[6] Contemporary elaboration of this insight has laid the foundation for a new understanding of administrative law, in which the rules and procedures that shape administrative governance are no longer limited to government rules that restrain government agencies. This broader conception of administrative law encompasses a wide array of norms – including constitutional doctrines, public laws, and private standards – that govern the activities of private entities.[7]

This chapter presents a case study of food safety regulation to illustrate the concept of risk regimes and the new administrative law that governs them. Food safety represents one of the oldest areas of health and safety governance and one of the most extensive. Food production is the world's largest industry, with a diverse array of sectors and global supply and distribution chains, which generate an estimated $7 trillion in annual revenues.[8] Within the area of food safety, the discussion below presents a detailed account of efforts to reduce microbial contamination of leafy greens in California's central valley. There are advantages and disadvantages to such a narrowly focused case study. Drilling down in one particular place yields a deeper analysis. However, any generalizations about the vast and varied terrain of health and safety governance must remain tentative.[9]

Before proceeding, an important caveat is in order. This chapter makes no claims about the efficacy or efficiency of either private standards or public regulation. Indeed, its conclusions will complicate attempts to evaluate efforts to advance health and safety. The focus is on how regulatory governance works, not on how well it works.

A. INDUSTRY GUIDELINES AND AGENCY GUIDANCE

Foodborne illness caused by microbial contamination is a significant public health concern in the United States. Researchers at the Centers for Disease Control and Prevention (CDC) estimate that each year in the U.S. foodborne pathogens cause 47.8 million cases of acute gastroenteritis, 128,000 hospitalizations, and 3,000 deaths.[10] According to a recent CDC report, contaminated fresh produce was responsible for 40 percent of reported foodborne illness cases.[11] Fresh produce presents a number of unique food safety challenges. It is grown in fields, where it is exposed to insects, feces from wildlife and livestock, and untreated water sources. Preventing

---

[4] Schepel 2005, 19–20; *see also* Salter 1988, 64.
[5] Freeman 2000, 816.
[6] Schepel 2005, 12–19. For a landmark study of the role of private standards in health and safety regulation, see Hamilton 1978.
[7] Freeman 2000, 854–858.
[8] IMAP 2010, 4.
[9] This case study is drawn from a more extensive account in Lytton 2019a.
[10] Scallan et al. 2011, 19.
[11] Centers for Disease Control and Prevention 2017, 7.

contamination in the field is especially important because fresh produce is frequently consumed raw, which forecloses the subsequent use of cooking to kill harmful pathogens during processing or home preparation.[12]

Food safety concerns about fresh produce are relatively recent. A 1985 National Academies report asserted that "raw fruits and vegetables are not common causes of foodborne illness in the United States," and that "there is little use for microbiological [safety standards] for fresh fruits and vegetables at the present time."[13] At that time, the U.S. Food and Drug Administration (FDA) had long possessed broad legal authority under the Federal Food, Drug and Cosmetic Act to prevent adulteration of any type of food sold in interstate commerce, but it had never developed implementing regulations for fresh produce as it had for processed foods.[14]

Complacency about the safety of fresh produce ended when, in the mid-1990s, public health officials began discovering foodborne illness outbreaks associated with fresh produce. Increased consumption of raw produce as part of changing dietary patterns that favored fresh salads over cooked vegetables likely contributed to a rise in outbreaks.[15] Simultaneously, improvements in foodborne illness surveillance and tracing enhanced the ability of public health officials to connect outbreaks to particular products and companies.[16]

In response to growing concern about the safety of fresh produce, several industry associations coordinated efforts to develop technical standards – known as Good Agricultural Practices (GAPs) – aimed at reducing the risk of microbial contamination during growing and harvesting.[17] In one such effort, the Western Growers Association and the International Fresh-Cut Produce Association launched the Food Safety Initiative. They assembled a steering committee consisting of representatives from five trade associations, six grower-processors, two cooling companies, a shipper, a private food safety laboratory, and a county agricultural commissioner. In addition, they convened a nineteen-member technical committee composed mostly of academics and industry experts with PhDs in food science, crop science, microbiology, virology, and toxicology. They also included in discussions and deliberations government officials from the FDA, the U.S. Department of Agriculture (USDA), the California and Arizona departments of agriculture, and the California department of health.[18]

In the summer of 1997, the Western Growers Association and the International Fresh-Cut Produce Association published a thirty-five-page booklet, *Voluntary Food Safety Guidelines for Fresh Produce*. That same year, the United Fresh Fruit and Vegetable Association published a similar twenty-eight-page booklet, *Industrywide Guidance to Minimize Microbiological Food Safety Risks for Produce*, and academics at Cornell University published a tri-fold pamphlet, *Prevention of Foodborne Illness Begins on the Farm*.[19]

For the most part, these early GAPs merely highlighted potential problems without providing specific procedures or metrics for reducing risk. For example, with regard to irrigation water, the *Voluntary Food Safety Guidelines for Fresh Produce* encouraged growers "to identify and review the source of water used on the ranch" and suggested that "the water may be tested for contaminants on a periodic basis. The frequency of testing may be determined by the water

---

[12] Bach & Delaquis 2009, 45; Niemira et al. 2009, 421.
[13] National Academy of Sciences 1985, 257–58.
[14] Burrows 2008; Shekhar 2010, 269, 273; Telephone interview with David Gombas by author (2016).
[15] Kohnke 2007, 499–500.
[16] FDA 2008, 3.
[17] For a more detailed description of GAPs, see Gravani 2009.
[18] International Fresh-cut Produce Association & Western Growers Association 1997, iv–v.
[19] International Fresh-cut Produce Association & Western Growers Association 1997; United Fresh Fruit and Vegetable Association 1997; Rangarajan et al. 1997.

source. Testing may be considered for *E. coli* and total coliforms." In some areas, the guidelines offered slightly more direction: "growers are encouraged to clean and sanitize or disinfect tables, baskets and mechanical harvesters on a daily basis." The guidelines in a few instances referred growers to government regulations. For example, with regard to field sanitation, they stated that "the number, condition and positioning of toilets must meet all local, state and federal guidelines." The authors of the guidelines openly acknowledged the need for further scientific research and subsequent standards development to support more specific instructions to growers, stating that "the guidelines are not 'final,' as they will be revised periodically as experience, new research and new technology may suggest."[20]

In October 1997, President Clinton announced a government Food Safety Initiative, which promised new federal guidance on good agricultural practices for fresh produce. The FDA and USDA officials charged with developing the new federal GAPs guidance for fresh produce relied heavily on the earlier efforts of industry associations and academics. "This is probably a really good example of leveraging the work of other people," recalls FDA official Michelle Smith, who played a leading role in developing the guidance. "We quickly found guidance that had been jointly developed by the Western Growers Association and the International Fresh Cut Produce Association, another guidance by United Fresh, and a third guidance put out by Cornell University. And so our first step was to take the best bits of each, weave them together, and present that as our working draft to stakeholder groups." The draft went through "various rounds of input and modification from industry and academia," recalls Trevor Suslow, one of the leading U.S. academic experts on food safety in fresh produce, who advised both industry groups and government agencies in the development of GAPs standards. In October 1998, the FDA published the *Guide to Minimize Microbial Food Safety Hazards for Fresh Fruits and Vegetables*.[21]

Like its industry and academic predecessors, the federal government's 1998 guidance highlighted areas of concern but lacked specific instructions. For example, the guidance advised that irrigation "water quality should be adequate for its intended use" and defined "adequate" as "that which is needed to accomplish the intended purpose in keeping with good practice." The guidance stated that "growers may elect to test their water supply for microbial contamination" but, as one commentator points out, did not specify "what to test for, what type of test to utilize, where to test, what the frequency of tests should be or any parameters upon which to evaluate the results of the tests." Also like its industry and academic predecessors, the federal government's 1998 guidance highlighted the inadequacy of scientific knowledge at the time and the need for additional research. In addition, like the industry and academic guidelines, the government's guidance was nonbinding. It merely represented "the current thinking" of its authors, and compliance with its suggestions was entirely voluntary.[22]

Continuing outbreaks associated with fresh lettuce and tomatoes led the FDA to issue a warning letter to these two industries in February 2004 urging companies to "review their current operations in light of the agency's guidance for minimizing microbial food safety hazards." In October, the FDA published the *Produce Safety Action Plan* for fresh produce, pledging to "develop, and assist in the development of … commodity-specific and practice-specific guidance." In a subsequent November 2005 warning letter to the California leafy greens industry, the agency urged companies "to begin or intensify immediately efforts" to "expedite

---

[20] International Fresh-cut Produce Association & Western Growers Association 1997.
[21] White House 1997; Telephone interview with Michelle Smith by author (2016); Telephone interview with Trevor Suslow by author (2016); FDA 1998.
[22] FDA 1998; Endres & Johnson 2011, 61–62.

completion of the industry-led lettuce and leafy green-specific supply chain guidance." Smith remembers that agency officials saw the warning letters as a way "to push our expectations for more action than we had been seeing up to that point."[23]

Hank Giclas of the Western Growers Association recalls a series of meetings between industry representatives and FDA officials during this time. "We were in a long series of iterative discussions with regulatory agencies at that point in time, both at the state and federal level." During the discussions, FDA officials focused on "high risk" crops – such as tomatoes and leafy greens – associated with continuing outbreaks. According to Giclas, agency officials insisted, "and we agreed with them: 'You in industry need to go back and look at what is unique about these crops, and decide if there are additional good agricultural practices that need to be created and put out there to try to reduce the frequency of these outbreaks.' And that was the genesis of the industry's work on commodity-specific guidance."[24]

In April 2006, the Western Growers Association, the International Fresh-Cut Produce Association, the United Fresh Fruit and Vegetable Association, and the Produce Marketing Association published *Commodity Specific Food Safety Guidelines for the Lettuce and Leafy Greens Supply Chain* with input from fifty leading food safety experts from industry, government, and academia. The foreword emphasized that the guidelines were voluntary and intended to merely "raise awareness" of "potential" food safety issues and to offer general suggestions for addressing them. Consequently, "it is the responsibility of individuals and companies ... to determine what actions are appropriate in their individual operations. ... This guidance document, as presented, is not sufficient to serve as an action plan for any specific operation but should be viewed as a starting point."[25]

The industry's commodity-specific GAPs did little to advance food safety in field operations beyond previous attempts. For example, the 2006 commodity-specific guidelines suggested that "water may be tested on a regular basis, treated or drawn from an appropriate source as a means of assuring it is appropriate for its intended purpose" without any specification of metrics, methods, or frequency of testing. "We stayed away from numbers because we wanted to remain flexible," recalls one of the industry experts involved in developing the guidelines. Moreover, "we were running into some opposition from growers who complained 'How *dare* you propose specific guidelines for fresh leafy greens! We've been growing these crops all our lives, and we know what to do.' So at the time, there was still some resistance to changing food safety practices, especially without the science to indicate 'this is exactly what you should be doing.'"[26]

Although the 2006 industry guidelines placed no specific demands on growers, the authors hoped that they would encourage growers to pay more attention to food safety. Industry leaders, believing that the new guidelines would be taken more seriously if they came from federal regulators, asked FDA officials to co-author the guidelines or to publish them as agency guidance. However, FDA officials, despite having participated extensively in the process of formulating the guidelines, were unwilling at that time to adopt them as their own without subjecting them to additional review within the agency. In August 2006, the agency collaborated with the State of California to launch the Leafy Greens Safety Initiative, which sent officials to farms to assess current practices with the aim of further refining existing guidance to reduce the risk of microbial contamination in what Smith characterizes as a "two-way educational" process

---

[23] FDA 2004a; FDA 2004b; FDA 2005.
[24] Telephone interview with Hank Giclas by author (2016).
[25] International Fresh-cut Produce Association et al. 2006, iv.
[26] International Fresh-cut Produce Association et al. 2006; Telephone interview with David Gombas by author (2016).

between regulators and growers. A few weeks later, the era of voluntary and vague guidelines in the California leafy greens industry came to an end.[27]

B. MARKETING AGREEMENTS AND GOVERNMENT REGULATIONS

In September 2006, public health officials linked a rapidly growing number of illnesses caused by the deadly pathogen E. coli O157:H7 to fresh spinach. The magnitude of the outbreak far surpassed that of previous outbreaks linked to leafy greens. Government reports eventually blamed the outbreak for more than 200 reported illnesses in twenty-six states. One hundred and three victims required hospitalization, thirty-one suffered kidney failure, and three died. FDA warnings early in the outbreak to avoid eating bagged spinach until the precise source of contamination could be identified devastated the industry. According to one estimate, California leafy greens producers suffered nearly $100 million in losses following the outbreak.[28]

Investigators obtained from outbreak victims bags of Dole baby spinach that tested positive for the outbreak strain of *E. coli* O157:H7 and traced their contents back to four growing fields. A mile from one of the fields, they found the outbreak strain of *E. coli* O157:H7 in samples that they collected from cattle feces, wild pig feces, and river water. Investigators speculated that the contamination could have been caused by the incursion of wild pigs into the spinach rows or the infiltration of contaminated river water into irrigation wells. They also noted that samples taken from the areas surrounding the other three fields in question yielded non-outbreak strains of *E. coli* O157:H7 which, along with the results of previous outbreak investigations, indicated "systematic contamination" of waterways throughout the Salinas Valley.[29]

The 2006 baby spinach outbreak prompted leafy greens industry leaders to develop a more rigorous approach to regulating food safety on farms. Motivated by a desire to win back consumer confidence and to preempt efforts by state legislators to impose new government regulations, a half-dozen food safety managers from leading companies met informally. Their discussions quickly expanded to include additional stakeholders – trade association representatives, federal and state regulatory officials, and academic researchers – who formed a working group and developed a draft proposal. Hank Giclas, of the Western Growers Association, organized meetings of leafy greens growers and processors throughout the state at which he presented the draft and obtained feedback, which the working group used to refine the proposal. By the spring of 2007, this process produced the California Leafy Green Products Handler Marketing Agreement (LGMA).[30]

The California Marketing Act of 1937 authorizes the creation of marketing agreements. A marketing agreement is a voluntary commitment among a group of producers or handlers of a specific food commodity that sets common standards for production volume, quality characteristics, or packaging, with the aim of stabilizing prices. Marketing agreements allow agricultural producers and handlers to organize in ways that might otherwise violate antitrust laws designed to prevent collusion and price-fixing.[31]

---

[27] Telephone interview with Robert Brackett by author (2016); Telephone interview with Michelle Smith by author (2016); U.S. Food and Drug Association 2013b, 3512.

[28] For detailed accounts of the outbreak and investigation described in this and the following paragraph, see Food Industry Center & National Center for Food Protection and Defense 2009; Lytton 2019a, ch. 5.

[29] California Department of Human Services, Food and Drug Branch & FDA 2007.

[30] Interview with Robert Whitaker by author (2016); interview with Hank Giclas by author (2016); California Department of Food and Agriculture, Marketing Branch 2015.

[31] California Marketing Act of 1937. On marketing agreements generally, see Wood 1961; Endres 2011, 67–72. On the exemption of state action from federal antitrust laws, see Jorde 1987; California Department of Food and Agriculture, Marketing Branch 2015, Art. XI, § A.

The LGMA founders created a marketing agreement under the California Marketing Act that sets food safety standards for leafy greens growers. The agreement, however, is among leafy greens handlers – defined as "any person who handles, processes, ships or distributes leafy green product for market." The agreement distinguishes handlers from growers, who produce greens, and retailers, who sell greens to the public. Thus, handlers are the link between growers and retailers. Handlers who sign the marketing agreement commit to purchasing leafy greens exclusively from growers who pass periodic food safety audits of their operations by California Department of Food and Agriculture (CDFA) inspectors using LGMA standards. In exchange, signatory handlers may display a certification mark on their products and their promotional materials indicating membership in the LGMA and CDFA certification of their products.[32] Signatory handlers who violate the terms of the agreement lose their certification and their right to use the mark. Unauthorized use of the mark constitutes an unfair trade practice in violation of state consumer protection law.[33]

Following public hearings, the CDFA approved the LGMA. To assist the CDFA in the administration of the agreement, the LGMA establishes the California Leafy Green Products Handler Advisory Board, consisting of handler signatories from different growing regions of the state and one representative of the general public, who must not be affiliated with any industry organization. The agreement authorizes the LGMA Board to contract with the CDFA to provide agency inspectors to perform on-farm audits that assess growers' compliance with LGMA food safety standards. These third-party government audits are paid for by handlers through an annual assessment that finances the operating costs of the agreement as a condition of LGMA certification.[34]

Thus, the LGMA Board is a public entity empowered to administer a voluntary agreement among private firms. The rules that govern administration of the agreement have been adopted by the California Secretary of Food and Agriculture as state regulations. However, the food safety standards by which the firms agree to abide are private industry standards. The CDFA's willingness to provide audits against those standards does not give the standards the status of agency regulations.[35]

The LGMA is more rigorous than earlier industry guidelines and government guidance because it provides specific standards for safety, makes implementation of them a practical necessity to gain entry into the national market, and relies on government inspection to monitor compliance. The LGMA founders attached quantitative measures, called "metrics," to the GAPs guidance criteria. For example, the LGMA metrics specified testing protocols and thresholds for generic *E. coli* levels in irrigation water. The LGMA founders took a "three-tier approach" to developing metrics. As the introduction to the LGMA standards explains, "a comprehensive literature review was conducted to determine if there was a scientifically valid basis for establishing a metric for the identified risk factor or best practice. If the literature research did not identify scientific studies that could support an appropriate metric, standards or metrics from authoritative or regulatory bodies were used to establish a metric. If neither scientific studies nor

---

[32] The LGMA certification mark is a U.S. registered certification mark. California Department of Food and Agriculture Marketing Branch 2015, Art. V, § A. For a discussion of the issuance and use of certification marks, see Chapters 12, 13, and 14 in this volume.
[33] California Department of Food and Agriculture Marketing Branch 2015, Art. VI, § A.
[34] California Department of Food and Agriculture, Marketing Branch 2015. In food safety, third-party audits generally refer to audits of a supplier conducted by an outside auditor other than a buyer. The auditor is a third-party to the supplier–buyer relationship. Second-party audits are audits of a supplier conducted by a buyer. First-party audits, also known as internal audits, are audits of a supplier conducted by the supplier itself. Hammar 2015.
[35] Telephone interview with Scott Horsfall by the author (2016).

authoritative bodies had allowed for suitable metrics, consensus among industry representatives and/or other stakeholders was sought to establish metrics."[36]

Given the dearth of scientific studies directly related to microbial contamination in farming operations, the LGMA relies heavily on established standards from other areas of regulation. For example, in developing the metric for irrigation water of "adequate quality for its intended use," the LGMA adopted the Environmental Protection Agency (EPA) standard for recreational water, reasoning that "if it's safe enough to swim in, it must be safe enough to irrigate with," according to one industry expert.[37]

The LGMA founders anticipated that the metrics would develop over time as the relevant science advanced. The LGMA standards guide, created by industry and accepted by the California Secretary of Food and Agriculture, "has been and continues to be an evolving and live document, as new information comes to light through scientific research or from other sources," explains Suslow. The LGMA Board established a technical committee, composed of food safety managers and consultants, to review proposed changes to the metrics and make recommendations to the Board.[38]

In response to criticism that the original LGMA leafy greens metrics were developed in unannounced, private meetings by a small, self-selected group of executives from large processing companies, the Western Growers Association implemented a process for developing new and revised standards that provides public notice at every stage of the process, encourages broad stakeholder input, responds to comments, provides written justification for decisions, subjects final proposals to open public hearings with a written record before the LGMA's technical committee, and includes two post-hearing reviews by the LGMA Board and the California Secretary of Agriculture before a change is approved.[39]

The LGMA has achieved nearly universal adoption of its standards among California leafy greens growers by making handlers the subjects of the marketing agreement. A small group of handlers has a particularly high stake in preventing outbreaks, and it commands a level of market power that gives it considerable influence over growers. Although outbreaks can affect everyone in the leafy greens industry, they pose the greatest threat to handlers who produce leading brands of fresh-cut bagged produce. These companies lack the anonymity among consumers that shields growers and handlers of unmarked whole produce. Packaging bearing a brand name makes it easier to identify a particular company as the source of an outbreak. A few of these leading brand name handlers dominate the market. In 2006, Fresh Express (owned by Chiquita) accounted for 41 percent of all bagged, fresh-cut salad sales in the United States, and Dole accounted for 31 percent. Along with the next two leading firms, Ready Pac and Earthbound Farms, four companies controlled 86 percent of the market. Thus, a small group of highly brand-sensitive handlers who dominated the market had both the motivation and the leverage to encourage widespread adoption of the new standards among growers. Six months after approval of the LGMA, fifty-one handlers, responsible for more than 99 percent of the leafy greens produced in California, had joined the LGMA.[40]

---

[36] California Department of Food and Agriculture, Marketing Branch 2016. Telephone interview with Drew McDonald by author (2016).
[37] California Department of Food and Agriculture, Marketing Branch 2016. Telephone interview with David Gombas by author (2016).
[38] California Department of Food and Agriculture Marketing Branch 2016.
[39] For a typical critique, see Stuart 2010. For a description of the process, see Western Growers Association 2010.
[40] Cohen 2008, 9–11; Endres 2011, 47–50; Shekhar 2010; Telephone interview with David Gombas by author (2016).

LGMA reliance on government inspectors paid for by handlers avoids problems associated with private third-party food safety audits of farms. Typically, buyers of fresh produce – such as handlers or distributors or retailers – insist that growers obtain private third-party food safety audits to ensure their compliance with GAPs, and they insist that the growers select and pay auditors directly, creating a conflict of interest that incentivizes auditors to cut corners and inflate audit scores to please growers. Moreover, high demand coupled with inadequate training and experience has created a shortage of qualified private auditors. The LGMA's system of paying government inspectors from handler assessments eliminates both of these problems.[41]

Ongoing high-profile foodborne illness outbreaks involving many different sectors of the food industry generated growing public pressure for more rigorous federal oversight of food safety. Growers' desire to avoid a patchwork of varying state and local requirements and retailers' desire to improve food safety practices among their suppliers prompted industry association support for federal legislation. Starting in 2008, a year after the rollout of the LGMA, various members of Congress introduced food safety reform legislation in both the House and the Senate. In the final days of December 2010, Congress passed the Food Safety Modernization Act (FSMA), which President Obama signed on January 4, 2011. Among its many provisions, the new law instructed the FDA to issue food safety regulations for the production of fresh produce – what became known as the FSMA Produce Safety Rule, which the agency issued in November 2015.[42]

In crafting standards and metrics for the new rule, the agency drew heavily on the "experience over time and the interactions we've had with industry," explains Smith. "Industry folks really put a lot of effort into educating us – for example, different groups provided us opportunities to tour farms." California LGMA founders, in particular, take credit for shaping the Produce Safety Rule. "FDA has, for many years, been involved in the industry," says one industry food safety expert, and consequently "FSMA, by and large, got it right. I mean, they were listening. They wrote up what many of us in the industry were already doing, the exact language if you really do a comparison. In the produce rule, they borrowed so much – and I take it as a compliment – from the leafy greens metrics. So they really got it right." According to another industry expert, "when the FDA created the Produce Safety Rule, they looked at all the different standards out there ... and the only one that had numbers was leafy greens. So when they were trying to figure out what is water of 'adequate quality,' the only one that had a standard was leafy greens, so they adopted the standard from leafy greens."[43]

The FDA's shift from voluntary to mandatory standards had roots in both industry and government. Smith explains that,

> the initial response to regulating the industry was guidance, and that was fine with everyone. Around the time of the [2006] spinach outbreak, some folks started shifting toward being supportive of regulation, including some industry groups who, in advance of FSMA, sent letters to Congress saying that they would support produce regulation because, when an outbreak happens, it negatively impacts the entire industry. So, over time, support for regulations dealing with best practices on farms was growing. And it was FSMA that gave us the final push and direction to actually do it.[44]

---

[41] For an extensive analysis of this system of private food safety auditing, see Lytton & McAllister 2014; Lytton 2019a; Lytton 2019b.

[42] Lytton 2019a, ch. 5; FDA Food Safety Modernization Act 2011; FDA 2015.

[43] Telephone interview with Michelle Smith by author (2016); Telephone interview with Drew McDonald by author (2016); Telephone interview with David Gombas by author (2016). The influence of private standards on government regulation frequently raises concerns about industry capture. For an extended discussion of capture theories in analyzing the evolution of food safety, see Lytton 2019a, ch. 3. On capture more generally, see Carpenter & Moss 2014.

[44] Telephone interview with Michelle Smith by author (2016).

FSMA's mandate that the FDA issue binding regulations for farming operations raised questions about the agency's capacity to monitor and enforce compliance. Historically, FDA inspectors had visited farms only as part of outbreak investigations. It seemed highly unlikely that Congress would appropriate sufficient funds to enable the agency to routinely inspect the more than 120,000 U.S. farms that cultivate fresh produce for sale.[45] The FDA responded to doubts about its capacity to enforce the Produce Safety Rule by explaining that FSMA created a new approach to industry regulation that would not require comprehensive government inspection or enforcement. "There is no reasonable expectation FDA will have the resources to make routine on-farm inspection a major source of accountability for compliance with produce safety standards," the agency explained in a 2014 publication. From the outset, the agency insisted, "Congress envisioned a different role for FDA on produce farms compared to food facilities." Whereas FSMA mandated specific inspection frequencies for FDA oversight of food processors, the legislation made no mention of inspection frequency for fresh produce growers. FDA Deputy Commissioner for Foods and Veterinary Medicine Michael Taylor explained in a 2014 speech to the United Fresh Produce Association that the Agency was focused on supporting "the vast majority of operators who want to produce safe food and to get compliance on a voluntary basis, and that's the outcome that matters. That's a fundamental reorientation of our approach to our oversight." In a posting on an agency blog, Taylor explained that the agency planned to work "in close collaboration with other government agencies (federal, state, local, tribal, and foreign), the food industry and other stakeholders" to supplement its limited inspection and enforcement resources. The agency would reserve its own inspection resources for "high-risk" industry sectors. In addition, the agency would issue new guidance to clarify standards and conduct "outreach and technical assistance to facilitate voluntary compliance." In explaining its proposed Produce Safety Rule in 2013, the agency wrote that "we anticipate that compliance will be achieved primarily through the conscientious efforts of farmers, complemented by the efforts of State and local governments, extension services, private audits and certifications, and other private sector supply chain management efforts."[46]

C. THE ROLE OF PRIVATE STANDARDS AND CONFORMITY ASSESSMENT IN RISK REGIMES

The development and implementation of food safety governance within the California leafy greens industry blurs the distinction between private ordering and government regulation. GAPs emerged out of an iterative process that began with private standards initially formulated by an industry-sponsored technical committee that included government officials. Over time, this process produced voluntary industry guidelines, nonbinding federal agency guidance, marketing agreement requirements, and government regulations. Throughout, rulemaking occurred within an ongoing conversation among a mix of industry executives, government officials, and academic experts, conducted in both private and public institutional venues. At times, other groups, such as farmers and consumer advocates, also participated. Implementation increasingly relied on collaboration between private and public entities. Monitoring and enforcement of GAPs has contributed to the further intertwining – what some scholars refer to as the "hybridization" – of private and public food safety governance.[47] The resulting infrastructure of actors, institutions, and activities constitutes a risk regime.[48]

---

[45] FDA 2017, 40.
[46] FDA 2014; Taylor 2014; Food Safety News 2014; FDA 2013, 3608; FDA 2015, 74373, 74519–21.
[47] Verbruggen & Havinga 2017.
[48] For further analysis of the concept of an infrastructure, see Edwards et al. 2012.

Individual companies and trade associations played a leading role in developing GAPs and gradually increasing their rigor. A combination of economic pressure, the prospect of state regulation, and increasing professionalization of food safety expertise motivated them. Foodborne illness outbreaks traced to leafy greens created economic pressure on firms to improve food safety throughout the industry. As the 2006 spinach outbreak so dramatically illustrated, an outbreak attributed to one firm threatened the profits of every firm in the sector.[49] In addition, the prospect of state regulation following the 2006 baby spinach outbreak motivated industry leaders to impose rigorous LGMA metrics on growers. Industry leaders feared that legislators responding to political pressure from voters for tougher food safety laws would impose costly government mandates unsupported by either science or expert consensus. Industry lobbying efforts derailed legislative proposals within the California legislature to impose new government regulations on the industry and, within industry, the association used the prospect of heavy-handed state intervention to secure acceptance of the LGMA and accelerate efforts to get it up and running.[50] Moreover, increasing professionalization of food safety within the fresh produce sector in the 1990s – in particular the arrival of PhD microbiologists in a field previously dominated by farmers and agronomists focused on pests and crop yields – helps explain the desire and capacity within industry to deal rationally with the uncertainty of newly emerging food safety risk by assembling committees of scientific experts to produce technical standards.[51]

Throughout the evolution of GAPs in the leafy greens sector, private standards have influenced government standards. Private standards provided the starting point for the drafting and elaboration of subsequent government standards. In particular, the initial industry guidelines analyzed GAPs into the categories of irrigation water, soil amendments, animal intrusion, worker hygiene, and harvesting equipment – a framework adopted by subsequent government guidance and regulation. Government guidance and regulation frequently incorporated private standards or adopted them with minor modifications.

Private entities have also played a leading role in the implementation of GAPs. Traditionally, neither federal nor state regulatory agencies responsible for food safety on farms have had sufficient resources to inspect growing operations except as part of investigations following foodborne illness outbreaks. Industry supply chain management has filled this void through private third-party food safety audits that assess growers' conformity to GAPs. Commercial buyers of fresh produce – processors, distributors, and retail sellers – have long relied on private third-party food safety audits of their suppliers, and these audits include, at a minimum, compliance with government guidance and regulations. The LGMA finances a system of fee-for-service audits by government inspectors to monitor compliance. Thus, in practice, farm-level compliance with food safety standards is driven by private supply chain management.

The analysis presented here emphasizes the role of private standards and conformity assessment within this risk regime. The aim is not to undervalue the contribution of government regulation, but rather to highlight its private underpinnings and its ongoing reliance on private forms of monitoring and enforcement. The distinction between private ordering and public regulation does not delineate alternative approaches to governance, but rather reveals interactions between highly integrated components of a common enterprise.

---

[49] For extensive analysis of how reputational interdependence among firms motivates industry support for regulation, see Rees 1996; Yue & Ingram 2012.
[50] For a more detailed account, see Lytton 2019a, Appendix D.
[51] On the role of professionalization in risk management, see Olshan 1993, 320, 324; specifically in food safety risk, see Lytton 2019a, ch 5; Demortain 2011.

D. CONCERNS ABOUT THE LEGITIMACY OF PRIVATE GOVERNANCE

Information about food safety risk is limited due to a combination of the high cost of collecting and analyzing relevant data, the complexity and opacity of causal connections between microbial contamination and harm, and the limits of current biomedical science. This means that the development of standards relies heavily on rough estimates and speculation, which may be controversial, even among experts.[52] Moreover, determining the appropriate level of risk reduction requires highly subjective judgments concerning the public's risk tolerance.[53] Discretionary decisions based on speculation and subjective judgments in the face of uncertainty run the risk of being considered illegitimate unless they emerge from procedures that allow for stakeholder participation and public accountability.[54]

In some ways, industry-sponsored efforts to develop safety standards for leafy greens sacrificed these indicia of legitimacy in pursuit of greater efficiency. Technical committees gathered in closed-door sessions to expedite the process of drafting standards. For example, Giclas recounts how beginning the process of developing the LGMA in a small group made it easier to advance the group's desire for more rigorous GAPs: "When we were developing the early draft, we had a smaller group in the room. They saw the problem, they were ramped up, and they were engaged. You can't do that with an entire industry. We would never have had a document if we tried to put everybody in the room at the same time."[55] Insularity fostered greater candor and reduced political posturing in meetings.

However, it is not true that stakeholders outside of industry had no voice in the deliberations of these technical committees. Government officials routinely participated in industry-sponsored technical committees to develop GAPs. Although there is no direct evidence, there is reason to believe that government agency officials may have been less inhibited in representing consumer interests in these industry-sponsored technical committees than they were in government-sponsored venues. When government agency officials convene a group to develop guidance or regulations, they are supposed to serve as impartial brokers between the interests of different stakeholders, including industry groups and consumer advocacy organizations. Agency officials are further constrained by a fear of running afoul of the diverse political agendas of their legislative and executive branch overseers. By contrast, when government agency officials participate in an industry-sponsored technical committee to develop private standards off of the public record, they can serve as more honest and zealous advocates for what they conceive to be the public interest.

The involvement of government officials notwithstanding, the lack of transparency may have made industry-sponsored technical committees less politically accountable than government-sponsored advisory committees would have been. Government-sponsored advisory committees are subject to open meeting and public record requirements under the Federal Advisory Committee Act. However, although industry technical committees were not subject to short-term political accountability, they saw themselves as subject to long-term market accountability if their efforts failed to avert subsequent outbreaks, prompting consumer dissatisfaction and, consequently, lost revenues and the prospect of government regulation. Hank Giclas of the

---

[52] On the costs of policy information, see Schuck 2014, 161–70.
[53] On the importance of risk perceptions on risk analysis, see Ericson & Doyle 2004.
[54] On legitimacy generally, see Suchman 1995; on legitimacy in private governance, see Bernstein & Cashore 2007; Maurer 2017, 147–64; on legitimacy in private food safety governance, see Fuchs, Kalfagianni & Havinga 2009; for an extended critique on these grounds of the LGMA, see Stuart 2010.
[55] Telephone interview with Hank Giclas by author (2016).

Western Growers Association recalls that, following the 2006 baby spinach outbreak, industry leaders feared these consequences if they did not establish more rigorous GAPs in the growing fields. "At Western Growers, we consider ourselves to be industry leaders. We saw the writing on the wall in the state if we did not act and do something."[56]

In the absence of specific baselines and metrics, assessing the legitimacy of institutions is often a matter of comparative analysis, in this case: How does private governance compare to the alternative of public regulation? Blurring the distinction between private ordering and government regulation complicates this type of comparative institutional analysis, which typically depends upon generalizations about distinct process-related features of private and public institutions – for example, the claim that private organizations are comparatively more efficient than government agencies but that they are less participatory and publicly accountable. As the evolution of food safety governance in the California leafy greens industry illustrates, industry increasingly emulated government notice-and-comment procedures in developing the LGMA metrics, and government has often sought to achieve greater efficiency through reliance on voluntary guidance and industry supply-chain pressure to incentivize regulatory compliance. The mimicry between industry and government efforts, further analyzed below, erodes categorical generalizations about comparative institutional virtues and vices.

Differences do remain, but capturing them requires leaving aside increasingly inaccurate generalizations in favor of more detailed analysis and specific metrics for measuring qualities such as participation and accountability. Comparative institutional analysis must find ways to determine, for example, the relative accountability of the Western Growers Association procedure for revising the LGMA metrics compared to the FDA's process for developing the Produce Safety Rule. The comparison is further complicated by the interdependence and intertwining of the two processes. If private standard-setting is an integral part of an iterative process that also involves government rulemaking, it becomes unclear where, exactly, industry process ends and government process begins.

E. THE ADMINISTRATIVE LAW OF PRIVATE GOVERNANCE

Conformity to the rule of law adds an additional dimension of legitimacy to regulatory governance, a function performed by administrative law. Private standard-setting and private third-party food safety auditing are constrained by a variety of norms that constitute the administrative law of private governance. Insofar as private standards are an integral part of risk regimes, this administrative law of private governance is an integral part of administrative law more generally. The "new" administrative law is, thus, an enlarged conception of the domain of administrative law that includes various types of norms governing private standard-setting and private third-party auditing within risk regimes.[57] These norms shape the development and implementation of private health and safety standards, although, in the case of food safety, this influence is somewhat subtle.

Some of the norms that govern private standard-setting and private third-party auditing arise out of constitutional norms that constrain government regulation. For example, the U.S. constitutional doctrine of nondelegation limits the scope of regulatory authority that a legislature may delegate to private entities. The federal nondelegation doctrine requires that Congress provide an "intelligible principle" to define the scope of any grant of legislative power to any

---

[56] Telephone interview with Hank Giclas by author (2016).
[57] Freeman 2000.

public agency or private entity. Some states have stricter nondelegation doctrines. For example, the doctrine in Texas requires, in addition to an intelligible principle, meaningful oversight by government of private entities delegated legislative power; fair representation of stakeholders in rulemaking; general rulemaking rather than application of rules to particular parties; requirements that decision-making be unbiased and untainted by conflicts of interest; limitation to non-criminal matters; narrow limits on the duration, extent, and subject matter of the delegated authority; and sufficient qualifications and training to perform the delegated tasks.[58] In practice, these doctrines have rarely been invoked to strike down legislative delegations to private entities, and they have little application in food safety governance – where government does not officially delegate rulemaking powers to private standard setters and government reliance on private third-party auditing is informal.

Public law is another source of norms that constrain private standards activity. For example, antitrust law limits the types of health and safety standards that an industry can attempt to impose on its members, as detailed in numerous chapters in the companion volume of this collection.[59] However, such antitrust concerns have played no appreciable role in structuring private food safety governance.

Legal restraints on government agency rulemaking regulate the incorporation of private standards, including food safety standards, into government regulations. These include provisions of the Administrative Procedures Act (APA) governing notice-and-comment rulemaking and executive orders requiring administrative regulations to satisfy cost–benefit analysis. The FDA conducted an extensive notice-and-comment process and cost–benefit analysis as the agency incorporated and modified LGMA and other private standards in the development of its Produce Safety Rule.[60]

In the case of food safety governance, these constitutional, public law, and administrative law norms have exerted influence on the process of private standard-setting primarily through modeling rather than through enforceable legal regulation of delegation, competition, or incorporation. For example, the desire of the Western Growers Association to bolster the legitimacy of the LGMA metrics in the eyes of both producers and consumers led the association to develop rulemaking procedures modeled on the APA's notice-and-comment requirements. Following criticism that the original LGMA leafy greens metrics were developed in unannounced private meetings by a small self-selected group of executives from large processing companies, the Western Growers Association developed a process for developing new and revised standards that provides public notice at every stage of the process, encourages broad stakeholder input, responds to comments, provides written justification for decisions, subjects final proposals to open public hearings with a written record before the LGMA's technical committee, and includes two post-hearing reviews by the LGMA Board and the California Secretary of Agriculture before a change is approved. The association and its members have thus sought to bolster the legitimacy and influence of the LGMA metrics by adopting these elements of government agency rulemaking associated with transparency, participation, and accountability.[61]

---

[58] Federal and state constitutional doctrines of due process impose similar requirements on the exercise of governance authority delegated by legislatures to private entities. For an elaboration of both of nondelegation and due process doctrines as applied to private governance, see Volokh 2014; Schepel 2005.

[59] See, e.g., Chapters 4–6 (companion volume). See also Volokh 2014; Schepel 2005; Cheit 1990, 187–90.

[60] For details, see Lytton 2019a, ch. 6. On the incorporation of private standards into government regulations more generally, see Chapters 2 and 6 in this volume.

[61] For an analysis of institutional isomorphism generally, see DiMaggio & Powell 1991; Olshan 1993; Meidinger 2006. For discussions of legality in private institutions, see Edelman & Suchman 2007; Esty 2006. For additional examples, see Halabi & Lin 2017.

Private standards that govern standard-setting and conformity assessment are another source of constraints on private governance.[62] For example, the International Organization for Standardization (ISO) has published a series of technical standards that prescribe principles, policies, and practices for standard-setting bodies, auditors, certifiers, and the accreditation bodies that oversee them.[63] In food safety, standards for processing equipment are set by standard-setting bodies, such as Underwriters Laboratories (UL), the National Sanitation Foundation (NSF), and 3-A Sanitary Standards, Inc. (3-A SSI), which are accredited by the American National Standards Institute (ANSI) under ANSI's "essential requirements for openness, balance, consensus, and due process," which are consistent with ISO standards.[64] ANSI, in turn, is accredited by the International Accreditation Forum, which conforms to ISO standards for accreditation bodies. Similarly, private third-party food safety auditors must conduct their operations in accordance with ISO conformity assessment standards to obtain ANSI accreditation.[65]

It may seem odd to some readers to consider stretching the domain of administrative law to include private standards that govern standard-setting and conformity assessment. However, socio-legal studies have long characterized institutionalized norms and bureaucratic routines as essential parts of the "law in action."[66] Socio-legal scholars use the term "legality" to include "the meanings, sources of authority, and cultural practices that are commonly recognized as legal, regardless of who employs them or for what ends."[67] Within the fresh produce industry, LGMA metrics, UL equipment specifications, food safety scheme audit criteria, ANSI accreditation requirements, and ISO standards all operate as legal constraints on standard-setting and conformity assessment.[68] Just as private standard-setting is an integral part of agency rulemaking, and private auditing is essential to regulatory compliance, so too, the private principles, policies, and practices for standard-setting and conformity assessment are part of the law that governs administrative regulation.

CONCLUSION

The history of food safety in the California leafy greens industry provides an example of the coevolution of industry standards and government regulation in health and safety governance. Analyzing this example using the concept of a risk regime highlights aspects of health and safety governance – namely the interdependence and intertwining of private and public efforts – that are obscured by a sharp distinction between private ordering and public regulation. Moreover, the concept of a risk regime illuminates how private standard-setting can be a first step and an integral part of administrative rulemaking, which supports the idea that the study and practice of administrative law should include the principles, policies, and practices that govern private standards making and conformity assessment.

---

[62] Schepel 2005, 5–8, 145–76; Schepel 2013a.
[63] *See, e.g.*, ISO/IEC 2017.
[64] ANSI 2018a; ANSI 2018e.
[65] International Accreditation Forum 2018.
[66] A classic example is the use of "rules of thumb" by insurance adjusters to settle tort claims (Ross 1980).
[67] Edelman & Suchman 2009, xiii (quoting Ewick & Silbey 1998, 22).
[68] Lytton & McAllister 2014.

4

Tort Liability for Standards Development in the United States and European Union

*Paul Verbruggen**

A.	General Aspects of Tort Liability for Standards Development	61
B.	Perspectives from the United States	64
	1. Negligence Actions in General	64
	2. A Duty of Care in Negligence for SDOs?	65
	3. The Voluntary Undertaking Rule	68
	4. Negligent Misrepresentation	72
C.	Perspectives from the EU	75
	1. The New Approach	76
	2. Liability Under the New Approach	77
	3. Liability Beyond the New Approach	79
D.	Comparative Analysis	82
	1. Duty Considerations in Negligence Law	82
	2. Factors Bearing on Breach	84

Standardization is typically cast in technocratic language. Beneath the technical veneer, however, there is politics.[1] While the development of standards brings about opportunities for innovation and market access for some firms, for others it entails significant switching costs. Product specifications may need to be changed, production processes and methods may require amendment or the manufacture of certain products might need to be abandoned completely. With so much at stake, there are strong incentives to influence standards development.

Political contestation around standardization may lead standards development organizations (SDOs) to adopt suboptimal standards: they may fail to take into account state-of-the-art research, underestimate certain risks, or worse, favor certain industry interests over safety concerns of potential end-users. Incomplete, inaccurate or plainly "bad" standards can cause harm to firms implementing them in business operations, as well as to consumers using products designed in compliance with them. Inevitably, then, the question of tort liability for standards development arises.

---

*   This contribution is part of the project "The Constitutionalization of Private Regulation" funded by the Netherlands Organisation for Scientific Research (NWO) under the Innovational Research Incentives Scheme (Grant no. 451-16-011). Further information is available at www.paulverbruggen.nl/projects. The author is grateful for the comments provided by Jorge Contreras and Tim Lytton on a previous draft of this chapter.

[1]   Büthe and Mattli 2011, 12.

This chapter addresses three interrelated questions concerning tort liability for private standards development. First, what theories of tort law govern civil liability for such an activity? Second, what factors and circumstances do courts consider significant when assessing liability for harm caused by inadequate standards? Third and finally, what is the exposure of SDOs to liability given the answers to the first two questions? In answering these questions, this chapter builds on case law and academic literature from the United States and European Union. Case law in these multi-layered jurisdictions is most developed, best documented and electronically searchable and accessible. Data was retrieved by systematic searches using case law databases and secondary sources, such as academic literature, government reports, and industry policy briefs.

This chapter will first draw attention to a number of general aspects of private standards development that scholars of regulation and governance have considered important attributes of standardization and that may impact on the liability of SDOs.[2] This discussion serves to further embed the research questions in the literature on standardization and civil liability, thus providing more focus to the analysis. In discussing these general aspects, *product* standards will be the point of reference. These standards set out technical specifications for the design, production and performance characteristics of manufactured goods. They may prescribe physical attributes for products (including dimensions, size and composition), require certain methods of production, construction and assembly, or concern requirements of what a product must be able to do.[3] Examples of such performance characteristics concern interoperability with other products, resistance to temperature exposure, the level of user safety, testing methods, and quality assurance. Along the category of product standards, standards for services and system management have come to play an important role in our contemporary "world of standards."[4] So far, however, very little case law has developed with respect to these complementary types of standards. Most of the civil litigation against SDOs to date concerns product standards. The maturity of this body of case law allows for a rich and coherent analysis and therefore this chapter is concerned primarily with product standards.

A. GENERAL ASPECTS OF TORT LIABILITY FOR STANDARDS DEVELOPMENT

Standards development is celebrated for providing a wide range of important benefits to individuals, firms, and society at large. Sometimes, however, it may harm the interests of individuals and firms. Firms that suffer economic loss either because standards limit competition, restrict market access or violate pre-existing intellectual property (IP) rights, will principally have to look to antitrust, trade or IP law for protection.[5] Tort law may instead provide a remedy to firms who suffer economic loss because they relied on incomplete, outdated or otherwise inadequate standards in their business operations, or to those who suffer physical harm (i.e. personal injury or property damage) because they used a product that was manufactured in conformity with such bad standards.

As a general rule in the United States and the EU, tort law imposes civil liability on an SDO when it fails to exercise reasonable care in its activities and that failure causes direct or foreseeable physical harm to another. Standards development does not ordinarily cause direct or foreseeable

---

[2] See, e.g., *Bay Summit Cmty. Ass'n* (Cal. App. 1996). The tort liability of individual participants involved in standards development, as discussed in *Bay Summit Community Ass'n*, is beyond the scope of this contribution. The focus is on the liability of the SDO as the actor that promulgated the allegedly inadequate private standards.
[3] Brunsson & Jacobsson 2001, 4–5; Schepel 2005, 3–4; Scott 2010, 107 and 109; Büthe and Mattli 2011, 5.
[4] Brunsson & Jacobsson 2001. For a recent perspective on the rise of system management standards, *see* Galland 2017 (discussing how the global certification industry is further pushing the adoption of these standards by SDOs and governments).
[5] These actions are discussed extensively elsewhere in this volume and in the companion volume.

harm to others, however. Harm occurs primarily after inadequate standards are relied upon in the business operations of the addressees of these standards, typically manufacturers or sellers, who design or construct, install and maintain products in accordance with the standards. If standards turn out to be inadequate, these actors, by complying with the standards, place on the market a defective product. Accordingly, they may be held primarily responsible under the strict liability rules of products liability law.[6]

However, there are valid reasons to bring a civil liability claim against the SDO as a tortfeasor secondary to manufacturers or sellers. These may include the moral consideration that the SDO's standards are the origin of the harm given that manufacturers or sellers routinely implement these standards in their business operations. More practical considerations to target the SDO involved include the insolvency of the manufacturer, the ability of the manufacturer to escape liability under the so-called "regulatory compliance defense,"[7] or the potentially "deeper pocket" of the SDO (e.g. because of its comprehensive insurance coverage). If a liability claim is to prevail, however, the plaintiff must show that the conduct of the defendant SDO created a risk of direct or foreseeable harm. Thus, a key question for the inquiry in the chapter is: What factors do courts consider relevant in constructing foreseeability of harm and a sufficiently close relationship between the SDO's activities and the plaintiff's harm? Such factors are likely to be addressed in relation to the existence of a duty of care in negligence and the breach of that duty (or any other equivalent concepts of national tort law). They may also be found in considerations around causation, however, by asking: Did the inadequate standards proximately cause the harm suffered by the plaintiff, without any significant interference by the standards' addressee? Viewed in this way, a plaintiff may establish liability by following the chain of causation all the way up to the negligent adoption of the inadequate standards.

This discussion on the relationship between standards development and the plaintiff's harm draws attention to the degree to which the contested standards are binding upon manufacturers. Within that context, a distinction is typically made between "technical regulations" and "voluntary standards." The first category, following the parlance of international economic law, involve standards that are adopted by public, state actors and that are mandated by law.[8] This chapter is only concerned with voluntary standards, which are standards developed by private, non-state actors. They are non-mandatory in that actors can choose to abide by them. This voluntariness can be compromised in various ways, of course.[9] Private standards can be *de facto* mandatory if they constitute a condition for market access or the ability to effectively compete on it. Moreover, SDO internal regulations (e.g. bylaws, company statutes and rules of association) may impose compliance with private standards on membership and may employ mechanisms of certification and accreditation to enforce that obligation.[10] In addition, supply chain partners may require compliance with standards via commercial contracts or procurement policies.[11] In

---

[6] Whether such strict liability exists depends, among other things, on the type of defect and the type of harm suffered.
[7] Manufacturers and sellers in the United States and the EU may be able to escape liability under this defense if compliance with the inadequate standards was mandated by public statute. For more on this defense and its relation to private standards, see Schepel 2005, 361–74.
[8] WTO 1995, Annex 1, Arts. 1–2. *See also* Directive 2015/1535/EU (European Union, Art. 1(f)), laying down a procedure for the provision of information in the field of technical regulations and of rules on Information Society services [2015] OJ L241/1. This definition does not exclude the possibility that private actors (including SDOs) participate in the development of a technical regulation. As noted, *supra* note 2, however, the liability of individual participants in standards development is beyond the scope of this contribution.
[9] *See* Cafaggi 2012, 22.
[10] For example, the American National Standards Institute (ANSI) requires its members to comply with its ANSI Essential Requirements (2018a) as a condition to have their standards accredited as American National Standards.
[11] Verbruggen 2017a, 312 (with further references).

the public law domain, legislative measures, public authorities and courts may encourage or demand compliance with such standards once they have been adopted by a particular SDO, thus mandating them *de facto* or *de jure*.[12] Clearly, such public intervention blurs the lines between public mandatory "technical regulations" and private, voluntary standards. This chapter takes the resulting hybridity into account by asking: To what extent does (the degree of) public recognition of privately developed standards affect the liability risk of SDOs? What difference exists, if any, if compared to liability for developing purely private standards?

A related issue concerns the legal form and institutional embedding of SDOs. Most SDOs are private, not-for-profit bodies. They may be organized as individual companies, but more frequently they are collective, membership-based organizations for business, civil society or combinations of these.[13] Sometimes, however, SDOs are established by public statute or have acquired a public law status because of a delegation of public law powers to them.[14] Alternatively, SDOs may be recognized as having a "public law function" through the exercise of its regulatory activities.[15] Acting as bodies governed by public law the question arises whether the rules of state liability apply to SDOs setting voluntary product standards and whether they can avail themselves of state immunity doctrines to escape liability. Heidt (2010, 1280–1284) has argued that, because of the governmental nature of SDO decision-making, courts should shield SDOs from overly burdensome liability by recognizing a qualified privilege. Such a privilege would protect SDOs from civil liability where their decisions are taken in good faith, but would simultaneously guard against abusive standards development should they act in bad faith.[16]

Heidt's suggestion should be read against the background of the inherently political nature of standards development. Setting standards implies the making of policy-bound trade-offs between the conflicting interests of the owners, users and potential beneficiaries of the standards. Concerns of health and safety need to be balanced against concerns of cost, inconvenience and consumer choice.[17] How is this balancing reflected in cases concerning liability for standards development? Do courts show (high) levels of deference when evaluating these policy choices, as they typically do in judicial review procedures concerning public policy and decision-making? More generally, to what extent is the way in which contentious standards were designed or governed part of the liability assessment?

What is more, SDOs fulfill an important societal function when they promulgate standards that intend to enhance the collective welfare in assistance or in the absence of government. Imposing liability on SDOs, it is argued, challenges this laudable function and may inhibit the deliberation of possible standards.[18] It has therefore been suggested that courts, in making the threshold determination whether a private association should be exposed to civil liability for standards development or other activities, must weigh conflicting considerations of policy and justice, including "any existing social interest in permitting the type of conduct of which the plaintiff complains, the burden which would be imposed on [private associations] by judicial intervention in similar cases in the future, the burden on courts were they to take cognizance

---

[12] The inclusion and reliance on private and technical standardization in statute is increasingly popular among state actors. For a U.S. perspective, see Mendelson 2014.
[13] Abbott & Snidal (2009) have shown that transnational standard-setting increasingly involves business and civil society actors, thus moving from a state-driven toward a multi-actor approach. For an overview of the international "ecosystem" in ICT-standardization, see companion volume, Chapter 2.
[14] For an overview of technical standardization bodies in Europe, see Schepel & Falke 2000, 62–68.
[15] This is the case for the national SDO for technical standardization in France called AFNOR. See *infra* note 107.
[16] Heidt 2010, 1280–84.
[17] *Id.* at 1227–32.
[18] *Id.* at 1278.

of such disputes, and the extent to which such intervention might interfere with other socially recognized values promoted by such associations."[19]

Finally, SDOs may not only be engaged in the setting of standards. At times they also pursue certification and/or accreditation activities. In the case of product standards, both activities in essence involve the assessment of a firm's compliance with a normative document, i.e. the product standard. If the assessment is positive the firm is typically awarded some form of endorsement, such as an approval, enlisting, certificate or accreditation of the product or of the firm itself.[20] These endorsements do not reveal the specific details of performance, yet offer an aggregate, discrete judgment on compliance.[21] The attestations therefore generally signal packaged information on compliance to specific audiences (either businesses, consumers or governments), which may come to rely on it in making decisions. Certification and accreditation activities clearly go beyond standards development *per se*. The question arises of whether these activities make SDOs more or less vulnerable to liability claims. A discussion of the liability of "pure" certification and accreditation activities, i.e. without any standards being developed by the certifier or accreditor, is beyond the scope of this chapter.

B. PERSPECTIVES FROM THE UNITED STATES

Individuals and firms in the United States have sought compensation for harm from SDOs based on several theories of tort law. Actions other than those alleging negligence have been unsuccessful for the most part.[22] Three actions grounded in negligence will be discussed here: negligence; an action based on the so-called "voluntary undertaking" rule; and an action for negligent misrepresentation. In each of these actions considerations around the existence of a duty of care owed by the defendant SDO to the plaintiff are central to the success (or defeat) of the claim.

1. *Negligence Actions in General*

The elements of a negligence action in U.S. common law are a duty owed by the defendant to the plaintiff, breach of that duty by the defendant, and damages proximately caused by that breach. In a negligence action a duty may be defined as an obligation, recognized and enforceable by law, to conform to a certain standard of behavior with respect to others.[23] U.S. common law normally imposes a duty on an actor when he directly or foreseeably creates a risk of physical harm for another, that is, personal injury and property damage.[24] When a duty is owed, the standard of care to be applied by the court is usually that of reasonable care under the

---

[19] Note, *Harvard Law Review* 1963, 990.
[20] For a more detailed discussion of certification, see Chapters 12–14.
[21] Bartley 2011, 443.
[22] An exception is the case of *Hall and Chance* (E.D.N.Y. 1972). In this case, which developed out of a series of separate incidents across the United States in which infants were injured by exploding blasting caps, a U.S. District Court in New York held that the industry trade association, which administered a safety program covering the use of warning labels for explosives, and the entire national blasting cap industry could be held jointly liable under a strict theory of "enterprise liability." *Hall and Chance* has not been followed by other courts: the theory of "enterprise liability" has been abandoned in products liability law and SDOs have not been considered subject to strict products liability law as they do not normally engage in selling, distributing or offering products in the stream of commerce. *See* Rockwell 1992, §3, §4a and 4b (with further references).
[23] *Cf.* Keeton et al. 1984, § 53, at 356.
[24] Dobbs et al. 2016, § 10.1, at 204 (with further references to case law and literature); *see also* Restatement (Third) of Torts 2010, § 7.

circumstances. In general terms, then, a successful damages action sounding in negligence against an SDO demands from the plaintiff that he demonstrate that he suffered a loss because the SDO breached a duty of care owed to him while developing its standards.

The element of duty is a threshold issue. If an SDO cannot be found to owe a duty to use reasonable care, it is not answerable under common law for any of the harm sustained by the plaintiff. The claim will thus be denied. Whether an SDO owes a duty to the plaintiff, and what standard of care is required from it, are questions of law. These questions are determined by the judge, not the jury.[25] An SDO may as a preliminary matter petition the judge, via a motion to dismiss or, after discovery, in a motion for summary judgment, to hold that it owes no duty to the plaintiff. If either motion is granted, the action is rejected before questions on breach or proximate cause are addressed by a jury in trial. If, however, a motion is denied and the judge considers that a duty is owed, liability does not automatically follow: also the other elements of a negligence action have to be established. The judge thus only exposes the SDO to potential civil liability for harm. There is a good chance that a final decision on liability may not follow in the end, as a duty decision can lead the defendant to settle the case before trial.

2. A Duty of Care in Negligence for SDOs?

To assess whether an SDO owes a duty of reasonable care in negligence, courts frequently balance competing considerations of policy and justice that determine the fairness of exposing it to civil liability for harm allegedly caused by its standards development. These considerations include the foreseeability of harm to the plaintiff as a result of the defendant's conduct, the closeness of the connection between the defendant's conduct and the plaintiff's harm, the moral blame attached to the defendant's conduct, the potential impact of imposing liability on preventing such harm in the future, the burden of liability on the defendant and the community, the availability and cost of insurance to cover the risk of liability involved, and the potential volume of litigation that liability would generate and its impact on the court system.[26] The weight of these factors may either be in favor or against imposing a duty.

The majority of the cases involving the liability of SDOs for standards development have been rejected through motions to dismiss or motions for summary judgment. Key in such "no-duty decisions" are considerations of policy and justice, together with due regard to the relationship between the defendant SDO and the users of its standards. In *Beasock v. Dioguardi Enterprises Inc.*, for example, the Supreme Court of Monroe Country, New York allowed the motion for summary judgment of the Tire and Rim Association (TRA) in a wrongful death action. An employee of one of TRA's members, a tire manufacturer, was fatally injured while inflating a truck tire that was mistakenly mounted on a bigger size rim. The plaintiff, the wife of the deceased employee, claimed that TRA was liable in negligence because it set dimensional standards which permitted mismatch injuries to occur. Leaving aside the factual question of whether TRA's standards were indeed inadequate, the Supreme Court considered that liability of associations such as TRA, which do not directly cause injury to others by the promulgation of their standards, is dependent on their authority to control compliance with their standards amongst the membership. As the court held in this case, even though TRA standards had

---

[25] The jury determines questions on fact, unless no reasonable person can differ as to the correct answer. These questions concern, most prominently, whether the duty is breached and whether that breach proximate caused the harm. U.S. common law thus typically assigns to the jury the determination of the other constitutive elements of a negligence claim. *See id.* at § 7, cmt. i.

[26] Dobbs et al. 2016, § 10.3, 208–09.

become industry standards, they were voluntary in nature and the defendant lacked the control over any culpable and fatal mismatch in the production process since it "neither mandates nor monitors the use of its standards by any manufacturer."[27]

This "control thesis" has emerged as a centerpiece in the judicial reasoning around the existence of an SDO's duty of care in negligence actions. Unless the SDO is in a position of authority to direct or control the implementation of the standards by the addressees, the harm of the plaintiff was not reasonably foreseeable for the defendant SDO and there is no sufficiently close relationship between the latter's conduct and the plaintiff's harm. In those situations, no duty of care is ordinarily owed in negligence to third parties suffering physical harm allegedly caused by inadequate standards.[28] Several courts have relied upon the thesis to give no-duty decisions in actions alleging negligent standards development.[29]

However, in one specific line of cases courts have used the control thesis as a principal argument to impose a duty of care on an SDO. These cases all concerned patients who contracted HIV/AIDS after receiving a blood transfusion with HIV contaminated blood. The defendant in these actions of personal injury or wrongful death was the American Association of Blood Banks (AABB), a private, not-for-profit trade association setting national standards for blood banking and blood transfusion services. It was alleged that AABB had failed to timely implement changes in its standards to ensure that its member blood banks employed surrogate testing or alternative practices that could prevent the collection and distribution of contaminated blood at the time it became clear that HIV could spread by transfusion.

The first in this line of cases, *Snyder v. AABB*, the New Jersey Supreme Court carefully assessed the role the SDO played in the blood-banking industry. The Supreme Court held that by the time the plaintiff received the contaminated transfusion AABB "exerted considerable influence over the practices and procedures over its member banks" and "[i]n many respects, the AABB wrote the rules and set the standards for voluntary blood banks."[30] Such dominance was fostered by AABB's annual inspection and accreditation of its members to assure compliance with its standards, its presentation as an industry leader in setting policy and standards of practice,[31] as well as the strong deference of federal and local governments to AABB standards and inspection results.[32] In holding that AABB owed a duty of care to recipients of blood transfusions the

---

[27] *Beasock* (N.Y. Misc. 1985, p. 979).
[28] *Cf.* Keeton et al. 1984, § 56, at 385 ("[i]n the absence of the [relationship of control], there is generally no duty to protect others against harm from third persons".) This discussion relates to the distinction between misfeasance and nonfeasance, see *infra* Section B.3.
[29] See *Bailey* (Ill.App. 1999) (a non-profit trade association that developed standards for the design and construction of wood trusses used for roof framing systems owed no duty to severely injured construction workers who relied on the its standards to install such systems since the association exercised no control over the manufacturer of the product, intended the standards as a guide, and could not require the manufacturer to follow its installation instructions; *Howard v. Poseidon Pools* (N.Y. Misc. 1986) (non-profit swimming pool trade association owed no duty to a swimmer who sustained diving injury for it had no authority to control the manufacturer of the pool); *Commerce and Industry Ins. Co.* (E.D.La. 1999) (non-profit trade association setting fire safety standards owed no duty to owners of property that was damaged in a warehouse fire because it had no control over which of its minimum standards were incorporated into mandatory municipal building codes or over any construction that purported to conform to its standards).
[30] *Snyder* (N.J. 1996).
[31] *Id.* at 1048 ("Society has not thrust on the AABB its responsibility for the safety of blood and blood products. The AABB has sought and cultivated that responsibility. For years, it has dominated the establishment of standards for the blood-banking industry. (...) By words and conduct, the AABB invited blood banks, hospitals, and patients to rely on the AABB's recommended procedures.").
[32] *Id.* at 1040 ("Both the state and federal government, as well as the blood-banking industry, generally accept AABB standards as authoritative. Consequently, blood banks throughout the nation rely on those standards"); *see also id.* at 1043 ("Thus, if a blood bank failed the annual AABB inspection on the taking of medical histories, that bank could

Supreme Court further gave weight to the fact that its standards were not only adopted for the benefit of the industry, but also for patients, who had to rely on those standards for the safety of donor blood.[33] The court also considered the risk of contracting HIV/AIDS through transfusions of contaminated blood both foreseeable and severe given the available government reports and scientific publications.[34] Considerations of policy and justice as raised by AABB could not trump the existence of a duty of care.[35] Accordingly, the Supreme Court held, the trial jury could have found that AABB had been negligent in not recommending in its standards surrogate testing and that this negligence was a substantial factor in causing the plaintiff to contract HIV/AIDS. AABB was held liable to pay damages in excess of $400,000.

Snyder was followed by courts in Louisiana, New York and Virginia.[36] It was rejected, however, by the California Court of Appeals in *N.N.V. v. AABB*.[37] In this case, which involved a minor who contracted AIDS after receiving a contaminated donor blood during surgery, the Court ruled that liability should not be imposed on AABB as a matter of public policy and fairness. In reaching that conclusion it, by and large, rejected all factors that were considered relevant in *Snyder* to establish a duty of care, and in particular AABB's dominance in the sector and patients' reliance on AABB standards for their safety. In *Snyder*, AABB had advanced the argument that it should not be found liable "for taking the 'wrong side' of a debate involving medical uncertainties and public policy."[38] The California Court of Appeals agreed and placed strong emphasis on the lack of medical or scientific consensus regarding the effectiveness of available methods and practices to reduce the risk of HIV/AIDS contamination via blood transfusion. Such absence made it not reasonably foreseeable that the promotion of new testing methods in its standards would have reduced the risk of AIDS contraction for the plaintiff. This state of evolving knowledge also led the court to hold that imposing liability on the SDO would not further the goal of preventing future harm under the circumstances.[39]

Moreover, the court considered in its no-duty decision, AABB had to balance the legitimate concern of the safety of blood supply against the equally legitimate concern of the availability of blood to needing patients and the costs of rejecting unaffected blood through new testing methods. As the implications for availability and costs of blood supply were unknown, AABB's conduct "warrants no moral blame."[40] The court also expressed the fear that AABB would be exposed to an extensive burden of litigation if a duty of care were to be imposed. Opening the floodgates would also have a chilling effect on the SDO and would be detrimental for the community in that the SDO would be held back to further pursue its standard-setting activities, which support otherwise laudable public policy goals such as health and safety.[41]

---

lose its [state] license to operate in New Jersey. In sum, (…) the AABB was not a mere advisory body. It exercised control of its member banks (…)").

[33] *Id.* at 1048 ("Blood banks, hospitals, and patients rely on the AABB for the safety of the nation's blood supply. A patient contemplating surgery cannot assure the safety of blood drawn from others. Of necessity, patients rely on others, including the AABB, for that assurance").

[34] *Id.* at 1048–49.

[35] *Id.* at 1049–50.

[36] *Weigand* (N.Y. Misc. 1997, p. 399) (AABB's motion to dismiss is denied); *Douglass* (La.App. 5th Cir. 1997) (overturning a summary judgment in favor of AABB); and *Jappell* (E.D.Va. 2001, p. 481) (AABB's motion to dismiss is denied).

[37] *N.N.V.* (Cal. Ct. App. 1999, pp. 1388–92).

[38] *Snyder* (N.J. 1996, 1049).

[39] *N.N.V.* (Cal. Ct. App. 1999, 1383).

[40] *Id.* at 1382–83. The *Snyder* court had dismissed this argument by holding that such concerns should not have diverted AABB from "its paramount responsibility to protect the safety of the blood supply." *Snyder* (N.J. 1996, 1050).

[41] *N.N.V.* (1999, p. 1384) ("If liability were imposed here, then the AABB and other similar medical associations could be faced with a significant burden of litigation that might be impossible to avoid"); *see also id.* at 1386–87 ("[W]e

Finally, the costs of taking out insurance against such liability could also be high.[42]

The previous analysis suggests that courts, in determining the threshold issue of duty in a negligence action, consider primarily the foreseeability of harm as a result of the SDO's conduct and the closeness of the connection between its standard-setting activities and the plaintiff's harm. The ability to control or direct compliance with its standards by the standards' addressees (e.g. by mandating compliance on SDO members or administering a certification and accreditation scheme for the purposes of monitoring compliance) will normally show such foreseeability and/or close connection. Alternatively, the fact that the standards enjoy government endorsement in (agency) regulations or guidelines and that the SDO represents itself to the public as an industry leader for the development of standards may serve to demonstrate the two factors.[43] Other considerations of policy and justice may nonetheless weigh against imposing on an SDO a duty to exercise reasonable care in the promulgation of its standards under the circumstances. Courts have, in similar wording as the California Court of Appeals in *N.N.V.*, drawn attention to the societal importance of promulgating standards and argued that this function should not be hindered by exposing SDOs to liability in order to support their no-duty decisions.[44]

3. *The Voluntary Undertaking Rule*

An alternative way to impose a duty on SDOs and subject them to potential tort liability is by applying the rules concerning the U.S. common law doctrine on affirmative duties. U.S. common law, like English law, makes a distinction between misfeasance and nonfeasance for the purposes of establishing whether the defendant owes a duty of care to the plaintiff. Whereas misfeasance – understood as active conduct working positive harm to others – generally creates a duty of care in relation to physical harm, nonfeasance – held to be passive inaction to protect from harm – does not.[45] Thus, if the defendant does not directly create the risk of harm for others, the failure to prevent or minimize that risk does not normally expose him to liability. Nonfeasance is not a tort, unless there is a duty to act imposed on the defendant in specific

---

believe imposition of liability here would have adverse consequences to the public by chilling scientific and medical debate on important issues (...) Additionally, we note imposition of liability could hinder reconsideration of established standards."); Feldmeier 1999, 795 (arguing that the result of cases like *Snyder* could be "an unwarranted expansion of liability that could have the detrimental effect of discouraging trade association standards setting"); Heidt 2010, 1254–55 (noting that cases like *Snyder* "herald an area of increased liability" and raise "the spector of unlimited liability once a duty was imposed"). *Contra*, *Weigand* (N.Y. Misc. 1997, p. 400), in which the Supreme Court of New York County held that "the parties who would be covered by a duty on the part of the industry trade association were specifically foreseeable, i.e., the recipients of blood collected and screened according to the trade association standards by member blood banks complying with those standards. Imposition on the trade association of a duty of care to those blood recipients would not expose the trade association to liability to the public at large and its liability would be within manageable limits."

[42] *N.N.V.* (Cal. Ct. App. 1999, p. 1388).

[43] See *Snyder* (N.J. 1996, nn.30–31) and *Prudential Property and Cas. Ins. Co.* (S.D.Fla. 1994, p. 3) (trade association developing standards for plywood roofing construction and nailing patterns owes a duty to exercise due care in promulgating it standards vis-à-vis homeowners who incurred extensive property damage as a result of a hurricane because these standards enjoyed wide public law recognition and the association had made representations to the public as the world leading expert body in the field).

[44] See, e.g., *Meyers v. Donnatacci* (N.J. Super. 1987, p. 404) (non-profit swimming pool trade association owed no duty to a swimmer who sustained diving injury for it had no authority to control the manufacturers of the pool and imposing such a duty would undermine the many laudable purposes that organizations such as these serve in society); *Bailey* (Ill.App. 1999, p. 183) (citing *Meyers* favorably in holding that a non-profit trade association setting standards for the design and construction of wood trusses used for roof framing systems owed no duty to severely injured construction workers). *See also Commerce and Industry Ins. Co.* (E.D.La. 1999); *infra* section B.4.

[45] Keeton et al. 1984, §56, at 373.

circumstances.[46] Put differently, affirmative duties (i.e. duties to protect others from pre-existing risk of harm) only exist in special circumstances. Courts have been able to shield SDOs from liability by reference to the distinction between malfeasance and nonfeasance. By strategically characterizing the plaintiff's allegations regarding the SDO's conduct as nonfeasance (or omission), some courts have argued that no duty of care was owed in negligence in the absence of any special circumstances.[47]

However, one of the special circumstances that has enabled courts to impose an affirmative duty on an SDO is when it voluntarily undertakes to perform an activity that is aimed at reducing the risk of harm for another caused by some other source. U.S. common law then allows the imposition of a duty of care on the SDO vis-à-vis the other or even to third parties. One articulation of this so-called "voluntary undertaking" rule is found in Section 43 of the Restatement (Third) of Torts:

> An actor who undertakes to render services to another and who knows or should know that the services will reduce the risk of physical harm to which a third person is exposed has a duty of reasonable care to the third person in conducting the undertaking if:
>
> (a) he failure to exercise reasonable care increases the risk of harm beyond that which existed without the undertaking,
> (b) the actor has undertaken to perform a duty owed by the other to the third person, or
> (c) the person to whom the services are rendered, the third party, or another relies on the actor's exercising reasonable care in the undertaking.[48]

This guideline was previously laid down in similar wording in Section 324A Restatement (Second) of Torts, which "has been widely recognized by the court."[49]

Plaintiffs have relied upon the voluntary undertaking rule to establish civil liability for standards development, frequently in parallel to actions in negligence.[50] The service that is rendered concerns the development of product standards (including warnings) aimed to prevent or minimize risk of physical harm caused by dangerous products. The situation described under (a) suggests that an SDO has a duty of reasonable care in standards development when that activity leads to "some physical change to the environment or some other material alteration" that increases the risk of physical harm.[51] In the absence of evidence to the contrary, courts have considered the risk to exist independently of any standards development. In *Rountree v. Ching Feng Blinds Industry Co. Ltd.*, for example, the U.S. District Court of Alaska held that the risk of physical harm of strangulation posed by cords of window coverings does not vary as a function of the allegedly wrongful safety standards the Window Covering Manufacturers Association had

---

[46] *See generally* Dobbs et al. 2016, §25.1, at 615; Restatement (Third) of Torts 2010, § 37.

[47] *See, e.g., Meyers* (N.J. Super 1987, p. 401) (New Jersey Superior Court interpreting the claim against the SDO as allegations concerning the failure to take action to prevent harm resulting from shallow water diving while being aware of the correlation between the two, and not that the standards the SDO undertook to set were inaccurate, false or improper); *see also People v. Arcadia Machine & Tool, Inc.* (Cal.Super. 2003, p. 21) (granting a motion for summary judgment by trade associations in the gun industry after holding that the claim is premised on nonfeasance and that the plaintiffs failed to present authority that these associations owed a duty to develop standards for gun safety design).

[48] Restatement (Third) of Tort 2010, § 43. The rule can be traced back to *Glanzer v. Shepard* (N.Y. 1922, p. 276) in which Justice Cardozo held: "One who assumes to act, even gratuitously, may thereby become subject to the duty of acting carefully, if he acts at all." The rule has therefore also been known as the "Good Samaritan" rule.

[49] Dobbs et al. 2016, §25.7, at 628 (with references to case law); *see also* Restatement (Third) of Torts 2010 § 43, cmt. c.

[50] In *N.N.V.* (Cal. Ct. App. 1999) the plaintiff relied on Section 324A Restatement (Second) of Torts in its appeal against AABB's summary judgment, which had been granted in first instance in relation to a negligence action.

[51] *Patentas* (3d. Cir. 1982, p. 717) (referring to Section 324A Restatement (Second) of Torts, cmt. c, Illustration 1).

developed to reduce the risk of injury to infants.[52] The SDO's failure to decrease that risk was not considered sufficient. This meant that even if the plaintiffs in this case, the parents of a deceased girl who got strangled in the inner cord of a window blind, would prove the inadequacy of the standards, a duty of care could not be imposed on the SDO following the rule under (a).[53]

Applied to the context of product standardization, the situation set out under (c) of Section 43 of the Restatement subjects an SDO to a duty of care when the plaintiff shows that the manufacturer of the product that caused the physical harm ("the other") relied on negligently developed standards in the production or sale of that product, or, alternatively, that plaintiffs themselves ("the third person") placed such reliance on the standards when buying or using that product. Plaintiffs relying on this rule have seen their claims frequently defeated because of their inability to show that they (or the manufacturer of the dangerous product) actually relied on the negligently developed standards.[54] In *Sizemore v. Georgia-Pacific Corp.*, for example, the plaintiffs sought damages for personal injuries resulting from a fire that occurred in their home. They alleged that the Hardwood Plywood & Veneer Association (HPVA), a non-profit trade association for plywood manufacturers, had been conducive in promoting and adopting wrongful fire safety standards, with which the plywood paneling installed in their home complied. It was clear from the file, however, that they had only learned about HPVA and the standards after the fire.[55]

Most of the substantive discussion on the question of whether an SDO owes a duty to exercise reasonable care in standards development concerns the situation under (b). Such a duty exists, the Restatement proposes, if the SDO has undertaken to perform a duty one of its business members (i.e. a manufacturer or seller) owed to the plaintiff. In the case of developing product standards, the SDO must thus have assumed the duty manufacturers or sellers have to individuals or firms to produce or sell safe products. In determining whether that duty was indeed assumed, courts have frequently relied on the "control thesis" discussed above and have made the determination of the duty element dependent on the SDO's ability to control compliance with its standards by its membership, or in the industry more broadly.[56] Again, the lack of such authority or control, for example due to the voluntary, non-binding legal status of the standards involved or the absence of any instruments to inspect and sanction non-compliance, is then frequently considered sufficient for a no duty decision.[57]

---

[52] *Rountree* (D.Alaska 2008, p. 808).

[53] *Id.* at 808 ("A standard or warning that explicitly accounted for the danger posed by the inner cord may have decreased the risk of injury to plaintiffs [but] it does not show that an inadequate standard *increased* the risk of harm to the third-party consumer" (emphasis as in original)).

[54] Negligent misrepresentation actions have for the very same reason been denied. However, where SDOs engage in certification or accreditation plaintiffs are more successful in showing reliance, namely on the certificate, accreditation or any other label or seal attesting compliance with the product standards. See *infra* section B.4.

[55] *Sizemore* (D.S.C. 1996, p. 8) ("plaintiffs did not rely upon any publication or other activity on the part of HPVA, nor were they even aware that HPVA existed prior to suffering their injuries."); see also, e.g., *Friedman* (E.D.Pa. 1989, p. 383) ("there is no evidence that plaintiffs relied on [the SDO's] performance (...) Plaintiffs state that they had not read any allegedly false or misleading information or publication concerning PCBs in well pumps prior to the date of the incident") (applying Section 323 Restatement (Second) of Torts).

[56] *Cf. Commerce and Industry Ins. Co.* (E.D.La. 1999, p. 4) ("Under the Restatement analysis advanced by plaintiffs, most courts have focused on the amount, if any, of control a trade association wields over the behavior of its members concerning, for example, the proper implementation of its standards").

[57] See, e.g., *Bailey* (Ill.App. 1999, p. 185) (a non-profit trade association developing standards for the design and construction of wood trusses used for roof framing systems owed no duty to severely injured construction workers since its "instructions were advisory" and it "could not force the carpenters to abide by its admittedly general instructions"; see also *Commerce and Industry Ins. Co.* (E.D.La. 1999, p. 4) (non-profit trade association setting fire safety standards owed no duty to owners of property that was damaged in a warehouse fire because it has no control over compliance with its standards as it "does not list, inspect, certify or approve any products or materials for compliance with its

In *King v. National Spa and Pool Institute, Inc.*, however, the lack of control did not withhold the Alabama Supreme Court from imposing on the NSPI, a non-profit trade association which promulgated standards for the size, shape and dimensions of residential swimming pools, a duty to exercise due care under the voluntary undertaking rule as laid out in Section 324A of the Restatement (Second) of Torts. In this case, the plaintiff's husband broke his neck after diving into his pool from the jump board. Some months later he died of pneumonia secondary to his injury. In previous claims involving diving injuries, courts in New Jersey and New York had forthrightly refused to accept that NSPI owed a duty to pool users based on the theory that it had no control over pool manufacturers or sellers.[58] The Alabama Supreme Court held differently. Reading the case as premised on malfeasance rather than nonfeasance, it considered that NSPI "had no statutorily or judicially imposed duty to formulate standards," but nonetheless did so voluntarily.[59] It furthermore held that the SDO developed its standards for swimming pools having in mind "the needs of the consumer" and had declared that safety was "one of the basic considerations upon which these design and construction standards are founded."[60] Under those circumstances the Supreme Court held that harm for consumers was foreseeable for NSPI if due care was not exercised in promulgating its standards.[61]

The approach in *King* was confirmed by the Washington Court of Appeals in *Meneely*, in which NSPI was held liable for rendering a young swimmer quadriplegic who dove from a jump board into a pool, while it knew that the combination of the specific pool and board at hand posed a risk for certain divers and failed to amend its safety standards accordingly.[62] While NSPI may not have had any formal control over compliance with its standards by the industry, NPSI members followed its standards out of economic imperative.[63] The damages award against NSPI of $6.6 million, along with settlements in other cases, sent the SDO into insolvency.[64]

Emerging from bankruptcy in 2004, NSPI was again faced with a personal injury action of an injured swimmer. In assessing the action, the courts in first instance and on appeal reaffirmed the control thesis, and held that NSPI owed no duty of care to the plaintiff. The U.S. District Court in Georgia found at first instance that the "standards are voluntary, consensus standards" and that the association "has no power to enforce compliance with those standards" and "had no control over [the contractor's] installation of the [plaintiff's family] pool or over whether [the contractor] complied with the NSPI Standard when installing the pool".[65] The Eleventh Circuit Court confirmed these findings on appeal and added that NSPI did not owe a duty to warn consumers about the danger of swimming pools and diving boards covered by its standards following

---

standards. It merely sets forth safety standards to be used as minimum guidelines that third parties may or may not choose to adopt, modify or reject").

[58] *See Meyers* (N.J. Super. 1987, p. 406) ("NSPI had no authority to mandate compliance nor did it attempt to force its members to comply. It acted merely as a secretariat for its members; a forum where those who chose to make suggestions could do so. There were no penalties for failing to respond to the survey"); *Howard* (N.Y. Misc. 1986, p. 55) ("NSPI did not have the duty or the authority to control the manufacturers who did produce the product here in question, viz., the swimming pool") (discussing the existence of a duty of care in an action sounding in negligence).

[59] *King* (Ala. 1990, p. 614).

[60] *Id.* at 615–16.

[61] *Id.* at 616. *See also Rountree* (D.Alaska 2008, p. 809) (considering that "It is of no consequence that [the SDO] did not have control over the blinds because [it] had control over the content of the warning. The warning itself provides a critical nexus between [the SDO], the manufacturer and the consumer"). Instead, the court focused its duty analysis on a number of public policy factors, including foreseeability. *Id.* at 810.

[62] *Meneely* (Wash.Ct.App. 2000) (applying the Washington voluntary rescue doctrine, which is broadly similar to the rules proposed in the Restatement).

[63] *Id.* at 57.

[64] *See* Heidt 2010, 1231 n.15.

[65] *Lockman* (N.D.Ga. 2010, p. 7).

Section 324A of the Restatement (Second) of Torts: it did not increase the risk of diving injuries for swimmers; sufficient proof of actual reliance on NSPI standards was missing, and NSPI did not undertake to perform a duty owed by pool manufacturers to swimmers.[66]

Applying the voluntary undertaking rule to impose a duty of care on an SDO finds it limit in the scope of the undertaking: What was it that the SDO voluntarily undertook to do?[67] Courts have given particular importance to the addressees of the standards and the purpose for which the standards are developed, using both factors to argue either in favor or against the imposition of a duty.[68] Thus, in no-duty decisions courts have pointed to a limited undertaking by noting that the SDO develop standards for the purposes of sharing knowledge amongst peers in the industry, that it sought to address its membership exclusively, and that its standards were minimum standards only.[69] In duty decisions, by contrast, courts have stressed the public interests involved in having adequate standards for third parties, namely for the health and safety of ultimate consumers of the products for which standards are set.[70]

A second important limit in applying the voluntary undertaking rule is found in the courts' sense of policy and justice. Even if a duty can be imposed on SDOs following the voluntary undertaking rule, considerations of policy and justice may still trump the existence of a duty of care.[71] Thus, again, considerations regarding the foreseeability of harm, the closeness of connection between the defendant's conduct and the plaintiff's harm, the moral blame attached to the defendant's conduct, the policy of preventing future harm, the burden on the defendant and the consequences to the community if a duty is imposed, and the availability and cost of insurance to cover the risk involved.[72]

4. Negligent Misrepresentation

Finally, plaintiffs who allegedly suffered harm caused by the standard-setting activities of SDOs have on several occasions brought a negligent misrepresentation action to recover their harms. Such action may enable plaintiffs who reasonably relied upon false information supplied to them by the defendant to obtain from it compensation for the physical or economic harm caused by that reliance. For those seeking to establish liability for physical harm the existence of the SDO's duty of care is usually supported by the rules of a general action in negligence.[73] The success of the claim, if recognized under state law,[74] then turns on the questions whether the

---

[66] *Lockman* (11th Cir. 2010, p. 474).

[67] *See, e.g., Bailey* (Ill.App. 1999, p. 184) ("Under the voluntary undertaking theory of liability, the duty of care to be imposed on a defendant is limited to the extent of the undertaking"); *Rountree* (D.Alaska 2008, p. 809) ("The court agrees that 'the scope of one's duty is limited by the scope of [their] undertaking'").

[68] *See generally* Dobbs et al. 2016, §25.6, at 627.

[69] *See, e.g., Meyers* (N.J. Super 1987, 406) ("Although NSPI rendered services to its member by providing a forum, NSPI did not assume the duty to warn consumers of the danger of shallow water diving which it recognized as necessary for the protection of a third party").

[70] *See King* (Ala. 1990, pp. 615–16 n.59); *Rountree* (D. Alaska 2008, p. 810) ("[T]he objective of the ANSI standard sponsored by WCMA was 'to reduce the possibility of injury, including strangulation, to young children from the bead chain, cord, or any type of flexible loop device used to operate the product.' This factor favors imposition of a duty").

[71] Dobbs et al. 2016, §25.7, at 630; Restatement (Third) of Torts 2010, § 43, cmt. b.

[72] *See, e.g., Rountree* (2008, pp. 810–11) (considering that these policy considerations do not weigh against the imposition of a duty on an association of manufacturers of window covering which undertook to develop an ANSI national safety standard intended to address the strangulation hazard of window blinds).

[73] Dobbs et al. 2016, § 43.3 (suggesting that actions to recover personal injury, property damage or emotional harm based on risks created by misrepresentation are best recognized as negligence actions).

[74] Not all states recognize an action of negligent misrepresentation resulting in physical harm. *Compare, e.g., Flynn* (Minn. Ct. App. 2001, p. 351) (explaining that Minnesota only recognizes negligent misrepresentation actions for

standards at issue were developed without exercising reasonable care and thus constituted false information, whether that information was actually and reasonably relied upon, and whether that reliance caused the physical harm.

For those claiming pure economic loss, a duty of care not to be negligent in supplying information will not normally exist for an SDO, unless it has undertaken to perform such a duty for the plaintiff, or there is a special relationship (e.g. a fiduciary or confidential relationship) between the parties that led the plaintiff to expect that reasonable care would be exercised for its interests.[75] Following the Restatement, liability for stand-alone economic harm is limited to those for whose benefit and guidance the misinformation was supplied or to those the SDO knew the recipient intends to supply it.[76] Once these elements are satisfied the questions regarding the inadequacy of the standards, actual and reasonable reliance, and causation must also be affirmatively answered if the claim is to prevail.

Courts hearing actions for negligent misrepresentation against SDOs have dismissed these actions primarily because of the plaintiffs' failure to establish that the SDO owed a duty to them, and that there was actual reliance on the standards. A case in point is *Commerce and Industry Ins. Co. v. Grinnell Corp*, which involved a fire that consumed an entire warehouse in New Orleans. The insurance company of a firm that had stored (and lost) its merchandise in the fire sought recovery of over $27 million it had paid to its insured. It thus brought a subrogation action against the National Fire Protection Association (NFPA), a not-for-profit, voluntary membership organization which developed and published model consensus codes and standards concerning fire safety. These standards are applied throughout the U.S. and frequently incorporated in federal and state safety regulations.

In this case, the plaintiff alleged that the NFPA fire safety standards led the warehouse sprinklers system to be ineffective as they failed to provide accurate information on the distance between that system and a potential fuel source for a fire. Interpreting this allegation as a negligent misrepresentation claim, the U.S. District Court in Louisiana considered that in the absence of a contract or fiduciary relationship, NFPA could only owe a duty to the plaintiff when the misinformation is directly communicated to the plaintiffs' insured, the insured was part of the limited group of persons for whose benefit and guidance the misinformation was supplied, and the insured actually relied on that information. However, there was no evidence that the plaintiff had any direct or indirect contact with NPFA, or that it even knew about the NFPA standards.[77] Actual reliance upon those standards in any business transaction the plaintiff undertook was therefore impossible.[78] The court further reasoned that policy considerations weigh against imposing a duty of care on NFPA vis-à-vis third parties which occupied a building that was built by others in compliance with its standards. More specifically, it held that:

> Promoting public safety by developing safety standards is an important, imperfect, and evolving process. The imposition of liability on a nonprofit, standards developer who exercises no control

---

pecuniary loss and not for risk of physical harm) *with Randi W.* (Cal. 1997, p. 593) (holding that California recognizes the action based on the conditions set out in Restatement (Second) of Torts (1965) § 311).

[75] Dobbs et al. 2016, § 43.5.

[76] Restatement (Third) of Torts 2012, § 5, which sets rules that are "largely identical" (Reporter's note) to Restatement (Second) of Torts (1979) § 552. Many courts have followed the Restatement analysis. For an extensive list, see *Kohola Agriculture* (Haw. 1997, p. 159).

[77] *Commerce and Industry Ins. Co.* (E.D.La. 1999, p. 3).

[78] *See also Howard* (N.Y. Misc. 1986, pp. 52–53) (negligent misrepresentation action against NSPI is denied because the plaintiff had neither alleged reliance on NSPI's activities when he dove in an above-ground pool, nor had he demonstrated that he belonged to the group of beneficiaries NSPI could reasonably have intended to rely on the information supplied, which presumably were only the manufacturers of pools).

over the voluntary implementation of its standards under circumstances like those presented here could expose the association to overwhelming tort liability to parties with whom its relationship is nonexistent and could hinder the advancement of public safety.[79]

Where SDOs engage in certification and accreditation activities, however, they are at greater risk of incurring liability in a negligent misrepresentation action. A case in point is *Hempstead v. General Fire Extinguisher Corp.*, which involved a fire extinguisher that exploded when put to use by an employee. An injured co-worker brought a claim in negligence and misrepresentation against the manufacturer and Underwriters' Laboratories (UL). The latter had tested, for a fee and upon the manufacturer's request, the type of fire extinguisher concerned. Using for that purpose its own standards for construction and performance, UL found the design of the extinguishers compliant and had publicly communicated this approval in its professional publications. UL also allowed the manufacturer to affix to the fire extinguishers a label declaring that it was UL tested and inspected.[80]

UL had thus approved the defective design of the products based on its own standards. Saying otherwise would be "straining at words," the U.S. District Court in Delaware held.[81] This meant that UL's standards failed to ensure the safe use of the products, whereas UL "knew or should have known of construction and materials which would be required if the hazards involved in the use of the extinguishers were to be avoided."[82] UL certification was "unquestionably" of aid to the manufacturer in selling the products and reliance on the certification was further bolstered by the statutory backing it had received in the local Fire Prevention Code.[83] Liability for negligent misrepresentation could thus follow.[84]

In *Hempstead* the court second-guessed the product standards UL had adopted. In other cases involving the liability of SDOs engaged in certification, courts have been more reluctant to review the substance of standards. Instead, their concerns have been with the accuracy of the certification process and the attestations of compliance that have been awarded.[85] In these cases, the rationale for holding SDOs liable under the theory of negligent misrepresentation is no different from the rationale underpinning liability of certification bodies and other sorts of endorsers under such theory.[86] That rationale is perhaps best expressed in *Hanberry v. Hearst Corp.*, a California case establishing the liability of a certifier that had awarded the "Good Housekeeping Seal" to ladies' shoes that were extremely slippery when worn on certain floor coverings, and had so caused severe personal injury:

> Since the very purpose of respondent's seal and certification is to induce consumers to purchase products so endorsed, it is foreseeable certain consumers will do so, relying upon respondent's representations concerning them, in some instances, even more than upon statements made by

---

[79] *Commerce and Industry Ins. Co.* (E.D.La. 1999, p. 3).
[80] *Hempstead* (D.Del. 1967, pp. 116–17).
[81] *Id.* at 117.
[82] *Id.*
[83] *Id.* ("The Fire Prevention Code authorized the Fire Prevention Supervisor to rely upon the services of any recognized testing authority, including Underwriters, to determine the suitability of a particular type of fire extinguisher, and a listing by any such authority permitted the Fire Prevention Supervisor to find such extinguisher suitable for installation").
[84] *Id.* at 118. The success of the negligent misrepresentation action is not determined by the court in its summary judgment. Rather, it holds that UL would be liable on the basis of the voluntary undertaking rule.
[85] *See, e.g., Benco Plastics, Inc.* (E.D.Tenn. 1974, p. 786); *Groppel Co., Inc.* (Mo.Ct.App. 1981, p. 66); *Rottinghaus* (Wash.Ct.App. 1983, p. 907).
[86] *See generally* Rockwell 1992; Belson 2017, 112–18 (each with further references to case law). For more on accreditation bodies, see Schuck 1994, 188–91.

the retailer, manufacturer or distributor. Having voluntarily involved itself into the marketing process, having in effect loaned its reputation to promote and induce the sale of a given product, the question arises whether respondent can escape liability for injury which results when the product is defective and not as represented by its endorsement.[87]

Thus, actions sounding in negligent misrepresentation have been largely defeated because of plaintiffs' inability to show actual and detrimental reliance on the standards involved.[88] This failure, as noted, has also led to the failure of actions based on the voluntary undertaking rule.[89] However, if SDOs combine standard-setting with certification activities, such as in *Hempstead*, the chances of such actions prevailing increase. After all, these activities provide public, expert-based representations on key characteristics of the certified product or producer itself that carry currency in commerce and serve to encourage individuals and firms to rely on its representations to buy or use the product.

C. PERSPECTIVES FROM THE EU

It is striking to observe just how little case law has developed in the EU compared to the United States on liability for the development of product standards. As Spindler notes, "it is surprising that there is almost no case to be found [in the EU] that holds standardising organisations liable for standards which have been exceeded by new knowledge".[90] Judicial control over private standards development in the EU has for the most part taken place in the context of EU internal market law (i.e. competition and free movement law),[91] and judicial review at both the European[92] and Member State level.[93] In addition, there is hardly any theorization in European legal scholarship about the civil liability of SDOs, how such liability relates to the liability of, for example, public regulators, individual professionals or collective associations engaged in standardization or certification, and what policy considerations should support or limit the imposition of liability on these actors.[94] This stance may be explained by the lack of case law on this issue, but also in part by the fact that tort law is principally regulated at the level of the EU Member States, where concepts and theories of liability vary notoriously along long-lasting national traditions of common and civil law, or mixes in between. In other words, no general EU framework exists that covers the liability of SDOs.

Nevertheless, there are recent developments in the case law of the Court of Justice of the EU that should be taken into consideration. To put these developments into perspective, this section will first briefly set out the legal framework that applies to EU standardization called the "New Approach." It will then discuss the liability of SDOs for activities pursued within that framework.

---

[87] *Hanberry* (Cal.Ct.App. 1969, p. 684). *See also United States Lighting Serv, Inc.* (N.D.Ohio 1992) (finding that UL is required to act with ordinary care in the conduct of its certification process given the reliance placed in its mark by consumers and suggesting that it may incur liability for economic loss under the theory of negligent misrepresentation).
[88] For a similar observation in relation to liability of accreditation bodies, see Schuck 1994, 188–91.
[89] *See supra* notes 53–54.
[90] Spindler 1998, 331.
[91] See Mataija 2016, 233–44.
[92] In the recent case of *James Elliott Construction Ltd. v. Irish Asphalt Ltd.* (C-613/14, ECLI:EU:C:2016:821), the Court of Justice of the EU held itself competent to review European harmonized standards developed within the legislative framework of the New Approach (*see infra* section C.1). This expansion of the Court's jurisdiction to the domain of technical standardization has triggered a lively debate on the desirability of judicial control over standards development in Europe. For a more detailed analysis of the case and its likely consequences, see Chapter 7; Volpato 2017.
[93] Schepel & Falke 2000, 131–34.
[94] For notable exceptions, see Spindler 1998; Schepel 2005, 384–87; Cafaggi 2006, 58–73.

Finally, we will look beyond the scope of the New Approach and consider liability for the development of market-based product standards.[95]

1. The New Approach

Voluntary product standards in the EU are developed within the framework of the "New Approach." This legislative program was developed in the 1980s to improve the free movement of goods within the internal market.[96] Within the program, the legislative institutions of the EU adopt secondary legislation that set out the "essential requirements" with which products have to comply to be lawfully traded in the EU. The precise technical specifications are then laid down in a European harmonized standard that is developed by European standardization organizations – CEN, CENELEC or ETSI.[97] After the European Commission has published a reference to this voluntary standard in the Official Journal of the EU, a presumption arises that products that comply with the standard also comply with the essential requirements of the relevant EU legislation. As such, establishing compliance with a European harmonized standard has become the principal way for manufacturers to show that their products comply with the law. Although it is possible for manufacturers to demonstrate legal compliance through other means, in practice most manufacturers opt to show compliance with the European standard.[98]

Regulation 1025/2012/EU, which since 2012 constitutes the legal framework underlying the New Approach, recognizes CEN, CENELEC and ETSI as the European standardization organizations.[99] These SDOs are no institution or agency of the European Union, however. CEN and CENELEC are private not-for-profit associations (*association internationale sans but lucrative*) under Belgian law.[100] ETSI is also a private non-profit association, but is incorporated in France.[101] This means that the liability of the three European standardization organizations is not governed by EU law, but by national tort law, subject to the rules of private international law.[102] The liability of national SDOs that are members of CEN, CENELEC and ETSI is equally

---

[95] Beyond the scope of inquiry is therefore the liability for certification activities under the New Approach. The breast implants scandal that unfolded around the French manufacturer of silicone breast implants Poly Implant Prothèse SA (PIP) has triggered various claims from victims against the certification body that inspected and approved PIP's manufacturing processes within the New Approach framework, yet failed to discover the illegal use of substandard silicone gel to manufacture the implants. In 2017, the Court of Justice of the EU held, in the case of *Elisabeth Schmitt v TÜV Rheinland LGA Products GmbH* (C-219/15, ECLI:EU:C:2017:128), that certification bodies conducting conformity assessments under the New Approach owe a general duty of care to end users of certified products "to act with all due diligence" when performing such assessments (para. 46). This implies that they have to be alert on non-compliance and must take appropriate action once they receive evidence that indicates that products may no longer be compliant. However, EU law does not offer a basis to hold liable these actors for breach of this duty and their liability must be established under the tort law regimes of the Member States. See Verbruggen & Van Leeuwen 2018.
[96] *See generally* Schepel 2005, 227–46; Hodges 2005, 53–73.
[97] CEN (European Committee for Standardization), CENELEC (European Committee for Electrotechnical Standardization) and ETSI (European Telecommunications Standards Institute) develop standards for different sectors.
[98] Schepel 2013b, 528.
[99] Article 2(8) read in conjunction with Annex I of EU Regulation No 1025/2012.
[100] CEN 2015; CENELEC 2015. CEN and CENELEC have as their membership national standardization bodies of the EU Member States and a number of additional European countries.
[101] ETSI 2017b. ETSI has over 800 members including standardization bodies, government representatives, trade associations and individual businesses.
[102] More specifically, Article 340 of the Treaty on the Functioning of the EU (TFEU) governs the tort liability of institutions or agencies of the EU. It reads: "In the case of non-contractual liability, the Union shall, in accordance with the general principles common to the laws of the Member States, make good any damage caused by its institutions or by its servants in the performance of their duties."

governed by national tort law. These national SDOs participate in the creation of European harmonized standards and implement them at the national level, that is, they translate the standards and make them available, usually upon payment of a fee. The national SDOs are free to engage in the development of standards outside the scope of New Approach. The development of such market-based standards in areas like cyber security, environmental sustainability and worker safety now constitutes an important business activity for many. In that domain they compete against trade associations, NGOs and other standards developers at both national and international levels.

2. Liability Under the New Approach

Only very few national courts in the EU have been concerned with claims involving the liability of SDOs, both within and beyond the New Approach. Strict liability for personal injury and property damage caused by defective products is not the proper basis for bringing such claims. In the EU, this domain of tort law is exclusively regulated by the Product Liability Directive, unless pre-existing special liability regimes apply.[103] The Directive, as implemented by the EU Member States, imposes such liability on business actors that fall within the scope of the "producer" concept as set out in Article 3 of the Directive. While this concept "embraces a wide range of actors," it does not extend to those that are not involved in the manufacturing, sale or distribution of products.[104] Accordingly, SDOs fall outside the scope of the Directive.[105] Similar to the United States, liability claims against these private actors in Europe must be brought under theories of negligence to prevail.

A comprehensive comparative study commissioned by the European Commission and the European Free Trade Association called "Legal Aspects of Standardisation" concluded as regards the potential of tort law to hold liable SDOs for negligent standard-setting "even though the theoretical possibility is open in all jurisdictions under discussion here, France and Italy seem to be the only Member States where it has actually happened.[106] The Italian case involved the alleged violation of intellectual property rights for the use of geographical denominations by the national standards body as it developed a new standard to compete with an existing one. The outcome of the case was unknown at the time of this writing.[107]

In France, the liability of the national SDO for technical standards called *Association Française de Normalisation* (AFNOR), is a matter for the administrative courts since AFNOR is considered to fulfill a public law function (*mission de service public*) when developing technical standards in fields covered by New Approach legislation.[108] The comparative study reports just one tort law claim brought against AFNOR. In the case, AFNOR had licensed a manufacturer of a certain type of concrete pavement to use its conformity mark "NF." After a very severe winter, however, these pavements had cracked. The manufacturer was held liable by the municipalities where the defective pavements had been placed and by the contractors that placed them there. The manufacturer enjoined AFNOR in the proceedings and sued for damages

---

[103] Council Directive 85/374/EEC (European Union 1985, OJ L 210, 7.8.1985, p. 29); Directive 1999/34/EC (European Union, OJ L 141, 4 June 1999, p 20, art. 13).
[104] Weatherill 2013, 175.
[105] Some commentators have presented arguments to suggest that standards could be seen as a "product" within the scope of the Product Liability Directive. By extension, SDOs could then be considered "producer." So far, none of these arguments have been considered by the Court of Justice of the EU in the interpretation of the Product Liability Directive. For further discussion, see Stuurman & Wijnands 2000, 617–18.
[106] Schepel & Falke 2000, 238.
[107] *See* Menchetti 2000, 540.
[108] Conseil d'État, No. 73230 (France 1992). *See also* Décret No. 2009–697 (France 2009).

for developing "inadequate" standards. The *Tribunal Administrative de Paris* denied the claim. First, it upheld AFNOR's exclusion clause included in the license contract for use of its NF mark, implying that it could not be held liability for all defects in products that were awarded that mark. Second, it considered AFNOR not to be at fault given that its standards cannot be held to cover all characteristics of a product. Moreover, once AFNOR became aware of the problems concerned, it amended the relevant standard.[109]

If the national SDO is awarded a specific legal status or special powers by national statute or decree, its liability for standardization and certification activities is typically governed by rules on state liability in so far as it acts within the scope of that status or powers. While immunity from liability is rarely accepted in Europe, policy considerations may put more stringent demands on the conditions of duty and breach (or any equivalent under national tort law) when SDOs make use of their public law status or powers.[110] These considerations may thus further limit the risk of liability these SDOs face.[111]

The apparent insignificance of the theme of SDO liability in the case law of national courts in the EU hides the fact that, in practice, SDOs are concerned about the risk of incurring liability for their standard-setting activities. The cited study on "Legal Aspects of Standardisation" reports that several SDOs operating under the New Approach have taken out liability insurance.[112] Others try to exonerate themselves in general terms of sale or service.[113] The Dutch NEN (*Nederlands Normalisatie Instituut*), takes a rather defensive approach and includes in its general conditions of sale sweeping indemnity clauses that require its contracting parties, for which NEN undertakes to perform services such as standards development or certification, to indemnify it for any civil liability vis-à-vis third parties caused by the performance of the contract, including violations of intellectual property rights, privacy laws or any other laws and regulations that are in force (Articles 5.3 and 12.6). NEN further limits its contractual liability by limiting the extent of damages to its insurance coverage (Article 12.2), excluding liability for indirect damages (Articles 12.3–12.4) and damages related to any printing errors in the materials provided by the contracting party (Article 12.5), and by setting the limitation period to three months after the damage manifested (Article 12.7).[114] The NEN internal regulations also include a general clause exonerating NEN from liability for direct or indirect damages against members caused by or in relation to its norms (Article 10.2.2).[115]

The British Standards Institute (BSI) seemingly admitted that it owes a duty of care to anyone relying on its standards in the first version of its "Standard for Standards" publication.[116] In the version currently in force, this magnanimous assumption of a duty can no longer be found.[117] The study on "Legal Aspects of Standardisation" also reported the German *Deutsches Institut für Normung* (DIN) to admit to a duty of care (*Garantenstellung*) to users of its standards in

---

[109] *Société Les Grands Travaux de l État c/ Pottier et Oth* (France 1993); see also Champigneulle-Mihailov 2000, 318–19.
[110] Van Dam 2013, 532.
[111] Schepel & Falke 2000, 239.
[112] *Id.* at 238.
[113] For ANFOR's terms and condition of sale, see ANFOR 2018, art. 9.
[114] NEN 2016.
[115] NEN 2005. The validity of these limitation and exclusion clauses may be questioned. In business-to-business relationships they may be allowed only where the extent to which the liability is limited is not disproportionate to the loss incurred. In business-to-consumer dealings, however, they are likely to be challengeable under EU consumer law, in particular Council Directive 93/13/EEC of 5 April 1993 on unfair terms in consumer contracts OJ L 95/29. For a discussion of this EU Directive, its implementation in commercial and consumer law in England and Wales, and the extensive case law developed on it by the Court of Justice of the EU, see Lawson 2017.
[116] BSI 1997, part 2, sec. 6.9.1.5.
[117] BSI 2017.

its ground rules for standardization that were previously in force.[118] Still, the reporters of the study considered, the risk of the British and German SDOs incurring liability is relatively low since they have put in place several procedural safeguards that would mitigate against a breach of the duty.[119] Such safeguards include ensuring participation of interested stakeholders and knowledgeable experts in standards development, having available to these actors all relevant technical and scientific information, and ensuring that standards are developed for the common good and not for individual commercial benefit.[120] The AFNOR case discussed above demonstrates that it is also helpful in this respect to have in place a review procedure once shortcomings have become clear.

3. Liability Beyond the New Approach

In the absence of a common legal framework on tort liability and the limited discussion in European legal scholarship about liability for standards development, the landscape regarding such liability can be said to be even sketchier beyond and within the New Approach framework. The reach of EU law is generally limited here and divergent national regimes of liability hold sway. While tort claims against SDOs have reached the supreme courts of (some) Member States, these claims first and foremost disputed the certification activities the SDOs were engaged in, rather than standards development.[121] Liability for standards development is extremely rare and plaintiffs may not be able to meet the elements that national tort laws require for their actions to prevail.

In English common law, for example, policy considerations around the existence of a duty of care are likely to defeat most claims, as they do in American common law. The leading case law of the Supreme Court on the tort of negligence and on negligent misstatements suggests that no such duty exists because of a lack of a sufficiently proximate relationship between the plaintiff and defendant SDO, or the absence of the assumption of a responsibility by the SDO on which the plaintiff reasonably relied.[122] Policy factors concerning the public role of SDOs in society as non-profit organizations promoting the collective welfare and the consequences in terms of liability exposure for SDOs and their public role if a duty were imposed would further militate against a duty being recognized, in particular if the plaintiff is suing for economic loss.[123]

---

[118] Schepel & Falke 2000, 240–41.
[119] *Id.* at 241–42.
[120] *See, e.g.*, BSI 2017; DIN 2013.
[121] *See, e.g., Marc Rich* (UK 1995) (holding that a classification society does not owe a duty of care to cargo owners arising from negligent inspections of a damaged ship); *Cour de Cassation, No. 06-19.521 (France 2007)* (holding that a certifier is not liable for economic losses caused by a defect that arose in a certified television within the period of warranty set by the producer); Bundesgerichtshof, VII ZR 36/14 (Germany 2017) (holding that a certifier is not liable for personal injury caused by defective breast implants if the manufacturer of the implants had used materials not intended to be used for manufacturing such medical devices and had fraudulently concealed that use from the certifier); Hoge Raad *Strawberry Mite* (Netherlands 2007) (holding that a certifier is liable for pure economic loss sustained by a strawberry farmer and caused by the violation of its own certification protocol for pest control in horticulture products).
[122] *Hedley Byrne & Co. Ltd.* (UK 1964); *Caparo Industries* (UK 1990); *NRAM Ltd.* (UK 2018); *Banca Nazionale del Lavoro SPA* (UK 2018).
[123] *Cf. Marc Rich* (UK 1995, *pp. 12–13, 28*) *(Per Lord Lloyd of Berwick and Lord Steyn)*. However, there is case law suggesting that, in the case of personal injury, the issues of proximity and policy factors do not stand in the way of imposing a duty of care on an SDO. *See* in particular *Watson* (UK 2000) (holding that a professional boxing association owes a duty of care in respect of the formulation of its rules and regulations for the provision of medical assistance during boxing matches to boxers, who reasonably rely upon that association to look after their safety in these matches); and *Wattleworth* (UK 2004) (holding that a private governing body for motor sports in the UK owes a duty of care to drivers in adopting standards that aim to ensure their safety on motor race tracks). *See also Perrett* (UK 1998) (holding than an aircraft inspector owes a duty to aircraft passengers to act with reasonable care so to ensure that they are not injured by reason of a defect in the aircraft's construction that was part of the inspection protocol).

In civil law countries, in particular those that may be considered to stand in the Napoleonic tradition (e.g. Belgium, France, Italy, the Netherlands, Spain), the duty element in negligence liability (or any equivalent concept used) has not triggered discussions as profound as in American or English common law. Nonetheless, considerations around the foreseeability of the type of plaintiff's harm, the closeness of connection between the SDO's conduct and the harm, and the societal function of standard-setting are likely to surface in the determination of breach and legal causation.[124] Accordingly, breach and causation serve as the main control mechanisms to guard against overly burdensome liability for SDO. These elements are, unlike in the United States, decided by judges only.

Importantly, however, violations of EU law may serve as a catalyst of liability claims against SDOs based on national tort law. The case of *Fra.bo v. DVGW*, a German case which concerns the civil liability for product standardization and certification activities, may serve to illustrate that role.[125] Fra.bo was an Italian manufacturer of copper fittings used for water and gas piping. These copper fittings, which fell outside the scope of the New Approach legislation regulating the sale of construction materials in the EU, serve to make piping water tight and airtight. To sell these fittings in Germany, Fra.bo applied for certification by a German non-profit association called DVGW (*Deutsche Vereinigung des Gas- und Wasserfaches eV*). DVGW adopts technical standards for the performance of construction materials used in the gas and water sector and certifies products on that basis. Initially DVGW awarded Fra.bo certification of its copper fittings for both the water and gas sector. This award essentially revolved around compliance of the fittings with DVGW's technical standard "Worksheet W534," which specified the norms that products that come in contact with water have to meet in order to attain certification. Fra.bo applied for DVGW certification since such certification would show conformity with mandatory national product safety law. While in theory other certifications were available, in practice DVGW was the only body Fra.bo could turn to have its fittings certified.

Fra.bo's certification was soon subject to a re-assessment procedure because a competitor had complained to DVGW that it was technically impossible to satisfy the quality standards for water and gas supply by one and the same type of fitting, as Fra.bo did. As a result of that procedure DVGW no longer accepted the positive test results provided by a state-accredited Italian laboratory upon the request of Fra.bo, whereas the same laboratory had also provided the test results that initially led DVGW to grant Fra.bo certification. Furthermore, DVGW amended its technical standard W534 by introducing a test consisting of exposing the copper fitting to a temperature of 110 degrees Celsius in boiling water for 3,000 hours, claiming this was needed to ensure a longer lifecycle for certified products. The conditions for certification as included in the contractual arrangement between DVGW and Fra.bo required that if a technical standard was amended, certificate holders must apply for a renewal of their certification. Fra.bo did not make such an application and as a result DVGW withdrew Fra.bo's certification. In response, Fra.bo brought a damages claim against DVGW for breach of contract and EU law. It argued, among other things, that the introduction of the 3,000-hour test was arbitrary and had no other goal than to limit access to the German market. Moreover, there was no reason to deny the Italian test results since these were produced according to the procedures DVGW had itself stipulated.[126] Accordingly, Fra.bo argued, DVGW violated EU rules on competition and free movement of goods in the performance of its obligations under the certification contract.

---

[124] *See generally* Van Dam 2013, 208–17 (discussing the different policies and control mechanisms used in English, France and Germany law to limit the scope of protection offered by tort law in the context of pure economic loss).

[125] *Fra.bo* (CJEU 2012). For a comprehensive overview of the academic literature on this case, see http://eur-lex.europa.eu/legal-content/EN/NOT/?uri=CELEX:62011CJ0171.

[126] *Cf. Landgericht Köln* (Germany 2008, paras. 31–32, 36).

The district court denied the claim. The court hearing the appeal referred several preliminary questions to the Court of Justice of the EU as it was unsure how to interpret and apply the EU law rules concerned. In delivering its judgment, the European Court of Justice held that the standardization and certification activities of DVGW are covered by the EU rules on free movement of goods, which prohibits the imposition of measures by Member States that limit the import of products from other Member States. Even though DVGW is a private association, the Court applied a functional approach and considered that it restricted the free movement of goods "in the same manner as do measures imposed by the State."[127] German product safety law indeed held that DVGW certification signified legal compliance. DVGW was also the only body capable of certifying Fra.bo's copper fittings for the application at issue, whereas the lack of such certification constituted a significant restriction for companies seeking to market their products in Germany.[128] Therefore, the Court concluded, DVGW "in reality holds the power to regulate the entry into the German market."[129]

The judgment of the Court of Justice has attracted significant scholarly attention for its importance regarding the internal coherency of EU free movement law,[130] for its implications on the New Approach framework,[131] and for the way in which the Court has strengthened judicial review in the field of technical standardization.[132] Our principal interest in this chapter – the civil liability of SDOs for standardization and certification activities – has been of far less concern to scholars.[133] In concrete terms, for DVGW the *Fra.bo* judgment meant that it needed to be able to justify the adoption of the 3,000-hour test and its refusal to recognize testing results from an accredited laboratory in another Member State. In more general terms, it was challenged to provide justifications for the adoption of stricter standards and (de)certification decisions that harm the economic interest of firms like Fra.bo. If it cannot provide these, liability for damages may arise, either in contract or in tort.

After the Court of Justice of the EU rendered its judgment, the referring court of appeal in Germany held that DVGW was liable vis-à-vis Fra.bo for breach of contract. The national court considered that the DVGW performance standards for product certification in the water sector, including the 3,000-hour test, were contrary to the free movement of goods, as these could restrict the import of goods otherwise lawfully traded in other Member States. DVGW could not make the continuity of Fra.bo certification dependent on the meeting of that test. Accordingly, the revocation of Fra.bo's certification was without any ground and unlawful.[134] Moreover, DVGW was wrong to discard the testing results provided by an accredited laboratory in another Member State since this is contrary to the mutual recognition principle underpinning EU free movement law.[135]

DVGW's breach of the rules on the free movement of goods, the court of appeal further reasoned, could not be justified. The protection of public health, as DVGW claimed, did not serve as an appropriate justification for the adoption of the 3,000-hour test. The SDO failed to provide evidence that the adoption of the new standard was instrumental to such protection, for example by offering a detailed risk analysis of the hazards it claimed to control by introducing the

---

[127] *Fra.bo* (CJEU 2012, para. 26).
[128] *Id.* at paras. 27–30.
[129] *Id.* at para. 31.
[130] *See, e.g.*, Van Harten & Nauta 2013; Van Leeuwen 2013; Mataija 2016, 246–50.
[131] *See, e.g.*, Chapter 7; Schepel 2013b.
[132] *See, e.g.*, Van Gestel & Micklitz 2013.
[133] *See* Verbruggen 2017a, 72–73.
[134] *Oberlandesgericht Düsseldorf* (Germany 2013, paras. 48–50).
[135] *Id.* at para. 54.

test, that is, bacterial contamination of water or gas explosions caused by failing copper fittings. Apparently, such risks did not play any role when DVGW adopted the new standard. Moreover, the decision to fix the duration of the test at 3,000 hours was unsubstantiated. DVGW did not sufficiently establish that the test is the accepted state-of-the-art, which might as well be shorter (or longer) than 3,000 hours.[136] Accordingly, DVGW unlawfully and negligently withdrew Fra. bo's certification, which likely caused the latter's (pure economic) losses consisting in the loss of profit it could have made the period in which it was cut off from the German market.[137]

The case of *Fra.bo* neatly demonstrates how national private law and EU public law complement each other in the regulation of technical standardization and certification in the EU. As shown, a civil damages claim gave rise to a discussion of whether EU rules applied and were violated. While in this case the rules at stake concerned free movement of goods, in others it may involve rules of competition law or non-discrimination. After the Court of Justice established that EU rules did apply, the national court held that these rules were violated in the performance of contractual obligations, thus giving rise to a remedy in private law. Clearly, in *Fra.bo* it was contract law that provided the plaintiff with a remedy against the SDO, but had a contractual relationship been absent between the two, as is usually the case in standards development, an action in tort could have provided the means for addressing any allegedly wrongful activities. More generally, any breach of EU law that is directly applicable to the activities of an SDO and that is protective of the interests of the actor affected by those activities (i.e. EU free movement law of persons and services, competition law or non-discrimination law), constitutes a ground to bring a claim in tort against the SDO.[138] Tort law constitutes a key branch of the law to privately enforce those EU law rules at the national level and can, as such, be said to contribute in significant ways to the regulation of standards development in the EU.

D. COMPARATIVE ANALYSIS

The previous discussions highlight a number of themes worthy of further comparative analysis. The research questions set out in the introduction, as further developed in Section A, guide the analysis.

1. Duty Considerations in Negligence Law

Liability for standards development in the United States and the EU is established exclusively on theories based in negligence. Central to all actions sounding in negligence, the voluntary undertaking rule or negligent misrepresentation in the United States are considerations around the existence of a duty of care. The duty element proves to be a formidable requirement that the plaintiffs in the majority of these actions fail to meet. Considerations to impose on the defendant SDO a duty to exercise reasonable care in promulgating standards have frequently turned on the question to what extent the SDO exercises control over the standards' addressees to comply with its standards. In these actions, control is then seen a necessary proxy for establishing the foreseeability of harm to the plaintiff as a result of the development of standards and/or the closeness of the connection between that activity and the plaintiff's harm.[139] Such control can follow from

---

[136] *Id.* at paras. 63–64.
[137] *Id.* at paras. 73, 78.
[138] Verbruggen 2017b, 59–71.
[139] The exponent of this position perhaps is *Meyers* (N.J. Super. 1987, p. 403), in which a New Jersey Superior Court granted summary judgment for NSPI because "the crucial element of foreseeability is lacking" upon the finding that the SDO "had absolutely no power to force a member to comply with its promulgated standards."

any legal arrangement (e.g. contracts, rules of association, bylaws) that enables the SDO to mandate the standards, or the SDO's administration of a certification or accreditation scheme that monitors compliance with its standards amongst addressees. The SDO's lack of such leverage over compliance with its standards usually leads to a no-duty decision.

An obvious criticism against this reasoning is that, in practice, members routinely follow SDO standards in their business operations. Even without formal control, compliance rates are usually high amongst SDO members. A number of courts in the United States have therefore rightly looked beyond the control thesis and have sought to establish a duty of care by reference to the degree to which the standards enjoy a high level of market uptake, receive government endorsement, and to public representations made by the SDO as regards its expertise in developing standards in the field.[140] Considerations of whether the standards serve the purpose of protecting third parties against personal injury or property damage have been further added to the mix of relevant circumstances that justify the imposition of a duty.[141] In the EU, the *Fra.bo* case has echoed this functionalism where public law support of the contested standards and the economic significance of complying with those standards were considered as arguments to apply EU law rules on the free movement of goods to a private standardization and certification activities. Accordingly, the defendant SDO was under a legal duty to comply with EU rules of mutual recognition of market regulations and non-discrimination of goods lawfully traded in other Member States.[142]

Other considerations of policy and justice may nonetheless militate against imposing a duty to exercise reasonable care in standards development in negligence. Some U.S. courts have awarded particular weight to the moral blame attached to the defendant's conduct, the potential impact of imposing liability on the policy of preventing plaintiff's harm in the future, and the consequences of exposing SDOs to liability on their important societal function of promulgating standards in a given domain.[143] The absence of any commercial interest of the SDO in developing standards may further be relevant.[144] Such considerations, next to the plaintiff's failure to show actual reliance on the allegedly inadequate standards or that the SDO undertook to perform a duty owed by its members to the plaintiff, have also barred the imposition of a duty of care on SDOs in actions based on negligent misrepresentation and the voluntary undertaking rule.[145] Similar considerations would appear to lead courts in England and Wales to refuse to

---

[140] See, e.g., *Meneely* (Wash.Ct.App. 2000, p. 56); *Snyder* (N.J. 1996, pp. 1040, 1048); and *Prudential Property and Cas. Ins. Co.* (S.D.Fla. 1994, p. 3). In *Beasock* (N.Y. Misc. 1985, p. 979), however, the court admitted that the SDO's dimensional standards for tires, rims and wheels had become industry standards, but nonetheless held that no duty was owed to the plaintiff. In *Commerce and Industry Ins. Co.* (S.D.Fla. 1999, p. 3), the court held that the incorporation of the allegedly inadequate NFPA fire safety standard in government construction regulations did not help to impose a duty of care on the NFPA since that incorporation made the relationship between NFPA and the plaintiff's insured too remote to warrant the imposition of a duty.

[141] See, e.g., *Snyder* (N.J. 1996, pp. 1048, 1050); *King* (Ala. 1990, p. 616); *Rountree* (D.Alaska 2008, p. 810).

[142] *Fra.bo* (CJEU 2012, paras. 27–30).

[143] See, e.g., *Meyers* (N.J. Super. 1987, p. 404); *N.N.V.* (Cal.Ct.App. 1999, pp. 1382–87).

[144] See, e.g., *Meyers* (N.J. Super. 1987, p. 403) (holding that the development of design and construction standards for swimming pools "is not a money-making operation"); see also *Commerce and Industry Ins. Co* (S.D.Fla. 1999, p. 4) ("The NFPA is not even a trade association which acts in the economic self-interest of its members. The organization consists of 68,000 individuals and over 80 organizations. It is not a trade group consisting of businesses with homogeneous economic interests."). In *Snyder*, however, the economic interests involved in the development of standards for the blood banking industry was an important consideration to impose a duty on AABB. See *Snyder* (N.J. 1996, p. 1050) ("Although the AABB's mission doubtless has altruistic overtones, the bottom line is that the AABB represents its interests and those of its members. At stake for its members was a substantial financial interest in the regulation of the industry. (…) Blood is big business"). Similar considerations emerge in relation to civil liability for negligent certification. See, e.g., *Hempstead* (D.Del. 1967); *Hanberry* (Cal.Ct.App. 1969); *Rottinghaus* (Wash.Ct.App. 1983).

[145] See, e.g., *Commerce and Industry Ins. Co* (S.D.Fla. 1999, p. 3).

expose SDOs to civil liability for standards development under the tort of negligence as far as economic loss is concerned.[146]

2. Factors Bearing on Breach

The use of foreseeability of harm and the moral blame attached to the SDO's conduct as factors to determine the existence of a duty of care in negligence can be criticized for confusing duty with breach.[147] Foreseeability, it is contended, first and foremost bears on the issue of breach and determines whether an SDO has acted with reasonable care under the circumstances.[148] Blameworthiness also speaks to the reasonableness of the SDO's activities in the light of the particular circumstances.[149] By confusing the duty with breach, courts invade the province of the jury, prevent a full legal analysis of the dispute, and effectively shield SDOs from being exposed to civil liability. To minimize this strategic behavior of courts the Restatement (Third) of Torts proposes, amongst others, that foreseeability is a factor to be considered only on the breach issue, not duty, and that moral blameworthiness is not a valid consideration of policy.[150]

Once an SDO is considered to owe a duty of care, it is held to exercise reasonable care in the development of its standards. That standard of care implies that it is required to avoid harm that was known to it or reasonably foreseeable. U.S. common law permits the plaintiff to present at trial a wide range of evidence to show that the defendant SDO breached its duty and that the process of standards development administered by it fell short of the level of care it was reasonably required to exercise. Such evidence generally includes internal company rules or rules of association, industry practice, private standards, statutes, government regulation and guidance, and cost–benefit analysis.[151] Accordingly, a violation of the SDO's own guidelines or bylaws for standards development can be considered as evidence showing breach, but also non-compliance with government or industry-endorsed principles on how standard-setting procedures should be organized in terms of due process or good governance may be used to show that the defendant SDO fell short of the level of care required.[152]

Courts in the cases reviewed here do not explicitly refer to these principles of due process or good governance in the determination of breach. In fact, there is very little consideration around the question of what factors may establish the reasonableness of the care that the defendant SDO exercised. In *Meneely* and *Snyder* – the only two U.S. cases resulting in a damages award against the SDOs involved – the issue of breach turned on the narrow question of whether the SDOs could have reasonably refused to amend their safety standards while being aware of the risk of physical harm these standards posed to others.[153] More generally, however, these two cases suggest that in establishing breach it is important that the SDO uses the knowledge gained from

---

[146] See the case law cited *supra* at note 123.
[147] See, e.g., Heidt 2010, 1256–58 (criticizing the approach in *Snyder*); N.N.V. (Cal.Ct.App. 1999, p. 1404) (Amos, J., dissenting as regards the majority's no-duty decision and criticizing the decision for confusing duty with breach).
[148] See Cardi 2005.
[149] Dobbs et al. 2016, §10.4, at 210.
[150] Restatement (Third) of Torts 2010, § 7, cmt. j. For further discussion, see Dobbs et al. 2016, 212–13 and (critically) Zipursky 2009.
[151] See generally Dobbs et al. 2016, §§12.1–12.10, at 263–89.
[152] Particularly important for this purpose is Circular No. A-119 (OMB 2016) (promoting the adoption of private standards by US Federal agencies provided they meet attributes of openness, balance of interest, due process, having an appeals procedure, and operate on the basis of consensus (at para. 4)) and the ANSI Essential Requirements (2018a) (further detailing the elements set out in Circular No. A-119). See for a detailed discussion of the potential of tort law to foster compliance with good governance principles in private standards development Verbruggen 2019.
[153] *Snyder* (N.J. 1996, p. 1038); *Meneely* (N.J. Super. 2000, p. 57).

experience with the implementation of its standards in practice to inform and direct its decision-making around the revision or adoption of new standards.[154]

Such considerations can also be found in the sparse European case law on the matter. In the ANFOR case the French court held that the defendant SDO could not be at fault in developing standards for concrete pavement because of the limited protective scope of the standards and the fact that the SDO swiftly amended these standards once inadequacies surfaced.[155] Likewise, the German court in *Fra.bo* considered the defendant SDO to have breached its duty under EU law since it failed to provide evidence that the adoption of the contentious new standard was necessary and proportionate to the protection of health and safety. Moreover, the SDO had refused to recognize available testing results from a state-accredited laboratory in another Member State.[156] Thus, whenever an SDO does not take into consideration the state-of-the-art when promulgating or revising its standards, or altogether fails to adopt new standards in the face of evidence showing the existence of apparent risks to others, it does not act with ordinary care. SDO compliance with important good governance attributes such as impact evaluation, responsiveness to new insights from practice and technology, and recursive learning may thus be rewarded in the assessment of breach.

Some courts in the United States have also shown appreciation of the SDO's efforts to ensure inclusive and transparent rulemaking. In *Meyers*, for example, the court drew attention to the practice of public solicitation of comments and suggestions of non-members on draft standards to ensure a fair representation of interests to argue that the element of foreseeability was lacking.[157] In *N.N.V.*, the plaintiff alleged that AABB's standard-setting procedure was biased toward the interests of private organizations concerned with blood products and transfusions and that there was no active participation of those representing other interests in the standards development. The California Court of Appeal discarded the argument by holding that there was no evidence to support the assertions and that the private organizations involved did not represent industry alone. Each had different classes of membership representing a variety of interests and many voices.[158] In *Snyder*, however, the New Jersey Supreme Court sanctioned the absence of inclusive and transparent procedures of the AABB, along with the SDO's commitment to promote the financial interests of the blood banking industry at the expense of patients' health and safety.[159] Clearly, the courts in these cases weigh the facts of the cases in a very different way. However, when read together, the judicial considerations involved do reveal that concerns around fair stakeholder participation and transparency in procedures for standards development, as well as other principles of good governance, can weigh in on the determination of whether the SDO reasonably decided on its standards under the circumstances.[160]

Importantly, the standard of reasonable care does not require a perfect decision from the defendant SDO, yet only one that is fair and reasonable at the time of consideration. Standards development typically is an "imperfect and evolving process."[161] While a delay in setting a

---

[154] *See also Commerce and Industry Ins. Co* (S.D.Fla. 1999, p. 4) (If the NFPA had owed a duty to plaintiffs, it would not have breached the duty because the plaintiffs did not provide evidence that the SDO knew or should have known of the alleged fire safety risk. Instead, NFPA periodically reviews and revises its standards "to keep current with new fire protection knowledge and technologies" and "to include fire safety lessons learned from significant fires").

[155] *See supra* note 108.

[156] *See supra* notes 134–35. *See also Watson* (UK 2000), at 117–21 (Lord Philips M.R.) and *Wattleworth* (UK 2004), at 141–63.

[157] *Meyers* (N.J. Super. 1987, p. 403).

[158] *N.N.V.* (Cal.Ct. App. 1999, pp. 1393–94).

[159] *Snyder* (N.J. 1996, p. 1050).

[160] *Compare* Marasco 2005 (arguing that ANSI-accredited SDOs should not be subject to civil liability when they meet ANSI's requirements for openness, consensus and other due process safeguards).

[161] *Commerce and Industry Ins. Co* (S.D.Fla. 1999, p. 3).

particular standard in relation to a known and foreseeable risk may be negligent, SDOs enjoy a certain level of discretion in making choices on what the standard is that it adopts, particularly in times of uncertain knowledge about risks.[162] Given the nature of decision making in standards development, which always involves the balancing of competing interests, courts (and juries in the United States) should not lightly second-guess the decisions of the SDO, but assess whether they, at the time they were made, were fair and reasonable to those affected by them.

In the light of the apparent difficulty of conducting such assessment having the bias of hindsight, some commentators have suggested that SDOs should be protected from such inquiries by awarding them a qualified immunity or privilege.[163] Such award would mean that SDOs are liable only if they act in bad faith. With that, it is suggested, the exposure of SDOs to civil liability does not distort the delicate decision-making process around standards development and the many laudable goals that SDOs seek thereby to serve. The counter argument is that granting (any form of) judicial immunity or privilege is to impute "power without responsibility" on private associations that, in their activities, are first and foremost concerned with the private interests of those they represent.[164] The award would furthermore undermine the regulatory potential for tort law to encourage SDOs to pursue public policy objectives rather than narrow private interests, adopt and review standards based on state-of-the-art scientific evidence, and engage in inclusive and transparent procedures of rulemaking.[165]

CONCLUSION: THE RISK OF TORT LIABILITY FOR STANDARDS DEVELOPMENT

What then is the risk of incurring tort liability for standards development? Based on the review of case law in the United States and EU, it must be concluded that this risk is relatively low. In the United States, the majority of the actions against SDOs have been rejected via motions to dismiss or motions for summary judgment with courts holding that the SDO involved did not owe a duty to exercise reasonable care in the promulgation of its standards to the plaintiffs. Accordingly, SDOs have frequently been shielded from civil liability for harm allegedly caused by their inadequate standards. In so holding, a number of courts have strategically played on the doctrinal complexities in distinguishing between the elements of duty and breach in negligence with the view to exclude a defendant's standard-setting activities from a jury inquiry. In those no-duty decisions considerations around the absence of a specific relationship between the standard-setting activities of the SDO and the plaintiff's harm (i.e. the foreseeability of harm and its closeness of connection with the SDO's conduct) and the consequences of exposing the SDO to liability on the important societal function of promulgating standards in a given domain have been particularly instrumental in the reasoning of the courts.

The U.S. cases in which a duty of care was imposed have for the most part turned on the question of whether the SDO was in a position of authority such that its standards were followed by businesses, either out of legal or economic imperative. Accordingly, the necessary relationship between the plaintiff and defendant SDO to sustain a duty could be constructed. All but one

---

[162] Cf. Jappell (E.D.Va. 2001, p. 481) ("Where delay in setting a particular standard would be negligent, the duty to act without negligence may require Defendant to make difficult choices somewhat earlier than it would prefer."). See also Amos, J. dissent in N.N.V. (Cal.Ct.App. 1999, p. 1404) (holding that "If a duty were imposed on AABB, it would not be breached if there was an ongoing debate and the state of knowledge in a particular area was still evolving").

[163] Feldmeier 1999, 796–97; Heidt 2010, 1079–84; see also Snyder (N.J. 1996, pp. 1056–57) (Garibaldi, J., Dissenting) (arguing that AABB should be granted a qualified immunity based on the quasi-governmental nature of its activities in regulating blood banks).

[164] Snyder (N.J. 1996, pp. 1052–53).

[165] Cf. Schepel 2005, 399–400.

of these cases concerned wrongful death actions or actions involving severe personal injury.[166] Liability for negligent standard-setting causing pure economic loss has not been accepted in the United States.[167]

In the EU, there has been very little civil litigation on the development of product standards, both within and outside the scope of the New Approach. Judicial control over standards development takes place primarily in the context of EU internal market law (competition law and free movement law), and judicial review in administrative law. However, as the case of *Fra.bo* shows, the breach of directly effective EU rules of internal market law may trigger civil litigation on standards development before Member State courts subject to national regimes of tort law. Such litigation may enable the recovery of personal injury and property damage, but also pure economic loss as was the case in *Fra.bo*. Accordingly, EU law may function as a catalyst for damages actions against SDOs in Europe.

The comparative analysis in this chapter has revealed that there are a number of circumstances related to the activities and governance of an SDO that affect its exposure to civil liability for standards development. These include:

- *Legal or* de facto *control to direct compliance with standards.* If the SDO enjoys a position of authority such that its standards are followed by those using them for business operations, i.e. manufacturers and sellers of products, it is more likely to be subject to civil liability than if it has no such position. Authority or control can exist either *de facto* or *de jure*, and may be evidenced by showing that the standards are followed out of imperative market demands, enjoy a strong degree of government recognition, or are coupled with mandatory periodic certification or accreditation inspections.
- *Intended purposes of developing standards.* If an SDO explicitly and actively commits to protect the interests of non-members or industry outsiders by developing standards, in particular if related to their physical health and safety, the failure to do so in an adequate way will more likely lead to civil liability than if the SDO only commits to develop standards to promote the (economic) interests of its industry membership.
- *Representations about expertise in standards development.* Similarly, public statements and promotions by an SDO concerning the importance and currency of its standards in economic, government or community practice makes the SDO more susceptible to tort liability when the standards it promulgates cause harm to others.
- *Commercial benefits.* If the SDO stands to gain commercial benefits from the development of standards or related certification and accreditation inspections, the failure to pursue these activities adequately make it more likely to be subject to civil liability if it carries out these activities without commercial interests.
- *Good governance.* Lastly, the failure of the SDO to observe accepted principles of good governance, such as inclusive and transparent rulemaking and adoption and review of standards based on state-of-the-art scientific evidence, makes it more prone to liability.

---

[166] The exception is *Prudential Property and Cas. Ins. Co.* (S.D.Fla. 1994) (involving extensive property damage caused by a hurricane).
[167] See, e.g., *Waters v. Autuori* (Conn. 1996) (professional association for accountants owes no duty in negligence to the plaintiff who lost money on investments in a failed limited partnership the accounts of which had been audited by a member accounting firm based on allegedly inadequate standards developed by the association); *Appalachian Power Co.* (S.D.N.Y. 1959) (professional association for accountants is not liable for the pure economic loss third parties could allegedly sustain as a result of the promulgation of accounting standards, which would adversely affect the third parties' ability to obtain credit).

Compliance with such principles may show that the SDO exercised reasonable care in developing its standards.

These circumstances underline the very basic idea that an SDO should be answerable for harm caused to individuals and firms when it possesses, or holds itself out to possess, the power to affect these parties' interests. With power comes responsibility. As the analysis in this chapter has shown, tort law should be considered a key legal mechanism through which individuals and firms can hold an SDO responsible for the harm they suffered as a result of influential, yet negligently developed standards.

PART III

Copyright and Standards

5

Questioning Copyright in Standards

*Pamela Samuelson and Kathryn Hashimoto**

A.	Copyright in Coding Systems?	92
B.	Standards May Be Unprotectable Systems Under Section 102(b)	97
C.	Standards May Be or Become Unprotectable by Copyright Under the Scenes a Faire or Merger Doctrines	100
D.	Privately Developed Standards Adopted as Laws	104
E.	Considering Incentives and Competition Policy Concerns about Copyrights in Standards	106

Throughout this volume, commentators agree that technical interoperability standards are essential to the operation of the Internet, the World Wide Web, cellular networks, and, indeed, to the modern information society. They are an integral part of the largely invisible infrastructure of the modern world that makes things work, including the rapidly expanding Internet of Things. With the rise of the global economy, copyright has become a prominent factor in the longstanding debate over intellectual property rights in standards, as standards developing organizations (SDOs) typically claim copyright protection to charge substantial fees for access to and rights to use their standards.

The critical importance of claims of copyright in standards is illustrated by a controversy about the intellectual property policy that the International Organization for Standardization (ISO) issued in July 2003. It would have required all software developers and commercial resellers of data who embedded data elements from ISO's standard country, language, and currency codes to pay an annual fee (or a one-time fee plus regular maintenance fees) for doing so.[1] Tim Berners-Lee, director of the World Wide Web Consortium (W3C), wrote a letter to ISO's president to object to this policy because of its negative impact on the evolution of the Web:

> These and similar codes are widely used on the Web. In particular, the language and country codes are of direct interest to W3C and the users of W3C Recommendations in the context of HTTP, HTML and XML and various other technologies. Language and country codes currently provide a single, standard way of identifying languages (and locales) throughout the Web.

---

* © Pamela Samuelson and Kathryn Hashimoto
[1] Cover 2003. ISO standard 3166, for example, represents Afghanistan as "AF," Albania as "AL," Australia as "AU," and Austria as "AT" within this code. ISO standard 639–2 represents the modern German language as "deu," modern Greek as "gre," Hawaiian as "haw," and Italian as "ita" within this code.

Multilingual Web sites and Web pages, as well as internationalization and localization features, would be particularly affected.

Any charges for the use of these standards are going to lead to fragmentation, delay in deployment, and in effect a lack of standardization. In particular, those users who depend upon multilingual or non-English language services will suffer....

Given that this policy would have profound impact not only on ISO, but also on industry and users of the Web at large, we urge ISO to further consider this policy and its broader implications and consequences, and to reassure the community as quickly as possible that there will be no charges for the use of these standards.[2]

The ISO policy would also have had devastating consequences for open source developers.[3] After several other organizations published statements of concern about the policy,[4] ISO tabled it. Yet ISO continues to charge substantial fees for downloads and reproduction of its standards.

This chapter considers whether standards such as these should be eligible for copyright protection as a matter of copyright law. It reviews several U.S. lawsuits that challenged copyrights in standards, which met with mixed success. Looking at the statutory exclusions under 17 U.S.C. § 102(b) and limitations on the scope of protection under the merger and scenes a faire doctrines, we argue that at least some standards ought to be, or become, unprotectable by copyright. Taking into account competition and other public policy concerns, this chapter concludes that standards organizations may not, as they sometimes claim, need copyright incentives to develop and maintain the industry standards they promulgate, particularly those whose use is required by law.

A. COPYRIGHT IN CODING SYSTEMS?

Copyright protection has sometimes been claimed in coding systems. These systems typically use numbers, abbreviations, or other symbols to represent certain data elements in accordance with rules or organizing principles. Sometimes such systems have been collectively drafted to serve as industry standards, although some systems drafted by one person or firm have become, or their drafters intended them to become, de facto standards in the market. In the late 1990s, competitors challenged copyrights in medical and dental industry codes devised to enable efficient communication.

One example is the American Medical Association (AMA) coding system for medical services. The AMA first began publishing its Current Procedural Terminology (CPT) document in 1966. It revises the CPT each year. The CPT identifies terms and descriptors for thousands of medical services and procedures and assigns a unique five-digit number to each for the purposes of enabling uniform reporting of medical services to insurance companies and billing for these services.[5] In the 1980s, the federal government's Health Care Financing Administration (HCFA), since renamed the Centers for Medicare & Medicaid Services, mandated use of the CPT as part of its Healthcare Common Procedure Coding System when reporting services for Medicare and Medicaid reimbursement. The CPT thus become a standard in two senses: AMA promulgated it to be a standard coding system for physicians and other health professionals and agencies, and

---

[2] Berners-Lee & Bratt 2003.
[3] Clark 2003. *See also* Chapters 10 and 11 discussing standards and open source code.
[4] Cover 2003. The Unicode Technical Committee, the International Committee for Information Technology Standards, and the Internet Architecture Board were among the other objectors.
[5] American Medical Association 2017.

the federal government mandated its use as a standard for doctors who wanted to be reimbursed by government agencies.

Practice Management Information Corp. (PMIC) wanted to publish the AMA code in one of its guides for medical compliance services. When AMA threatened legal action, PMIC sought a declaratory judgment that the code had become uncopyrightable after HCFA mandated its use or, alternatively, that AMA misused its copyright by granting an exclusive license with HCFA that forbade the agency to use any other system of medical procedure nomenclature for reporting physician services.[6] The U.S. Court of Appeals for the Ninth Circuit ruled against PMIC's challenge to AMA's copyright, although it lifted, on grounds of copyright misuse, the preliminary injunction against PMIC's publication that the trial court had issued.

PMIC's invalidity argument rested mainly on U.S. Supreme Court case law about the uncopyrightability of judicial opinions and statutes. In *Banks v. Manchester* (1888), for instance, the Supreme Court decided that judicial opinions could not be copyrighted because judges in their official capacity and as public servants do not have pecuniary or proprietary interests in the opinions they write. The Ninth Circuit in *PMIC* distinguished *Banks*, deciding that AMA, by contrast, was a private entity that claimed it needed copyright protection to provide incentives to creation and maintenance of the CPT.[7] PMIC pointed out that *Banks* had rejected copyright claims in judicial opinions on due process grounds, that is, on a theory that people should have unfettered access to the law. However, the court found that PMIC had failed to show that anyone was having difficulty accessing the CPT. Moreover, the AMA had no reason to limit or preclude access to the code.[8]

The Ninth Circuit expressed concern that if it invalidated AMA's copyright and determined that the CPT had entered the public domain once a government entity required its use, this would have negative effects not just on the AMA, but also on a wide range of privately authored model codes, standards, and reference works. It further noted that the Supreme Court had not considered whether private actors could enforce copyrights in rules they drafted after government adoption. In addition, two other courts had refrained from invalidating copyrights under similar circumstances.[9]

Nevertheless, the Ninth Circuit agreed with PMIC that AMA had misused its copyright by entering into an exclusive licensing deal with HCFA.[10] This misuse did not invalidate the copyright, but it limited AMA's right to enforce the right until the misuse had been purged.[11] PMIC now publishes guides that include the CPT codes.

On appeal, PMIC belatedly argued that the CPT code was uncopyrightable because the HCFA mandate caused the CPT to become an unprotectable "idea" under § 102(b) of the U.S. Copyright Act, the merger doctrine, and another Ninth Circuit precedent, *Sega Enterprises Ltd. v. Accolade Inc.* (9th Cir. 1993). The court relegated PMIC's argument to a footnote and offered no opinion on the 102(b)/merger theory, although that footnote distinguished *Sega* as having involved an effort to suppress creativity: "[T]he AMA's copyright does not stifle independent creative expression in the medical coding industry. It does not prevent [PMIC] or the AMA's competitors from developing comparative or better coding systems and lobbying the federal government and private actors to adopt them. It simply prevents wholesale copying of an existing

---

[6] *PMIC* (9th Cir. 1997).
[7] *Id.* at 518.
[8] *Id.* at 519.
[9] *Id.* The two cases discussed were *CCC* (2d Cir. 1994) and *BOCA* (1st Cir. 1980).
[10] *PMIC* (9th Cir. 1997, pp. 520–21)
[11] *Id.* at 520 n.9.

system."[12] This statement ignores that the very point of developing a standard coding system such as the CPT is to gain the benefits of uniformity.

PMIC apparently did not make the more straightforward argument that the CPT was an unprotectable coding *system* under § 102(b), which provides: "In no case does copyright protection ... extend to any idea, procedure, process, *system*, method of operation, concept, principle, or discovery, regardless of the form in which it is ... embodied in such work."[13] This is curious given that AMA and the Ninth Circuit repeatedly referred to the CPT as a "system."[14] As a practical matter, the federal mandate requiring use of the CPT for Medicaid and Medicare reimbursements made the use of alternative systems infeasible, which meant that PMIC's merger defense had more substance than the Ninth Circuit recognized.[15]

Section 102(b) played a somewhat more prominent role in a sister case to *PMIC* that arose after Delta Dental published a book containing standard dental procedure nomenclature and associated numbers from the Code on Dental Procedures and Nomenclatures developed by the American Dental Association (ADA). ADA sued Delta for copyright infringement and sought an injunction to stop Delta from publishing ADA's code, as well as for money damages for past infringements.

The trial judge ruled against the copyrightability of the ADA code, holding that it did not qualify for copyright protection because it comprehensively cataloged a field of knowledge rather than creatively selected information about it.[16] Although the Code's arrangement of the code data was creative, the arrangement was systematic and highly useful and, hence, unprotectable under § 102(b). The code was, moreover, the collaborative work product of a committee, not an expression of an author. Indeed, Delta had participated in the drafting of the ADA standard, which further supported its right to reuse the ADA code.

Judge Easterbrook, writing for the U.S. Court of Appeals for the Seventh Circuit, disagreed. In his view, ADA's "taxonomy" of dental procedures was creative enough to qualify for copyright protection. Easterbrook's opinion goes into considerable detail about his perception of creativity in the ADA's numbering system.[17] Because there are many different ways to name and organize types of dental procedures, the way chosen by ADA was a creative expression not dictated by functional considerations. The usefulness of a taxonomy did not disqualify it from protection, in Easterbrook's view, because only pictorial, sculptural, and graphic works were disqualified from copyright on account of their utility.[18] Furthermore, the trial court's reasoning would imperil copyrights in many other works, such as standards promulgated by the Financial Accounting Standards Board (FASB), the West key numbering system, the uniform system of citation for legal materials, and even computer software.

To Delta's argument that § 102(b) rendered ADA's system unprotectable, Judge Easterbrook flippantly responded: "But what could it mean to call the Code a 'system'? This taxonomy does

---

[12] *Id.* at 520 n.8.
[13] 17 U.S.C. § 102(b) (emphasis added).
[14] The Ninth Circuit referenced coding systems thirteen times in its *PMIC* opinion. See *PMIC* (9th Cir. 1997).
[15] *See, e.g.*, Samuelson 2016c.
[16] *ADA* (N.D. Ill. 1996, p. 1725).
[17] *ADA* (7th Cir. 1997, p. 979). Judge Easterbrook was so taken with the creativity of the ADA code that he opined that the name of each procedure and the number assigned to it were themselves original works of authorship entitled to copyright protection. *Id.* Justin Hughes has criticized *ADA* for treating names of dental procedures and associated numbers as "microworks" of authorship in contravention of the long-standing copyright policy of not allowing copyright protection for titles, short phrases, and the like (Hughes 2005, 595–96).
[18] *But see* Samuelson 2016a, pp. 335–55 (giving examples of compilations denied copyright protection on account of their functionality).

not come with instructions for use, as if the Code were a recipe for a new dish. ... The Code is a taxonomy, which may be put to many uses. These uses may be or include systems; the Code is not."[19]

Judge Easterbrook seemed to think that § 102(b) made unprotectable only those systems presenting a danger of monopolization of a widely used practice such as bookkeeping, as in *Baker v. Selden* (1880) in which the Supreme Court denied copyright protection to forms embodying the novel system Selden had developed. Judge Easterbrook perceived no danger that ADA would monopolize dental practices. Under § 102(b), according to the ADA decision, dentists were free to use ADA code in their forms and Delta was free to create and distribute forms on which dentists could enter those codes; but Delta could not copy the code or prepare a derivative work based on the code without infringing ADA's copyright.[20]

Thus it was that both the AMA and ADA coding systems were held protectable by copyright. In more recent cases, however, courts have not been persuaded by the *PMIC* or *ADA* decisions. In the decade following these rulings, other courts rejected copyright claims in similar name and numbering systems. The reasoning of these cases undermines the copyrightability rulings in the *PMIC* and *ADA* cases.

One such case was *Southco, Inc. v. Kanebridge Corp.* (3d Cir. 2004). Southco, a manufacturer of hardware products such as screws and fasteners, sued its competitor, Kanebridge, for copyright infringement because Kanebridge included in its competing catalog the same nine-digit product serial numbers it took from Southco's catalog. Kanebridge did so in order to allow customers to compare its products and Southco's and to indicate the interchangeability of Southco and Kanebridge parts. Southco relied heavily on the *ADA* case in support of its copyright claim.

Writing for the U.S. Court of Appeals for the Third Circuit, Judge Samuel Alito (now a Justice of the U.S. Supreme Court) held that Southco's parts numbers were not copyrightable, because they were merely the mechanistic results of its numbering system, and therefore unprotectable.[21] In addition, the court found the individual numbers analogous to short phrases and titles, which are excluded from copyright protection.[22] The numbers, the court concluded, were "purely functional."[23] It accepted that Southco had exercised some skill and judgment in identifying and classifying the product characteristics and assigning respective numbers or symbols to each, but "[o]nce these decisions were made, the system was in place, and all of the products in the class could be numbered without the slightest element of creativity."[24] Insofar as any originality could be discerned, it lay in Southco's development of rules for the numbering system, not in the pairing of numbers and products.

A second name-and-numbering system case was *ATC Distribution, Inc. v. Whatever It Takes Transmissions & Parts, Inc.* (6th Cir. 2005). ATC tried to distinguish its parts numbering system from Southco's and take cover under *ADA* by characterizing its system as a "taxonomy." As

---

[19] ADA (7th Cir. 1997, pp. 980–81) (citation omitted).
[20] Id. at 981. Professor Hughes has observed that the ADA decision "may follow our intuitions on unfair competition and seems to give the ADA an [INS]-like quasi-property right against competitors, but not against individuals. Yet the distinction makes a hash out of § 106 rights; it would be more sensible to say that an individual practitioner's form-filling never produces a work substantially similar to the ADA Code as a whole" (Hughes 2005, 597 (citing 17 U.S.C. § 106)). Judge Easterbrook, however, considered each number to be an original work of authorship. *See supra* note 16 and accompanying text. Under this view, entry of each number in a form, whether by a dentist or by Delta, would arguably be infringement unless saved by fair use. Easterbrook thus makes a hash of § 102(b), as well as of § 106.
[21] *Southco* (3d Cir. 2004, pp. 282–83).
[22] Id. at 286.
[23] Id. at 284.
[24] Id. at 282.

in *Southco*, ATC alleged that its competitor, Whatever It Takes Transmissions & Parts, Inc. (WITTP), infringed copyright because it copied ATC's transmission parts numbers from ATC's catalog. ATC claimed creativity in its numbering scheme, including the various decisions and choices it made in categorizing and numbering the parts.

The U.S. Court of Appeals for the Sixth Circuit accepted that ATC exercised at least some creativity in its decision-making, but it ruled against the copyrightability of the taxonomy because the creative aspects of ATC's classification scheme lay in its ideas. Ideas, no matter how original, are not copyrightable under § 102(b).[25] Further, the court found that "[f]or almost all of the types of creativity claimed by ATC, there is only one reasonable way to express the underlying idea," and so the idea and its expression had merged.[26]

Nor was the court persuaded that the numbers themselves were original works of authorship entitled to copyright protection. Characterizing Judge Easterbrook's rationale for a similar holding in *ADA* as "rather opaque,"[27] the Sixth Circuit doubted its soundness. The court concluded that the part numbers used by ATC did not evince sufficient creativity to merit copyright protection. The numbers were essentially the products of a random process, "serving only to provide a useful shorthand way of referring to each part."[28]

The court expressed concern that upholding copyright in part numbers "would provide a way for the creators of otherwise uncopyrightable ideas or works to gain some degree of copyright protection through the back door simply by assigning short numbers or other shorthand phrases to those ideas or works (or their component parts)."[29] The real competition between ATC and WITTP, after all, was in sales of uncopyrightable transmission parts, not in sales of catalogs or licensing of the part numbers.

The four copyright claims discussed in this Section rested on their plaintiffs' assertions that they could claim copyright in the pairing of particular numbers with particular phenomena (i.e., medical and dental procedures, as in *PMIC* and *ADA*, or hardware parts, as in *Southco* and *ATC*) in accordance with rule-based systems for efficiently organizing information for a specific purpose. AMA and ADA developed uniform standard names and numbers for medical and dental procedures to enable more accurate and efficient recordkeeping and information processing for these procedures. These standards promoted interoperability of data among professionals in their respective fields for exchanging information on a regular basis. In addition, HCFA mandated use of the CPT to lower its costs for processing Medicare and Medicaid claims, standardize payments to doctors for the same procedures, and avert fraud arising from nonuniform reporting procedures. Facilitating efficient recordkeeping is among the reasons that copyright law precludes protection of blank forms.[30] This rationale reinforces the soundness of denying copyright to numbering systems. Most of these systems were, moreover, promulgated with the intent that they would become industry standards.

We believe that the Ninth and Seventh Circuits in *PMIC* and *ADA* erred in not seriously analyzing the § 102(b) challenges to these systems. The Third Circuit in *Southco* and the Sixth Circuit in *ATC* correctly recognized that systematic ways of assigning numbers to phenomena are unprotectable by copyright law. The *Southco* and *ATC* precedents would have been more powerful had the courts invoked the long history of copyright cases denying protection to systems

---

[25] ATC (6th Cir. 2005, p. 707).
[26] *Id.*
[27] *Id.* at 708.
[28] *Id.* at 709.
[29] *Id.*
[30] *See* 37 C.F.R. § 202.1(c) ("Material not subject to copyright").

and had they discussed various policy rationales for excluding systems and their component parts from the scope of copyright protection.[31]

B. STANDARDS MAY BE UNPROTECTABLE SYSTEMS UNDER SECTION 102(B)

The first U.S. Supreme Court copyright case to appreciate the desirability of standardization as a rationale for limiting the scope of copyright was *Perris v. Hexamer* (1878). In that case, the Court ruled that copyright did not protect a symbol system for representing specific types of information on maps of urban areas prepared to assess fire insurance risks. Perris, a civil engineer who had mapped structures in parts of New York City, sued Hexamer for copyright infringement because Hexamer used the same symbol system as Perris in a later map of urban Philadelphia.

The Supreme Court concluded:

> The complainants have no more an exclusive right to use the form of the characters they employ to express their ideas upon the face of the map, than they have to use the form of type they select to print the key. Scarcely any map is published on which certain arbitrary signs, explained by a key printed at some convenient place for reference, are not used to designate objects of special interest, such as rivers, railroads, boundaries, cities, towns, &c.; and yet we think it has never been supposed that a simple copyright of the map gave the publisher an exclusive right to the use upon other maps of the particular signs and key which he saw fit to adopt for the purposes of his delineations. That, however, is what the complainants seek to accomplish in this case. The defendant has not copied their maps. All he has done at any time has been to use to some extent their system of arbitrary signs and their key.[32]

The Court implicitly recognized that the comprehensibility of maps would be impeded if subsequent mapmakers had to use entirely different symbol systems for each map. *Perris v. Hexamer* presents an example of a system held unprotectable by copyright law notwithstanding the fact that its component parts were not dictated by functional considerations, as the Seventh Circuit in *ADA* seemed to think was necessary for a system to be ineligible for protection under § 102(b).[33]

In explaining why bookkeeping and other useful systems should be outside the bounds of copyright law, the Supreme Court in *Baker v. Selden* (1880) observed that to give the author of a book an exclusive right in a useful art, such as a bookkeeping system, depicted in the book "would be a surprise and a fraud upon the public. That is the province of letters-patent, not of copyright."[34] This was relevant in *Baker* because Charles Selden had sought, but apparently not obtained, a patent on his novel bookkeeping system. The Court refused to allow Selden to misuse his copyright by getting patent-like protection for the system through the copyright in his book. Selden could protect his description of the system through copyright, but not the system itself.

Although useful arts can generally "only be represented in concrete forms of wood, metal, stone, or some other physical embodiment," the principle that copyright doesn't protect useful systems applies even when, as with Selden's forms, they are embodied in a book.[35] In *Baker*, the selection and arrangement of headings and columns was deemed too useful to be protected by

---

[31] For a discussion of the origins of the exclusions of methods and systems from copyright protection, see Samuelson 2007.
[32] *Perris* (U.S. 1878, p. 676).
[33] *ADA* (7th Cir. 1997, p. 980).
[34] *Baker* (1880, p. 102).
[35] *Id.* at 105.

copyright. Because some systematic organizations of information have been patented,[36] *Baker's* concerns about possible misuses of copyright to obtain patent-like protection may have some significance in information systems cases.

Many cases after *Baker* followed its exclusion of systems from the scope of copyright protection. Especially pertinent to the numbering system cases are *Griggs v. Perrin* (C.C.N.D.N.Y. 1892) and *Brief English Systems, Inc. v. Owen* (2d Cir. 1931). In these cases, the plaintiffs sued authors of competing books on the shorthand systems each plaintiff had devised. Both systems involved the assignment of particular abbreviations and symbols to represent particular letters, words, phrases, and the like for such purposes as stenographic transcription. The courts ruled against the copyright claims in both cases, citing *Baker*.[37] These cases are notable because in neither case was the particular shorthand system at issue dictated by specific rules or functionality.

When faced with assessing whether a particular information artifact is an uncopyrightable "system," courts should start by recognizing that systems, by their nature, consist of interdependent, interrelated parts that are integrated into a whole scheme. This is true not only of bookkeeping systems (*Baker*) and shorthand systems (*Griggs* and *Brief English Systems*), but also of burial insurance systems,[38] systems for teaching how to play musical instruments,[39] systems for reorganizing insolvent life insurance companies,[40] systems for issuing bonds to cover replacement of lost securities,[41] systems for consolidating freight tariff information,[42] systems for teaching problem-solving techniques,[43] and rules and strategies for playing games,[44] among others.

Mathematical formulae and the periodic table of chemical elements are other examples of systematic arrangements of information that are unprotectable under § 102(b).[45] Considerable originality may underlie formulae, but mathematical precision and comprehensibility of mathematical ideas are better served by standardizing the language elements of formulae. The periodic table is a useful tool for teaching students about the fields of chemistry and physics precisely because of its standardized representation of atomic phenomena. Gratuitous differences in the fields of mathematics and science would impede effective communication.

Elsewhere, one of this chapter's authors has argued that computer languages, such as the macro command language at issue in *Lotus Development Corp. v. Borland International, Inc.* (1st Cir. 1995), are unprotectable systems under copyright law.[46] In an earlier lawsuit involving Lotus 1-2-3, a trial court recognized that "the exact hierarchy – or structure, sequence and organization – of the menu system is a fundamental part of the functionality of the macros"[47] and an integral part of the Lotus macro command language. Use of exactly the same command terms

---

[36] *See, e.g.*, U.S. Patent No. 6,446,061, Taxonomy Generation for Document Collections (filed June 30, 1999) (issued September 3, 2002).

[37] *Griggs* (C.C.N.D.N.Y. 1892, p. 15) ("complainant has no right to a monopoly of the art of shorthand writing"); *Brief English* (2d Cir. 1931, p. 556) ("the plaintiff's shorthand system, as such, is open to use by whoever will take the trouble to learn and use it").

[38] *Burk v. Johnson* (8th Cir. 1906); *Burk v. Relief* (D. Haw. 1909).

[39] *Jackson v. C. G. Conn* (W.D. Okla. 1931).

[40] *Crume v. Pacific Mutual* (7th Cir. 1944).

[41] *Continental Casualty v. Beardsley* (2d Cir. 1958).

[42] *Guthrie v. Curlett* (2d Cir. 1929).

[43] *Kepner-Tregoe v. Carabio* (E.D. Mich. 1979).

[44] *Downes v. Culbertson* (N.Y. Sup. Ct. 1934).

[45] The periodic table of elements is in the public domain and is widely available on the Internet. *See, e.g.*, Seely 1998. Professor Hughes agrees that mathematical formulae are uncopyrightable subject matter (Hughes 2005, 599).

[46] *See* Samuelson 1992a. *See also* Amicus Brief in *Borland* – U.S. Supreme Court 1994; Amicus Brief in *Borland* – 1st Circuit 1995; Samuelson 1992b. Languages and their component parts are essential inputs to expression that copyright law ought not to protect.

[47] *Lotus v. Paperback* (D. Mass. 1990, p. 65).

in exactly the same order and hierarchical structure as in 1-2-3 was necessary for users to be able to reuse macros constructed in the Lotus macros language for commonly executed sequences of functions when using other programs. User investments in their macros and their desire to reuse those macros with Borland's software was a factor in the First Circuit's ruling that the Lotus command hierarchy was unprotectable under § 102(b).[48]

Judge Easterbrook may be right that merely calling an intellectual artifact a "system" should not automatically disqualify it from copyright protection.[49] However, if plaintiffs characterize it as a system, as the AMA did in its contract with HCFA and the Ninth Circuit did in *PMIC*, and it fits standard definitions of "system," courts should at least consider whether the artifact is the kind of system that should be ineligible for copyright protection. Likewise, merely calling a numbering system a "taxonomy" shouldn't avert the inquiry. Taxonomies are, by definition, systematic classifications of information that group subcomponents into logical categories based on similarities in clusters of phenomena.[50] The Sixth Circuit in *ATC* recognized the interchangeability of "taxonomy" and "system" in connection with the numbering scheme at issue there.

Revisiting the claimed creativity in the ADA's "taxonomy" in light of *ATC*, it is evident that the creative endeavor underlying the ADA code ("the fundamental scheme,"[51] as Judge Easterbrook called it), as in *ATC*, subsisted in the creation of a system. Even though the ADA decision went to considerable lengths to tout the creativity of the ADA code in terms of such things as deciding which number to assign or whether to use a leading zero in the five-digit code, what it described, in essence, was a system of identification. The decision-making process in classifying and designating strings of numbers to dental procedures and nomenclatures is little different from developing a transmission parts numbering system, which the Sixth Circuit characterized as reasonable, useful, and not protectable under copyright.

The ADA code, moreover, drew substantially from a pre-existing code. The naming and numbering of dental procedures in ADA's code were thus products of an incremental collaborative effort of skilled practitioners in the field with the intention that these were (or should be) standard names for dental procedures organized by logical class. Judge Easterbrook may be right that "[b]lood is shed in the ADA's committees about which [procedure name] is preferable,"[52] but shedding blood is no more a sign of original expression under U.S. copyright law than expenditure of sweat has been in the aftermath of *Feist Publications, Inc. v. Rural Telephone Service Co.* (1991), which ruled that white pages listings of telephone directories, even if the product of "sweat of the brow" industrious compilations, lack sufficient originality of expression to be copyrightable.

In keeping with the reasoning in *Baker* and *Feist*, industry standard codes promulgated by organizations such as the AMA and the ADA should be unprotectable systems under § 102(b). Such codes and other systematic organizations of information are certainly uncopyrightable if dictated by rules or functionality. Among the other factors that may be relevant to whether systematic organizations of information should be unprotectable under § 102(b) are these: (1) when the system is a useful art and copyright in it would give patent-like protection; (2) when

---

[48] *Lotus v. Borland* (1st Cir. 1995, pp. 817–18). The First Circuit, however, characterized the Lotus menu command hierarchy as an unprotectable "method of operation" under § 102(b). *Id.* at 818.

[49] Computer programs, for example, may literally be "processes," but they are copyrightable under legislation passed by Congress. See, e.g., *Apple v. Franklin* (3d Cir. 1983) (operating system programs held copyrightable).

[50] *Webster's Third New International Dictionary* (1993) defines "taxonomy" as "systematic distinguishing, ordering, and naming of type groups within a subject field."

[51] *ADA* (7th Cir. 1997, p. 979).

[52] *Id.* Standards often emerge from tough negotiations. Bowker & Starr 2000, 9 (decades of negotiations were required to standardize sizes and capacities of CDs, and the speed, electrical settings, and amplification rules for CD players).

second-comers need to use the system to compete or communicate effectively; (3) when systematizing information is necessary to achieve efficiencies; (4) when the system is incidental to uncopyrightable transactions or processes; and (5) when systematizing the information will produce social benefits from uniformity and the social costs of diversity would be high. Standard systems of this sort are born uncopyrightable.

C. STANDARDS MAY BE OR BECOME UNPROTECTABLE BY COPYRIGHT UNDER THE SCENES A FAIRE OR MERGER DOCTRINES

Section 102(b)'s exclusion of systems from copyright protection is not the only limiting doctrine under which standards may be excluded from this law's protection. The scenes a faire and merger doctrines and policies that underlie them are alternative theories for concluding that industry standards should be ineligible for copyright protection. The scenes a faire doctrine, originally developed to recognize that certain plot structures are to be expected from works exploring certain literary or dramatic themes,[53] has been adapted, especially in the software copyright case law, to recognize that expressive choices of subsequent authors may become constrained over time by the emergence of industry standards. The merger doctrine holds that if there is only one or a small number of ways to express an idea, copyright protection will generally be unavailable to that way or those ways in order to avoid protecting the idea.[54] While many merger cases involve creations whose plaintiffs had no or few choices when developing its work, some courts have held that an initially copyrightable work may be disqualified for copyright protection over time. This section will first discuss cases in which scenes a faire defenses were given credence and then those in which merger defenses prevailed.

In *Southco*, a concurring opinion stated that the scenes a faire doctrine was a plausible alternative basis for ruling that Kanebridge's catalog did not infringe Southco's copyright.[55] Southco had "selected characteristics for its system based on customer demand," and once these characteristics had been chosen, "values – such as screw thread sizes, screw lengths, or ferrule types – were determined by industry standards rather than through any exercise of originality by Southco."[56] Other values, such as finishes, were limited by the parts themselves rather than any exercise of creative expression. Judge Becker in his concurrence relied on the Tenth Circuit's instructive analysis of scenes a faire in *Mitel, Inc. v. Iqtel, Inc.* (10th Cir. 1997).

Mitel manufactured call controllers, a type of telecommunications hardware used to automate the selection of a particular long distance carrier and perform other tasks. Mitel developed an instruction set of four-digit command codes to enable activation of features of its call controllers. It also published an instruction manual on how to use these command codes.

At the time Iqtel began manufacturing its call controllers, Mitel controlled a large share of the call controller market. Iqtel initially devised its own call controller instruction set, but ultimately decided that it could compete with Mitel only if its controllers were compatible with Mitel's, since "technicians who install call controllers would be unwilling to learn Iqtel's new set of instructions in addition to the Mitel command code set and the technicians' employers would be unwilling to bear the cost of additional training."[57] So Iqtel programmed its controllers to accept the Mitel command codes and translate them into Iqtel codes. Iqtel's manual included

---

[53] *See, e.g.*, Kurtz 1989.
[54] *See, e.g.*, Goldstein 2017 supplement, 1:§2.3.2 at 2:36–2:37.
[55] *Southco* (3d Cir. 2004, pp. 287–89) (Becker, J., concurring).
[56] *Id.* at 288.
[57] *Mitel* (10th Cir. 1997, p. 1369).

an appendix that listed and cross-referenced the Iqtel and Mitel command codes. It thus copied parts of Mitel's command codes for the call controllers' common functions.

The U.S. Court of Appeals for the Tenth Circuit affirmed the district court's denial of a preliminary injunction, concluding that Mitel had failed to show that its command codes were copyright-protectable. The court questioned the originality of the Mitel command codes insofar as the symbols either were arbitrarily assigned to functions or exhibited de minimis creativity.[58] To the extent some Mitel codes were original, the Tenth Circuit concluded that they were unprotectable under the scenes a faire doctrine, which excludes "those elements of a work that necessarily result from external factors inherent in the subject matter of the work," such as "hardware standards and mechanical specifications, software standards and compatibility requirements, computer manufacturer design standards, industry programming practices, and practices and demands of the industry being serviced."[59]

According to the court, the scenes a faire doctrine "plays a particularly important role [as to functional aspects of a work] in ensuring that copyright rewards and stimulates artistic creativity in a utilitarian work 'in a manner that permits the free use and development of non-protectable ideas and processes' that make the work useful."[60] Applying this doctrine to the Mitel command codes, the Tenth Circuit concluded that "much of the expression in Mitel's command codes was dictated by the proclivities of technicians and limited by significant hardware, compatibility, and industry requirements."[61] The Mitel codes embodied industry standards, and were thus unprotectable by copyright law.

Similar concerns about customer demands for compatibility caused a Cisco competitor, Arista, to use many parts of Cisco's command-line interface (CLI) for software embedded in its competing networking equipment. Cisco sued Arista for copyright infringement, and Arista asserted scenes a faire, among others, in its defense. It argued that Cisco's CLI included many terms that were industry standards whose creation was guided less by creativity than by using terms familiar to those in the industry.

The jury was instructed that in order to prove scenes a faire, "Arista must show that, at the time Cisco created the user interfaces ... external factors other than Cisco's creativity dictated that Cisco select, arrange, organize and design its original features in the manner it did."[62] The jury returned a verdict in favor of Arista, finding that the command lines were scenes a faire. Relying in part on *Mitel*, the district court denied Cisco's post-trial motions for judgment as a matter of law, finding that the evidence on networking industry protocols and preexisting networking systems "fall squarely in *Mitel*'s list of factors that could support a scenes a faire defense."[63] The court pointed to evidence that at least some of Cisco's decisions in forming its command line were constrained by functionality, driven by device features and preexisting standards, and dictated by customer requirements.[64] Therefore, a jury could reasonably have found that the parts of Cisco's CLI that Arista utilized contained elements that flowed from external factors such as "widely accepted programming practices within the computer industry."[65]

---

[58] *Id.* at 1373–74.
[59] *Id.* at 1375. In support of this conclusion, the court cited *Gates Rubber* (10th Cir. 1993, p. 838), *CAI v. Altai* (2d Cir. 1992, pp. 709–12), and *Plains Cotton* (5th Cir. 1987, p. 1262).
[60] *Mitel* (10th Cir. 1997, p. 1375) (quoting *Altai* (2d Cir. 1992, p. 711)).
[61] *Id.*
[62] *Cisco* (N.D. Cal. 2017, p. 7) (Order Denying Motions for Judgment As a Matter of Law and Motion for a New Trial).
[63] *Id.* at 15.
[64] *Id.* at 8–11.
[65] *Id.* at 7 (quoting *Altai* (2d Cir. 1992, p. 710)). Cisco appealed the district court's denial of its post–jury verdict motion for judgment as a matter of law on copyright infringement. As with *Oracle v. Google*, discussed later in this chapter,

Industry standards serve an important function by allowing those in the industry or field to use the standard for effective communication. The interoperability case law, of which *Mitel* is one instance, recognizes that the design of computer program interfaces may be the product of considerable skill and judgment, and thus might seem to qualify for copyright protection.[66] However, in creating an interface, functional considerations and industry requirements and expectations may undercut the expressive nature of the resulting creation. Further, once an interface has been developed, the parameters it establishes for the effective communication of information between one program and another constrain the design choices of subsequent programmers. The interface thus is or becomes an unprotectable functional design,[67] and the scenes a faire doctrine and the merger doctrine are often invoked in decisions coming to such conclusion.[68]

Paul Goldstein has analogized the copyright case law on industry standards to trademark law's genericide doctrine.[69] Under that doctrine, a once-viable trademark may become unprotectable because widespread public use of the mark as a common name for a product or service causes it to lose its source significance. Some of the software copyright cases demonstrate that industry standards may become unprotectable over time.

The Java Application Program Interface (API), for example, systematized names of commands in the Java programming language in a very efficient way, which was a key reason Java became a popular programming language. In ruling on Oracle's claim that Google's use of parts of the Java API was copyright infringement, a district court decided that the functionality of the Java API elements were inextricably interconnected with any expression they might be said to contain. That court accepted that Google was constrained in its design choices by the rules of Java as to names of Java methods and classes and as to the structure of the API command structure.[70] To compete effectively and to enable ongoing innovation, a second-comer, such as Google, needed to use the same API designs.

However, the U.S. Court of Appeals for the Federal Circuit overturned the ruling that the parts of the Java API that Google used in its Android software were excluded from copyright protection under § 102(b) or the merger doctrine.[71] Instead, the Federal Circuit stated that there was a triable issue of fact as to whether Google's use of the Java API elements might be fair use and remanded for further proceedings on the fair use issue.[72] After a two-week trial, Google prevailed with its fair use defense, apparently persuading the jury that it had used only as much of the Java API as was necessary for the transformative purpose of developing a novel smartphone platform.[73] The district court denied Oracle's motion for judgment as a matter of law as

---

this appeal went to the Court of Appeals for the Federal Circuit because the original suit included patent claims. The Federal Circuit is supposed to apply the law of the regional circuit in which the district court that decided the case sits. The Federal Circuit heard oral argument in June 2018.

[66] *See, e.g., Altai* (2d Cir. 1992, pp. 697–98) (describing the considerable judgment involved in the process of computer program design).

[67] *See, e.g., id.* at 709–10. *See also* Samuelson et al. 1994, 2402 (program interfaces are "information equivalents to the gears that allow physical machines to interoperate").

[68] The similarities and distinctions of the merger and scenes a faire doctrines, and how they are sometimes confused by courts, is discussed in Samuelson 2016c, 447–50.

[69] Goldstein 2017, 1:§2.3.2.1 at 2:41. Some courts reject merger defenses if there were more than a few expressive choices when the plaintiff's work was created. However, other courts, notably the Second Circuit, "appear hospitably inclined to the proposition that merger should be tested at the time the expression was copied rather than at the time it was created." *Id.* at 2:40. *See also* Chapter 12 (this volume), Part A.IV (discussing genericide).

[70] *Oracle* (N.D. Cal. 2012, pp. 998–1000).

[71] *Oracle* (Fed. Cir. 2014, pp. 1359–68).

[72] *Id.* at 1372–77. The fair use doctrine is codified in Section 107 of the U.S. Copyright Act. *See* 17 U.S.C. § 107.

[73] *Oracle* (N.D. Cal. 2016, p. *9).

to fair use.[74] Oracle once again appealed its loss to the Federal Circuit. Despite its earlier ruling that there was a triable issue of fact about Google's fair use defense, including whether the use was transformative, the same panel of that court once again reversed the district court and held that Google's use of the Java API could not as a matter of law be fair use.[75] With these decisions on the Java APIs, the Federal Circuit has called into question the utility of fair use as well as § 102(b) and merger defenses for unlicensed reuses of APIs or other functional designs, thereby ignoring decades of precedent and policy.[76]

The principle that a second-comer's use of even program code might be constrained by a first comer's use was first recognized in 1980 by the National Commission on New Technological Uses of Copyrighted Works (CONTU). It concluded that "when specific instructions, even though previously copyrighted, are the only and essential means of accomplishing a given task, their later use by another will not amount to an infringement."[77]

Also relevant to determining whether copyright should protect industry standards is the extent of user investments in the standard. In ruling against Lotus's lawsuit against Borland for copying the command hierarchy of 1-2-3, the First Circuit emphasized the significant investments users had made in developing macros with Lotus's macro command language.[78] Although Judge Boudin was not fully persuaded by the majority's § 102(b) analysis, he concurred in its holding, observing:

> Requests for the protection of computer menus present the concern with fencing off access to the commons in an acute form. A new menu may be a creative work, but over time its importance may come to reside more in the investment that has been made by *users* in learning the menu and in building their own mini-programs – macros – in reliance upon the menu. Better typewriter keyboard layouts may exist, but the familiar QWERTY keyboard dominates the market because that is what everyone has learned to use.[79]

User investments in a standard constrained the design choices of subsequent users in much the same way that Iqtel felt constrained by Mitel's command codes. Iqtel believed it could compete with Mitel, which enjoyed a considerable market lead time, by developing compatible call controllers that technicians had already learned to use. Similarly, Google reimplemented 37 Java API packages in independently written code but retained the names for method headers to identify specific functions that it believed Java programmers would want to reuse. Google did not want to risk confusing and possibly alienating Java programmers by requiring them to learn a new dialect of Java to write apps for the Android platform. Compelling programmers to program in a different way just to avoid infringement is not only an inefficient use of their time and effort, but also may keep them from optimally expressing themselves in the command language they know well.[80]

Thus, industry standards may be unprotectable by copyright law under the scenes a faire or merger doctrines, even though recent decisions by the Federal Circuit have threatened to disrupt two decades of seemingly settled prior case law. Considerations that may affect such decisions include (1) whether industry demand or practices effectively constrain expressive

---

[74] *Id.* at *1.
[75] *Oracle* (Fed. Cir. 2018, p. 1186). As of this writing, Google is requesting a rehearing *en banc* to challenge the panel's ruling.
[76] *See, e.g.*, Samuelson & Asay 2018.
[77] CONTU 1979, 20.
[78] *Lotus v. Borland* (1st Cir. 1995, p. 818).
[79] *Id.* at 819–20) (Boudin, J., concurring).
[80] For a more in-depth discussion of the *Oracle* case, see Samuelson 2016b.

choices of subsequent developers; (2) whether reuse of the standard is necessary for effective competition; (3) whether user investments in the standard are substantial enough to give rise to the right to reuse the standard; and (4) whether the government mandates use of the standard or has embodied the standard in its legal code.

D. PRIVATELY DEVELOPED STANDARDS ADOPTED AS LAWS

Whether a privately drafted standard, such as a model building code, retains copyright protection after governmental enactment of it as law has been the subject of numerous lawsuits.[81] Some courts have found the standard to become uncopyrightable upon enactment as law under the merger doctrine, as happened in *Veeck v. Southern Building Code Congress International* (5th Cir. 2002).[82] In *Veeck*, the U.S. Court of Appeals for the Fifth Circuit, sitting *en banc*, held that governmental enactment of a privately drafted standard caused the code as law and its expression to merge.

Southern Building Code Congress International (SBCCI), a standards organization, was formed to develop model building codes. It encourages towns to enact its codes into law. The towns of Anna and Savoy, Texas, adopted SBCCI's Standard Building Code as the law governing construction of buildings in those towns, whereupon Peter Veeck, who ran a website providing information about north Texas, purchased an electronic copy of SBCCI's code and posted these building codes online. When SBCCI objected, Veeck sought a declaratory judgment that SBCCI's code had become uncopyrightable upon its adoption as law. Although a trial court granted SBCCI's motion for summary judgment, the Fifth Circuit Court of Appeals reversed that ruling, holding that "as *law*, the model codes [have] enter[ed] the public domain and [we]re not subject to the copyright holder's exclusive prerogatives."[83]

The Fifth Circuit gave three reasons for this ruling. First, withholding copyright from enacted codes was consistent with Supreme Court decisions that laws are not subject to copyright protection. Second, upon its adoption as law, the ideas expressed in SBCCI's code had merged with its expression, and the code had, for purposes of copyright law, become an uncopyrightable "fact." Third, both relevant case law and relevant policies supported its ruling. After enactment, the only way to express the building code laws of Anna and Savoy was by uttering the precise text of SBCCI's code.[84] The merger doctrine then foreclosed SBCCI's claim of copyright in the enacted code. *Veeck* calls into question the Ninth Circuit's ruling in *PMIC* because federal law required use of the AMA's standard, thereby limiting the range of choices of codes that could be used by medical and health professionals.

The ruling in *Veeck* was recently called into question in lawsuits brought by the American Society for Testing and Materials (ASTM), the American Educational Research Association, and four other standards organizations. They sued Public.Resource.Org for posting online copies of standards promulgated by these organizations that had been incorporated by reference into law.

---

[81] For a further discussion of these cases and the issues associated with "incorporation by reference" (IBR) of standards into statutory enactments, *see* Chapter 6 (United States) and Chapter 7 (Europe) of this volume.

[82] *See also BOCA* (1st Cir. 1980) (vacating preliminary injunction because of doubts about the copyrightability of a model code adopted by Massachusetts).

[83] *Veeck* (5th Cir. 2002, p. 793). A Fifth Circuit panel initially ruled to affirm, but upon rehearing, the majority *en banc* voted to reverse. *Id.* at 793–94. Six judges dissented. *See id.* at 806–08 (Higginbotham, J., dissenting); *id.* at 808–15 (Wiener, J., dissenting).

[84] *Id.* at 802.

The district court found in favor of the SDOs and enjoined Public Resource from distributing, displaying, or reproducing the works.[85]

The district court found that the SDOs did not lose copyright protection and their works did not enter the public domain after having been incorporated by reference into the law.[86] Congress, the court reasoned, could have but did not explicitly provide for the loss of copyright in such circumstances. Apparently persuaded more by *PMIC* than by *Veeck*, the court determined that the SDOs needed copyright incentives to create standards and that due process concerns were not at issue because the public has at least some access to the standards. In addition, the court was unpersuaded that the copyrights that the law initially granted to these standards were revocable under the scenes a faire or merger doctrines.[87] Finally, the court concluded that Public Resource's scanning and posting of the standards in their entirety, which the court characterized as "for the direct purpose of undermining [the SDOs'] ability to raise revenue," could not be a fair use.[88]

The U.S. Court of Appeals for the D.C. Circuit reversed the district court's grant of summary judgment against Public Resource, ruling that the record was not fully developed and did not support the district court's fair use analysis.[89] The court vacated the injunction and remanded the case for the district court to again consider Public Resource's fair use defense.[90] It left "for another day" the question of whether the Constitution permits copyright to persist in works incorporated by reference into law.[91]

After first observing that as a matter of law there was reason to believe Public Resource's reproduction of certain standards was a fair use, the D.C. Circuit then directed the district court to further develop the factual record and more fully consider the variety of incorporated standards at issue.[92] The court reviewed each of the fair use factors. For the first factor, the purpose and character of the use, the D.C. Circuit found fault with the district court, stating that it had ignored Public Resource's stated purpose of educating the public about specifics of the law and instead had erroneously concluded that Public Resource's purpose was commercial because it undermined the SDOs' market share.[93] The court also found that the district court had "failed to adequately consider whether, in certain circumstances, distributing copies of the law for purposes of facilitating public access could constitute transformative use," an important facet of factor-one analysis.[94] For the second factor, the nature of the copyrighted work, the court discerned standards incorporated by reference into law as "at best, at the outer edge" of copyright protection.[95] The D.C. Circuit criticized the district court for failing to engage in a thorough third-factor analysis, regarding the amount and substantiality of the taking, as to each of the standards at issue; if Public Resource copied only as much as necessary in light of its purpose to inform the public, the court instructed, then this factor should weigh heavily in favor

---

[85] *ASTM* (D.D.C. 2017) (consolidated opinion).
[86] *Id.* at *9–14.
[87] *Id.* at *14–15.
[88] *Id.* at *15–18.
[89] *ASTM* (D.C. Cir. 2018, p. 441).
[90] *Id.* at 458.
[91] *Id.* at 447. In a separate case involving Public Resource's republication of the State of Georgia's official annotated code, the U.S. Court of Appeals for the Eleventh Circuit held that the official codification of Georgia's laws as well as annotations in the official code are not copyrightable. See *Code Revision Commission* (11th Cir. 2018).
[92] *ASTM* (D.C. Cir. 2018, pp. 448–49).
[93] *Id.* at 449.
[94] *Id.* at 450–51.
[95] *Id.* at 451–52.

of fair use.[96] Finally, for the fourth factor, the harm to the market for the work, the court found that the district court had incorrectly inferred that Public Resource's use was commercial and caused commercial harm, and it directed the district court to gather evidence about particular economic harms caused by Public Resource's use of the standards at issue.[97] The case will go back to the district court to once again perform its fair use analysis consistent with the D.C. Circuit's opinion.

While the D.C. Circuit's reversal in *ASTM* provided a significant course correction, we believe that decisions such as *PMIC* and the district court's opinion in *ASTM* remain worrisomely flawed because they give inadequate consideration to the public's interest in unfettered access to information resources that either are the law or are required by law.[98] Providing access to the law or material that is required by law only through commercial transactions undermines meaningful access for the public, particularly in the internet age where almost all things of import are available in digital form and online. Charging a fee to get access to the law or to what the law requires may be too high a price for many citizens to pay in order to be on notice of regulations to which they are subject. The Founders did not intend for copyright law to be a tool to allow copyright owners to decide where and in what form the law should be available. Because due process concerns under the Fifth and Fourteenth Amendments, as well as the First Amendment right to receive information, are implicated in cases such as *ASTM* and *Veeck*, it is well within the purview of the courts, rather than Congress, to circumscribe the reach of copyright in matters involving the text of laws or to what the law requires. It is regrettable that the D.C. Circuit in *ASTM* chose not to take up the constitutional and copyrightability questions arising when standards are incorporated into law.[99] Subsequent to *ASTM*, however, another federal appellate court has held that a state's Official Code, including its annotations, are "attributable to the constructive authorship of the People" and "free for publication by all."[100] Hopefully more courts will clearly articulate, and not just as to one defendant at a time, the public's interest in and right to accessing and sharing a wide variety of information resources that either are the law or are required by law.

E. CONSIDERING INCENTIVES AND COMPETITION POLICY CONCERNS ABOUT COPYRIGHTS IN STANDARDS

The principal argument in favor of copyright protection for industry standards is the claim SDOs make that they need copyright incentives to develop standards. The Supreme Court's *Feist* (1991) decision, however, rejected an incentives-based argument for granting copyright protection to information artifacts just because they are products of industrious efforts and their developers assert the need for copyright incentives. Several considerations reinforce our doubts about the utility of incentive-based arguments for copyright in standards.

---

[96] *Id.* at 452.
[97] *Id.* at 452–53.
[98] In support of Public Resource on appeal, two members of the U.S. House of Representatives filed an amicus brief urging the appellate court to "safeguard public access to the law and the integrity of the lawmaking process." *See* "Brief of *Amici Curiae* Members of Congress In Support of Defendant-Appellant and for Reversal" p. 2, *ASTM* (D.C. Cir. 2018).
[99] In a concurring opinion in *ASTM*, Judge Katsas included the First Amendment, the Due Process Clause of the Fifth Amendment, and Section 102(b) of the Copyright Act, in addition to fair use, as legitimate bases justifying the republication of incorporated standards. *See ASTM* (D.C. Cir. 2018, pp. 458–59).
[100] *Code Revision Commission* (11th Cir. 2018, p. *20).

First, SDOs generally have ample incentives to develop standards for use by professionals in their fields.[101] It is simply not credible to claim that organizations like the AMA and ADA would stop developing standard nomenclature without copyright protection. The fields they serve need these standards for effective communication with other healthcare providers, insurers, and government agencies.

Second, SDOs themselves generally do not develop the standards in which they claim copyrights. Rather, they typically rely upon volunteer service by experts in the field to develop standards and require these volunteers to assign any copyright interests to the SDOs. The community development of a standard is a reason to treat the standard itself as a shared resource.

Third, SDOs generally use the revenues they derive from selling or licensing the standards to subsidize other activities of their organizations, rather than to recoup investments in the making of the standard. Even without copyright in the standards, SDOs can derive revenues from sales of print materials embodying the standard and value-added products or services.[102]

Fourth, the Internet and World Wide Web now make it very inexpensive and easy to disseminate standards. Given the rise of volunteer information posting on the Web, there is reason to be confident that users of a successful standard will put the standards online for all to use.

Fifth, once a standard has achieved success through widespread adoption, this success provides an opportunity for the SDO to charge monopoly rents for use of or access to the code.[103] The availability of copyright protection for standards may give SDOs excess incentives to invest in the creation of standards to get monopoly rents.

Sixth, copyrighting standards may create perverse incentives for SDOs to invest in persuading governments to mandate use of their standards. *Veeck* (5th Cir. 2002) illustrates this temptation. Under the deal SBCCI offered, local governments such as Anna and Savoy got royalty-free rights to use the code and one or more copies of the code, which they could make available to any members of the public who visited city hall offices. However, SBCCI charged a substantial fee to anyone else who wanted a copy of the code or access to it. Moreover, building inspectors and other public officials referred many prospective users of the codes to SBCCI, in effect making these public employees into a free sales force for SBCCI. The perverse incentives problem is of particular concern because of the increasing frequency with which governments are actively encouraging government adoption of privately drafted industry standards.

The long-term credibility of SDOs depends principally on their ability to produce sound standards. They should be saved from the temptation to develop standards in which they have such a strong financial interest that the standards become a cash cow to milk all those who rely upon and need to use the standards. Developers should not be able to invoke copyright to control access to standards, especially those that have been enacted into law or are required by law. Not only are recognizing copyrights in standards bad public policy, but also this control may run afoul of First Amendment and due process rights guaranteed by the U.S. Constitution.

---

[101] *See, e.g.*, Goldstein 2017, 1:§2.5.2.1 at 2:59 ("[I]t is difficult to imagine an area of creative endeavor in which copyright incentive is needed less. Trade organizations have powerful reasons stemming from industry standardization, quality control, and self-regulation to produce these model codes; it is unlikely that without copyright they will cease producing them."). *See also Veeck* (5th Cir. 2002, pp. 805–06).

[102] *See, e.g., Veeck* (5th Cir. 2002, p. 806).

[103] For example, the U.S. government paid $32.4 million for a perpetual license to use and allow U.S.-based private organizations to use SNOMED (an acronym for Systematized Nomenclature for Medicine) clinical terminology for documentation and reporting. *See* NLM 2003. In 2007, the International Health Terminology Standards Organisation acquired the rights to SNOMED CT, and it establishes and collects fees for the use of SNOMED terminology. *See* SNOMED International 2017.

6

Integrating Technical Standards into Federal Regulations: Incorporation by Reference

*Daniel J. Sheffner**

A.	Overview	109
B.	Legal Background	110
	1. 5 U.S.C. § 552(a)(1)	110
	2. Regulations of the Office of the Federal Register	112
C.	Copyright and Public Access to Incorporated Materials	114
	1. The Public-Access Problem	114
	2. Scope of Copyright Protection for Standards Incorporated by Reference	115
D.	Public and Private Solutions to the Public-Access Problem	119

As discussed in Chapter 2, federal law and policy direct U.S. federal agencies to use, when practical, technical standards developed by private standards development organizations (SDOs) instead of government-created standards. To comply with this directive, agencies often utilize a regulatory drafting technique known as "incorporation by reference" (sometimes abbreviated as "IBR"). Through this practice, an agency may integrate into regulations materials that have been published elsewhere simply by *referring* to the extrinsic materials in the text of its regulations. An extremely useful tool for federal agencies that frequently lack the resources and expertise necessary to develop adequate technical standards themselves, the practice has nonetheless faced criticism that it impedes access to the law. This is because SDOs commonly claim copyright in the standards they develop and, therefore, reserve the right to charge for access, even when their standards are incorporated into federal regulations.

This chapter provides an overview of incorporation by reference. It considers the reasons agencies engage in the practice, its legal foundations, and the procedural requirements agencies must follow to successfully incorporate standards and other materials by reference into their regulations. It also discusses the public-access problem engendered by incorporation by reference and public and private attempts to increase the accessibility of incorporated standards.

---

* The views expressed in this chapter are the author's and do not necessarily represent the views of the Congressional Research Service or the Library of Congress. In addition, although portions of the cited material in this chapter are derived from Administrative Conference reports and recommendations, any expressions of opinion are attributable to the author and do not necessarily reflect those of the Administrative Conference or its members (including the Chairman, Council, and Committees).

A. OVERVIEW

Access to and notice of the law are enduring values in the U.S. legal system.[1] In the context of federal administrative law, these values are embodied, in part, by the publication requirements that govern federal agencies' promulgation of legally binding regulations (also called "rules"). Under the Administrative Procedure Act (APA), agencies must submit for publication in the Federal Register – the official daily federal bulletin – proposed and final rules of general applicability, as well as other important pronouncements and information.[2] Final rules are eventually codified in the Code of Federal Regulations (CFR), a "special edition" of the Federal Register that "present[s] a compact and practical code" for public consumption.[3] The Federal Register and CFR are available in print and online.[4]

While the centralized Federal Register publication scheme ensures that regulated entities are afforded notice of the requirements imposed on them by the vast array of federal regulations,[5] by 1966, roughly 30 years after the establishment of the Federal Register, Congress had become concerned that the proliferation of agency regulations and other materials would eventually render the Federal Register unmanageable in length.[6] In that year, Congress significantly amended the APA through passage of the Freedom of Information Act (FOIA). One particular FOIA provision, which would eventually be codified as a standalone paragraph in 5 U.S.C. § 552(a)(1), was crafted with the specific goal of preventing the Federal Register and CFR from bursting at the seams (See S. Rep. 1964, 4; Bremer 2013a, 134). The provision attempted to accomplish this feat by authorizing agencies to incorporate certain types of extrinsic publications into their regulations merely by referring to such publications in the text of regulations, as opposed to reprinting them. That drafting technique is known as "incorporation by reference."

Federal agencies engage in incorporation by reference with a high degree of frequency. As of the time of writing, a public database operated and periodically updated by the National Institute of Standards and Technology – a component of the Department of Commerce – indicates that the CFR contains over 23,000 references to standards.[7] Voluntary consensus standards authored by private SDOs are not the only category of standards agencies incorporate by reference; the CFR also contains references to private industry, government, and international standards.[8] In addition, agencies incorporate by reference many other types of materials, including state laws, U.S. Government Publishing Office publications, and private technical manuals.[9]

Agencies incorporate by reference when integrating private technical standards into their regulations for a number of reasons. Graphs, charts, and like materials may not fit easily within the Federal Register and CFR.[10] And printing long, complex technical standards may render regulations impenetrable to non-experts.[11] Incorporation by reference permits agencies to use private technical standards in the face of these obstacles. Beyond these concerns, many SDOs

[1] *Cf.* Bremer 2015, 283.
[2] *See* 5 U.S.C. §§ 552(a)(1)(D), 553(b); Bremer 2015, 283.
[3] 1 C.F.R. § 8.1(a); Bremer 2013a, 133 n.1; *see generally* 44 U.S.C. § 1510.
[4] *See* 44 U.S.C. § 4101(a)(2); www.federalregister.gov; www.ecfr.gov. The "e-CFR," however, "is not an official legal edition of the CFR." https://gov.ecfr.io/cgi-bin/ECFR. *See* Bremer 2015, 284 n.26.
[5] Bremer 2013a, 157 n.114. Accordingly, publication constitutes constructive notice of a regulation. A regulation that is not published in the Federal Register is not enforceable, barring actual notice of the rule. 5 U.S.C. § 552(a)(1).
[6] *See* S. Rep. 1964, 4; Bremer 2013b, 3.
[7] Standards Incorporated by Reference Database, www.nist.gov/standardsgov/what-we-do/federal-policy-standards/sibr.
[8] Bremer 2015, 296.
[9] Bremer 2013a, 145–47.
[10] *Id.* at 153–54.
[11] *See id.*

claim that their standards are protected by copyright and, therefore, may not be reprinted in the text of regulations without permission.[12]

Issues of length, fit, and complexity aside, if an agency wants to state in full the technical standards that it adopts in its regulations, could it not simply avoid the copyright problem by creating its own technical standards and eschewing use of the privately drafted variety? Agencies opt to use private technical standards for a variety of reasons, not least of all because they do not typically possess enough personnel, resources, and, often, expertise to easily create their own.[13] Most significantly, as discussed in Chapter 2, federal law and policy *direct* agencies to use a specific type of private technical standards – voluntary consensus standards – when it is legal and practical to do so. This directive can be found in Office of Management and Budget (OMB) Circular A-119 – first published in 1982 – and the National Technology Transfer and Advancement Act of 1995 (NTTAA).[14] OMB Circular A-119, which was most recently revised in 2016, instructs agencies to "use voluntary consensus standards in lieu of government-unique standards in their procurement and regulatory activities, except where inconsistent with law or otherwise impractical."[15] Section 12(d) of the NTTAA also embraces this directive.[16] In addition, the Circular requires that agencies "observe and protect the rights of … copyright holder[s],"[17] which many agencies seek to accomplish through the use of incorporation by reference.

B. LEGAL BACKGROUND

This Section offers an overview of the legal basis for incorporation by reference and the procedures that govern federal agencies' use of the tool. As discussed above, agencies use incorporation by reference to comply with the NTTAA and OMB Circular A-119; however, the legal authority for the practice stems from a different source – the standalone paragraph within 5 U.S.C. § 552(a)(1) (also mentioned above). Additionally, regulations promulgated by the Office of the Federal Register (OFR) prescribe the procedural requirements agencies must satisfy before they may incorporate materials by reference.

1. 5 U.S.C. § 552(a)(1)

Originally an amendment to the APA via FOIA, the standalone paragraph in 5 U.S.C. § 552(a)(1) is composed of two sentences. The first sentence stipulates the penalty for an agency's failure to publish regulations in the Federal Register, providing that, "[e]xcept to the extent that a person has actual and timely notice of the terms thereof, a person may not in any manner be required to resort to, or be adversely affected by, a matter required to be published in the Federal Register and not so published." The second sentence, however, provides that "matter required to be

---

[12] *Id.*; *see* Chapter 5 for a discussion of the arguments supporting and against the recognition of copyright in standards.
[13] Bremer 2015, 300.
[14] Additionally, as noted in Bremer (2015, 307), "the policy is echoed in myriad, narrower contexts through executive directives and statutory provisions that require individual agencies to use private standards, participate in private standards development, and otherwise collaborate with the private sector on standards issues."
[15] OMB Circular A-119, ¶ 5.
[16] Bremer 2015, 296. If using a specific voluntary consensus standard would be illegal "or otherwise impractical," an agency is permitted to use a government-unique standard. In that event, however, it must submit an explanation of its reasons for doing so to OMB. 15 U.S.C. § 272 note; OMB Circular A-119, ¶ 5.
[17] OMB Circular A-119, ¶ 5(g).

published" need not necessarily be set out in full in the Federal Register in order to be successfully integrated into a regulation. Instead, that sentence stipulates that "matter reasonably available to the class of persons affected thereby is deemed published in the Federal Register when incorporated by reference therein with the approval of the Director of the Federal Register."

Section 552(a)(1), therefore, authorizes the use by agencies of incorporation by reference. It does not, however, afford agencies limitless discretion to engage in the practice. The second sentence of § 552(a)(1)'s standalone paragraph imposes two conditions on agencies seeking to incorporate by reference. First, the materials an agency wishes to incorporate must be "reasonably available to the class of persons affected thereby."[18] Second, an agency may not incorporate anything by reference before securing "the approval of the Director of the Federal Register."

Congress did not supply a definition for the term "reasonably available." FOIA's legislative history, however, may offer some insight into its meaning.[19] The report supporting the Senate's 1964 bill[20] seems to indicate that to be "reasonably available" under 5 U.S.C. § 552(a)(1), incorporated publications must be relatively easy to locate and, if offered for sale, not unduly expensive.[21] Although free access is certainly preferable, materials need not be obtainable for free.[22] The report emphasized that incorporation by reference serves the salutary purpose of ensuring the Federal Register is held to a "manageable size."[23] Because, as maintained by the report, many agencies' "activities are thoroughly analyzed and publicized in professional or specialized services, such as Custom Clearing House, West publications, etc." and, therefore, are "readily available to interested members of the public," full publication of such materials in the text of regulations was deemed unnecessary.[24] The report, therefore, suggests that Congress acknowledged that individuals may have to purchase at least some materials that have been incorporated by reference.[25] Such materials, however, would have to be "readily available."[26]

Agencies and SDOs ensure that standards incorporated into federal law are reasonably available in a variety of ways. Both promulgating agencies and OFR maintain copies of materials incorporated into federal regulations for public inspection in their offices (which are generally located in the Washington, D.C.-area).[27] Some commentators, however, believe that

---

[18] While the statute applies the "reasonable-availability" requirement to "the class of persons affected" by the incorporated material, the Administrative Conference of the United States, in Recommendation 2011–5, *Incorporation by Reference*, ¶ 1, 77 Fed. Reg. 2257, 2258 (January 17, 2012), urged agencies to make incorporated material reasonably available to "regulated and other interested parties." (Recommendation 2011–5 was based on a research report authored by Professor Emily Bremer, who was then an attorney advisor with the Administrative Conference. The report (Bremer (2011)) formed the basis for Bremer (2013a).) OFR encourages this approach. See OFR (2018a, 8). Its incorporation-by-reference regulations require that agencies include in their rules a discussion of "the ways that [incorporated materials] are reasonably available to interested parties and how interested parties can obtain the materials." 1 C.F.R. § 51.5(b)(2). OFR's regulations are discussed in the next subsection. The Administrative Conference and Recommendation 2011–5 are discussed in Section D.

[19] See ACUS Response to OFR Petition 2012b, 3

[20] S. Rep. 1964. The Senate passed S. 1666 in 1964, "but sufficient time did not remain in [the 88th] Congress for its full consideration by the House." S. Rep. 1965, 4. The bill that became FOIA, S. 1160, was passed by both houses in the subsequent Congress. See *Renegotiation Board v. Bannercraft Clothing Co.* (U.S. 1974), 18 n.18. As noted in the Senate's 1965 report, S. 1160 "was substantially S. 1666." S. Rep. 1965, 4.

[21] See ACUS Response to OFR Petition 2012b, 3.

[22] See Bremer 2015, 287.

[23] S. Rep. 1964, 4.

[24] *Id.*; ACUS Response to OFR Petition 2012b, 3.

[25] ACUS Response to OFR Petition 2012b, 3.

[26] S. Rep. 1964, 4. The Attorney General's 1967 memorandum on the FOIA (*see* Clark 1967) comports with this latter point. It interpreted the "reasonably available" standard to require that private materials incorporated into regulations by reference "be readily available to the class of persons affected thereby, and *not be difficult for them to locate*" (emphasis added).

[27] *See* 1 C.F.R. §§ 5.2, 51.9(b)(4); Bremer 2013a, 136, 143, 153.

the definition of "reasonably available," no matter what it was at the time of FOIA's drafting, changed with the advent of the Internet Age.[28] Specifically, they contend that advances in digital technologies militate in favor of requiring that all materials incorporated by reference be made freely available online.[29] In its most recent amendments to its regulations, however, OFR refused to impose such a requirement, asserting that doing so "would compromise the ability of regulators to rely on voluntary consensus standards, possibly requiring them to create their own standards, which is contrary to the NTTAA and the OMB Circular A-119."[30] That said, SDOs, agencies, Congress, and others have offered various approaches aimed at increasing the availability of incorporated materials through electronic means, while respecting copyrights. These approaches are discussed in Section D, below.

To successfully incorporate by reference, therefore, agencies must guarantee that incorporated materials are "reasonably available." But reasonable availability alone is not sufficient to ensure the legal validity of an incorporation by reference. In addition, 5 U.S.C. § 552(a)(1) requires that agencies obtain "the approval of the Director of the Federal Register." The next subsection considers the regulatory scheme OFR has developed to evaluate proposed incorporations by reference.

2. Regulations of the Office of the Federal Register

The steps agencies must take to obtain the Director's approval to incorporate by reference are laid out in regulations and guidance issued by OFR, a component of the National Archives and Records Administration (NARA). OFR's incorporation-by-reference regulations are codified in 1 C.F.R. part 51. First adopted in 1982, the regulations were most recently updated in 2014.[31] Important guidance is detailed in OFR (2018a), which is available on NARA's website.[32]

OFR regulations provide that, in evaluating agency requests to incorporate by reference, the Director assumes that incorporation "is intended to benefit both the Federal Government and the members of the class affected" and "[i]s not intended to detract from the legal or practical attributes" of the Federal Register and governing publication requirements.[33] Beyond establishing the general policy of incorporation, OFR's regulations and guidance also stipulate the manner in which agencies are to seek OFR's approval, the language agencies must use when drafting rules incorporating materials by reference, and those documents that are eligible for incorporation.

An agency seeking to incorporate materials by reference must send a formal request to OFR before submitting a rule for publication in the Federal Register. Simply publishing a rule containing an incorporation by reference in the Federal Register "does not of itself constitute an approval of the incorporation by reference by the Director."[34] An agency's request package must include, *inter alia*, a copy of the draft final rule and "[e]nsure" that copies of all materials to be incorporated are "on file at the [OFR]."[35] The preamble of the draft rule must summarize

---

[28] Bremer 2015, 296–97.
[29] *See, e.g.*, Incorporation by Reference, 77 Fed. Reg. 11,414, 11,414 (February 27, 2012) (petition for rulemaking); *see also* Strauss 2013; Mendelson 2014.
[30] Incorporation by Reference, 79 Fed. Reg. 66,267, 66,268 (November 7, 2014).
[31] *See generally id.*
[32] www.archives.gov/files/federal-register/write/handbook/ibr.pdf. In addition, OFR issues general drafting guidance in the form of OFR (2018b). OFR (2018b) is also available on NARA's website. www.archives.gov/files/federal-register/write/handbook/ddh.pdf.
[33] 1 C.F.R. § 51.1(c)(1), (2); *see* Bremer 2013a, 141–42.
[34] 1 C.F.R. § 51.1(e).
[35] *Id.* § 51.5(b)(4), (5). *See also id.* § 51.3(b)(4) ("The Director will formally approve the incorporation by reference of a publication in a final rule when … [t]he publication is on file with [OFR].")

the incorporated materials and explain "the ways ... the materials it incorporates by reference are reasonably available to interested persons" and how such parties can access the materials.[36] The "language of incorporation" in the rule must be "precise, complete, and clearly state that the incorporation by reference is intended and completed by the final rule document."[37] Once OFR receives an agency's request package, it has twenty business days to inform the agency of its approval or disapproval.[38]

Not every publication may be incorporated into a regulation by reference. As discussed above, agencies incorporate many types of materials by reference other than voluntary consensus standards, including government publications and standards, as well as private standards not developed by SDOs. No matter their origin, however, OFR regulations stipulate that only publications that consist of "published data, criteria, standards, specifications, techniques, illustrations, or similar material" and "[d]o[] not detract from the usefulness of the Federal Register publication system" are eligible for incorporation by reference.[39]

Further, OFR regulations not only restate (without defining) 5 U.S.C. § 552(a)(1)'s requirement that incorporated materials be "reasonably available," but also mandate that such materials be "usable."[40] OFR determines usability by considering the publication's "completeness and ease of handling" and "[w]hether [the publication] is bound, numbered, and organized, as applicable,"[41] factors that, as others have noted, harken back to the regulations' 1980s-origins.[42]

Certain federal government materials are subject to additional requirements. "Material published previously in the Federal Register" may not be incorporated by reference. This same prohibition applies to the contents of the U.S. Code.[43] Additionally, agencies are generally prohibited from incorporating their own materials into regulations. As explained by OFR in its most recent amendments to 1 C.F.R. part 51, "[o]therwise, the Federal Register and CFR could become a mere index to material published elsewhere."[44] However, materials "produced by [an] agency may be approved, if, in the judgment of the Director," the materials (1) comply with incorporation by reference policy and the above-stated requirements pertaining to publication-type, reasonable-availability, and usability, and (2) "possess[] other unique or highly unusual qualities" or "cannot be printed using the Federal Register/Code of Federal Regulations printing system."[45]

In addition, OFR regulations prohibit dynamic incorporation.[46] If a publication from which materials were incorporated is updated or revised post-incorporation, the agency must amend its regulations if it wants to include the update or revision.[47] If the agency does so, it must again acquire OFR's approval.

---

[36] *Id.* § 51.5(b)(2)–(3).

[37] *Id.* § 51.9(a).

[38] *Id.* § 51.3(c); *see also id.* § 51.5(b)(1) (providing that an agency's formal request letter must be sent "at least 20 working days before the agency intends to submit the final rule document for publication").

[39] *Id.* § 51.7(a)(2)(i)–(ii); *see also id.* § 51.3(b)(1). Incorporated material must also comply with incorporation by reference policy, as laid out in § 51.1. *See id.* § 51.7(a)(1).

[40] *Id.* § 51.7(a)(3).

[41] *Id.* § 51.7(a)(3)(i)–(ii);

[42] Bremer 2013b, 3; *see* Strauss 2013, 557.

[43] *Id.* § 51.7(c)(1)–(2).

[44] Incorporation by Reference, 79 Fed. Reg. 66,267, 66,268 (November 7, 2014); *see also* Bremer 2013a, 142. ("This rule prevents agencies from pulling regulations out of the CFR, publishing them elsewhere (for example in a pamphlet or on the agency's website), and then incorporating them by reference.")

[45] 1 C.F.R. § 51.7(a)–(b).

[46] Bremer 2013a, 184.

[47] 1 C.F.R. § 51.1(f). This, in turn, may require the initiation of notice-and-comment rulemaking proceedings.

The discussion so far has been in reference to final agency rules. As a general matter, before an agency may issue a rule, it must first publish a proposed rule in the Federal Register and solicit public comments.[48] In the interest of efficiency, an agency may wish to ensure a proposed rule satisfies OFR's requirements.[49] While OFR does not officially approve proposed rules, it does nonetheless informally review proposed rules that incorporate materials by reference upon their submission for publication in the Federal Register.[50] A proposed rule will be informally approved if its preamble discusses the ways in which the incorporated materials are reasonably available – or else "how [the agency] worked to make those materials reasonably available" – and summarizes the materials to be incorporated.[51] OFR will return any proposed rule that does not satisfy these requirements to the promulgating agency.[52]

Agencies must satisfy these procedural requirements or else run the risk of unnecessarily delaying the publication process.[53] But compliance with OFR's regulatory regime is not the reason incorporation by reference – a seemingly routine regulatory drafting technique – has become a controversial subject in recent years. That is the topic of the next section.

C. COPYRIGHT AND PUBLIC ACCESS TO INCORPORATED MATERIALS

Although incorporation by reference is a valuable regulatory drafting tool, its use by federal agencies in the context of privately-authored standards places limits on public access to the full text of many regulations. SDOs generally claim copyright in the standards they develop, and many – although not all – charge for access to their standards, even if they are incorporated by reference into federal regulations. Several observers have expressed concern over the cost of incorporated standards. However, fears of widespread price gouging are not universal, and SDOs credit revenues from the sales of standards with funding standards-development.

This section examines the public-access problem, as well as important considerations from selected judicial decisions concerning – but not providing answers on – the scope of copyright protection for standards incorporated by reference.

1. The Public-Access Problem

Incorporation by reference provides substantial benefits to agencies, the public, regulated entities, and the U.S. private standards-setting regime.[54] Through use of the tool, agencies are able to leverage the technical knowledge and resources of SDOs in the drafting of a wide range of regulations. In doing so, they are able to further the goals of the NTTAA and OMB Circular A-119. But for all the benefits it affords, the practice of incorporation by reference also places restrictions on the availability of the law, at least in regard to the incorporation of privately drafted standards. This public-access problem stems from the fact that nearly all SDOs claim copyright protection in the standards they develop and many reserve the right to charge for access to the texts of voluntary consensus standards incorporated into federal law.[55] And yet, free

---

[48] *See* 5 U.S.C. § 553(b)–(c).
[49] OFR 2018a, 16.
[50] *Id.* at 3 n.5, 17.
[51] 1 C.F.R. § 51.5(a)(1)–(2); *see also id.* § 51.3(a)(1).
[52] *Id.* § 51.3(a)(2) (citing *id.* § 2.4). These requirements also apply to advanced notices of proposed rulemakings. *See* OFR 2018a, 16.
[53] ACUS Recommendation 2011–5, 77 Fed. Reg. 2257, 2258 (January 17, 2012).
[54] Bremer 2013b, 5.
[55] *See* Mendelson 2014, 743.

and open access to the law is a critically important principle in the U.S. legal system. Bremer summarizes the problem succinctly:

> The greatest challenge presented by incorporation by reference is that it impedes access to the law. In all cases, the practice requires interested parties to find material outside of the CFR in order to view an entire regulation. In some cases, if the incorporated material is copyrighted and sold by a private party, incorporation by reference may even require interested parties to pay to see the law.[56]

Some commentators argue that copyright protection allows SDOs to engage in monopoly pricing. They claim that some SDOs charge exorbitant prices – far more than the cost of developing their standards – for access to standards incorporated by reference.[57] Others dispute that monopoly pricing is a common practice.[58] Prices vary from standard to standard, from tens and hundreds to even thousands of dollars. For example, a PDF copy of the 1995 edition of the National Fire Protection Association's (NFPA) *Standard on Types of Building Construction*, which supplies the definition for "[n]oncombustible material" as that term is used in certain federal manufactured housing regulations, costs $31.[59] On the other hand (and as discussed below), the American Petroleum Institute (API) supplied a quote to a congressional staffer of $1,195 for a standard incorporated into federal pipeline regulations by the Pipeline & Hazardous Materials Safety Administration (PHMSA).[60] In any event, while certainly not all SDOs charge for access to the standards they develop,[61] the fact that some do even after those standards become incorporated by reference into federal regulations is controversial.[62]

Copyright protection certainly affords benefits to SDOs and the public. SDOs maintain that revenues realized from the sale of standards or other related fees ultimately fund the standards-development process.[63] Without the ability to charge for access to their standards, SDOs would necessarily raise or impose membership fees and perhaps other costs and, ultimately, pass on the cost of standards development to consumers,[64] a troubling prospect given that standards serve multiple important purposes, including those of setting minimum quality or safety levels and enabling interoperability between products.[65] However, given the significance of the public-access problem, we may ask ourselves whether there are limits to the scope of copyright protection for private standards incorporated into public law. That question is taken up next.

2. Scope of Copyright Protection for Standards Incorporated by Reference

Closely related to the question of copyright's applicability to incorporated standards is the question whether the law is generally subject to copyright protection. Statements of the law

---

[56] 2013a, 153.
[57] See, e.g., Strauss 2013, 510; Chapter 5.
[58] See Bremer 2015 *passim*.
[59] NFPA Catalog, https://catalog.nfpa.org/NFPA-220-Standard-on-Types-of-Building-Construction-P1239.aspx?icid=D729; 24 C.F.R. § 3280.202. A PDF, e-book, or physical copy costs $42. NFPA Catalog, https://catalog.nfpa.org/NFPA-220-Standard-on-Types-of-Building-Construction-P1239.aspx?icid=D729.
[60] See *infra* Section D.
[61] For example, the Internet Engineering Task Force (IETF) and World Wide Web Consortium (W3C), prominent Internet SDOs, have always offered free online access to their standards. See IETF, http://ietf.org/; W3C, www.w3.org/.
[62] Bremer 2013b, 5.
[63] Mendelson 2014, 743 & n.33.
[64] Bremer 2015, 294.
[65] Blind & Kahin 2018, 9.

are in fact generally *not* amenable to copyright protection. In *Wheaton v. Peters* (U.S. 1834), the Supreme Court announced this basic principle in regard to judicial opinions. The Court in *Wheaton* held that the official reporter of the Supreme Court's decisions could not claim copyright in the actual opinions of the Court (as opposed to the annotations and any other original contributions of the reporter).[66] Significantly, the Court declared that it was the unanimous opinion of the members of the Court "that no reporter has or can have any copyright in the written opinions delivered by this court; and that the judges thereof cannot confer on any reporter any such right."[67] The Court faced a similar issue roughly fifty years later in *Banks v. Manchester* (U.S. 1888). In rejecting the copyright claim asserted by a reporter in the decisions of the Supreme Court of Ohio, the Court in *Banks* announced that "there has always been a judicial consensus, from the time of ... *Wheaton v. Peters* ... that no copyright could under the statutes passed by Congress, be secured in the products of the labor done by judicial officers in the discharge of their judicial duties."[68]

But does the principle embodied by *Wheaton* and *Banks* apply to standards incorporated by reference into federal regulations? A Fifth Circuit decision potentially calls into question the availability of copyright protection for incorporated standards.[69] In *Veeck v. Southern Building Code Congress International, Inc.* (5th Cir. 2002), the Fifth Circuit, sitting *en banc*, held that an individual who had posted on his non-commercial website a privately-authored model building code that had been formally adopted by two Texas municipalities had not infringed the copyright of the code's institutional author. Peter Veeck maintained a website devoted to publishing information about north Texas. In 1997, he sought to post the building codes of two north Texas towns on his website. The towns had adopted as their respective building codes the 1994 edition of the *Standard Building Code*, a product of the non-profit Southern Building Code Congress International, Inc. (SBCCI). Veeck acquired an electronic copy of the 1994 edition from SBCCI for $72 and pasted the code onto his website. The website indicated that the codes were the building codes of the two Texas towns. It did not credit SBCCI as the author of the model code.[70]

Based in large part on its understanding of *Wheaton* and *Banks*, the Fifth Circuit held that Veeck did not infringe SBCCI's copyright in the *Standard Building Code* when he posted the code on his website. The court asserted that "*Banks* represents a continuous understanding that 'the law,' whether articulated in judicial opinions or legislative acts or ordinances, is in the public domain and thus not amenable to copyright."[71] Thus, while acknowledging that SBCCI retained a valid copyright in its model buildings codes *as model building codes*, the court held that the organization's copyright did not extend to the republication of its codes as law.[72]

The court in *Veeck* did not extend its analysis outside the context of copyright's applicability to model codes. Several SDOs submitted a brief as amici for SBCCI in *Veeck* "out of fear that their copyrights may be vitiated simply by the common practice of governmental entities' incorporating their standards in laws and regulations."[73] In response, the court made clear that its decision was limited to the role of copyright protection for privately-authored model codes adopted

---

[66] *Wheaton* (U.S. 1834, p. 668); *see also Veeck* (5th Cir. 2002, p. 795).
[67] *Wheaton* (U.S. 1834, p. 668).
[68] *Banks* (U.S. 1888, p. 253).
[69] Bremer 2015, 291; Bremer 2013a, 167.
[70] *Veeck* (5th Cir. 2002, p. 793).
[71] *Id.* at 797, 800.
[72] *Id.* at 793; *see* Bremer 2013b, 4 (writing that the Fifth Circuit "held that [SBCCI] could not claim copyright in the code *qua* law").
[73] *Veeck* (5th Cir. 2002, pp. 803–04).

as law and created for that purpose.[74] Incorporation by reference, the court reasoned, was a distinct issue that required a different mode of analysis.[75]

Veeck, therefore, did not explicitly answer any questions concerning the scope or extent of copyright protection for private standards incorporated by reference. Even so, some commentators and advocates maintain that the decision calls into question the ability of SDOs and others to charge for access to incorporated standards, at least when the standards constitute mandatory rules.[76] Others, however, see significant distinctions between the private materials at issue in Veeck and voluntary consensus standards, maintaining that Veeck is inapplicable to incorporation by reference. Bremer, for instance, contends that while SBCCI intended for its *Standard Building Code* to be adopted by municipalities, adoption into law is generally *not* the primary reason for voluntary consensus standards' development.[77] Bremer additionally maintains that "agencies do not adopt [voluntary consensus] standards as law, but rather incorporate them by reference – in whole or in part, and often with substantial modification or addition – to support substantive requirements of federal regulations."[78] Thus, while not directly on point, Veeck is sure to remain controversial for the time being.[79]

While Veeck is persuasive authority for those who favor limiting the scope of copyright protection for incorporated standards, SDOs and their supporters can locate support in *Practice Management Information Corporation v. American Medical Association*, a 1997 (pre-Veeck) decision of the Ninth Circuit. In *Practice Management*, the court considered whether the American Medical Association's (AMA) copyright in its medical procedure coding system survived the system's adoption by the federal Health Care Financing Administration (HCFA).[80] The AMA granted HCFA "a non-exclusive, royalty-free, and irrevocable license to use, copy, publish and distribute" the codes, and the agency agreed to use no other codes for identifying physician services and to require use of the codes in its programs.[81] HCFA included the codes in its Common Procedure Coding System. Further, by regulation, the agency mandated their use in connection with Medicaid reimbursement claims.[82] Practice Management Information Corporation (Practice Management) sued the AMA, claiming that its copyright in the coding system was rendered invalid when HCFA required its use by Medicaid reimbursement claimants.[83]

The Ninth Circuit rejected Practice Management's claim, asserting that to declare invalid an entity's copyright in a publication simply because it has been adopted by a government agency "could ... prove destructive of the copyright interest[] in encouraging creativity, a matter of particular significance in this context because of the increasing trend of state and federal adoptions of model codes."[84] In addition, the court opined that no barriers to access to the AMA's coding system were engendered by the AMA's copyright.[85] The court, therefore, held

---

[74] *Id.* at 804–05.
[75] *Id.* at 804. The court included a citation to OMB Circular A-119 after referencing "the common practice" described by the SDO amici. *Id.* at 804 n.20; *see* Bremer 2015, 291.
[76] *See, e.g.*, Incorporation by Reference, 77 Fed. Reg. 11,414, 11,415 (February 27, 2012) (petition for rulemaking).
[77] Bremer 2013a, 169. *See also supra* text accompanying note 66; Blind & Kahin (2018), 9.
[78] Bremer 2013a, 169–70.
[79] Bremer 2015, 292.
[80] *Practice Management* (9th Cir. 1997, p. 517). HCFA is now the Centers for Medicare & Medicaid Services.
[81] *Id.* at 517–18 (internal quotation marks omitted).
[82] *Id.* at 518 (citing 42 C.F.R. § 433.112(b)(2)).
[83] *Id.*
[84] *Id.* at 518 (internal citation and quotation marks omitted).
[85] *Id.* at 519.

that the AMA's copyright in its coding system had not been abrogated upon its adoption by HCFA.[86]

More recently, SDOs initially found success in the since partially reversed and remanded decision of the U.S. District Court for the District of Columbia in *American Society for Testing & Materials v. Public.Resource.Org*. In that case, several SDOs sued Public.Resource.Org (Public Resource), a non-profit organization devoted to increasing the accessibility of legal information to the public, for copyright and trademark infringement. Public Resource, founded and run by Carl Malamud, seeks to shed light on local, state, and federal laws deemed to be insufficiently accessible to the public by posting those laws on its website.[87] In 2013, ASTM International, NFPA, and the American Society of Heating, Refrigerating, and Air-Conditioning Engineers sued Public Resource for violating their copyrights in 257 voluntary consensus standards that had been incorporated by reference into law after the non-profit disseminated the standards on its website without plaintiffs' permission.[88] A year later, the American Educational Research Association, American Psychological Association, and National Council on Measurement in Education also sued Public Resource for posting the 1999 edition of the organizations' collaboratively-authored *Standards for Educational and Psychological Testing* on its website.[89]

In an opinion consolidating the two cases, the district court granted plaintiffs' motions for summary judgment and permanently enjoined Public Resource from further infringing the plaintiffs' copyrights.[90] Public Resource had argued, in part, that copyright protection for plaintiffs' standards had been revoked upon the standards' incorporation by reference. The court was unpersuaded by this argument. As a preliminary matter, the court acknowledged that, under the Copyright Act, copyright protection does not extend to "any work of the United States Government."[91] It noted, however, that, pursuant to the Act, "any work of the United States Government" means "a work prepared by an officer or employee of the United States Government as part of that person's official duties."[92] Based on its reading of the Act's legislative history, the court asserted that, "[f]or *other types of work*, such as those commissioned by the government or created under government contract by private parties, Congress chose to make case-by-case decisions and leave the determination of whether private copyright should exist to the federal agency that commissioned or contracted for the work."[93]

In the court's estimation, Congress had not chosen to eliminate copyright protection for privately authored standards incorporated by reference into regulations, as evidenced by its silence on the issue through the successive enactments of FOIA, the Copyright Act, and the NTTAA. The court explained that, although Congress had authorized incorporation by reference in 1966 through passage of FOIA, it "made no mention of these incorporated works" ten years later when it passed the Copyright Act.[94] And Congress's silence persisted when, roughly twenty years

---

[86] *Id.* at 520. The court was influenced, in part, by the Second Circuit's decision in *CCC Information Services, Inc. v. Maclean Hunter Market Reports, Inc.* (2d Cir. 1994), which upheld the publisher's copyright in the *Red Book*, a publication containing used car valuations that had been incorporated by many states.

[87] See www.public.resource.org.

[88] *See Am. Soc'y for Testing & Materials* (D.D.C. 2017, pp.*13–14); Bremer 2015, 293.

[89] *See Am. Soc'y for Testing & Materials* (D.D.C. 2017, pp.*14–15); Bremer 2015, 293.

[90] *Am. Soc'y for Testing & Materials* (D.D.C. 2017, pp.*84–85). The motion of the American Educational Research Association, American Psychological Association, and National Council on Measurement in Education was granted in part. *Id.* at *5.

[91] *Id.* at *31 (quoting 17 U.S.C. § 105) (internal quotation marks omitted).

[92] *Id.* (quoting 17 U.S.C. § 101) (internal quotation marks omitted).

[93] *Id.* (emphasis added)

[94] *Id.* at *34.

after the Copyright Act's passage, it encouraged the use of incorporation by reference to integrate technical standards into federal regulations in the NTTAA.[95]

On appeal, the Court of Appeals for the D.C. Circuit vacated the district court's injunctions, reversed its grant of summary judgment, and remanded the case to the district court.[96] The court limited its review to the district court's determination (not discussed above) that Public Resource's reproduction of the petitioners' standards did not constitute fair use under the Copyright Act or qualify under the "nominative fair use" exception to trademark infringement,[97] "leaving for another day the far thornier question of whether standards retain their copyright after they are incorporated by reference into law."[98] On the fair use question, the court instructed the district court to develop a fuller record in regard to "the nature of each of the standards at issue, the way in which [the standards] are incorporated, and the manner and extent to which [the standards] were copied by [Public Resource]."[99]

The scope of copyright protection for private technical standards incorporated by reference into federal law, therefore, is still an open question. But while we await clearer guidance from the courts, the federal government, SDOs, and other stakeholders have proposed several solutions to the public-access problem engendered by copyright that generally attempt to balance the public's interest in free access to the law and SDOs' interests in the protection of their copyrights.

D. PUBLIC AND PRIVATE SOLUTIONS TO THE PUBLIC-ACCESS PROBLEM

Several institutions and individuals have offered solutions to the public-access problem. These initiatives come in the form of non-binding resolutions by governmental or non-profit organizations, congressional action, advocacy by interested individuals and organizations, or attempts by SDOs themselves – sometimes in collaboration with federal agencies – to increase the availability of standards incorporated by reference through free, electronic means.

In 2011, the Administrative Conference of the United States issued a non-binding recommendation on how incorporating agencies and OFR can ensure incorporated materials are reasonably available to regulated entities and other interested parties.[100] The Administrative Conference is an independent agency in the Executive Branch that is tasked with recommending improvements to administrative procedure. Along with several other discrete recommendations, Recommendation 2011–5 proposes that, when considering whether to incorporate material by reference, agencies "should work with … copyright owner[s] to ensure the material will be reasonably available to regulated and other interested parties both during rulemaking and following promulgation."[101] One way to do so, the recommendation advises, is to request copyright holders'

---

[95] Id. at *35.
[96] Am. Soc'y for Testing & Materials (D.C. Cir. 2018, p. 458).
[97] See Chapter 12, which discusses the nominative fair use exception.
[98] Am. Soc'y for Testing & Materials (D.C. Cir. 2018, p. 441).
[99] Id. at 448–49. To assist in developing a fuller record, the court of appeals asked the district court to consider three issues on remand: (1) the extent to which Public Resource's reproduction of the SDOs' standards causes additional harm in light of the fact that the SDOs post the standards in freely accessible online reading rooms; (2) where only specific portions of a standard are incorporated into federal law, whether reproduction of only those portions would leave "a vibrant market for the standard[] in [its] entirety"; and (3) whether Public Resource's reproduction of old editions of standards is harmful to the market for new and non-incorporated standards. Id. at 453.
[100] The recommendation also provides guidance on how to update regulations containing incorporated materials, navigate procedural requirements, and resolve drafting difficulties. See ACUS, Incorporation by Reference, https://acus.gov/research-projects/incorporation-reference.
[101] ACUS Recommendation 2011–5, ¶ 3, 77 Fed. Reg. 2257, 2258 (January 17, 2012).

consent in making incorporated materials freely available in an electronic format.[102] Barring such consent, the recommendation suggests that "agencies … work with [copyright holders] and, through the use of technological solutions, low-cost publication, or other appropriate means, promote the availability of the materials while respecting the copyright owner's interest in protecting its intellectual property."[103]

Congress entered the fray around the same time in its effort to increase the accessibility of pipeline safety standards incorporated into regulations by PHMSA, a component of the Department of Transportation. In 2012, President Obama signed into law the Pipeline Safety, Regulatory Certainty, and Job Creation Act of 2011. The Act was a response to several tragic and destructive pipeline accidents, including, most prominently, the 2010 pipeline explosion in San Bruno, California, which resulted in eight deaths and fifty-eight injuries, as well as the destruction of thirty-eight homes.[104] Relevant for our purposes, section 24 of the Act prohibited PHMSA from "issu[ing] guidance or a regulation … that incorporates by reference any documents or portions thereof unless the documents or portions thereof are made available to the public, free of charge, on an Internet Web site." The provision was apparently inserted after a representative from API cited a price of $1,195 for a copy of one of its incorporated standards in response to an inquiry from a congressional staffer.[105]

PHMSA spent a substantial amount of time and resources attempting to comply with section 24.[106] While the agency successfully reached agreements with several SDOs to begin providing online access at no cost to the agency's incorporated standards, in 2013, Congress amended section 24 in a manner that lessened the provision's "uncompromising free access mandate."[107] Significantly, although section 24 still requires that incorporated materials be made freely available, pursuant to the amendment, it now no longer mandates that they be published "on an Internet Web site."[108] As Bremer notes, it is unclear whether section 24 now requires that PHMSA do anything beyond allow public inspection of its incorporated materials (as all agencies are required to do pursuant to OFR regulations).[109]

In addition to government initiatives, private groups have urged legislative, regulatory, or judicial fixes to the public-access problem. Public Resource's ongoing litigation, discussed above, is one prominent example. Also important was the 2012 petition for rulemaking that prompted OFR's subsequent 2014 amendments to its incorporation-by-reference regulations. The petition, which was filed by several administrative law scholars and practitioners, as well as Carl Malamud of Public Resource, requested that OFR amend its regulations to require that incorporated materials be made available in read-only formats online for free.[110] OFR ultimately refused to impose such a requirement, but the petition was nonetheless a significant contribution to the public-access debate.

---

[102] *Id.* ¶ 3(a), at 2258.
[103] *Id.* ¶ 3(b). Recommendation 2011–5 has been implemented by several agencies, including OFR.
[104] Nat'l Transp. Safety Bd. 2011, 1; Seifter 2018, 159.
[105] Strauss 2013, 508. Bremer (2013a, 175) reports that the House staffer called API's sales office instead of its government affairs office. Had he or she called the latter, API would presumably have offered the staffer a copy free of charge, as "SDOs ordinarily provide free copies [of their standards] to legislators." *Id.*
[106] Bremer 2015, 324–25.
[107] *Id.* at 324–25, 281–82.
[108] Availability of Pipeline Safety Regulatory Documents, Pub. L. No. 113–30, § 1, 127 Stat. 510, 510 (2013). Pursuant to the amendment, section 24 also no longer requires that guidance documents containing incorporated materials be made freely available. *Id.*
[109] Bremer 2015, 325–26.
[110] Incorporation by Reference, 77 Fed. Reg. 11,414 (February 27, 2012) (petition for rulemaking).

And in 2016, the American Bar Association's (ABA) House of Delegates adopted Resolution 112, which sought a legislative solution to the public-access problem. In Resolution 112, the ABA recommended passage of legislation that would compel agencies to make their incorporated standards available to the public for free (while ensuring they receive required authorizations from relevant copyright holders).[111] Importantly, it urged that any such legislation require that "public access ... include at least online, read-only access" to incorporated standards, "including availability at computer facilities in government depository libraries."[112] The resolution is reproduced in full below.

American Bar Association
Resolution 112
August 2016

1 RESOLVED, That the American Bar Association urges Congress to enact legislation that
2 requires the following when a federal agency proposes or issues a substantive rule of general
3 applicability that incorporates by reference any portion of a standard drafted by a private
4 organization:
5 (a) The agency must make the portion of the standard that the agency intends to
6 incorporate by reference accessible, without charge, to members of the public.
7 (b) If the material is subject to copyright protection, the agency must obtain authorization
8 from the copyright holder for public access to that material.
9 (c) The required public access must include at least online, read-only access to the
10 incorporated portion of the standard, including availability at computer facilities in
11 government depository libraries, but it need not include access to the incorporated
12 material in hard-copy printed form.
13 (d) The legislation should provide that it will have no effect on any rights or defenses
14 that any person may possess under the Copyright Act or other current law.
15 FURTHER RESOLVED, That the American Bar Association urges Congress to permanently
16 authorize agencies subject to these provisions to enter into agreements with copyright holders to
17 accomplish the access described above.
18 FURTHER RESOLVED, That the American Bar Association urges Congress to require each
19 agency, within a specified period, to:
20 (a) identify all privately drafted standards and other content previously incorporated by
21 reference into that agency's regulations;
22 (b) determine whether the agency requires authorization from any copyright holder in
23 order to provide public access to the materials as described above; and
24 (c) establish a reasonable plan and timeline to provide public access as described above,
25 including taking any necessary steps (i) to obtain relevant authorizations, or (ii) to amend
26 or repeal the regulation to eliminate the incorporation by reference.

These governmental and public interest initiatives have influenced and, in many ways, spurred the public-access debate. Perhaps as a result, several SDOs have begun offering free, electronic access to their incorporated standards. Many SDOs do so in collaboration with individual

---

[111] ABA Resolution 112, lines 5–8.
[112] *Id.* at lines 9–12.

agencies on an individual basis during or after the rulemaking process.[113] And some sell licenses to agencies that authorize the latter to distribute copies of standards they are in the process of incorporating or have already incorporated.[114]

Either in conjunction with or independent of these public–private collaborations, many SDOs offer online access to some or all of their incorporated standards for free. For example, ASTM International, which, as the largest American SDO, has over 3,000 standards incorporated by reference into federal regulations,[115] allows users to read all of its incorporated standards from an online reading room accessible from its website.[116] And, in 2013, the American National Standards Institute (ANSI) launched the "ANSI IBR Standards Portal." The portal offers for viewing, at no cost, read-only copies of the incorporated standards of several participating SDOs, including the Acoustical Society of America, American Welding Society, International Electrotechnical Commission, and International Organization for Standardization.[117] In addition, the portal offers links to the websites of SDOs that independently provide free online access to their incorporated standards, including API, the Institute of Electrical and Electronics Engineers, and Underwriters Laboratories, Inc.[118]

Such free access is generally governed by digital rights management technologies and the standards made available are frequently read-only.[119] In addition, many organizations reserve the right to rescind access for violation of governing license agreements or for any other reason.[120] For example, users seeking to access standards directly from ANSI's online portal are asked to "agree that ANSI may terminate [their] access to the Licensed Materials at any time and for any reason, including [their] failure to comply with the terms of [the] license or any license agreement incorporated herein."[121] Organizations may also require users to waive their rights to pursue copyright challenges.[122]

Any viable consensus-based solution to the public-access problem will likely need to balance the principle of free access to the law with SDOs' interests in the protection of their copyrights.[123] For the most part, the initiatives described in this section attempt to strike that balance.

CONCLUSION

Incorporation by reference is an extremely useful tool for federal agencies. Through its use, agencies may take advantage of the vast amounts of resources and technical expertise that SDOs

---

[113] Bremer 2013a, 178–79.

[114] *Id.* at 178.

[115] Standards Incorporated by Reference Database, https://standards.gov/sibr/query/index.cfm?fuseaction=rsibr.total_regulatory_sibr; Bremer 2015, 311.

[116] ASTM 2018c.

[117] ANSI 2018c; Bremer 2015, 330–31.

[118] ANSI 2018c.

[119] *See, e.g.,* ASTM 2018c (providing, in part, that "[t]he ASTM Document is designed to be viewed online only – there are no "print," "save," or "cut and paste" options – and the license granted to you by this agreement does not include the right to download, reproduce, store in a retrieval system, modify, make available on a network, use to create derivative works, or transmit the content of the ASTM Document in any form or by any means, electronic, mechanical, photocopying, recording, scanning, or otherwise").

[120] Mendelson 2014, 743 n.30.

[121] ANSI 2018c.

[122] *See* Mendelson 2014, 743 n.30, 753. Not all SDOs, however, impose such restrictions. *See, e.g.,* All PPI Publications, http://plasticpipe.org/publications/index.html.

[123] *See* Bremer 2015, 330 (writing that "agencies should work with standards developers in pursuit of the ideal of free online access, but with the willingness to compromise when doing so is necessary to promote other important administrative values and fulfill regulatory responsibilities, including protecting public health and safety").

bring to bear in the standards-development process in the formulation of a diverse array of regulations, assuming they adhere to OFR's procedural requirements. The tool, however, places limits on the availability of the law by requiring interested individuals to resort to additional sources and perhaps even pay a fee in order to access the full text of many regulations. But while the precise scope of copyright protection for incorporated standards is unknown, entities from the public and private sectors, including SDOs, have proposed many creative solutions to the public-access problem, most of which seek to balance SDOs' intellectual property rights with the important U.S. legal principle of free, unfettered access to the law.

7

Public Law, European Constitutionalism and Copyright in Standards

Björn Lundqvist

A.	The Origins of the European System of European Standards	126
B.	Standards and Business Conduct in the New Economy	128
C.	The *James Elliot* Case: Testing the Boundaries of Copyright Protection in the EU Standardization Process	129
D.	The Wider Implications of the *James Elliott* Case: The Applicability of Competition Law Rules to the Standard-Setting Procedure	132
E.	The Interface Between Free Trade Rules and Competition Law	134

Should technical standards decided and published by official Standards Development Organizations (SDOs) and referred to in Regulations, Directives or, generally, in EU law be regarded as "law" that must be accessible to the public, or could these standards still be private goods, licensed for royalties and, indeed, only accessible by a few? Access to technical standards may be the next hot topic for the European Standard Setting Organisations (SSOs) and the EU Commission. Some SSOs, as a way to finance their activities to develop technical standards, may charge firms or third persons to access and make use of the technical standards produced. The charges are based on the copyright protection of said standards and may range from low to high depending on the SSO and the market penetration of the standard in question.[1] However, with increasing action by legislators of incorporating standards by reference into legal acts, the question is whether claiming copyright and, thus, charging for access to such technical standards, is still feasible. If technical standards, which are being used to interpret or fill in norms contained in laws and regulations have to be regarded as law, then their content should, according to the general consensus, belong to the public domain. According to several Member States' Copyright regimes and general legal thinking, laws and regulations should be publicly accessible free of charge since only free access complies with basic standards of democracy, rule of law and transparency.[2] If instead technical standards are not to be regarded as law, but as products of private intellectual, creative production, access may have to be paid for, by way of buying a license or by otherwise paying the price for the product of the standardization effort.[3]

---

[1] Strauss 2013, 497–509 et seq.; Bremer 2015, 279, 317 et seq.
[2] Van Gestel & Micklitz 2013, 145–181; *Knooble* (The Hague 2008).
[3] Van Gestel & Micklitz 2013, 145–181.

The EU procedure to create technical standards, the so-called 'New Approach', is a *sui generis* intertwined procedure where the EU Commission plays a large role, but where *de facto* the technical standards are drawn up through collaborative self-regulation by firms under the supervision of a European SDO. Some European standards can achieve the status of harmonized standards through the New Approach, where the standard is included through reference in the relevant EU legal act. The *de facto* material rule to be followed is, generally, included in the harmonized standard, and not in the legal act, while the legal act is a short document that primarily refers to the technical standard document in question. Harmonized standards are not binding, but products manufactured in compliance with harmonized standards benefit from a presumption of conformity with the corresponding essential requirements, and thus with the right to be freely circulated in the EU.

So, in these situations, can the technical standards be copyright protected? Stating this, perhaps this question is, indeed, wider: Is the issue whether the standard-setting process is a legislative procedure creating laws, or, whether is it something else, a private procedure? And, what consequences may this have for the copyright protection of EU technical standards for the benefit of the SSOs? These are the issues which this chapter intends to address.[4]

This chapter is sparked by the recent *James Elliot* case[5], where the European Court of Justice (ECJ) stated that European harmonized standards should be considered part of EU law. However, the larger issue will be also be addressed. Indeed, the issue of copyright protection is a (major) sub-issue to the question of whether European harmonized standards constitute EU law, or not, and what that implies. The issue whether standards constitute 'law' may not only have consequences for whether ESOs may charge royalties for accessing standards. It may also have consequences on the issue of whether to judge the standard-setting process and the result of that process under competition law, or under the rules of free movement. Competition law under Article 101 TFEU regulates undertakings taking part in collaborations and there are cases where collaborations by undertakings in standard-setting bodies were considered self-regulation to the point of establishing cartels.[6] When the ECJ in *James Elliot* states that Harmonized Standards are part of EU law, is the Court thereby stating that harmonized standards are not the result of undertakings taking part in collaborations? They are instead the result of a public legislative procedure and should be governed by constitutional rules and principles? Indeed, neither national nor EU laws are, normally, addressed under EU Competition law. Moreover, there are some cases, most recently the *Fra.bo* case, that suggest that SSO-produced technical standards can be judged under Article 34 TFEU. Whether technical standards are law or the result of self-regulation is an issue to be discussed under EU constitutional, Trade and Competition Law.

Initially, a general background to the EU system of creating European standards is presented, as well as the practice of referencing to standards in legislative acts. Second, the modern business practice of developing technical standards is discussed. Thereafter, the copyright problem connected to these standards is discussed and presented, and the *James Elliott* case is analysed. Third, the interface between European harmonized standards, trade and competition law is discussed. In the end, I present my view on whether technical standards should continue to be protected under Member States' Copyright Acts, or whether they belong in the public domain.

---

[4] For an earlier version, *see* Lundqvist 2017, 421–436.
[5] *James Elliott Construction* (CJEU 2016).
[6] *Pre-insulated Pipe Cartel* (E.C. 1998); *EMC Development* (CJEU 2011); *EN 197-1 Standard* (E.C. 2005). "The Pre-insulated Pipes cartel" where 'ABB's internal documentation confirms that compliance with standards was being used as a means of keeping up price levels.

A. THE ORIGINS OF THE EUROPEAN SYSTEM OF EUROPEAN STANDARDS

The general perception is that, in the United States, standard-setting organizations are mostly private sector-specific organizations, while in Europe the general model consisted of, and to some extent still comprises, centralized national private non-profit associations enjoying public recognition and (monopoly) power, elaborating and promulgating standards according to a rather homogeneous and harmonized procedure.[7]

The European Standardization Committee (CEN) has a somewhat central position in the landscape of European standard-setting. CEN was established in 1961 by several national standards bodies and acts as an umbrella organization. CEN's national members are the National Standards Organizations of the 28 European Union countries and Macedonia, Serbia and Turkey, plus the three countries of the European Free Trade Association (Iceland, Norway and Switzerland). There is a one member per country policy. The European Commission is a counsellor to CEN and there are also a number of associated members, i.e. representatives of organizations at the European level, e.g. the European Environmental Citizens Organization for Standardization (ECOS).[8]

CEN's national members have exclusive voting rights in the general assembly and on the administrative board of CEN, and they provide delegations to the technical board and the technical bodies of CEN. The technical bodies of CEN are the working units that draw up standards and are, thus, the *de facto* important organs when drawing up the technical specifications for the standard. The persons included in the national delegations are normally from the relevant industry, as are the persons making up the technical bodies. Indeed, it is the composition of the technical bodies that creates *de facto* self-regulation by the industry.

It is the responsibility of the CEN national members to implement European standards as national standards. The National Standard Setting Organisations (NSOs) distribute for remuneration (license/sells) the implemented European standards, and, generally, claim copyright protection for the implemented standards. The NSOs thus claim that the representatives who participate in a technical committee or working group that prepared the standard are the authors of a collective copyright-protected work and the NSO has obtained through contract the exclusive and permanent right to utilize the so-called financial rights connected to the work, i.e. the standard.[9] Indeed, since most standards take the form of written documents, it is generally understood that they are considered copyrightable works of authorship and protected by copyright law, though this can be disputed.[10] Generally, under the Member States Copyright regimes there are exemptions from copyright for legal and administrative acts, while a narrower exemption may also be found in the EU InfoSoc directive.[11]

When deciding on a European standard, the NSOs are obliged to remove any pre-dating conflicting national standards.[12] Thus, there is a harmonization effort of standards under CEN under the so-called New Approach. CEN standards not only have precedence and primacy over national standards, they might also be recognized in the EU as European standards, and even as harmonized standards.[13]

---

[7] Schepel 2005, 101.
[8] For further details, see CEN's website: www.cen.eu/cen/pages/faq.aspx
[9] See, e.g., the Swedish Standards Institute explanation regarding copyright: www.sis.se/en/standards/generalterms andconditions/copyright/
[10] On the contrary, see Chapter 5; Samuelson 2007.
[11] Art. 5 *InfoSoc*; Art. 2 sect, 4 *Berne Convention for the Protection of Literary and Artistic Works*; WIPO, p. 30.
[12] CEN/CENELEC 2018a.
[13] Id.

The so-called New Approach was an EU effort to deal with several perceived inefficiencies with the EU system of developing technical standards or product requirements, whether the standard originated with public organizations, e.g. Member States, or private NSOs. The 'old approach', where the EU or the Member States produced technical standards, was considered too slow and created technical standards of suboptimal quality. Member State-produced standards could also violate EU free trade rules by restricting trade between Member States.[14] Self-regulation by the industry, through standard-setting organizations on an EU level, incorporating the interested parties, seemed to be a more effective way to create – and to update – technical standards and to implement the internal market. Indeed, the technical expertise did not exist within the public authorities to create high quality, up-to-date, standards for the creation of the internal market, while such expertise did exist within EU private firms ('undertakings'). In essence, the New Approach was and still is a regulatory technique and strategy for de-regulation, first laid down by the Council Resolution of 1985 on the new approach to technical harmonization and standardization.[15] It was the starting point of 'outsourcing' the creation of product requirements to the industry on an EU level through self-regulation under standard-setting organizations.[16]

The New Approach established the following principles: (i) legislative harmonization in the EU is limited to essential requirements that products and services placed on the Community market must meet if they are to benefit from free movement within the Community; (ii) the essential requirements are set out in (annexes to the) relevant directives concerning the product. Although no detailed manufacturing specifications are included in the essential requirements, the degree of detailed wording differs between directives; (iii) the technical specifications of products meeting the essential requirements set out in the directives are laid down in harmonized standards drafted and produced by organizations competent in standard-setting. Application of harmonized or other standards remains voluntary, and the manufacturer may always apply other technical specifications to meet the requirements; however (iv) products manufactured in compliance with harmonized standards benefit from a presumption of conformity with the corresponding essential requirements, and thus with the right to be freely circulated in the EU.[17]

Harmonized standards are a specific category amongst standards. They ensure that products meet the essential requirements of harmonized EU legislation and they are prepared in accordance with the general guidelines agreed upon between the Commission and the European standards organizations, and follow a mandate issued by the Commission after consultation with the Member States. The terminology used in New Approach directives is a legal qualification of technical specifications existing as 'European standards', but to which a special meaning has been given by the relevant directives.[18] Harmonized standards are according to Regulation 1025/2012 '… a European standard adopted on the basis of a request made by the Commission for the application of Union harmonisation legislation'.[19] Other European standards are adopted outside EU legislation on the initiative of private firms or other stakeholders.[20] The New Approach was updated in 2008 and 2012 with a number of regulations, but without altering these basic premises.[21]

---

[14] See *Dassonville* (European Commission 1974); *Cassis de Dijon* (European Commission 1979).
[15] CJEU 1985.
[16] For further development, see Lundqvist 2018.
[17] European Commission 2017, 27 et seq.
[18] Id.
[19] European Commission 2012, Art. 2 (1) (c).
[20] European Commission 2011c, 1 et seq.
[21] European Commission 2008; European Commission 2013; European Commission 2012.

Under the New Approach, the Commission formally requests the European standards organizations (e.g. CEN) to develop harmonized standards by issuing a mandate. The European Standards Organizations, e.g. CEN will formally take a position on a mandate from the Commission in conformity with their internal regulations. Acceptance of the mandate and the subsequent work programme of these organizations initiate the stand-still period as provided in their internal regulations and in EU Regulation 1025/2012.[22] The stand-still period was implemented due to the 'standards war' over colour TV in the 1960s.[23] Thus, formally, the Commission may initiate the process, but creating a harmonized standard is an ESO matter and, *de facto*, the initiative comes normally from industry.

CEN is one of the three ESOs with the primary objective of removing trade barriers within the EU. However, in order to promote European standards in a globalized world, CEN cooperates more and more with CENELEC, the European Committee for Electrotechnical Standardization, and ETSI, the European Telecommunication Standards Institute. CENELEC is responsible for standardization in the electrotechnical engineering field. It was created in 1973 as a result of the merger of two previous European organizations: CENELCOM and CENEL.[24]

CENELEC's set-up is similar to that of CEN and they share the same internal regulations for governance and for drafting and implementing standards.[25] CEN and CENELEC are recognized under Regulation 1025/2012, Annex I as ESOs.

The New Approach and its implied methodology for 'outsourcing' the creation of product requirements to the industry through self-regulation under standard-setting organizations has in several aspects been successful. Several well-functioning standards have been established and disseminated, not only in the EU but also globally. The EU has become a global leader in technical standards. However, the EU system is facing problems. From a constitutional viewpoint the system is under pressure, with the increasing political importance of the technical standards produced. Technical standards increasingly regulate markets that are not only sources of economic wealth, but also reflect current and future infrastructure for societies at large, e.g. technical standards for telecommunication.[26] With increased importance comes calls for ensuring that the standard-setting procedure absorbs features from public rule making in order to be considered as legitimate and trustworthy.[27] However, the New Economy and the increased importance of interoperability also puts strain on the system underlying the New Approach.

B. STANDARDS AND BUSINESS CONDUCT IN THE NEW ECONOMY

Interestingly, the New Approach by the EU caters to the old economy and the old model of standardization, inter alia promoting the dissemination of already well understood and used technical solutions by consensus among the parties in relevant industries.[28] As such, the New Approach contributes to competition in downstream markets, the creation of internal markets without technical barriers to entry, transparency, lessening transaction costs and increased compatibility among products. It is an efficient way to establish 'the' technology for an industry that is already well adapted for the same.[29]

---

[22] *Id.*
[23] Austin & Milner 2001, 411, 423.
[24] CENELEC.
[25] CEN/CENELEC 2018b, part 1 et seq.
[26] For further development, *see* Lundqvist 2014.
[27] Hettne 2017, 409–20.
[28] Ullrich 2017.
[29] *Id.*

However, the new mode for standardization is different. Technical standards, especially technical standards for interoperability in the ICT industry, today represent unilateral or joint innovation projects, often by the leading firm(s) in a market. The innovation process and standardization in these industries are connected – intertwined – to quickly generate innovations, achieve rapid market penetration and to win (tip) network driven markets. Indeed, the standard may very well exist before the market. The question is whether this change should be taken into consideration when analysing the New Approach from an EU Constitutional law perspective.

Indeed, technical interoperability standards have become competitive tools and the official SDOs have become competitive arenas. The idea is to have the technology implemented to establish markets, however, also, among other things, to create a barrier to entry for other competing technologies. Should this standard business conduct be taken into consideration when analysing whether European Standards should be considered EU law? That the legislative procedure in the SDO is, indeed, an arena for rivalry, competition, collusion and abuse of dominance in the form of self-governance *ex ante* the market is established. These issues will be addressed below.[30]

From the above general description of the procedure to develop technical standards in the EU under the New Approach, a relevant issue has been whether it is a private self-regulatory procedure or whether it is a legislative procedure, or both. Is it a procedure for creating laws or something else, and, thus, do regular constitutional checks and balances apply to technical standards, or not? Indeed, are, for example, European Standards, in general, and harmonized standards, in particular, reviewable by the EU courts? And, if harmonized standards form part of EU law and may be interpreted by the ECJ, can they benefit from copyright protection, or for that matter can the procedure to establish the standards be judged under competition law, if the standard is EU law? Or, are technical standards trade rules that should be reviewed under the free movement rules of the internal market? The recent *James Elliot* case does not answer all of these questions, but gives us some clues and hints regarding how the ECJ might decide future cases.

C. THE *JAMES ELLIOT* CASE: TESTING THE BOUNDARIES OF COPYRIGHT PROTECTION IN THE EU STANDARDIZATION PROCESS

The critical issue in the *James Elliot* case is whether the ECJ may accept a request for preliminary ruling under Article 267 TFEU for interpreting a European harmonized standard, while the 'sticking point' is whether a harmonized standard is an act that the ECJ can interpret under Article 267 of the TFEU. Indeed, implicitly, the ECJ, by accepting the case, acknowledged that harmonized standards have some kind of legal standing within the EU legal system.[31]

The case arose from a contractual dispute and whether a breach of contract could be established. James Elliott Construction was to construct a youth facility in Dublin (Ireland), where the specifications given required that the internal floors of the building were to be built *inter alia* in accordance with a harmonized standard. For that purpose, Irish Asphalt supplied James Elliott Construction with a product (concrete) designated in accordance with that standard. When the floor eventually collapsed, the issue was whether Irish Asphalt had breached the contract by not supplying the right concrete with, according to the technical standard, the right content. The Irish Supreme Court eventually heard the case and requested a preliminary ruling from the ECJ

---

[30] *See also* Chapter 6 (EU Competition Law and Standards) in the companion volume.
[31] *James Elliott Construction* (CJEU 2016, p. 32 et seq.).

to ask, *inter alia*, whether the interpretation of a harmonized standard is a matter upon which a preliminary ruling may be sought from the ECJ pursuant to Article 267 TFEU.

The ECJ confirmed that it has jurisdiction to interpret non-binding EU acts, while also clarifying that acts adopted by bodies that cannot be described as 'institutions, bodies, offices or agencies of the Union' still might be within the Court's reach under Article 267 TFEU. Indeed, at least harmonized standards created through ESOs, while not considered institutions, bodies, offices or agencies of the Union, may now, according to *James Elliot*, be reviewable under Article 267 TFEU. According to the ECJ, such jurisdiction being justified by the very objective of Article 267 TFEU, which is to ensure the uniform application and interpretation,[32] throughout the EU, of all provisions forming part of the EU legal system.[33] Moreover, the fact that the measure of EU law has no binding effect does not preclude the Court from ruling on its interpretation in proceedings for a preliminary ruling under Article 267 TFEU.[34]

The Court stated that while the development of a harmonized standard is indeed entrusted to an organization governed by private law and is non-binding, it is nevertheless a necessary implementation measure which is strictly governed by the essential requirements defined by the relevant directive, initiated, managed and monitored by the Commission, and its legal effects are subject to prior publication by the Commission of its references in the 'C' series of the *Official Journal of the European Union*. The Court also specifically stated that a harmonized standard forms part of EU law, since it is by reference to the provisions of such a standard that it is established whether or not the presumption laid down in Article 4(2) of Directive 89/106 applies to a given product.[35]

The ECJ clarifies that the presumption created through conformity with the essential requirements of Directive 89/106 and the 'CE' marking,[36] is for the ability to freely circulate and market products within the EU. The objective of a harmonized standard is, thus, limited to the removal of obstacles to trade, not seeking to harmonize the specific conditions and rules for the use of construction products at the time of their incorporation in construction and civil engineering works, but the rules governing market access in respect of those products. Indeed, the ECJ is careful to state that the material technical specifications of the standard create a presumption for free circulations of goods in the EU which cannot bind a national court when establishing what constitutes 'merchantable quality' and 'fit for purpose' according to the Sale of Goods Act of the Member State.

The court follows Advocate General Campos Sánchez-Bordona's opinion to a large extent, establishing that European standards adopted under the New Approach may fall under the ECJ's jurisdiction. However, the ECJ did not submerge itself in the issue of lawful or non-lawful delegation of power under the *Meroni* doctrine[37]. Moreover, the ECJ did not follow the AG's opinion in reference to the origin of the standards. While Advocate General Campos Sánchez-Bordona argued in favour of equating harmonized standards to 'acts of the institutions, bodies, offices or agencies' under Article 267 TFEU,[38] the Court bases its ability to give a preliminary ruling on the interpretation of harmonized standards on the established case law relating to

---

[32] *Sevince* (CJEU 1990); *Deutsche Shell* (CJEU 1993).
[33] *Sevince* (CJEU 1990, p. 11).
[34] *James Elliott Construction* (CJEU 2016, p. 34 et seq); *Deutsche Shell* (CJEU 1993, p. 18).
[35] *James Elliott Construction* (CJEU 2016, pp. 38, 40, and 43).
[36] CE marking is a certification mark that indicates conformity with health, safety, and environmental protection standards for products sold within the European Economic Area (EEA).
[37] The *Meroni* criteria stipulates a test for the delegation of power: *Meroni* (CJEU 1958); *United Kingdom v. EU* (CJEU 2014).
[38] *James Elliott Construction* (CJEU 2016, p. 40).

Article 267 TFEU, which allows for the interpretation of measures other than those listed in the Treaty, or from other sources.[39] This is a material difference. Indeed, the Court seems to imply that the standards are created under private law by SSOs, while the Commission has oversight and a control function over the standards. The Court at least left unanswered the question whether standards should be considered originating from the Commission, while the ESO only acts as a preparatory organ.

By neither discussing whether there is a formal delegation of power to ESOs when establishing harmonized standards or whether harmonized standards should be considered adopted by the Commission, the ECJ makes the issue of copyright protection difficult to answer, *de lege lata*.

The Advocate General took a more bold approach and emphasized that the Commission exercises significant control over establishing harmonized standards. First, the AG pointed out that a harmonized technical standard is always drawn up pursuant to a mandate given by the Commission. Without such a mandate the standard in question would not have been developed. Second, the AG emphasized that reference to harmonized technical standards must be published in the *Official Journal of the European Union*. That is a requirement for ensuring that such standards have the main effect attributed to them by the directive, namely the presumption that conformity with a standard implies compliance with the directive itself and guarantees freedom of movement for the product within the European Union.[40] The AG continued that only reference is made to the harmonized standard, and its full content is not published, while harmonized technical standards adopted by CEN are drafted in English, French and German. Based on this, it seemed that the AG would consider harmonized standards being law and hence without Copyright protection. However, the AG refused to take a stand in reference to the copyright issue, stating:

> national bodies hold the intellectual property rights in the respective national versions of harmonised technical standards and charge for their distribution, a fact which has led to varying case-law in certain Member States on the necessity of official publication of technical national standards when legislatures make a reference to those standards. For the purposes of this reference for a preliminary ruling, I do not consider it essential to examine in more detail the important question of whether the complete official publication of harmonised technical standards is necessary in order for those standards to have legal effect and for the principle of the publication of legislation to be observed. That requirement would have a very significant impact on the European standardisation system, and in particular on the sale of harmonised technical standards by national standardisation bodies. [footnotes omitted][41]

Third, the AG noted that the Commission, the European Parliament and the Member States have the option to object to the standards developed by CEN, and the Commission is even obliged to do this *ex ante*, i.e. before the standard is published. Moreover, decisions relating to the publication of harmonized technical standards, decisions adopted by the Commission concerning formal objections to harmonized technical standards raised by the Member States or the European Parliament are legal acts against which an action for annulment may be brought. Based on this, the AG concluded that harmonized standards should be regarded as drafted under a controlled delegation of legislative power.[42]

---

[39] Volpato 2017, 591–603.
[40] *James Elliott Construction* (CJEU 2016, pp. 47–55).
[41] Van Gestel & Micklitz 2013, 145–82.
[42] *James Elliott Construction* (CJEU 2016, pp. 47–55).

The AG made reference to Member State case law regarding copyright protection. In the famous *Knooble* case[43] from the Netherlands, the Dutch Supreme Court seems to argue that reference to standards in the relevant legal document pulls these into the public domain and makes them generally applicable but does not turn the standards into law. An essential condition for this is missing according to the Supreme Court: standards are not based on delegation by a public authority of law-making powers, but rely on private agreements.[44] In Germany, the highest civil court (*Bundesgerichtshof*) has held that standards should not be copyright protected due to the fact that they were produced pursuant to delegation and they yield external effect and are not only for internal use within the Government. The requirement for this finding is that governmental organizations accept and incorporate the content of the standards into their decision-making.[45]

Notwithstanding this, the AG refused to take a stand in reference to the Copyright issue. The ECJ seems instead to have followed the national courts' line of reasoning, and connects delegation of public power with the elimination of copyright. It is not certain why restricting access to a document that forms part of EU law needs to hinge upon whether the proper delegation of public power needs to be at hand. One could argue that as long as the document is encompassed by the notion of EU law, the EU should have an obligation to make it generally available to the public.

In conclusion, it seems that the ECJ has left unanswered the question whether the control exercised by the European Commission through the mandate and through the publication in the Official Journal is sufficient or insufficient to transfer responsibility for standards from the SSO to the Commission,[46] and the issue whether there has been a delegation of rule making power when establishing harmonized standards has not been fully determined. Indeed, we do not know yet whether harmonized standards should be considered copyright protected or not.

D. THE WIDER IMPLICATIONS OF THE *JAMES ELLIOTT* CASE: THE APPLICABILITY OF COMPETITION LAW RULES TO THE STANDARD-SETTING PROCEDURE

The *James Elliott* case is not only interesting for the important yet narrow issue of copyright protection for standards. The case also opens the door for a broader discussion regarding which EU rules should be utilized when scrutinizing standard-setting procedures. Should standard-setting be seen as a private initiative governed by property rights and competition law, or is it a public procedure governed by constitutional principles for creating rules, e.g. transparency, participation etc.; indeed, for creating rules for the free movement part of the internal market legal system.

It seems that *James Elliot* implies that the ECJ may not only interpret harmonized standards, but also may invalidate harmonized standards under Article 267 TFEU.[47] As Hettne points

---

[43] *Knooble* (The Hague 2008)
[44] *Cf.* Medzmariashvili 2013; *Knooble* (The Hague 2008); *Hoge Raad* (Netherlands 2007).
[45] Medzmariashvili 2013.
[46] Volpato 2017, 591–603.
[47] In this context, it should be pointed out that the 2012 Regulation on European Standardization provides rules regarding the standard-setting procedure and the quality of the standard as regards when consortia-created standards should be identified for incorporation in public procurement procedures. Indeed, this is a legal basis for addressing standards under the EU Court system based even on quality, i.e. that the standard adopted is not the "best" technology. Regulation (EU) No 1025/2012 of the European Parliament and of the Council of the 25 October 2012 on European standardisation, OJ L 316 of 14 November 2012, Art 13 and Annex II. It should be pointed out that establishing a standard is not a rigorous, scientific process driven by identifying the "best" technology in a particular field. Rather,

out, it could for instance be claimed that a harmonized standard which does not fully respect the limits of the mandate from the Commission or is in conflict with fundamental procedural requirements could be invalidated under Article 267 TFEU. However, these fundamental procedural requirements that Hettne refers to must, without implying that Hettne stated this, be derived from the general principles of the Treaties, while some may also be implied or derived from the Regulation for European standardization, such as Article 10 of the Regulation.[48] Indeed, European standardization and, hence, the Regulation is founded on principles of coherence, transparency, openness, consensus, voluntary application, independence from special interests and efficiency ('the founding principles'),[49] which in several ways reflect values that may be used to nullify a standard when such standard was adopted with a procedure that did not meet such values.

Notwithstanding the possible applicability of the EU's general principles to the European standardization procedure, we also do have 'good governance' procedural rules regarding *inter alia* openness, right to participation and transparency for standard-setting in the realm of competition law. In particular, for an SSO to be able to benefit from the 'safe harbour' for standard setting under Article 101 TFEU, it needs to fulfil the procedural soft law contained in the EU Horizontal Guidelines.[50] The Commission in the Horizontal Guidelines states that European standardization bodies recognized under Regulation 1025/2012 and Directive 98/34/EC of the European Parliament and of the Council of 22 June 1998 laying down a procedure for the provision of information in the field of technical standards and regulations[51] are subject to competition law to the extent that they can be considered to be an 'undertaking' (i.e., a private firm) or an association of undertakings within the meaning of Articles 101 and 102 TFEU.[52] As a starting point, this position implies that competition law could be applicable in relation to these organizations, or to the undertakings that *de facto* collaborate under their supervision, for the creation of technical standards.

The Commission acknowledges a broad safe harbour in the Horizontal Guidelines. Any SSO can make use of the safe harbour, and, thus, not worry about the Commission initiating an investigation into whether Article 101 TFEU has been breached, provided that certain procedural requirements are met. Thus, if participation in standard-setting is unrestricted and the procedure for adopting the standard in question is transparent, the standard does not contain any obligation to comply with the standard, and access to the standard is provided on fair, reasonable and non-discriminatory terms, the standard-setting will, according to the Guidelines, normally not restrict competition within the meaning of Article 101(1) TFEU.[53] Transparency implies that the standard-setting organization must be open and the SSO needs *de facto* to inform all stakeholders of upcoming endeavours to form new standards. However, if these good governance procedural rules are not met, the prohibitions under Competition law may become applicable.

In light of the above, there might be a concern about regulatory overlap, as to whether standards adopted by an ESO should conform to good governance rules under constitutional

---

technology is included in a standard through a collaborative process. It draws heavily on prior R&D, standards, and may involve evaluation of, or selection and even compromise among competing technical approaches. *See, e.g.,* Rubin 2007.

[48] Hettne 2008.
[49] European Commission 2012.
[50] European Commission 2011, 1.
[51] European Commission 2011 (Horizontal Guidelines), para. 258.
[52] *Höfner* (C-41/90); *Selex Sistemi* (C-113/07).
[53] European Commission 2011 (Horizontal Guidelines), para. 280; *SCK and FNK* (EGC 1997).

rules and principles of the Treaties and in the general legal principles (General Principles[54]), or under competition law, or both. Indeed, the standard could, at least in theory, be invalided under both systems of law.

A collaboration leading up to a European standard originating from CEN has been scrutinized under EU competition law by the EU Commission and the EU courts. In the *EMC* case,[55] the Commission and later the Courts found that a standard developed within the Europeans standard system under CEN at least could be addressed under Article 101 TFEU, providing that the requirements stipulated, *inter alia* that the participants take part in a collaboration akin to an agreement and that there is an economic activity with EU and possible anticompetitive effects. The Commission, and the ECJ, left unanswered whether the work of a technical committee under an SDO can be regarded as an agreement between firms (undertakings).[56] However, the Commission acknowledged that not only are the members of the technical committees experts representing firms, but also national delegations to CEN are staffed with members who originate from the relevant industry. It seems that they, in their capacity as members of technical committees, still conduct an 'economic activity', and do not lose their standing as 'undertakings' under EU competition law. The Commission made an analysis of all the requirements for the safe harbour and found it applicable to CEN and the technical committee and the adjoining standard-setting trade association. Since the procedural 'good governance' rules in the Horizontal Guidelines had been adhered to, the Commission did not even address the difficult issue of whether the conduct of a technical committee can be considered an agreement under Article 101 TFEU.[57]

James Elliott provides an opening to judge standards under the constitutional rules and principles of the Treaties. The *EMC* case seems to imply that the standard-setting procedure can also be analysed under competition law. Perhaps, both legal systems should to some extent be available, but then be used in reference to the harm they were enacted to govern. Generally, constitutional rules and principles are a better place for judging standard-setting procedure, while competition law should focus on the result of the standard-setting process. Competition law should ask whether the agreement on the technology making up the standard is an anticompetitive agreement. Does it exclude competitors or inhibit innovation to the extent that anticompetitive effects can potentially appear. Indeed, we need to acknowledge the new role of standards for the New Economy, as a market facilitator, and that competition may take place before the markets are established. However, the fundamental procedural rules regarding the standard-setting procedure have more of a constitutional character and should be derived from the general principles and under general EU law, and not from competition law.

E. THE INTERFACE BETWEEN FREE TRADE RULES AND COMPETITION LAW

Private technical standards have also, historically, been presumed immune to the reach of e.g. Article 34 TFEU, while public technical regulations, in cases like *Dassonville*[58] and *Keck*,[59] have been under attack for preventing access to markets.

---

[54] Hettne 2008.
[55] *EMC Development* (CJEU 2011); *EN 197-1 Standard* (E.C. 2005).
[56] *EN 197-1 Standard* (E.C. 2005).
[57] However, interestingly, if the NSO does claim that copyright protection for standards originates from a *collective* effort of the undertakings involved then that would imply that there is an agreement between undertakings under Article 101 TFEU.
[58] *Dassonville* (CJEU 1974).
[59] *Keck and Mithourd* (CJEU 1993).

While the dichotomy between public regulations and private standards is still relevant, the recent *SELEX*,[60] *Fra.bo*[61] and *OTOC*[62] cases have, at least, opened up a small opportunity to use Article 34 TFEU in connection with privately produced standards and SSOs.

In the *SELEX* case,[63] first the General Court and then the ECJ shed some light on the standard-setting process and the interaction between research and development and standards. The Court had to scrutinize an international standard-setting body, the European Organization for the Safety of Air Navigation (Eurocontrol),[64] which primarily sets standards in the area of air navigation to enable the participating states to create a uniform system for Air Traffic Management (ATM). Eurocontrol was set up by contracting States, and the ECJ describes its role as being akin to that of a minister, who, at the national level, prepares legislation or regulatory matters which are then adopted by the government. The second area of activity was research and development. The research activity consisted of spearheading joint studies of new technologies in the ATM sector. It acquires and develops prototypes of ATM equipment and systems, for example radar systems, with a view to using that equipment and knowledge to validate and define new standards and technical specifications. Under its research activity, Eurocontrol created a regime of intellectual property rights in relation to the prototypes purchased under research contracts from firms. Access to these rights becomes important for competing firms should the prototype lead to enactment of a standard. Access to these rights was however dependent on whether Eurocontol or the developer of the prototype held the necessary rights in question. The applicant, SELEX, accused the Commission of not taking action against Eurocontrol and the regime of intellectual property rights developed under its research of prototypes. Eurocontrol's research created, according to SELEX, factual monopolies in the systems that eventually became standards, and the firms that provided the prototypes were therefore in a particularly advantageous position compared to their competitors. This situation was all the more serious because Eurocontrol did not use a transparent, open and non-discriminatory system for the acquisition of the prototypes and, thus, for establishing the standards.

The case regarding non-action of the Commission was based on the applicability of Article 102 TFEU and not Article 101 TFEU. Nevertheless, some interesting conclusions may be drawn. First, the General Court concluded that Eurocontrol's standardization activities could not be regarded as economic activities and the EU competition rules were therefore not applicable.[65] The General Court carefully distinguished between researching, developing and adopting standards and, initially, scrutinized each activity individually. According to the General Court there was no market for a technical standardization service in the sector of ATM equipment. Thus, Eurocontrol could not be regarded as offering a service. Secondly, the General Court stated that the research and development activities could not be regarded as economic activities, since the acquisition did not involve the offering of goods or services on a given market. This was further supported by the fact that the intellectual property rights developed under the research were made available to anyone concerned at no cost. Only some confidential information held by the firm which sold the prototype to Eurocontrol was not available to competitors. The intellectual property rights pool was also considered ancillary to 'non-economic' research and

---

[60] *Selex Sistemi* (EGC/CJEU 2006/2009).
[61] *Fra.bo SpA* (CJEU 2012).
[62] *OTOC* (CJEU 2013).
[63] *Selex Sistemi* (EGC/CJEU 2006/2009).
[64] *SAT Fluggesellschaft* (CJEU 1994).
[65] *Selex Sistemi* (CJEU 2009, para. 59 et seq.).

development activity.[66] The Court continued that even if it were established that Eurocontrol did not have a system in place for distinguishing between rights and technologies, e.g. source code, developed under the research contracts and background software, it did not make the intellectual property rights regime economic in nature.

The ECJ went beyond the findings of the General Court and struck down the General Court's dichotomy between different forms of conduct by Eurocontrol. According to the ECJ the adoption of standards could not be separated from the production of the same, and preparation and production of standards could not be separated from the public task (or the expression of public power) vested in Eurocontrol of managing air space and developing air safety.[67] Therefore, Eurocontrol was not to be considered an undertaking (private firm).

The Eurocontrol case dealt with an international public body, while the issue is whether the ECJ in this case relieves all SDOs, such as CEN and CENELEC, and also their handling of intellectual property rights and R&D, from the ambit of EU competition law, when assigned to develop European Standards.[68] Clearly, the case opens up an avenue for arguing that SDOs made up of officials from national public bodies with the public task of producing standards may not be judged under competition law. Somewhat alarming is the way the ECJ did not stop with such a conclusion, but, instead, disregarded the General Court's division of conduct in preparation, production and adoption of standards. The ECJ's method or test for tying the conduct together, and finding that it all fell under the 'public power and thereto connected conduct' exemption, not only seems to be redefining the boundaries between an undertaking and the exercise of public power set out in earlier case law,[69] it also makes it more difficult to argue that members of technical committees of SDOs, even those representing firms (undertakings), may violate EU competition law when creating a standard that may possibly restrict competitors or exclude competing technical solutions. Nonetheless, the *SELEX* case seems to establish an exemption under EU law, which effectively exempts publicly derived SDOs and their handling of technologies and of intellectual property rights from the ambit of competition law. However, at least in theory, the EU free movement rules may become applicable vis-à-vis the national rules of an EU Member State that might be derived from Eurocontrol.

In the recent *Fra.bo*[70] case the ECJ takes a new but expected step in the direction established in the *SELEX* judgment and actually finds that an SSO, and standards, can be scrutinized under Article 34 TFEU. The background of the case is as follows: According to a German Regulation on general conditions of water supply, copper parts of water pipes must comply with recognized rules (standards) for the supply of water. Copper components labelled with the German review and standard body DVGW brand were assumed to fulfil these rules.

DVGW is an SSO, a private non-profit organization made up of members which may be utilities, gas-and-water sector companies, public institutions and independent individuals focusing on the promotion of the gas and water sector. Fra.bo, on the other hand, was an Italian company which produced and sold copper parts. In 2000 Fra.bo was granted the right to label its products

---

[66] The Court also distinguishes Eurocontrol from collective societies since they, according to the Court, collect fees for their members and therefore do conduct an economic activity. See *Selex Sistemi* (CJEU 2009, para. 78).
[67] *Selex Sistemi* (CJEU 2009, para. 89 et seq.).
[68] According to the Horizontal Guidelines, the European standardization bodies recognized under Directive 98/34/EC of the European Parliament and of the Council of 22 June 1998 laying down a procedure for the provision of information in the field of technical standards and regulations and on rules on Information Society services (2) are subject to competition law to the extent that they can be considered to be an undertaking or an association of undertakings within the meaning of Articles 101 and 102 (3). European Commission 2011 (Horizontal Guidelines), para. 258.
[69] *Belasco* (CJEU 1989).
[70] *Fra.bo SpA* (CJEU 2012).

with the DVGW mark for a period of five years. Following a complaint from a third party, DVGW reconsidered its decision to grant Fra.bo the right to use the brand. DVGW performed new tests on the copper parts. The copper parts could not pass some of the tests and Fra.bo was given three months to submit a report showing that the copper parts satisfied the technical requirements stipulated. Fra.bo submitted a report from an Italian laboratory, but this was not adopted because the laboratory was not an 'approved' laboratory according to DVGW. In the meantime, DVGW introduced new tests under the standard for copper parts. Manufacturers of certified copper parts were given three months to submit reports on whether their products met the new standards. In 2005, DVGW withdrew the certificate it had issued for Fra.bo in 2000, as Fra.bo had not submitted a report regarding the new tests. Fra.bo appealed the DVGW decision to the Cologne Regional Court, arguing that the decision on revocation of the certificate presented an obstacle to the free movement of goods under Article 34 TFEU or a violation of Article 101 TFEU. The court dismissed the complaint. The ruling was appealed to the Oberlandesgericht Düsseldorf in 2011, which requested a preliminary ruling by the ECJ.

The ECJ considered several factors when analysing whether to use Article 34 or 101 TFEU. The main thrust of the analysis focused on DVGW's special position: it being mentioned in the German Regulation, being *de facto* the only body able to certify copper fittings, and, thus, being able to restrict the marketing and market of products which are not certified by the body. The ECJ concluded therefore that Article 34 TFEU was applicable and breached. The ECJ therefore did not need to establish whether Article 101 TFEU was applicable, or not.

The *Fra.bo* case is an interesting development. In line with case law development in the other areas of free movement (e.g. the *Laval* case[71]), it also provides an opening to judge standards not only in the light of the objectives and aims acknowledged under competition law, but possibly also under other public policy objectives recognized and easily applicable under the Free Trade rules. Clearly, European SDOs risk violating Article 34 TFEU under the *Fra.bo* case.

In a recent case[72], the ECJ touched upon these issues again. Now in reference to an association for Chartered Accountants in Portugal: Ordem dos Técnicos Oficiais de Contas (the OTOC). The OTOC had set up a system of compulsory training for chartered accountants. It seemed clear to the ECJ that even though allowing competing training bodies to provide compulsory training, the OTOC claimed certain courses exclusively.

The ECJ established that OTOC was regulated under public law and held a public service mission. However, this was immaterial, given its wide discretion vis-à-vis the State in setting up this training. It only held a non-exclusive right to provide training under the law, and the OTOC *de facto* was acting in a relevant market for the professional training of chartered accountants. The relevant rules under OTOC by-laws were found in the end to have violated Article 101 TFEU, since they reflected an exclusionary agreement among its members to exclude competing course providers.

In many ways this case follows the older case law concerning exclusionary certifications. However, it seems clear that SDOs connected to trade associations, i.e. consortia and fora, would be considered associations of undertakings according to Article 101 TFEU under *OTOC*.[73] The evaluation includes a test with respect to the freedom to decide what to decide about, and whether SDOs act in a standard-setting market. However, the outstanding issue, even after

---

[71] *Laval un Partneri* (CJEU 2007).
[72] *OTOC* (CJEU 2013).
[73] See, e.g., *SCK and FNK* (EGC 1997).

OTOC, is still whether collusion within technical committees in the more official SDOs may be addressed under EU competition law.

It seems clear that the SDOs themselves were exempted under the *SELEX* doctrine. Furthermore, under *Fra.bo* these SDOs may be scrutinized under Article 34 TFEU. The *EMC* case, discussed *supra*, sheds more light on the issue of whether to use Article 34 TFEU or 101 TFEU, and against what entities. According to the Commission in *EMC*, CEN is a recognized standard body under Directive 98/34/EC and therefore a body entrusted with the general economic interest. This would not totally exclude the possibility of EU competition law being applied to CEN, while Article 106 TFEU would possibly need to be applied if the members of CEN were proven to consist of 'undertakings'. However, neither the EU courts nor the EU Commission have yet made a final decision about whether the members of the technical committees may be scrutinized under Article 101 TFEU. Moreover, a plaintiff could utilize the Regulation on European Standardisation[74] horizontally vis-à-vis ESOs that are not, for example, transparent. Also, governments making use of ICT consortia-derived standards that do not live up to the requirements in Annex II of the Regulation on public procurement procedures may be challenged.[75] Thus, a plaintiff that would like to bring an action against CEN does better to use both Article 34, including the Regulation of European Standardisation, and Article 101/102 TFEU.

Private standards have, for a long time, been regarded as immune from the reach of e.g. Article 34 TFEU. It should be acknowledged that the ECJ, has however broadened the definition of the state in several cases, e.g. *Buy Irish*, which could imply that NSOs under EU law could benefit from the application of Article 34 TFEU. Schepel, referring to research conducted in Germany, indicates that standards originating in several NSOs – the Irish, French and the Greek standard bodies – could be capable of being measured under Article 34 TFEU. On the other hand, some NSOs – the German, British and Danish (DIN, BSI and DS) – could not. The respective Member States do not have a dominant influence over these NSOs and the NSOs do not conduct or hold public power in this regard.[76]

A bold approach would be to apply Article 34 TFEU directly to SDOs. In an isolated obiter dictum in *Dansk Supermarked*, the ECJ held in 1981 that 'it is impossible in any circumstances for agreements between individuals to derogate from the mandatory provisions of the Treaty on the free movement of goods'.[77] Even though the ECJ has subsequently ignored this statement, it gives support to a general principle under free trade rules. The ECJ accepted this reasoning regarding the free movement of workers and services as early as 1974.[78] The ECJ has furthermore confirmed the principle in *Bosman*,[79] *Wouters*[80] and *Laval*.[81] If this principle also applies to the free movement of goods, it could be applicable to standards, given their ability to inhibit free movement of goods and access to markets. Nonetheless, whether this principle also applies to the free movement of goods should be judged in the light of the interface between Article 34 TFEU and the competition rules. The *Dassonville*[82] formula originates from *Consten and*

---

[74] European Commission 2012.
[75] Whether a government making use of a harmonized standard that does not live up to the requirements in Annex II may also be sued under the EU law generally and the Regulation specifically is presumably a matter for the ECJ to decide.
[76] Schepel 2005, 43 et seq.
[77] *Dansk Supermarked* (CJEU 1981).
[78] *Walrave* (CJEU 1974).
[79] *Bosman* (CJEU 1995).
[80] *Wouters* (CJEU 2002).
[81] *Laval* (CJEU 2007).
[82] *Dassonville* (CJEU 1974).

Grundig[83] and *Leclerc*,[84] and the ECJ lays down similar goals for both the rules of free movement of goods and the competition rules.

In the recent *Fra.bo* case,[85] the ECJ therefore took a new, but expected, step and actually found that SDOs, and SDO-created standards and certifications, can be scrutinized under Article 34 TFEU.

The ECJ considered several factors when analysing whether to use Article 34 or 101 TFEU in *Fra.bo*. The main thrust of the analysis was on the SDO's special position because it was mentioned in the German Regulation, was *de facto* the only body able to certify products under the standard, and, thus, was able to exclude the marketing and market for products which were not certified by the body. The ECJ concluded, therefore, that Article 34 TFEU was applicable and, if one read between the lines, had also been infringed.

The SDO in *Fra.bo* was organized as a limited company but was structured as a consortium, with members from the relevant industry. It held some powers under German law, especially concerning certification. Nonetheless, it seems that *Fra.bo* could also have been judged under Article 101 TFEU, especially if the plaintiff had also included the members of the organization in the suit.[86]

Fra.bo provides an opening to judge standards not only in the light of the objectives and aims acknowledged under competition law, but possibly also under other public policy objectives recognized and readily applicable under free trade rules. In fact, under the free movement of goods regulation, in conjunction with the Regulation on European Standards, it seems clear that a court could actually judge the content, quality, and whether a standard should be implemented in the first place.[87] Moreover, does Article 34 TFEU require a showing of anti-competitive effect in these cases? That is highly unlikely. In fact, Article 34 TFEU utilizes a per se doctrine from a competition law perspective. Clearly, European SDOs risk violating Article 34 TFEU under the *Fra.bo* case, especially if they connect the standard to a certification system.

Furthermore, the Regulation on European Standardization stipulates rules for the standardization process and, to a limited extent, specifies the quality and substance of consortia-derived standards.[88] Indeed, under the *James Elliot* doctrine perhaps these principles may be used by the ECJ as an inspiration when scrutinizing the procedure for creating technical standards under Article 267 TEFU, i.e. when a plaintiff claims that the technical standard should be declared null and void due to being adopted under a wrongful procedure.

From a free movement of goods perspective, *Fra.bo* is a natural step for the ECJ to take. Similar cases exist under the free movement of workers, of service, and the right to establish.[89] But from a standard-setting perspective, is it a good development that SDOs should be bound by free trade rules? Was not the whole idea of the New Approach precisely to have standards decided outside the public sphere? Normally, competition agencies and courts refrain from intervening in the substance of standards, but the courts may intervene under the rules of free trade in these circumstances. However, from a free trade perspective, the response might be that

---

[83] *Consten and Grundig* (CJEU 1966).
[84] *Leclerc* (CJEU 1985).
[85] *Fra.bo SpA* (CJEU 2012).
[86] The organizational structure of the SSO in *Fra.bo*, for example, seems similar to the SSO in the German EU competition law case from the Federal Supreme Court (Bundesgerichtshof): *Standard-Spundfass* (Germany 2009).
[87] See, for example, the rules in Annex II of the Regulation of European Standards regarding identifying ICT consortia created standards for public procurement procedures. Here, the court clearly can be forced to judge the technical quality of standards.
[88] European Commission 2012.
[89] *Bosman* (CJEU 1995); *Wouters* (CJEU 2002); *Laval* (CJEU 2007); *Dassonville* (CJEU 1974).

entities that create infrastructure hold power – perhaps not private power over relevant markets, but public power, creating barriers to entry – and they need therefore to be held accountable for these activities. While their economic conduct should be judged under competition laws, possibly their conduct representing public power should be judged under general constitutional principles (and the Regulation) under the *James Elliot* doctrine. This sounds good in theory, and, given the fact that the scope for scrutiny of standard setting is less under competition law, it is likely that the system will not be held up to closer scrutiny by utilizing only competition law. Some standards, and even firms' conduct in SDOs, can be scrutinized under the free trade rules under *Fra.bo* and, when applicable, the Regulation of European Standards and general principles now under *James Elliot*.

Furthermore, the application of free movement of goods rules is different from that of competition rules. The notions of restriction of trade and discrimination are based on nationality, while the competition rules mainly turn on whether competition has been restricted. Hence, Article 34 TFEU would seldom be applicable to the EU-wide SDOs, e.g. CEN and ETSI. The notion of restriction of trade or discrimination based upon nationality may exist, but more predominant would perhaps be restriction of trade or restriction of access to markets. However, the general principles of EU law and EU constitutional rules, and the Regulation on European Standardization might be applicable in these circumstances. This is perhaps what *James Elliot* is telling us. For example, SMEs will not be able to get their innovations recognized by SDOs adequately, and this would constitute a breach of stakeholder participation under the Regulation.[90] But these rules are not about discrimination or restriction of trade based on nationality. Instead, they concern restrictions to accessing the regulatory procedure and markets and trade. In other words, they are principles equivalent to the rules and principles under *James Elliot*, but also regarding 'good governance' found in the Horizontal Guidelines. In fact, there may be some overlap in the regulation of SDOs between, on one hand, the *James Elliot* doctrine, Regulation on European Standardization and, on the other hand, the rules for the 'safe harbour' in the Horizontal Guidelines. It depends on the definition of undertaking under competition law, the origin of the standard under the *James Elliot* case and the position of the standard setter under *Fra.bo*. Indeed, it is possible that the Regulation and the principles making up the rules under that Regulation offer more benefits to private plaintiffs than the competition rules.[91]

It seems that the EU legislature needs to make a choice how to regulate SDOs and their members. Clearly, given the *Fra.bo*, *EMC* and *SELEX*[92] decisions, the legislature will have a difficult choice. The SDOs may be scrutinized under the free movement rules, while economic conduct in SDOs, consortia and the members of technical committees, and thereby indirectly the SDOs, may be judged under the competition rules. These entities fulfil the requirement for an 'undertaking', while ETSI, CEN and even IEEE should, presumably, be judged particularly under Article 34 TFEU.

While it is at best uncertain whether it is possible to use Article 34 TFEU against SDOs, the application of the somewhat equivalent rule in the United States, the dormant commerce

---

[90] The regulation on European Standardization is far from clear. Thus, it is possible that the Regulation may not have direct effect, while still such a rule may be regarded when ECJ would apply Article 267 TFEU.
[91] The public interest exemptions in Art. 36 TFEU, and under the doctrine of mandatory requirements of Cassis de Dijon, are furthermore less forgiving than Art. 101(3) TFEU in exempting rules on the basis of the procedure of the organization in question. Art 36 TFEU is focused on public policy exemptions such as the environment, public health etc. which are difficult to fit inside a competition law analysis. Cf. *Rewe-Zentral AG vs. Bundesmonopolverwaltung für Branntwein* (CJEU 1979).
[92] *Selex Sistemi* (EGC/CJEU 2006/2009).

clause[93] vis-à-vis a standard from an SDOs that is a barrier to trade between U.S. states, is unlikely, or even alien, to American jurists. Similar case law to *Dassonville* may be found in the United States under the dormant commerce clause; see *Minnesota v. Clover Leaf Creamery Co.*[94] and *Bibb v. Navajo Freight Lines.*[95] Furthermore, the 'state action' exemption under U.S. antitrust law, first established in *Parker*[96] immunizes federal and state government and agencies from antitrust scrutiny. This implies that, for these agencies, other rules apply, such as, possibly, the dormant commerce clause.

Actually, very few commentators in the U.S. academic debate have ever approached the dormant commerce clause from this point of view. Nonetheless, in several antitrust standard-setting cases, the *Noerr* defence was raised and the defendants argue that the SSO should be regarded as a public body.[97] The Courts have been reluctant to accept that line of reasoning.[98] However, if courts did allow the *Noerr* doctrine to be applicable, would that imply that the dormant commerce clause might be available vis-à-vis the SDO? In the United States, delegation of Federal power is benign from a constitutional perspective, while state courts may have a different opinion. The heavy use of private standards by public agencies triggered the so-called non-delegation doctrine, i.e. that public power to legislate cannot be delegated to private parties under (state) constitutions.[99]

Notwithstanding the above, in the EU it is clear that economic conduct that falls within the exemption for conduct that reflects activities in accord with the concept of public power, i.e. act of public power and thereto connected activities, will not be scrutinized under competition law, while it is possible that such conduct can now be judged under both EU constitutional principles and rules, and under the free trade doctrine. In addition, when deciding when competition law is applicable, the variable that competition law regulates markets needs to be taken into consideration. Indeed, pre-competition conduct when selecting technologies, or, for that matter, when construing infrastructure standards should only be regulated under competition law if an anti-competitive harm and effect can be identified.[100] Otherwise, a plaintiff needs to utilize other regulations, such as the free trade rules or general EU constitutional principles, under the *James Elliot* precedent.

Indeed, the *James Elliot* case should be embraced if it implies that standards can now be analysed by EU courts in light of EU fundamental procedural law, while, before this case, it seemed that several forms of conduct, by firms and others, in reference to an SDO, neither fell under competition law, nor under free movement rules. Now we see the contours of a dichotomy: procedural rules for the SDOs can be derived from the general EU legal system for the internal market, i.e. the general principles, rules and doctrines under the free movement of goods and services, and the Regulation for European standardization. Indeed, even the content

---

[93] See Chemerinsky 2013, 455–56 ('The "dormant Commerce Clause" is the principle that state and local laws are unconstitutional if they place an undue burden on interstate commerce. There is no constitutional provision that expressly declares that states may not burden interstate commerce. Rather, the Supreme Court has inferred this from the grant of power to Congress in Article I, §8 to regulate commerce among the states'). In reference to standards, the dormant commerce clause might in theory be applicable should a state in law refer to a technical standard if that standard would 'improperly discriminate against interstate commerce'.
[94] *Clover Leaf Creamary Co.* (U.S. 1981).
[95] *Navajo Freight Lines* (U.S. 1959).
[96] *Parker* (U.S. 1943).
[97] Noerr-Pennington doctrine. See *Noerr Motor Freight, Inc.* (U.S. 1961); *United Mine Workers of America*, (U.S. 1965).
[98] *Union Oil Co. of Cal.* (FTC Dkt. No. 9305); Ohlhausen 2006.
[99] Rice 2017.
[100] Drexl 2012, 507.

of a harmonized standard can, to some extent, be reviewed under these rules and doctrines, while anticompetitive effects of the firms collaborating within an SDO may be judged under EU competition law.

CONCLUSION

It is obvious that the ECJ and the EU legislature want both to obtain the benefits of self-regulation, while still upholding the possibility of judicial review of standards and standard-setting from constitutional, trade and competition law perspectives. Indeed, under the EU system, a plaintiff may make use of different lines of argument, which may prove contradictory, if it wishes to bring an action regarding a standard, an SSO or the members (of the technical committee) of an SSO under EU law. Article 34 TFEU could best be utilized for addressing the MS standard and vis-à-vis the NSO if the matter is seen as connected to the State (see *Fra.bo*[101]), while Article 101 TFEU could be applied to the members of the technical committees, should they be undertakings (firms). We now know that harmonized standards form part of EU law, and may be interpreted by the ECJ, and could very likely also be scrutinized under Article 267 TFEU.[102] Indeed, this implies that standards and standard-setting procedure can also be scrutinized in light of the general principles of EU law, some of which can be implied from the Regulation for European standardization. This seems to be the distinction that the Commission and the courts have carved out in the *EMC*, *Fra.bo* and now *James Elliott* cases. The question is whether this dichotomy between form, content and authorship can also be applicable in reference to the copyright issue discussed in this chapter.

It seems clear that the content and authorship for many technical standards lie with the SDO and the private firms that develop the standards in technical committees, while legal effects of harmonized standards in the EU clearly reflect the result of public power. The right solution could be that the harmonized standards, or at least the part of the standards that reflect law, should not be copyright protected, while access to the standard with possible connected comments and guidelines can, mainly, be achieved through databases connected to the IT, where the SDO (perhaps through the Commission) could still obtain fees reflecting its marginal cost for creating, developing the standard and maintaining and upholding the databases (see to that effect the PSI directive[103]). That would possibly be a just compromise for the few standards that actually become harmonized standards.

---

[101] *Fra.bo SpA* (CJEU 2012).
[102] Volpato 2017, 591–603.
[103] European Commission 2003; Directive 2013/37/EU of the European Parliament and of the Council of 26 June 2013 amending Directive 2003/98/EC on the re-use of public sector information Text with EEA relevance.

8

Termination of Copyright Transfers and Technical Standards[*]

Jorge L. Contreras and Andrew T. Hernacki

A.	How Section 203 Can Apply to Technical Standards	144
	1. Technical Standards and Copyright	144
	2. Implications of Section 203 Termination on Technical Standards	145
B.	Exceptions Under Section 203 and Technical Standards	147
	1. Technical Standards as Joint Works	147
	2. The Works-Made-For-Hire Exception	150
	3. The Derivative Works Exception	153
	4. Underlying Policy Consideration	154

In 1938 Jerry Siegel and Joseph Shuster, the creators of the Superman comic book character, sold their copyright to the predecessor of DC Comics for $130.[1] Siegel and Shuster died in the 1990s, virtually penniless,[2] while Superman earned heroic sums for his corporate owners over many decades.[3] Similar scenarios have arisen for literary authors, songwriters, and visual artists. In each case, young and unknown creators, eager to secure their first commercial contract, sell their rights in important early works to a publisher or record label for a pittance, and are then unable to profit from the work's later success.

Stories like these led to the enactment of Section 304,[4] and later Section 203, of the U.S. Copyright Act.[5] These statutory provisions give the author of a copyrighted work the right to terminate the grant of any license or assignment of that work between thirty-five and forty years after the license or assignment was first made.[6] Following such a termination, any transferred rights in the copyright revert to the author or his or her heirs.[7] To prevent publishers and record labels from requiring that this right be waived at the time of the initial grant, the statute provides that the reversionary right is not waivable by contract or otherwise.

---

[*] This chapter is based on Contreras & Hernacki (2014).
[1] Busch 2012.
[2] *Id.*
[3] *Id.* DC Comics' owner, Warner Brothers, spent a decade in litigation with the heirs of Seigel's and Shuster's estates.
[4] 17 U.S.C. § 304 (2006).
[5] *See* Loren 2010, 1342–46; Menell & Nimmer 2010, 804–08.
[6] 17 U.S.C. § 203(a) (2006).
[7] *Id.* § 203(b).

Termination rights under Section 203 are not absolute, and there are several exceptions that exempt certain types of works from its reach.[8] For example, grants covering works-made-for-hire are exempt from termination,[9] and if a single work has multiple authors, a majority of the authors must exercise the termination.[10] Moreover, termination under Section 203 only prohibits further exploitation of the original copyrighted work, but not of any authorized derivative work.[11] These exceptions, however, are poorly defined within the statute and largely untested in the courts.

Despite its origins in the publishing and music industries, Section 203 has the potential to affect other copyrighted works including software, architectural drawings, technical designs, and technical standards documents. This chapter examines how Section 203 may impact standards documents in the context of the following doctrines: (1) the creation of standards as joint works, (2) application of the work-made-for-hire exception, and (3) the derivative works exception. We argue that the underlying purpose of the Section 203 termination right – protecting novice artists against unremunerative transfers – is inapplicable in light of the non-remunerative nature of submissions to standards development organizations (SDOs). Accordingly, we suggest that technical standards be legislatively or judicially exempted from the Section 203 termination right to avoid significant disruption in technology markets.

A. HOW SECTION 203 CAN APPLY TO TECHNICAL STANDARDS

1. Technical Standards and Copyright

By most accounts, the documents setting forth technical standards are works of authorship that are protected by copyright in the United States and other countries adhering to the Berne Convention.[12] Most of these standards are developed not by single authors, but by multiple collaborators within SDOs that operate in particular technical domains.[13] These collaborators are typically technical experts who are full-time employees of corporations, government agencies, and research institutions having an interest in the standardized technology. For example, the 802.11 (Wi-Fi) wireless networking standards were developed by engineers from dozens of different companies working under the auspices of the Institute of Electrical and Electronics Engineers (IEEE), and the standards that underlie the Internet were developed through the loosely-organized Internet Engineering Task Force (IETF) and Worldwide Web Consortium (W3C).

Individuals collaborating in an SDO may either submit a complete document to an SDO for consideration as a standard or interact with other SDO participants to create a joint document. In either case, such contributions are generally modified and evolved by one or more working groups within the SDO as they progress along the "standards track," until such time as they are

---

[8] *Id.* § 203(a)–(b).
[9] *See id.* § 203(a).
[10] *See id.* § 203(a)(1).
[11] *Id.* § 203(b)(1) ("A derivative work prepared under authority of the grant before its termination may continue to be utilized under the terms of the grant after its termination, but this privilege does not extend to the preparation after the termination of other derivative works based upon the copyrighted work covered by the terminated grant").
[12] *But see* Chapter 5 (questioning this assumption). For purposes of this discussion, we will assume that standards documents are copyrightable works.
[13] For a general description of the entities and processes involved in the development of technical interoperability standards, *see* the companion volume, Chapter 2. In this chapter we do not focus on standards produced by single companies such as Adobe's Portable Document Format (PDF) or Microsoft's .doc format. While such standards are undeniably important to the market, the copyright termination issues discussed herein are generally not applicable to such standards.

approved by the requisite body within the SDO. To facilitate the standards development process, SDOs often employ administrative staff. But SDO employees are usually non-technical personnel who assist with document formatting and editing. SDO employees do not generally contribute technical content or intellectual property to the standard.

SDO policies and membership agreements typically set forth the copyright rights that participants must grant to the SDO. The individuals who make technical contributions to an SDO and their employers typically assign or license the copyright in those contributions to the SDO for purposes of standards development, evolution, publication, and dissemination.[14] In almost all cases, this "transfer" of copyright is made without monetary consideration, and neither individual standards developers nor their employers (who typically fund their participation in SDO activities) receive any financial compensation for this work.[15] The copyright in the collective work that comprises a standard is often owned by the SDO, but individual contributors or, more frequently, their employers, retain ownership of the copyrights in their underlying contributions.[16]

2. Implications of Section 203 Termination on Technical Standards

Suppose that a foundational data communications standard developed at SDO-X was published in 1984 based largely on the technical contributions of John Q. Engineer, an employee of Bigdata Corp. Like all participants in SDO-X, John (or Bigdata, if John has assigned the copyright to Bigdata under his employment agreement or the work-made-for-hire doctrine) has granted SDO-X a perpetual, irrevocable, worldwide, royalty-free license under the copyright in his contributions.[17] Since 1984, the standard has continued to evolve and is now an integral part of the global telecommunications infrastructure. However, notwithstanding the irrevocable license that John/Bigdata granted to SDO-X in 1984, beginning in 2019 either John or Bigdata (depending on their initial allocation of copyright ownership) could conceivably terminate that license under Section 203.[18]

The implications of such a termination could be serious. First, SDOs often charge modest fees for the sale and downloading of technical standards.[19] These fees help to support the administrative budgets of SDOs, which typically operate as non-profit corporations or membership associations.[20] If SDOs were required to fund copyright litigation, not to mention royalties to regain terminated rights, these costs would most likely be passed through to their members and, ultimately, to consumers. More importantly, the termination of SDO grants to technical contributions would prevent SDOs from further distributing those contributions, and from

---

[14] *See, e.g.*, IEEE 2013, § 6.3.1(A)(7) ("Prior to publication by the IEEE, all authors or their employers shall transfer to the IEEE in writing any copyright they hold for their individual papers. Such transfer shall be a necessary requirement for publication, except for material in the public domain or which is reprinted with permission from a copyrighted publication").

[15] *See, e.g., id.* § 6.3.1(A)(8) ("In return for the transfer of authors' rights, the IEEE shall grant authors and their employers' permission to make copies and otherwise reuse the material"). This no-charge transfer is entirely reasonable in the standards context, as participants in standards development projects wish to develop standards rapidly and efficiently in order to more quickly develop products that implement the standards or to seek patent royalties on such products.

[16] *See infra* note 39 and accompanying discussion.

[17] *See* IETF 2008, 10.

[18] *See* 17 U.S.C. § 203(a)(3) (2006) ("Termination of the grant may be effected at any time during a period of five years beginning at the end of thirty-five years from the date of execution of the grant…").

[19] *See* ANSI 2018g; *see also* Chapter 5.

[20] *See id.*

modifying or creating further derivative works of them. The adverse impact on enterprises depending on affected standards could be significant, as those standards could no longer evolve to accommodate future technological developments (e.g., the shift from 4G to 5G mobile communications, the upgrading of computer operating systems, or the introduction of new technologies).

Given these consequences, why would John, a dedicated engineer who originally made a voluntary technical contribution to SDO-X, suddenly decide to disrupt the technological infrastructure thirty-five years later? There are several possible reasons. First, John may opportunistically wish to profit from the widespread adoption and success of the standard. As discussed in the companion volume, the holder of intellectual property rights covering a technical standard gains the ability to charge elevated rents after the standard has been widely adopted by the industry.[21] This "hold-up" phenomenon is usually associated with patents, but could apply equally to a copyright owner who had the ability to impede the public utilization of a standard.[22] Thus, while John, as an aspiring young engineer, may have been inclined to grant an initial license to SDO-X without charge when the standard was in development and its success uncertain, he may now wish to capitalize on the broad adoption of the standard in the marketplace and renegotiate a license at a higher (i.e., non-zero) rate.[23] Moreover, after thirty-five years, it is possible that John is deceased and John's heirs may feel no loyalty to SDO-X and simply wish to maximize the value of his estate's assets. They may have no qualms about terminating license grants that he made to SDO-X under Section 203 in the hope of renegotiating for increased compensation.[24] But the termination of customary royalty-free copyright licenses granted by contributors to SDOs could significantly disrupt the standardization process and impose a substantial new cost on industries that are standards-dependent (a cost that would most likely be passed on to consumers).

In a recent article, Professor Timothy Armstrong observes, in a similar vein, that Section 203 terminations could adversely affect open source code software by enabling individual software developers to terminate their copyright grants to open source projects, thereby disrupting the many downstream uses of that software.[25] Professor Armstrong expresses concern that Section 203 terminations could adversely impact important open source projects and "chill the vibrant creative environment that presently surrounds the development and use of open-content works."[26] His concern is well-founded. However, open source software is a relatively recent development.[27] The first version of the first widely used open source code license, the GNU General Public License (GPL), was originally published in 1989. Thus, the first Section 203 termination of a GPL license could not occur until 2024. The far more common GPL v.2 was released in 1991, meaning that no GPL v.2 license could be terminated until 2026, at the

---

[21] See companion volume, Chapter 7.
[22] See Pacelli 2008, 1239–40. Copyright has typically not factored into the standards hold-up analysis due to the perpetual, irrevocable license grants that are usually made by contributors to technical standards. Section 203 has the potential to alter this balance.
[23] Given that most SDOs are thinly-staffed non-profit entities, the financial burden of such royalty demands would likely fall on other implementers of the standard (product vendors), and eventually be passed through to consumers.
[24] This chapter will discuss the ability of corporate "authors," such as Bigdata, to exercise Section 203 termination rights. See infra Part II.
[25] Armstrong 2010, 405–09; Phelps 2010, 261–62 (if open source code licenses are terminable under Section 203, the open source software movement could be negatively affected; the Section 117 safe harbor for software copies could avoid termination problems while permitting continued open source code development).
[26] Armstrong 2010, 363.
[27] See Perens 2002, 172.

earliest. In the realm of standards, however, the risk of termination exists today.[28] Many technical standards that were first published in 1983 (thirty-five years prior to 2018) or before are still in use. Moreover, the number of standards produced each year has grown steadily, and with each year that passes the number of standards potentially subject to Section 203 termination will increase.

It is important to note that only the author of a work (or his heirs) is entitled to exercise the right of termination under Section 203.[29] Thus, subsequent transferees and assignees of the author's rights do not have standing to terminate under Section 203, nor, arguably, do corporate successors in interest to a corporate author.[30]

B. EXCEPTIONS UNDER SECTION 203 AND TECHNICAL STANDARDS

Section 203 contains a number of exceptions and exclusions that could potentially be applied to limit the potential impact of copyright termination on technical standards.

1. Technical Standards as Joint Works

One of the key provisions of Section 203 addresses the way in which joint authors of a single copyrighted work can terminate a prior transfer of that joint work.[31] The Copyright Act defines a "joint work" as "a work prepared by two or more authors with the intention that their contribution be merged into inseparable or interdependent parts of a unitary whole."[32] Joint authors must share a common design and each author must contribute at least a minimal amount of creative expression beyond mere editorial revisions.[33] Joint authors each own an undivided interest in the entire joint work, enabling each joint author to grant nonexclusive licenses to third parties, provided the licensor accounts for profits to his joint authors.[34] Section 203 requires that a majority of the authors who executed a grant in a joint work act together to terminate that grant.[35] Thus, to the extent that a standard is considered a joint work, a single author (or his employer or heirs) acting alone could not terminate the grant of rights under Section 203.[36]

a) Joint or Collective?

A joint work should not be confused with a collective work, defined as "a work, such as a periodical issue, anthology, or encyclopedia, in which a number of contributions, constituting separate and independent works in themselves, are assembled into a collective whole."[37] Collective works

---

[28] See Phelps 2010, 265.
[29] 17 U.S.C. § 203(a) (2006).
[30] See id.
[31] Id. § 203; see also Nimmer 1977, 963–67 (describing requirements for termination by joint authors).
[32] See 17 U.S.C. § 101 (2006 & Supp. V 2012). Notably, the Act does not explicitly define "joint author." However, as Nimmer points out, this definition practically serves as establishing the circumstances under which joint authors create a joint work, not the parameters for joint ownership. See Nimmer & Nimmer 2013, § 6.01.
[33] See Childress v. Taylor (2d. Cir. 1991, 509) ("helpful advice" is insufficient to establish joint authorship, and expounding the idea that "[c]are must be taken to ensure that the true collaborators in the creative process are accorded the perquisites of co-authorship and to guard against the risk that a sole author is denied exclusive authorship status simply because another person rendered some form of assistance").
[34] Id. at 505; Erikson v. Trinity Theatre (7th Cir. 1994, 1068) ("[E]ach author as co-owner has the right to use or to license the use of the work, subject to an accounting to the other co-owners for any profits").
[35] 17 U.S.C. § 203(a)(1) (2006). Section 203(a)(2) addresses the scenario in which one or more joint authors have died, imposing the same majority requirement as Section 203(a)(1) but permitting statutory survivors to work as a "unit" in order to reach the necessary 51 percent mark. Id. § 203(a)(1)–(2).
[36] Id. § 203(a)(1).
[37] 17 U.S.C. § 101 (2006 & Supp. V 2012).

lack the merger and unity requirements of joint works and represent instead an aggregation of independent works into a single collection. Though the individual authors of contributions to a collective work retain ownership of the copyrights in their contributions (absent contractual terms to the contrary), a separate copyright exists in the collective work itself, which is owned by the compiler (usually the editor or publisher of the collective work).[38]

Though Section 203 requires that the majority of authors of a joint work act together in order to terminate a copyright grant made with respect to that joint work, no such requirement exists for collective works.[39] Thus, a contributor to a collective work can independently terminate a grant with respect to his individual contribution to the collection. This distinction makes it important to determine whether technical standards should be classified as joint works or collective works for the purposes of Section 203.

Some SDOs seek to treat finalized standards documents as collective works and claim ownership of the copyright in those collective works, while acknowledging that individual contributors retain copyright in their individual contributions.[40] If a standard is considered a collective work, then Section 203 would permit an author, or his heirs, to terminate a license to his individual contribution to the collection, potentially rendering the standard incoherent.

b) Joint Authorship of Standards

While it is possible that in some cases standards may represent compilations of individual contributions, the typical standards-development process appears far more likely to result in joint works. Standards are often written or substantially reviewed by committee, and each committee member who meaningfully participates in the drafting or revision of a standard likely has a claim as a joint author.[41] The key to joint authorship is intent, and while the parties need not work together physically or have an express collaboration agreement, they must have a common design to merge their contributions into an inseparable, unitary work.[42] Joint authorship status, however, depends on the level of contribution made by individual contributors.[43] An individual who simply attends meetings of a standardization committee, for example, but does not actually participate in writing or revising the standard, may have difficulty proving the required level of contribution.[44] On the other hand, one who can prove contribution through meeting notes, e-mail exchanges, or online postings will have a much stronger claim.[45]

---

[38] 17 U.S.C. § 201(c) (2006).

[39] *Id.* § 203(a)(1).

[40] *See, e.g.*, IETF 2008, § 5.9 ("Subject to each Contributor's (or its sponsor's) ownership of its underlying Contributions … each Contributor hereby acknowledges that the copyright in any RFC in which such Contribution is included … shall be owned by the IETF Trust").

[41] It is unlikely, however, that editorial or formatting contributions by an SDO employee would rise to the level of expressive contribution necessary to qualify the SDO as a joint author of the underlying standard, though some "thin" copyright may exist in these superficial contributions.

[42] 17 U.S.C. § 101 (2006 & Supp. V 2012).

[43] *Childress v. Taylor* (2d Cir. 1991, 507) ("It seems more consistent with the spirit of copyright law to oblige all joint authors to make copyrightable contributions, leaving those with non-copyrightable contributions to protect their rights through contract"). Some scholars and courts have taken the position that anything more than a *de minimis* contribution is sufficient to qualify for joint authorship status, reasoning that the lower threshold incentivizes collaboration, rewards authors, and permits contracts designed to circumvent a default joint authorship rule through assignment of rights or work for hire agreements. *See Gaiman v. McFarlane* (7th Cir. 2004, 658–61). However, some courts have determined that the mere contribution of independently copyrightable expression is still insufficient to establish joint authorship. *See Aalmuhammed v. Lee* (9th Cir. 2000, 1232–34) (control, in addition to intent, is central to a determination of joint authorship).

[44] *See Cabrera v. Teatro Del Sesenta* (D.P.R. 1995, 767–68) (mere regular attendance at meetings with the author does not raise one's level of contribution to that of a joint author).

[45] *See id.* at 764–65 (describing the spectrum of contribution required to establish authorship status).

Several cases have recognized joint authorship in standards developed by committee. In *American Dental Ass'n v. Delta Dental Plans Ass'n*,[46] the Seventh Circuit overruled an Illinois District Court's holding that the ADA's billing guidelines, the "Code on Dental Procedures and Nomenclature," was not copyrightable because it was created by a committee.[47] The Seventh Circuit rejected the lower court's reasoning that committees are categorically incapable of achieving the requisite level of creativity to qualify the work as copyrightable.[48] The court went on to explain that committees are, in fact, capable of original authorship and therefore entitled to copyright protection, noting that "[b]lood is shed in the ADA's committees about which [billing] description is preferable."[49]

The Court of Federal Claims addressed similar arguments in *Herbert v. United States*.[50] In *Herbert*, a committee of the National Academy of Sciences developed a report entitled *10th Recommended Dietary Allowances*.[51] The committee held regular meetings and reviewed numerous drafts "line-by-line."[52] Though the committee members did not have final editorial control over the report, the court held that the entire committee as a whole, and not just the individual authors, had control over the draft manuscript; and therefore the report qualified as a joint work.[53] Accordingly, each committee member had a valid claim as a joint author.[54]

If a copyright grant to the SDO was made collectively by joint authors, then termination under Section 203 would require the action of a majority of the joint authors or their heirs.[55] Given the long periods required between the grant and termination (thirty-five to forty years), it will probably be difficult for multiple authors or heirs to coordinate the exercise of termination rights under Section 203, particularly since individuals may be deceased and their employers may be defunct, acquired, or substantially reorganized since initial grants were made.[56] Moreover, the fact that initial grants to SDOs are without compensation means that such grants will generally not be recorded in corporate books of account, tracked for royalty purposes or, in many cases, retained in written form by the author. Thus, if technical standards are viewed as joint works in which copyright grants have been made collectively by the contributors, the likelihood of successful Section 203 termination will probably be low.

c) Individual Grants in Joint Works

But even assuming that a committee-drafted technical standard is, in fact, a joint work, it is not necessarily the case that the contributors have jointly granted rights to the SDO for purposes of Section 203. Though the statute contemplates a scenario, common in the music and publishing industries, in which joint authors jointly grant rights to a publisher or record label, this approach is generally not used in the standards context.[57] Rather, each individual author or firm typically grants a license to the SDO with respect to its contributions on an individual basis. The co-authors of a standard seldom execute a joint assignment or license.

---

[46] *Am. Dental Ass'n v. Delta Dental* (7th Cir. 1997).
[47] *Id.* at 977–78.
[48] *Id.* at 978–79.
[49] *Id.* at 979.
[50] *Herbert v. United States* (Fed. Cl. 1996, 306–09).
[51] *Id.* at 302.
[52] *Id.* at 309.
[53] *Id.*
[54] *Id.* at 310.
[55] 17 U.S.C. § 203(a)(1) (2006).
[56] *Id.* § 203(a)(3).
[57] *See* Barritt 2009.

Scorpio Music S.A. v. Willis[58] illustrates how a court may view attempts to terminate by a single author of a joint work. Willis, the original lead singer of the popular musical group Village People, sought to terminate his post-1977 grants of thirty-three musical compositions to Can't Stop Music (CSM), the exclusive U.S. publisher of compositions owned by Scorpio Music.[59] Copyright registrations for the songs listed Willis as one of *several* composers.[60] In a series of separate agreements between 1977 and 1979, however, Willis independently transferred his copyright interest in the songs to CSM – who in turn assigned these rights to Scorpio – in exchange for royalties of 12 percent to 20 percent.[61] In January 2011, Willis served on CSM and Scorpio a notice of termination under Section 203 for all thirty-three songs, and Scorpio challenged the termination's validity.[62]

Scorpio's main argument was that in order to effect a valid termination under Section 203, a majority of all authors who transferred their interests in the joint work (whether separately or in a single transaction) must join the termination.[63] Accordingly, Scorpio argued that Willis' termination notice was invalid because Willis was the only author named.[64] However, the court reasoned that Willis was the sole party to his own contracts with CSM – his co-authors had entered into separate agreements – and his termination notice was valid based on the clear statutory allowance that "[i]n the case of a grant executed by one author, termination of the grant may be effected by that author."[65] The court therefore concluded that a "joint author who separately transfers his copyright interest may unilaterally terminate that grant."[66]

If a contributor's grant of his interest in a joint work was *individually* made to an SDO then, under the reasoning of *Scorpio*, it is likely that the individual contributor may terminate his individual grant in the joint work under Section 203. This situation could result in more terminations than the scenario described in Part III.B.2 above, in which co-authors of a joint work *jointly* make a grant to the SDO, requiring a majority of their number to effect a termination under Section 203. But even this result may not be catastrophic to SDOs, as any joint author has the right to grant the SDO a license under the joint copyright.[67] Thus, if other non-terminating joint authors continue to license the SDO, a single joint author's termination would have no practical effect.

2. The Works-Made-for-Hire Exception

The work-made-for-hire exception is arguably the most important and least clear element of the Section 203 termination right. The Section expressly applies to "any work *other than* a work made for hire."[68] Thus, to the extent that a work can be characterized as a work-made-for-hire, it will not be subject to the termination provisions of Section 203.[69]

---

[58] *Scorpio v. Willis* (S.D. Cal. 2012, *1).
[59] *Id.*
[60] *Id.*
[61] *Id.*
[62] *Id.* at *1, *5.
[63] *Id.* at *1.
[64] *Id.*
[65] *Id.* at *1–2.
[66] *Id.* at *2, *4.
[67] See *supra* note 35 and accompanying text.
[68] 17 U.S.C. § 203(a) (2006) (emphasis added). A similar exclusion for works made for hire appears in Section 304 governing termination of pre-1978 grants or transfers. *Id.* § 304(c)–(d).
[69] See *id.* § 203(a); see also Burrows 2010 (questioning work-for-hire clauses in the recording industry); Davis 2000 (discussing the work-made-for-hire doctrine and Section 203 termination in the context of studio pitches); Molinaro 2004 (discussing the dispute over whether the author of the Captain America comics created them as a work-made-for-hire and the impact of that determination on his termination rights under Section 203).

Section 101 of the Copyright Act defines a "work made for hire" as: "(1) a work prepared by an employee within the scope of his or her employment,"[70] or "(2) a work specially ordered or commissioned" and falling into one of nine specific categories.[71] When a work-made-for-hire is created, the employer is automatically deemed to be the "author" of the work, and the employee never obtains ownership of any copyright interest.[72] A key rationale behind the exclusion of works-made-for-hire from Section 203 was to assure employers that works created by their employees would not subsequently be recaptured.[73] In effect, the statute recognizes that an employee's wages should be sufficient compensation for works produced within the scope of employment, and does not allow the employee or his heirs to terminate such rights years later in the hope of receiving additional compensation. Thus, even if an employee produced a work while earning the minimum wage, and even if that work later became wildly successful and earned the employer enormous profits, the employee would have no right under Section 203 to terminate the assignment and renegotiate for greater remuneration. The employer is considered the work's author from the moment it is created, and Section 203 simply does not apply.[74]

Despite the seemingly straightforward statutory language and underlying rationale, the Section 203 exclusion of works-made-for- hire leaves open several questions. Most importantly, does the Section 203 exclusion apply to (1) any work that is a work-made-for-hire *for the grantee* (that is, the rights-holder against which the 203 termination right is exercised), or (2) any work that is a work-made-for-hire *at all*? This distinction is critical. Scenario 1 appears to have been contemplated by Congress when it sought to protect employers from subsequent terminations by their employees.[75] Scenario 1 is illustrated in Figure 8.1.

In Scenario 1, the application of the Section 203 exclusion is straightforward. An employee creates a script for her employer (a television producer). The script is within the scope of her employment and thus constitutes a work-made-for-hire. Under Section 203, the employee script writer is not permitted to terminate the transfer of copyright to her employer.[76] Scenario 2, however, is also included within the literal wording of Section 203. It is illustrated by Figure 8.2.

---

[70] 17 U.S.C. § 101 (2006 & Supp. V 2012). The Supreme Court addressed the question whether an independent contractor can constitute an "employee" for purposes of the work-made-for-hire doctrine in *CCNV v. Reid* (U.S. 1989). In CCNV, the Court found that a contractor engaged by the city to create a sculpture was not an employee, even though the city directed his work. The Court instead relied on a number of factors weighing in favor of finding that the contractor was independent, such as the skilled nature of the work, the contractor's independent ownership of tools and studio space, the one-time nature of the project, and the relatively short time period of the work. *Id.* at 752–53.

[71] 17 U.S.C. § 101 (2006 & Supp. V 2012). More specifically as to the second prong, the work must be "specially ordered or commissioned for use as a contribution to a collective work, as part of a picture or other audiovisual work, as a translation, as a supplementary work, as a compilation, as an "instructional text," as a test, as answer material for a test, or as an atlas, if the parties expressly agree in a written instrument signed by them that the work shall be considered a work made for hire. For the purpose of the foregoing sentence, a "supplementary work" is a work prepared for publication as a secondary adjunct to a work by another author for the purpose of introducing, concluding, illustrating, explaining, revising, commenting upon, or assisting in the use of the other work, such as forewords, afterwords, illustrations, maps, charts, tables, editorial notes, musical arrangements, answer material for tests, bibliographies, appendixes, and indexes, and an "instructional text" is a literary, pictorial, or graphic work prepared for publication and with the purpose of use in systematic instructional activities." *Id.*

[72] 17 U.S.C. § 201 (2006).

[73] *See* H.R. Rep. No. 94-1476 (1976, 124) (Section 203 should include a provision that protects authors against unremunerative transfers due to the "unequal bargaining position of authors"). *See id.* at 121 ("[t]he [presumption] that initial ownership rights vest in the employer for hire is well established in American copyright law").

[74] *Id.*

[75] *See id.* at 127.

[76] 17 U.S.C § 203 (2006); *see* H.R. Rep. No. 94-1476 (1976, 125) (providing that "the right of termination would not apply to 'works made for hire'"); *see also* Palmieri 2012, 1176–77 ("U.S. copyright law grants to an author of a work other than a work made for hire a right to terminate any transfers (except testamentary transfers) she has made of her copyright, with the result being that ownership of the copyright reverts to the author of the work. This termination right is a

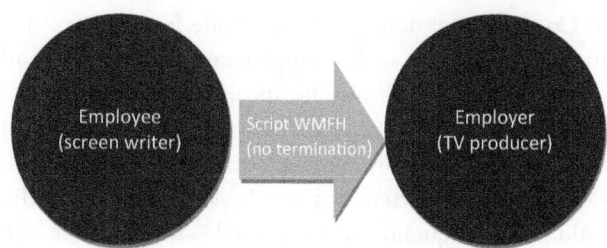

FIGURE 8.1 Scenario 1: Work-made-for-hire for grantee (no termination)

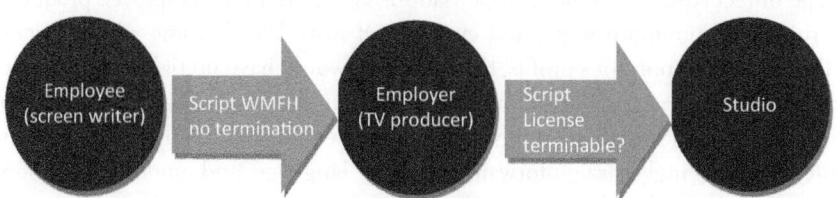

FIGURE 8.2 Scenario 2: Work-made-for-hire for grantee (no termination)

In Scenario 2, the employee produces the same script for her employer, a producer. It is a work-made-for-hire, and the employee has no right to terminate her transfer under Section 203. However, sometime after receiving the script, the employer licenses it to a studio. Can the employer, which is deemed to be the author of the script under the work-made-for-hire doctrine, terminate the license to the studio under Section 203? Ordinarily, one might think this termination would be possible, as the script was not made by an employee of the *studio* (i.e., it was not a work-made-for-hire for the grantee (the studio). However, the script *was* a work-made-for-hire for the producer. Under Section 203, does the fact that a work was originally a work-made-for-hire forever brand it as a work-made-for-hire as to which Section 203 does not apply? Or is Section 203 intended to exclude from termination only works-made-for-hire *for the grantee*? This question, which is highly relevant to the standards development context, appears to be unanswered by the legislative history of Section 203 as well as the case law.

The typical standards-development arrangement (engineer – employer – SDO) resembles the three-party example illustrated in Figure 8.2 (screen writer – producer – studio). An individual engineer creates a contribution to a standard within the scope of his employment, that contribution is treated as a work-made-for-hire, and his employer is therefore recognized as the contribution's author. The employer then grants the SDO a license to that contribution. The contribution was made by the engineer for his employer, but it is clearly not a work-made-for-hire for the SDO.[77] Is the initial character of the contribution as a work-made-for-hire enough to exempt the contribution from the termination right under Section 203?

As noted, the statute is ambiguous in this regard. However, we believe that the policy considerations leading to the enactment of Section 203 militate *against* allowing a corporate author

---

powerful one; it is inalienable and the author retains the right to terminate transfers 'not withstanding any agreement to the contrary'").

[77] An SDO neither employs engineers nor commissions work from them in the statutory sense, as the SDO pays nothing for the work and does not specify the parameters of the work, as the commissioner of a work typically would. And even if work could be construed as commissioned, technical standards do not fall into one of the nine statutory categories under which commissioned (i.e., non-employee) works will be deemed works-made-for-hire. *See* 17 U.S.C. § 101 (2006 & Supp. V 2012).

to terminate a copyright grant with respect to works made by its employees. There are several reasons for this conclusion. First, the plain language of the statute excludes all works-made-for-hire from the scope of Section 203.[78] Nothing in the legislative history indicates that any particular varieties of works-made-for-hire should be immune from this exclusion.[79] Second, corporate authors were clearly not the class of persons that Section 203 sought to protect.[80]

As demonstrated in its legislative history, Section 203 was intended to benefit relatively unknown authors who sold significant works to far more powerful publishers and thereby failed to reap the financial benefits of their work.[81] Section 203 was not intended to give corporations the right to terminate commercial licensing arrangements simply because their employees created the works at issue.[82] In fact, the statutory mention of authors' deaths and heirs, and the lack of any mention of corporate authors, indicates that the termination right granted under Section 203 was intended to be exercised by individuals, and not by corporate "persons."[83]

Finally, if employees themselves are not permitted to take advantage of the termination right under Section 203 after their works-made-for-hire are transferred to their employers, employers should not be permitted to protect their own financial interests by terminating downstream license grants with respect to those very employee-created works.[84] Employers were intended to be protected by the works-made-for-hire exception under Section 203, but only to prevent subsequent terminations by employees long after works had been created.[85] The employer's protection should not be doubled by also enabling it to exercise its own termination right under Section 203 with respect to downstream grants. Accordingly, we believe that the works-made-for-hire exclusion of Section 203 should prevent employers from terminating copyright grants in their employees' contributions to technical standards.

3. The Derivative Works Exception

Another key exception of Section 203 permits grantees to continue to exploit derivative works even after the grant in an underlying work is terminated.[86] However, this exception does not authorize the creation of *new* derivative works based on the original contribution after the grant has been terminated.[87] Thus, the right to exploit existing derivative works created under the authority of a grant is non-terminable, while the right to create new derivative works *is* terminable.[88]

Section 101 of the Copyright Act defines a derivative work as a work that is "based upon one or more preexisting works."[89] Examples of derivative works include: a movie based on a play, a sculpture based on a drawing, and a drawing based on a photo.[90]

---

[78] See *supra* note 70 and accompanying text.
[79] See *supra* note 76 and accompanying text.
[80] H.R. Rep. No. 94–1476 (1976, 124).
[81] *Id.*
[82] See *id.* at 125.
[83] See 17 U.S.C. § 203 (2006); H.R. Rep. No. 94–1476 (1976, 124–25).
[84] H.R. Rep. No. 94–1476 (1976, 124–28).
[85] *Id.* at 127–28.
[86] 17 U.S.C. § 203(b)(1) (2006) ("A derivative work prepared under the authority of the grant before its termination may continue to be utilized under the terms of the grant after its termination, but this privilege does not extend to the preparation after the termination of other derivative works based upon the copyrighted work covered by the terminated grant"). See Nimmer, *supra* note 32, at 961–63 (describing termination rights as to derivative works).
[87] 17 U.S.C. § 203(b)(1) (2006).
[88] See *id.*
[89] 17 U.S.C. § 101 (2006 & Supp. V 2012).
[90] U.S. Copyright Off. 2013.

The Supreme Court addressed the issue of the derivative works exception to the termination right under Section 304 (mirroring the language of Section 203)[91] in *Mills Music v. Snyder*.[92] In *Mills Music*, Ted Snyder, author of the copyrighted song *Who's Sorry Now*, granted the copyright, including Snyder's renewal interest, to music publisher Mills Music. Mills Music then licensed the song to over 400 record companies, who in turn hired separate artists to record variations of the song. Snyder's heirs subsequently sought to exercise their statutory right of termination, but Mills Music claimed that this termination did not apply to the *derivative* versions of the song recorded by other artists. The Court agreed with Mills Music, determining that a publisher may continue to share in the royalties generated from the licensing of derivative works even after termination of the underlying grant by the original author. The Court focused its interpretation on the meaning of "utilized under the terms of the *grant* after its termination," concluding that the derivative sound recordings were prepared under the authority of the original grant.[93]

Turning to technical standards, the derivative works exception will apply in the standards context if a standard can be characterized as a derivative work of the individual contributions on which it is based.[94] This characterization may be more or less accurate depending on the specific facts of each case. For example, a standard could represent a synthesis of three independent technical contributions or it could simply be a reformatted version of an already-mature document by a single contributor. In the first case, it is likely that the standard would be considered a derivative work of each underlying contribution. But in the latter case, treatment as a derivative work is less likely.

If a standard were considered a derivative work of an underlying contribution, then if the contributor terminated the SDO's grant to that contribution, the SDO could no longer publish that contribution or any *new* modifications, updates, or standards "based upon" the original contribution.[95] The SDO could only continue to distribute versions of the standard that were published at the time of termination. Given that standards are frequently updated, corrected, modified, and improved, an SDO's right to distribute only pre-termination versions of a standard could present a serious problem.

4. Underlying Policy Considerations

Moving beyond the specific language of the statute, it is useful to consider the original policy goals of Section 203 when evaluating its application to technical standards. As discussed in the Introduction, Section 203 was enacted to ensure that authors and artists who granted their copyrighted works to large publishers and record labels for low initial sums could terminate those grants and renegotiate their financial returns if the works were still successful thirty-five years later. Thus, the underlying goal of the statute is to secure fair financial returns to the creators of copyrighted works, even though they may have lacked sufficient bargaining power at the time of their initial grants.

---

[91] *See supra* note 5 (discussing termination under Section 304).

[92] *Mills Music v. Snyder* (U.S. 1985).

[93] *Id.* at 164–65; *see also Woods v. Bourne* (2d. Cir. 1995, 987–88) (determinations of derivative work status in the context of the termination right requires an examination of the rights to which each party was entitled *before* the point of termination).

[94] *See* 17 U.S.C. § 101 (2006 & Supp. V 2012) (defining a derivative work as "a work based upon one or more preexisting works").

[95] 17 U.S.C. § 203(b)(1) (2006); *cf. Mills Music* (U.S. 1985, 173 & n.40) (applying similar statutory language to a derivative work and finding that only previously existing derivative works are excepted).

The scenario could not be more different in the case of technical standards. First, there is no imbalance of power in the negotiation of standards-related copyright licenses. The firms that employ engineers engaged in standardization are among the largest in the world, and SDOs are typically organizations formed and run by their members. Thus, there is no need to protect the authors of standards documents from unfair bargains, as there is with young and unknown authors and artists.

Second, firms engaged in standardization willingly contribute copyrighted material to SDOs without compensation. There is no expectation that the copyright transfer will ever be remunerative. The firms that participate in SDOs do so in order to influence the technical direction of future products, to ensure that their products will be interoperable with others, and to gain valuable market intelligence regarding the technical direction of the industry. These motivations differ from those of individual authors and artists, whose sole reward for the transfer of their copyrights is typically the remuneration received from the grantee publisher or record label. Thus, the motivation for Section 203, which allows an author to increase his compensation for a work that was difficult to value at the time of its initial exploitation, does not exist in the standards context.

Finally, the entire market relies on the system of no-compensation, perpetual copyright licenses granted with respect to technical standards. Allowing authors to revoke copyright grants thirty-five years after they are made could wreak havoc with a voluntary consensus standards system that itself is the source of substantial economic benefits and social welfare.

CONCLUSION

Both the formal permissibility and the technical feasibility of terminating copyright grants under Section 203 in the context of technical standards are dubious. In order to effect such a termination, either a copyrighted contribution to an SDO must be an individual contribution, or a majority of the authors must act in concert, which is unlikely after four decades. During that time, authors may die or lose track of their commitments. Section 203 expressly prohibits termination in the case of works-made-for-hire, which likely represent the majority of standards contributions.[96] And even if a Section 203 termination were successfully invoked against a contribution to a standard, the standard itself could continue to be distributed as a derivative work of the underlying contribution.

Nevertheless, the outcomes described above may be achieved only after litigation and the expenditure of significant time and money. And, as with all litigation, such outcomes are subject to the vagaries of the facts before the court (reflecting the old adage "bad facts make bad law"). Thus, it may be preferable for Congress to clarify in a categorical fashion that Section 203 does not apply to voluntary consensus standards.[97] We believe that such clarification is necessary to avoid the disruption and uncertainty that could be caused by the attempted termination of long-ago copyright grants under Section 203.

---

[96] 17 U.S.C. § 203 (2006).
[97] In this recommendation we join Professor Armstrong, who has expressed a similar view in order to correct similar inequities in the potential application of Section 203 to the termination of open source code licenses (Armstrong 2010, 416–19).

PART IV

Standards and Software

9

Open Standards

Jay P. Kesan

A.	Definition	159
	1. Early Definitional Attempts	160
	2. Definitional Consistency	163
	3. American Governmental Definitions	164
	4. Non-U.S. Governmental Definitions	165
B.	Problems in Definitional Attempts	167
C.	Government Policies for Adopting Open Standards	168
D.	Vendor Lock-In	172
E.	Open Standards and Technical Interoperability	173
F.	Multiple Implementations and Running Code	175

"Open standards" is a fluid term encompassing those standards which are available to be employed to develop multiple implementations compatible with the standard. No single definition can encompass what makes up an open standard, although there are many consistencies between experts, scholars, and lawmakers in their attempts to define the term. The main reasons behind governments adopting open standards are to reduce costs by preventing vendor lock-in and promoting interoperability between different implementations and technologies. However, achieving interoperability between multiple independent implementations that are compliant with a particular standard remains a significant challenge.

A. DEFINITION

Many scholars and experts have tried to define "open standards," but the term has remained somewhat nebulous despite various attempts to do so. Other attempts at creating a definition simply narrow down specific requirements or principles a standard must embody before being considered truly open. In general, "open standards" are standardized specifications, rules or guidelines that are widely and freely available for public and commercial use. Using an open standard, manufacturers located on different continents can potentially create products with a reasonable likelihood of interoperability and compatibility, despite never interacting in any meaningful way. Compared to "closed," otherwise known as "proprietary" standards, open standards have the potential to lower costs, as an "off the shelf" solution exists for implementation of certain product features, while also increasing overall interoperability and compatibility between technologies. Open standards have been in use in many industries, when open standards relating to high-tech applications entered the scene *en masse* during the early 2000s, and organizations around the globe and scholars alike submitted their ideas on what constitutes open standards. Over time, certain constants have repeated themselves and seem to be the core of what open standards embody.

1. Early Definitional Attempts

Perhaps one of the first attempts to include principles for what constitutes an open standard was undertaken by Bruce Perens.[1] Perens offered six principles that should be considered when considering what makes a standard "open":

1) Availability: Open Standards are available for all to read and implement.
2) Maximize End-User Choice: Open Standards create a fair, competitive market for implementations of the standard. They do not lock the customer in to a particular vendor or group.
3) No Royalty: Open Standards are free for all to *implement*, with no royalty or fee. *Certification* of compliance by the standards organization may involve a fee.
4) No Discrimination: Open Standards and the organizations that administer them do not favor one implementer over another for any reason other than the technical standards compliance of a vendor's implementation. Certification organizations must provide a path for low- and zero-cost implementations to be validated, but may also provide enhanced certification services.
5) Extension or Subset: Implementations of Open Standards may be extended, or offered in subset form. However, certification organizations may decline to certify subset implementations, and may place requirements upon extensions (see *Predatory Practices*).
6) Predatory Practices: Open Standards may employ license terms that protect against subversion of the standard by *embrace-and-extend* tactics. The licenses attached to the standard may require the publication of reference information for extensions, and a license for all others to create, distribute, and sell software that is compatible with the extensions. An Open Standard may not othe[r]wise prohibit extensions.

Perens became the early benchmark for what should be included in any definition of an open standard. The first four principles would become jumping off points for other scholars, government agencies, and standard-setting organizations (SSOs) to follow in the future.

In 2004, the European Commission, the European Union's executive body,[2] through the Interchange of Data between Administrations (IDA) agency, made an attempt to attach "minimal characteristics that a specification and its attendant documents must have to be considered an open standard."[3] The IDA prescribed four separate characteristics to open standards:

1) The standard is adopted and will be maintained by a not-for-profit organization, and its ongoing development occurs on the basis of an open decision-making procedure available to all interested parties ...

---

[1] Perens 2002.
[2] European Commission 2016.
[3] European Commission 2004.

2) The standard has been published and the standard specification document is available either freely or at a nominal charge. It must be permissible to all to copy, distribute and use it for no fee or at a nominal fee.
3) The intellectual property ... [of] the standard is made irrevocably available on a royalty- free basis.
4) There are no constraints on the re-use of the standard.

Those four characteristics would become a common theme throughout future attempts at defining open standards, though future authors and organizations would add other requirements or put more focus on certain characteristics.

After the IDA released its definition, Tsilas noted that this definition already had its detractors.[4] He noted that "contrary to the IDA definition, the intellectual property rights (IPR) policies of ETSI, IEEE, IETF, ISO/IEC, ITU, OMA, ANSI, ECMA, and other leading standards organizations do not mandate royalty-free licensing or prohibit other 'constraints on the re-use of the standard.'" It was at this point a split began between whether open standards should be required to have royalty-free licensing or rather a policy of reasonable and non-discriminatory (RAND) licensing. Under RAND (or FRAND, which includes that the licensing must also be fair), the licensing scheme does not have to be royalty-free.

That same year, the Berkman Center for Internet and Society at the Harvard Law School included representatives from thirteen national governments and leading technological companies to create a report[5] presented at the World Bank in an effort to promote open standards. The group focused on only two requirements for open standards[6]:

1) The standard is not propriety, or owned by a single company.
2) The standard is published and freely available for use by developers.

The Berkman Center report eventually led to the Massachusetts state government adopting an open standards policy, discussed below.

The simple definition by the Berkman Center can be contrasted with one of the most robust definitional attempts undertaken soon afterwards by Krechmer.[7] Krechmer gives ten requirements for open standards, which all relate to what he recognized as the three perspectives an open standard may be seen from – recognized SSOs, "an implementer of an existing standard," and "the user of an implementation of the standard." The ten requirements he recognizes are:

1) Open Meeting – all may participate in the standards development process.
2) Consensus – all interests are discussed and agreement found, no domination.
3) Due Process – balloting and an appeals process may be used to find resolution.
4) Open IPR – how holders of IPR related to the standard make available their IPR.
5) One World – same standard for the same capability, world-wide.
6) Open Change – all changes are presented and agreed in a forum supporting the five requirements above.
7) Open Documents – committee drafts and completed standards documents are easily available for implementation and use.

---

[4] Tsilas 2005.
[5] Berkman Center 2005.
[6] Lohr 2005; Weil 2005.
[7] Krechmer 2006.

8) Open Interface – supports proprietary advantage (implementation); each interface is not hidden or controlled (implementation); each interface of the implementation supports migration (use).
9) Open Access – objective conformance mechanisms for implementation testing and user evaluation.
10) On-going Support – standards are supported until user interest ceases rather than when implementer interest declines.

Krechmer's requirement for Open Meetings incorporated several previously-used requirements. The IDA desired standards that incorporated "open decision-making procedure available to all interested parties."[8] The IDA also includes the sentiments of the Berkman Center that no single company own the standard. If a company were creating a standard, it would not want open meetings with its own competitors or to allow other parties not connected to the company to control the direction of the product. Krechmer saw economic barriers as the main threat to open meetings within SSOs, noting that "[p]articipation expenses, unless quite low, are part of real barriers to participation for students, many users and even start-up companies in the field."[9]

Consensus and Due Process also encompass the need to not have one company control a standard. Krechmer's view of Consensus "requires that no single stakeholder group constitutes a majority of the membership of an SSO." Similarly, Due Process "requires that prompt consideration be given to the written views and objections of all participants." Both of these assume that one company would not control the setting of an open standard and all participants would have an equal opportunity for input into the process.

One World (or Open World) is a new requirement that Krechmer added to the discussion. A One World requirement was "supported by the WTO to prevent technical barriers to trade." The key is for an SSO to have a jurisdiction over as large an area as possible so that it "does not favor[] divergent regional or national standards."

Krechmer's requirement of Open IPR (*i.e.*, how holders of IPR related to the standard make available their IPR) contemplates a RAND regime instead of just a royalty-free regime. Open Change harkens back to the original IDA definition and requires that "ongoing development" occur with all interested parties having a chance to be involved. Open Documents also echoes the IDA definition with its requirement to make the "standard specification document is available either freely or at a nominal charge."

Open Interface was another new concept that Krechmer included as a requirement for open standards. It is described as requiring a standard that "supports compatibility to previous systems (backward compatibility) and to future systems (forward compatibility) that share the same interface." This feature of interoperability is often seen as a benefit of open standards, but has rarely been seen as a requirement for the definition of open standards.

Open Access relates back to the user, ensuring that the user is able to access the implementation, and is divided into two classes: "physical access (*e.g.*, access by people with disabilities) and defined access (*e.g.*, CE or UL mark indicating equipment is safe to use)." This requirement will not be used by any future definitional attempt discussed here, and open access became one of the key problems with the Massachusetts implementation of an open standards policy, as discussed below. Finally, On-going Support relates back to Open Change, except that it includes users' ability to receive support regarding the standard.

---

[8] European Commission 2004.
[9] Krechmer 2006.

2. Definitional Consistency

After 2006, attempts to define open standards became simpler. The United Nations' International Telecommunication Union Telecommunication Standardization Sector (ITU-T) by 2007 defined open standards based on only two criteria: "standards made available to the general public and are developed (or approved) and maintained via a collaborative and consensus driven process."[10] The ITU-T continued to use that definition until at least 2016.[11]

These kinds of definitions become more common over the next decade, as scholars begin to narrow definitions down to the few actual requirements they consistently recognize as necessary for open standards. Scholars and governmental organizations became much less likely to require open standards to include a feature that could more commonly be seen as a benefit, such as technical interoperability. However, DeNardis makes an argument for interoperability as one of her four requirements for "maximal openness in a standard," saying that the standard must "allow[] technical interoperability between heterogeneous products, enable[] multiple competing implementations, and preclude[] users from being locked into a single vendor's products."[12]

However, this technical interoperability is normally seen as a usual byproduct of what will result from having an open standard defined by other, simpler standards. Three requirements for inclusion in the definition of open standards that were cited most frequently through scholarly work are:

1) Specifications are made public at little or no charge.
2) Public participation in development of the standard.
3) A RAND/FRAND licensing scheme; with a royalty-free licensing scheme as a minority approach.

The advantages of standard specifications being made public at little or no charge were detailed by Shah and Kesan:

> When standards are open and freely available, it becomes possible for anyone to develop an interoperable implementation. This reduces the ability of vendors to tie a standard to the purchase of other products ... This in turn facilitates multiple interoperable implementations, thus providing users with choice. Choice typically brings with it lower costs and technological variation.[13]

The ability to have standards free to all possible participants in the market ties in with many of the other proposed inclusions into the definition of open standards. Instead of having to require technical interoperability as part of what makes a standard "open," having standards freely available to all participants in the market means that they are working with the same information and will be able to make products interoperable with each other. Also, one market participant cannot create a monopoly on the standard and control the market because any competitor may use the same standard to create a comparable product. Therefore, it is clear why this is often considered one of the key requirements for what makes an open standard.

Open, public participation in the development of a standard is the second most-commonly cited requirement for an open standard to be considered so. There are advantages and

---

[10] ITU 2016.
[11] *Id.*
[12] DeNardis 2008/2009.
[13] Shah & Kesan 2009.

disadvantages to this requirement. As Werbach states, "The more open and informal the process, the greater the range of views that can be taken into account. On the other hand, such openness can lead to delay and other inefficiencies."[14] However, DeNardis encapsulates why more participation in the process of creating a standard is desirable:

> The legitimacy of Internet standards governance has, in part, depended upon the institutional processes being open to participation by various stakeholders… Standards-setting organizations with open membership policies, despite any barriers, at least allow for the possibility of developing country input into standards policy decisions. In the standards-setting process itself, institutions wishing to have global legitimacy should be open to anyone wanting to participate regardless of membership status, institutional affiliation, credentials, or government or corporate backing.[15]

Finally, there has been a movement away from royalty-free licenses and into RAND licensing from patent holders of necessary technology for open standards. One disadvantage to a RAND system was described by Greve: "One common criticism of (F)RAND terms is the lack of a definition of what is reasonable and for whom."[16] However, market participants who put assets into creating the intellectual property and research in order to get a patent on the material want to get a return on their investment. The easiest way to do this is to charge what would be deemed a "reasonable" licensing fee, as well as competitors taking advantage of each others' patents, even if it has the side effect of non-related parties also having access to those same patents.[17]

3. American Governmental Definitions

Governments began seeking open standards policies in order to preserve electronic government documents for future generations. In order to create a policy favoring open standards, governments would necessarily have to define what makes up an open standard in the process.

The first U.S. government entity to attempt the adoption of open standards was the state of Massachusetts in 2003. In their policy document, the state defined open standards as "specifications for systems that are publicly available and are developed by an open community and affirmed by a standards body."[18] With those three requirements, Massachusetts embraced in 2006 what the open standards community two of the main three requirements later scholars would fully embrace as the most important requirements for open standards in having the standards publicly available and developed with public participation. However, the state also included the third requirement of being affirmed by a standards body, which would show up again in 2013.[19]

That same year, Texas introduced a similar bill to require open standards, which ultimately failed.[20] The Texas bill was similar to the Massachusetts definition in that specifications should be publicly available, but did not include an SSO or public participation requirement. Instead, Texas desired no royalties, that no implementer would be favored over another, and that standards be freely implementable; all of which requirements have been seen in scholarly articles.[21] Texas also included the requirement that the specifications "do not lock the user into

[14] Werbach 2009.
[15] DeNardis 2008/2009.
[16] Greve 2008a.
[17] West 2005.
[18] Shah et al. 2007.
[19] Greve 2008a.
[20] S.B. 1579 (Tex. 2003).
[21] DeNardis 2008/2009; Shah & Kesan 2007; Contreras 2019.

a particular vendor or group."[22] This requirement of no vendor lock-in is generally seen as a byproduct of open standards, and is likely redundant with the additional requirement that the specifications "not favor one implementer over another for any reason."[23]

In 2006, Minnesota made a similar effort but defined open standards with many more criteria for a specification to be considered an open standard. Minnesota joined Massachusetts and Texas in requiring publicly-available specifications ("has a specification available for all to read, in a human-readable format, written in commonly accepted technical language"), but only shared two other requirements in part with Texas.[24] Both states required no royalties and that the specifications are freely implementable. Minnesota also included that open standards must allow technical interoperability, which, like Texas' requirement against vendor lock-in, is normally simply a byproduct of using open standards. Similar to Texas, Minnesota's bill failed to pass through the state legislature.

4. Non-U.S. Governmental Definitions

The international community became interested in mandating open standards at around the same time as U.S. state governments. Denmark became one of the first countries to define what it considered to be open standards in 2004. The Denmark National IT and Telecom Agency joined with virtually all scholars and other governments at the time requiring publicly available specifications ("all aspects of the standard are transparent and documented…").[25] Denmark also required the standard be "accessible to everyone free of charge" and that it remains that way – "owners renounce their options, if indeed such exist, to limit access to the standard at a later date…"

In 2010, Denmark followed up on what it considered open standards once again, as its parliament "decided on a set of rules to which open document formats must adhere if they are to be used by state authorities…"[26] They kept the requirement for specifications to be publicly available, but changed their other requirements. Denmark joined Massachusetts in necessitating that open standards must be "recognized by an internationally known standards body." SSO-recognition, as will be seen below, became a common point between international governments in how they saw open standards. It also required that open standards must be able to work on multiple implementations, which followed in the footsteps of only South Africa, seen below.

South Africa put out a definition of open standards in 2007, with its Handbook on Minimum Information Interoperability Standards.[27] The South African government also mandated that specifications be publicly available to all: "[A]ll may access committee documents, drafts and completed standards free of cost or for a negligible fee." In addition, everyone should be able to "copy, distribute and use the standard free of cost" and the intellectual property should be available royalty-free. South Africa did take the unusual step for a government entity at the time, mandating that the creation and development of the standard be "open to all interested parties." This had been a key feature in a majority of scholarly works, but South Africa became the first nation to recognize its importance in open standards. After development, the standard should also be "maintained by a non-commercial organization," harkening back to Massachusetts's

---

[22] S.B. 1579 (Tex. 2003).
[23] Id.
[24] H.F. 3971 (Minn. 2006).
[25] OECD 2010.
[26] Ricknäs 2010.
[27] South Africa 2007.

requirement that the standard be affirmed by an SSO. Finally, the standard should be freely implementable and be used by multiple implementations – the requirement Denmark would also adopt three years later.

The government of New Zealand was very clear in stating that there would likely be no concrete definition of open standards, so it "accepts that a definition of 'open standards' needs to recognise a continuum that ranges from closed to open, and encompasses varying degrees of 'openness.'"[28] New Zealand chose to focus on only three properties. First, it required, like all other governments, that "all aspects of the standard should be transparent and documented." Borrowing from Denmark's original definition four years prior, New Zealand also required that owners of the standard "should renounce their options, if any, to limit access to the standard at a later date." Finally, it required that no royalty be attached to the standard, and that it "[b]e accessible to everyone free of charge."

India followed in the footsteps of these other nations, but instead of using a broad definition of what "open standards" should encompass, it decided to impute mandatory and desirable characteristics for what it accepts as open standards.[29] Among the mandatory requirements are those accepted by other governments, such as the documentation being freely (or with a nominal fee) available and the intellectual property royalty-free. India also borrowed from Denmark and South Africa, mandating the standards be "maintained by a not-for-profit organization" in which "all stakeholders can opt to participate in a transparent, collaborative and consensual manner." The standards must also be "recursively open as far as possible," which seems to mirror New Zealand and Denmark's 2004 definition that a standard owner may not limit access at a later date. Finally, India also included two unique requirements: that the standard have "technology-neutral specification" and "be capable of localization support, where applicable, for all Indian official Languages for all applicable domains."

Desirable characteristics of open standards, according to the Indian government, would be used to whittle down between different standards that met all of the required characteristics but only one could be chosen for governmental purposes. In this case, India desired that: (1) the standard have "multiple implementations from different agencies"; (2) the standard be "widely used in India for which technical expertise and support exists in India"; and (3) the standard "has Extensions and / or Subsets meeting [the] mandatory characteristics."

India also allowed for a scenario where no standard meets every mandatory requirement, and so included a list of characteristics that would be relaxed in order to have an acceptable standard, listed in order. The first would allow the intellectual property owner to license under RAND/FRAND conditions but without a royalty payment. Next, the requirement for a not-for-profit organization adopting and maintaining the standard would be relaxed. Third, the government would allow for royalty payments on a RAND/FRAND basis. Finally, it would allow for other characteristics in general to be relaxed on a case-by-case basis.

The United Kingdom added its own unique definition of open standards in 2012. While supporting certain requirements also adopted by other governments – publicly available specifications, public participation in development of the standard, royalty-free licensing, no renunciation of intellectual property, and that the standard is adopted by an SSO – the UK also included two other requirements.[30] It joined Texas in being the only governments scrutinized here to require that no entity controls the standard, or that it is "independent of any individual

---

[28] New Zealand 2008.
[29] India 2010.
[30] GUK 2012.

supplier." It also added a new requirement of "Market Support," which says that "other than in the context of creating innovative solutions, the standard is mature, supported by the market and demonstrates platform, application and vendor independence." This definition remained consistent through 2015.[31]

Although governments differ on the exact specifications of what makes up an open standard, they usually agree on most of the key points. Each government takes into account what works best with their specific case and uses their judgment to determine what requirements best suit their populace. There is perhaps no perfect definition of open standards, but through these definitions we can see the running themes and what are seen as the most important pieces of what we consider to be open standards.

B. PROBLEMS IN DEFINITIONAL ATTEMPTS

Tsilas has found that many of these governmental definitional attempts above presented problems to the open standards community.[32] One of the main problems, Tsilas observed, was that these definitions of open standards were not made in a way that looked for the most efficient and economical outcomes for each government. Instead, these definitions represented "a desire, largely by proponents of 'open source software' (OSS) such as Linux, to remove patents, royalties, and licensing restrictions from standards implementations ... so as to avoid incompatibilities with RAND licensing created by certain OSS licenses." This may explain why royalty-free intellectual property is such a popular feature among governmental definitions – i.e. Texas, Minnesota, Denmark, South Africa, New Zealand, and India[33] – but a RAND/FRAND royalty structure is more popular among scholars,[34] and a royalty-free structure is usually seen as an alternative.[35] In addition, "it is inconsistent with the approach taken in the IPR [Intellectual Property Rights] policies of leading open standards organizations worldwide which expressly acknowledge the right of patent holders to charge reasonable royalties."[36] Many SSOs, including the "ITU, W3C, IETF, and the WiFi Alliance, among many others, make clear that such terms are acceptable RAND provisions."[37]

While we may hope that state governments would choose the most efficient and effective definitions to further their objectives of using open standards, one cannot discount the effect that outside stakeholders and interested parties may lobby a governmental body in order to change the definition to their liking. By requiring royalty-free licensing, governments may actually "deter key patent holders from participating in and contributing to the standards development process" which "would deprive such standards of the best technical solutions and would allow the key patent holders (who would not be subject to the organization's IPR policies) either to refuse to license their essential technology or to impose unreasonable terms and conditions on implementers of the standard."[38]

In a similar vein, only a few governments required public participation in the development of a standard (i.e. Massachusetts,[39] South Africa,[40] India[41]). By not requiring participation open

---

[31] GUK 2015.
[32] Tsilas 2005.
[33] S.B. 1579 (Tex. 2003); H.F. 3971 (Minn. 2006); OECD 2010; South Africa 2007; New Zealand 2008; India 2010.
[34] Shah & Kesan 2007; Contreras 2019.
[35] DeNardis 2008/2009; Werbach 2009; An 2009; Heiner 2011.
[36] Tsilas 2005.
[37] Id.
[38] Id.
[39] Shah et al. 2007.
[40] South Africa 2007.
[41] India 2010.

to all interested parties, governments could allow standards made by private parties, such as Microsoft's OOXML, which appear to meet most (if not all) other requirements for an open standard, but interoperability between other implementations outside of Microsoft products is lacking.[42] This also runs contrary to nearly every definition given by scholars and experts on the subject, as noted above.

C. GOVERNMENT POLICIES FOR ADOPTING OPEN STANDARDS

In 2003, Massachusetts became the first U.S. state government to openly consider adopting an open standards policy. Eric Kriss, the Secretary of Finance and Administration, "released a memo to Chief Information Officers (CIOs) of Massachusetts's state agencies that advised them of a summary of a plan to move toward increased use of open standards in the state's information technology (IT) systems."[43] The following year, a policy brief was released whereby the Massachusetts Information Technology Division (ITD) "rationalized the new position by explaining that it wanted to prevent vendor lock-in, keep maintenance and acquisition costs down, and gain the ability to switch to differing software suites without having to concern itself with cumbersome switch-over costs resulting from proprietary issues."[44]

The move started promisingly, as the ITD "engaged with all stakeholders, including major proprietary software companies, and weighed the interests of industry, the administration, and the citizens of Massachusetts."[45] Later in 2005, the ITD "released a draft of a policy initiative" in August and then amended it in September, resulting in the requirement that "all documents saved after January 1, 2007 to meet the Adobe PDF file or the Open Document Format (ODF) standard."[46] By specifying the exact standards the state would find acceptable, Massachusetts became "the only state to specify a file format for state records."[47] The argument for the move was backed by reports of saving money in long-term projections as well as keeping government electronic documents viable for decades into the future as they could be opened by various implementations based around the adopted open standard.[48]

The state soon became a battleground between different corporate lobbies, with Sun Microsystems (which played a large part in the development of the ODF standard, which was based upon Sun's XML file format),[49] IBM, and Novell supporting the move to the ODF standard while Microsoft opposed. Two members of the Massachusetts administration resigned soon afterwards – one directly attributable to the open standards conflict – both of whom supported the move to the ODF format.[50] Within the next two months, Microsoft released OOXML and submitted it to two SSOs for approval, intending for it to replace ODF in the open standards battle.

The move to an ODF standard was dealt a major blow in 2006, when the realities of the situation became fully known. While the ODF standard had potential benefits for the state, "disability advocates publicly voiced strong concerns over the planned switch away from Microsoft

---

[42] Shah & Kesan 2012.
[43] Shah et al. 2007.
[44] Commonwealth of Massachusetts 2004.
[45] Ghosh & Schmidt 2006.
[46] Shah et al. 2007.
[47] Peterson 2007.
[48] Shah et al. 2007.
[49] OASIS 2006.
[50] Shah et al. 2007.

Office to an ODF compliant office suite." Microsoft Office had features that aided disabled state workers in doing their jobs on computers, and "[d]isabled workers depend[ed] on extra technologies, such as dictation applications and readers that convert text into Braille for the blind."[51]

Despite the pushback, Massachusetts Governor Mitt Romney remained supportive of the plan, but the state did announce "that third-party plug-in software which allowed Microsoft Office users to open and save files in the ODF format would meet the state's January 1, 2007 deadline for using open standard electronic document formats."[52] Microsoft seemingly accepted this concession and "announc[ed] on July 6 that it would completely conform to the ODF standard."[53] It was at this time that the international community saw the Massachusetts scenario as a success. Ghosh and Schmidt saw it so positively they wrote: "[t]he example of shows that open source software and open standards are not solutions primarily for developing countries. Open standards have now been endorsed by one of the richest and most advanced states of the richest country in the world."[54]

However, the January 1, 2007 deadline passed without full implementation of the open standard. Instead, in July of that year, "Massachusetts released a draft of a new policy that would support Microsoft's Office Open XML (OOXML) as a document format for the government's agencies."[55] This sudden change in policy "infuriated ODF supporters, pleased backers of OOXML and left unclear the question of whether state governments are the right environment for settling these kinds of arguments." Due to the backlash against the state's actions and the hardships it took against the politicians and administrative members involved, "most CIOs have steered clear of the controversy."

Massachusetts, despite its promising start in the move to open standards, "never made the full switch to ODF or OOXML."[56] In fact, so little was done in the way of converting files to meet the open standards that as of January 2008, Shah and Kesan "identified 17,300 DOC files [the default file type for Microsoft Word], 31 ODT files based on ODF, and no DOC files based on OOXML."[57]

Massachusetts's journey, thought it ended without true implementation of an open standards policy, went much further than any other state government. Following Massachusetts's initial success, a Minnesota representative "introduced an open-formats bill in early 2006, but the bill didn't get passed out of committee."[58] The following year, the bill passed through the committee, but after merging with a similar bill from the Minnesota Senate, the "open-format 'bill' that emerged from the legislative process was a much-thinned version of the original." By the time the bill passed as part of a larger budget bill, all that it allowed for open standards was to provide that "the CIO, in consultation with the state archivist and legislative reference librarian, 'shall study how electronic documents and the mechanisms and processes for accessing and reading electronic data can be created, maintained, exchanged and preserved by the state in a manner that encourages appropriate government control, access, choice and interoperability.'"[59]

Texas also sent a bill mandating open standards in 2007, but it "lacked sufficient votes to make it out of committee and proceed to a vote on the House floor." The next time the bill came up

[51] Id.
[52] Id.
[53] Id.
[54] Ghosh & Schmidt 2006.
[55] Peterson 2007.
[56] Shah & Kesan 2009.
[57] Id.
[58] Peterson 2007.
[59] Minnesota 2007.

before the Texas legislature was in the 2009–2010 legislative session before the Senate, where it "died in chamber" as well.[60]

While Denmark released a definition of open standards in 2004, Brazil became one of the first governments to push toward open standards in the international community.[61] Beginning in 2005, the Brazilian government "has published an evolving set of interoperability standards for electronic government known as the e-PING program, which 'address technical, semantic, and organizational issues, as well promote open standards and public or free software.'"[62] The program "issued an interoperability policy establishing the adoption of open standards for technology used within the executive branch of the federal government."[63] It was also somewhat narrow in scope, and "is limited to internal government communications and information exchanges with citizens and specifically states that the policies cannot be imposed upon the private sector, citizens, or on government agencies outside of the federal government."

South Africa released its plan to adopt open standards in its Handbook on Minimum Information Interoperability Standards (MIOS).[64] While also giving their own definition of open standards (discussed above), it gave the main goal of the program to "adopt the Internet and World Wide Web standards for all government systems" and "adopt Extensible Markup Language (XML) and Extensible Stylesheet Language (XSL) as the core standard for Data interoperability and management of presentational data." This goal, which was admitted to be long-term, was done for the stated reasons of "reduc[ing] cost and risk for government systems whilst aligning them to the global information society revolution."[65]

The Standardization Administration of the People's Republic of China (SAC) released its country's interoperability plan in 2009. The SAC "proposed standardization interoperability rules (interim draft regulations) governing the disposition of patents involved in the development or revision of both compulsory and voluntary national standards."[66] However, this plan was much stricter regarding the intellectual property rights of patent holders for the standards used. According to the rules presented:

> only patented technology that is "essential" to the implementation of a voluntary national standard may be incorporated into its development. Once deemed "essential," a patented technology may be included in a voluntary national standard only if the patentee chooses to license on a free-of-charge, reasonable and nondiscriminatory basis or on a reasonable and nondiscriminatory basis at a price significantly lower than the normal royalties.

In the case of a "compulsory national standard" having to use a patent:

> the patentee shall grant a license free of charge [i.e., royalty-free] or shall enter into licensing negotiations with the appropriate administrative authorities. If the patentee and the authorities fail to enter into a mutually agreeable licensing arrangement, the compulsory national standard's release will be temporarily withheld or the patent will fall subject to a compulsory license by force of law."[67]

---

[60] Texas 2009.
[61] Kogan 2011.
[62] Id.
[63] DeNardis 2008/2009.
[64] South Africa 2007.
[65] Id.
[66] Kogan 2011.
[67] Id.

Following the release of the plan, the U.S. International Trade Commission announced that the plan was "in conflict with those followed by standards developing organizations in other countries."[68]

In 2010, Russia also joined the growing international community when "Prime Minister Vladimir Putin signed an executive order setting forth specific guidelines that mandate the complete transition from proprietary to free software by all Russian federal executive bodies and agencies during 2011–2015."

India began its journey toward using open standards in 2008, when it released a new draft policy that aimed to:

> promote interoperability among the technologies used by multiple agencies within the Indian government; to provide greater technological choices; to ensure that public documents are accessible in the long term; to promote local innovation and entrepreneurship; and to minimize the potential for the government to become locked into using a single vendor for critical public services.[69]

By late 2010, the policy was finalized. The Indian government was very careful with their implementation of open standards, noting that "Europe's equivalent European Interoperability Framework had been hijacked by rights holders."[70] Afraid that allowing royalties would give rights-holders too much power, India "joined Brazil in becoming the second country in the developing world to mandate 'open' royalty-free, and effectively, proprietary-free standards in e-governance."

Smaller countries also produced similar results to the larger players on the world stage. For instance, Malaysia put out its Malaysian Government Interoperability Framework for Open Source Software (MyGIFOSS) in 2006 "as a supplement to the Malaysian Government Interoperability Framework version 1.0 (MyGIF), August 2003" in order to, in part, address "compliance to published open standards where applicable."[71] Three of the five main objectives of the MyGIFOSS related to open standards, including "[t]o promote and foster the adoption of open standards that enables the exchange of data between applications," "[t]o promote vendor-neutral and technology-neutral implementations, with the adoption of open standards, for all Government information systems," and "[t]o reduce the total cost of ownership of Government information systems, with the adoption of open standards." In the conclusion to the document, the Malaysian government also included a note that "the importance of open standards have been repeatedly emphasised, simply because the adherence to these standards, do more than any other measures that can be taken to ensure interoperability."[72]

Various countries around the world addressed using open standards during this time, each in their own unique and individuals ways, responding to their own needs and what policies were the most effective in previously enacted policies that they could learn from. Due to each country's relative technological advancement and political structure, no singular standards policy would work for all in the international community; rather, each had to find their own way to enact such a policy to encourage meeting their own stated objectives. For a full list of governmental open source policies, which includes open standards – although "[w]hile there is general consensus that 'open' standards are best … there is less consensus on what qualifies as open."[73]

[68] Id.
[69] India 2008.
[70] Kogan 2011.
[71] Malaysia 2006.
[72] Id.
[73] See Lewis 2010.

D. VENDOR LOCK-IN

One of the most-cited objectives in adopting open standards is the avoidance of vendor lock-in. Lock-in generally "refers to a situation in which economic agents' equilibrium decisions regarding standards adoption yield lower social welfare than an alternative."[74] Alternatively, lock-in has been defined as any time when the market cannot be corrected to accept a more efficient technology because the more inefficient technology has been in use for long enough that switching to the more efficient technology is not economically feasible, even with a government subsidy.[75] Simply, keeping with the status quo regarding a technology is actually less efficient than it would be to adopt other alternatives. There is perhaps no more well-known example of vendor lock-in than the QWERTY keyboard.

The QWERTY style keyboard is used for most (if not all) Latin languages, originally invented for typewriters to slow typing and thereby prevent jamming of keys.[76] However, after the advent of the computer, key jamming was no longer an issue, and "the argument is that superior alternatives to the QWERTY design exist in terms of learning costs and ultimate typing speed, and that the costs of switching are vastly outweighed by the benefits. This implies that the market is locked in to an inferior standard."[77] However, consumers are used to the QWERTY keyboard design and would undoubtedly resist a change despite any purported benefits to efficiency, so the market is locked-in to this particular keyboard.

The effect of vendor lock-in on software is much like that of hardware in the QWERTY example. In the case of software:

> if the provider of software that accounts for the major part of the market has the exclusive right to use technologies especially related to interoperability and interfaces (and even more so if these technologies have been standardized), factors such as economies of scale and high cost of migration to another platform tend to result in a long-lasting monopolistic market and generate adverse effects on innovation because of inhibited competition.[78]

By adopting open standards, the hope is that vendor lock-in can be avoided. Contemporary lock-in may occur through "the artificial acquisition of monopoly power."[79] However, "[w]hen standards are open and freely available, it becomes possible for anyone to develop an interoperable implementation. This reduces the ability of vendors to tie a standard to the purchase of other products."[80] Opening up the market "facilitates multiple interoperable implementations, thus providing users with choice. Choice typically brings with it lower costs and technological variation."[81]

In modern technological practice, governments are mostly attempting to avoid the use of proprietary systems that they would then be forced to use for years in order to continue accessing older electronic files. When Massachusetts established its open standards policy, "it was made clear that the greatest incentive for the change was overcoming vendor lock-in."[82] In Massachusetts's case, they were attempting to avoid being perpetually tied to Microsoft's

---

[74] Stango 2004.
[75] Arthur 1989.
[76] David 1985.
[77] Stango 2004.
[78] Commerce and Information Policy Bureau 2005 (Japan).
[79] Devlin 2009.
[80] Shah & Kesan 2009.
[81] Id.
[82] Shah et al. 2007.

products by using open standards. Therefore, "[t]he fact that Microsoft initially came out in vigorous opposition to Massachusetts's policy should not come as a surprise as past research has shown that vendors lean towards closed control of standards when they maintain a disproportionate share of the market."[83] By moving to a system that uses open standards, government files and documents could be saved in a format where it would not matter what implementation is being used to open, view, and edit the files, as opposed to having to use proprietary software in order to access certain files.

E. OPEN STANDARDS AND TECHNICAL INTEROPERABILITY

Interoperability, like many of the terms discussed in this chapter, can have many different definitions attached to it. For the most part, interoperability can be seen as "the ability to transfer and render useful data and other information across systems ... applications, or components"[84] or the "[a]bility of people, organizations, and systems to interact and interconnect so as to efficiently and effectively exchange and use information."[85] The Institute of Electrical and Electronics Engineers attempted a more formal definition of "the ability of two or more systems or components to exchange information and to use the information that has been exchanged."[86]

Interoperability is a concept as old as man. In order to communicate, "[t]here must always be agreement between the sender of information and the receiver as to protocol (including social concepts such as cooperation), semantics, and even the technology relied upon such as drums, voice, or digital telephony to achieve communication."[87] When translated to the world of technology, the concept becomes known as technical interoperability. Technical interoperability standards are "are sets of protocols and design parameters that enable products manufactured by different vendors to work together with minimal user intervention."[88] Technical interoperability is desirable because "interoperability 'enhances variety by allowing consumers to mix and match (differentiated) components from various systems,' which is a necessary (albeit not sufficient) precondition for flexible personal use of content."[89]

Historically, vendors tried to avoid technical interoperability in order to get users locked-in using that particular vendor's products.[90] As Baird explains, "information silos [IT systems with no ability to interoperate] may occur by design as an aspect of segregation of divisions within an enterprise, computing silos came about primarily because of the structure of the computer industry at the time the systems we now describe as 'legacy' were built." However, the industry evolved to the point where technical interoperability became more desirable, so those companies began evolving with it and provided products able to work and communicate with each other. It was not always the entrenched vendors who favored interoperability, however. Instead, even "'[a]n entrant who has a superior technology may be the one that opposes compatibility,' as it will be interested in breaking the incumbent's hold and benefit from the network market."[91]

The technology industries found that the "'closed innovation' model, i.e., all research and development occurred within the walls of a company and was commercialized and supported

---

[83] Id.
[84] Melendez-Juarbe 2009.
[85] Baird 2009.
[86] IEEE 1990.
[87] Baird 2009.
[88] Contreras 2019.
[89] Melendez-Juarbe 2009.
[90] Baird 2009.
[91] Melendez-Juarbe 2009.

exclusively by that company," was not the best way to go about business.[92] Instead, they began using open innovation, whereby "companies should use outside ideas as well as internal research, and should use external avenues to the market to both advance their own technologies and maximize value from internal research." Baird identifies five common industry approaches "used by industry to achieve technical interoperability, particularly in the modern fields of electronics and computing." Among these approaches is:

> 4. Technical standards, whether formal (i.e., adopted for standardization by a Standards Development Organization ("SDO") such as the International Standards Organization), established by consortiums (industry groups that organize to develop a technology), or adopted by users as de facto; this category includes both "open standards," i.e., those submitted to a SDO for adoption, and broadly accessible proprietary technologies, i.e., those developed by a company or group of companies, and although not submitted for formal adoption as a standard, have been very widely implemented.[93]

As industries evolved on interoperability, so did governments around the world. Since "[n]early any business or government can now have a global reach. This drives a need for greater interoperability between the services and products across national borders." This kind of growth of interoperability systems results in what can be called an "interoperability ecosystem." When efficient, this ecosystem can aid governments by "result[ing] in more efficient service to citizens in almost all areas of government service, including better healthcare, education, economic development opportunities, emergency services, and national defense."[94]

As addressed above, interoperability is one of the main draws of adopting an open standards policy. In addition to avoiding vendor lock-in, "[s]ome governments are concerned about the transparency ensured by free information flow between governments and citizens due to the interoperability of IT systems."[95] To address this concern, "the Netherlands and Denmark have mandated an open standards policy in public information systems to ensure interoperability for public IT systems at reasonably low costs."[96]

Interoperability and open standards also intersect in the area of patents. SSOs generally hold the view that the effect of patents regarding interoperability should be limited in order to have the maximum public benefit allowable. Free Software Foundation Europe "has insisted that because 'both patents and standards derive their justification from the public benefit' and '[the] upholding [of] one deprives the other of its function,' 'patents which limit or prevent interoperability should be [rendered legally] unenforceable.'"[97] The European Committee for Interoperable Systems endorsed a similar view looking toward the largest public benefit possible and "ensur[ing] against 'overbroad patent protection that frustrates interoperability in the ICT sector'" meaning that "patents cannot be used as a means of confining users to a particular technology by closing off full interoperability."[98]

Shah and Kesan attempted to test the leading open standards of word processing files (ODF and OOXML) against Microsoft's DOC file format in terms of operability in different implementations.[99] The formats were scored on how well different implementations could

[92] Baird 2009.
[93] Id.
[94] Id.
[95] An 2009.
[96] Id.
[97] Kogan 2011.
[98] ECIS 2012.
[99] Shah & Kesan 2012.

"read the test documents," "how well they can read and then write documents," and how well they preserved the metadata of the document. For the ODF file, only OpenOffice.org (the system it was designed from) was 100 percent across the board. Five other implementations, including Microsoft Word 2007 and StarOffice, earned above 90 percent in every category, while another six implementations fell lower. For OOXML, only Office 2007 was able to hit 100 percent in every category (Office 2008 on Mac was 99 percent in read only but 100 percent elsewhere). Only OpenOffice.org was above 90 percent in every category and the other five implementations tested were either below 90 percent or did not have the capability to write OOXML documents. The DOC file worked similarly to OOXML, except that the programs which could not write OOXML could write DOC files, resulting in more implementations tested being able to use the proprietary DOC format rather than the open standard-based OOXML format. This study shows that "[t]he lack of independent implementations that can offer good performance is troubling," and work needs to be done in the area.

Technical interoperability is one of the key features that open standards offers for governmental entities willing to adopt such a scheme. Coupled with avoiding vendor lock-in and avoiding being forced to use one implementation in order to access files, government systems can work together via interoperability, creating a much more efficient system. However, the current state of interoperability between leading formats may leave much to be desired and work to be done before governments begin to see the full benefit of adopting open standards.

F. MULTIPLE IMPLEMENTATIONS AND RUNNING CODE

Adopting open standards can bring about a benefit to governments who choose to do so; and one of the main reasons such a scheme is adopted is to cut costs (i.e. South Africa's 2010 adoption would "serve[] as a basis for reducing the costs and risks associated with carrying out major IT projects").[100] However, to ensure the full benefits of open standards are achieved, governments should ensure that there are multiple implementations capable of using the open standard, as to not fall into the same situation as using a proprietary format. Whereas a proprietary format can likely only be used by one implementation with the same owner as the format itself, if an "open" standard only has one implementation that can use the standard, despite its openness, no real benefit can be gained. The need for multiple implementations is called running code.

Running code has been defined as "multiple actual and interoperable implementations of a proposed standard must exist and be demonstrated before the proposal can be advanced along the standards track."[101] The concept came about in the 1990s, when the Internet Engineering Task Force (IETF) "require[d] that a standard be implemented by two independent vendors before it can be considered an open standard."[102] That view was not adopted by the International Organization for Standardization or World Wide Web Consortium, who were concerned "that an emphasis on running code may influence how a standard develops."

Shah and Kesan see the requirement of running code as necessary.[103] For example, had Massachusetts lawmakers adopted a requirement for running code during their attempt to adopt an open standards policy, it "would have led Massachusetts to defer adopting ODF." Instead of requiring the state to conform to ODF standards by a set date, the state would have instead

---

[100] Satyanarayana 2004.
[101] Russell 2006.
[102] Shah & Kesan 2009; Bradner 1996.
[103] Shah & Kesan 2009.

waited until multiple implementations could support the format. While no perfect interoperable implementation existed years later for ODF,[104] multiple implementations received nearly 100 percent scores in that study. While the Massachusetts policy ultimately failed, "[t]he open formats policy was critical in influencing Microsoft's decision to make its OOXML standard an open standard and to support ODF."[105]

While most governments have not included a running code requirement in their definitions for open standards, the United Kingdom is an outlier. As an update to its requirement for open standards to have "market support,"[106] the UK government announced its "criteria for compulsory open standards in government IT is based on the European Common Assessment Method for Standards and Specifications."[107] Included in those "core questions that are considered by a challenge owner when assessing standards in proposals" for market support includes: "Has the formal specification been used for different implementations by different vendors/suppliers?"[108] This would appear to indicate that the British government is looking as part of one of its requirements for an open standard at running code, as that would satisfy this question (among several) for the market support requirement.

Most governments and many SSOs have not made running code a requirement for open standards. However, running code has the capability of providing a larger safety net for governments, ensuring that they are not beholden to a single implementation for a format/standard which otherwise meets all other requirements of an open standard.

---

[104] Shah & Kesan 2012.
[105] Shah & Kesan 2009.
[106] GUK 2012.
[107] GUK 2015.
[108] GUK 2014.

10

Standardization, Open Source and Innovation: Sketching the Effect of IPR Policies

*Martin Husovec**

A.	Two Ecosystems	178
	1. Standardization	179
	2. Open Source	181
	3. Comparison	184
B.	Interactions	185
	1. From Specification to Implementation	186
	2. From Implementation to Specification	186
	3. Co-Development of Specification and Implementation	187
C.	Frictions Among IPR Rules	188
	1. Scenario by Scenario	188
	2. Legal Incompatibility	190
	3. Business Inconsistencies	192
D.	Innovation Ecosystem	193

Open Source and standardization can be described as two "stewards of innovation."[1] Although practically two different ecosystems with diverging sets of rules and objectives, they, however, meet in their purpose to push the frontier of innovation. The latest technological developments are increasingly incentivizing firms and individuals participating in these ecosystems to work more closely together. However, under whose rules? And with what consequences for the innovation ecosystem? In this contribution, I try to sketch answers to these and related questions.

Firms engaging in research activities routinely face a choice between opening up of parts of their R&D efforts by contributing it to the building blocks of the industry, or preserving market exclusivity. The trade-off is that while exclusivity might mean higher rents, it also means lower diffusion. Sharing, on the other hand, might mean lower rents, but higher diffusion. But even within technological sharing, there are a number of ways that such choices can be made. Committing parts of technology to standardization represents the most typical and usually less intensive way of opening up. It means losing exclusivity, but preserving IP rights (mostly patents) and potential royalties. But potential royalties are of little use if markets do not adopt

---

* The author thanks the following for their invaluable comments on earlier drafts of this chapter: Mirko Boehm, Jorge Contreras, Carlo Piana, Mark Schankerman, McCoy Smith and the attendees of TILEC weekly seminars.
[1] Kappos 2017.

technology. Therefore, firms naturally also explore new and more intensive ways of defining the shared building blocks of their new products which might further accelerate the process of entry to the market. Open Source offers such an alternative. Depending on the project rules, it may, however, limit the appropriation strategies of firms much more severely than standardization.

Open Source deals with software products and standardization with basic specifications on which those products are based. They are not the same. Conventional description of their interaction would be that firms cooperate on specifications through standardization, thus creating a common level-playing field, and then compete on the product implementations.[2] Only when they wish to deepen their involvement, they *additionally* invest in co-development of such implementations through Open Source projects. So why then compare the two, since they seem to produce something very different?

The argument put forward in this chapter is that the conventional roles assigned to the implementation/specification phase are becoming increasingly blurred. Open Source and standardization activities represent only different ways how to express *technological choices*. Through a set of concrete examples, I will try to convince the reader that Open Source and standardization are in a growing number of cases less separated than one would expect. The activities taking place between two ecosystems will be conceptualized in three scenarios usually used in the literature: (1) from specifications to implementation; (2) from implementation to specification; and (3) parallel co-development of specifications and implementations. Depending on the scenario, the standard and Open Source production can be said to play complementary, overlapping or even identical roles.[3] It is argued that these dynamics, more than anything else, influence also the types of tensions or misunderstandings that arise, in particular in the area of intellectual property rights. From the perspective of the future innovation ecosystem in the ICT, parallel co-development of specifications and implementations is likely to represent a profound change in the innovation production ecosystem. Since such co-production can be influenced by policy choices of organizations involved, we discuss these along with potential trade-offs that are associated with them.

A. TWO ECOSYSTEMS

The driving force behind convergence of Open Source and standardization activities is a simple one. Ever more technological choices are embodied in the software instead of hardware. In the area of networking technologies, for instance, a big part of development today happens in the Open Source projects.[4] Virtual private networks turn the entire classes of network node functions into digital building blocks that may connect, or chain together, to create communication services. This allows firms to substitute custom hardware appliances by software development. As a consequence, we observe that different types of innovations resulting from distinct types of open processes are embedded together in the overall ecosystem.

---

[2] In the recent OMA Survey, from 419 respondents, 70 percent were of the view that open standards play "an entirely different" role than Open Source; only 10 percent of participants disagreed and the remaining 20 percent were "neutral" toward the claim (OMA SpecWorks 2016).
[3] *See also* Eisape et al. (forthcoming).
[4] *See* IETF 2016.

1. Standardization

In the area of ICT, standardization is a process of specification of the technical design features, which mostly allow different products of multiple vendors to work together. The traditional view has been that standards and firm innovation are in conflict.[5] Therefore network externalities, efficiency in the supply chains, economies of scale or the reduction of transaction costs would be cited as more obvious economic benefits.[6] However, increasingly, the catalyst role of standards is getting more attention.[7] This is because in many modern industries, standardization is becoming an essential prerequisite for the *diffusion* of innovative technology.[8] In the literature,[9] it is recognized that standardization can help to: (a) build a focus, cohesion and critical mass of firms to launch an emerging technology;[10] (b) act as an effective technology transfer,[11] including by facilitating licensing of patent rights;[12] and (c) spur innovation by enabling compatibility and competition within and between technologies.[13] Among these, coordination is viewed as the main feature in the area of ICT.[14]

Nowadays, it seems equally relevant to emphasize their role as *platforms for open innovation*[15] because besides selection and codification of knowledge in standards, an important "exchange of tacit knowledge takes place during the standardization process."[16] This dimension is not merely theoretical, as exchange of knowledge seems to attract firms to standardization process itself.[17] Hence, arguably, standards facilitate all the stages of the innovation process: search for innovations, their coordination, codification and subsequent diffusion. The projects like 3GPP are a good example of this.[18]

The European Commission distinguishes three categories of standards development organizations (SDOs): (1) those that are formally recognized by governments (e.g. ISO, IEC, ITU, ETSI); (2) "quasi-formal" groups that are typically large and well-organized and share many of the characteristics of the first group, but lack official governmental recognition (e.g. IEEE, IETF, W3C); and (3) smaller, privately organized consortia.[19] The governance structure of these SDOs differs significantly because, among other things, they are subject to different external legal constrains. Although formal membership can be sometimes restricted, participation in the technical committees is usually open to all interested parties. In SDOs, standards are developed in the technical committees which adopt them by a consensus. The resulting documents then have to be subsequently approved by further organs of the SDO, e.g. its membership, director or board of directors. The process of drafting standards in the technical committees is guided and regulated by a number of SDO policies. The rules on intellectual property rights (IPR) are among the most crucial policies.

---

[5] Blind 2009.
[6] Swann 2000.
[7] Blind 2006; Blind 2009; Choi et al. 2011.
[8] Baron & Schmidt 2017.
[9] Blind 2017.
[10] Choi et al. 2011; Featherston et al. 2016.
[11] Choi et al. 2011; Narayanan & Chen 2012.
[12] Bekkers et al. 2016.
[13] Cabral & Salant 2014; Baron et al. 2016; Blind & Mangelsdorf 2016.
[14] Foray & Lundvall 1998; Egyedi 2000a.
[15] Chesbrough 2003. This paradigm of standardization has yet to attract more research. Blind 2017.
[16] Blind 2006; Blind 2009.
[17] Blind & Mangelsdorf 2006.
[18] Lopez-Berzosa & Gawer 2014.
[19] European Commission 2014. (This report was prepared by third parties for the European Commission. The information presented therein does not necessarily reflect the official opinion of the European Commission.)

Specifications resulting from the standardization process are described in standardization documents which are usually copyright protected.[20] Some SDOs charge for access to the standardization documents in order to support their work (e.g. ISO, national SDOs, IEEE). The copyright policies are becoming much more important in the area of software standards, such as those developed by IETF, OASIS or W3C, because the code is becoming a way to formulate specifications themselves. As a response, some SDOs adopted also more explicit copyright licensing policies for software specifications (e.g. ETSI,[21] OASIS,[22] IETF,[23] or W3C[24]). In the SDOs where no explicit policies exist for software specifications (e.g. IEEE), the usual rules regarding specifications arguably apply.[25]

To facilitate the diffusion of technologies and to prevent patent hold-up, SDOs adopt policies which regulate situations when standards include patent rights of its participants. The patent policies usually require disclosure of standard-essential patents and specify basic terms for their availability to other market players. Depending on the industry, the presence of patented technologies can be significant. Incorporating patented technology in the standards allows the patent holders to capitalize on the value of their inventions through licensing, while they are contributing the underlying technology to the common building blocks. At the same time, it creates additional cost in the diffusion phase of standards. Some SDOs try to prevent this by formulating a preference against inclusion of patented technology or by requiring royalty-free licensing.

In the last two decades, many SDOs adopted rules requiring commitments to license standard essential patents (SEPs) on specified, most often FRAND terms (Baron and Spulber 2015). The exact meaning of such commitments was subject to extensive debate before the courts and in the literature.[26] They do not constitute a license, but only a type of pledge.[27]

To be sure, the concept of FRAND, like Open Source, is better viewed as a category or a range, rather than a single, defined entity. The exact wording, and thus definitions and permissions, may differ from SDO to SDO, though the variability is usually less significant as in cases of different Open Source licenses. The most widely adopted wording of FRAND commitment is a "Common Patent Policy for ITU-T/ITU-R/ISO/IEC."[28] This FRAND commitment only obliges the patent holder to be willing to negotiate licenses "with other parties on a non-discriminatory basis on reasonable terms and conditions," including an option to declare willingness to engage in royalty-free licensing if it wishes.[29] Such negotiations then take place outside of an SDO. Some SDOs specify additional features of such commitment, such as define how royalties should be calculated (IEEE)[30] or ask SEP owners to specify their maximum future fees or royalties and the most restrictive license terms for licenses (VITA).[31] Instead of simply requiring FRAND commitment from participants, some SDOs require royalty-free licensing (W3C)[32] or

---

[20] Hamburg Case No. 3 U 220/15 (2017) (standardization documents can be subject to copyright protection).
[21] See ETSI 2017a, sec. 9.
[22] See OASIS 2018a.
[23] See IETF 2015.
[24] See W3C 2015.
[25] Li 2017, 2.
[26] Bekkers & Updegrove 2012; NAS 2013; Pentheroudakis & Baron 2017.
[27] For more, see Contreras 2015.
[28] See ITU 2018.
[29] Id.
[30] See IEEE 2018.
[31] See VITA 2018.
[32] See W3C 2004a.

provide a broader choice of licensing options (OASIS).[33] IETF is one of the few SDOs that has no obligatory licensing commitment and relies only on an extensive disclosure policy.[34]

2. Open Source

Open Source is a prototype of open innovation. It allows unaffiliated firms or individuals to develop products in a collaborative process. Its popularity is best illustrated by the fact that all major technology firms are today involved in its production. According to one survey conducted back in 2008, 85 percent of companies use Open Source and the remaining 15 percent are expecting to use it in the next 12 months.[35] The software is so omnipresent that a Samsung representative recently exclaimed that: "[t]oday, you can't build a product without using Open Source."[36]

Although there are many definitions of Open Source, the most authoritative is one maintained by the Open Source Initiative (OSI), a private certification authority. Its definition is composed of ten criteria,[37] such as free distribution, availability of source code, freedom to carry out modifications and non-discrimination. As explained by Shane Curcuru, "OSI-approval is not a magic stamp; however it does show licenses that are so widely used – and reviewed by lawyers – that there is seen as less risk to everyone else in consuming software under an OSI license."[38] In order to gain an approval, each license is scrutinized against the set of ten criteria. In the context of co-existence with FRAND commitments, in particular the requirement of free distribution is without problems.

An Open Source license may not only differ in terms, but also in its coverage. We can observe three categories of licenses: (1) copyright-only licenses, where the scope of permissions is explicitly limited to copyrights (e.g. GNU Free Documentation License); (2) copyright and patent license (hybrid license), where the scope of permissions explicitly extends to both copyright and patents (e.g. Apache2, GPLv3); and (3) in between licenses (unclear licenses), where the copyright permissions are explicit, but patent grants are not articulated and thus subject to ongoing controversy (e.g. BSD, MIT, GPLv2).[39] One of the issues in the Open Source world is that it has to deal with a great proliferation of licenses. Only OSI certified 83 licenses to this day,[40] and there are many other licenses that don't qualify despite calling themselves "Open Source," or would qualify, but are not yet certified.

OSI-approved licenses generally do *not* seem to favor patent royalty-bearing licenses, but OSI's stance is not entirely consistent. Stakeholders often perceive OSI's stance as not certifying patent agnostic licenses. This would mean that all the certified licenses either have explicit or (assumed) implicit patent grant (e.g. BSD). At a closer look, it is less clear that they always do. This issue was hotly debated during the certification of CC0 license (2012), which clearly carved out patents,[41] and MXM license (2009),[42] which included very limited non-assertion pledge for non-commercial uses. Neither of the two licenses are certified. However, as was explained by

---

[33] *See* OASIS 2018b.
[34] *See* IETF 2017. For a discussion of the history of this approach, *see* Contreras 2016.
[35] Kempa 2009.
[36] *See* King 2014.
[37] *See* OSI 2018a.
[38] *See* Curcuru 2017.
[39] For more debate, *see* Haapanen 2015.
[40] *See* OSI 2018b.
[41] *See* OSI 2018c.
[42] *See* OSI. 2018d.

the OSI Board itself, "CC0 was not explicitly rejected, but the License Review Committee was unable to reach consensus that it should be approved, and Creative Commons eventually withdrew the application."[43] The most serious of the concerns were the explicit patent carve-outs. OSI explains this dilemma as follows: "While many open source licenses simply do not mention patents, it is exceedingly rare for open source licenses to explicitly disclaim any conveyance of patent rights, and the Committee felt that approving such a license would set a dangerous precedent, and possibly even weaken patent infringement defenses available to users of software released under CC0."[44] MXM was not certified either. Its example is even more interesting given that its context had directly to do with a formal standard. It originated from ISO/IEC 23006 MPEG eXtensible Middleware (MXM) standard and the license was intended to cover its future reference implementation. Stakeholders were, however, entirely clear, even in the license itself, that they want to collect patent royalties on patents covering the standard and its implementation by means of patent pools. Eventually, the implementation was released under BSD license.[45]

Non-certification of these two licenses would suggest consistency. In 2017, however, OSI certified W3C Software and Document License (2015),[46] despite appearing as copyright-only,[47] without any implicit patent permissions. The license was unanimously approved by the Board.[48] It seems that this certification was made under impression of W3C's (separate) royalty-free patent policy and the limited reach of the license.[49] Some would argue it would have normally been expected at OSI that newly certified licenses deal with patent rights, but this was less of a concern in this case. Therefore the situation is less clear-cut and only the future will tell whether OSI will maintain its critical stance toward copyright-only licenses.

The project licenses are crucial also for another reason. Apart from the governance structure, it is the main organizing principle of any Open Source project, which influences the entire surrounding ecosystem. In terms of governance, Open Source projects may be supported by a separate legal entity, but they don't have to be. For instance, the world's most famous project, Linux, was not hosted by any organization between 1991 and 2000. Today, it is supported by the Linux Foundation. Apart from The Linux Foundation, there are a few generalist organizations, such as the Apache Software Foundation or the Eclipse Foundation that host multiple projects by providing them with organizational, legal, and financial support. At the same time, we also observe a number of project-specific foundations, such as the Document Foundation hosting LibreOffice, Open Course Ware Consortium hosting Open Course Ware software, or OpenStack Foundation hosting Open Stack cloud operating system.

The default in the Open Source world is that individual developers or their employers retain their ownership of copyrights and patents. This means that ownership is decentralized through the project license. Licensor–licensee relationship is between developers and users, and there is no middle-man. This set-up empowers more original contributors of the project, but also creates

---

[43] See OSI. 2018c.
[44] Id.
[45] See MPEG 2018.
[46] At the time of writing, OSI was listing the old name of the same license ("Software Notice and License") on its website.
[47] The license does not explicitly deal with patents, but also does not explicitly limit the grants to copyright law, despite few references to the copyright holder.
[48] See OSI 2017c.
[49] See OSI 2017d.

a risk of decentralized enforcement, which can be misused.[50] Increasingly, however, foundations, where they exist, step in by centralizing copyright and patent permissions of its members. Such foundations then ask their contributors to sign contributory licensing agreements (CLAs) with them. For instance, Apache Software Foundation asks its contributors for a specified "a perpetual, worldwide, non-exclusive, no-charge, royalty-free, irrevocable" copyright and patent license.[51] This set-up allows the hosting organizations to re-license the project, if necessary, and more easily enforce the project's license. The downside of CLAs are transaction costs, potential antagonization of the community base of developers and potential abuse by foundations.[52]

Copyright / Patent	Patent royalty-free	Patent royalty-allowing		
	Explicit	If implicit	If not implicit	Explicit
Permissive copyright license	Apachev2; UPLv1; MPL-2.0; BSD-2-Clause-Patent;	BSD; MIT	BSD; MIT	BSD & patent carve-out
Copyleft copyright license	GPLv3	GPLv2	GPLv2	n/a

Apart from the patent grants included in the Open Source licenses, another important element are so-called *patent retaliation clauses*, which can be (a) weak or (b) strong. Patent retaliation clause is an in-built license mechanism, the purpose of which is to withdraw licensing authorizations toward potential licensees that assert their own patent rights against the licensor. The difference between weak and strong retaliation clauses is in their breath. While weak retaliation clauses are usually limited to patent licenses pertaining to the underlying software (e.g. GPLv2), strong clauses cover broader range of actions (e.g. Apache v2) or terminate even copyright permissions (e.g. MPL 2.0). The best example of such clause is a recent controversy around Facebook's React project which was licensed under BSD-3-Clause license text, which is OSI-approved, but accompanied by Facebook's own custom-written patent declaration. This declaration effectively meant that suing Facebook over patent rights, even if unrelated to the React project, would automatically revoke Facebook's own royalty-free patent grants to such plaintiff.[53] The controversy surrounding this clause was so strong that Facebook eventually decided to relicense the project under the MIT license after seeing an increase in the number of communities opting to not use the project's code.[54]

In contrast to Facebook's clause, according to the Apache v2 license, which also includes a stronger patent retaliation clause, each contributor grants royalty-free license to its patents

---

[50] *See, e.g.*, Meeker 2017 (a controversy surrounding enforcement by Patrick McHardy which triggered a response in the form of community enforcement guidelines: (1) The Principles of Community-Oriented GPL Enforcement (SFConservancy 2018); (2) Linux Kernel Community Enforcement Statement (Kroah-Harthman et al. 2017); (3) Statement of netfilter project on GPL enforcement (Netfilter 2016) and (4) unilateral common cure rights commitments by firms (Redhat 2017)).
[51] *See* Apache Software Foundation 2018.
[52] For discussion, *see* Kuhn 2014.
[53] See Github 2015. ("The license granted hereunder will terminate, automatically and without notice, if you (or any of your subsidiaries, corporate affiliates or agents) initiate directly or indirectly, or take a direct financial interest in, any Patent Assertion: (i) against Facebook or any of its subsidiaries or corporate affiliates, (ii) against any party if such Patent Assertion arises in whole or in part from any software, technology, product or service of Facebook or any of its subsidiaries or corporate affiliates, or (iii) against any party relating to the Software.")
[54] *See* Wolff 2017.

concerning the project. Moreover, its retaliation clause creates a defensive mechanism under which a trigger is pulled by a litigation instituted by any licensee against "*any* entity (...) alleging that the Work or a Contribution incorporated within the Work constitutes direct or contributory patent infringement."[55] Any patent licenses granted to such work will automatically terminate. The wording assures that any third-party patents against anyone over the project will be retaliated by termination of any inward patents licenses received. It also acts as a trigger deactivating the entire royalty-free patent "shield" over the project against such a firm. As a consequence, all the patent owners are free to enforce their patents against it.

In its effects, we witness reliance on a similar mechanism also as an add-on practice that accompanies Open Source licensing from the outside. Open Invention Network (OIN) is the most famous defensive patent pool which first obtains patents of its members and then licenses them to its members and the outside world for free under its OIN License Agreement.[56] The license includes a retaliation clause which automatically terminates granted *patent* permissions in case a licensee files a claim against any of its licensees "for making, having made, using, importing, or distributing any Linux System." In the enforcement realm, we can also observe defensive *copyright* strategies. For instance, older GPL licenses include automated termination of copyright permissions upon a single violation of the license.[57] This rather harsh defensive mechanism was later revised in the latest GPLv3 license, which includes a cure clause that reinstates the permission under some circumstances. Because earlier licenses are still in use and can potentially discourage use of the licensed software, the industry is slowing softening the mechanism by means of unilateral commitments that externally embed the cure period into them.[58]

3. Comparison

In a way, standards and Open Source projects are not comparable. While standards provide basic specifications which can support products commercialized via a multitude of business models, Open Source *is* a set of more limited business opportunities. The idea of standardization is to cooperate on the basic building blocks, and compete on their product implementation. Therefore while standards leave the choice of appropriation strategies wide open, Open Source licensing of implementations greatly limit them. While Open Source licenses that cover patents and copyrights significantly limit licensing-based business models, copyright-only licenses leave patent-licensing intact. That being said, the view of standardization as business model agnostic can be challenged if the SDO's IPR policy is more prescriptive. For instance, W3C's IPR policy requires royalty-free patent licensing.[59] The outcome is that appropriation strategies for standard-essential patents shrink, but are still left open for any non-essential specifications and product-related elements. In the end then, Open Source is more limiting for appropriation strategies not only because of its default IPR position, but also due to the fact that it covers also technology of non-essential specifications and product elements.

At the same time, Open Source and standards share some features. According to Douglas Heintzmann from IBM, "[t]he similarity [of Open Source] to open standards lies in the development-by-community approach, which makes the process visible to all interested

---

[55] Apache Software Foundation 2004 (emphasis added).
[56] *See* Open Invention Network 2012.
[57] *See* GNU 2017, sec. 4.
[58] *See* Levine 2018.
[59] *See* W3C 2004b.

parties."[60] The open way of production is, however, far from identical. Standards are adopted by SDOs after deliberations of participants in the technical committees which reach a *consensus*. Open Source projects, on the other hand, are usually administered by their maintainers. Some projects also pre-announce in their guidelines how a contribution is reviewed and what types of contributions are accepted.[61] The governance is often more informal and decentralized. It is driven more by meritocracy than a stakeholder consensus.[62] Different projects can rely on different governance models.[63] Consensus, for instance, can be built differently. Exit options, too, can differ. For instance, if community cannot agree on some contributions or the general trajectory, some members might decide to split the project and continue to develop it separately (so-called "fork"). This is different from standardization, where lack of consensus usually leads to no standard being produced. Although participants can try to change the forum to a different SDO and seek consensus in a narrower constituency, the costs of doing so once the project is ongoing might be prohibitive.

This leads to another important distinction. Versions of a standard are more stable than releases of Open Source projects. As explained by Lundell and others (2014), "releases of OSS occur at more or less arbitrary points in time. Standards, on the other hand, are by and large static, or perhaps semi-dynamic". Standards are valued exactly because they codify industry knowledge and provide firm reference points. Open Source is more volatile in this regard. As will be shown, however, this aspect can drive synergies between two ecosystems by providing means of pre-testing or showcasing standards. Egyedi points out that many SDOs neglect implementation issues and concludes that "[w]here interoperability is concerned, standard development and implementation issues cannot be meaningfully separated."[64] She therefore calls on SDOs in the area of ICT "to shift their emphasis from standard development to a more systematic inclusion of implementation concerns, both at the technical level of standard committees and at the policy level of standard organizations." Moreover, the exchange of working techniques can bring a new transparent way to improve the standardization process. For instance, Lundell and others show that the practice of tracking is a governance feature from the Open Source world that was adopted by SDOs such as W3C, IETF, and OASIS.[65] The ecosystems therefore undoubtedly borrow from each other, but their make-up remains distinct.

B. INTERACTIONS

The previous discussion organically leads to the question of how Open Source projects and standards interact in practice. According to Lundell and Gamalielsson, we can broadly distinguish the following three situations: (1) "standard first;" (2) "software implementation first;" and (3) "standard and implementation of standard in parallel."[66] Daniel Veillard from RedHat offers similar categorization calling it: (1) "late implementor;" (2) "early implementor;" and (3) "software and stand in parallel."[67] In the following section, we will use this established classification to discuss some basic interactions.

[60] ETSI 2005.
[61] *See, e.g.*, Jekyll 2018.
[62] *See* Eisape et al. (forthcoming).
[63] Jensen & Scacchi 2010; Egyedi 2000b.
[64] Egyedi 2007.
[65] Lundell et al. 2014.
[66] Lundell & Gamalielsson 2017.
[67] Veillard 2012.

1. From Specification to Implementation

The most typical scenario recalled by many when thinking about interaction between Open Source projects and standardization is when Open Source projects are the means of standard implementation. Open Source implementation then competes with other implementations on the market. For instance, the famous IEEE 802.11 standard is a set of specifications defining wireless local area network computer communication in specific frequencies. It is naturally also implemented in Open Source-based operating systems, including those using Linux kernel.[68] While typically such implementations are produced independently by firms active on the market or communities, increasingly, SDOs themselves are interested in designing their own reference implementations along with standard specifications.

There are several reasons for this. First, SDOs developing specifications connect participants that possess lot of knowledge in the area, so it is natural to offer them a platform for the further development of the technology. Second, specifications are often too abstract and thus there is no guarantee of seamless implementation without an authoritative reference implementation.[69] A great example of this are problems encountered by two Open Source projects when trying to implement ISO standards.[70] West explains this as follows:

> for complex digital systems standards, the formal specification is inherently incomplete and the actual standard is defined both through the written specification and through actual implementations ... for any firm trying to implement a standard, knowledge of both the formal specification and existing implementations is valuable.[71]

For these reasons, for instance, IETF requires multiple interoperating implementations before adopting any standard.[72]

Third, SDOs which are able to offer reference implementation are more likely to see successful market diffusion of their standards since such references test specifications and save investments in the implementation phase. As pointed out by West, "[o]therwise, the implementer faces an extended trial-and-error process as it seeks to discover how other firms have resolved specification ambiguities."[73]

2. From Implementation to Specification

The second, perhaps less frequent, scenario is when an Open Source project develops technological design which is then codified through specifications in the actual standard. An example is offered by JavaScript, which is one of the core World Wide Web technologies, along with HTML and CSS. JavaScript was first released by Netscape and Sun Microsystems in 1995. Already in the original announcement, the two companies wrote:

> Netscape and Sun plan to propose JavaScript to the W3 Consortium (W3C) and the Internet Engineering Task Force (IETF) as an open Internet scripting language standard. JavaScript will be an open, freely licensed proposed standard available to the entire Internet community. Existing Sun Java licensees will receive a license to JavaScript. In addition, Sun and Netscape

---

[68] See Lisovy et al. 2014.
[69] Egyedi 2007.
[70] Gamalielsson & Lundell 2013.
[71] West 2004.
[72] See IETF 1996.
[73] West 2004.

intend to make a source code reference implementation of JavaScript available for royalty-free licensing, further encouraging its adoption as a standard in a wide variety of products.[74]

Eventually, unlike HTML and CSS that were standardized with W3C, the standardization work for JavaScript commenced at ECMA International under the name ECMAScript.[75] ECMAScript was released under the BSD license text applicable to all the software,[76] however, with an explicit patent carve-out. The decision clearly was meant to assure that patent licensing is not limited by the standardization efforts. For patents essential to the standard which are contributed by "any party participating in a technical committee," regular ECMA patent policy applies.[77] Since the ECMA Code of Conduct in Patent Matters allows for royalty-free or FRAND licensing, contributors are free to choose.[78] The standard is nowadays implemented by a number of firms, such as Adobe, Apple, Google, Microsoft and the Mozilla Foundation. Each of the firms then determines its own licensing commitments.

Another example of this scenario is a standardization project called Linux Standard Base (LSB). It is a joint effort of several Open Source projects hosted by the Linux Foundation. Its goal is to develop and promote set of specifications that will increase compatibility among different operating systems (distributions) based on Linux. The results of the standardization work are published as ISO/IEC 23360–1:2006 standard.[79] The IEC website does not list any related patent declarations.[80]

As the two examples show, this scenario seems to mostly arise in situations when an existing product serves as a starting point for a new standardization work or when a family of similar products seeks to find a common building block in order to increase their mutual interoperability. Depending on the timing of contribution and of the feedback loops, it can overlap with the third scenario.

3. Co-Development of Specification and Implementation

While the first and second scenarios appear to be almost linear, the third scenario certainly is not. It covers situations when work on standardization and implementation are undertaken in parallel. This can take place by either (1) affiliated, or (2) unaffiliated projects.

The typical case of the latter is when during the standardization work an early Open Source reference implementation work is developed in order to explore the functioning of the specifications in action. Gamalielsson and Lundell report on interesting evidence in this regard.[81] They study mutual interactions between an Open Source community, Drupal, and a standardization community at W3C concerning RDFa technology, which is a set of extensions necessary for embedding rich metadata within web documents. Through a quantitative study of Drupal

---

[74] See Netscape 1995.
[75] There is an interesting trademark history behind this choice of name. See Krill 2008.
[76] See ECMA Int'l 2011. ("All Software contained in this document ('Software') is protected by copyright and is being made available under the 'BSD License,'" included below. This Software may be subject to third party rights (rights from parties other than Ecma International), including patent rights, and no licenses under such third party rights are granted under this license even if the third party concerned is a member of Ecma International.")
[77] See ECMA Int'l 2016.
[78] According to the registry, for instance, Intel and salesforce.com decided to grant royalty-free licenses. See ECMA 2018.
[79] See ISO 2012. ("International Standard ISO/IEC 23360-1 was prepared by the Free Standards Group and was adopted, under the PAS procedure, by Joint Technical Committee ISO/IEC JTC 1, Information technology, Subcommittee SC 22, Programming languages, their environments and system software interfaces.")
[80] See IEC 2018.
[81] Gamalielsson & Lundell 2013.

and W3C trackers for RDFa, they find clear evidence of reciprocal actions between the two communities. Gamalielsson and Lundell summarize this as follows: "standards can influence implementations of standards, implementations of standards can influence standards, and that implementations of standards can influence other implementations of standards."[82] Moreover, according to their findings, this set-up seems to have attracted new pool of participants to the standardization project at W3C. In a way, even two earlier scenarios can lead to co-development in the long run.

The example of an *affiliated* Open Source project is MANO Open Source (OSM) project hosted by ETSI. In 2016, an ETSI director created an Open Source Group OSM, the goal of which was to create Open Source reference implementations for ETSI's specifications in the area of network virtualization known as ISG NFV architectural framework.[83] According to its terms of reference, which also include a number of governance agreements: "OSG OSM will provide an opportunity to capitalise on the synergy between standardization and Open Source approaches by accessing a greater and more diverse set of contributors and developers than would normally be possible. This maximises innovation, efficiency and time to market and ensures a continuing series of true (conformant) reference implementations."[84] ETSI explicitly recognizes that "essential feedback" to standardization work is one of its goals. The OSM project is licensed under Apache v2, a permissive OSI-certified license, with royalty-free licensing of patents and a stronger patent retaliation clause. The governance of the hosted project is assured through a web of contractual agreements among ETSI and the participants, which creates a rigid structure from the perspective of a future change.

The distinction between affiliate and unaffiliated Open Source projects is important also because while both provide feedback to the standardization process, only the former might be viewed as an authoritative co-definition of the standard in situations where the language of specifications is ambiguous. Therefore, a choice of standardization-participants not to participate in an affiliated Open Source implementation is effectively less free if they want to influence the resulting standard. On the other hand, even unaffiliated projects can have spill-over effects on the specifications due to market power and/or acceptance.

C. FRICTIONS AMONG IPR RULES

When standardization and Open Source projects interact, frictions between their accompanying rules can arise. This part explores what types of frictions we see, and what their consequences are.

1. Scenario by Scenario

To begin with, let's look at the late implementor scenario. Since implementation only comes after specifications are adopted in the standardization process, the main question is whether Open Source licensing can be applied to specifications containing SEPs with FRAND commitment. This is usually presented as the main point of potential friction. It is argued that while standardization community primary is after *fair* access, Open Source community usually mandates *free* access. In fact, this friction has two main components: (a) legal compatibility and (b) business

---

[82] Id.
[83] See ETSI 2016b.
[84] Id.

consistency. As will be shown, with many Open Source projects, the business inconsistency is the key issue.

In the *late implementor* scenario, patent holders usually do not need to worry. After all, competitors will have to license any of their used patents anyway, regardless of whether such project is Open Source or not. Actually, the Open Source character can improve the chances of detection of an infringement. Their concerns start when the project is being developed as a reference implementation by an SDO itself. In these cases, they face a choice of whether to participate or not. If they do, depending on the project's license, they might need to license SEPs, and even non-essential patents, claiming the reference implementation. Moreover, they might expose themselves to patent retaliation clauses which, again depending on the wording of the license, could be used as a leverage even in other cases, where they may seek royalties.

From the implementer's side, however, non-licensed patents represent a ticking threat. First, individual licensing of patents disrupts the licensing model, where no separate permissions are needed for the software production and re-use. Given that many projects start with an informal and decentralized governance structure, seeking ex-ante project licensing might be difficult. Unless the industry practices some form of centralized end-product licensing, such as in the case of smartphones, it might be hard to arrange the licensing along the value chain. Second, due to uncertainty about which patents are reading on the technological implementation, the developers, or their firms, might be dissuaded from investing in the follow-on innovation. These concerns are well illustrated by the studies which tried to map licensing of patents in the context of Open Source implementations.[85]

As regards copyrights, code of the Open Source project has to be compliant with the licensing terms of specifications. This might be particularly important when copying specifications verbatim in the code or the accompanying documentations. Given that some standard specifications are sold by SDOs, there might be a risk of committing a copyright infringement, unless one of the statutory exceptions and limitations applies (e.g. quotation). That being said, SDOs can avoid these problems in case they recognize value of such specifications upfront.

In the *early implementor* scenario, the project license can influence the viability of the follow-on standardization in two ways. If a standardization project is initiated and the project license did not include any grants concerning patents reading on the implementation, the standardization process will need to take care of all the patents that remain essential to the standard-specifications. The exact way would depend on a particular SDO and its policy, of course. However, the lack of participation by original developers in the follow-on standardization could endanger its viability as they are neither obliged to consent to inclusion of their patents to a standard, nor to provide a FRAND commitment. In a way, they could prevent widely used Open Source projects from being successfully standardized into building blocks. Naturally, if the original Open Source project license includes a royalty-free patent grant, the follow-on standardization is easy to arrange to the extent that newly minted SEPs are already covered by it. In these cases, the project license basically serves as a substitute for such standardization-specific commitment.

As regards copyrights, if the code from the original project becomes part of the specifications, two copyright policies need to be legally, but also business compatible. For SDOs that earn for their operations by selling standards, the decision to include Open Source code could mean that particular standards, or their parts (depending on the Open Source license), have to be available free of charge. They might be thus legally constrained in introducing pay-walls for

---

[85] Lundell et al. 2014; Gamalielsson & Lundell 2013.

their standardization documents. In addition, their standard contributor copyright policies in the technical committees need to be compatible with the original project license.

In the *co-development* scenario, the interactions of the first two scenarios are only accelerated. The flow of exchange between specifications and implementations goes both ways and at much higher speed. Consistency of two sets of rules and legal certainty is then highly important for successful standardization efforts and clear understanding of the rules between participants of two communities. Naturally, if the participants in Open Source project and standardization work are identical, all problems can be easily mitigated. But when such membership is not identical, two ecosystems might contain stakeholders with both overlapping and antagonistic interests. For instance, Open Source developers might be interested to assure absolutely (copyright and patent) royalty-free diffusion of implementations, while selected standardization contributors may want to capitalize on their investment embodied in the included technologies. Although both parties desire diffusion, they do so under different conditions, and with different business models in mind. In these cases, close "knitting" of technology by a back-and-forth between standardization and open source production, without any synchronization, might inhibit innovation in the long run. It would therefore be advisable to determine the applicable IPR rules together (ex-ante), so that technical contributions can be fully exploited on the market. This can be done either directly through organizations, often SDOs, hosting such efforts, or by organizing outside umbrella initiatives such as patent pools.

2. Legal Incompatibility

In the last couple of years, it was often debated whether Open Source is (legally) compatible with FRAND. Much of the debate seems hard to follow as the authors even disagree on *when* two systems are incompatible. Kesan, for one, for instance says that: "[o]pen source licenses cannot be categorically described as conflicting with a FRAND-based standards license unless each term of each Open Source license is examined and tested against the FRAND model."[86] In other words, according to his definition, as long as there is a single Open Source license out there, in his case certified by OSI, that is compatible with an unspecified type [sic] of FRAND commitment, one cannot say that two systems are incompatible. Some broaden this further by suggesting that there are moreover many "Open Source" licenses that are not OSI-certified and would be compatible. Others argue that the mere fact that the patent holders are not able to collect royalties means that the two are inherently incompatible.[87] The result of this is that while one camp claims that "an empirical examination of all OSS licenses approved by the OSI reveals that there is no inherent conflict between OSS and FRAND,"[88] the other camp disagrees by saying that FRAND is incompatible most of the time.[89] Who is right?

Firstly, the problem is definitional. Two *licenses* are *legally incompatible* only if their obligations cannot be reconciled at the same time. For instance, once one license requires disclosure of a component and another prohibits it, it is clear that there is an incompatibility. However, if two licenses can be respected at the same time, by settling for the least common denominator, then there is no *legal* incompatibility. So for instance, if a commitment to be fair is rivaled by a commitment to not charge anything, there is no conflict between the two

---

[86] Kesan 2011.
[87] *See* Moodey 2016.
[88] Kesan 2011.
[89] *See* FSFE 2016a; FSFE 2016b.

as one can simply not charge anything and thus remain also fair. In these situations, one may speak of (business) inconsistency, or frictions, but hardly about legal incompatibility. In the debates, this distinction often gets lost. Moreover, as was explained earlier, there are hundreds of Open Source licenses and dozens of versions of FRAND commitments. One can answer any legal compatibility question only with reference to two specific legal texts. This also means that answering the question about compatibility between Open Source and FRAND in general is a pointless rhetoric exercise. It simply depends on the exact wording.

Second, the problem also seems interpretational. For at least some types of conflicts, reasonable minds might disagree about the proper construction of the text of the license. Open Source licenses are notoriously ambiguous, and can be subject to diverging community interpretations. For instance, many authors agree that the GPL family of licenses is incompatible with royalty-bearing licensing due its strong safeguards against non-free use.[90] In particular, according to "The Liberty or Death" clause, if recipient cannot distribute freely by transmitting third-party authorizations downstream, it cannot distribute at all. In the words of the Free Software Foundation (FSF), a non-profit behind the GPL family of licenses, this allows the license to "kill the program" and thus prevent "enslaving it" for the patent licensing purposes.[91]

The "Liberty or Death" mechanism effectively prevents co-existence with royalty-bearing FRAND patent licensing which is usually negotiated individually. However, even such legal compatibility is only *conditional*. In this case, conditional upon feasibility of the necessary licensing solutions. The patent settlement between RedHat and Firestar surrounding GPLv3-licensed products shows that even this incompatibility can be solved if a firm is willing to absorb the cost for the entire downstream and upstream ecosystem and obtain a patent license for the entire community.[92] Other solutions to the "Liberty or Death" clause could include direct buy-outs of strong patents, invalidation of weak ones, or institution of some kind of (inverted) patent pools, where the "obstacle patents" are purchased or licensed by a group of firms that pools resources and then licenses or sub-licenses them to the entire community. In a way, the "Liberty and Death" clause, rather than being an impossible impediment, asks for an action. To the extent that the software that it purports to kill is valuable for the industry, it asks for a *collective* action from the entire community to assure royalty-free distribution. As long as the "obstacle patents" are SEPs that are committed under FRAND, the problem has a number of solutions. This is because these patent holders are unable to invoke their exclusivity, and thus have to be willing to license. The situation might prove much more difficult if the "obstacle patents" are strong and not committed under FRAND terms. If the patent holders invoke exclusivity, this may effectively kill the developed software. This demonstrates, however, that even a subset of the real *legal* compatibility issues is again conditional upon the business context.

A different example of an interpretational problem concerns the downstream copyright licensing architecture of the reciprocal obligation known as copyleft. Copyleft is an obligation according to which follow-on modifications by a licensee have to be usually distributed under a compatible license. Kappos argues that legal incompatibility of Open Source licenses "predominantly stem[s] from copyleft licenses."[93] However, it is not obvious that the copyleft mechanism per se, as opposed to GPL's version of it, constitutes really a problem. For instance, copyleft could be only limited to copyright permissions, or even if covering also patents, simply

---

[90] Mitchell & Mason 2011; Kesan 2011.
[91] See FSFE 2018.
[92] See Tiller 2008.
[93] Kappos 2017.

not extend to third-party rights (e.g. Section 2 of the EUPL license). In the former case, patent rights are not implicated at all. In the latter, this not a legal issue, but one of a business nature.

Last but not least, it should be reminded that even a royalty-free patent component is not a guarantee of a FRAND-compatible scheme. For instance, a strong firm-centered patent retaliation clause such as Facebook's React clause that unduly favors one of the parties could be objected to on the basis of a discrimination requirement. Therefore, even if the patent license would be royalty-free, but subject to discriminatory patent retaliation clause or a similar provision, it might be objectionable from the perspective of the FRAND commitment. The outcome would again depend on the exact wording and its interpretation.

3. Business Inconsistencies

Standardization allows firms to cooperate on specifications and compete on their implementations. Where firms are not vertically integrated on the product markets, they can simply earn by licensing their patents. Naturally, this strategy is heavily constrained if the SDO IPR policies require them to license standard-essential patents on a royalty-free basis. For pure R&D firms, i.e. non-integrated up-stream firms, such licensing arrangement can significantly reduce their appropriation strategies. Open Source licensing that includes royalty-free patent clauses leads to comparable business outcomes, although the scope and therefore impact of thereby licensed patents differs. The opposition to patent royalty-free SDO policies thus logically also extends to patent royalty-free Open Source licenses. The argument against such licenses is broader because Open Source licensing might limit appropriation strategies for technology *and* products. Although firms might still invent-around and on top of the reference implementation, it might be hard to beat on the market as an early royalty-free competing product.

Moreover, strong patent retaliation clauses which sanction any enforcement also concerning project-unrelated patents can have impact on a collection of royalties before the courts. Under such clauses, pure R&D firms that find themselves licensing their broad patent portfolios to many firms might risk that their litigation efforts that are unrelated to technology essential to an Open Source implementation, or standard specifications, will trigger retaliation under such project. If such project is important to them, this can then create a leverage in negotiations against such patent holders.

At the same time, we should be reminded that in practice, many firms already decide to engage in various defensive activities outside of the world of FRAND commitments and Open Source licenses. One of such defensive mechanisms, Open Invention Network (OIN), aggregates firm patent portfolio in order to create a defensive patent pool. The pool then licenses relevant patents free of charge, but under a condition of patent enforcement cease fire. In the effect then, such defensive patent pools are just more centralized versions of decentralized royalty-free licenses with strong patent retaliation clauses or aggregated stand-alone patent commitments.[94] What these strategies have in common is that they are *external* to the projects/standards themselves. As was pointed out, even the hardest compatibility issues, such as "The Liberty or Death" clause of GPL licenses, can have external solutions to them, such as umbrella licensing or buy-out arrangements. Compared to SDO IPR policies or Open Source license texts, they are not ex-ante in-built in the ecosystem, but require ex-post individual or collective action to materialize. One could even say that similar to FRAND, they leave a number of issues open to delay the answer of the industry.

[94] *See, e.g.,* IBM 2005.

Last but not least, business inconsistency can also take place on the side of SDOs. For those SDOs which sells standards in order to support their work, the challenge might be to earn money and engage Open Source communities at the same time. Although this issue might seem marginal, it can be important in the long run because standardization requires resources to be invested by firms and basic architecture to be provided by SDOs. At the moment, there are many SDOs in ICT which all want to attract standardization work. With the technological shift, they have to increasingly compete for new work (and funding) not only among themselves but also with other Open Source projects.

D. INNOVATION ECOSYSTEM

Open Source and standardization both express technological choices. They usually complement each other. In the "standardization first" scenario, Open Source offers just one of the ways how to more openly implement the specifications with some trade-offs. In the "implementation first" scenario, standardization helps to stabilize quickly moving technology and ensure its interoperability. However, the ecosystems of production can also compete with each other. Competition takes two forms: (1) Open Source as a co-definition of standardization specifications (intra-competition) and eventually (2) Open Source as a substitute to standardization specifications (inter-competition).

In the first case, it is used to further define specifications in a technological direction which was not or could not be agreed upon in the standardization process. Open Source projects in these circumstances serve a purpose similar to consortia. Consortia are often alliances formed by likeminded firms outside of the standardization process in order to influence or complement its outcomes (Pohlmann 2014). This can be both before adoption of the standard, for instance to settle conflicts or streamline its finalization, or ex-post, for instance to de facto further develop technology based on specifications (e.g. WiFi Alliance). According to the existing research, standards related to consortia are characterized by a more fragmented ownership of intellectual property rights and a strong degree of technological rivalry.[95] At the moment, we can observe IoT as one of the areas where many consortia, Open Source projects and SDOs actively compete even in the same knowledge areas.[96] In this competition, Open Source project licenses can be an important factor. This can be already observed for instance in a recent change of policy by ALLSeen Alliance after it merged with the Open Connectivity Foundation, which prompted change in its license. Instead of a copyright-only license, ISC, combined with a limited patent non-assertion pledge, they switched to Apache v2, a patent and copyright royalty-free license with a strong patent retaliation clause.[97]

In the second case, Open Source is used *instead* of standardization to produce the common building blocks. It might be that such production is still complemented by parallel writing of specifications to compensate for volatility of the code, but the main coordination of technological choices remains in the realm of software. An example of this effort is the Telecom Infra Project (TIP) which is a collaborative telecom community launched in 2016 with the goal of accelerating the pace of innovation in the telecom industry.

In the previous parts, we have concluded that legal incompatibility can only be assessed on the level of the text of the exact Open Source license and FRAND commitment. At the same

---

[95] Baron & Pohlmann 2013.
[96] *See* AIOTI 2016.
[97] *See* Open Connectivity 2016; AllSeen Alliance 2017.

time, we see that some instances of at least conditional legal incompatibility exist. In the literature, Kesan argued that: "[o]f the eight most popular OSS licenses, only the GPL and the Lesser GPL license conflict with the FRAND model. And only a small fraction of the remaining 59 OSI-approved licenses have any conflict with FRAND."[98] Even if one would completely agree with his legal analysis of the licenses and side-step the issue of conditional compatibility, this appears to be a very optimistic statement in a situation when GPLv2 and GPLv3 licenses account for more than one fourth of the used licenses according to some estimates.[99] This conditional incompatibly might remain an issue for many GPL-licensed projects that implement basic building blocks subject to royalty-bearing FRAND.

It should be remembered, however, that although FRAND constitutes a default in the standardization world, this is not necessarily the case for all the technologies. On one hand, application layer of Internet technologies standardized by W3C and IETF is usually subject to royalty-free patent licensing.[100] On the other hand, the infrastructure technologies standardized at SDOs such as ETSI or IEEE remain predominantly subject to FRAND royalty-bearing commitments. This licensing rift creates an interesting split for the functioning of the Open Source projects. While the former with royalty-free patent regime is more accommodating for Open Source production, the latter potentially conflicts with a use-intensive subset of its licenses, such as GPL-family. Is this a problem for the innovation ecosystem? And what *can* and *should* SDOs do about this?

SDO IPR policies have an important role to play in shaping the innovation ecosystem. Such choices are usually generated bottom-up from their constituency, but can be also steered from the top by SDO leadership. Broadly speaking, there might be two effects on innovation: encouragements and discouragement. Standards help with finding, coordinating and diffusing new technologies. SDOs acting as platforms have to clearly attract both firms committing their technology and firms building upon it to achieve its dual goals. If SDOs dissuade the first constituency, or its part, it might risk producing inferior or no standards. Firms can always try to opt for proprietary strategies. If SDOs dissuade the second constituency, or its part, they risk producing standards that will not be used on the market. At the same time, SDOs are exposed to external competition from other fora such as Open Source projects which can overtake part of their work if they are not satisfying either of two demands on the market. Already from the above analysis, it is clear that SDO's choices have consequences for the innovation ecosystem. They incentivize or disincentives different sets of innovators to participate in the standardization process.

According to theory, emphasis on royalty-free patent licensing is likely to discourage "pure innovators" from participating in either of two ecosystems. It might potentially limit technologies of new generations brought to SDOs by these firms since it restrains their appropriation strategies. It might push some "pure innovators" outside of the standardization system or incentivize them to either vertically integrate or negotiate with such integrated firms. Inclusion of royalty-free patent licensing on implementations only further deepens this expected effect. At the same time, royalty-free policies are capable of accelerating diffusion and facilitating more decentralized follow-on innovation.[101] This is especially so if mere royalty-free specifications are coupled with royalty-free reference implementations as implementations provide a valuable

---

[98] Kesan 2011.
[99] *See* Black Duck Software 2018.
[100] Contreras 2016.
[101] Contreras 2011.

way of testing standards and of providing building blocks which further save resources for follow-on users and innovators.

The evidence for the discouragement effect is ambiguous. Following W3C's 2002 change to a default royalty-free policy, it was reported in the media that large patent holders such as IBM, SAP, and Microsoft decided to channel some of their standardization work concerning Web technology to OASIS, which had more favorable policy at the time. They all, however, later returned back to W3C (Contreras 2016). Empirical evidence for this type of discouragement can be found in the studies which look at the ecosystem changes after SDOs revise their IPR policies in this way. Very illustrative work is a study conducted by Stoll who empirically examines effects of IPR policy change by OASIS in 2005.[102] He finds that the change from FRAND to policy allowing working groups to opt for royalty-free (RF) or non-assertion regime is correlated with a significant decrease in the overall membership. However, at the same time, he finds that the composition re-shapes following the change as the share of non-profit research organizations and systems integrators significantly increases in the aftermath. Pohlmann and Contreras offer two similar empirical studies *without* finding similar effects.[103] However, both of them focus on SDO changes at IEEE and VITA concerning what constitutes fair, reasonable and nondiscriminatory licensing *rates*.

The discouragement of pure R&D firms is not the only effect, however. SDO choice of a particular Open Source license can also activate a new pool of innovators, i.e. software developers, to enter the co-development process. As shown by Belenzon and Schankerman (2008), Open Source developers strongly sort by license type, project size and corporate sponsorship due to heterogeneity of their motivations. In their empirical study they find that highly restrictively licensed projects (e.g. under GPL) attract almost exclusively developers who contribute only to projects with such restrictive licensing. On the other hand, contributors to projects with permissive licenses (e.g. Apache, BSD, MIT) are more likely to contribute to larger projects and to those that are sponsored by corporations. This reveals a split in the underlying motivation of the Open Source developers.

Highly restrictive (strong copyleft) licenses seem to attract motivated developers who are dedicated to the movement's ideology, while permissive licenses attract developers who want to improve their career prospects by building up their own reputation. Moreover, Belenzon and Schankerman find that developers contributing to restrictive projects are more likely to be involved in projects close to the end consumer, while developers contributing to unrestrictive projects are more likely to be involved in developer-oriented projects. In other words, their findings suggest that more fundamental infrastructure research R&D takes place within permissively licensed projects whose developers are motivated by the careers prospects within the industry. Based on this, the innovation opportunity costs of SDOs choosing permissive Open Source licenses would be very low – which is an important finding for the standardization ecosystem as it would suggest that basic infrastructure projects that are not user-oriented are anyway less likely to attract developers with preferences for strong copyleft licenses. It remains to be tested, however, to what extent such permissive licenses when adopted by SDOs for their reference implementations attract also firms that previously were *not* involved in the standardization work.

Although we lack comparable studies for self-selection of individual developers or firms depending on the underlying patent policy of projects, there is some anecdotal evidence

---

[102] Stoll 2014.
[103] Pohlmann 2017; Contreras 2013.

suggesting that some patent features, such as broad retaliation clauses, might discourage some innovators from adopting or further developing technologies. In 2017, Facebook faced this problem with respect to a broad patent retaliation clause in its React project license which was permissive. This customized clause would automatically terminate authorization to use any of Facebook's React-relevant royalty-free licensed patents if any potential user wants to enforce any of its own patents against Facebook. The company faced strong backlash from the community and eventually decided to re-license its project because a number of the Open Source projects announced that they would not use the technology or build upon it.[104]

Last but not least, even copyright policies of SDOs regarding its standard documents can have an impact on innovation. A number of developers seem to be discouraged by pay-walled standardization documents. They might feel discouraged to contribute to further development of such standards, as they view it contrary to the main Open Source idea, namely that of openness. Moreover, copy and pasting such specifications in the implementation phase for the purpose of discussion or referencing can be viewed as violation of SDO's copyright. How strong these effects are really, however, remains an open question for a further research.

CONCLUSION

The most significant type of future interactions between Open Source and standardization are beyond simple "standard first" scenario in which specifications are implemented in a number of products, including ones under an Open Source license. Open Source should be rather viewed as a mode of production. Embracing it offers a number of important synergies. In particular, it helps to remove specification ambiguities and provide a fast-track ground for specification testing. SDOs have an important role in facilitating this collaboration. If SDOs fail to react in the area of ICT standards, their activities might be increasingly "emptied" in favor of post-specification Open Source projects or consortia-like organizations emulating their role entirely or partially outside of the standardization ecosystem.

Clarification of the IPR issues definitely constitutes one of the important barriers to seamless collaboration of two ecosystems. At the same time, answering the question about compatibility between Open Source licenses and FRAND in general is a pointless rhetoric exercise. No other answer can be given than the lawyerly "it depends." Open Source licenses and FRAND commitments come in a number of forms, and the answers depend on too many details. That being said, the royalty-free feature of OSI-certified licenses per se does not lead to a *legal* conflict. However, some other provisions of Open Source licenses can. Most typically, GPL-family of licenses is conditionally legally incompatible due to a set of safeguards known as the "Liberty or Death clause." Also, strong patent retaliation clauses that sometimes accompany royalty-free licensing in Open Source licenses can be legally incompatible under some circumstances. Their main impact, however, usually would be on enforcement strategies concerning royalties from patents that remain outside of the project remit. The most common tension between two ecosystems is of a business nature – a demand to give up on patent royalties.

Based on the outlined trade-offs for the innovation ecosystem, a number of specific points can be offered. First of all, patent and copyright royalties may discourage use of standards within Open Source projects. For patent royalties, these effects can be also addressed outside of the standardization process by means of defensive and licensing patent pools or aggregated individual commitments. Even the most restrictive license conditions may be incompatible only

[104] *See* Wolff 2017.

conditionally. Often, there are external solutions to them too. Therefore, it depends on the cost and benefits of a particular project whether such solutions should be in-built ex-ante or created externally ex-post.

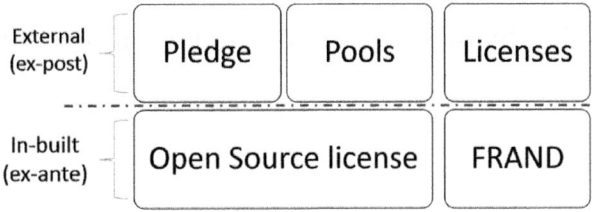

Second, Open Source licenses with royalty-free patent grants might accelerate diffusion of specifications, especially if done within the reference implementations of SDOs, and encourage a new set of innovators to join the process. At the same time, it might discourage a set of pure R&D firms which heavily rely on royalties to recoup the investment. SDOs steering the process might want to consider the likely pool of innovators on both sides when launching a project. Third, given that we observe that both royalty-free and royalty-bearing layers are able to sustain innovation investments in the ICT, neither of the two approaches seems inherently superior. However, the choice can influence the make-up of innovators and technological trajectories. From this perspective, they both have their place in the innovation ecosystem. SDOs should, therefore, promote a choice between them on a project basis.

11

OSS and SDO: Symbiotic Functions in the Innovation Equation

David J. Kappos

A.	Standards and OSS Both Advance Innovation	198
B.	FRAND Works, for Both Patents and OSS	199
C.	Open Source Software is Compatible with FRAND	200
D.	SDO Policies Should Not Be Amended to Address False Conflicts	201
E.	When Open Means Closed	202

Two groups – industry standards development organizations (SDOs) and the open source software (OSS) community – have contributed enormously to the breathtaking technological achievements of recent decades that permit anyone almost anywhere in the world to catch a Pokémon on a $100 smartphone. SDOs have been remarkable stewards of this innovation, developing principles and processes of self-governance, such as FRAND ("fair, reasonable and non-discriminatory") licensing, as well as catalyzing the inclusion of the best available technology from their applicable fields, in the standards they set. Meanwhile, the OSS community, with its strong ethos of sharing and an organic, social network, has accelerated the pace of software innovation. However, the intersection of their jurisdictions, OSS embedded *in* standards, has become a contentious subject. Some critics now question the compatibility of OSS with FRAND licensing, contending instead that standards using OSS should be royalty-free.

As SDOs consider again whether OSS can appropriately be licensed under FRAND terms, it is important to recognize that both OSS and standards are good for innovation, can and do coexist with the right choice of license, and indeed complement one another. SDOs should not lightly undertake modifications to their policies and practices that are unnecessary, and will likely have serious negative repercussions on the quality of technology contributed to their standards.

A. STANDARDS AND OSS BOTH ADVANCE INNOVATION

An important precipitating factor in the recent wave of innovation has been the creation and adoption of industry standards.[1] In the telecommunications industry, widely adopted, highly

---

[1] For an in-depth discussion of the standards development ecosystem and the role of SDOs in it, see companion volume, Chapter 2.

innovative standards such as 3G and 4G have created vastly improved technical capabilities. The technology behind these standards is often protected by standard essential patents (SEPs), which are accepted into a technical standard by SDOs. An important balance has long been maintained by leading SDOs such as ETSI and ITU, recognizing the need to reward innovators by compensating them for giving access to their patented inventions, while also recognizing the need to make standardized and interoperable technology that requires such inventive contributions available for implementers of standards to use at a reasonable cost.[2] As evidenced by the enormous technical advances in standardized technology in fields like mobile telecommunications, the standardization process based on FRAND licensing has served and is serving humanity well, providing huge consumer value through both innovation and reasonably priced products.

OSS also provides efficiencies and network effects crucial to innovation. OSS, unlike proprietary software, gives developers access to the source code of computer programs developed by others working on a given open source project, and enables developer communities to share tools and build on common infrastructure. In recent years, OSS has been critical in shaping cloud computing, big data and mobile technology.[3] The community-based development process for OSS has also allowed it to organically develop a cohesive social network.[4] This social element has been an important driver in the adoption of OSS by industry. In order to take advantage of OSS-enabled technological infrastructure in their own products and services, commercial entities have had to adapt their internal processes to comply with the software licenses and other requirements of open source communities, as well as provide funding and engineering talent to contribute to and even to lead open source projects.

Properly managed, companies engender goodwill with programmers and customers through investments in open source[5] and reduce development and maintenance expense by sharing software costs across the applicable open source community, redeploying the saved funds on more investments in innovation rather than recreating duplicative infrastructure, while customers enjoy highly innovative, stable, low-cost software.

B. FRAND WORKS, FOR BOTH PATENTS AND OSS

Many SDOs have long required that members agree to the FRAND system of licensing in order to participate in the standard development process. The "fair, reasonable and non-discriminatory" tenets of FRAND require SEP holders to abide by licensing terms that are pro-competitive, include reasonable terms and conditions, and treat similarly situated licensees similarly.[6] SDO

---

[2] In contrast, the Institute of Electric and Electronics Engineers (IEEE), an SDO which previously developed one of the most successful standards of all time (802.11 or Wi-Fi) under policies very similar to those of ETSI and ITU, made drastic policy changes in 2015, systematically ignoring the concerns of patent holders. Its policy will likely impact the willingness of innovators to contribute leading-edge technology to IEEE standards, versus standards development efforts of other standards bodies that have maintained a balance to encourage contribution of the best available technology as well as affordable license rates for implementers. IEEE 2014 (comments of Dina Kallay, Director for IP and Competition, Ericsson) ("Ericsson believes the proposed text will retard innovation and directly compromise IEEE standards by negatively influencing the willingness of patent holders to participate in IEEE standard-setting process.").

[3] Pillay 2014; Niazi 2014.

[4] Taulli 2015.

[5] Lerner & Shankerman 2010.

[6] For a detailed discussion of these terms, see companion volume, Chapters 10, 12, 16–21 and 23.

guidelines historically also accommodate licensing of software generally (including OSS) under FRAND principles, rendering the two systems compatible by definition.[7]

For a number of years some critics have argued that FRAND was "broken," and the "monopolies" conferred by SEPs would result in "patent holdup" and "royalty stacking" as SEP holders exploited the sunk costs of standards implementers.[8] However, as FRAND-based industries such as mobile telecommunications have matured and large bodies of data have become available showing the actual economics of the industry over 20-plus years, empirical studies and other scholarly works have sharply refuted the earlier dire predictions.[9] In fact, industries such as mobile telecommunications are thriving under the FRAND licensing regime, providing additional marketplace data that undermines the previously plausible concerns of patent holdup and royalty stacking.

In the meantime, critics have more recently begun airing a new argument: that FRAND is discriminatory toward OSS and inherently incompatible with OSS.[10] As was the case with holdup and royalty-stacking theories, there is no real-world indication of any incompatibility or discrimination, and the predominant view is that the marketplace has developed solutions to incorporating FRAND principles in licensing OSS.[11]

C. OPEN SOURCE SOFTWARE IS COMPATIBLE WITH FRAND

Contributors and SDOs are readily able to ensure that OSS contributions are compatible with FRAND by simply choosing compatible OSS licenses for contributions.

The Open Source Initiative (OSI), a standards body of sorts and arbiter of the "open source definition," lists over 70 different licenses that have been reviewed and approved under its License Review Process.[12] Broadly speaking, these licenses fall into one of two categories, permissive or copyleft. Copyleft licenses require the licensed software and any modifications to be redistributed with the same set of rights (*i.e.*, under the same copyleft license), thus preventing the software from becoming proprietary.[13] Claims of incompatibility of open source licenses with FRAND licensing predominantly stem from copyleft licenses and the conflation of open source software with free software. The original copyleft license, the General Public License (GPL), was designed by Richard Stallman, founder of the Free Software Foundation, an organization that continues to advocate for free software.[14]

Permissive licenses, on the other hand, do not place restrictive terms on software redistribution, providing an opportunity for innovators to benefit financially from their modifications to applicable open source software. The only requirements accompanying redistribution under a Berkeley Software Distribution (BSD) license, for instance, are to provide the copyright notice, reproduce the license language and refrain from using the original software developer's name

---

[7] ETSI 2016a.
[8] Galetovic & Haber 2017.
[9] Harkrider 2013, 10.
[10] Kesan 2011, 19.
[11] Muller 2011.
[12] OSI 2017a.
[13] Making matters more complicated, OSS contributions can implicate non-SEPs such as patents that may be used (but are not mandatory) to facilitate implementation of a particular standard. Given this likelihood, the contribution of OSS under restrictive copyleft licenses can compel innovators to relinquish innovations beyond those essential to the standard, forcefully discouraging contributions at all levels for fear of having valuable investments reduced to giveaways.
[14] Lerner & Shankerman 2010, 37.

in any derivative works without written permission.[15] Other popular permissive licenses include the MIT license and the ISC license.

A few other licenses can be categorized as neither permissive nor copyleft. For example, the Apache 2.0 license does not require distribution under the same license for any modifications or derivative works, but does require distribution under the same license for any unmodified components. Apache 2.0 also differs from many permissive licenses in its grant of a royalty-free patent license.[16] The Apache License's grant of a royalty-free patent license on all contributions to Apache licensed software does conflict with FRAND principles, because it does not give innovators an avenue for fair compensation.[17] However, this problem only arises from a small subset of OSS licenses.

Permissive licenses account for the vast majority of OSI's approved licenses and are fully compatible with FRAND licensing. An empirical study of all available OSI approved licenses in 2011 showed that only two of the eight most popular OSS licenses and seven of the 67 then approved OSS licenses had terms conflicting with FRAND.[18] These statistics flatly contradict any contention that OSS cannot be reconciled with FRAND. To the contrary, OSS is readily compatible with FRAND by simply choosing a permissive open source license for code submitted to standards bodies developing FRAND standards.

D. SDO POLICIES SHOULD NOT BE AMENDED TO ADDRESS FALSE CONFLICTS

SEPs and OSS spur innovation, both together and separately. Moreover, there are clearly many viable open source licenses that allow SDOs to utilize OSS without a resulting conflict between the open source license and the FRAND license. So why are critics claiming the systems are incompatible?

The answer is in part ideological, but is mostly about business models. The ideological component is driven by the free software movement, which sprang from the early "hacker" culture of software engineering that has advocated for free software since the early 1980s. The free software community opposes any royalty-based licensing or proprietary software on principle and believes software developers should instead seek economic incentives through warranties, maintenance or other non-royalty based channels.[19] Many of the copyleft licenses incompatible with FRAND licensing were developed within this community and, some have argued, explicitly to frustrate FRAND licensing.[20]

However, another potent force in propagating the myth of FRAND and OSS incompatibility has been interested parties who seek to reduce their licensing costs.[21] The ubiquity of OSS in standards means that any policy removing OSS components from being factored into a royalty-bearing license would significantly reduce implementer component costs and thus improve the bottom line for implementers. This is a natural competitive point of view and not objectionable per se – every implementer of technology wants to reduce its input costs. But for those SDOs seeking to maintain the delicate balance that encourages innovators to contribute cutting-edge technology, the gambit must be taken for what it is – economic self-interest by those seeking

---

[15] OSI 2017b.
[16] Apache 2004.
[17] This becomes a key difficulty where such software must be modified by innovators so that it can be used by others to implement a standard.
[18] Kesan 2011.
[19] FSF 2017.
[20] Kesan 2011, 19.
[21] Kesan 2011, 20.

access to others' innovation investments for free. To take this bait will inevitably drive innovators away and leave standards to the moribund contributions of those who don't, or can't, innovate.

Some see OSS as the next opportunity to devalue SEPs after successfully pushing through the controversial amendments to the Institute of Electrical and Electronics Engineers (IEEE)'s patent policy.[22] A major change, and one vehemently protested by some SEP holders, was the prohibition of SEP holders from seeking an injunction against infringers until after the conclusion of first-level appellate review, significantly tilting the balance between innovators and implementers, and emboldening implementers to infringe the patents of innovators rather than taking licenses.[23] While the amendment's long-term effects remain to be seen, there is widespread concern that cheapening the value of SEPs will result in less investment in and development of effective standards.[24]

Likewise, amending SDO policies to require the use of FRAND-incompatible OSS licenses could also result in less innovative standards and a diminished industry role for the SDO. When SDOs are considering specific software submissions for inclusion in standards, it is natural that software associated with highly innovative features will include proprietary licenses. Furthermore, many of these software submissions will be adjunct to highly innovative hardware, circuitry or algorithms. Insistence on a FRAND-incompatible license will prevent the adoption of both highly innovative software and its associated technology, sending a message that the SDO is willing to prioritize "free" over innovation.

The answer to the false choice between OSS and FRAND in standard development is simple: continue to allow, as has historically been the practice, contributors of OSS to make their contributions under permissive open source licenses. To those seeking to create an innovation-hostile climate in SDO operations by forcing software under copyleft licenses or licenses with royalty-free patent grants, just say no.

E. WHEN OPEN MEANS CLOSED

The recent press to weaken innovation incentives in standards development by changing the approach to accepting OSS code comes cloaked in pleasantries such as "open" and "free." Policy makers, however, should remain wary. Terms like "open standards," "free" and "sharing" evoke egalitarian ideals that belie a more complicated truth. The current FRAND licensing system has been remarkably successful in balancing the needs of OSS users and developers with the interests of SEP holders through appropriate permissive licenses.

In contrast, moving to incompatible licenses for FRAND standards submissions weakens innovation incentives and discourages innovators from participating in standardization efforts. For standards development organizations, this means abdicating technical leadership to those who prioritize commodity implementations above innovative standards.[25]

Before SDOs change their historically successful policies on the treatment of OSS in standards, they should consider the evidence of whether their policies are actually broken. The kid with the $100 smart-phone playing Pokémon Go would say, probably not.

---

[22] See supra note 2.
[23] IEEE 2017.
[24] Kesan 2011, 24–25.
[25] In addition, impairing the FRAND paradigm would shift the economics of innovation away from a patent disclosure-based regime to favor a trade-secret based regime. A trade secret regime with its barriers to sharing can cause secrecy-shrouded exclusivity in perpetuity and tragically inefficient allocation of resources, a giant step backwards for innovation and the downfall of standards development, which relies so heavily on disclosure, transparency and sharing.

PART V

Trademarks, Certification and Standards

12

Trademarks, Certification Marks and Technical Standards

Jorge L. Contreras[*]

A.	Background – Trademarks and Certification Marks	206
	1. Basic Attributes of Trademarks	206
	2. Certification Marks and Product Certification	208
	3. Infringement	211
	4. Genericism and Genericide	212
	5. Trademark Licensing: Quality Control and Stylistic Guidelines	213
	6. Nominative Fair Use	214
B.	How Trademarks and Certification Marks are used in Standardization	217
	1. House Marks	217
	2. Standard-Names	218
C.	SDO Approaches to Authorizing the Use of Standard-Names	224
	1. Caveat Emptor	224
	2. Member Certification	226
	3. License Agreements and Conduct Restrictions	227
	4. Third-Party Certification	227
	5. Genericide	229

When a consumer shops for a new smartphone, she will likely check whether different models implement a range of common standards such as Wi-Fi, Bluetooth, and 4G (soon 5G). Likewise, the typical consumer knows that when she switches from a phone that is charged using a microUSB connector to one that uses Apple's "Lightning" connector or the more recent USB-C connector, she will need to replace her charging cables as well. Most consumers have only the vaguest notion of how the standards behind these technologies work. Nevertheless, consumers are familiar with the functionality associated with these simple trade names. The names of technical standards thus fulfill a critical informational role for consumers.[1]

---

[*] The author thanks Carter Eltzroth, Yvette Liebesman, Earl Nied, Gil Ohana and Clark Silcox for valuable comments and feedback on this chapter, and Brad Biddle for an advance look at his empirical results on the use of trademarks by SDOs.

[1] For example, the term *Bluetooth* conveys to the consumer a host of functional details such as the types of products that are generally connected using this technology (phones, computers, headphones and portable speakers), the range over which it works (within a large room, not across the country) and whether or not it is necessary for the application at hand (some consumers may be just as happy connecting headsets to their music players with physical cords and 3.5mm jacks).

Standards, and the names given to them, are generally created either by firms that develop a proprietary technology that eventually becomes an industry standard (e.g., Adobe's Portable Document Format (PDF)) or, more often, by voluntary industry associations known as standards development organizations (SDOs).[2] As discussed in Chapter 2 (companion volume), SDOs come in many shapes and sizes, from small single-purpose consortia to large multinational organizations. This diversity is also reflected in the range of policies, approaches and attitudes of SDOs toward trademarks. Yet relatively little has been written about the use of trademarks by SDOs or in the context of standardization more generally.[3] This chapter seeks to identify the divergent approaches to trademark management and licensing taken by different SDOs and to explain their development and effect on the overall goals of standardization and interoperability.

A. BACKGROUND – TRADEMARKS AND CERTIFICATION MARKS

This section offers a brief overview of the doctrinal principles of trademark and certification mark law that are most relevant in the context of technical standards. Though the emphasis of this section is on U.S. and EU law, many of these principles apply throughout the world.

1. Basic Attributes of Trademarks

a) Scope

A trademark is a word, name, symbol or other device that is used to identify the source of a particular product or service.[4] While most trademarks are words and phrases, represented either in plain textual form (the broadest form of coverage) or with a stylized appearance (e.g., the novel fonts in which marks such as Coca Cola and IBM are rendered), logos, designs, colors, shapes, scents, and sounds can also be trademarks in the United States. To be a valid trademark, the mark must be used in commerce, distinctive and must not be confusingly similar to a mark that is already in use.[5] While registration provides some extra benefits, in the United States registration is not required in order to have trademark protection. One must merely use the trademark in commerce in connection with goods or services as a source indicator[6] prior to anyone else who might use a similar mark in a confusingly similar manner. In order to have trademark protection outside the United States under the Madrid Protocol, however, the trademark must be registered.[7]

The degree of distinctiveness exhibited by a word or other device affects its ability to be used as a mark, its eligibility for registration, and its enforceability (see Infringement, below). Distinctiveness is generally classified along a five-point scale laid out in *Abercrombie and Fitch Co. v. Hunting World, Inc.*[8] Marks that are *fanciful* (entirely invented words such as Lexus, Exxon and Prozac) and *arbitrary* (common words applied in an unfamiliar way, such as Apple for computers and Prince for spaghetti) are the strongest and inherently distinctive.[9]

---

[2] The principal focus of this chapter will be on SDO-developed "voluntary consensus standards," though it is also important to understand the role of single-firm "de facto" standards.
[3] For some early discussions of this topic, *see* ANSI 2008; Contreras & Updegrove 2016.
[4] 15 U.S.C. § 1127.
[5] 15 U.S.C. § 1052(d).
[6] 15 U.S.C. § 1127.
[7] *See infra* Section A.1.c.
[8] *See Abercrombie* (2d Cir. 1976) (establishing four-tier scale for trademark distinctiveness).
[9] *Id.* at ¶12.

Marks that are *suggestive* (words that require "imagination, thought, and perception to reach a conclusion as to the nature of goods"),[10] are also distinctive (such as Coppertone for sunscreen and PlayStation for a video game platform). However, words that are merely *descriptive* of the good or service they name may not be trademarks without an additional showing of secondary meaning (i.e., that they have come to identify the source of the goods or services in the public eye).[11] Marks that could be classified as descriptive include Best Buy (for a discount retailer), Dial-a-Mattress (for a mattress vendor), and CitiBank (for a New York-based bank). In some of these cases, where the mark has come to be associated in the public eye with the supplier of goods or services rather than the item described, the mark may be protected as a trademark (e.g., the name CitiBank today is likely associated with a particular bank rather than a general description of a metropolitan bank). And, finally, terms that are *generic*, connoting a general category to which a particular product belongs (e.g., car, savings bank, lawnmower) but which give no specific indication of the product's source, receive no protection whatsoever.[12]

While unregistered trademarks enjoy protection wherever there is market penetration, when a trademark registration is granted, it provides the registrant constructive nationwide market penetration, and, with some exceptions, an exclusive right to use the mark to identify its goods or services throughout the granting jurisdiction.[13] This right includes the right to use the trademark on product labeling, packaging and advertising. In some jurisdictions, including the United States, a particular trademark registration only extends to certain classes of goods and services. The classes of protected goods and services must be identified by the applicant in its trademark application. The applicant must also demonstrate actual use of the mark in the requested classes or have a bona fide intent to use the mark in those classes; the latter is limited to three years before either use must be demonstrated or their priority in the mark is canceled. Accordingly, the same mark may be used and/or registered to different owners in different classes of goods and services. For example, the mark "PRINCE" is registered in the United States, among others, to Prince Minerals, Inc. (for specialty mineral products), Buck Knives, Inc. (for pocket knives), New World Pasta Company (for pasta) and Prince Sports Group, Inc. (for tennis equipment). Many countries, however, do not require the specification of a particular class of goods or services to obtain trademark protection. Trademarks in these countries cover all classes of goods and services.

b) Duration

Trademark protection is generally of unlimited duration, provided that the mark owner continues to use the trademark in commerce and, if registered, pay required renewal and maintenance fees. In the United States, for a registered mark, a Declaration of Use attesting to the registrant's use of the mark must be filed between the fifth and sixth years following registration, and a combined Declaration of Use and Application for Renewal must be filed between the ninth and tenth years following registration, and every ten years thereafter.[14]

---

[10] *Id.* at ¶18.
[11] *See id.* at ¶6 and 15 U.S.C. § 1052(f).
[12] *Abercrombie*, at ¶12. For further discussion, *see infra* Sections A.4 and C.4.
[13] In some cases, prior users of a registered trademark may be permitted to continue their use after the mark is registered and even prevent use of a later-registered mark within their geographical market.
[14] 15 U.S.C. §1058–1059.

c) International Treaties

Every sovereign nation, and some regional groups (e.g., the European Union, which offers a community-wide trademark or "EUTM"),[15] has its own trademark registration system. Trademarks recognized by one country, with some exceptions, are typically not recognized or enforceable in other countries. However, since the nineteenth century, treaties have been established to foster international coordination of trademark registrations. The 1883 International Convention for the Protection of Industrial Property (the "Paris Convention") requires that member countries grant "national treatment" to parties from other member countries. That is, they must permit residents of all member countries to file applications for protection on the same basis as their own citizens. In addition, if an application for a trademark in a member country is filed within six months of the application filed in the owner's home country, the second application will have the benefit of the original application's filing, or priority, date.

The most significant international trademark treaty today is the Madrid Protocol of 1989,[16] an adjunct to the 1890 Madrid Registration of Marks Treaty to which the United States never became a party. The United States, however, did join the Madrid Protocol in 2002.[17] Currently more than ninety countries are members of the Madrid Protocol.[18] The Madrid Protocol allows a trademark applicant to file in multiple countries by submitting a single international application to the International Bureau of the World Intellectual Property Organization[19] (WIPO). Following receipt, WIPO submits the international application to the individual trademark offices of the countries designated in the application. The designated countries then examine the application in accordance with their own procedures for national trademarks, ultimately leading to separate and distinct nationally registered trademarks in each country.[20]

Thus, while registration is not required for trademark protection in the United States, a mark owner who wishes to take advantage of trademark protection through the Madrid Protocol must have a validly registered mark in the United States in order to do so.

2. Certification Marks and Product Certification

A certification mark is, generally speaking, a species of trademark. However, unlike true trademarks, which are intended to indicate to the consumer the *source* of a particular product or service, certification marks are intended to identify particular *characteristics* of a product, typically when those characteristics are not easily discernable from an inspection of the product.[21] As discussed in Chapters 3, 13, and 14, certification may be used to indicate that a product has met specified requirements regarding safety, reliability or manufacturing process. Perhaps the best-known certification mark is the world is Underwriters Laboratories' "UL" certification. Underwriters Laboratories claims that its mark appears on 22 billion products per year, ranging from kitchen appliances and hoverboards to fire extinguishers and industrial carpet. UL

---

[15] Prior to March 23, 2016, the term "Community Trade Mark" or "CTM" was used to refer to a mark registered in the European Union.
[16] Madrid Protocol 1989.
[17] Madrid Protocol Implementation Act 2002.
[18] WIPO 2018.
[19] Id.
[20] PTO 2018.
[21] For example, a mark identifying a product as a banana is probably not particularly useful to the average consumer, but a mark identifying a product as an organic, "fair trade" banana would be useful to consumers who value those qualities.

tests and certifies products for compliance with its own standards and for standards developed by others.[22]

a) Registration

In the United States, certification marks may be registered with the U.S. Patent and Trademark Office (PTO) in a manner similar to trademarks, though they differ from trademarks in several important regards.[23] Whereas trademarks are used to indicate the origin of a product or service and thereby to assure its quality to the consumer, certification marks are used to indicate compliance by a product or service with a particular standard, without regard to its origin. Certification marks are generally subject to the same requirements regarding distinctiveness as ordinary trademarks, except in the case of certifications as to geographic origin (e.g., GROWN IN IDAHO for potatoes).[24]

Certification marks may be applied to goods or services by any organization adhering to the relevant standard but may *not* be applied by the mark's owner.[25] For example, thousands of new buildings around the world display the Leadership in Energy and Environmental Design (LEED) certification owned by the U.S. Green Building Council (USGBC). Though USGBC developed and administers the LEED rating system, it does not itself construct buildings bearing the LEED mark.[26] Importantly, the holder of a certification mark must allow any organization that complies with the relevant standard to apply the mark on a nondiscriminatory basis.[27] Violation of the foregoing requirements can result in cancelation of the certification mark.[28]

Interestingly, at least according to one recent Second Circuit opinion, the determination of a certifying body as to a product's compliance with the standards for certification appears to carry more weight than objective evidence introduced by a competitor that the product does *not* comply with those standards. In *Board-Tech v. Eaton*, Eaton's decorative light switches were certified by Underwriters Laboratories to comply with the UL 20 electrical safety standard.[29] Board-Tech conducted its own test of Eaton's switches, however, and determined that they were not compliant with UL 20. Board-Tech brought a claim against Eaton for false advertising under the Lanham Act, among other things. The district court dismissed Eaton's complaint, and the Second Circuit affirmed, reasoning (somewhat metaphysically) that Eaton's display of the UL 20 mark on its switches signified only that the switches had been certified by UL, which was true, but *not* that they objectively complied with the UL 20 standard.[30] This holding significantly increases the importance of certification bodies in the realm of certified products.

Certification marks are distinct from collective marks, which generally signify membership in a particular group or origin from a particular geographic region (e.g., the REALTOR® mark and "R" logo used by members of the National Association of Realtors).[31] Collective marks are

---

[22] UL 2018a. Obtaining a UL certification is viewed as a commercial necessity for many product categories in the United States. *See Board-Tech* (2d Cir. 2018, p. 1) ("to be commercially viable, light switches in the United States must undergo certification by Underwriters Laboratories").
[23] For a more detailed summary of the law relating to certification marks, *see, e.g.*, Chon 2018; Belson 2017; Chapter 13.
[24] *See Institut National* (TTAB 1998); Beebe 2017, Sec. 1, p. 27; Belson 2017, 60.
[25] 15 U.S.C. § 1064(5)(B).
[26] *See* Contreras & McManis 2013 (discussing LEED, among other building standards).
[27] 15 U.S.C. § 1064(5)(D). *See also* McCarthy 2008, § 19:92; Belson 2017, 63.
[28] 15 U.S.C. § 1064.
[29] *Board-Tech*, at p. 2.
[30] *Id.*
[31] 15 U.S.C. § 1027; Belson 2017, 1. The designation of products originating from particular geographic regions (e.g., Champagne sparkling wine and Scotch whiskey) is a complex and developing area of law, a discussion of which is beyond the scope of this chapter.

registrable in the United States, EU and numerous other jurisdictions. In the EU, prior to the 2017 adoption of a formal certification mark regime, compliance with standards could be signified through use of collective marks obtained by an SDO "for the benefit of its members."[32] Given that the introduction of certification marks to EU law is recent, many SDOs continue to use collective marks for certification purposes and will likely do so for the foreseeable future.[33]

Certification marks may be registered in a number of countries in addition to the United States, including Australia, Brazil, China, Egypt, India, and the United Kingdom, and, as of October 2017, the European Union.[34] In other jurisdictions such as France, Germany, Mexico, and the Philippines, certification marks are still treated as collective marks.[35] And some jurisdictions, most notably Japan, provide no system for the registration of certification marks.[36]

b) Product Certification

As noted above, the owner of a certification mark may authorize manufacturers to place the mark on their products that comply with the owner's requirements for usage. Depending on the standard, the owner of a certification mark may establish different processes to authorize the application of its certification mark to products. As explained by Contreras and McManis in the context of SDOs:

> *First-party certification*, or *self-certification*, occurs when a product manufacturer declares that its own products meet the requirements of a standard. There is an inherent conflict of interest in self-certification, but it also has the virtue of being relatively inexpensive and quick to achieve. *Second-party certification* occurs when an SDO certifies that a product meets the requirements of its own standard. While viewed as more reliable than first-party certification, second-party certification remains somewhat suspect due to the SDO's inherent interest in increasing the number of products certified to its standard. *Third-party certification* occurs when an outside certification organization certifies that a product meets the requirements of a standard. Because the certifier is independent of both the SDO and the manufacturer, third-party certification is generally seen as the most objective form of certification in this field, though even independent certification groups may be susceptible to market pressure to certify as many products as possible.[37]

Some commentators have argued that the complexity and limited transparency of the certification process can result in consumer confusion as well as unscrupulous and overzealous use of certification marks, particularly in the area of "green" standards and ecolabels.[38] To address this and other concerns, a range of adjustments to the statutory framework governing certification marks have been proposed, including requirements that more information about the standards underlying certification marks be disclosed; applying the doctrines of trademark "abandonment"

---

[32] See Belson 2017, 80–81.
[33] See, e.g., ETSI 2018 ("we have registered the following wordmarks and figurative marks for the benefit of our members"); Belson 2017, 81 (noting American Petroleum Institute's EU collective mark AMERICAN PETROLEUM INSTITUTE CERTIFIED).
[34] See Belson 2017, 33–36; Webster 2017. The EU certification mark was introduced under the EU Trademark Directive in 2017.
[35] Webster 2017.
[36] Id.
[37] Contreras & McManis 2013, 494. In addition to the classification structure laid out in this paragraph, alternative definitions of first- second- and third-party certification exist. See, e.g., ISO/IEC 17000:2004, Sec. 2.2–2.4 (defining first- second- and third-party conformity assessment).
[38] Chon 2009, 2316; Contreras et al. 2011. For further discussion of potential issues with third-party certification, see Chapters 3 and 13.

and misuse to certification marks; and allowing consumer protections actions to be brought against both holders of certification marks and the entities using those marks.[39]

3. Infringement

Under the Lanham Act, a person who makes commercial use of a trademark, or any reproduction, counterfeit, copy or colorable imitation of that mark, without the consent of the owner, in a manner that is likely to cause confusion, mistake or deception, is liable for infringement and/or false designation of origin.[40] Liability extends to false advertising and "passing off" – either by the defendant attaching the plaintiff's trademark to the defendant's goods (often referred to as "counterfeiting"), or by the defendant labeling the plaintiff's goods with the defendant's mark.[41] Over the years, courts have developed an eight-factor test to assess the likelihood of confusion arising from the use of a mark. While each circuit's description of these factors varies, the Second Circuit's statement in *Polaroid Corp. v. Polarad Electronics Corp.*[42] is representative of the general approach taken throughout the United States. The factors to be taken into consideration under the *Polaroid* test include:

(1) strength of the allegedly infringed mark;
(2) similarity of the infringed and infringing marks;
(3) proximity of the products and their competitiveness with one another;
(4) evidence that the mark owner may "bridge the gap" by developing a product for sale in the market of the alleged infringer's product;
(5) evidence of actual consumer confusion;
(6) evidence that the infringing mark was adopted in bad faith;
(7) respective quality of the products; and
(8) sophistication of consumers in the relevant market.[43]

The factors are weighed, and some are given more significance than others. For example, strength of a mark is important, as a weak mark receives less protection than a strong mark. The above analysis is conducted whether an alleged infringer is using an exact copy of the registered mark (e.g., counterfeit goods) or a purportedly different mark that bears some degree of similarity to the registered mark. For example, in the context of technical standards, the mark BLUETOOTH is registered to the Bluetooth SIG, the SDO that developed the Bluetooth standard for short-range wireless connectivity.[44] Bluetooth SIG actively enforces its mark against manufacturers of devices that use the term BLUETOOTH without authorization.[45] These "passing off" cases typically involve an exact copy of the mark, as the manufacturer of the "counterfeit" product wishes to deceive consumers into believing that the product is a "genuine" Bluetooth product (i.e., a product certified by Bluetooth SIG as conforming to the Bluetooth Standard (see Section C.3

---

[39] *See* Chapter 13; Chon 2009, 2348–49; Contreras et al. 2011.
[40] 15 U.S.C. 1114, 1125(a)(1)(A) & (B). Section 1114 applies to registered marks; section 1125(a)(1)(A)) covers both registered and unregistered marks as well as passing off, and section 1125(a)(1)(B) applies to false advertising. In addition to claims for infringement, trademark owners may have claims against the users of confusingly similar marks that sound in dilution. *See* 15 U.S.C. 1125(c). Because dilution claims are less germane in the context of technical standards, they will not be addressed in this chapter.
[41] §1125(a)(1)(A).
[42] *Polaroid* (2d Cir. 1961).
[43] *Id.*
[44] U.S. Reg. No. 2,909,356 (December 14, 2004).
[45] *See, e.g.*, Bluetooth SIG 2008.

below)), though the bad faith intent of the defendant is only one factor that the courts consider, and even if adopted in bad faith, if there is no likelihood of customer confusion, then there is no actionable infringement liability.

In other cases, products may not bear exact replicas of the BLUETOOTH mark, but may bear marks that are similar enough at least to suggest to consumers that Bluetooth SIG may have endorsed or authorized the use. For example, in 2008 an individual sought a U.S. trademark registration for the mark BLACKTOOTH for "MP3 Player Sunglasses."[46] In 2009, Bluetooth SIG filed a Notice of Opposition with the Trademark Trial and Appeals Board (TTAB) against the BLACKTOOTH application.[47] Bluetooth SIG argued, among other things, that allowing the mark BLACKTOOTH to be used on wireless sunglasses would suggest to consumers that Bluetooth SIG had endorsed, sponsored or approved those products.[48] While this case involved an opposition to the registration of a mark, the analysis with respect to infringement would be comparable.

A final infringement scenario that is relevant to standardization is the use of a registered mark as part of a compound name (also known as a composite mark). For example, one well-known TTAB decision involved the rejection of a registration for the name DARJEELING NOUVEAU for tea, where the name DARJEELING was already registered.[49] The TTAB rejected the new mark even though it was not disputed that the applicant's product consisted entirely of certified Darjeeling tea.[50] Another such case arose with the attempted registration of the mark CANADIAN MIST AND COGNAC, which incorporated the pre-existing certification mark COGNAC.[51] The TTAB again rejected the application on the ground that it could cause confusion with the original mark.[52] Thus, as explained by McCarthy, "even where a defendant's product contains ingredients which have been certified by the owner of a certification mark, the defendant's incorporation of that certification mark into its own composite trademark might be likely to cause confusion as to sponsorship, affiliation or connection."[53]

Various remedies exist if a trademark is found to have been infringed. In the United States, both injunctive relief to prevent further infringement, as well as monetary relief to redress past harm, are available. Under the federal Lanham Act, damages that may be recovered by the owner of an infringed mark include lost profits and other actual damages, an accounting of the infringer's profits, attorneys' fees and legal costs. Actual damages may be computed on the basis of injury to or loss of reputation or goodwill, lost sales or revenue, lost profits, and the expense of preventing further customer confusion (including remedial advertising).[54]

4. Genericism and Genericide

As discussed in Section A.1.a above, a mark that connotes a general category to which a particular product belongs (e.g., car, savings bank, lawnmower) but which gives no specific indication of the product's source, is considered *generic* and is not protectable as a trademark.[55] A mark may be

---

[46] U.S. Trademark Application Ser. No. 77/506993 (June 24, 2008).
[47] *Bluetooth SIG v. Chisholm* (TTAB 2009).
[48] *Id.* at 7.
[49] *Tea Bd. of India* (TTAB 2006).
[50] *Id.*
[51] *Institut Nat'l* (TTAB 1998).
[52] *Id.*
[53] McCarthy 2008, §19:92.50 (citing *Institut Nat'l*).
[54] *Id.*
[55] *Abercrombie*, at ¶12.

deemed to be generic either initially, when registration is refused by the PTO,[56] or after registration, if the mark no longer identifies a source of goods. This latter circumstance is commonly known as "genericide" and results in the cancelation of the mark found to be generic. There is a long list of U.S. trademarks that have been revoked as a result of genericide: ASPIRIN, BRASSIERE, ESCALATOR, LINOLEUM, THERMOS and TRAMPOLINE to name just a few.[57]

Though genericism is typically discussed in terms of trademarks for products and services, certification marks may also be the subject of genericide. For example, in *Community of Roquefort v. William Faehndrich, Inc.*, the court observed that "if an indication of regional origin, registered as a certification mark, becomes a generic term for a certain type of goods coming from any region, then the mark is subject to cancellation."[58]

Generic terms can, of course, be included as components of distinctive marks. For example, the mark GRIZZLY COFFEE for a chain of coffee shops is likely arbitrary under the *Abercrombie* framework (given the lack of any logical connection between grizzly bears and coffee), and thus a strong mark. Yet the term COFFEE for a coffee shop is clearly generic. Thus, to avoid any implication that the owner of GRIZZLY COFFEE could claim rights in the word COFFEE itself, the PTO often requires that generic terms included within registered marks be *disclaimed* as to separate use of the generic term.[59] Thus, the owner of GRIZZLY COFFEE would potentially have an infringement claim against Grizzly Cafés, but not against Caribou Coffee.

5. Trademark Licensing: Quality Control and Stylistic Guidelines

Like other intellectual property rights, trademarks may be licensed by their owners to others. In the United States, a trademark owner who licenses a mark must ensure that the goods and services produced and sold by the licensee that bear the licensed mark meet the quality standards of the trademark owner. The owner's failure to impose quality control restrictions, and to police or monitor the quality of the licensed goods or services can be deemed to constitute so-called "naked" licensing and can form the basis for a claim that the mark has been abandoned by its owner.[60] As a result, most trademark owners impose some degree of quality control measures on the products and services that are branded with the licensed marks. At one extreme, business franchisors often specify quality and service requirements for their franchisees at an extreme level of detail, often running to hundreds of pages, while SDOs often require only that licensed marks be applied exclusively to products and services that comply with the relevant standard.

It is important to distinguish between quality control requirements and stylistic guidelines for the use of trademarks. Independently of, and in addition to, quality control requirements, many trademark owners impose restrictions on how their marks are to be presented and used (as opposed to requirements pertaining to the quality of the goods and services to which the marks are applied). These requirements are intended not only to preserve the consistent appearance and image of the licensed mark, but also to prevent uses that could cause the mark to become generic. While the precise requirements vary, below is a non-exhaustive list of stylistic restrictions imposed by trademark owners (and SDOs in particular) on the use of licensed marks[61]:

---

[56] *See, e.g.*, Beebe 2017, x (listing numerous examples).
[57] *See, e.g.*, Folsom & Teply 1980, 1324 (citing relevant decisions for each mark).
[58] *Community of Roquefort* (2d Cir. 1962, p. 497).
[59] *See* PTO 2017, Sec. 1213.03(c) ("If a mark is comprised in part of matter that, as applied to the goods or services, is generic or does not function as a mark, the matter must be disclaimed to permit registration…").
[60] *See, e.g.*, *Barcamerica* (9th Cir. 2002, pp. 595–98).
[61] For an extensive example of such requirements, *see* Oracle 2016.

- Marks must be reproduced according to specified color, size, font and placement guidelines (often including the mandatory use of a downloadable graphics file to reproduce a logo).
- Prohibition on use of a mark as a verb (e.g., "I am going to Xerox these papers").
- Prohibition on use of a mark as a noun (e.g., "DECT" is necessary in this configuration).
- Prohibition on altering the mark or combining it with other marks.
- Prohibition on using the mark in a demeaning, derogatory or misleading manner.
- Prohibition on registering or using the mark as, or as part of, a trade name, domain name, metatag or similar device (e.g., Bluetooth Consultants, Bluetooth-users.org).
- Prohibition on using the mark in, or as, a pun.[62]
- The mark must be accompanied by the ® or ™ symbol and acknowledged as the property of the mark owner.

6. Nominative Fair Use

Despite a trademark owner's exclusive right to use, and authorize others to use, its marks, there are certain situations in which others are free to use trademarks without permission of the owner. An important category of exceptions to a trademark owner's exclusivity is broadly termed "fair use." Under U.S. law, several fair use trademark defenses are embodied in the Lanham Act, but the most relevant doctrine in the context of technical standards, "nominative" fair use, has developed primarily through judicial decisions.[63]

Nominative fair use allows a third party to use another's trademark in a manner that is nondeceptive and that does not imply endorsement by the mark owner when referring to the products or services of the mark owner.[64] For example, in considering the case of an automotive repair shop that advertised that it repaired Volkswagen automobiles by using the word "Volkswagen" in its advertising, the Court of Appeals for the Ninth Circuit held that "[In] advertising the repair of Volkswagens, it would be difficult, if not impossible, to avoid altogether the use of the word Volkswagen or its abbreviation 'VW', which are the normal terms which, to the public at large, signify [the mark owner's] cars."[65] Thus, the use of a trademark is permitted when the user is referring factually to the mark owner's products or services.

As noted above, such uses must not imply that the mark owner has endorsed or approved the products or services offered by the user of the mark. In order to take advantage of the nominative fair use defense, one may use only so much of the mark as is necessary to convey the relevant factual information, but no more. Thus, an auto repair shop may use the words "Volkswagen" or the letters "VW," but probably not the distinctive circular Volkswagen logo.

The American National Standards Institute (ANSI) recommends that users of third-party marks in standards documents make it clear that the owners of the marks have not endorsed the standard. To do this, ANSI recommends that such marks be used strictly as adjectives, and not as

---

[62] This unusual requirement was adopted by ETSI, perhaps due to the inherently satiric nature of standards engineers. See ETSI 2018 ("Our trademarks represent our standards, the symbols of ETSI goodwill worldwide. They should be treated with respect as valuable assets. Accordingly, they should not be used as the object of puns").

[63] See generally, McGeveran 2008, 88–104. A similar doctrine has been recognized in countries outside the United States. See, e.g., BMW v. Technosport London (UK 2017).

[64] See McCarthy 2008, § 23:11.

[65] Volkswagen v. Church (9th Cir. 1969).

nouns or verbs, that marks not be used in the possessive sense, and that marks not be combined, shortened or abbreviated.[66]

Nominative fair use is also applicable to the resale of goods. If someone is selling genuine Sony headphones that are either used, repackaged, or merely being resold, then the seller may truthfully advertise the goods using their correct brand name. Thus, the person who is selling unused Sony headphones may advertise them as such; a person selling golf balls retrieved by a nearby golf course may advertise them for sale and indicate them by their origin, but must indicate that they are used, to distinguish them from new/unused and thus avoid confusion with regard to the quality of the goods.

The doctrine of nominative fair use has also been applied to certification marks. Most recently, in *International Information Systems Security Certification Consortium, Inc. v. Security University LLC*,[67] the International Information Systems Security Certification Consortium (ISC²) owned the registered certification mark CISSP® (Certified Information Systems Security Professional), signifying an individual "who has met certain requirements and standards of competency in the information security field, including passing the CISSP® certification examination that ISC² administers."[68] Security University (SU) offered a preparation class for the CISSP examination. As noted by the court,

> It is undisputed that SU is allowed to use the CISSP® certification mark to indicate that its services are directed at preparing students for the CISSP® certification examination. Furthermore, given the nature of ISC²'s certification mark, SU instructors may accurately identify themselves as being CISSP®-certified, so long as they follow ISC²'s regulations governing the use of the mark.[69]

The dispute arose over SU's use of the term CISSP to describe one of its instructors as a "Master CISSP" and a "CISSP Master," which, ISC² alleged, implied that it offered or endorsed SU's classes.[70] In considering ISC²'s claim, the Second Circuit first noted that the test for trademark infringement is "whether the defendant's use is likely to cause confusion not just as to source, but also as to sponsorship, affiliation or connection."[71] The court emphasized that "nominative fair use is not an affirmative defense to a claim of infringement under the Lanham Act," but is rather a set of facts that can impact the existing "likelihood of confusion" analysis for trademark infringement.[72] It then fashioned a new test for assessing whether a particular nominative use of a certification mark would likely cause confusion, adding the following three factors to the Second Circuit's traditional eight-factor test for confusion under trademark law[73]:

(1) whether the use of the plaintiff's mark is necessary to describe both the plaintiff's product or service and the defendant's product or service, that is, whether the product or service is not readily identifiable without use of the mark;
(2) whether the defendant uses only so much of the plaintiff's mark as is necessary to identify the product or service; and

---

[66] ANSI 2008, 4–5.
[67] *Security University* (2d Cir. 2016).
[68] *Id.* at 7 (slip op.).
[69] *Id.* at 8.
[70] *Id.* at 9.
[71] *Id.* at 19 (quoting McCarthy 2008, § 23:76.
[72] *Id.* at 5.
[73] *Id.* at 5–6 (citing *Polaroid* (2d Cir. 1961)).

(3) whether the defendant did anything that would, in conjunction with the mark, suggest sponsorship or endorsement by the plaintiff holder, that is, whether the defendant's conduct or language reflects the true or accurate relationship between plaintiff's and defendant's products or services.[74]

The Second Circuit remanded the case for further proceedings in line with this guidance.

Another recent case to address nominative fair use in the context of technical standardization was *ASTM v. Public.Resource.Org* (2018). In *ASTM*, the defendant, Public.Resource.Org (PRO), copied and posted certain technical standards online without the consent of the relevant SDOs.[75] In identifying the copied standards, PRO used the names of the standards and, in some cases, the relevant SDO's logo. In analyzing whether PRO's use may have constituted nominative fair use, the DC Circuit considered the three factors previously identified by the Second Circuit in *Security University*. As to the first factor, the court reasoned that if reproducing the relevant standards was permitted under copyright law, then identifying such standards by name would likely be necessary.[76] However, with respect to the second factor, the court speculated that PRO may have "overstepped when it reproduced both ASTM's logo and its word marks."[77] Finally, as to the third factor, the court considered as relevant PRO's written statements disclaiming any endorsement or sponsorship by the relevant SDOs.[78] The court thus remanded the case to the district court for further consideration whether PRO's use of the relevant marks constituted nominative fair use.

Interestingly, the DC Circuit went on to note that even if the district court found that PRO infringed the SDOs' marks, it should "consider whether its previous grant of an injunction barring all unauthorized use is still warranted or whether it may order defendants to modify their use of the mark[s] so that all three factors are satisfied and a narrower remedy would suffice."[79]

It is worth noting that the judicial doctrine of nominative fair use is in some disarray in the United States. At least four different circuits (the 1st, 2nd, 3rd and 9th) have each developed a different test for nominative fair use, some considering it an affirmative defense to a claim of trademark infringement (Third), some incorporating it into the test for infringement (Second, Ninth), and at least one which has adopted reasoning that does not appear to follow either of these approaches (First).[80] The DC Circuit in *ASTM* did not reach the question of which approach to follow, as the district court below failed to consider any nominative fair use factors at all, which was reversible error.[81]

Another species of nominative fair use arises in the context of comparative advertising. In the United States, competitors are permitted to compare their products to the competition in advertising, so long as that comparison accurately identifies the source of each product and does not mislead consumers.[82] Thus, McDonald's and Burger King, Coke and Pepsi, and AT&T and Verizon are free to name each other in competing ads comparing food taste, beverage popularity and network coverage so long as the information conveyed is accurate and not misleading.

---

[74] *Security Univ.* at 38–39.
[75] For a discussion of the copyright implications of this case, *see* Chapter 5.
[76] *ASTM* (D.C. Cir. 2018, p. 35).
[77] *Id.* at 35–36.
[78] *Id.* at 36.
[79] *Id.* at 36–37 (internal quotation marks and citations omitted).
[80] *See ASTM* (D.C. Cir. 2018, pp. 34–35) (discussing circuit discrepancies).
[81] *Id.* at 35.
[82] *See Pizza Hut* (5th Cir. 2000); Dornis & Wein 2016, 424–26. The use of comparative advertising is significantly more restricted in the European Union. *See* Dornis & Wein 2016, 430–39.

While most competition today in the high technology sector is among different standardized *products* (e.g., Apple and Samsung smartphones, each of which implements the latest Wi-Fi, 4G and Bluetooth protocols) rather than among different standards, competition among standards was prominent in the "standards wars" of the past (e.g., VHS v. Betamax, HD-DVD v. Blu-ray, OpenXML v. ODF).[83] In these settings, advertising that compared the features of competing standards could have been warranted and may even have assisted consumers in making purchasing decisions. As new technologies such as the Internet of Things emerge, it is again possible that standards will compete for market share and the use of standard-names in advertising may increase.

B. HOW TRADEMARKS AND CERTIFICATION MARKS ARE USED IN STANDARDIZATION

Trademarks and certification marks play an important role in the standardization ecosystem. SDOs identify themselves and their work through their organizational names, also known as "house marks." For example, APPLE is the house mark of Apple Inc. In addition to its house mark, Apple Inc. has registered additional marks, such as IPAD and MACBOOK, for particular products. In a similar manner, many SDOs select unique names for individual standards, sometimes incorporating the SDO's house mark and sometimes not. The names of standards (referred to in this chapter as "standard-names"[84]) serve as the primary mechanisms by which consumers identify and differentiate the standardized technologies that are implemented in a broad range of products. Around the world, even young children can immediately identify the distinguishing features of a USB drive versus a DVD disc and the pros and cons of connecting headphones to a computer using a wireless Bluetooth link versus a wired 3.5mm jack. Yet the ways that different SDOs regulate the use of their trademarks vary dramatically, sometimes with potential implications for market adoption and usage.

1. House Marks

Every SDO has a house mark, and in most cases this mark is registered as a trademark in at least the jurisdiction in which the SDO is based.[85] In addition, many SDOs that operate internationally register their house marks in multiple jurisdictions where they or their members conduct significant operations. ISO, for example, claims that it has registered its name and principal logo in more than 100 countries.[86]

The most comprehensive form of trademark protection exists in the block text version of a mark (also referred to as "standard characters" and "typed drawing"). Most corporate names, including SDO names, are registered in this fashion (Figure 12.1a).[87] In addition to their names, many SDOs have also registered stylized designs or logos. These may include the SDO name in a distinctive script (Figure 12.1b)[88] or accompanied by one more fanciful design elements

---

[83] *See* Shapiro & Varian 1998.
[84] For purposes of this chapter, I hyphenate the term "standard-names" when referring to the names of technical standards, as opposed to unhyphenated "standard names" – names that are commonplace or standardized in some manner.
[85] *See* Biddle et al. 2017 (finding that 33 of 40 SDOs studied have registered their house mark as a trademark).
[86] ISO 2018b.
[87] U.S. Trademark Reg. No. 3,249,072 (June 5, 2007) (IETF).
[88] U.S. Trademark Reg. No. 4,079,772 (January 3, 2012) (ASTM).

IETF

Fig. 12.1a   Fig. 12.1b   Fig. 12.1c   Fig. 12.1d
Typed drawing   Word with design   Word with design   Design only

FIGURE 12.1 Standards and trademarks

(Figure 12.1c).[89] Finally, some SDOs have also obtained trademark protection for stand-alone designs, such as the Bluetooth "Runic B" (Figure 12.1d).[90]

2. Standard-Names

While some SDOs such as IETF protect only their house marks, other SDOs also seek trademark protection for the names of the standards that they release.[91] At one level, standard-names are necessary to differentiate one standard from another and to signify different versions of standards as they evolve over time. But trademark coverage for standard-names can also enhance an SDO's reputation, improve consumer recognition, and help an SDO combat piracy of its standards. The seriousness with which SDOs take the selection of standard-names should not be underestimated. As Judge Easterbrook colorfully noted in ADA (7th Cir. 1997, p.979), "blood is shed" over the naming and numbering of protocols as seemingly anodyne as dental procedures. SDOs have taken several different approaches to creating and protecting standard-names, including the choice between seeking trademark and certification mark protection. Some of the approaches that SDOs have taken to the selection and protection of standard-names are summarized below.

a) House Marks

Particularly in the case of SDOs that are small consortia focused on the development of a single standard or set of standards, the SDO's house mark may also be used as the name of the resulting standard. Examples include the *Bluetooth* standard released by the Bluetooth Special Interest Group, the *HDMI* standard released by the HDMI Users Forum and the *USB* standard now maintained by the USB Implementers Forum.[92] What's more, many SDOs that utilize alpha-numeric designations for their standards (see Section B.2.c below) also attach their house mark to the name of the standard (e.g., ISO 9001 and IEEE 802.11ab). As discussed above, many SDOs have obtained trademark registrations for their house marks. Thus, the names of standards that incorporate an SDO's house mark may have a degree of built-in protection.

b) Descriptive Titles

In many cases, SDOs designate standards using descriptive titles. For example, ISO's well-known ISO 9001:2015 standard is blandly titled "Quality Management Systems – Requirements" and

---

[89] U.S. Trademark App. S/N 89/000874 (filed July 31, 1996) (ITU).
[90] U.S. Trademark Reg. No. 3,389,311 (February 26, 2008) (technically, the "B" is registered as a word mark consisting of a single letter in stylized script).
[91] *See, e.g.,* Biddle et al. 2017 (of 40 SDOs studied, 33 registered a house mark and 20 of these registered at least one additional mark).
[92] The Uniform Serial Bus (USB) standard was originally developed in 1994 by a group of seven firms: Compaq, Digital, IBM, Intel, Microsoft, NEC and Nortel. The maintenance and evolution of the standard has since been assumed by the USB Implementers Forum, a non-profit organization.

IETF's foundational standard for the Internet, RFC 791,[93] is simply named "Internet Protocol." These textual titles, which describe the nature of the standard in technical terms, are likely to be considered descriptive or generic in nature under the *Abercrombie* framework and unlikely to be eligible for trademark protection. Moreover, from a practical standpoint, they are often long and jargon-laden (e.g., IEEE's 139–1988 standard "Recommended Practice for the Measurement of Radio Frequency Emission from Industrial, Scientific, and Medical (ISM) Equipment Installed on User's Premises"), which, even if protectable, would be of limited use in labeling compliant products in a convenient and consistent manner.

c) *Alphanumerical Designations*

As noted above, in addition to an SDO's house mark and a descriptive textual "title," many standard-names include an alphanumerical designation: ISO 9001, IEEE 802.11ac, RFC 791. In rare cases, this alphanumerical designation may be descriptive of some feature of a standard. For example, the term 3G was used to describe a range of third generation wireless communication protocols. In this case, the term "3G" signifies the third generation standard. A similar situation might arise if a standard's designation were tied to a particular transmission speed (e.g., 512 gigabits per second) or encryption level (e.g., 512-bit encoding). Finally, as in the case of ISO 9001:2015, part of a numerical designation may indicate a release year or version number. In these cases, the alphanumerical portion of the standard-name is likely to be considered descriptive for trademark purposes and would be difficult to protect.

However, in many cases a standard's alphanumerical designation is simply an indication of the sequence in which the standard was published (e.g., IETF's standards are numbered as RFCs in roughly the sequential order of their publication), or an arbitrary numerical designation, like a part number in a piece of machinery. As such, under the *Abercrombie* hierarchy, such alphanumerical designations could be considered arbitrary and hence amenable to registration.[94] Several famous numerical trademarks exist, including Boeing's registrations of the numerals 737, 747, etc. for aircraft[95] and Levi's registration of 501 for jeans.[96] In the context of standards, IEEE has registered the numerical designation 802[97] for "publications, namely, pamphlets of standards and specifications for local and metropolitan area networks."[98] It is likely that other arbitrary alphanumeric designations forming portions of standard-names could also be registered as trademarks.

This being said, most SDOs elect not to register the alphanumerical designations of their standards. There are likely several reasons why they do not. First, SDOs often release large numbers of standards[99] and seeking to register them all could result in a significant cost and resource burden. Second, most standards that are released by SDOs do not gain significant market adoption and seeking registrations for the numerical designations of these standards would probably not be a good use of resources. Third, it is unlikely, except in rare instances, that consumers will recognize, let alone build up loyalty to, any particular standard's numerical designation, again making a trademark registration of questionable value. Finally, the most common form of infringement faced by SDOs is the unauthorized sale or distribution of their standards,

---

[93] "RFC" is an abbreviation of "Request for Comments" and is the customary nomenclature for IETF standards.
[94] Numerals may be registered as trademarks in Europe and other jurisdictions as well. *See Seven SpA v. OHIM* (CJEU 2011).
[95] U.S. Trademark Reg. No. 857,824 (October 1, 1968) (737); U.S. Trademark Reg. No. 905,785 (January 12, 1971) (747).
[96] U.S. Trademark Reg. No. 1552985 (August 22, 1989) (501).
[97] The 802 series of IEEE standards include 802.11 (wireless networking also known as "Wi-Fi") and 802.3 (Ethernet). As discussed below, the term "Wi-Fi" is not owned by IEEE, but by the Wi-Fi Alliance.
[98] U.S. Trademark Reg. No. 2,342,235 (January 25, 2000) (802).
[99] *See, e.g.,* ASTM 2018d (claiming that more than 12,000 ASTM standards are currently in use around the world).

often by offshore entities.[100] While this practice undoubtedly involves infringement of the SDO's copyrights and other potential claims, it is not clear that a claim for trademark infringement will be available if the copyist is simply distributing the SDO's own work.[101] Thus, while IEEE may have deemed it worthwhile to register 802 as a trademark for its pervasive networking standards, most SDO numerical designations do not appear to warrant formal protection.[102]

d) Acronyms

Many standard-names are acronyms for longer descriptions of one or more principal functional features of the standard. For example, the following acronyms are arguably well-known abbreviations for functional descriptors of standards:[103]

CDMA	Code Division Multiplex Access (Qualcomm)
PDF	Portable Document Format (Adobe)
MP3	Moving Picture Experts Group (MPEG) Layer-3 Audio (ISO/IEC)
TCP	Transmission Control Protocol (IETF)
HDMI	High Definition Multimedia Interface (HDMI Forum)
USB	Uniform Serial Bus

Under U.S. law, an acronym or abbreviation will generally be considered descriptive or generic if the terms that it abbreviates are themselves descriptive or generic and consumers would understand the acronym to be "substantially synonymous" with the terms that it abbreviates.[104] However, if such an acronym develops secondary meaning and comes to be associated in the public eye with a particular source of goods or services, then the acronym may be deemed distinctive. For example, the mark IBM, which is well-known as an acronym for International Business Machines Corp., is likely registered on the basis that IBM is associated in the minds of consumers with IBM Corp. and has thus acquired secondary meaning.

Acronyms may also be registered as trademarks in Europe. However, as in the United States, the EUIPO explains that "[a]bbreviations of descriptive terms are in themselves descriptive if they are used in that way, and the relevant public, whether general or specialized, recognizes them as being identical to the full descriptive meaning."[105] Thus, according to one commentator,

---

[100] For example, see the following Reddit post by "StandardsPirate" in April 2018:

> If anyone reading this is able to get a hold of pristine standards documents or other technical rules, please get in touch with me (PM). Maybe your employer, university or local library has network licenses or a DVD lying around somewhere? Maybe you are even able to scan some documents for which no PDF exists?
>
> I'm part of a small group of people that specializes in standards piracy and we are always on the lookout for new sources. We are proficient in watermark removal, so don't let those deter you. National or international standards, English or foreign language, official translations, historical/withdrawn documents, drafts. All are welcome. www.reddit.com/r/Piracy/comments/8bfdnb/where_to_find_iso_en_and_din_standards/

[101] Simply redistributing a manufacturer's branded product without consent may violate one or more agreements and/or constitute an unfair business practice, but under the doctrine of nominative fair use, it is unlikely to be trademark infringement. *See Swarovski v. Building #19* (1st Cir. 2013).

[102] Notwithstanding the likely unavailability of trademark protection for alphanumerical designations in standard-names, some degree of copyright protection may be available for SDO numbering systems/series. *See Feist* (U.S. 1991).

[103] Note that not all acronyms abbreviate English words. GSM, for example, the principal 2G wireless telephony standard adopted in Europe, originally stood for the French term "Groupe Spécial Mobile." Today, however, the acronym GSM is generally understood to stand for "Global System for Mobile communication."

[104] PTO 2017, § 1209.03(h). *See, e.g., In re Thomas Nelson* (TTAB 2011) (acronym "NKJV" is descriptive because it is substantially synonymous with the term "New King James Version," a descriptive term for a type of Bible).

[105] EUIPO 2017, 12.

TABLE 12.1 *Distinctiveness of standard-names*

Standard-name	Description	Distinctiveness Level*
Internet Protocol	IETF packet switching	descriptive
Blu-ray	high-resolution video discs and players	suggestive
Lightning	device charging and data connectivity	suggestive
FireWire	IEEE 1394 serial bus interface (Apple)	suggestive
i.Link	IEEE 1394 serial bus interface (Sony)	suggestive
Lynx	IEEE 1394 serial bus interface (Texas Instruments)	suggestive
Gopher	Internet-based file transfer protocol	arbitrary
Java and coffee cup logo	programming environment	arbitrary
Bluetooth	short-range wireless connectivity	arbitrary
Zigbee	Internet of Things (IoT) framework	fanciful
802.11	IEEE wireless local area networking	fanciful or arbitrary
Wi-Fi	IEEE 802.11 wireless local area networking	fanciful or suggestive

* These classifications are based on the author's initial estimates only, without reference to any external sources or data.

if the term AAC is understood by industry participants to mean "Advanced Audio Coding," it would not be registrable even if, standing alone, it might seem to be distinctive.[106] This being said, ETSI claims to have registered certain acronym standard-names in Europe, including LTE (for the "Long Term Evolution" 4G wireless telecommunications standard) and UMTS (for the "Universal Mobile Telecommunications System" 3G wireless telecommunications standard).

e) *Distinctive Standard-Names*

In some cases, the names of standards are not merely descriptive acronyms or alphanumeric designations, but suggestive, fanciful or arbitrary terms. Table 12.1 lists a number of standard-names and their possible distinctiveness level under the *Abercrombie* framework.

As discussed above, suggestive marks are those that may suggest the nature of the marked product or service, but require "imagination, thought and perception to reach a conclusion" as to its actual nature.[107] For example, the mark BLU-RAY, which is used for a high-definition video disc standard, reflects the use of laser light in the blue-violet frequency band, offering shorter wavelengths, and thus higher storage capacity, than prior generation red laser light. Some highly sophisticated consumers would be aware of the superiority of blue-violet light over red light to store and read data on a physical medium. However, even if this were the case, the BLU-RAY mark for video discs and players would at most be suggestive (unlike, for example, the use of the mark for a flashlight with a blue beam). Thus, under the *Abercrombie* framework, BLU-RAY is likely to be a suggestive mark and thus distinctive. Similar arguments can be made for Apple's LIGHTNING protocol (suggesting a fast data transfer rate) and the trade names that Apple, Sony and Texas Instruments, respectively, devised for the IEEE 1394 serial bus standard (FIREWIRE, suggesting a fast/hot speed, I.LINK, suggesting device connectivity, and LYNX, also suggesting connectivity).

Arbitrary marks are common words that are applied in a unfamiliar or novel context. For example, the GOPHER data transmission protocol was named for the Golden Gopher, the mascot of the University of Minnesota, where it was developed.[108] Thus, like a toucan representing

---

[106] Graver-de-Looper 2016.
[107] *Abercrombie* (2d Cir. 1976, ¶18).
[108] Kozierok 2005, 1431–32.

University of Minnesota's "Golden Gopher", borrowed for the GOPHER protocol

King Harald Bluetooth, borrowed for the BLUETOOTH standard

Sun Microsystems' JAVA logo

FIGURE 12.2 Arbitrary standard-names and designs

a breakfast cereal,[109] the name of a small rodent as an Internet protocol is fairly arbitrary. Sun Microsystems' use of the mark JAVA and a steaming cup of coffee for a programming language and application development environment are similarly arbitrary.

But perhaps the most curious standard-name in recent times is that of the BLUETOOTH protocol for short-range wireless connectivity that connects peripherals such as headsets and speakers to computers, phones and tablets. Lore abounds regarding the origin of this mark, but the following explanation seems more than plausible:

> Ericsson originally called their technology "Bluetooth" after Harald Bluetooth, who was king of Denmark between 940 and 981. During his rule, Denmark and Norway were Christianised and united, so Ericsson used the analogy that he "allowed greater communication between people" when naming their wireless communication protocol.[110]

Clearly, even with this remote association with "communication," using the name of an ancient Viking king to designate a technological protocol is rather arbitrary,[111] thus making the BLUETOOTH mark quite strong on the *Abercrombie* scale.

Finally, fanciful marks – coined words with no ordinary language connotation – are considered to be the most distinctive category of marks on the *Abercrombie* scale. Zigbee Alliance's mark "ZIGBEE," used to describe a framework specification for the Internet of Things, likely qualifies as fanciful, as Zigbee is not an ordinary word in the English language nor an abbreviation or acronym. Another potentially fanciful standard-name is WI-FI, which designates IEEE's 802.11 family of wireless local area networking standards. The significance of the name WI-FI is subject to some debate. IEEE released the first version of 802.11 in 1998. In 1999, the Wireless Ethernet Compatibility Alliance (WECA) was formed to test and certify products for 802.11 compliance. According to one of the founders of WECA, shortly after its formation WECA engaged the marketing firm Interbrand (the creator of blockbuster brands such as "Prozac" and "Compaq") to re-brand 802.11 along more colloquial lines.[112] From ten candidate names

---

[109] *See Kellogg v. Toucan Golf* (6th Cir. 2003) ("Toucan Sam" is arbitrary, and hence a strong trademark).
[110] Thompson 2011.
[111] Note that the "runic B" that is also used in connection with the Bluetooth standard (see Figure 12.1.d) also evokes this Viking heritage.
[112] Doctorow 2005.

TABLE 12.2 *Standard-mark types of registration*

Mark	Owner	Type
BLUETOOTH	Bluetooth SIG	Certification Mark
DVD	DVD Format/Logo Licensing Corp.	Trademark
GSM	GSM MOU Corp.	Trademark
HDMI	HDMI Licensing	Trademark
HTML	W3C	Not registered (declared generic)
LTE	ETSI	Trademark/Service Mark
UMTS	ETSI	Trademark (EU)
USB	n/a	Not registered
WI-FI	Wi-Fi Alliance	Certification Mark

proposed by Interbrand, WECA chose "Wi-Fi." According to some sources, WI-FI was intended as a pun evoking an earlier era's "Hi-Fi" (high fidelity) sound recording technology. Early on, however, WECA decided to add a tag-line to the new logo: "The Standard for Wireless Fidelity." This tag-line led many to believe that WI-FI was simply an abbreviation for the term "wireless fidelity," though one WECA founder denies this.

The mark WI-FI could thus be classified in several different ways under the *Abercrombie* framework. First, if WI-FI is generally understood to be an abbreviation for "wireless fidelity," then WI-FI should have no greater distinctiveness than the term "wireless fidelity" itself. Wireless fidelity, however, does not indicate precisely what type of product it applies to. Certainly, the word "wireless" implies wireless functionality of some kind, but this could be a television signal, a satellite broadcast or a handsfree speakerphone. Thus, while "Wireless Fidelity" could suggest a wireless LAN, it is not necessarily descriptive of a wireless LAN, and would, most likely, be a suggestive mark. In that case, WI-FI would also be considered suggestive. If, on the other hand, WI-FI is not generally understood to be an abbreviation for "wireless fidelity," then the mark WI-FI, which has no ordinary English language meaning, could be considered fanciful under the *Abercrombie* framework. In either case, it is likely that the mark WI-FI would be distinctive.

f) Standard-Names as Certification Marks

The standard-names discussed above have generally been registered as trademarks or service marks. In some cases, however, SDOs register standard-names as certification marks. There appears to be little pattern regarding the decision to register a standard-name as a trademark/service mark or a certification mark. Table 12.2 above provides examples of standard-names that have been registered as trademarks, service marks and certification marks, as well as some standard-names that have no U.S. registrations whatsoever.

One might question why some standard-names are treated as trademarks rather than certification marks. SDOs that create standards have little use for standard-names other than to designate and identify their standards to product manufacturers. Admittedly, some SDOs support themselves through the sale of paper or electronic copies of their standards documents. However, unlike a breakfast cereal or a video game, the name of a technical standard seems unlikely to affect purchasing decisions in any meaningful way.

Thus, the principal market function for standard-names appears to be enabling product manufacturers to inform consumers that their products incorporate particular technical features (e.g., a smartphone that has Wi-Fi, Bluetooth and 4G LTE capabilities is clearly distinguishable from one that has only 3G UMTS capabilities). Almost certainly a consumer will have little preference for a standard developed by IEEE versus ITU versus Bluetooth SIG, as these organizations are virtually unknown to the general populace. Thus, the function of a standard-name is oriented more toward third-party product manufacturers than the SDO that developed the standard. As such, it is more intuitive that standard-names be treated as certification marks rather than trademarks. But even when standard-names function as certification marks, some SDOs impose rigorous certification and qualification requirements on manufacturers wishing to indicate that their products are standard-compliant. The range of SDO requirements regarding third party use of standard-name trademarks and certification marks are discussed in the following section.

g) Use of Existing Marks

As noted above, it may be permissible under the doctrine of nominative fair use to use a third party's trademark in a standards document when referring to that party's services or products (e.g., "this protocol is compatible with Apple IOS 11.8"). However, some SDOs may expressly prohibit the use of third-party marks in standard-names or the body of a standard's text. ANSI recommends that SDOs that reference third-party marks either do so in accordance with nominative fair use principles (i.e., non-endorsement by the mark owner) or seek permission of the mark owner.[113] Some SDOs, however, do not expressly prohibit the use of third-party marks in standards documents, but instead seek to educate standards developers regarding the consequences of doing so (see discussion of IETF in Section C.1, below).

C. SDO APPROACHES TO AUTHORIZING THE USE OF STANDARD-NAMES

In addition to a variety of distinct approaches to naming standards and protecting standard-names, SDOs also have a range of approaches toward authorizing others to use standard-names on products and services that are compliant with the relevant standards. Several of these approaches are summarized below.

1. Caveat Emptor

IETF is an organized activity of the Internet Society (ISOC), a District of Columbia non-profit corporation based in Reston, Virginia.[114] Prior to becoming part of ISOC, IETF was a loosely coordinated group connected with the early development of the Internet.[115] IETF is responsible for numerous key Internet standards including IP (Internet Protocol), TCP (Transmission Control Protocol), and HTTP (hypertext transport protocol).

IETF holds its intellectual property, including trademarks, domain names and copyrights, through the IETF Trust, an independent Virginia trust that operates for the benefit of the IETF community. The IETF Trust maintains trademark registrations for the IETF mark in multiple countries, and for its logo in the United States. It holds additional registered trademarks relating to the Internet Assigned Number Authority (IANA) function overseen by IETF. These can all be considered house marks.

---

[113] ANSI 2008, 4.
[114] While this description is accurate as of this writing, IETF is currently engaged in a formal review of its organizational structure.
[115] See Contreras 2016.

IETF permits the use of its house marks for descriptive purposes without prior approval, provided that such use conforms to IETF's published style guidelines.[116] Other uses of the marks, including use on t-shirts, social media platforms, conference posters and the like, require approval of the IETF Trust and the execution of a short-form license agreement.[117]

IETF does not, however, register the names of particular standards as trademarks. If a contributor to an IETF standard includes one or more trademarked terms in its technical contribution, IETF and all IETF participants obtain a royalty-free, perpetual license to use, reproduce and publish those terms in draft and final IETF standards documents.[118] Thus, if BigCo submits a draft standard to IETF entitled "The WHIZBANG® Standard for Internet Security," IETF and its participants are entitled to reproduce and publish the trademark WHIZBANG® in the documentation relating to the development of that standard, as well as in the final published standard.

However, neither IETF nor its participants obtain any license to use the trademarked term "in connection with any product or service offering."[119] Thus, the license that IETF participants obtain to use the term WHIZBANG® in the IETF standardization process does not extend to the use of WHIZBANG® to name their own product or service offerings, even if they implement the WHIZBANG® standard. Instead, each contributor to an IETF standard is "requested to state specifically what conditions apply to implementers of the technology relative to the use of such trademarks."[120] That is, on what terms would the owner of the WHIZBANG® trademark permit an implementer to market a product as the "WhizBang Kitchen Network Adaptor"? In some cases, the owner of the mark may wish to allow such use, so long as the implementer conforms to the WHIZBANG® standard. In some cases, the owner of the mark may wish to charge a royalty for use of the mark. And in some cases, the owner of the mark may not wish to authorize such use at all (e.g., suppose that instead of WHIZBANG®, the mark were MICROSOFT or APPLE). It is for these reasons that IETF requests that a mark owner disclose its licensing intentions with respect to the WHIZBANG® mark. Thus, if the terms on which the mark owner intends to license the mark are onerous, of if the owner does not wish to license the mark at all, then the relevant working group within IETF would be well-advised to avoid using the term WHIZBANG® in the name of the final standard.[121] But the onus for determining whether a mark used in an IETF standard will become problematic for implementers of IETF standards is left entirely to IETF participants and implementers. The SDO itself adopts a deliberately hands-off approach to all trademark usage issues beyond those involving the IETF house marks.

In summary, IETF controls only its house marks (the names/logos for IETF and IANA). It takes no action regarding standard-names other than requesting that owners of marks included in contributions to IETF standards disclose their intentions, if any, with regard to licensing of those marks. This approach can be broadly termed *caveat emptor* ("buyer beware"). Implementers of IETF standards are on their own to assess the risks and potential costs of using marks contained within IETF standards. While nominative fair use, in jurisdictions where it is recognized, will permit the manufacturers of standardized products to truthfully represent that their products are compliant with relevant IETF standards, other uses of protected marks in advertising and

---

[116] IETF Trust 2018c, Item 4 ("What usage is OK without a license?").
[117] IETF Trust 2018a; IETF Trust 2018b.
[118] IETF 2008, § 5.3(d).
[119] *Id.* at § 3.4.
[120] *Id.* at § 5.8.
[121] Readers may recognize many of these considerations as also arising in the context of patents covering standards. But while the use and licensing of patents covering industry standards has received significant attention, these issues have been underappreciated in the context of trademarks.

product names are not likely to be shielded from liability. This situation requires that IETF working groups pay attention to potential trademark issues in standard-names before standards are approved and adopted, and suggests that they take action (e.g., altering the names of draft standards to avoid protected marks and/or opposing such marks through available administrative routes (e.g., oppositions at the EUIPO or the U.S. TTAB)) prior to such approval.[122]

2. Member Certification

Unlike IETF, many SDOs seek trademark protection for standard-names. Many of these SDOs wish to permit implementers of their standards to use these names in relatively straightforward manner. For example, ETSI, which has registered standard-names including UMTS (3G wireless communications)[123] and LTE (4G wireless communications),[124] authorizes (and encourages) its members to use ETSI trademarks "in an appropriate and approved manner on, or in relation to, standard-compliant equipment and/or services," provided that they adhere to a set of customary stylistic and usage guidelines.[125] Non-members may also use ETSI trademarks on the same terms, provided that they obtain prior authorization from ETSI.

As noted above, ETSI permits the use of its marks on "standard-compliant equipment and/or services." Yet the determination whether a product is compliant with a particular ETSI standard is generally made by the product's manufacturer, not by ETSI. As discussed in Section A.2.b, this arrangement is referred to as self-certification or "first party" certification, and generally offers the lowest certitude with respect to compliance of the branded product.

The Bluetooth SIG has also adopted a members-only usage policy for the BLUETOOTH certification mark and associated logo (see Figure 12.1.d). While membership in the Bluetooth SIG is cost-free, Bluetooth SIG imposes fees (generally below US$25,000) in connection with the certification of products. In order to use the Bluetooth marks, licensees must execute a trademark license agreement with Bluetooth SIG which, when combined with the attached style guidelines, is over thirty pages in length.[126] Written license agreements are required by a number of other SDOs, including, for example, the USB Interoperability Forum (USB-IF) and the GSM Association.

The practice of limiting usage of certification marks to members of an SDO could raise questions regarding the mark owner's compliance with the non-discrimination requirement associated with certification marks. As noted in Section A.2.a, above, certification marks in the United States and Europe must be licensed to any party that complies with the relevant certification standard. Some SDOs that require membership in order to use a certification mark, such as Bluetooth SIG, do not charge for membership, thus alleviating this concern to some degree. However, SDOs that both require membership in order to use a certification mark and charge more than a nominal fee to join the SDO, or which charge excessive fees for product testing and certification, may risk the cancelation of their certification marks.[127]

---

[122] Again, the need to "work around" proprietary positions that are not available for licensing on acceptable terms also occurs in the context of patents, particularly at IETF, which imposes no affirmative obligation on IETF participants to grant licenses under standards-essential patents. See Contreras 2016 (describing IETF patent policies); NRC 2013, 73 (discussing the use of disclosures to enable standards working groups to work-around particular patents).

[123] UMTS does not appear to be registered in the United States. It is the subject of European trademark No. 797,688 (February 20, 2001).

[124] U.S. Trademark Reg. No. 3,922,100 (February 22, 2011) (trademark/service mark).

[125] ETSI 2018.

[126] Bluetooth SIG 2016.

[127] See Belson 2017, 64–65.

Like most SDOs, Bluetooth SIG requires that its marks be used only on Bluetooth-compliant products. However, the qualification procedure for Bluetooth products is more complex than for ETSI-compliant products. Products may be certified as compliant with the Bluetooth standard either by a product manufacturer (provided that it is recognized by Bluetooth SIG as a Bluetooth Recognized Test Facility (BRTF)) or by a third party recognized by Bluetooth SIG as a Bluetooth Qualified Test Facility (BQTF).[128] Bluetooth SIG charges fees for recognizing BRTFs and BQTFs, and for accepting manufacturers' designation of their products as Bluetooth-compliant.[129] BRTFs are permitted to perform certification testing only on their own products, and not for third parties. BQTFs, on the other hand, are authorized to provide certification testing for third-party products.

While many SDOs make it relatively easy for implementers of their standards to use the associated marks on standard-compliant products, there have been instances in which mark owners have sought to leverage their ownership of a standard-mark for commercial advantage. Egyedi, for example, describes Sun Microsystems' alleged refusal in the late 1990s to permit Microsoft to use its Java Compatible mark as part of a commercial dispute between the companies.[130]

3. License Agreements and Conduct Restrictions

Some SDOs that license their trademarks to members and others include restrictions on conduct in their license agreements that go well beyond conformity to the relevant standards. One common form of restriction seeks to prohibit licensees from challenging the validity of the licensed marks (a "no-challenge" clause). While the enforceability of no-challenge clauses in patent licenses has been significantly limited by the courts,[131] the same does not hold true for trademark or certification mark licenses, in which such prohibitions have been upheld.[132]

Another form of contractual restriction seeks to prohibit the licensee from engaging in conduct that could tend to damage the reputation of the mark owner. For example, the trademark license agreement used by the DVB Project requires the user to represent and warrant that it does not "engage in any audiovisual piracy" or "manufacture products that are intended principally to allow circumvention of a technological measure."[133] If a licensee does engage in one of these prohibited activities, the trademark license may be terminated. Though the prohibited activities (AV piracy and circumvention) do not strictly relate to a licensee's compliance with DVB standards, such activities could arguably tarnish DVB's reputation if a licensee were associated with DVB through the display of its trademark. In a sense, prohibitions of this nature are akin to termination rights commonly associated with celebrity endorsement arrangements, in which an agreement may be terminated if the celebrity engages in conduct suggesting moral turpitude.

4. Third-Party Certification

As discussed in Section B.2.e above, IEEE's 802.11 series of wireless local area networking standards is generally known by the term "Wi-Fi." The WI-FI mark[134] is owned by Wi-Fi Alliance,

---

[128] Bluetooth SIG 2018a.
[129] Bluetooth SIG 2018b.
[130] Egyedi 2001, pp. 19–20.
[131] *Lear v. Adkins* (U.S. 1969).
[132] Idaho Potato Comm'n (2d Cir. 2003) (upholding prohibition on challenges to certification mark).
[133] DVB 2018, § 3(d).
[134] U.S. Trademark No. 2525795 (January 1, 2002).

FIGURE 12.3 The Wi-Fi Certified logo

an independent testing and certification organization that is not formally related to IEEE. WI-FI is a certification mark that is intended to "certify that goods manufactured by authorized persons comply with interoperability standards." Wi-Fi Alliance has also registered a number of related certification marks, including WI-FI CERTIFIED, WI-FI CERTIFIED VANTAGE, WI-FI TIMESYNC, and WI-FI PASSPORT.

Wi-Fi Alliance conducts an active product certification program. It claims that over 40,000 different products have been certified to its standards. Product testing is conducted through a network of twelve independent Authorized Test Laboratories in North America, Europe and Asia.[135] In addition, Wi-Fi Alliance makes available a free, open source test suite that enables any manufacturer to test its products for standards compliance.[136] However, running this free test suite is not sufficient to obtain Wi-Fi Alliance certification, which is available only to Wi-Fi Alliance members through its Authorized Test Laboratories. In addition, a full software test suite is available to members. As noted in Section C.2 above, an SDO that does not permit all manufacturers of products complying with its standards to apply the relevant certification marks on a non-discriminatory basis may risk cancelation of its marks.[137]

Products certified by Wi-Fi Alliance may display the WI-FI CERTIFIED logo or one of the many additional certification marks licensed by Wi-Fi Alliance. Interestingly, the mark WI-FI itself, which is registered to Wi-Fi Alliance as a certification mark, is not one of the marks expressly authorized for use on certified products. This notable absence raises some questions regarding the status of the WI-FI mark. Perhaps Wi-Fi Alliance believes that it would have limited success regulating the use of the term Wi-Fi to signify products that implement IEEE's 802.11 standards. Certainly, under the nominative fair use doctrine, it would seem difficult for Wi-Fi Alliance to prevent manufacturers from truthfully advertising that their products implement the standard. But this could be achieved, presumably, by advertising a product as conforming to IEEE 802.11a, b, g, n, etc.[138] The term "WI-FI" is not strictly necessary to convey the fact that a product is compliant with an 802.11 standard, just as an auto repair shop that services Volkswagen automobiles may be permitted, as nominative fair use, to display the terms "Volkswagen" and "VW" but not Volkswagen's tag line "Fahrvergnügen" (a German neologism meaning "joy of driving"). This distinction is even more clear when the additional term is owned not by the owner of the principal mark but by a third party. So why does Wi-Fi Alliance retain its registration of WI-FI but not authorize or restrict its use? Is it possible that the term Wi-Fi has effectively become generic and available for all to use? This possibility is discussed at greater length in the following section.

---

[135] WFA 2018a.
[136] WFA 2018b.
[137] Implementers of Wi-Fi Alliance standards may become members for annual dues of $5,000 ($2,500 for small businesses). WFA 2018c.
[138] The question whether IEEE could police and/or prevent this usage using its trademark in the numerical designation "802" is a separate one. However, under the doctrine of nominative fair use, it seems unlikely that IEEE could prevent a product manufacturer from truthfully advertising that its product implements the relevant 802.11 standards.

5. Genericide

As discussed in Section A.4 above, terms that identify a general category of goods, rather than the particular source of those goods (e.g., car, café and computer versus Toyota, Starbucks and MacBook), are generic and cannot be registered or enforced as trademarks. Given the large investments that many firms make in building brand identity and goodwill, trademark owners often go to great lengths to prevent their marks from becoming generic.[139] For example, Xerox Corporation is well-known for appealing directly to the public in advertisements, pleading with readers not to use the word XEROX as a synonym for "photocopy."[140]

But, surprisingly, some SDOs have taken a divergent approach. Instead of seeking to prevent their standard-names from becoming generic, they have affirmatively stated that certain standard-names *are* generic. For example, the USB Interoperability Forum (USB-IF) is the owner of several trademarks and certification marks pertaining to the Uniform Serial Bus (USB) standard[141] (e.g., CERTIFIED USB[142]). Yet USB-IF does not hold a registration for the term USB itself. While USB, as an acronym for a relatively well-known descriptive term (Uniform Serial Bus), would likely be deemed descriptive under the *Abercrombie* framework, it is possible that the mark USB, which has been in use for more than twenty years, has developed secondary meaning and thus acquired distinctiveness. As such, it is not a term without potential value.

Nevertheless, USB-IF has publicly declared that the term USB is generic. For example, in a 2008 opposition proceeding before the TTAB, USB-IF opposed a third party's attempted registration of the mark USB-HOUSE (which lacked any disclaimer of the term USB) on the ground that the term USB is generic.[143] In the proceeding, the President and Chairman of USB-IF submitted a declaration stating that the term USB "is the common generic term used to describe a computer port that can be used to connect keyboards, mice, game controllers, printers, scanners, digital cameras, and removable media drives."[144] USB-IF also noted that there were more than eighty records in the U.S. Patent and Trademark Office's trademark database containing the term USB (e.g., USB NOW, USB REALTIME, FLEXIUSB, etc.), all of which contained a disclaimer of the term USB standing alone. USB-IF was successful in having the registration for USB-HOUSE denied.

Even more notable is the practice of the Worldwide Web Consortium (W3C). W3C is the primary standardization body for the Worldwide Web and is responsible for fundamental Internet application layer protocols including Worldwide Web (www), Hypertext Markup Language (HTML), and Extensible Markup Language (XML).[145] The acronym W3C is a registered trademark in a number of jurisdictions.[146] W3C also holds registered and unregistered trademarks in a number of project names including P3P (the Platform for Privacy Preferences Project) and the Amaya web browser/editor. Yet on its website, W3C expressly identifies twenty additional terms (including HTML, XML and HTTP) that it considers to be generic.[147] In doing so, W3C

---

[139] *See, e.g.*, Johnson 2017.
[140] Xerox Corp., Advertisement, ABA Journal, February 2008 (reproduced in Loren & Miller (2017, p. 515)).
[141] It is worth noting that the USB series of standards was not developed by USB-IF. Rather, the technical standards were developed by a group of promoter firms that later created USB-IF to manage and administer the standard and its associated trademarks. Intel (n.d.).
[142] U.S. Trademark No. 2,592,682 (July 9, 2002).
[143] *In re USB-HOUSE* (TTAB 2008).
[144] *Id.* at Ex. C.
[145] *See* Contreras 2016.
[146] Because W3C is not an incorporated entity, its intellectual property, including trademarks, is held by MIT.
[147] W3C 2018.

likely precludes itself from exercising control over the use of these standard-names. And while a self-declaration of genericism is not itself dispositive of the status of these terms (as genericism is a question of fact that can only be determined definitively through applicable legal processes, either at the TTAB or the courts), such a self-declaration by the creator of the relevant standard is likely to be viewed as strong evidence of the marks' genericism, should any other organization seek to establish proprietary rights over them.

CONCLUSION

Trademarks and certification marks are critical in identifying the thousands of technical standards that are in use today. SDOs have taken a variety of approaches to protecting standard-names, from the registration of dozens of marks throughout the world, to the registration of none. Likewise, SDO approaches to authorizing others to apply their marks to products vary considerably, from rigorous product testing requirements available only to SDO members to manufacturer self-certification to virtually no requirements at all. In this final category, some SDOs have even gone so far as to declare their own standard-names to be generic terms, a declaration that is still of uncertain legal significance.

But even without a declaration of genericness, there may be limits to the authority of SDOs that create standard-names to prevent product manufacturers from publicly declaring that their products implement the relevant standard. Many standard-names, particularly those that consist merely of descriptive titles and alphanumeric designations, are relatively weak in terms of trademark distinctiveness. And even for distinctive marks such as Bluetooth and Wi-Fi, the doctrine of nominative fair use in the United States and other countries permits a product manufacturer to refer to the mark owner's product or service (i.e., the standard) in a truthful manner that does not imply endorsement. Thus, some SDOs, in following corporate models of brand protection, may be over-protecting marks that are, in the end, intended primarily to assist consumers and product designers in understanding the interoperability features of today's complex products.

The same may be said of standard-names that are classified as certification marks. While in many ways a standard-name adheres more closely to the function of a certification mark than a trademark (i.e., indicating that a product meets certain technical criteria rather than that a standard was produced by a particular SDO) the strict certification criteria (and monetary charges) imposed by some mark owners may go beyond what is necessary to enable product manufacturers to inform consumers that a particular product implements a common standard. What's more, the registration, maintenance, licensing and policing of trademarks and certification marks are not cost-free, and the firms that have developed, and financially support, costly trademark programs for otherwise commonplace standard-names may wish to consider the value that is provided by such programs.

13

The Unregulated Certification Mark(et)*

*Jeanne C. Fromer***

A.	The Certification Mark as a Species of Trademark	232
	1. The Similarities	233
	2. Statutory Differences	234
	3. Consumer Perceptions of Certification Standards	235
B.	Exclusive Certification or Certification Exclusion? The Case of Swiss Watches	236
C.	Counterproductive Certification Marks	239
	1. Certifier Incentives	239
	2. Counterproductive Worries	240
D.	Fixing Certification Marks	244
	1. Substantive Regulation	245
	2. Procedural Regulation	246
	3. Antitrust Scrutiny	250

Certification mark law – a branch of trademark law – itself enables consequences that undermine the law's own goals through inadequate regulation or oversight. Because the law allows certification standards to be kept vague, high-level, and underdeveloped, a certifier can choose to exclude certain businesses inconsistently or arbitrarily, even when those businesses' goods or services would seem to qualify for the certification mark (particularly to consumers). Moreover, even when a certification standard is clear and complete, certifiers can wield their marks anticompetitively. They can do so through redefinition – something certification mark

---

* A version of this work previously appeared in Fromer (2017).
** For their gold-standard comments, I am grateful to David Abrams, Amy Adler, Arnaud Ajdler, Barton Beebe, Christopher Buccafusco, Emiliano Catan, Harlan Cohen, Julie Cohen, Adam Cox, Jorge Contreras, Graeme Dinwoodie, Rochelle Dreyfuss, Harry First, Eleanor Fox, Dev Gangjee, Kristelia Garcia, Jim Gibson, Eric Goldman, Michael Avi Helfand, Scott Hemphill, Laura Heymann, Jake Linford, Mark McKenna, Alexandra Mogyoros, Paul Ohm, Lucas Peeperkorn, Lisa Ramsey, Edward Rock, Albert Rosenblatt, Daniel Rubinfeld, Zahr Said, Jason Schultz, Victoria Schwartz, Jeremy Sheff, Christopher Sprigman, Katherine Strandburg, Neel Sukhatme, Rebecca Tushnet, Philip Weiser, and Katrina Wyman, as well as participants at workshops at Georgetown University, New York University, Oxford University, and University of Colorado law schools and at the fourteenth annual Intellectual Property Scholars Conference. I thank Emily Ellis, Andrew Hunter, Jordan Joachim, James Salem, and Russell Silver-Fagan for excellent research assistance. I also gratefully acknowledge support from the Filomen D'Agostino and Max E. Greenberg Research Fund.

law currently allows without oversight – to ensure that certain businesses' goods or services will not qualify for the mark. Both of these forms of certification mark manipulation undermine the goals of certification marks: to protect consumers by providing them with succinct information on goods' or services' characteristics and to promote competition by ensuring that any businesses' goods or services sharing certain characteristics salient to consumers qualify for a mark certifying those characteristics. The law should be restructured to curb this conduct. I advocate for robust procedural regulation of certification standard-making and decision-making that would detect and punish poor certification behavior. Moreover, for anticompetitive behavior that nonetheless slips through the regulatory cracks, I suggest attentive antitrust scrutiny to catch it.

A. THE CERTIFICATION MARK AS A SPECIES OF TRADEMARK

Under U.S. law, the Lanham Act provides for federal protection of trademarks, including certification marks. According to the statute, a certification mark is

> any word, name, symbol, or device, or any combination thereof ... [intended] to certify regional or other origin, material, mode of manufacture, quality, accuracy, or other characteristics of [a] person's goods or services or that the work or labor on the goods or services was performed by members of a union or other organization.[1]

Examples of certification marks abound: Underwriters Laboratories' UL mark certifies the safety of a vast range of products (including fire extinguishers, band saws, and carts powered by electric batteries);[2] the Orthodox Union's OU mark certifies that food is kosher according to rabbinic standards;[3] the IDAHO and GROWN IN IDAHO certification marks are used by the Idaho Potato Commission to signify potatoes that were grown in the state of Idaho;[4] the G, PG, PG-13, R, and NC-17 movie ratings are employed by the Motion Picture Association of America (MPAA);[5] and the GOOD HOUSEKEEPING seal of approval is used to warrant that tested products "perform as intended."[6]

This regime contemplates that certifiers themselves establish the particular standard that products or services must meet to be certified.[7] Consumers who see a certification mark on a good or that is associated with a service can reasonably infer that the good or service meets the certification's established standard.[8]

Although there are some crucial differences, the certification mark is a species – or perhaps a sibling – of the trademark.[9] In the following sections, I explain how the certification mark fits into, and diverges from, trademark law and theory.

---

[1] 15 U.S.C. § 1127.
[2] UL Registration; UL 2018b.
[3] OU Registration; Orthodox Union 2018.
[4] GROWN IN IDAHO Registration; IDAHO Registration; Idaho Potato Commission 2018.
[5] G Registration; PG Registration; PG-13 Registration; R Registration; NC-17 Registration; MPAA & NATO 2010, art. II, § 3.
[6] GOOD HOUSEKEEPING PROMISES LIMITED WARRANTY TO CONSUMERS REPLACEMENT OR REFUND IF DEFECTIVE Registration; Good Housekeeping 2014.
[7] McCarthy 2017, § 19:91.
[8] Id.
[9] 15 U.S.C. § 1054.

1. The Similarities

Trademarks identify and distinguish particular sources of goods or services.[10] A focus on fair competition drives trademark law.[11] According to one classic take, trademarks bolster trade by "identify[ing] a product as satisfactory and thereby ... stimulat[ing] further purchases by the consuming public."[12] Per this notion, producers of trademarked goods will be encouraged to invest in the goods' quality because consumers will use the trademark as a way to identify a desirable good only if their past experiences with a particular producer's goods reliably forecast the good's worth.[13] Protecting against trademark infringement, from this vantage point, thus prevents others from trading on the goodwill that is represented by the trademark and helps consumers be certain they can easily find the products they seek.[14] In all of these ways, trademarks reduce consumers' otherwise steep search costs – the expenditures they must make to discern important but hard-to-ascertain qualities of goods or services – by conveying this information succinctly.[15] Trademarks, then, ought to promote trade and enable consumer decision-making. To achieve these goals, trademark law guards against use of a too-similar mark that causes consumer confusion as to goods' or services' origins.[16]

Certification marks serve a similar role in providing shorthand information to consumers that certified goods or services comply with standards about which they might care, such as complex religious rules for being kosher. Margaret Chon theorizes that certification marks – if implemented properly by "represent[ing] accurately the standards purported to be embodied within the products (and services) being purchased by consumers" – can "facilitate consumer protection and access to quality market information."[17] Certification marks can facilitate consumer trust in buying compliant goods or services from sources they do not otherwise know (or those that are distantly located).[18] Like trademarks, certification marks can also encourage purveyors of goods and services to provide quality goods or services that conform to those marks' standards, to the extent that consumers care about them. Similarly, prohibiting certification mark infringement safeguards the investments of both certifiers and businesses with certified goods or services and protects consumers from experiencing confusion in the marketplace as to certification. One can – but need not – register a trademark or certification mark with the U.S. Patent and Trademark Office (PTO) to protect it.[19] Nonetheless, the law encourages the registration of marks by providing incentives to do so, such as enhanced remedies in federal court.[20] To qualify for registration, a trademark must be distinctive of the source of the goods or services with which it is used; used in commerce; and not otherwise barred by statute from protection, such as because it is confusingly similar to an already-registered mark or is deceptive.[21]

---

[10] 15 U.S.C. § 1127.
[11] McKenna 2007, 1840–41.
[12] Schechter 1927, 818.
[13] Landes & Posner 1987, 269.
[14] Bone 2006, 549; Dogan & Lemley 2004, 778.
[15] Beebe 2004, 623. *But see* McKenna 2012, 71–72.
[16] Dinwoodie 1999, 614.
[17] Chon 2009, 2312.
[18] *Id.* at 2318.
[19] 15 U.S.C. §§ 1052, 1114, 1125(a).
[20] *Id.* §§ 1057(c), 1072, 1117(b), 2065.
[21] *Id.* §§ 1051, 1127.

2. Statutory Differences

Ostensibly, then, the statutory framework for certification marks seeks to further trademark law's twin goals of consumer protection and promotion of competition. There are, however, crucial differences. A major difference, already noted, is definitional. Trademarks indicate the source of a good or service, whereas certification marks indicate that the marked good or service meets the certifying standard.[22] Both types of marks might help consumers choose among goods or services, but they provide different information. As such, registrants for certification marks must provide information that those registering trademarks need not provide, including "a copy of the standards that determine whether others may use the certification mark on their goods and/or in connection with their services."[23]

Additionally, a certification mark owner may not "discriminately refus[e] to certify or to continue to certify the goods or services of any person who maintains the standards or conditions which such mark certifies."[24] This requirement creates a regime akin to compulsory licensing of certification marks.[25] By contrast, a trademark owner can generally refuse to license the use of its mark to others.[26]

Each of these two types of marks, by taking opposite approaches, acts to promote competition: businesses employing a trademark for their goods or services can help lower search costs for consumers and be encouraged to invest in the quality of their goods or services. These goals are achievable only if businesses can decide not to let others use their trademark. By contrast, certification marks serve to mark a good or service as complying with a standard that matters to consumers, so allowing all businesses whose goods or services conform to that standard helps consumers and promotes competition.

Additionally, unlike a trademark, which is used by its owner, a certification mark is registrable under the Lanham Act only if its owner does not itself "engage[] in the production or marketing of any goods or services to which the certification mark is applied."[27] Certification marks are treated differently because of the fear that a certifier competing in the marketplace with the goods or services it is certifying would no longer be able to certify objectively based on the certification standard.[28] That is, a certifier in that position might decide to deny certification to qualifying goods or services merely because they compete with the certifier's products or services. Such denials would undermine the utility of the certification mark by denying useful information to consumers and harming competition.

Finally, certification marks can remain registered unless the mark holder "does not control, or is not able legitimately to exercise control over, the use of such mark."[29] This condition is similar to trademark law's general rule that trademark owners have abandoned their rights in their trademark if they engage in naked licensing – a "grant of permission to use [the] mark without attendant provisions to protect the quality of the goods or services provided under the licensed mark."[30] As the Federal Circuit has explained, "the risk of misleading the public may be ... great[] because a certification mark registration sets forth specific representations about

---

[22] *Id.* § 1127.
[23] 37 C.F.R. § 2.45(a).
[24] 15 U.S.C. § 1064(5)(D).
[25] McCarthy 2017, § 19:92.
[26] Holmes 2012, § 11:2.
[27] 15 U.S.C. § 1064(5)(B).
[28] *Idaho Potato Commission* (2d Cir. 2003, p. 138); McCarthy 2017, § 19:94.
[29] 15 U.S.C. § 1064(5)(A).
[30] *Exxon* (5th Cir. 1997, p. 1075).

the manufacture and characteristics of the goods to which the mark is applied."[31] If a certification mark is being used on goods or services that do not meet the certification standard due to the certifier's lack of control, then the mark's major purpose is fundamentally undermined. This was recently found to be the case with the MADE IN USA certification, which was being conferred on businesses without any certifier oversight as to where the marked goods were made.[32]

3. Consumer Perceptions of Certification Standards

Underpinning these statutory differences is the premise that consumers have an accurate sense of the standard represented by a certification mark. This issue is less obviously relevant for trademarks writ large, which do not certify a specific standard and might instead merely convey a general sense of quality.

There can be significant mismatches between consumers' perceptions of a certification standard and the actual standard being applied. The harm caused by these mismatches can be substantial. To take a stylized example, if a certifier purports to apply a certain rule or standard (such as "lighter than five pounds, with packaging"), it would defeat the law's goals if the certifier were to approve of goods or services that do not comply with that purported rule or standard (in the example, products weighing five pounds or more, with packaging). If consumers truly care whether goods fall below this threshold weight, they would be misled by inaccurately certified goods. Moreover, competition could also be harmed. If consumers have misplaced faith in the certification standard, they might end up buying inaccurately certified products in a way that hurts those companies that produce accurately certified products (perhaps even at greater expense). Additionally, if consumers grow to distrust this certification standard, sales of accurately certified goods could also suffer, thereby harming competition.

There can be more complex mismatches between consumers' perceptions and the actual standard. Consumers might mistake a flexible certification standard for a clear-cut certification rule, or vice versa. For example, consumers might mistakenly think that the GOODLITE certification mark affixed to a product signifies the rule that the product is "lighter than five pounds, with packaging" when in fact it indicates the standard that the product weighs less than other similar goods. These consumers are not wrong about the certification's gist – indicating a light product – but are mistaken about the approach to measuring lightness – a standard instead of a rule. Whenever the GOODLITE certification is affixed to a product that weighs five pounds or more but in fact weighs less than other similar products, these consumers will mistakenly think the product weighs less than five pounds.

As a general matter, consumers might miscomprehend the particular boundaries of a certification rule or standard. They might, for instance, think that the GOOD HOUSEKEEPING seal of approval certification mark indicates that certified products are generally good products worthy of purchase, whereas the mark actually demonstrates that the certified products perform as intended. Or consumers might mistakenly believe that a particular kosher food certification signifies rabbinical approval of all aspects of a food, including its packaging, rather than just the food's ingredients and preparation. Consumers' misperceptions of a certification mark's signification – whatever the sort – can sometimes diminish or extinguish the

---

[31] *Midwest Plastic Fabricators* (Fed. Cir. 1990, p. 1572).
[32] Federal Trade Commission 2014.

mark's utility. They can do so by failing to recognize the mark's intended standard – or, even worse, be counterproductive by presuming a standard at odds with or distinct from the mark's intended standard.[33]

These mismatches are problematic only if consumers will not readily deduce that the certification standard is not what they think it is, either because they have been affirmatively misled or because of confusion as to the actual standard. In some circumstances, consumers will observe that certified goods or services do not conform to the specified standard, such as if a product certified to be blue is actually red.[34] But in many – perhaps most – circumstances, even the most astute consumers will not detect mismatches between perceived and actual certification standards. Sometimes consumers are unable to observe what is being certified, such as when the certified characteristic is the production process for goods or services or invisible components of goods.[35] At other times, the certification standard itself might be hard to ascertain or grasp precisely because of complexity or obscurity.

This is all to say that undetected mismatches can cause great mischief for the goals of certification marks. Precision, or at least consistency, and consumer perception of certification marks are both crucial to the marks' operating as designed. After introducing a case study of certification, this chapter analyzes how current certification mark law allows mismatches between consumer perceptions of certification standards and actual certification standards.

B. EXCLUSIVE CERTIFICATION OR CERTIFICATION EXCLUSION? THE CASE OF SWISS WATCHES

Many certification marks are used indisputably as the law intends: to promote fair competition and lower consumers' search costs for goods or services conforming to certain standards that are marked by the certification. But some certifiers behave questionably in employing their marks. In the case study that follows – the geographical indication for Swiss watches – a certifier is invoking its certifying standard to exclude certain providers of goods and services or to impose changes upon their businesses. The certifier is dominant in its domain (and might have power over the relevant certification market or even the downstream market in which it certifies). Its imprimatur thus carries significant weight for consumers who care about the certification. Query whether this certifier is deploying its certification properly to ensure that the products it is certifying meet its ideal standard or instead is manipulating the certification standard to exclude certain businesses at the expense of helping consumers and promoting fair competition.

Consider a geographical indication for Swiss watches. A geographical indication (GI) is a certification whose mark corresponds to a particular geographic region and certifies that the product bearing it has specific characteristics owing to its geographic region of origin or location.[36] In the United States, GIs are protected principally through certification marks of regional origin, oftentimes coupled together with product quality characteristics.[37]

---

[33] Misperceptions will not always cause harm to consumers or competition. Some misperceptions might be principally irrelevant. For example, that would be the case if the GOODLITE certification actually signifies products of less than 5.0003 pounds, but consumers think the mark signifies products of less than 5 pounds and in practice no certified product weighs 5 pounds or more.
[34] Meidinger 2008, 267.
[35] Id. at 268.
[36] Hughes 2006, 305–06.
[37] Id. at 308–11.

The Swiss government has instituted regulations for all watchmakers who would like to call their watches SWISS MADE. They care about this GI because Swiss watches have a (perhaps deserved) reputation of being of high quality.[38] In fact, Swiss watches generate half of the value of the $40 billion international watch market despite representing only 3 percent of the world's watches.[39] The SWISS MADE GI is thus clearly economically desirable. The Federation of the Swiss Watch Industry – which polices whether companies comply with the SWISS MADE certification criteria – protects this GI in the United States with a registered certification mark whose standard "certifies geographical origin of [watches] in Switzerland."[40]

Although one might reasonably think that a watch is Swiss made only if fully made in Switzerland, this is not the case. It is considerably more complicated. A watch is SWISS MADE according to Swiss law and the Federation of the Swiss Watch Industry if its movement is Swiss, its movement is cased up in Switzerland, and the manufacturer's final inspection takes place in Switzerland.[41] For a movement to be considered Swiss, among other things, it has to have components of Swiss manufacture that account for at least 60 percent – formerly at least 50 percent – of the movement's total value, without the cost of assembly.[42] This increase to 60 percent came in response to pressure from watchmakers in Switzerland fearing "foreign" competition that qualifies for the SWISS MADE certification under the 50 percent standard.[43] In fact, Swiss companies had been advocating for an increase to a requirement that at least 80 percent of the watch's total value come from Swiss components.[44]

These requirements – and the push to change them – are notable for three connected reasons: how malleable the standard is, how consumers are served by the standard, and how competition is affected by the standard. First, although GIs are renowned for maintaining static standards – even to the detriment of innovation – the example of Swiss watches shows, quite to the contrary, the malleability of a GI's standard. Against expectation, the SWISS MADE certification does not refer to watches wholly made in Switzerland. Rather, the definition is more nuanced, based on certain parts of the watch being Swiss or assembled in Switzerland and a certain percentage of the watch movement's value coming from Swiss components. One watch executive in Switzerland has noted that "[i]f everything in a watch really had to be Swiss-made, a large part of the Swiss industry would already have been destroyed."[45] Even though this GI standard has well-defined boundaries, those boundaries can be changed, as they recently were.

Second, it is open to debate whether consumer interests are well served by the SWISS MADE standard and its modification. Does the standard optimally capture what consumers care about or ought to care about with regard to a watch being Swiss made? Perhaps consumers care more about, say, the number of Swiss parts in the watch than the total value or that the watch was engineered in Switzerland. Regardless, how accurate is the consumer's understanding of the standard as it existed both before and after modification? Recall the problems that mismatch between perception and standard can cause for consumer welfare.

---

[38] *Swiss Watch Int'l* (T.T.A.B. 2012, p. 1742).
[39] Minder 2012.
[40] SWISS MADE Registration.
[41] Schweizerisches Zivilgesetzbuch 1971.
[42] *Id.* art. 2.
[43] Soon 2013.
[44] Minder 2012.
[45] *Id.*

Finally, what is the effect of this modification on competition? Most watchmakers in Switzerland that would undoubtedly qualify under a more stringent 60 or 80 percent value standard have been the ones advocating for a narrowed definition.[46] Such an arrangement would undoubtedly risk excluding smaller watchmakers in Switzerland. The bigger companies maintain that to protect consumers and maintain high quality, the certification standard must be constricted.[47] The president of the Federation of the Swiss Watch Industry, for instance, has stated that "[t]he 'Swiss Made' label confers a certain status in the marketplace. When you think watch, you think Swiss. It is to our advantage to preserve its value and credibility and to protect consumers who buy Swiss products."[48] The bigger companies articulate that given the nuanced SWISS MADE definition, businesses they do not think qualify as making Swiss watches had nonetheless been gaming the definition to qualify: for instance, by designing watches outside Switzerland but buying their movements from Switzerland, or by assembling a watch outside of Switzerland and then bringing it into Switzerland to put in the last screw and case up the movement.[49]

Smaller watchmakers in Switzerland think exclusion is what motivates the stricter standard. They worry that they will no longer qualify to apply the SWISS MADE certification to their watches because of increased expense. To stay competitive, these watchmakers rely on some cheaper foreign components that they import to Switzerland for assembly.[50] They maintain that many watch components made in Switzerland, like dials, are no better than foreign-made components but cost more in Switzerland because of higher labor costs there.[51] They fear an inability to remain competitive if they have to buy more Swiss-made components and at a heavier price to satisfy the stricter standard. They also worry that dominant Swiss movement manufacturers, like Swatch, will suppress the supply of movements, further reducing their chances of qualifying their watches as Swiss made.[52] One Swiss movement maker stated: "[T]his Swiss-made campaign is … about weakening rivals within Switzerland…"[53] Perhaps most troubling of all is the admission of one watchmaker in Switzerland that, in an age of globalization, the Swiss no longer have better watchmaking technology than anyone else in the world.[54] There seems to be a suspicious implication that the SWISS MADE standard is being manipulated to exclude competitors, not to indicate quality differences between watches. In a context in which the SWISS MADE certification is economically significant, that suggestion is dangerous for competition.

The SWISS MADE certification is suggestive of possibly troublesome exclusionary behavior. Are new entrants and smaller players being excluded from the GI's certification so that those who remain can charge supracompetitive rents? Or are excluded firms failing to meet an appropriately and increasingly demanding and exclusive certification standard? And how is the consumer affected by these standards and their modification? The next Part steps back from the specific example to analyze generally the confluence of circumstances under which certification marks can come to be used in ways that are counterproductive to the very purpose of certification marks.

---

[46] Id.
[47] Id.
[48] Lankarani 2009.
[49] Minder 2012; Soon 2013.
[50] Lankarani 2009.
[51] Id.
[52] Minder 2012.
[53] Id.
[54] Lankarani 2009.

C. COUNTERPRODUCTIVE CERTIFICATION MARKS

This Part builds an analytical framework to show that one cannot be sanguine that certification marks will have only positive or benign effects on competition and consumer welfare. Owing to the incentives of certifiers and the current state of certification mark law, certification marks can be counterproductive. Moreover, their negative potential is generally more worrisome than the negative potential within trademark law generally.

1. *Certifier Incentives*

A certifier typically earns money (and reputational success) through certification.[55] Thus, the more widely a certification is adopted, the more successful the certification tends to be. There are two prevalent paths to success for a certifier. First, if a business's consumers widely care about the standard the certifier is providing and the business trusts this certifier in particular, that business would reasonably seek out and pay for the certifier's certification for its goods or services.[56] Second, if a centralized body – typically a government – decides that a particular standard ought to be required for particular goods or services, certifiers of that standard can stand to play an important and lucrative role in assessing whether products comply with that standard.[57] Frequently, for both pathways, the certifier uses advertising or lobbying to convince consumers, businesses, or centralized bodies that the standard and the certification it provides ought to be important to them.[58] Taken together, then, consumers, businesses, or a centralized body must decide both that the certifier's standard is important and that the certifier is to be trusted in verifying that businesses' products or services meet the certifier's standard.

In light of these basic incentives, certifiers might become beholden to certain businesses seeking their certification at the expense of others. Although it seems that certifiers would want to maximize the number of businesses using them to certify, they may actually want to maximize their business by preferring certain businesses and excluding others. This differential treatment might occur out of a reputational or financial desire to keep the certification exclusive – by making sure some businesses get excluded – or because they can charge more overall if they give preferential treatment to certain businesses. For example, bigger businesses will tend to be more important clients of certifiers than smaller businesses. The price charged for a certification is typically proportional to the size of the business.[59] Moreover, bigger businesses tend to have more goods or services to certify and can pay accordingly. Therefore, bigger businesses are usually more critical to a certifier's success. Similarly, all other things being equal, certifiers might prefer businesses that already use a particular certifier – particularly for a long time – over those that are mere prospects. Certifiers might readily have this preference to protect their financial security and preserve their extant relationship with the existing business.

Certifiers' preferential treatment of some businesses over others can readily transpire even when certifiers are organized as nonprofit entities (which many of them are), despite scholarship suggesting otherwise. Jonathan Barnett stresses that certifiers that organize in the constrained nonprofit form do so to guard against being beholden to interests that pay them.[60] By design,

---

[55] Contreras & McManis 2013, 496. *See also* Chapter 14.
[56] Lytton 2013, 60–61.
[57] Contreras & MacManis 2013, 498–502.
[58] McCarthy 2017, §§ 19:91, 19:94.
[59] Amit 2014.
[60] Barnett 2012, 507; and Chapter 14.

nonprofit entities cannot distribute profits to managers, members, or other controlling parties and cannot compensate managers beyond a reasonable amount.[61] According to the conventional account, these constraints keep nonprofit entities honest.[62] Nonetheless, concerns about certifiers' preferences for some businesses over others are still present in substantial ways for nonprofit certifiers. As Jeffrey Brennan and Paul Cuomo note when discussing whether merging nonprofit entities should undergo antitrust scrutiny, "nonprofits are managed by people who – like their for-profit colleagues – have natural human and economic incentives to maximize their employer's welfare by increasing revenues to fund quality improvements, attract superior [employees], and similar goals."[63] The funds earned from certification can support the nonprofit organization's activities, including those unrelated to certification. Therefore, these entities still would rationally tend to be more responsive to certain businesses over others to the extent that maximizes their business interests, as with for-profit entities.[64] Just as they might support businesses that provide them with more money, they might also prefer businesses whose reputation better accords with the overarching mission of the certifying organization.

2. Counterproductive Worries

Although it is rational for certifiers to prefer certain businesses over others, that alone does not raise red flags that a certifier is going to be able to act in ways that undermine certification marks' purposes. This section explores the conditions under which the law ought to be worried about certifiers acting counterproductively: (1) when a certifier's standard is subjective, fluid, or vague; and (2) when the certifier has market power, either in the certification market or something this chapter calls "downstream market power." These conditions are problematic because they allow a certifying organization to manipulate its certification standard to exclude goods or services from certification in ways that can hurt competition and are contrary to consumers' understanding of the certification standard. Both of these effects undermine what certification marks seek to do: promote competition and consumer welfare.

a) Flexible Standards

Recall that the law of certification marks is premised on these marks' availability to every business whose goods or services satisfy the certifying standard. That open availability is thought to protect consumers who care about the certifying standard and promote competition by enabling businesses providing qualifying goods or services to obtain that certification.

In practice, however, certification standards are not fixed in any comprehensive sense. Registrants of certification marks must provide the PTO with information about the certifying standard, but the degree of detail is not mandated.[65] Standards tend to be articulated at the most general or abstract level, leaving room for their manipulation down the line. Take the example elucidated in the previous Part. The registration for the SWISS MADE certification mark for watches has as its certifying standard that the "geographical origin of [the watches is] in Switzerland." Vague – or at least capacious – standards plausibly give certifiers room to maintain that watches with over 50 or 60 percent of their value originating in Switzerland geographically originate in Switzerland.

---

[61] Hopkins 2007, 5, 559–61.
[62] Hansmann 1980, 843–45.
[63] Brennan & Cuomo 1999, 14.
[64] Brody 1996, 460.
[65] 37 C.F.R. § 2.45(a).

Certifiers have preserved these flexible standards in two ways. First, some certifiers do not publicly release much concrete and comprehensive information about the certification standard. And third parties cannot easily ascertain a certification standard based on which goods and services are certified and which are not.[66] Second, certifiers might make public more precise and complete certification standards, as in the case of Swiss watches. They then remain free to change those standards to other precise and complete standards that cohere with the more flexible registered certification standard, as the Swiss authorities did.

In light of a certifier's incentives to entrench its own certification mark, one can see why a certifier would want to keep its certifying standard flexible. Certifiers' success depends in large part on how much consumers and businesses trust the certifier. An aspect of that trust is how well the certifier's certifying standard appears to accord with the values these consumers and businesses have with regard to certification. Therefore, a certifier might reasonably want to ensure that its standards are kept flexible so that it can respond to requests to certify in light of the complete factual context based on its overarching certifying goals. This allows the certifier to maintain an intact reputation with its consumer and business base. For example, the certification standards specified in the registrations for the SWISS MADE mark are sufficiently elastic to accommodate these concerns.

This flexibility to define what a mark represents is native to trademark law generally. A company deploying a trademark, which signifies a cluster of values, can decide internally at any point that it wants the trademark to represent something different as a way to improve or refocus its business. Consider Burberry – the British fashion company – which became renowned as a luxury brand in the early to mid-twentieth century for its trench coats. It began using its now-iconic check print on these trench coats in 1924. About seventy years later, the check print became ubiquitous in mainstream culture, causing a "downmarket association" for Burberry's brand, according to one commentator.[67] In the early twenty-first century, however, in an effort to reclaim the brand's luxury meaning, Burberry executives chose to remove the check pattern from about 90 percent of its items to catapult Burberry back among the top few luxury brands.[68]

That said, certification mark standards are not intended to be internal to a business, as trademark "standards" are. Rather, they are to be specified and publicly available. And for good reason. Certification standard flexibility can undercut the goals of promoting competition and protecting consumers. For one thing, flexibility to redefine certification standards undercuts the benefits of standard stability over time. If consumers already understand a certification mark to stand for a particular standard, changes to that standard might be hard for consumers to detect, especially if consumers continue to see only the unchanging certification mark. In that regard, many consumers might come to hold incorrect, outdated views of the certification standard. As discussed above, such a mismatch undermines the goals of certification mark law. Relatedly, certification specification helps consumers learn the standard, and these benefits are more easily achieved if the standard is not changing.

Certification standard flexibility can also empower certifiers to carve out less-preferred businesses from their certification as a way to improve their standing with their preferred businesses or to prioritize other interests. Taking the example from the previous Part: were smaller watchmakers in Switzerland excluded from the constricted SWISS MADE certification standard to benefit larger watchmakers in Switzerland? If so, that indicates how certification standard flexibility can

---

[66] Contreras et al. 2011, 4–7.
[67] Day 2004.
[68] Hass 2010, 52.

undercut the goals of certification mark law of promoting competition and protecting consumers. As to competition, flexibility can lead to the unfair exclusion of certain businesses as a way to prefer other businesses or protect interests separate from the certification standard. This exclusion is unfair because it hurts competition by withholding the certification standard at issue from businesses not because of failure to meet the standard but for other reasons. To the extent the certification standard's presence or absence on goods or services enhances the business of the purveyor, the excluded purveyor is hurt competitively while the included purveyor is boosted competitively. Yet the certification standard's competitive value is supposed to derive directly from its providing shorthand information on a standard's presence or absence for particular goods and services – nothing more and nothing less. When the certification standard provides value to or withholds value from businesses for other reasons via certification standard manipulation, the certification mark has been improperly wielded. It constitutes unfair competition, plain and simple. For certifiers to nonetheless have the protection of federal trademark law enhancing their marks' value by preventing unauthorized use perverts trademark law's goal of promoting fair competition.

Sometimes the marketplace might be able to resolve this problem on its own. If a party detects a certification standard's misuse, that party might decide to enter the marketplace, offering an alternative certification that does not bend flexibly in favor of preferred businesses. Companies might then flock to the newer certification standard and away from the older one, all to the benefit of competition. If and when this market correction happens, there is less worry for certification mark law in terms of competition.[69]

That said, this market correction is unlikely to occur. For one thing, in the face of flexible standards with opaque, or at least complex, certification goals, it might be too hard for third parties to notice something amiss with a certification standard. The inconclusive nature of the Swiss-watch example, even with a potential whiff of misconduct, underscores how hard it is to detect and repair certification problems with new certifications. This opacity is not reduced by the fact that many certifiers do not publish concrete and comprehensive certification standards. Additionally, existing certifiers often have power in the marketplace, in the sense that they add value to certified goods and services. Even if certifiers do not have full-fledged market power, there are typically sufficient barriers to entry in the certification market preventing significant competition from emerging, as discussed below. Furthermore, when a certifier has downstream market power and wields flexible certification standards, the certifier might exercise control over a whole industry in ways that are particularly detrimental to competition.

Just as competition can suffer from flexible certification standards, consumers can also suffer by not having an accurate sense of what a certification represents. As discussed above with regard to the goals of certification marks, if consumers have an incorrect understanding of what a certification standard signifies, they will not benefit from the certification mark and might even be led astray in their purchases. The law seems to presume, without more, that consumers know what a certification that matters to them truly represents.[70] But that is often far from the case, as suggested by the technical complexity of the Swiss-watch certification standard. When certifiers deploy a standard in ways inconsistent with consumer perceptions, which is possible due to the standard's flexibility, this mismatch becomes worrisome. When there is a salient mismatch between consumer perception of a certification standard and the standard's actual reach, the values of consumer protection and promotion of competition are both undermined.

---

[69] That said, the proliferation of certification marks can also lead to consumer confusion and inability to compare product features. Contreras et al. 2011, 4–7.
[70] *Swiss Watch Int'l* (TTAB 2012, p. 1743).

This counterproductive use of flexible certification standards is worrisome. Before returning to a discussion of how to separate out the tolerable forms of standard flexibility from the less acceptable forms, this chapter turns to another counterproductive possibility for certification marks, when there is market power.

b) Certifier and Downstream Market Power

The incentives that certifiers might have to certify certain businesses and exclude others can be exacerbated by the ability to effectuate those goals when certifiers wield market power. Certifiers can have market power in two ways: first, simply in the market for certification of that kind, and second, perhaps even more concerning, in the downstream market for certified goods or services. The first kind of market power is straightforward. For example, if the Federation of the Swiss Watch Industry could charge more for its certifications than would prevail under conditions of competition in the market for watch certification, there is strong evidence that it has market power. Yet this market power does not necessarily stymie competition among certified goods or services in the downstream market. The second kind of market power – downstream market power – is more unusual and will occur only when there is already certifier market power: The certifier has enough market power over a certification of products or services about which consumers care that it confers market power in the downstream market of certified goods and services. That is, in light of the Federation of the Swiss Watch Industry's exclusive role in certification of SWISS MADE watches, which represent a disproportionate amount of profit to the watch industry, there is reason to suspect it might possess downstream market power.

Both sorts of market power are worrisome and can cause certification marks to operate counterproductively in ways that perhaps rise to the level of anticompetitive behavior forbidden by antitrust and competition law. Each situation can enable a certifier to take advantage of its competitive might and exclude select businesses from certification. It can do this in a number of ways, as discussed in the previous section, owing to certification standard flexibility: by maintaining a vague or incomplete standard so as to pick and choose in each instance which goods or services get certified or by setting or changing its standard to a clear and comprehensive one that matches the businesses whose goods or services it wants to certify.

A certifier with market power ought not to be able to use its power in the certification market to act anticompetitively – including by flexing its muscle to manipulate standards as a surgical tool for exclusion of some businesses and inclusion of others. This is the precise allegation that smaller watchmakers in Switzerland made as the Swiss organization constricted its standard for the SWISS MADE certification by increasing the percentage of watch movement value that must be Swiss: they alleged that they were being excluded from the SWISS MADE certification for the benefit of the larger watchmakers in Switzerland. Downstream market power is particularly troublesome because it can give the certifier power over the entire space of goods or services for which it offers certification.

Worth noting is that in many ways, the anticompetitive worries here are similar to those that antitrust scholars address with regard to standard-setting. As discussed in the companion volume, when there are patents that are essential to the implementation of standards, such as those enabling wireless telecommunications, competition will be negatively affected if some businesses are denied the possibility of using a standard necessary to compete.[71] Similarly, to the extent that a particular certification matters to consumers, those businesses excluded from

---

[71] *See* companion volume, Part II (discussing potential antitrust and competition issues in the United States and Europe arising from standardization).

the certification will find it harder, if not impossible, to compete. If this certification standard is deployed anticompetitively, the effect on competition can be both great and unfair. In the context of patents for industry standards, antitrust scholars maintain that the anticompetitive problem can be solved by licensing the patents on fair, reasonable, and nondiscriminatory terms.[72] The next Part takes up analogous proposals for certification marks.

How likely are these scenarios in which certifiers obtain one of these forms of market power, enabling them to act anticompetitively? Real-world conditions are ripe to enable certifiers to achieve market power. In particular, achieving meaningful competition in the certification market – which would eliminate certifier market power – is hard. There are two major barriers to entry for certifiers hoping to compete against existing certifications. First, there are supply-side barriers to entry. For a certification to be successful, it needs to garner a strong enough reputation to compete with established certifiers.[73] As discussed above, this reputation is hard to achieve, whether sought by building up a base in the marketplace (with businesses that might wish to adopt the certification or with their consumers), by establishing legal requirements or other standards that necessitate a particular certification, or both. Certifications have network effects; they tend to become yet more valuable as more businesses use them and more consumers rely on them. Building a sufficient reputation with regard to certification standards – typically informationally opaque by design – is costly and can take a long time.[74] Moreover, establishing a reliable network of certification agents can be difficult.[75]

There are also demand-side barriers to entry for certifiers. Businesses that wish to adopt a type of certification need to evaluate the possible certifiers' reliability and other qualities, which can be hard to do without using them but instead relying solely on readily available information.[76] If a business is already using a particular certification, it will thus be relatively costly to switch from the certifier the business has already evaluated through experience to one that is less assessable.[77] Additionally, businesses bear the cost of learning a certifier's process of collecting and assessing certification information about the business, a cost that weighs against switching certifiers.[78]

D. FIXING CERTIFICATION MARKS

This Part considers what might be done to keep certifiers from wielding their certification marks counterproductively. In short, there needs to be more regulation of the currently underregulated certification mark(et). This Part evaluates two possible forms of regulation internal to trademark law to temper the counterproductive behavior that stems from permitting flexible standards: substantive and procedural regulation of certification marks. Although a substantive approach – having the federal government define certifiers' standards – would put a damper on the misuse of certification standard flexibility, such an approach is generally undesirable because it undermines certification mark goals in other ways.[79] The preferable approach to

---

[72] *Id.*
[73] Barnett 2012, 478–79.
[74] *Id.* at 488.
[75] *Cf.* Lytton 2014, 558 (discussing how improving certifier reliability requires intensive efforts to "increas[e] expertise and accountability").
[76] Barnett 2012, 489.
[77] *Id.*
[78] *Id.*
[79] It also interferes with express government policies in the United States and Europe stating that privately developed interoperability standards should be used in agency regulation and procurement. *See* Chapter 2.

curbing the counterproductive behavior that stems from permitting flexible standards is instead procedural: to regulate private certifiers' process of crafting, disclosing, revising, or applying certification standards to safeguard against the misuse of flexibility. Moreover, to solve the problems that certifier and downstream market power can cause, there ought to be more attentive antitrust scrutiny external to trademark law.

1. Substantive Regulation

One straightforward approach to addressing the worries raised by certifiers' incentives to keep their standards flexible and then wield them counterproductively is to make sure those standards are not flexible in the first instance. Under this approach, certification standards would be clearly defined and perhaps unable to be changed over time. As this section contends, this approach would directly thwart flexible certification standards and the problems they enable but at the too-heavy price of the benefits that can also come from certification standard flexibility: agility and awareness to respond to changing or unexpected conditions out of responsiveness to consumer welfare and competition, the precise goal of protecting certification marks in the first place.

As I have previously explored with regard to other forms of intellectual property, articulating the bounds of the "thing" protected by an intellectual property right requires thinking up front and globally about all sorts of situations or manifestations that ought to be covered by the right.[80] This is no different for certification tests, if they are to be articulated up front and clearly. Great cost and care must be taken to define the certification test to account for the range of situations to which it might apply.

If the government were to undertake, or at least oversee, the ex ante fixing of certification tests, that would counteract the problems enabled by currently flexible certification tests because they would no longer be malleable. Although there are many ways in which this fix could occur, the most extreme way would be for the government itself to set the standard for each registered certification, likely through interacting with the certifier and possibly also with affected businesses and consumers. Having the government set standards for every certification mark is obviously less than realistic and is more of a thought experiment than a serious proposal. That said, sometimes the federal government has set such standards. Consider the federal government's certification for "organic" food. In 1990, Congress passed the Organic Foods Production Act to create a national standard for organic food certification in response to the states' different organic food labeling requirements.[81] After over a decade of wrangling with the public and interested industries over the standard for the "organic" certification, the Department of Agriculture issued detailed rules governing the process of growing, harvesting, raising, and preparing foods.[82]

The organic certification standard is clear and detailed, so it is not manipulable as an exclusionary tool. Yet it also has significant potential downsides as a certification test. For one thing, as with governmental ex ante rules generally, there is a fear that detailed rules can become ossified. Ossification can happen both because the certification test does not address situations that arise after the test is crafted and also because the test's details fall out of step with evolved norms and values of society. Warranted or not, ossification seems to be a large part

---

[80] Fromer 2009a, 757.
[81] Organic Foods Production Act of 1990.
[82] U.S. Department of Agriculture 2002.

of the criticisms that have been directed at the "organic" certification standard. For example, critics want to exclude wild-harvested seafood from certification[83] and make changes to the certification's dairy standards.[84] It is costly and sometimes politically implausible to redefine government-set tests to accommodate new circumstances, so in many instances, out-of-date rules remains standing.

Moreover, government-crafted substantive standards that are inflexible in practice would likely not improve the current state of certification mark law. While there may be problems with flexible certification standards, they can be useful in allowing certifiers to make appropriate decisions at the moment of certification, all in service of the goals of certification mark law. Conversely, inappropriate invocations of flexibility do just the opposite by confusing consumers and excluding businesses from certification in ways that undermine competition and consumer welfare. Therefore, it is not flexibility per se that trademark law needs to eliminate in certification tests but rather counterproductive deployments of flexibility.

Another concern with governmental substantive regulation is that the government is often poorly situated to establish certification tests. The government can be out of touch with consumers and the competitive marketplace or, at the very least, less connected to these entities than those operating in the marketplace, namely private certifiers and consumers. This aspect may cause ossification or a bad certification standard from the start, another critique that has been aimed at the federal government's "organic" certification standard.

Finally, though possibly not fully applicable to the "organic" certification standard, there is a colossal worry about the state's substantive involvement in many types of certification tests that are religious or cultural in nature. Should the government be involved in crafting rules for kosher certification? For movie ratings? For ethically sourced products? As trademark scholarship has demonstrated in varied contexts, trademarks can be used to certify and express something that is religious or cultural in nature, not just commercial information.[85] From this vantage point, having the state's hand draw the boundaries of certification tests raises constitutional worries about government involvement in areas – religion and speech, in particular – designed to be left to private groups.[86]

2. Procedural Regulation

Procedural regulation is more realistic and desirable. This section proposes that the law ought to require private certifiers to install some combination of procedural protections to minimize the possibility that certifiers can subvert the goals of certification marks and act counterproductively to exclude businesses from certification. Certifiers' implementation of one or more forms of procedural oversight would minimize their counterproductive behavior by giving the PTO and businesses seeking to be certified better traction to detect this behavior and thus diminish certifiers' incentives to act counterproductively in the first place. Effectively, the federal government ought to offer certifiers the substantial benefits of its protection under trademark law only in exchange for bolstering – rather than undermining – the law's goals, by certifying in a neutral and consistent way at any point in time.

---

[83] Carroll 2004, 140.
[84] Kruse 2006, 529–31.
[85] Dreyfuss 1990, 412–24; Katyal 2010, 1602–09.
[86] U.S. Const. amend. I; *cf.* Tam 2017, 757–60.

a) Regulation of Certification Standard-making

Drawing on administrative law principles of rulemaking, this section first turns to procedural rules governing the contents of a certification test itself: namely, disclosure of the certification test, review of test clarity, and notice-and-comment standard-making and revisions.

i. Disclosure of the Certification Test

As the Swiss-watch example suggests, the PTO currently permits certifiers to secure certification mark protection by exposing a wisp of information in vague and general terms. That ought to change. The advantage of requiring or incentivizing certifiers to reveal their certification test in detail is great. If businesses and consumers have access to a certifier's detailed test, they can often monitor whether the certifier's practices diverge from the articulated test. If so, that divergence confers a legal basis for the government to withdraw protection from the certification mark.[87] That threat ought to bolster the certifier's incentive to certify according to its articulated test, just as trademark law dictates, and not diverge from it to behave counterproductively.

That said, it is not necessarily the case that the certification standard ought to be pinned down in advance in excruciating detail. Not only is that costlier to do, but it just might be that some certifications do and should turn on the totality of the circumstances and their context, which is too hard to articulate in rule-like detail in advance of application.

Just as some laws are better expressed as rules and some as standards, some certification tests are relatively straightforward to articulate as comprehensive rules and others are sufficiently complicated or nuanced that a standard to be refined in application is preferable. Because of this heterogeneity among certification tests, there needs to be room in certification mark law for flexibility.

Where does this heterogeneity and complexity leave the notion of heightened disclosures of certification tests? First, whether better described in a standard or rule, the PTO is currently satisfied with too little disclosure from certifiers as to their certification tests. Pertinently, while the PTO contemplates the fluidity of certification tests,[88] it does not impose any heightened disclosure requirements as to certification tests. The PTO can and should ask for more than highly abstract and general short statements representing a certification test. The PTO ought to impose a requirement that certifiers set forth the content of their certification tests in much greater detail than is currently required. There are multiple ways to secure this more detailed information about certification tests. One way, for instance, is to have the law insist on disclosure of certifying organizations' operating manuals for their certifying agents. Another is to require that these certification tests be disclosed to the PTO in the first instance.

Second, the certifier is usually the best placed to determine whether its certification test is better articulated as a detailed rule or a standard to be fleshed out in its application. Perhaps the PTO should require highly detailed certification rules from those certifiers that think it best for their certification test. And for those certifiers that think their certification test would be best elaborated in application, the PTO should not require the same level of detail up front but should instead ramp up its procedural regulation of the certifier's decision-making – as discussed below – to ensure that the certifier is fleshing out its standard consistently with trademark law's goals. Third, as analyzed above, even a requirement of well-defined and disclosed certification tests should allow for the possibility that certification standards might have good, procompetitive reasons to change over time. Any regulation of disclosed tests must account for the possibility of

---

[87] 15 U.S.C. § 1064(5)(D).
[88] 15 U.S.C. §§ 1058–1059; 37 C.F.R. §§ 2.161, 7.37.

certification test revision as new and pressing situations arise, such as when technology evolves, consumer tastes change, and supply chains shift.

ii. Review of Standard Clarity and Comprehensiveness

Requiring augmented disclosure of certification tests would be of little value if the PTO does not also review these disclosures to make sure they are sufficiently clear and comprehensive.[89] Otherwise, certifiers could submit a too-flexible test to the PTO and then wield that test in ways that undercut the goals of certification mark law. Review of submitted tests might be hard for PTO examiners to conduct properly on their own, as they are almost surely not experts in each of the certifications submitted for their review, not to mention the underlying businesses relying on the certification. Nonetheless, to improve this review, the PTO could share submitted disclosures with the public, so as to seek comment by interested businesses and consumers on whether the disclosures are sufficiently clear and comprehensive or whether there are neglected situations or aspects that ought to be addressed.[90]

iii. Notice-and-Comment Standard-making and Revisions

Central to review of certification tests for clarity and comprehensiveness, as discussed above, is a recognition of the expert knowledge possessed by businesses and consumers of goods and services that fall within the ambit of a certification. It might prove useful for procedural regulation of certification standards to rely on this expertise more generally and broadly. Just as the government invites interested members of the public to comment on proposed administrative rules by giving them notice and an opportunity to comment,[91] it would be beneficial to give businesses and consumers affected by certification an opportunity to comment on the substance of certification tests. There could be opportunity for notice and comment when a certifier is establishing its test for the first time and whenever it revises its certification test.

Notice-and-comment opportunities could buoy trademark law's goals by providing a more direct, comprehensive, and documented connection between consumers, businesses, and certifiers. Consider first the direct and comprehensive connection it would create between certifiers and third parties. There are likely informal opportunities for businesses and consumers to communicate with certifiers about the content of their certification tests. Nonetheless, certifiers have the incentive to pay attention to certain businesses and consumers over others, in line with the rational preferences they will have for those certain businesses and consumers. Creating a forum of notice and comment to which any interested businesses and consumers can contribute levels the playing field in some sense by democratizing the opportunity to share thoughts on certification tests. That is not to say that certifiers now have to incorporate all of these submitted comments into their ultimate test. However, they would have an obligation to review them, perhaps more than they would have done for some of these comments based on their rational discriminating incentive.

This opportunity to comment on certification tests in turn advances the goals of trademark law. It improves the possibility that certifiers have information from businesses and consumers about what consumers think their certification standard covers or should cover and from businesses about the practical effects of different plausible certification tests. As discussed

---

[89] The United Kingdom currently reviews certification regulations for clarity and compliance with the certification mark requirements (Dawson 1988, 30–35). The government must also consent to alteration of the certification standard (Id. at 42–43).

[90] Cf. Fromer 2009b, 591–92; Ouellette 2016; Peer to Patent 2018.

[91] 5 U.S.C. § 553.

previously, certification marks are supposed to help consumers identify goods and services that possess certain characteristics about which consumers care. The ability to communicate with certifiers to minimize the differences between consumer perceptions of the certification test and the actual test is thus beneficial.

A notice-and-comment opportunity would also encourage the accomplishment of certification marks' goals through enhanced documentation. Via the process of notice and comment, consumer and business comments are memorialized and become part of a record of third-party reactions to a certifier's proposed tests. If one collects a certifier's proposed test, third-party comments, and the certifier's ultimately adopted test, one can measure how responsive the certifier was to certain businesses or groups of consumers over others. This total record can then provide additional evidence when certifiers exclude businesses from certification to clarify the currently murky waters of whether certifiers are behaving counterproductively to trademark law.

Finally, procedural regulation can also be cautious about certification test revisions. As discussed, there are some positive reasons to enable revisions as a way to promote certification flexibility, but there are also critical reasons to discourage this flexibility and instead encourage certification stability. It might be worthwhile for the PTO to presume that all certification test revisions are counterproductive to certification mark law's goals of promoting fair competition and consumer welfare. The PTO might then allow certification tests to be revised only if the certifier can overcome this presumption by articulating a plausible productive reason for the revision.

b) Regulation of Certification Decision-making

Procedural rules can also be used to encourage proper certification decision-making. Assuming that the regulations for certification standard-making discussed in the previous section are adopted, counterproductive behavior with regard to decisions to certify goods or services will still be possible. Whether the certifier's test is a more detailed and comprehensive rule or a more flexible standard, there are opportunities to exclude for reasons unconnected to the certification at hand because there will always be some – even minimal – flexibilities in any certification test. This possibility is more worrisome the more flexible the certification test, thereby suggesting that regulation of certification decision-making is most important to apply with force to certifiers with more flexible standards than to certifiers with more comprehensive rules.

i. Disclosure of Certification Decisions and Reasoning

A direct way to ensure that certifiers are undertaking their certifications fairly, consistently, and in line with the purposes of certification mark law is to require certifiers to disclose their certification decisions, and possibly requiring them to include the reasoning behind each decision. This body of certification "precedent," so to speak, would be helpful to businesses seeking certification for two related reasons: They can learn why certification decisions were made, giving them the ability to assess whether the decisions are in line with the certification test. They can also see if those decisions are consistent with previous decisions for other businesses that are similarly situated. If a certification decision is out of line either with the certification test or with prior certification decisions, the business seeking certification can legitimately complain that the certifier has contravened trademark law. That is, according to the law, a certification mark owner may not "discriminately refuse[] to certify or to continue to certify the goods or services of any person who maintains the standards or conditions which such mark certifies."[92] By

---

[92] 15 U.S.C. § 1064(5)(D).

refusing a certification to goods or services that deserve to be certified in accordance with the certification standard or prior certification decisions, the certifier is not carrying out the compulsory licensing scheme trademark law conceives for it and is not deserving of certification mark protection. Disclosure of certification decisions and reasoning can thus help identify certifiers that are behaving counterproductively. In this way, disclosure can discipline certifiers to behave in accordance with trademark law's goals and detect and punish those who are not.

Requiring certifying organizations to divulge how they interpret and apply their certification tests would be akin to the clarifying effect that public case law applying legal standards in varied factual contexts has on communicating the scope of legal standards. Case law ruling on a legal standard might need to be more elaborate to explain how to apply the standard to the particular factual situation at hand. Case law explicating a legal rule, on the other hand, might be able to tersely apply the elaborate rule. Similarly, certification decisions based on a certification rule will generally not need as much reasoning to explain these decisions; a pointer to the rule, or subrule, at hand will often suffice. By contrast, certification decisions based on a certification standard typically ought to include more reasoning to apply the standard to the facts at hand and explain the certification decision. Over time, the body of certification decisions applying a certification standard can yield more predictability.

ii. Certification Audits

A second way to protect the integrity and fairness of certification decision-making is to ensure that there is some reasonable probability of detection of certifiers deploying their certification standards to exclude some businesses counterproductively. One tried-and-true technique to do so, as is frequently recognized in the context of income tax compliance, is for government officials to conduct random audits of certification decisions and penalize those who fail these audits. The most natural penalty is already a part of trademark law: certifiers that are found to be inappropriately applying their standard in counterproductive ways can be said to no longer be deserving of certification mark protection for having "discriminately refus[ed] to certify or to continue to certify the goods or services of any person who maintains the standards or conditions which such mark certifies."[93]

All in all, these possible forms of procedural regulation – be they improved disclosure of certification tests, review of test clarity and comprehensiveness, and notice-and-comment standard-making and revision as ways to regulate certification standard-making, or disclosure of certification decisions and reasoning and certification audits as approaches to regulate certification decision-making – are intended to start a conversation about how best to bring some productive regulation to oversee the unregulated certification mark(et). Some of these forms of regulation might prove wiser and more effective than others in practice.

3. Antitrust Scrutiny

As shown above, certification marks can be used anticompetitively in ways that antitrust law is designed to police and to which it ought to be attentive. To address this, there ought to be attentive scrutiny of a certifier's behavior in situations in which its behavior is consistent with anticompetitive action, when the certifier has certification or downstream market power. The

---

[93] 15 U.S.C. § 1064(5)(D). This consequence might also punish the public and industry because the certification mark will no longer have protection and can likely be used by others without any quality control. This is a consequence that ought to be avoided, perhaps by transferring rights in the certification mark to a new entity.

federal government – be it through the Department of Justice or the Federal Trade Commission – should be emboldened to institute investigations of and enforcement actions against certifiers in these circumstances.

One of the most important actions to undertake in this regard is to make these enforcement agencies aware that there are substantial antitrust concerns with regard to the deployment of certification marks.

CONCLUSION

This chapter has explored the underpinning justifications of certification mark law: promoting fair competition and consumer welfare. These two overarching goals align with trademark law's key goals. Yet owing to the ways in which certification marks are designed to be different from trademarks, there are important distinctions. The statutory rules for certification marks are more restrictive. The need for consumers to perceive the certification standard signified by the corresponding certification mark is heightened. Moreover, there are grave concerns that the mostly unregulated certification mark has led to and can lead to certifier behavior that is at cross-purposes with the law's goals of promoting fair competition and consumer welfare. The law can diminish the possibility of this behavior through better procedural regulation of certifiers as a quid pro quo for receiving certification mark protection and in greater antitrust scrutiny of certifiers.

14

The Certification Paradox

*Jonathan M. Barnett**

A.	Certification Intermediaries: The Conventional View	254
B.	Certification Intermediaries: An Alternative View	257
	1. The Virtues of Certifier Oligopolies	257
	2. Entry Barriers in Certification Markets	259
	3. Rational Certifier Shirking	260
C.	Regulatory Intervention in Certification Markets	261
	1. Increased Certifier Liability	261
	2. Reduced Entry Barriers	262
D.	Organization as Commitment: Self-Imposed Limitations on Certifier Shirking	263
	1. Nonprofit Entities	264
	2. General Partnerships (Financial Services Markets)	265

Private certification intermediaries reduce the costs of trade by assessing the quality of firms' products or processes and, in many cases, establishing a standard for making those quality assessments.[1] That cost reduction occurs whenever certification intermediaries mitigate information asymmetries that would otherwise distort trade or block trade entirely. The result is a clear efficiency gain: a repeat-play intermediary supplies its reputational capital and evaluation expertise to sellers who cannot make credible commitments to, or buyers who cannot make independent evaluations of, product quality at a comparable cost.[2] In the capital markets, a "Big Four" accounting firm certifies the accuracy of a public firm's financial statements by reference to "generally accepted accounting principles" (GAAP). That service lowers the evaluation costs that potential purchasers of the firm's securities would otherwise have to incur, which in turn reduces the firm's cost of capital. In consumer goods markets, Underwriters Laboratories (UL) has developed over 1,500 safety standards[3] and provides a recognized "stamp of approval" to firms that meet those standards. This service reduces the costs that an uninformed consumer

---

[*] This chapter draws on my earlier discussion of these topics in Barnett (2012). I am grateful for helpful comments from Jorge Contreras and Brian Galle.
[1] This chapter is confined to private certification intermediaries. For a brief discussion of certification by public tax-funded certification entities, *see infra* note 43.
[2] Gilson & Kraakman 1984.
[3] UL Standards 2017.

would otherwise have to incur in order to assess the quality of an unfamiliar product, which in turn expands markets and supports accurate pricing of competing goods and services.

This account both explains the ubiquity of certification intermediaries and has a normative implication: namely, if markets already widely use certification intermediaries to relieve information asymmetries, then government regulation for that same purpose may be redundant or counterproductive. This point is emphasized in law-and-economics scholarship that expresses skepticism concerning government intervention to address information deficiencies in the securities and financial services markets.[4] However, this account does not satisfactorily explain apparent certification "failures" – that is, either fraud by a certifier or, more commonly, failure by a certifier to detect fraud, misrepresentation or other material deficiencies by a certified firm. These failures are not infrequent and sometimes result in injury or dramatic economic losses, raising doubts concerning the reliability of even well-established certification intermediaries. These concerns, which became especially salient in connection with the Enron scandal in 2002[5] and the financial crisis of 2007–08,[6] raise important questions concerning the appropriate scope of legal intervention to address information asymmetries in markets that are already serviced by certification intermediaries. In connection with those concerns, some law-and-economics scholars have expressed doubts concerning the informational value of routinely used certification instruments in the financial services markets, including legal opinions,[7] fairness opinions,[8] audit reports,[9] credit ratings,[10] and stock exchange listings.[11]

In this chapter, I argue that certification intermediaries – both in the financial services sector and beyond – are prone to periodic failure but that such failure is inherent to reasonably well-functioning markets for certification services. The rationale behind this paradox is as follows. Mature certification markets are characterized by dominant providers occupying secure market shares. This is the cause of both the general success, and periodic failure, of well-developed certification markets. A small number of certifiers is necessary in order to maximize transacting parties' savings in evaluation costs as compared to independent quality assessment. High concentration levels are also necessary to generate the rents that induce certifiers to make efforts to safeguard reputational capital through robust evaluation and monitoring efforts. But dominant certifiers' market shares are protected by competitors' high entry costs and users' high switching costs, which induce certifiers to shirk through limited reductions in certification effort. Given users' switching costs, dominant certifiers can periodically reduce investment in information-gathering and verification activities without inducing user migration. Historically, certifiers have sought to commit against shirking and other forms of opportunism by adopting "constrained" organizational forms that limit a certifier's profit-taking opportunities, which reduces the gains from relaxing certification effort. This suggests that certifier performance may be indirectly enhanced through regulatory action that influences certifiers' organizational choices, rather than legal penalties, which are prone to induce both over- and

---

[4] See, e.g., Mahoney 2005, 110–11, 118–20; Easterbrook & Fischel 1996, 276–314; Goldberg 1988, 312. Some of these scholars ultimately support limited retention of some disclosure requirements and other forms of legal intervention in the financial services markets.
[5] Coffee 2002, 2004; Macey 2003.
[6] Macey 2010.
[7] Barnett 2006.
[8] Bebchuk & Kahan 1989.
[9] Eisenberg & Macey 2004.
[10] Partnoy 2002.
[11] Macey 2010.

undercertification, or lowering entry barriers, which reduces the rents that support incentives to maintain robust certification efforts.

Discussion proceeds as follows. In Section A, I present the conventional account of certification intermediaries and its implications concerning legal intervention to correct information asymmetries. In Section B, I present an alternative view that accounts for both the general success, and periodic failure, of certification intermediaries. In Section C, I analyze conventional regulatory options to improve certifier performance. In Section D, I describe organizational mechanisms by which certification intermediaries commit against opportunism. I briefly conclude.

A. CERTIFICATION INTERMEDIARIES: THE CONVENTIONAL VIEW

It is widely recognized that certain markets exhibit information asymmetries that advantage better-informed transacting parties. Information asymmetries are most severe in markets for experience goods, whose quality can only be ascertained during consumption, and credence goods, whose quality can never be fully ascertained.[12] To a lesser but still substantial extent, these asymmetries are present in markets for search goods, whose quality can be assessed prior to consumption but at a positive cost. As Akerlof showed in his famous "lemons" problem, information asymmetries inefficiently pool high-quality and low-quality sellers, which ultimately results in a market in which all but the lowest-quality sellers are compelled to exit.[13] As Akerlof also observed (and as Spence elaborated in the labor market context[14]), this outcome can be avoided or mitigated so long as higher-quality sellers have incentives and capacities to alleviate information asymmetries by sending costly "signals" that lower-quality sellers cannot mimic.[15] Some of these signaling devices include contractual guarantees of quality provided by creditworthy sellers or reliable evaluations of product quality provided by external entities. Third-party certification lowers transaction costs whenever the certifier can provide buyers with a credible signal of product quality at a lower cost than any individual seller can do so independently. When that condition is satisfied, certification induces an efficient separating equilibrium at the lowest feasible cost, thereby maximizing the net social value generated by the underlying transaction.

The literature on certification entities distinguishes between first-party certification, in which a transacting party "self-certifies" the quality of its own products or services, and third-party certification, in which an independent entity undertakes that function on behalf of a transacting party.[16] In theory, there are several reasons to believe that third-party certification outperforms self-certification. First, a repeat-play third-party certifier has limited incentives to misrepresent quality to favor any individual firm or product. The third-party certifier seeks to maximize revenues from a pool of products sold by multiple firms, including existing and

---

[12] On information asymmetries, experience goods and credence goods, see Jahn et al. (2005).
[13] Akerlof 1970. More specifically, Akerlof showed that, in a market in which buyers cannot distinguish between high-quality and low-quality sellers (or, equivalently, sellers cannot make credible commitments to product quality), buyers are compelled to assess a discount against all sellers. Assuming that high-quality sellers incur higher production costs than low-quality sellers, the former rationally exit the market (or, equivalently, cease to make investments in quality), resulting in an inefficiently narrow market that consists entirely of products located at the lowest point on the product-quality distribution (hence, the analogy to "lemons" in the used-car market).
[14] Spence 1973. Spence also identified circumstances in which parties overinvest in signaling, with adverse net welfare consequences. This qualification has some relevance in my subsequent discussion of legal interventions that may induce overcertification (see page 000).
[15] Akerlof 1970.
[16] Tanner 2000, 415.

future clients over an indefinite time period. Knowing this, any potential buyer concludes that the profit-maximizing, repeat-play certifier would be unlikely to risk future expected revenues from its client portfolio in order to save evaluation costs on, or fabricate the evaluation for, a single client. Second, certification may exhibit scale economies insofar as the development of quality standards, and processes for testing conformity with those standards, requires fixed-cost investments that can be amortized across a pool of products sold by multiple firms. Relatedly, as product characteristics or other relevant factors change, a repeat-play certification intermediary can draw on its accumulated stock of intellectual capital and efficiently make adjustments to its testing technology. Third, in the case of a new seller, only an established third-party certifier holds a stock of reputational capital that can be "pledged" to counterparties in order to send a credible quality signal. A new or unfamiliar seller lacks any comparable stock of reputational capital, which means that buyers cannot determine whether the seller is a one-off or repeat-play transacting party and must apply a quality discount that discourages entry (or encourages exit) by higher-quality sellers. This inefficient pooling equilibrium – the "lemons" problem described by Akerlof[17] – converts to an efficient separating equilibrium when new or unfamiliar sellers can "rent" the reputational collateral held by an established certifier who has known incentives to maximize total expected revenue from its accumulated goodwill.

This understanding of certification intermediaries, which has predominated in a body of law-and-economics scholarship pioneered by Gilson and Kraakman,[18] implies that information asymmetries are not likely to be a regular source of market failure and therefore do not provide a strong basis for regulatory intervention. To the extent that information asymmetries exist, competitive forces induce certification intermediaries to supply transacting parties with efficient inspection and monitoring technologies to reduce the costs of trade. In the most stylized market setting, this self-correction mechanism is expected to result in a perfectly separating equilibrium in which prices accurately reflect product quality and fully informed transactions implement efficient resource allocation. Given technological constraints that limit the accuracy of a certifier's testing technology, a more realistic setting anticipates that markets would converge on a partially separating equilibrium in which certifiers sometimes fail to detect quality deficiencies.[19] Absent willful misrepresentation by the seller, however, any such certification "failure" is not necessarily inefficient. Certifiers rationally identify, verify and supply product quality information subject to a marginal cost-benefit constraint, which is a function of both the certifier's information-gathering costs and the value that transacting parties place on incremental information. This implies that some positive level of certification "failure" can be consistent with market efficiency. Absent collusion or other market distortions, any regulatory intervention to reduce information asymmetries would then be redundant and, with respect to undetected quality deficiencies, would demand investment in inefficiently high levels of certification accuracy.

This conventional understanding implies that certification failure should be a limited occurrence and confined to circumstances in which supplying additional certification effort

---

[17] Akerlof 1970.
[18] Gilson & Kraakman 1984, 613–21. In later work, Gilson and Kraakman recognize limitations to the view that reputational intermediaries typically successfully ameliorate information asymmetries (Gilson & Kraakman 2003).
[19] Choi (1998) identifies multiple circumstances where certifiers may fail to fully correct for information asymmetries due to limits on screening accuracy (as mentioned above), certifiers' incentives to provide false information and other relevant factors. In more stylized settings, the theoretical economics literature has identified other circumstances in which certification induces a partially pooling equilibrium. For example, Albano and Lizzeri (2001) show that a monopolist certifier will extract rents from more efficient sellers, which then induces those firms to underinvest in quality, and Lizzeri (1999) shows that a monopolist certifier will strategically underinvest in certification effort, so that buyers only know whether sellers exceed a minimum quality threshold.

TABLE 14.1 *Selected certification "failures"*

Year	Certified Firm(s)	Certifier	Certifier Type
1991	Bank of Credit and Commerce Intl.	PricewaterhouseCoopers	Auditor
1991	Bank of Credit and Commerce Intl.	Ernst & Young	Auditor
2002	Worldcom	Arthur Andersen	Auditor
2002	Enron	Arthur Andersen	Auditor
2002	Enron	Vinson & Elkins	Law firm
2007–08	Issuers of subprime mortgage-backed securities	Moody's	Credit rating agency
2007–08	Issuers of subprime mortgage-backed securities	Standard & Poor's	Credit rating agency
2009*	Taylor Bean & Whitaker; Colonial Bank	PricewaterhouseCoopers	Auditor

* This entry refers to two related lawsuits against PricewaterhouseCoopers in connection with the auditor's alleged failure to detect fraud at Taylor Bean, a mortgage lender that went bankrupt in 2009, and Colonial Bank, which also went bankrupt in 2009, in one of the country's largest bank failures. The suit concerning Taylor Bean was settled, *see* Fitzgerald (2016); a second suit by the Federal Deposit Insurance Corporation, which had insured Colonial, resulted in a finding of liability against the auditor, *see* Frankel (2018).

would fail a marginal cost–benefit test. While cogent in theory, this optimistic account of certification markets does not clearly account for historical cases of at least ostensibly dramatic certification failures even in well-developed markets, each of which resulted in billions of dollars in losses for investors and other market participants. (Again, to be precise, even these apparently dramatic failures may not necessarily be inefficient given the cost–benefit considerations described above.) Headline examples abound in the history of the financial services industry, some of which are shown below.

In each of these cases, the apparent failure by a certification intermediary to detect fraud or other deficiencies at the certified firm resulted in substantial losses to investors and other market participants following the certified firm's collapse, and, in the case of Arthur Andersen (which was initially found guilty on criminal obstruction of justice charges[20]), precipitated the collapse of the certifier itself. Additionally, doubts concerning the conventional account are raised by empirical studies that reach mixed results when assessing the added information value of widely-used certification instruments in the financial services markets.[21] Outside the financial services industry, empirical studies have identified deficiencies at leading accreditation services in agricultural production[22] and e-commerce privacy assurance services[23] and limited information value attributable to accreditation services in the childcare market.[24] The press has reported similar concerns about allegedly lax practices at well-established accreditors in the hospital services,[25] legal education,[26] and general business[27] sectors.

---

[20] The conviction was later overturned by the U.S. Supreme Court. *Arthur Andersen LLP v. U.S.*, 544 U.S. 696 (2005). The decision was practically moot, however, since the firm had largely disbanded by that time.
[21] *See* Barnett 2006, 102–06 for a review of the empirical studies.
[22] Albersmeier et al. 2009.
[23] Edelman 2010.
[24] Xiao 2010.
[25] Armour 2017.
[26] Kelderman 2011.
[27] Segal 2011.

B. CERTIFICATION INTERMEDIARIES: AN ALTERNATIVE VIEW

The periodic occurrence of apparent certification failure challenges the conventional account of certification intermediaries (although, given that the conventional account anticipates some positive level of certification failure even under the most feasibly efficient conditions, it does not necessarily dismiss that account). In fact, certification markets exhibit certain structural characteristics that may cause certifiers to persistently fall short in correcting informational asymmetries in the certified product market.

The difficulty arises from the fact that Akerlof's lemons problem, and the underlying information asymmetries between transacting parties, applies not only at the level of the product market, but *again* at the level of the certification market. Just as buyers have doubts concerning the quality of any particular product, so too buyers have doubts concerning the quality of any particular certifier, which is akin to a credence good that cannot be easily evaluated even after consumption. In theory, this n-order information asymmetry requires an iterated stack of certification entities, each of which inspects and, using its accumulated reputational capital, vouches for the quality of the certifier located "below" it. Consistent with this intuition, certification markets often exhibit a stacked organizational structure, in which local and regional certifiers are certified by a national entity, which is then certified by an umbrella international entity. For example, the Forest Stewardship Council (US) (FSC-US) accredits multiple entities to verify compliance by certified firms with FSC-US standards; FSC-US is in turn accredited by FSC (International); and FSC (International) operates subject to the standards set forth by the International Standardisation Organization and the International Social and Environment Accreditation and Labeling Alliance.[28] However, without some limit on this iterative process, certification intermediaries would ultimately not offer any appreciable cost advantage relative to direct inspection of quality by buyers, contractual guarantees of quality by sellers, or other signaling mechanisms.

Second-order information asymmetries at the level of the certification market are typically resolved by converging on a concentrated market populated by a handful of leading intermediaries and, in some cases, only one. Table 14.2 depicts selected certification markets and the dominant providers in each market. As indicated by these entities' founding dates (in parentheses), they have serviced each relevant market for considerable periods of time and, presumably, have therefore accrued deep stocks of reputational capital. As discussed in detail below, this reputational asset is the source for the "certification paradox" that underlies the general success and periodic failure of mature certification markets. While established certifiers' stock of reputational capital generates rents that preserve incentives to generally maintain high levels of investment in information collection and verification, it implies entry costs for competitors and switching costs for users that periodically induce incumbents to reduce investment in those same activities.

1. The Virtues of Certifier Oligopolies

This oligopolistic or monopolistic market structure, combined with the long lives of dominant intermediaries, that characterizes most mature certification markets has several efficiency virtues.

---

[28] Barnett 2012, 517–18.

TABLE 14.2 *Selected certification markets**

Certification Market	Dominant Provider(s); Year(s) Founded
Bond ratings	Moody's (1909), Standard & Poor's (1860), Fitch (1913)
Business credit reports	Dun & Bradstreet (1841)
Consumer credit reporting	Experian (1970), Equifax (1899), TransUnion (1841)
Financial audits (large public corporations)	Ernst & Young (1903), Deloitte (1880), PWC (1865), KPMG (1870)
Electrical appliances	Underwriters Laboratories (1894), Intertek (1885)
Gas appliances	AGA Laboratories (1918)
Ship vessels	DNV GL (1864)**, Lloyd's Register (1876), American Bureau of Shipping (1862), Nippon Kahi Kyokai ("ClassNK") (1899)
Agricultural seeds	Association of Official Seed Certifying Agencies (1919)
Higher education institutions	Council for Higher Education Accreditation (1996)
Law schools	American Bar Association (1900)
Hospitals	The Joint Commission (1951)

* Year indicated reflects the year of founding of the oldest progenitor entity active in approximately the same area of business activity. Leading firms in each certification market identified based on review of relevant trade and scholarly literature. For detailed sources on all entities except the American Bar Association, *see* Barnett (2012, Appendix). On the American Bar Association, *see* Katcher (2006, 364).

** This is the year of the founding of Det Norske Veritas, which merged in 2013 with Germanischer Lloyd, to form DNV GL.

a) Incentives to Maintain Certification Efforts

A secure expectation of market rents induces a certifier to rationally invest in the costly inspection efforts that preserve the value of its reputational capital, without which it cannot supply a credible quality signal. Following Klein and Leffler[29] and Shapiro,[30] marginal-cost pricing cannot support investments in product quality since a firm must expect a future stream of market rents in order to rationally forfeit immediate gains from underperformance. The same logic applies at the level of the certification market: a perfectly competitive market would convert a certification intermediary into a short-term market player with little incentive to accumulate and preserve a stock of reputational capital through robust inspection efforts. Rather, the certifier would act as a one-shot player and rationally engage in various forms of short-term profit-taking, such as shirking, taking bribes for fabricated evaluations, or otherwise colluding with certified firms. Concentrated market structures generate rents that preserve the dominant certifier's incentives to maintain a strong track record of quality inspection and monitoring, which in turn maintains the value of the certifier's stock of reputational capital.

b) Maximize Search-Cost Savings

The cost savings generated by a well-established certifier, which enables a buyer to avoid incurring search and investigation costs through direct evaluation of the relevant product or service, would be substantially eroded in a certification market populated by multiple providers. In that case, a buyer would partially replace search and investigation costs at the level of the product market with search and investigation costs at the level of the certification market. Consistent with this proposition, nascent certification markets exhibit concerns about excessive numbers of standards or certifiers and consumer confusion over certification accuracy.[31] Contreras, Lewis

---

[29] Klein & Leffler 1981.
[30] Shapiro 1983.
[31] Barnett 2012, 491.

and Roth describe this state of affairs in the "sustainable building" industry, in which there are multiple, inconsistent and sometimes imprecise standards and accompanying certifications.[32] As those reports illustrate, low levels of concentration detract from the cost-savings that consumers can enjoy by relying on a certifier's recognized stamp of approval in lieu of independent quality evaluation.

c) Economies of Scale

Certification markets exhibit economies of scale insofar as certifiers must invest fixed costs in establishing product quality standards and developing the technology for measuring conformity to those standards by any particular product. If the marginal costs of evaluating a particular product are substantially lower than the fixed costs to develop the standard and testing methodology, then the market naturally converges on a handful of certification entities or even a single certification entity. Relatedly, a repeat-play certifier that services a large pool of certified firms is likely to accumulate a deep stock of intellectual capital on which it can draw to readily adjust standards and testing methodologies in response to changes in market conditions, regulations and other relevant factors.

2. Entry Barriers in Certification Markets

The long life of most dominant certification entities suggests that those entities' high market shares are protected to some extent by entry barriers. There are two barriers. On the supply side of the market, any potential entrant faces a considerable time lag in accumulating a comparable stock of reputational capital (often conveyed in the marketplace through the certifier's trademark) that it can offer to transacting parties. That inherent time lag means that any potential entrant into a certification market must contemplate a sustained period of negative returns before it has acquired a sufficient stock of reputational capital that it can pledge to clients at an above-market premium. On the demand side of the market, buyers and sellers face switching costs when migrating to a new and unfamiliar certification provider. For buyers and sellers, switching to a new certifier imposes costs insofar as neither party has substantial information concerning the quality of the new provider as compared to the incumbent. For a seller, switching to a new certifier imposes learning costs to adapt its data-collection and reporting infrastructure to the new provider. For a buyer, switching to a new certifier implies learning costs in understanding how to interpret the information delivered by the new provider. In some markets (especially, the financial services markets), buyers incur inflated switching costs (and new certifiers incur inflated entry costs) due to regulations that mandate use of designated incumbent certifiers in order to show compliance with certain legal requirements.[33] The combination of high entry costs and high switching costs may explain why even major certification failures, such as the Enron accounting scandal in 2002 and concerns over performance of the credit ratings agencies in the event preceding the financial crisis of 2007–08, have not induced substantial entry into those certification markets (public-firm auditing and credit ratings, respectively).[34] Similarly,

---

[32] Contreras et al. 2011.

[33] The best-known example of this is the "nationally recognized securities rating organization" designation for incumbent credit rating agencies in connection with certain securities law requirements. Similar practices are followed by the U.S. Department of Education, the U.S. Department of Health and Human Services, the U.S. Occupational Safety and Health Administration, and the U.S. Department of Agriculture. For additional details, see Barnett (2012, 488 n.44).

[34] Fitch has acquired significant additional market share in the credit-ratings market since the mid-2000s. See Becker & Milbourn 2010, 2–3, Figure 2. However, this predates the 2007–08 financial crisis, in connection with which the

those factors may explain why, with the exception of Arthur Andersen (which was targeted by a criminal prosecution[35]), none of the certification intermediaries associated with recent headline scandals in the financial services industry (see Table 14.1) appear to have suffered any long-lasting loss in market share.

3. Rational Certifier Shirking

The time-lag obstacle to successful entry by a new certifier, combined with the switching costs borne by users when moving to a new certifier, have countervailing effects on dominant certifiers' incentives to invest in certification effort. Assume that a certifier can elect to invest greater or lesser resources in information collection and verification, which results in more or less accurate evaluations of product quality. Following the standard account, large market shares combined with entry protections generate a large expected stream of rents, which encourages certifiers to preserve reputational capital and forego short-term cost savings by opportunistically cutting back on certification effort. However, this line of argument implicitly assumes that, whenever a certifier is perceived to have reduced its certification efforts, buyers and sellers will punish the certifier by immediately switching to a competitor (or reverting to self-certification). But this is not clearly users' dominant response to certifier failure if users bear high switching costs in moving to another certifier. If switching costs are sufficiently large, a one-time observed failure by an incumbent certifier will not induce customer departures. Rather, users will rationally tolerate certifier shirking so long as the costs incurred as a result do not exceed the costs expected to be incurred by moving to a new provider.[36]

This observation has a key implication. Contrary to the standard account, an incumbent certifier may rationally maximize profits (equal to (i) the sum of short-term gains and the discounted present value of all long-term gains, *less* (ii) certification costs) by relaxing its certification efforts to a certain extent on particular occasions. User tolerance of certifier shirking will be enhanced further to the extent that a single case of certification failure is observationally ambiguous and can be reasonably attributed to inadvertent error, in which case the certifier will suffer little loss of goodwill or can rapidly restore goodwill through a follow-on period of strong performance. Certifier shirking may be especially difficult to detect in environments where, as Contreras, Lewis and Roth emphasize, market participants cannot easily assess the accuracy of a particular standard or a certifier's methodology in evaluating compliance with a given standard.[37] Paradoxically, as the costs of ascertaining quality in the first-order product market increase, demand for reliable third-party certification services increases; at the same time, this implies that any quality-assessment methodology is not likely to be amenable to evaluation for accuracy in the second-order certification market.

This revised understanding of certification entities yields an account that more closely matches observed performance in real-world markets. Largely consistent with the conventional account, this revised understanding anticipates that well-established certification intermediaries

---

two leading credit rating agencies' performance was widely viewed as having been deficient. At least as of 2016, S&P, Moody's, and, to a lesser extent, Fitch continue to dominate the ratings market. *See* Ramakrishnan & Scipio 2016.

[35] *See supra* note 22.

[36] I am aware of two related contributions on this point. Biglaiser & Friedman (1994) posits that an intermediary's incentive to terminate its relationship with a producer is sensitive to the cost of locating a substitute for the producer's good. More generally, Horner (2002) observes that, in the case of a producer with a reputation for high quality, whether delivery of a low-quality product induces customers to terminate depends on customers' patience.

[37] Contreras et al. 2011.

will *generally* invest substantially in quality inspection efforts, thereby delivering a steady flow of information that mitigates information asymmetries and reduces the costs of trade. To do otherwise would place at risk the certifier's valuable stock of reputational capital and the associated stream of future rents. However, the revised understanding observes that an established certifier's typically strong track record relies on a market structure that induces it to periodically make limited reductions in certification effort. So long as switching costs and entry costs are sufficiently high, and especially if certification failures give rise to ambiguous interpretations, dominant certifiers will necessarily engage in limited and periodic reductions in certification effort.[38] Given these countervailing tendencies, the revised understanding anticipates that even well-established certification markets will periodically result in failures to detect product deficiencies, reflecting a dominant certifier's election to make limited reductions in certification effort.

C. REGULATORY INTERVENTION IN CERTIFICATION MARKETS

The revised understanding of certification markets conforms more closely to market outcomes in which certification failure arises periodically and, as evidenced most clearly by the 2007–08 financial crisis, sometimes with dramatic effect. This naturally invites re-consideration of the normative implications of the conventional account, which casts doubt on the necessity for legal intervention to correct information asymmetries given that certification intermediaries pursue the same objective. Below I consider two forms of governmental intervention (excluding direct provision of certification services by the government[39]) that can potentially enhance certifier performance. In both cases, I assess the "error costs" associated with each mechanism, specifically taking into account the informational constraints faced by regulators in assessing the socially efficient level of certifier effort.

1. Increased Certifier Liability

The state can institute a regulatory framework that identifies and penalizes certifiers who fail to identify fraud or other deficiencies at a certified firm. Legal penalties can be understood to encompass all monetary or other penalties to which certifying entities could be subject as a result of litigation or enforcement actions brought by government agencies or private plaintiffs under applicable statutes, regulations or common-law tort causes of action. Legal penalties complement existing reputational penalties that are administered in the market through customer defections (or adjustments to fees or other terms that are required to retain customers) in response to perceived certification failures. Certifier obligations and accompanying liability exposure have been regularly expanded in the wake of major scandals in the U.S. financial markets. The 1929 stock market crash led to passage of the Securities Act of 1933,[40] which imposed liability on underwriters and other advisors in connection with public offerings of securities; the Enron collapse led to passage of the Sarbanes-Oxley Act of 2002,[41] which empowered the SEC to

---

[38] It may be objected that far-sighted users would anticipate this behavior and demand an appropriate discount on certification fees to reflect this risk. Subsequently I show that certifiers seek to reduce this discount by adopting organizational forms that limit their incentives to engage in future opportunism (*see infra* Part C.2).

[39] Under the public option (for example, the Food & Drug Administration), the state would enjoy a *de jure* or *de facto* monopoly over certification services for the relevant market. As a result, it would not be subject to competitive discipline, which would exacerbate the risk of both over- and under-certification, as discussed in this Part with respect to private certification entities.

[40] Securities Act of 1933.

[41] Sarbanes-Oxley Act of 2002.

further regulate auditors of public companies; and the financial crisis of 2007–08 led to passage of the Dodd-Frank Wall Street Reform and Consumer Protection Act in 2010,[42] which expanded credit rating agencies' exposure to legal liability under certain circumstances.

These politically popular policy actions, which impose monetary and other penalties on top of the reputational penalties to which certifiers are already subject as a result of market discipline, inherently carry the risk that regulators or courts will impose a total level of liability exposure that induces certifiers to invest excessively, from a social welfare perspective, in information gathering and verification. As noted previously, some positive level of certification "failure" is efficient so long as certification is a positive-cost activity subject to technological constraints, which implies that some incremental level of certification effort will no longer yield net positive marginal welfare gains. In response to legal obligations and penalties that demand increased investment in information gathering and verification efforts, certifiers will seek to pass on the increased costs to users. This raises the possibility of two inefficient outcomes. If some users do not sufficiently value the additional information being delivered by the certifier (which suggests that the legal requirement is inducing overcertification), then consumption of the certifier's services will decline. If not enough users sufficiently value the "improved" but more costly certifier service, then the certifier will be forced to exit since it is legally foreclosed from offering any less costly certification service. In both cases, increasing certifier liability results in *less* information being provided to the market.

The possibility that increased certifier liability can lead to certifier exit, whether partial or complete, is far from theoretical. A few examples can illustrate. In 1972, the SEC targeted certain prominent law firms that had allegedly issued opinion letters in connection with a "sham" transaction. Subsequently, corporate law firms apparently shifted toward issuing opinion letters that were heavily qualified and conveyed little incremental information – effectively, a form of partial market exit.[43] In 2002, the Sarbanes-Oxley Act required that accounting firms register with the Public Company Accounting Oversight Board in order to audit public companies and increased such firms' liability exposure to claims relating to alleged accounting misstatements. In response, smaller auditing firms elected to exit the public accounting market.[44] In 2010, Congress enacted the Dodd-Frank Act, which eliminated the exemption under the securities laws that had previously shielded rating agencies from liability as an "expert" in connection with a securities offering by a public company. Thereafter, the SEC attenuated or effectively suspended regulations that required the inclusion of credit ratings in public offering documents (and would have exposed the rating agencies to liability under the securities laws), in response to indications by the rating agencies that they would exit certain market segments.[45]

2. Reduced Entry Barriers

The state can intervene to lower entry barriers into certification markets and thereby impose increased competitive discipline on incumbent certifiers that are otherwise protected by entry time-lag and user switching costs. This approach was undertaken by the Occupational Safety & Health Administration in 1988, when it sought to accredit multiple nationally recognized testing laboratories in order to facilitate entry into markets dominated by the incumbent certifier,

---

[42] Dodd-Frank Wall Street Reform and Consumer Protection Act (2010).
[43] Barnett 2012, 498–99.
[44] Reynolds 2005, 30.
[45] Barnett 2012, 499–500; Securities and Exchange Commission 2010.

Underwriters Laboratories.[46] A similar approach was implemented in the Credit Rating Agency Reform Act of 2006 and the Dodd-Frank Act of 2010, which sought to reduce the exclusive use of Moody's and Standard & Poor's ratings for a wide range of regulatory purposes in securities and financial services regulations. This approach, which commentators have widely advocated in the credit ratings market,[47] suffers from an important weakness that could lead to counterproductive outcomes. As argued above, a dominant certifier's incentives to invest efforts in inspection and monitoring activities rely on the certifier's expectation that doing so will preserve its stock of reputational capital and the stream of market rents that it enjoys as a result. If that is the case, then endangering a dominant certifier's market position could reduce its incentives to undertake those efforts by limiting the rents that it can expect to accrue as a result. Contrary to standard intuitions, relieving market concentration may increase entry but reduce the total volume of certification effort, potentially resulting in a net social loss due to reduced information flow, increased information asymmetries, and increased costs of trade. Consistent with these arguments, researchers have found that decreasing concentration in certain segments of the credit ratings markets correlates with declines in ratings' predictive accuracy, as measured by the correlation between the ratings supplied by incumbent rating agencies and the market-implied yields of the rated securities.[48] Similarly inverse relationships between increased entry and decreased certification rigor have been demonstrated in the market for auto emissions testing services.[49]

D. ORGANIZATION AS COMMITMENT: SELF-IMPOSED LIMITATIONS ON CERTIFIER SHIRKING

Both types of traditional regulatory responses to certification failure – legal penalties and reduced entry barriers – are unattractive options that carry high risks of regulatory error and counterproductive market outcomes. Absent other regulatory options, it may then follow that the normative implications of the conventional account in the law-and-economics literature are correct, even if it is imprecise as a positive matter. That is: shirking by dominant certifiers, and periodic certification "failures," are inherent to the most feasibly efficient market mechanism for inducing third-party certification. In fact, this "do nothing" position is largely consistent with the common law's treatment of certification intermediaries, which has generally declined to impose liability through tort law and has resisted overriding contractual disclaimers of certifier liability. In 1995, the English House of Lords rejected a claim against a "classification society" (a certifier of a ship's seaworthiness), stating: "In England no classification society, engaged by owners to perform a survey, has ever been held liable to cargo-owners on the ground of a careless conduct of any survey."[50] The Court justified its ruling by specific reference to concerns over potential overdeterrence and certifier exit, stating that, if a "duty of care" were imposed on the certifier, "there is a risk that classification societies might be unwilling from time to time to survey the very vessels which more urgently require independent examination."[51] Consistent with this "do nothing" approach, U.S. courts have similarly generally declined to impose liability on certification entities,[52] standards development

---

[46] Barron 2007, 422–23.
[47] Macey 2010, 434–35; Hill 2004, 45.
[48] Becker & Milbourn 2010.
[49] Bennett et al. 2013.
[50] *Marc Rich & Co. AG v. Bishop Rock Marine Co.* (1995) (U.K.).
[51] *Id.*
[52] Goldberg 2002, 245–76.

organizations,[53] accreditation entities[54] and, with respect to credit rating agencies in particular, have mostly shielded them under the protective umbrella of the First Amendment.[55]

Notwithstanding the absence of any significant exposure to legal liability as a general matter, it would be incomplete to conclude that certification markets rely entirely on reputational effects in order to discipline certifier opportunism. A somewhat surprising legal tool appears to mitigate shirking behavior in certification markets. Specifically, certification markets regularly use organizational forms to limit dominant certifiers' opportunities and incentives to shirk. Certifiers typically operate (or, in some markets, have historically operated) under "constrained" organizational forms, such as non-profits and general partnerships, that limit managers' ability to extract gains earned through shirking and other forms of opportunism, as compared to "unconstrained" entities such as the traditional stock corporation. This organizational preference is consistent with rational self-interest: certifiers that can most credibly commit against shirking minimize the discount assessed by buyers and sellers on their "stamp of approval" and, in the case of new certifiers, are more likely to induce transacting parties to make the learning and other investments required to use the certifier's services. Put differently: organizational form provides a mechanism by which to induce at least a partially separating equilibrium in the second-order certification market, which can then induce separation effects among transacting parties in the associated first-order products and services markets.

1. Nonprofit Entities

Nonprofit forms have historically been used by leading private certification entities in various markets, including (among others) electrical appliances, gas appliances, water treatment, shipping, seed certification, lumber, automotive parts, higher education, hospitals and healthcare facilities, "sustainable" wood and paper products, kosher food, and "green" construction.[56] Nonprofit entities typically operate under two key constraints: (i) the inability to make cash distributions to managers, members or any other controlling entity, and (ii) a reasonableness standard that places some limit on the size of managerial compensation.[57] Additionally, a nonprofit entity cannot raise equity capital, which therefore limits the cash resources available to its managers. These limitations make it difficult for a non-profit certifier's managers (as compared to the managers of a for-profit corporation) to extract profits earned through cutbacks on certification effort or other forms of opportunism. As Hansmann observed, these self-imposed constraints limit the gains from opportunistic behavior and can therefore operate as commitment devices against such conduct in circumstances above and beyond contractual or reputational

---

[53] In this volume, Verbruggen (Chapter 4) describes decisions by U.S. courts that have imposed liability on standard development organizations in connection with consumer injury. However, he notes that the most aggressive decisions (under theories of strict product liability) are no longer "good law" and ultimately concludes that these organizations' liability risk under U.S. law is "relatively low."

[54] Schuck 1994, 187.

[55] See, e.g., *Compuware Corp. v. Moody's Investors Services* (6th Cir. 2007). Rating agencies' liability exposure is probably greater since the 2007–08 financial crisis. In 2015, Standard & Poor's agreed to pay approximately $1.5 billion in fines in connection with lawsuits brought by various states in connection with the 2007–08 financial crisis (Martin and Grossman 2015).

[56] Barnett 2012, App. Consistent with this historical pattern, leading entities in these markets mostly continue to use nonprofit organizational forms. One important exception is Underwriters Laboratories, the dominant certifier for electrical appliances and other consumer products, which converted in 2012 to the corporate form.

[57] Barnett 2012.

devices.[58] Consistent with these arguments, multiple studies have found that banking entities organized as mutuals[59], as compared to entities organized as stock corporations, experienced lower failure rates during the 1980s' savings and loan crisis.[60]

2. General Partnerships (Financial Services Markets)

In the financial services market, certifiers have mostly tended toward the general partnership, a less aggressively, but still moderately, constrained organizational form as compared to the stock corporation. (The exceptions to this tendency are the stock exchanges, which historically used other constrained forms, the mutual and nonprofit entities, and the credit rating agencies, which used, and continue to use, the unconstrained corporate form.) Until the early 1990s, national accounting firms, corporate law firms and investment banks typically operated as general partnerships. While a general partnership can distribute cash to its members (unlike a nonprofit), it still operates under substantial impediments that do not exist in the stock corporation (or in more recent types of partnership entities that have certain "corporate" characteristics): (i) partners are exposed to unlimited personal liability on a joint and several basis, and (ii) partnership interests are illiquid since they are generally not transferable without the other partner's consent. Like a nonprofit, these constraints limit a partnership's ability to raise capital from outside investors and preclude partners from easily liquidating their ownership interests. These widely-noted "deficiencies" in the traditional partnership may operate to the partners' long-term economic interests by sending a credible signal of certifier trustworthiness. Partners' liability exposure and "lock-in" support incentives to deliver high performance and forego opportunistic action – as well as to monitor other partners' conduct – that could place partnership capital at risk. Given these observable limits on the risk of opportunism, the market reduces the discount that would otherwise be assessed on the certifier's services and transacting parties are more readily induced to make costly investments in entering into relationships with the certifier.[61]

Remarkably, in the years leading up to the 2007–08 financial crisis (which, as noted, might be deemed a certification "failure"), virtually every key type of "Wall Street" certification intermediary abandoned these constrained forms of organization,[62] as shown in Table 14.3.

Law firms and accounting firms largely abandoned the general partnership form, which had exposed partners to unlimited personal liability, for limited liability partnerships, which removed such liability. Investment banks (which act as certification intermediaries in IPOs and other financing transactions) mostly abandoned the partnership form for the corporation, which

---

[58] Hansmann 1996, 229–30; Hansmann 1980, 841–45. Galle (2017) identifies potential limitations to Hansmann's assertion, arguing specifically that managers at nonprofit entities may have reduced incentives to operate efficiently or otherwise promote the entity's objectives due to the absence of equity compensation and the difficulty in measuring the performance of non-profit-seeking tasks. While there is certainly merit to this observation, it would nonetheless appear that, as a general matter, the structural constraints inherent to the nonprofit form at least provide more limited avenues for opportunistic action as compared to for-profit entities. Empirical study may shed further light on this point in specific contexts.

[59] While a mutual can distribute cash to its members (unlike a nonprofit), it cannot raise equity capital and members cannot freely transfer their interests. Additionally, a mutual typically commits to deliver its services at cost. None of these constraints typically exist in a public corporation.

[60] Hansmann 1996: 256–58; O'Hara 1981, 327–28.

[61] This is not to say that certifiers' interest in credibly committing against future opportunism entirely or even primarily motivated these entities' selection of "constrained" organizational forms such as the general partnership. A richer analysis would identify tax-related and other considerations that may have historically driven certifier entities toward these organizational forms.

[62] Barnett 2012, 510; Macey 2010, 24; Ribstein 2010, 207.

TABLE 14.3 *Organizational choices of certification entities in financial services markets**

Entity Type	Dominant Organizational Form (Historical)	Dominant Organizational Form (Current)	Approximate Time of Change in Organizational Form
Credit reporting agencies	Corporation	Corporation	n/a
Accounting firms	General partnership	Limited liability partnership	1990s
Leading investment banks	General partnership	Corporation	1990s
Stock exchanges	Mutual; nonprofit	Corporation	2000s
Law firms	General partnership	Limited liability partnership	2000s

* All supporting sources listed in Barnett (2012, Tbl. II).

substantially expanded their ability to raise capital from outside investors. While I am not aware of evidence demonstrating a causal connection between this shift in organizational form and the subsequent surge in certification failure, the close sequencing of these two events at least preliminarily suggests considering regulatory interventions that influence certifiers' choice of organizational form, which may then provide dominant certifiers with fewer opportunities to extract rents from users through shirking.[63] This approach has some precedents. In the United Kingdom, trademark authorities had historically limited registrations of a certification mark (a trademark that certifies the quality of a third party's product or service) to non-profit entities.[64] In the United States, banking regulations had once mandated or favored the use of nonprofit or mutual forms.[65] These interventions are not free from a substantial risk of regulatory error: for example, the banking regime's constraints on organizational forms limited intermediaries' access to outside capital, potentially resulting in limited investment in scale and innovation.[66] As a more modest variant of this approach, it may be possible to improve certifier performance, while still preserving market choice over organizational forms, by supplying certifiers with the broadest feasible set of legally recognized organizational forms, which certifiers can then customize to commit against future opportunism in response to competitive pressures. In the more general context of business organizations law, Delaware and other states have adopted this menu-expanding approach and substantially increased the organizational options from which businesses can select in the entity formation process.[67]

---

[63] It could be objected that this override of market choice lacks justification so long as the market will assess a discount against certifiers that adopt organizational forms that provide greater shirking opportunities. Market signals would then elicit an efficient mix of organizational choices. Even excluding any limitations on market capacities to accurately price organizational choices, these regulatory interventions to reduce certifier shirking may still be justified on two efficiency grounds: (i) a certifier may underinvest in certification quality given that it is at least a partially excludable good; and (ii) a certifier may mistakenly "overshirk" and excessively deplete its goodwill stock, thereby imposing unexpected (and therefore unpriced) losses on both users and itself.
[64] Belson 2002, 33.
[65] Barnett 2012, 519; Hansmann 1996, 257–58.
[66] For this reason, some commentators have opposed arguments in favor of reinstating regulations that mandate non-corporate forms of organization in the banking sector. See Barnett 2012, 519–21.
[67] Whereas businesses were once confined to the choice between the corporation and the general partnership, U.S. states now typically offer several intermediate options, such as the limited liability corporation, the limited partnership, the limited liability partnership, and various combinations of those forms. Consistent with historical tendencies, Delaware has been among the states that have granted business organizers the greatest latitude in selecting among, and customizing, these options. For the leading account, see Ribstein (2010).

CONCLUSION

Private certification intermediaries play a critical role in alleviating information asymmetries in various markets. Conventional accounts of certification intermediaries make the valuable observation that competitive forces drive intermediaries to make substantial investments in certification effort, resulting in a regular flow of information that efficiently reduces the costs of trade. Nonetheless these accounts cannot readily explain periodic and occasionally dramatic cases in which established certifiers have apparently neglected to identify fraud and other deficiencies at certified firms. The "certification paradox" explains why certification markets mostly succeed but periodically fail. The future expected stream of market rents both induces robust certification effort but, given switching costs and entry costs, induces certifiers to expend reputational capital through limited cutbacks on certification effort. It may be difficult to improve upon this state of affairs simply by expanding certifiers' exposure to fines and other legal penalties in the event of a perceived failure to detect malfeasance by certified firms. While politically popular, these conventional forms of regulatory intervention to deter certifier shirking carry a high risk of error by inducing both over- and underinvestment (including market exit) by certification intermediaries. Certifiers' choice of organizational form may offer a more attractive mechanism for mitigating shirking and enhancing the information collection and verification functions played by certification markets. While further empirical inquiry is merited, both theory and evidence suggest that the constrained organizational forms that are (or once were) common in certification markets may limit dominant certifiers' capacities and incentives to reduce investments in certification effort. Legal interventions that target certifiers' choice of organizational form, rather than certifiers' level of diligence, may offer an indirect mechanism for improving certifier performance at a reduced risk of regulatory error.

References

CASES

United States

Aalmuhammed v. Lee, 202 F.3d 1227 (9th Cir. 2000).
Abercrombie and Fitch Co. v. Hunting World, Inc., 537 F.2d 4 (2d Cir. 1976).
American Society for Testing & Materials v. Public.Resource.Org, Inc., No. 13-cv-1215, No. 14-cv-0857 (D.D.C. Feb. 2. 2017).
American Society for Testing & Materials v. Public.Resource.Org, Inc., 896 F.3d 437 (D.C. Cir. 2018).
American Dental Ass'n v. Delta Dental Plans Ass'n, 39 U.S.P.Q.2d (BNA) 1714 (N.D. Ill. 1996), *rev'd*, 126 F.3d 977 (7th Cir. 1997).
Appalachian Power Co. v. American Institute of Certified Pub. Accountants, 177 F.Supp. 345 (S.D.N.Y.), *aff'd per curiam*, 268 F.2d 844 (2d Cir.), *cert. denied*, 361 U.S. 887 (1959).
Appalachian Power Co. v. Envtl. Prot. Agency, 566 F.2d 451 (4th Cir. 1977).
Apple Computer, Inc. v. Franklin Computer Corp., 714 F.2d 1240 (3d Cir. 1983).
Apple Inc. v. Motorola, Inc., 757 F.3d 1286 (Fed. Cir. 2014).
ATC Distribution, Inc. v. Whatever It Takes Transmissions & Parts, Inc., 402 F.3d 700 (6th Cir. 2005).
Bailey v. Hines, 719 NE.2d 178 (Ill.App.1999).
Baker v. Selden, 101 U.S. 99 (1880).
Banks v. Manchester, 128 U.S. 244 (1888).
Barcamerica International USA Trust v. Tyfield Importers, Inc., 289 F.3d 589 (9th Cir. 2002).
Bay Summit Community Ass'n v. Shell Oil Company 51 Cal.App.4th 762 (1996).
Beasock v. Dioguardi Enterprises Inc., 494 NYS.2d 974 (N.Y. Misc. 1985).
Benco Plastics, Inc. v. Westinghouse Elec Corp., 387 F.Supp. 772 (E.D.Tenn. 1974).
Bibb v. Navajo Freight Lines, Inc., 359 U.S. 520 (1959).
Bluetooth SIG, Inc. v. Chisholm, Notice of Opposition (TTAB, March 11, 2009).
Board-Tech Electronic Co. v. Eaton Corporation, Cooper Wiring Devices, Inc., 2018 WL 2901336, No. 17-3829-cv (2d Cir. 2018).
Brief English Systems, Inc. v. Owen, 48 F.2d 555 (2d Cir. 1931), *cert. denied*, 321 U.S. 785 (1931).
Building Officials & Code Administrators v. Code Technology, Inc., 628 F.2d 730 (1st Cir. 1980).
Burk v. Johnson, 146 F. 209 (8th Cir. 1906).
Burk v. Relief & Burial Ass'n, 2 Haw. 388 (D. Haw. 1909).
Cabrera v. Teatro Del Sesenta, Inc., 914 F. Supp. 743 (D.P.R. 1995).
CCC Information Services, Inc. v. Maclean Hunter Market Reports, Inc., 44 F.3d 61 (2d Cir. 1994).
Childress v. Taylor, 945 F.2d 500 (2d. Cir. 1991).
Cisco Systems, Inc. v. Arista Networks, Inc., No. 14-cv-05344-BLF (N.D. Cal. May 10, 2017), *argued*, No. 17-2145 (Fed. Cir. June 6, 2018).
Code Revision Commission v. Public.Resource.Org, Inc., 244 F. Supp. 3d 1350 (N.D. Ga. 2017), *rev'd in part, vacated in part, & remanded*, No. 17-11589, 2018 WL 5093234 (11th Cir. Oct. 19, 2018).

Cohen v. United States, 578 F.3d 1 (D.C. Cir. 2009).
Commerce and Industry Ins. Co. v. Grinnell Corp, 1999 WL 508357 (E.D.La. 1999).
Community for Creative Non-Violence v. Reid, 490 U.S. 730 (1989).
Community of Roquefort v. William Faehndrich, Inc., 303 F.2d 494, 497 (2d Cir. 1962).
Computer Associates International, Inc. v. Altai, Inc., 982 F.2d 693 (2d Cir. 1992).
Compuware Corp. v. Moody's Investors Services, 499 F.3d 520, 526 (6th Cir. 2007).
Continental Casualty Co. v. Beardsley, 253 F.2d 702 (2d Cir. 1958).
Crume v. Pacific Mutual Life Insurance Co., 140 F.2d 182 (7th Cir. 1944), cert. denied, 322 U.S. 755 (1945).
Ctr. for Auto Safety v. Nat'l Highway Traffic Safety Admin., 452 F.3d 798 (D.C. Cir. 2006).
Douglass v. Alton Ochsner Medical Foundation 696 So.2d 136 (La.App. 5th Cir. 1997).
Downes v. Culbertson, 275 N.Y.S. 233 (N.Y. Sup. Ct. 1934).
E. R.R. Presidents' Conference v. Noerr Motor Freight, Inc., 365 U.S. 127 (1961).
E.G.L. Gem Lab Ltd. v. Gem Quality Inst., Inc., 90 F. Supp. 2d 277 (S.D.N.Y. 2000).
Erikson v. Trinity Theatre, Inc., 13 F.3d 1061 (7th Cir. 1994).
Exxon Corp. v. Oxxford Clothes, Inc., 109 F.3d 1070 (5th Cir. 1997).
Fed. Crop. Ins. Corp. v. Merrill, 332 U.S. 380 (1947).
Feist Publications, Inc. v. Rural Telephone Service Co., Inc., 499 U.S. 340 (1991).
Flynn v. Am. Home Prods. Corp., 627 N.W.2d 342 (Minn. Ct. App. 2001).
Friedman v. F.E. Myers Co., 706 F.Supp 376 (E.D.Pa. 1989).
Gaiman v. McFarlane, 360 F.3d 644 (7th Cir. 2004).
Gates Rubber Co. v. Bando Chemical Industries Ltd., 9 F.3d 823 (10th Cir. 1993).
Gen. Elec. Co. v. EPA, 290 F.3d 377 (D.C. Cir. 2002).
Glanzer v. Shepard, 135 NE.275 (N.Y. 1922).
Griggs v. Perrin, 49 F.15 (C.C.N.D.N.Y. 1892).
Groppel Co., Inc. v. United State Gypsum Co., 616 S.W.2d 49 (Mo.Ct.App. 1981).
Guthrie v. Curlett, 36 F.2d 694 (2d Cir. 1929).
Hall and Chance v. E.I. DuPont de Nemours & Co, Inc. 345 F.Supp 353 (E.D.N.Y. 1972).
Hanberry v. Hearst Corp., 276 Cal.App.2d 680 (1969).
Hempstead v. General Fire Extinguisher Corp., 269 F.Supp. 109 (D.Del. 1967).
Herbert v. United States, 36 Fed. Cl. 299 (Fed. Cl. 1996).
Howard v. Poseidon Pools 133 Misc.2d 50 (N.Y.Misc. 1986), aff'd in part and rev'd in part on other grounds, 522 NYS.2d 388 (1987).
Idaho Potato Comm'n v. M & M Produce Farm & Sales, 335 F.3d 130 (2d Cir. 2003).
In re Thomas Nelson, Inc., 97 USPQ2d 1712, 1715 (TTAB 2011).
In re. Application S/N 79013672 for the Mark USB-HOUSE, Notice of Opposition (TTAB 2008).
Institut Nat'l Des Appellations d'Origine v. Brown-Forman Corp., 47 U.S.P.Q.2d 1875 (TTAB 1998).
International Information Systems Security Certification Consortium, Inc. v. Security University LLC, 823 F.3d 153 (2d Cir. 2016).
Jackson v. C. G. Conn Ltd., 9 U.S.P.Q. (BNA) 225 (W.D. Okla. 1931).
Jappell v. American Ass'n of Blood Banks, 162 F.Supp.2d 476 (E.D.Va. 2001).
Kellogg Co. v. Toucan Golf, Inc., 337 F.3d 616 (6th Cir. 2003).
Kepner-Tregoe, Inc. v. Carabio, 203 U.S.P.Q. (BNA) 124 (E.D. Mich. 1979).
King v. National Spa and Pool Institute, Inc., 570 So.2d 612 (Ala. 1990).
Kohola Agriculture v. Deloitte & Touche, 949 P.2d 141 (Haw. 1997).
Larson v. Warner Bros. Entm't, Inc., No. 2:04-cv-08400-ODW (RZx), 2013 WL 1694448 (D.D.C. 2013).
Lear v. Atkins, 395 U.S. 653 (1969).
Lockman v. S.R. Smith, LLC, 4:07-CV-0217-HLM, 2010 WL 11566367 (N.D.Ga. 2010).
Lockman v. S.R. Smith, LLC, 405 Fed.Appx. 471, (11th Cir. 2010) (per curiam) WL 5158571.
Lotus Development Corp. v. Borland International, Inc., 49 F.3d 807 (1st Cir. 1995), aff'd by an equally divided court, 516 U.S. 233 (1996).
Lotus Development Corp. v. Paperback Software International, 740 F. Supp. 37 (D. Mass. 1990).
Meneely v. S.R. Smith, Inc., 5 P.3d 49 (Wash.Ct.App. 2000).
Meyers v. Donnatacci, 531 A.2d 398 (N.J.Super. 1987).
Midwest Plastic Fabricators, Inc. v. Underwriters Labs. Inc., 906 F.2d 1568 (Fed. Cir. 1990).
Mills Music, Inc. v. Snyder, 469 U.S. 153 (1985).

Minnesota v. Clover Leaf Creamary Co, 449 U.S. 456 (1981).
Mitel, Inc. v. Iqtel, Inc., 124 F.3d 1366 (10th Cir. 1997).
N.N.V. v. American Ass'n of Blood Banks, 75 Cal.App.4th 1358 (1999)
Nat'l Ass'n of Home Builders v. Norton, 415 F.3d 8 (D.C. Cir. 2005).
Oracle America, Inc. v. Google LLC, 886 F.3d 1179 (Fed. Cir. 2018).
Oracle America, Inc. v. Google Inc., 750 F.3d 1339 (Fed. Cir. 2014).
Oracle America, Inc. v. Google Inc., 872 F. Supp. 2d 974 (N.D. Cal. 2012).
Parker v. Brown, 317 U.S. 341 (1943).
Patentas v. United States, 687 F.2d 707 (3d. Cir 1982).
People v. Arcadia Machine & Tool, Inc., 2003 WL 21184117 (Cal.Super. 2003).
Perris v. Hexamer, 99 U.S. 674 (1878).
Pizza Hut, Inc. v. Papa John's Int'l, Inc., 227 F.3d 489 (5th Cir. 2000).
Plains Cotton Cooperative Ass'n v. Goodpasture Computer Service, Inc., 807 F.2d 1256 (5th Cir. 1987).
Polaroid Corp. v. Polarad Electronics Corp., 287 F.2d 492 (2d Cir. 1961).
Practice Management Information Corp., Inc. v. American Medical Ass'n, 121 F.3d 516 (9th Cir. 1997).
Prudential Property and Cas. Ins. Co. v. American Plywood Ass'n 1994 WL 463527 (S.D.Fla. 1994).
Randi W. v. Muroc Joint Unified Sch. Dist., 929 P.2d 582 (Cal. 1997).
Renegotiation Bd. v. Bannercraft Clothing Co., 415 U.S. 1 (1974).
Rottinghaus v. Howell, 666 P.2d 899 (Wash.Ct.App. 1983).
Rountree v. Ching Feng Blinds Industry Co. Ltd., 560 F.Supp.2d 804 (D.Alaska 2008).
Scorpio Music S.A. v. Willis, No. 11cv1557 BTM(RBB), 2012 WL 1598043 (S.D. Cal. 2012).
Sega Enterprises Ltd. v. Accolade, Inc., 977 F.2d 1510 (9th Cir. 1993).
Sizemore v. Georgia-Pacific Corp., 1996 WL 498410 (D.S.C. 1996).
Snyder v. American Ass'n of Blood Banks, 676 A.2d 1036 (N.J. 1996).
Southco, Inc. v. Kanebridge Corp., 390 F.3d 276 (3d Cir. 2004) (en banc).
Swarovski Aktiengesellschaft v. Building No. 19, Inc., 704 F.3d 44 (1st Cir. 2013).
Swiss Watch Int'l, Inc. v. Fed'n of the Swiss Watch Indus., 101 U.S.P.Q.2d (BNA) 1731 (T.T.A.B. 2012).
Tea Bd. of India v. Republic of Tea, Inc., 80 U.S.P.Q.2d 1881 (TTAB 2006).
United Mine Workers of America v. James Pennington, 381 U.S. 657 (1965).
United States Lighting Serv, Inc. v. Llerad Corp., 800 F.Supp. 1513 (N.D.Ohio 1992).
Veeck v. Southern Building Code Congress Int'l, Inc., 293 F.3d 791 (5th Cir. 2002) (en banc).
Volkswagen v. Church, 411 F.2d 350 (9th Cir. 1969).
Waters v. Autuori, 236 Conn. 820 (1996).
Weigand v. University Hospital of New York, 659 NYS.2d 395 (N.Y. Misc. 1997).
Wheaton v. Peters, 33 U.S. 591 (1834).
Woods v. Bourne Co., 60 F.3d 978 (2d Cir. 1995).

European Union

B.N.O. Walrave and L.J.N. Koch v. Association Union Cycliste International (Case 36/74), EU:C:1974:140 (CJEU 1974).
Cassis de Dijon Rewe-Zentral AG v. Bundesmonopolverwaltung für Branntwein (Case 120/78), EU:C:1979:42 (CJEU 1979).
Dansk Supermarked A/S v. A/S Imerco (Case 58/80), EU:C:1981:17 (CJEU 1981).
Deutsche Shell (Case 188/91), EU:C:1993:24 (CJEU 1993).
Elisabeth Schmitt v. TÜV Rheinland LGA Products GmbH (Case 219/15), EU:C:2017:128 (CJEU 2017).
EMC Development v. Commission (Case 367/10 P), EU:C:2011:203 (CJEU 2011).
EN 197-1 Standard – EMC/European Cement, Case COMP/F-2/38.401 (E.C. 2005).
Établissements Consten S.à.R.L. and Grundig-Verkaufs-GmbH v. Commission (Joined Cases 56 and 58/65), EU:C:1966:41 (CJEU 1966).
Fra.bo v. Deutsche Vereinigung des Gas- und Wasserfaches eV (Case 171/11), EU:C:2012:453 (CJEU 2012).
Henri Cullet v. Centre Leclerc à Toulouse (Case 231/83), EU:C:1985:29 (CJEU 1985).
Inter-Environnement Wallonie v. Région Wallone (Case 129/96), EU:C:1997:628 (CJEU 1997).

J. Wouters, v. Algemene Raad van de Nederlandse Orde van Advocaten (Case 309/99), EU:C:2002:98 (CJEU 2002).
James Elliot Construction Ltd v. Irish Asphalt Limited (Case 613/14), EU:C:2016:821 (CJEU 2016).
Keck and Mithouard (Joined Cases 267/91 and 268/91), EU:C:1993:905 (CJEU 1993).
Klaus Höfner and Fritz Elser v. Macrotron GmbH (Case 41/90), EU:C:1991:161 (CJEU 1991).
Laval un Partneri Ltd v. Svenska Byggnadsarbetareförbundet (Case 341/05), EU:C:2007:809 (CJEU 2007).
Meroni & Co, Industrie Metallurgiche SpA v. High Authority (Case 10/56), EU:C:1958:7 (CJEU 1958).
OTOC v. Autoridade da Concorrencia (Case 1/12), EU:C:2013:127 (CJEU 2013).
Pre-insulated Pipe Cartel, Case No IV/35.691/E-4 (E.C. 1998).
Procureur du Roi v Benoît and Gustave Dassonville (Case 8/74), EU:C:1974:82 (CJEU 1974).
SAT Fluggesellschaft v. Eurocontrol (Case 364/92), EU:C:1994:7 (CJEU 1994).
SC Belasco v. Commission (Case 246/86), EU:C:1989:301 (CJEU 1989).
SCK and FNK v. Commission (Joined Cases 213/95 and 18/96), EU:T:1997:157 (EGC 1997).
SELEX Sistemi Integrati v. Commission (Case 113/07 P), EU:C:2009:191 (CJEU 2009).
SELEX Sistemi Integrati v. Commission (Case 155/04), EU:T:2006:387 (EGC 2006).
Seven SpA v. OHIM (Case 176/10), EU:T:2011:577 (EGC 2011).
Sevince v. Staatssecretaris van Justitie (Case 192/89), EU:C:1990:322 (CJEU 1990).
Union des associations européennes de football (UEFA) v. Jean-Marc Bosman (Case 415/93), EU:C:1995:463 (CJEU 1995).
United Kingdom of Great Britain and Northern Ireland v. European Parliament and Council of the European Union (Case 270/12), EU:C:2014:18 (CJEU 2014).

France

Conseil d'État, Section S, 17 February 1992, No. 73230.
Cour de Cassation 2 October 2007 (Chambre civil 1), Case no. 06-19.521, Bulletin 2007, I, N° 315.
Société Les Grands Travaux de l État c/ Pottier et Oth, Tribunal Administrative de Paris, 9 March 1993, not reported.

Germany

Bundesgerichtshof, 22 June 2017, VII ZR 36/14.
Decision of the Court of Appeals in Hamburg (2017), Case No. 3 U 220/15.
Gesundbeter, DIN, BVerfGE, 29 July 1998, ZUM 1998.
Landgericht Köln, 12 March 2008, 28 O (Kart) 529/07, (28. Zivilkammer).
Oberlandesgericht Düsseldorf, 14.08.2013, VI-2 U 15/08 (Kart), (2. Kartellsenat).
Standard-Spundfass, Case No. KZR 40/02 *(Federal Sup. Ct. of Germany 2009).*

Netherlands

Hoge Raad, 29 June 2007, ECLI:NL:HR:BA0895 (*Strawberry Mite*).
Knooble B.V./De Staat der Nederlanden, HR 22 juni 2012, NJ 2012, 397 m.nt.
Knooble, The Hague District Court Decision of 31 December 2008, LJN:BG8465.

United Kingdom

Banca Nazionale del Lavoro SPA v. Playboy Club London Ltd. & others [2018] UKSC 43.
Bayerische Motoren Werke AG (BMW) v. Technosport London Ltd., EWCA (Civ.) (UK), No. A3 2016, 1801 (June 21, 2017).
Caparo Industries plc v. Dickman [1990] 2 AC 605.
Hedley Byrne & Co. Ltd. v. Heller & Partners Ltd. [1964] A.C. 465.
Marc Rich & Co. AG v. Bishop Rock Marine Co. (The Nicholas H) [1995] 3 All E.R. 307.
NRAM Ltd (formerly NRAM plc) v Steel [2018] UKSC 13.

Perrett v. Collins [1998] 2 Lloyd's Rep 255 (CA).
Watson v. British Boxing Board of Control [2000] EWCA Civ 2116.
Wattleworth v. Goodwood Road Racing Company Ltd. and others [2004] EWHC 140 (QB).

LEGISLATIVE AND AGENCY MATERIALS

United States

1 C.F.R. §§ 2, 5, 8, 51.
5 C.F.R. §§ 8.1(a), 8.2.
10 C.F.R. § 50.55a.
24 C.F.R. § 3280.202.
37 C.F.R. §§ 2.161, 2.45, 7.37, 202.1.
42 C.F.R. §§ 433.112.
49 C.F.R. §§ 195.132.
5 U.S.C. §§ 552, 553.
6 U.S.C. § 747.
15 U.S.C. §§ 272, 1051, 1052, 1054, 1057, 1058, 1059, 1064, 1072, 1114, 1117, 1125, 1127, 1151, 1193, 1262, 2054, 2056, 2058, 2065.
17 U.S.C. §§ 101, 102, 105, 107, 201, 203, 304.
42 U.S.C. §§ 6294a, 16194.
44 U.S.C. §§ 1510, 4101.
Admin. Conf. of the U.S. (ACUS). 1979. "Recommendation 78-4, Federal Agency Interaction with Private Standard-Setting Organizations in Health and Safety Regulation." *Federal Register* 44(4): 1357–1359.
Admin. Conf. of the U.S. (ACUS). 2011. "Recommendation 2011–5, Incorporation by Reference," *Federal Register* 77(10): 2257–2259.
Admin. Conf. of the U.S. (ACUS). 2012a. "Recommendation 2011–5, Incorporation by Reference," *Federal Register.* 77(1): 2257, 2257.
Admin. Conf. of the U.S. (ACUS). 2012b. Response to Office of Federal Register Petition (June 1, 2012). www.acus.gov/sites/default/files/documents/Final-ACUS-Response-to-OFR-Petition-6-1-12.pdf
California Department of Food and Agriculture, Marketing Branch. 2015. California Leafy Green Products Handler Marketing Agreement. www.cdfa.ca.gov/mkt/mkt/pdf/LeafyGreensProductsHandlerMktAgmt.pdf
California Department of Food and Agriculture, Marketing Branch. 2016. Commodity Specific Food Safety Guidelines for the Production and Harvest of Lettuce and Leafy Greens. www.lgma.ca.gov/wp-content/uploads/2014/09/California-LGMA-metrics-01-29-16-Final1.pdf
California Department of Human Services, Food and Drug Branch & U.S. Food and Drug Administration. 2007. Investigation of and Escherichia coli O157:H7 Outbreak Associated with Dole Pre-Packaged Spinach. www.cdc.gov/nceh/ehs/docs/investigation_of_an_e_coli_outbreak_associated_with_dole_pre-packaged_spinach.pdf
California Marketing Act of 1937. 21 Cal. Food & Agric. Code §§ 58601–58624.
Centers for Disease Control and Prevention. 2017. *Surveillance for Foodborne Disease Outbreaks, United States 2015.* Atlanta, Georgia: US Department of Health and Human Services.
Commonwealth of Massachusetts. 2004. Enterprise Open Standards Policy. www.mass.gov/anf/research-and-tech/policies-legal-and-technical-guidance/it-policies-standards-and-procedures/ent-pols-and-stnds/
Copyright Office. 2013. Circular No. 14.0713, Copyright in Derivative Works and Compilations 1. www.copyright.gov/circs/circ14.pdf
Department of Agriculture. 2002. Veneman Marks Implementation of USDA National Organic Standards (October 10, 2002).
Dodd-Frank Wall Street Reform and Consumer Protection Act. 2010. 124 Stat. 1376, codified at 15 U.S.C. § 78.
Electronic Code of Federal Regulations. 2018. www.ecfr.gov/cgi-bin/ECFR?page=browse
ENERGY STAR. 2018. ENERGY STAR Overview. www.energystar.gov/about
FDA Food Safety Modernization Act of 2011. Pub. L. No. 111–353, 124 Stat. 3885.

Federal Trade Commission (FTC). 2005. Statement in the *Matter of Union Oil Company of California*. Dkt. No. 9305.

Federal Trade Commission (FTC). 2014. Made in USA Brand, LLC Agrees to Drop Deceptive Certification Claims. www.ftc.gov/news-events/press-releases/2014/07/made-usa-brand-llc-agrees-drop-deceptive-certification-claims

Food and Drug Administration (FDA). 1998. Guidance for Industry: Guide to Minimize Microbial Food Safety Hazards for Fresh Fruits and Vegetables. www.fda.gov/downloads/Food/GuidanceRegulation/UCM169112.pdf

Food and Drug Administration (FDA). 2004a. Letter to Firms that Grow, Pack, or Ship Fresh Lettuce and Fresh Tomatoes. https://wayback.archive-it.org/7993/20170404002726/www.fda.gov/Food/GuidanceRegulation/GuidanceDocumentsRegulatoryInformation/ProducePlantProducts/ucm118896.htm

Food and Drug Administration (FDA). 2004b. Produce Safety from Production to Consumption: 2004 Action Plan to Minimize Foodborne Illness Associated with Fresh Produce Consumption. https://wayback.archive-it.org/7993/20171103205748/www.fda.gov/Food/FoodborneIllnessContaminants/BuyStoreServeSafeFood/ucm129487.htm

Food and Drug Administration (FDA). 2008. Guidance for Industry: Guide to Minimize Microbial Food Safety Hazards of Fresh-cut Fruits and Vegetables. www.fda.gov/Food/GuidanceRegulation/GuidanceDocumentsRegulatoryInformation/ProducePlantProducts/ucm064458.htm

Food and Drug Administration (FDA). 2013. Standards for Growing, Harvesting, Packing, and Holding Produce for Human Consumption, Proposed Rule, 78 Fed. Reg. 3504 (January 16, 2013).

Food and Drug Administration (FDA). 2014. Operational Strategy for Implementing the FDA Food Safety Modernization Act (FSMA). www.fda.gov/Food/GuidanceRegulation/FSMA/ucm395105.htm

Food and Drug Administration (FDA). 2015. Standards for Growing, Harvesting, Packing, and Holding Produce for Human Consumption, Final Rule, 80 Fed. Reg. 74354 (November 27, 2015).

Food and Drug Administration (FDA). 2017. Standards for the Growing Harvesting, Packing, and Holding Produce for Human Consumption, Final Regulatory Impact Analysis. Archived at http://perma.cc/9U6F-M7RB

H.F. 3971, 84th Leg., Reg. Sess. (Minn. 2006).

H.R. Rep. No. 94–1476, at 124 (1976), *reprinted in* 1976 U.S.C.C.A.N. at 5659.

IHS Markit Standards Store. 2018. ASME NQA-1. https://global.ihs.com/doc_detail.cfm?&input_search_filter=ASME&item_s_key=00011834&item_key_date=900400&input_doc_number=%26quot%3BNQA-1%26quot%3B&input_doc_title=&org_code=ASME&origin=HISC

Madrid Protocol Implementation Act of 2002. Public Law 107–273, 116 Stat. 1758, 1913–1921.

Madrid Protocol to the 1891 Madrid Agreement Concerning the International Registration of Marks and the Protocol Relating to that Agreement; adopted June 27, 1989, Madrid, Spain; amended on October 3, 2006 and November 12, 2007. 15 U.S.C. § 1141a(b).

Minnesota, State of. 2007. *Preserving the Present: Creating, Accessing and Maintaining Minnesota's Electronic Documents*. https://mn.gov/mnit/images/gov_lr_2008_0115_Legislative_Report.pdf

National Archives and Records Administration (NARA). 2012. *Incorporation by Reference*, 77 Fed. Reg. 11,414, 11,414 (February 27, 2012).

National Archives and Records Administration (NARA). 2014. *Incorporation by Reference*, 79 Fed. Reg. 66,267, 66,267 (November 7, 2014).

National Archives and Records Administration (NARA). 2017. IBR Handbook. www.archives.gov/files/federal-register/write/handbook/ibr.pdf/

National Archives and Records Administration (NARA). 2018. Federal Register. www.federalregister.gov/

National Commission on New Technological Uses of Copyrighted Works (CONTU). 1979. Final Report. Washington, DC: Library of Congress.

National Institute of Standards & Technology (NIST). 2018. Standards Incorporated by Reference (SIBR) Database, Regulatory SIBR (P-SIBR) Statistics. https://standards.gov/sibr/query/index.cfm?fuseaction=rsibr.total_regulatory_sibr

National Library of Medicine (NLM). 2003. SNOMED Clinical Terms to Be Added to UMLS Metathesaurus. www.nlm.nih.gov/research/umls/Snomed/snomed_announcement.html

National Technology Transfer and Advancement Act of 1995 (NTTAA). 2016. Pub. L. No. 104–113, 110 Stat. 775 (codified at 15 U.S.C. § 3701 et seq.).

National Transportation Safety Board. 2011. NTSB/PAR-11/01, Pipeline Accident Report, Pacific Gas and Electric Company Natural Gas Transmission Pipeline Rupture and Fire, San Bruno, California, September 9, 2010 (August 30, 2011).

Office of Management and Budget (OMB). 1998. "Circular A-119: Federal Participation in the Development and Use of Voluntary Consensus Standards and in Conformity Assessment Activities." *Federal Register* 63: 8546.

Office of Management and Budget (OMB). 2016. OMB Circular A-119: Federal Participation in the Development and Use of Voluntary Consensus Standards and in Conformity Assessment Activities. www.nist.gov/sites/default/files/revised_circular_a-119_as_of_01-22-2016.pdf

Office of the Federal Register (OFR). 2018a. Incorporation by Reference (IBR) Handbook. www.archives.gov/files/federal-register/write/handbook/ibr.pdf/

Office of the Federal Register (OFR). 2018b. Document Drafting Handbook. www.archives.gov/files/federal-register/write/handbook/ddh.pdf

Organic Foods Production Act of 1990. Pub. L. No. 101–624, 104 Stat. 3935 (codified as amended at 7 U.S.C. §§ 6501–6522).

Patent & Trademark Off. (PTO). 2017. Trademark Manual of Examining Procedure (TMEP).

Patent & Trademark Off. (PTO). 2018. *The Madrid Protocol Frequently Asked Questions by U.S. Trademark Owners Seeking International Rights.* www.uspto.gov/trademarks/law/madrid/madridfaqs.jsp

S. 1160, 89th Cong. 1965.

S. 1666, 88th Cong. 1964.

S. Rep. No. 1219. 1964.

S. Rep. No. 813. 1965.

S.B. 1579, 78th Leg., Reg. Sess. (Tex. 2003).

Sarbanes-Oxley Act of 2002. 116 Stat. 745 (codified in Titles 15, 18, 28 and 29 U.S.C.).

Securities Act of 1933. 48 Stat. 74 (codified at 15 U.S.C. § 77a et seq.).

Securities and Exchange Commission (SEC). 2010. Response of the Office of Chief Counsel, Division of Corporate Finance, Re: Ford Motor Credit Company LLC. www.sec.gov/divisions/corpfin/cf-noaction/2010/ford072210-1120.htm

Texas, State of. 2009. "Texas Senate Bill 266." https://legiscan.com/TX/bill/SB266/2009

Trade Agreements Act of 1979. Pub.L. 96–39, 93 Stat. 144 (codified at 19 U.S.C. § 2501 et seq.).

U.S. Const. amend. I.

White House. 1997. President Clinton Announces Initiative to Ensure the Safety of Imported and Domestic Fruits and Vegetables. https://clintonwhitehouse4.archives.gov/WH/New/html/19971002-8886.html

European Union

Directive 85/374/EEC of 25 July 1985 on the approximation of the laws, regulations and administrative provisions of the Member States concerning liability for defective products (OJ L 210, 7.8.1985, p. 29), as last amended by Directive 1999/34/EC of the European Parliament and of the Council (OJ L 141, 4 June 1999, p 20).

Directive 2001/29/EC of the European Parliament and of the Council of 22 May 2001 on *the harmonisation of certain aspects of copyright and related rights in the information society.*

Directive 2003/98/EC of the European Parliament and of the Council of 17 November 2003 on *the re-use of public sector information.*

Directive 2013/37/EU of the European Parliament and of the Council of 26 June 2013 *amending Directive 2003/98/EC on the re-use of public sector information Text with EEA relevance.*

Directive No. 2015/2436, codified under EU Regulation No. 2015/2424 (European Trademark Directive).

Directive 2015/1535/EU of the European Parliament and of the Council of 9 September 2015 laying down a procedure for the provision of information in the field of technical regulations and of rules on Information Society services [2015] OJ L241/1.

EU Intellectual Prop. Office (EUIPO). 2017. Guidelines for Examination of European Union Trade Marks, Part B – Examination.

European Commission. 1985. Council Resolution (85/C 136/01) of 7 May 1985 on a *new approach to technical harmonization and standards* – OJ C 136 of 4 June 1985.

European Commission. 1986. Decision 86/399 of 10 July 1986 relating to a *proceeding under Article 85 of the EEC Treaty* (1986) OJ L 232 /15.
European Commission. 1992. COM(92) 445, Communication from the Commission, Intellectual Property Rights and Standardization.
European Commission. 2003. General Guidelines for the Cooperation between CEN, Cenelec and ETSI and the European Commission and the European Free Trade Association, 2003 O.J. (C 91).
European Commission. 2004. European Interoperability Framework for Pan-European eGovernment Services. http://ec.europa.eu/idabc/servlets/Docd552.pdf
European Commission. 2008. Decision 768/2008 of 9 July 2008 on a *Common Framework for the Marketing of Products* OJ L 218 (13 August 2008).
European Commission. 2011a. "Communication: A strategic vision for European standards: Moving forward to enhance and accelerate the sustainable growth of the European economy by 2020," COM(2011) 311 final, 1 June 2011.
European Commission. 2011b. Staff Working Paper, "Executive Summary of the Impact Assessment," SEC (2011) 672 final, 1 et seq.
European Commission. 2011c, "Communication: Guidelines on the applicability of Article 101 of the Treaty on the Functioning of the European Union to horizontal co-operation agreements," *Official Journal* C11, 14.1.2011, p. 1.
European Commission. 2012. Commission Regulation 1025/2012, On European Standardisation, 2012 O.J. (L 316).
European Commission. 2014. Patents and Standards: A modern framework for IPR-based standardization. A study prepared for the European Commission.
European Commission. 2016a. "Communication: Standardisation package: European standards for the 21st century," COM(2016) 358 final, 1 June 2016.
European Commission. 2016b. About the European Commission. http://ec.europa.eu/about/index_en.htm
European Commission. 2017. Publication of an update to the list of national standardisation bodies pursuant to Article 27 of Regulation (EU) No 1025/2012 of the European Parliament and of the Council on European standardization, O.J. (C 351), p. 13–16.
European Commission. 2018. General framework of European standardisation policy. https://ec.europa.eu/growth/single-market/european-standards/policy/framework_en
Regulation (EU) No. 1025/2012 of the European Parliament and of The Council of 25 October amending *Council Directives 89/686/EEC and 93/15/EEC and Directives 94/9/EC, 94/25/EC, 95/16/EC, 97/23/EC, 98/34/EC, 2004/22/EC, 2007/23/EC, 2009/23/EC and 2009/105/EC of the European Parliament and of the Council and repealing Council Decision 87/95/EEC and Decision No 1673/2006/EC of the European Parliament and of the Council.*
Regulation 764/2008 of 9 July 2008 *Laying down Procedures Relating to the Application of Certain National Technical Rules to Products Lawfully Marketed in Another Member State* OJ L 218, 13 August 2013.
Regulation No 765/2008 of 9 July 2008 *Setting Out the Requirements for Accreditation and Market Surveillance Relating to the Marketing of Products* OJ L 218, 13 August 2008.

France

Décret No. 2009–697 of 16 June 2009 relatif à la normalisation.

Malaysia

Malaysian Public Sector Open Source Software (OSS) Initiative. 2006. The Malaysian Government Interoperability Framework for Open Source Software (MyGIFOSS).

New Zealand

State Services Commission, New Zealand. 2008. New Zealand E-government Interoperability Framework (NZ e-GIF). www.ict.govt.nz/assets/Guidance-and-Resources/eGIF-v3.3.pdf

India

India. 2008. *Policy on Open Standards for E-Governance*, Ministry of Communications & Information Technology Department of Information Technology. http://nisg.org/files/documents/A03020001.pdf

Department of Information Technology, Ministry of Communications & Information Technology, Government of India. 2010. Policy on Open Standards for e-Governance. www.gswan.gov.in/PDF/Policy%20on%20Open%20Standards%20in%20eGovernance.pdf

Japan

Commerce and Information Policy Bureau, Ministry of Economy, Trade and Industry, Government of Japan. 2005. Interim Report of "Study Group on the Legal Protection of Software and Promotion of Innovation" (Tentative Translation).

South Africa

Office of the Government CIO-South Africa. 2007. Handbook on Minimum Information Interoperability Standards (MIOS). http://unpan1.un.org/intradoc/groups/public/documents/cpsi/unpan026787.pdf

Switzerland

Schweizerisches Zivilgesetzbuch [ZBG], *Ordinance Governing the Use of the Appellation "Swiss" for Watches*, Code Civil [CC], Codice civile [CC] [Civil Code] December 23, 1971, RO 1915 (Switz.).

United Kingdom

Cabinet Office (GUK). 2012. Open Standards Principles: For software interoperability, data and document formats in government IT specifications. http://webarchive.nationalarchives.gov.uk/20140904135420/www.gov.uk/government/uploads/system/uploads/attachment_data/file/78892/open-standards-principles-final.pdf

Cabinet Office (GUK). 2014. Government Digital Service: Core Assessment Questions. www.gov.uk/government/organisations/government-digital-service

Cabinet Office (GUK). 2015. Policy Paper: Open Standards Principles (UK). www.gov.uk/government/publications/open-standards-principles/open-standards-principles

World Intellectual Property Organization

World Intellectual Property Organization (WIPO). 2018. *How to file your application: Basic Requirements.* www.wipo.int/madrid/en/how_to/file/requirements.html

World Trade Organization

Committee on Technical Barriers to Trade (TBT Committee). 1993. World Trade Organization, Communication from the ISO/IEC, TBT/W/178, 15 December 1993.

Committee on Technical Barriers to Trade (TBT Committee). 1995. World Trade Organization, "Negotiating History of the Coverage of the Agreement on Technical Barriers to Trade with Regard to Labelling Requirements, Voluntary Standards, and Processes and Production Methods Unrelated to Product Characteristics," WT/TBT/W/11, 29 August 1995.

Committee on Technical Barriers to Trade (TBT Committee). 2000. World Trade Organization, "Decision of the Committee on Principles for the Development of International Standards, Guides and Recommendations with Relation to Articles 2, 5 and Annex 3 of the Agreement," G/TBT/9 (13 November 2000).

Committee on Technical Barriers to Trade (TBT Committee). 2001. World Trade Organization, "Decisions and Recommendations Adopted by the WTO Committee on Technical Barriers to Trade Since 1 January 1995," Note by the Secretariat, G/TBT/1/Rev.10 (9 June 2001).
Committee on Technical Barriers to Trade (TBT Committee). 2016. World Trade Organization, "List of Standardizing Bodies that Have Accepted the Code of Good Practice for the Preparation, Adoption and Application of Standards Since 1 January 1995," G/TBT/CS/2/rev.22, 29 February 2016.
World Trade Organization (WTO). 1994a. Agreement on Trade Related Aspects of Intellectual Property Rights, 1869 U.N.T.S. 299 (April 15, 1994).
World Trade Organization (WTO). 1994b. Marrakesh Agreement Establishing the World Trade Organization.
World Trade Organization (WTO). 1994c. The WTO Agreement on the Application of Sanitary and Phytosanitary Measures (SPS Agreement).
World Trade Organization (WTO). 1995. Agreement on Technical Barriers to Trade.
World Trade Organization (WTO). 2001. Appellate Body Report, *EC – Measures Affecting Asbestos and Products Containing Asbestos*.
World Trade Organization (WTO). 2002a. Appellate Body Report, *EC – Trade Description of Sardines*.
World Trade Organization (WTO). 2002b. Panel Report, *EC – Trade Description of Sardines* (2002b).
World Trade Organization (WTO). 2008a. Appellate Body Report, *China – Measures Affecting Imports of Automobile Parts*.
World Trade Organization (WTO). 2008b. Appellate Body Report, *EC – Bananas III (Article 21.5 – Ecuador II)*.
World Trade Organization (WTO). 2011a. Panel Report, *United States – Certain Country of Origin Labeling (COOL) Requirements*.
World Trade Organization (WTO). 2011b. Panel Report, *US – Tuna II*.
World Trade Organization (WTO). 2012a. Appellate Body Report, *US – Certain Country of Origin Labeling (COOL) Requirements*.
World Trade Organization (WTO). 2012b. Appellate Body Report, *US – Measures Affecting the Production and Sale of Clove Cigarettes*.
World Trade Organization (WTO). 2012c. World Trade Report.
World Trade Organization (WTO). 2014. Appellate Body Report, *EC – Seal Products*.
World Trade Organization (WTO). 2015. Appellate Body Report, *US – Tuna II* (2015).

International Agreements

Vienna Convention on the Law of Treaties (VCLT), concluded on 23 May 1969.

ORGANIZATIONAL MATERIALS

AFNOR. 2018. Terms and Condition of Sale (available in English). www.boutique.afnor.org/resources/c98c56a0-e973-4790-aca2-17f3f8417b4c.pdf
Alliance for Internet of Things Innovation (AIOTI). 2016. IoT LSP Standard Framework Concepts. Release 2.6. https://docbox.etsi.org/SmartM2M/Open/AIOTI/!!20160530Deliverables/AIOTI%20WG3_sdos_alliances_landscape_-_iot_lsp_standard_framework_concepts_-_release_2_v6.pdf
AllSeen Alliance. 2017. IP Policy. https://web.archive.org/web/20171125000858/https://identity.allseenalliance.org/about/governance/ip-policy
American Medical Association. 2017. CPT Purpose and Mission. www.ama-assn.org/practice-management/cpt-purpose-mission
American National Standards Institute (ANSI). 2008. *ANSI Guidelines on Embedded Trademark*.
American National Standards Institute (ANSI). 2018a. ANSI Essential Requirements: Due Process Requirements for American National Standards. www.ansi.org/essentialrequirements/
American National Standards Institute (ANSI). 2018b. Domestic Programs (American National Standards) Overview. www.ansi.org/standards_activities/domestic_programs/overview?menuid=3
American National Standards Institute (ANSI). 2018c. IBR Standards Portal: Standards Incorporated by Reference. https://ibr.ansi.org/

American National Standards Institute (ANSI). 2018d. Introduction to ANSI. www.ansi.org/about_ansi/introduction/introduction

American National Standards Institute (ANSI). 2018e. ISO Programs Overview. www.ansi.org/standards_activities/iso_programs/overview

American National Standards Institute (ANSI). 2018f. Overview of the U.S. Standardization System. www.standardsportal.org/usa_en/standards_system.aspx

American National Standards Institute (ANSI). 2018g. Why Charge for Standards? www.ansi.org/help/charge_standards.aspx

American Petroleum Institute. 2018. Publications, Programs, Services. www.api.org/~/media/Files/Publications/2018_Catalog/2018_Pubs_Catalog_final_sm.pdf

Apache Software Foundation. 2004. Apache License. www.apache.org/licenses/LICENSE-2.0

Apache Software Foundation. 2018. Software Grant and Corporate Contributor License Agreement. www.apache.org/licenses/cla-corporate.txt

ASTM International. 2018a. Benefit-Cost Analysis of Committee F37 on Light Sport Aircraft to the Light Sport Aircraft Community and the FAA. www.astm.org/COMMIT/LSA_Case_Study.pdf

ASTM International. 2018b. Committee F37 on Light Sport Aircraft. www.astm.org/COMMITTEE/F37.htm

ASTM International. 2018c. Reading Room. www.astm.org/READINGLIBRARY/

ASTM International. 2018d. Standards Products, www.astm.org/Standard/index.html (last accessed June 15, 2018).

ASTM International. 2018e. Subcommittee F37.10 on Glider. www.astm.org/COMMIT/SUBCOMMIT/F3710.htm

ASTM International. 2018f. Subcommittee F37.70 on Cross Cutting. www.astm.org/COMMIT/SUBCOMMIT/F3770.htm

Black Duck Software. 2018. Top Open Source Licenses. www.blackducksoftware.com/top-open-source-licenses

Bluetooth SIG. 2008. Thousands of Products Infringing on Bluetooth Trademark Seized. www.bluetooth.com/news/pressreleases/2008/12/15/thousands-of-products-infringing-on-bluetooth-trademarks-seized

Bluetooth SIG. 2016. Bluetooth Trademark License Agreement (E-Sign Version 1.3 – Last Revised December 14, 2016).

Bluetooth SIG. 2018a. Qualification Fees. www.bluetooth.com/develop-with-bluetooth/qualification-listing/qualification-listing-fees

Bluetooth SIG. 2018b. Qualification Test Facilities. www.bluetooth.com/develop-with-bluetooth/qualification- listing/qualification-test-facilities

BSI. 1997. BS 0: 1997 – A Standard for Standards.

BSI. 2017. Rules for the Structure and Drafting of UK standards. www.bsigroup.com/Documents/standards/guide-to-standards/Rules-for-structure-and-drafting-of-UK-standards-2017.pdf

CEN. 2015. Statutes. ftp://ftp.cencenelec.eu/CEN/AboutUs/Governance/Statutes/Statutes_CEN-EN.pdf

CEN/CENELEC. 2018a. European Standardization. www.cencenelec.eu/standards/Pages/default.aspx

CEN/CENELEC. 2018b. Internal Regulation, part 1. https://boss.cen.eu/ref/IR1_E.pdf

CENELEC. 2015. Articles of Association. ftp://ftp.cencenelec.eu/CENELEC/ArticlesOfAssociation/1_CLCArticlesOfAssociation2015_EN.pdf

Classification & Rating Administration (CARA). 2010. Classification and Rating Rules. www.filmratings.com/downloads/rating_rules.pdf

DIN. 2013. DIN 820–1. Normungsarbeit – Teil 1: Grundsätze. www.din.de/de/ueber-normen-und-standards/din-norm/grundsaetze

DVB Services Sárl. 2018. DVB Trademark Authorised User Agreement. www.dvbservices.com/dvb_logo/agreement/

ECMA International. 2011. ECMAScript® Language Specification. www.ecma-international.org/ecma-262/5.1/

ECMA International. 2016. ECMA Code of Conduct in Patent Matters. Version 2. www.ecma-international.org/memento/codeofconduct.htm

ECMA International. 2018. ECMA List of Patent Statements. www.ecma-international.org/publications/files/ECMA-ST/Ecma%20PATENT/EcmaListofPatentStatements.htm

European Telecommunications Standards Institute (ETSI). 2005. Open Source impacts on ICT standardization. www.etsi.org/website/document/workshop/sosinterop/sosinteropiiibackground01.pdf
European Telecommunications Standards Institute (ETSI). 2016a. ETSI Rules of Procedure Annex 6: ETSI Intellectual Property Rights Policy. www.etsi.org/images/files/IPR/etsi-ipr-policy.pdf
European Telecommunications Standards Institute (ETSI). 2016b. Terms of Reference of the Open Source Group on 'Open Source MANO' (OSG OSM). https://portal.etsi.org/Portals/0/TBpages/OSM/Docs/ETSI_OSG_OSM_ToR_2016-02-09.pdf
European Telecommunications Standards Institute (ETSI). 2017a. ETSI IPR Policy. www.etsi.org/images/files/IPR/etsi-ipr-policy.pdf
European Telecommunications Standards Institute (ETSI). 2017b. Statutes https://portal.etsi.org/directives/37_directives_apr_2017.pdf
European Telecommunications Standards Institute (ETSI). 2018. Use of ETSI Trademarks.
European Committee for Interoperable Systems (ECIS). 2012. *ECIS patent consultation contribution*. http://ec.europa.eu/internal_market/indprop/docs/patent/hearing/vinje_ecis_en.pdf
Food Industry Center & National Center for Food Protection and Defense. 2009. Natural Selection: 2006 *E. coli* Recall of Fresh Spinach. http://ageconsearch.umn.edu/bitstream/54784/2/Natural%20Selection.pdf
Free Software Foundation (FSF). 2017. What is free software? www.gnu.org/philosophy/free-sw.html
Free Software Foundation Europe (FSFE). 2016a. EU jeopardises its own goals in standardisation with FRAND licensing. https://fsfe.org/news/2016/news-20160428-02.en.html
Free Software Foundation Europe (FSFE). 2016b. Why is FRAND bad for Free Software? https://fsfe.org/activities/os/why-frand-is-bad-for-free-software.en.html#fn1
Free Software Foundation Europe (FSFE). 2018. Transcript of Richard Stallman at the 2nd international GPLv3 conference; April 21, 2006. https://fsfe.org/campaigns/gplv3/fisl-rms-transcript.en.html
Github. 2015. Patents. https://github.com/facebook/react/blob/b8ba8c83f318b84e42933f6928f231dc0918f864/PATENTS
GNU. 2017. GNU General Public License, version 2. www.gnu.org/licenses/old-licenses/gpl-2.0.en.html
Good Housekeeping. 2014. About the GH Limited Warranty Seal. www.goodhousekeeping.com/institute/about-the-institute/a22148/about-good-housekeeping-seal
IBM. 2005. IBM Statement of Non-Assertion of Named Patents Against OSS. www.ibm.com/ibm/licensing/Patents/pledgedPatents.pdf
Idaho Potato Commission. 2018. Ask Dr. Potato: Top 5 Frequently Asked Questions. www.idahopotato.com/frequently-asked-questions
IETF Trust. 1996. The Internet Standards Process – Revision 3. https://tools.ietf.org/html/rfc2026
IETF Trust. 2008. RFC 5378 – Rights Contributors Provide to the IETF Trust.
IETF Trust. 2015. IETF TRUST Legal Provisions Relating to IETF Documents. https://trustee.ietf.org/documents/IETF-TLP-5_001.html
IETF Trust. 2016. IETF Trends and Observations. www.ietf.org/archive/id/draft-arkko-ietf-trends-and-observations-00.txt
IETF Trust. 2017. Intellectual Property Rights in IETF Technology. www.ietf.org/rfc/rfc8179.txt
IETF Trust. 2018a. Trademark Usage Guidelines. https://trustee.ietf.org/trademark-usage-guidelines.html.
IETF Trust. 2018b. General Trademark License Agreement. https://trustee.ietf.org/docs/IETF_General_TM_License.pdf
IETF Trust. 2018c. FAQ for use of the IETF Acronym and Logo. https://trustee.ietf.org/ietf-logo-acronym.html
Institute of Electrical and Electronics Engineers (IEEE). 1990. IEEE Standard Computer Dictionary: A Compilation of IEEE Standard Computer Glossaries 114.
Institute of Electrical and Electronics Engineers (IEEE). 2013. IEEE Policies. www.ieee.org/documents/ieee_policies.pdf
Institute of Electrical and Electronics Engineers (IEEE). 2014. IEEE-SA Standards Board Patent Committee, IEEE-SA Patent Policy: Draft Comments ID No. 38. http://grouper.ieee.org/groups/pp-dialog/drafts_comments/PatCom_sort_by_commentID_040314.pdf
Institute of Electrical and Electronics Engineers (IEEE). 2017. IEEE-SA Standards Board Bylaws: Clause 6. http://standards.ieee.org/develop/policies/bylaws/sect6-7.html

Institute of Electrical and Electronics Engineers (IEEE). 2018. IEEE-SA Standards Board Bylaws. http://standards.ieee.org/develop/policies/bylaws/sect6-7.html

International Accreditation Forum. 2018. About Us. www.iaf.nu//articles/About/2

International Electrotechnical Commission (IEC). 2018. Patent Database. http://patents.iec.ch/iec/pa.nsf/pa_h.xsp?v=0#

International Fresh-cut Produce Association & Western Growers Association. 1997. Voluntary Food Safety Guidelines for Fresh Produce. Alexandria, VA: International Fresh-cut Produce Association.

International Fresh-cut Produce Association, Produce Marketing Association, United Fresh Fruit and Vegetable Association, and Western Growers. 2006. Commodity Specific Food Safety Guidelines for the Lettuce and Leafy Greens Supply Chain. Alexandria, VA: International Fresh-cut Produce Association.

International Standardization Organization (ISO). 2012. ISO/IEC 23360–1:2006. www.iso.org/standard/43781.html

International Standardization Organization (ISO). 2018a. ISO Members. www.iso.org/iso/home/about/iso_members.htm

International Standardization Organization (ISO). 2018b. ISO Name and logo. www.iso.org/iso-name-and-logo.html

International Telecommunication Union (ITU). 2016. Definition of "Open Standards." www.itu.int/en/ITU-T/ipr/Pages/open.aspx (last accessed October 21, 2016).

International Telecommunication Union (ITU). 2018. Common Patent Policy for ITU-T/ITU-R/ISO/IEC. www.itu.int/en/ITU-T/ipr/Pages/policy.aspx

Internet Engineering Task Force (IETF). 2008. RFC 5378 – *Rights Contributors Provide to the IETF Trust* (Scott Bradner & Jorge Contreras eds., November 2008). http://tools.ietf.org/pdf/rfc5378.pdf

Internet Engineering Task Force. 2018. http://ietf.org/

ISEAL Alliance, ISEAL Code of Good Practice – Setting Social and Environmental Standards v5.0, 2010.

ISO/IEC 17000:2004 – Conformity Assessment.

ISO/IEC Directives (ISO/IEC Dir 1), Part 1, Edition 10.0, 2013-10, clause 2.5.6.

ISO/IEC Guide 2: 2004.

ISO/IEC. 2017. ISO/IEC 17011:2017 Conformity Assessment – Requirements for Accreditation Bodies Accrediting Conformity Assessment Bodies. www.iso.org/standard/67198.html

Jekyll. 2018. *Contributing.* https://jekyllrb.com/docs/contributing/

Kroah-Harthman, Greg, Chris Mason, Rik van Riel, Shuah Kahn, and Grant Likely. 2017. Linux Kernel Community Enforcement Statement. http://kroah.com/log/blog/2017/10/16/linux-kernel-community-enforcement-statement

Motion Picture Association of America, Inc. (MPAA) & National Association of Theatre Owners, Inc. (NATO). January 1, 2010. Classification and Rating Rules. https://filmratings.com/Content/Downloads/rating_rules.pdf

Moving Picture Experts Group (MPEG). 2018. MXM License. https://mpeg.chiariglione.org/docs/mxm-license

National Fire Protection Association. 2018. NFPA 220: Standard on Types of Building Construction. https://catalog.nfpa.org/NFPA-220-Standard-on-Types-of-Building-Construction-P1239.aspx?icid=D729

NEN. 2005. Statuten en Huishoudelijk Reglement. www.nen.nl/web/file?uuid=088db660-6abe-47ec-b0aa-03e4ca3eeb78&owner=ffb94002-6f6e-4bdf-98ad-d18724cf33ce

NEN. 2016. Algemene Verkoopvoorwaarden Diensten Normontwikkeling. www.nen.nl/Home/Algemene-voorwaarden-2.htm

Netfilter. 2016. Statement of Netfilter Project on GPL Enforcement. www.netfilter.org/files/statement.pdf

Netscape. 1995. Netscape and Sun Announce Javascript, The Open, Cross-Platform Object Scripting Language for Enterprise Networks and the Internet. https://web.archive.org/web/20070916144913/http://wp.netscape.com/newsref/pr/newsrelease67.html

OASIS. 2006. Open by Design: The Advantages of the OpenDocument Format (ODF). www.oasis-open.org/committees/download.php/21449/oasis_odf_advantages_10dec2006.odt

OASIS. 2015. Open Standards, Cover Pages. http://xml.coverpages.org/openStandards.html (last updated September 27, 2015).

OASIS. 2018a. Open Repositories. www.oasis-open.org/policies-guidelines/open-repositories

OASIS. 2018b. Intellectual Property Rights (IPR) Policy. www.oasis-open.org/policies-guidelines/ipr

OMA SpecWorks. 2016. Open Standards and Open Sources. www.omaspecworks.org/open-standards-and-open-source/

Open Connectivity Foundation. 2016. Unification Will Combine the Best of Both Organizations under Open Connectivity Foundation Name and Bylaws. https://openconnectivity.org/announcements/allseen-alliance-merges-open-connectivity-foundation-accelerate-internet-things

Open Invention Network. 2012. OIN License Agreement. www.openinventionnetwork.com/joining-oin/oin-license-agreement/

Open Source Initiative (OSI). 2017a. The Open Source Definition. https://opensource.org/osd

Open Source Initiative (OSI). 2017b. The BSD 2-Clause License. https://opensource.org/licenses/bsd-license.php

Open Source Initiative (OSI). 2017c. Fall 2017 Face to Face Meeting Minutes. https://opensource.org/minutes2017FallF2F

Open Source Initiative (OSI). 2017d. For Approval: W3C Software and Document License. http://lists.opensource.org/pipermail/license-review_lists.opensource.org/2017-August/003081.html

Open Source Initiative (OSI). 2018a. The Open Source Definition (Annotated). Version 1.9. https://opensource.org/osd-annotated

Open Source Initiative (OSI). 2018b. Licenses by Name. https://opensource.org/licenses/alphabetical

Open Source Initiative (OSI). 2018c. FAQ. https://opensource.org/faq#cc-zero

Open Source Initiative (OSI). 2018d. April 2009 Archives by thread. http://lists.opensource.org/pipermail/license-review_lists.opensource.org/2009-April/thread.html#723

Oracle Corp. 2016. Java Licensing Logo Guidelines. www.oracle.com/us/technologies/java/java-licensing-logo-guidelines-1908204.pdf

Organisation for Economic Co-operation and Development (OECD). 2010. *Efficient e-Government for Smarter Public Service Delivery*, Denmark.

Orthodox Union. 2018. Basics of Certification. https://oukosher.org/kosher-overview/how-does-ou-kosher-certification-work

Public.Resource.Org. (n.d.) https:// public.resource.org/

Plastics Pipe Institute. 2018. All PPI Publications. http://plasticpipe.org/publications/index.html

Redhat. 2017. Technology Industry Leaders Join Forces to Increase Predictability in Open Source Licensing. www.redhat.com/en/about/press-releases/technology-industry-leaders-join-forces-increase-predictability-open-source-licensing

SNOMED International. 2017. Licensing. www.snomed.org/snomed-ct/get-snomed-ct

Software Freedom Conservancy (SFConservancy). 2018. The Principles of Community-Oriented GPL Enforcement. https://sfconservancy.org/copyleft-compliance/principles.html

Underwriters Laboratories (UL). 2017. UL Standards. https://ulstandards.ul.com (last accessed December 3, 2017).

Underwriters Laboratories (UL). 2018a. Marks and Labels. www.ul.com/marks/

Underwriters Laboratories (UL). 2018b. Standards Catalog. https://standardscatalog.ul.com

United Fresh Fruit & Vegetable Association, 1997. Industrywide Guidance to Minimize Microbiological Food Safety Risks for Produce. Archived at https://perma.cc/4FLG-YTGM

VITA. 2018. Disclosure. www.vita.com/Disclosure

Western Growers Association. 2010. About the Process – Nine Things You Need to Know. www.leafygreenguidance.com/node/118

Wi-Fi Alliance (WFA). 2018a. Authorized Test Laboratories, www.wi-fi.org/certification/authorized-test-laboratories

Wi-Fi Alliance (WFA). 2018b. Wi-Fi Test Suite, www.wi-fi.org/certification/wi-fi-test-suite

Wi-Fi Alliance (WFA). 2018c. Membership. www.wi-fi.org/membership

World Economic Forum (WEF). 2012. *The Global Enabling Trade Report 2012 – Reducing Supply Chain Barriers.*

Worldwide Web Consortium (W3C). 2004a. W3C Patent Policy. www.w3.org/Consortium/Patent-Policy-20040205/

Worldwide Web Consortium (W3C). 2004b. Overview and Summary of W3C Patent Policy. www.w3.org/2004/02/05-patentsummary.html

Worldwide Web Consortium (W3C). 2015. W3C Software and Document Notice and License. www.w3.org/Consortium/Legal/2015/copyright-software-and-document

Worldwide Web Consortium (W3C). 2018. W3C Trademarks and Generic Terms. www.w3.org/Consortium/Legal/2002/trademarks-20021231

BOOKS, ARTICLES AND ONLINE MATERIALS

4iP Council. 2016. "The European Commission and the value of patents for 5G and IoT," April 26, 2016.

Abbott, Kenneth W. and Duncan Snidal. 2001. "International 'Standards' and International Governance," *Journal of European Public Policy* 8(3): 345.

Abbott, Kenneth W. and Duncan Snidal. 2009. "The Governance Triangle: Regulatory Standards Institutions and the Shadow of the State" in W. Mattli and N. Woods, eds., *The Politics of Global Regulation*. Princeton, NJ: Princeton University Press.

Acemoglu, Daron, Gino Gancia, and Fabrizio Zilibotti. 2012. "Competing engines of growth: Innovation and standardization," *Journal of Economic Theory* 147: 570.

Akerlof, George A. 1970. "The Market for 'Lemons': Quality Uncertainty and the Market Mechanism," *Quarterly Journal of Economics* 84(3): 488–500.

Albano, Gian Luigi and Alessandro Lizzeri. 2001. "Strategic Certification and Provision of Quality," *International Economic Review* 42(1): 267–83.

Albersmeier, Friederike, Holger Schulze, Gabriele Jahn, and Achim Spiller. 2009. "The reliability of third-party certification in the food chain: From checklists to risk-oriented auditing," *Food Control* 20: 927–35.

American Bar Association. 2016. House of Delegates Resolution 112.

Amicus Curiae. Brief Amicus Curiae of Copyright Law Professors in Support of Respondent. 1995. Reprinted as "Brief Amicus Curiae of Copyright Law Professors in *Lotus Development Corp. v. Borland International, Inc.*" *Journal of Intellectual Property Law* 3(1): 103–34 ("Amicus Brief in *Borland* – U.S. Supreme Court").

Amicus Curiae. Brief Amicus Curiae of Copyright Law Professors. 1994. Reprinted as "The Nature of Copyright Analysis for Computer Programs: Copyright Law Professors' Brief Amicus Curiae in *Lotus v. Borland*" in *Hastings Communications and Entertainment Law Journal* 16(4): 657–80 ("Amicus Brief in *Borland* – 1st Circuit").

Amit, Hagai. 2014. "The Incredibly High Cost of Keeping Your Food Kosher," *Haaretz*, February 21, 2014.

An, Baisheng. 2009. "Intellectual Property Rights in Information and Communications Technology Standardization: High-Profile Disputes and Potential for Collaboration Between the United States and China," *Texas International Law Journal* 45: 175.

Appleton, Arthur. 2005. "The Agreement on Technical Barriers to Trade" in P. Macrory, A. Appleton, and M. Plummer, eds., *The World Trade Organization: Legal, Economic and Political Analysis*. Leiden: Martinus Nijhoff, p. 371.

Armour, Stephanie. 2017. "Hospital Watchdog Gives Seal of Approval, Even After Problems Emerge," *Wall Street Journal*. September 8.

Armstrong, Timothy K. 2010. "Shrinking the Commons: Termination of Copyright Licenses and Transfers for the Benefit of the Public," *Harvard Journal on Legislation*. 47: 359.

Arthur, W. Brian. 1989. "Competing Technologies, Increasing Returns, and Lock-in by Historical Events," *Economic Journal*. 99: 116.

Austin, Marc T. and Helen V. Milner. 2001. "Strategies of European Standardization," *Journal of European Public Policy* 8: 411, 423.

Bach, Susan and Pascal Delaquis. Milner. 2009. "The Origin and Spread of Human Pathogens in Fruit Production Systems." In Xuetong Fan, Brenda A. Niemira, Christopher J. Doona, Florence E. Feeherry, and Robert B. Gravani, eds., *Microbial Safety of Fresh Produce*. Ames, IA: Wiley-Blackwell.

Baird, Stacy. 2009. *Government Role and the Interoperability Ecosystem*, ISJLP 5: 219.

Barnett, Jonathan M. 2006. "Certification Drag: The Opinion Puzzle and Other Transactional Curiosities," *Journal of Corporation Law* 33: 95–150.

Barnett, Jonathan M. 2012. "Intermediaries Revisited: Is Efficient Certification Consistent with Profit Maximization?," *Journal of Corporation Law* 37(3): 475–527.

Baron, Justus and Daniel F. Spulber. 2018. "Technology Standards and Standard Setting Organizations: Introduction to the Searle Center Database," *Northwestern Law & Econ Research Paper* No. 17-16, https://papers.ssrn.com/sol3/papers.cfm?abstract_id=3073165

Baron, Justus and Julia Schmidt. 2017. "Technological Standardization, Endogenous Productivity and Transitory Dynamics." Working Paper.

Baron, Justus and Tim Pohlmann. 2013. "Who cooperates in standards consortia – rivals or complementors?," *Journal of Competition Law & Economics* 9(4): 905–29.

Baron, Justus, Tim Pohlmann, and Knut Blind. 2016. "Essential patents and standards dynamics," *Research Policy* 45: 1762–73.

Barritt, Keith. 2009. *Copyright Ownership of Voluntary Consensus Standards*, Fish & Richardson (August 13, 2009), www.fr.com/Copyright-Ownership-of-Voluntary-Consensus-Standards/

Barron, Mark R. 2007. "Creating Consumer Confidence or Confusion: The Role of Product Certification Marks in the Market Today," *Marquette Intellectual Property Law Review* 11(2): 414–42.

Bartley, Tim. 2011. "Certification as Mode of Social Regulation" in D. Levi-Faur, ed., *Handbook on the Politics of Regulation*. Cheltenham, UK: Edward Elgar.

Bebchuk, Lucian Arye and Marcel Kahan. 1989. "Fairness Opinions: How Fair Are They and What Can Be Done About It?," *Duke Law Journal* 27(1): 27–53.

Becker, Bo and Todd Milbourn. 2010. "How did increased competition affect credit ratings?," *National Bureau of Economic Research*, Working Paper No. 16404. September.

Beebe, Barton. 2004. "The Semiotic Analysis of Trademark Law," *UCLA Law Review* 51(3): 621–704.

Bekkers, Rudi and Andrew Updegrove. 2012. "A Study of IPR Policies and Practices of a Representative Group of Standard Setting Organizations Worldwide." Presented at National Academies of Science Symposium on Management of IP in Standards-Setting Processes. http://sites.nationalacademies.org/xpedio/groups/pgasite/documents/webpage/pga_072197.pdf

Bekkers, Rudi, Christian Catalini, Arianna Martinelli, Cesare Righi, and Tim Simcoe. 2016. "Essential patents and standard dynamics," *Research Policy* 45(9): 1762–73.

Belenzon, Sharon and Mark Schankerman. 2008. "Motivation and Sorting in Open Source Software Innovation," *LSE STICERD Research Paper No. EI47*. https://ssrn.com/abstract=1401776

Belson, Jeffery. 2002. *Special Report Certification Marks*. London: Sweet & Maxwell.

Belson, Jeffrey. 2017. *Certification and Collective Marks. Law and Practice*. Cheltenham, UK; Northampton, MA: Edward Elgar.

Bennett, Victor Manuel, Lamar Pierce, Jason A. Snyder, and Michael W. Toffel. 2013. "Customer-Driven Misconduct: How Competition Corrupts Business Practices," *Management Science* 59(8): 1725–42.

Berkman Center for Internet & Society. 2005. *Roadmap for Open ICT Ecosystems*. https://cyber.harvard.edu/publications/2005/The_Roadmap_for_Open_ICT_Ecosystems

Berners-Lee, Tim and Steven R. Bratt. 2003. Email to Dr. Oliver Smoot, President, International Organization for Standardization, September 18, 2003. http://lists.w3.org/Archives/Public/www-international/2003JulSep/0213.html

Bernstein, Steven and Benjamin Cashore. 2007. "Can non-state global governance be legitimate? An analytical framework," *Regulation and Governance* 1: 347–71.

Biddle, Brad, Frank Curci, Matt Dodson, and Molly Edwards. 2017. "Standards Setting Organizations and Trademark Registration: An Empirical Analysis" (working paper October 18, 2017).

Biglaiser, Gary and James W. Friedman. 1994. "Middlemen as guarantors of quality," *International Journal of Industrial Organization* 12(4): 509–31.

Black, J. 2009. "Legitimacy, Accountability and Polycentric Regulation: Dilemmas, Trilemmas and Organisational Response." In A. Peters, L. Koechlin, T. Förster, and G. Fenner Zinkernagel, eds., *Non-State Actors as Standard Setters*. Cambridge: Cambridge University Press, 241.

Blind, Knut. 2006. "Explanatory Factors for Participation in Formal Standardization Processes: Empirical Evidence at Firm Level," *Economics of Innovation and Technology* 15(2): 157–70.

Blind, Knut. 2009. "Standardisation as a Catalyst for Innovation," *ERIM Report Series Reference No. EIA-2009-LIS*.

Blind, Knut. 2017. "The economic functions of standards in the innovation process." In Richard Hawkins, Knut Blind, and Robert Page, eds., *Handbook of Innovation and Standards*. London: Edward Elgar.

Blind, Knut and A. Jungmittag. 2008. "The Impact of Patents and Standards on Macroeconomic Growth: A Panel Approach Covering Four Countries and 12 Sectors," *Journal of Productivity Analysis* 29: 51.

Blind, Knut and Brian Kahin. 2018. "Standards and the Global Economy," in J. Contreras, ed., *The Cambridge Handbook of Technical Standardization Law: Competition, Antitrust, and Patents*. Cambridge: Cambridge University Press, 7–16.

Blind, Knut and Axel Mangelsdorf. 2006. "Motives to Standardize: Empirical Evidence from Germany," *Technovation* 48–49: 13–24.
Bone, Robert G. 2006. "Hunting Goodwill: A History of the Concept of Goodwill in Trademark Law," *Boston University Law Review* 86(3): 547–622.
Bowker, Geoffrey C. and Susan Leigh Star. 2000. *Sorting Things Out: Classification and Its Consequences*. Cambridge, MA: MIT Press.
Boyle, Alan and Christine Chinkin. 2007. *The Making of International Law*. Oxford: Oxford University Press.
Bradner, Scott. 1996. "The Internet standards process – Revision 3" (October), Request for Comments (RFC) 2026, www.ietf.org/rfc/rfc2026.txt
Breitenberg, Maureen A. 2009. "NISTIR 7614, The ABC's of Standards Activities." www.nist.gov/sites/default/files/nistir_7614.pdf
Bremer, Emily. 2011. "Incorporation by Reference in Federal Regulations," *Administrative Conference of the United States*.
Bremer, Emily. 2013a. "Incorporation by Reference in an Open-Government Age," *Harvard Journal of Law & Policy* 36(1): 131–210.
Bremer, Emily. 2013b. "Technical Standards Meet Administrative Law: A Primer on an Ongoing Debate," *Standards Engineering* 65(2): 1–6.
Bremer, Emily. 2015. "On the Cost of Private Standards in Public Law," *Kansas Law Review* 63(2): 279–333.
Bremer, Emily. 2016. "American and European Perspectives on Private Standards in Public Law," *Tulane Law Review* 91(2): 325–70.
Brennan, Jeffrey W. and Paul C. Cuomo. 1999. "The 'Nonprofit Defense' in Hospital Merger Antitrust Litigation," *Antitrust*, Spring 1999: 13–19.
Brody, Evelyn. 1996. "Agents Without Principals: The Economic Convergence of the Nonprofit and For-Profit Organizational Forms," *New York Law School Law Review* 40(3): 460–536.
Brunsson, Nils and Bengt Jacobsson, eds. 2001. *A World of Standards*. Oxford: Oxford University Press.
Burrows, Emily. 2010. "Termination of Sound Recording Copyrights & the Potential Unconscionability of Work for Hire Clauses," *Review of Litigation*. 30: 101.
Burrows, Vanessa K. 2008. *FDA Authority to Regulate On-Farm Activity*. Washington, DC: Congressional Research Service.
Busch, Richard. 2012. "Fighting for the Right to Superman's Copyright: More Brutal than Anything Lex Luther Could Have Imagined," *Forbes*, November 1, 2012. www.forbes.com/sites/richardbusch/2012/11/01/truth-justice-and-the-american-way-fighting-for-the-right-to-supermans-copyright-more-brutal-than-anything-lex-luthor-or-the-legion-of-doom-could-have-ever-imagined/.
Büthe, Tim. 2008. "The Globalization of Health and Safety Standards: Delegation of Regulatory Authority in the SPS Agreement of 1994 Establishing the World Trade Organization," *Law and Contemporary Problems* 71: 219.
Büthe, Tim and Walter Mattli. 2003. "Setting International Standards – Technological Rationality or Primacy of Power?" *World Politics* 56: 1.
Büthe, Tim and Walter Mattli. 2011. *The New Global Rulers. The Privatization of Regulation in the World Economy*. Princeton, NJ: Princeton University Press.
Cabral, Luis and David Salant. 2014. "Evolving technologies and standards regulation," *International Journal of Industrial Organization* 36: 48–56.
Cafaggi, Fabrizio. 2006. "Rethinking Private Regulation in the European Regulatory Space" in F. Cafaggi, ed., *Reframing Self-Regulation in European Private Law*. Alphen aan den Rijn: Kluwer Law International.
Cafaggi, Fabrizio. 2012. "New Foundations of Transnational Private Regulation," *Journal of Law and Society* 38(1):20–49.
Cardi, W. Jonathan. 2005. "Purging Foreseeability," *Vanderbilt Law Review* 58(3): 739–809.
Carpenter, Daniel and David A. Moss. 2014. *Preventing Regulatory Capture: Special Interest Influence and How to Limit It*. Cambridge: Cambridge University Press.
Carroll, Claire S. 2004. "What Does 'Organic' Mean Now?: Chickens and Wild Fish Are Undermining the Organic Foods Production Act of 1990," *San Joaquin Agricultural Law Review* 14: 117–41.
Champigneulle-Mihailov, Jeanne. 2000. "Les Aspects Juridiques de la Normalisation en France" in H. Schepel and J. Falke, eds., *Legal Aspects of Standardisation in the Member States of the EC and EFTA, Volume 2: Country Reports*. Luxembourg: Office for Official Publications of the European Communities.

Cheit, Ross H. 1990. *Setting Safety Standards: Regulation in the Public and Private Sectors.* Berkeley, CA: University of California Press.
Chemerinsky, Erwin. 2013. *Constitutional Law*, 4th ed. New York: Wolters Kluwer Law & Business.
Chesbrough, Henry. 2003. *Open Innovation: The New Imperative for Creating and Profiting from Technology.* Boston: Harvard Business School Press.
Chiao, B., J. Lerner and J. Tirole. 2007. "The Rules of Standard-Setting Organizations: An Empirical Analysis," *RAND Journal of Economics* 38: 905–30.
Choi, Dong Geun, Heesang Lee, and Tae-kyung Sung. 2011. "Research profiling for standardization and innovation," *Scientometrics* 88(1): 259–78.
Choi, Stephen S. 1998. "Market Lessons for Gatekeepers," *Northwestern University Law Review* 92: 916–66.
Chon, Margaret. 2009. "Marks of Rectitude," *Fordham Law Review* 77: 2311.
Chon, Margaret. 2018. "Certification and Collective Marks in the United States" in Jane Ginsburg and Irene Calboli, eds., *Cambridge Handbook on International and Comparative Trademark Law.* Cambridge: Cambridge University Press.
Clark, Kendall Grant. 2003. "ISO to Require Royalties?" *XML.com*, September 24, 2003. www.xml.com/pub/a/2003/09/24/deviant.html
Clark, Ramsay. 1967. Attorney General's Memorandum on the Public Information Section of the Administrative Procedure Act (July 4, 1967).
Coffee, John C. Jr. 2002. "It's About the Gatekeepers, Stupid," *Business Lawyer* 57(4): 1403–20.
Coffee, John C. Jr. 2004. *Gatekeepers: The Professions and Corporate Governance.* New York: Oxford University Press.
Cohen, Daniel. 2008. *The History, Politics & Perils of the Current Food Safety Controversy.* Davis, CA: Community Alliance with Family Farmers. www.perishablepundit.com/docs/CAFF.Policy.Guide.l.pdf
Contreras, Jorge L. 2011. "An Empirical Study of the Effects of Ex Ante Licensing Disclosure Policies on the Development of Voluntary Technical Standards." *NIST*, No. GCR 11–934.
Contreras, Jorge L. 2013. "Technical Standards and Ex Ante Disclosure: Results and Analysis of an Empirical Stud," *Jurimetrics* 53(1): 163–211.
Contreras, Jorge L. 2015. "Patent Pledges," *Arizona State Law Journal* 47(3): 543–608.
Contreras, Jorge L. 2016. "A Tale of Two Layers: Patents, Standardization, and the Internet," *Denver University Law Review* 93(4): 853–95.
Contreras, Jorge L. 2019. "Patents, Technical Standards and Standards-Setting Organizations: A Survey of the Empirical, Legal and Economic Literature" in Peter Menell and David Schwarz, eds., *Research Handbooks on the Economics of Intellectual Property Law, Vol. 2 – Analytical Methods.* Cheltenham, UK: Edward Elgar.
Contreras, Jorge L. and Andrew Hernacki. 2014. "Copyright Termination and Technical Standards," *University of Baltimore Law Review* 43: 221–53.
Contreras, Jorge L., Meghan Lewis, and Hannah Roth. 2011. "Toward a Rational Framework for Sustainable Building Materials Standards," *Standards Engineering* 63(5): 1–7.
Contreras, Jorge L. and Charles R. McManis. 2013. "Intellectual Property Landscape of Material Sustainability Standards," *Columbia Science & Technology Law Review* 14: 485–513.
Contreras, Jorge L. and Andrew Updegrove. 2016. "A Primer on Intellectual Property Policies of Standards Bodies" in Kai Jacobs, ed., *Effective Standardization Management in Corporate Settings.* Hershey, PA: IGI Global, pp. 215–35.
Cover, Robin. 2003. "Standards Organizations Express Concern About Royalty Fees for ISO Codes," *Cover Pages*, Sepember 20, 2003.
Curcuru, Shane. 2017. "Three Reactions to the Facebook Patents License." Medium.com. https://medium.com/@shanecurcuru/three-reactions-to-the-facebook-patents-license-b64e6942012b
David, Paul A. 1985. "Clio and the Economics of QWERTY," *American Economics Review* 75: 332.
Davis, Michael H. 2000. "The Screenwriter's Indestructible Right to Terminate Her Assignment of Copyright: Once a Story is 'Pitched,' A Studio Can Never Obtain All Copyrights in the Story," *Cardozo Arts & Entertainment Law Journal.* 18: 93.
Dawson, Norma. 1988. *Certification Trade Marks: Law and Practice.* London: Intellectual Property Publishing Ltd.
Day, Julia. 2004. "Burberry Doffs Its Cap to 'Chavs,'" *The Guardian*, November 1, 2004.

Delaney, Helen and Rene van de Zande. 2000. "NIST Special Public 951, A Guide to EU Standards and Conformity Assessment."

Delimatsis, Panagiotis. 2011. "Protecting Public Morals in a Digital Age : Revisiting the WTO Rulings on *US – Gambling* and *China – Publications and Audiovisual Services*," *Journal of International Economic Law* 14(2): 257.

Delimatsis, Panagiotis. 2018. "Global Standard-Seting 2.0: How the WTO Spotlights ISO and Impacts the Transnational Standard-Setting Process," *Duke Journal of Comparative and International Law* 28: 101.

Delimatsis, Panagiotis and Olia Kanevskaia. 2018. "Exit, Voice and Loyalty in Standards Development Organizations: Strategic Behaviour in IEEE" (working paper).

Delimatsis, Panagiotis (ed.). 2015. *The Law, Economics and Politics of International Standardization*. Cambridge: Cambridge University Press.

Demortain, David. 2011. *Scientists and the Regulation of Risk: Standardizing Control*. Cheltenham, UK: Edward Elgar Publishing.

DeNardis, Laura. 2008/2009. "Open Standards and Global Politics," *International Journal of Communications Law & Policy* 13: 168.

Devlin, Alan. 2009. "Standard-Setting and the Failure of Price Competition," *NYU Annual Survey of American Law* 65: 217.

DiMaggio, Paul J. and Walter W. Powell. 1991. "Introduction," in Paul J. DiMaggio and Walter W. Powell, eds., *The New Institutionalism in Organizational Analysis*. Chicago: The University of Chicago Press.

Dinwoodie, Graeme B. 1999. "The Death of Ontology: A Teleological Approach to Trademark Law," *Iowa Law Review* 84(4): 611–752.

Dobbs, Dan B., Paul T. Hayden, and Ellen M. Bublick. 2. 2016. *Hornbook on Torts*. St. Paul, MN: West Academic Publishing.

Doctorow, Cory. 2005. "WiFi isn't short for Wireless Fidelity," *BoingBoing*, November 8, 2005, https://boingboing.net/2005/11/08/wifi-isnt-short-for.html

Dogan, Stacey L. and Mark A. Lemley. 2004. "Trademarks and Consumer Search Costs on the Internet," *Houston Law Review* 41(3): 777–838.

Donnelly, C. 2007. *Delegation of Governmental Power to Private Parties – A Comparative Perspective*. Oxford: Oxford University Press.

Dornis, Tim W. and Thomas Wein. 2016. "Trademarks, Comparative Advertising and Product Imitations: An Untold Story of Law and Economics," *Pennsylvania State University Law Review* 121: 421.

Drexl, Josef. 2012. "Anti-competitive Stumbling Stones on the Way to a Cleaner world: Protecting Competition in Innovation without a Market," *Journal of Competition Law & Economics* 8: 507.

Dreyfuss, Rochelle Cooper. 1990. "Expressive Genericity: Trademarks as Language in the Pepsi Generation," *Notre Dame Law Review* 65(3): 397–424.

Easterbrook, Frank H. and Daniel R. Fischel. 1996. *The Economic Structure of Corporate Law*. Cambridge, MA: Harvard University Press.

Edelman, Benjamin. 2010. "Adverse selection in online 'trust' certifications and search results," *Electronic Commerce Research and Applications* 10(1): 17–25.

Edelman, Lauren B. and Marc C. Suchman. 2007. "Introduction" in Lauren B. Edelman and Marc C. Suchman, eds., *The Legal Lives of Private Organizations*. Hampshire, UK: Ashgate.

Edwards, Paul N., Steven J. Jackson, Melissa K. Chalmers, Geoffrey C. Bowker, Christine L. Borgman, David Ribes, Matt Burton, and Scout Calvert. 2012. "Knowledge Infrastructures: Intellectual Frameworks and Research Challenges." http://pne.people.si.umich.edu/PDF/Edwards_etal_2013_Knowledge_Infrastructures.pdf

Egan, Michelle. 2001. *Constructing a European Market: Standards, Regulation, and Governance*. Oxford: Oxford University Press.

Egyedi, Tineke. 2000a. "Institutional Dilemma in ICT Standardisation: Co-ordinating the Diffusion of Technology?," in Kai Jakobs, ed., *Information Technology Standards and Standardisation: A Global Perspective*. London. Idea Group Publishing.

Egyedi, Tineke. 2000b. "Compatibility Strategies in Licensing, Open Sourcing and Standardisation: The case of JavaTM," in Heide Coenen, Manfred J. Holler, and Esko Niskanen. eds., *5th Helsinki Workshop on Standardization and Networks*. Helsinki: Government Institute for Economic Research.

Egyedi, Tineke. 2001. "Beyond Consortia, Beyond Standardisation? New Case Material and Policy Threads – Final Report for the European Commission."

Egyedi, Tineke. 2007. "Standard-compliant, but incompatible?!," *Computer Standards & Interface* 29(6): 605–13.
Eisape, Davis and Mirko Boehm. 2018 "Standard Setting Organisations and Open Source Communities – Partners or Competitors?" Open Source Summit, Vancouver, BC (August 30).
Eisenberg, Theodore and Jonathan Macey. 2004. "Was Arthur Andersen Different? An Empirical Examination of Major Accounting Firm Audits of Large Clients," *Journal of Empirical Legal Studies* 1(2): 263–300.
Endres, Bryan and Nicholas Johnson. 2011. "Integrating Stakeholder Roles in Food Production, Marketing, and Safety Systems: An Evolving Multi-Jurisdictional Approach," *Journal of Environmental Law and Litigation* 26: 29–108.
Ericson, Richard V. and Aaron Doyle. 2004. *Uncertain Business: Risk, Insurance, and the Limits of Knowledge*. Toronto: University of Toronto Press.
Esty, Daniel C. 2006. "Good Governance at the Supranational Scale: Globalizing Administrative Law," *Yale Law Journal* 115: 1490–562.
Ewick, Patricia and Susan Silbey. 1998. *The Common Place of Law: Stories from Everyday Life*. Chicago: The University of Chicago Press.
Farrell, Joseph and G. Saloner. 1988. "Coordination through Committees and Markets," *RAND Journal of Economics* 19: 235.
Farrell, Joseph and Timothy Simcoe. 2012. "Choosing the Rules for Consensus Standardization," *RAND Journal of Economics* 43: 235.
Featherston, Charles, Jae-Yun Ho, Laure Brevignon-Dodin, and Eoin O'Sullivan. 2016. "Mediating and catalyzing innovation: a framework for anticipating the standardization needs of emerging technologies," *Technovation* 48–49: 25–40.
Feldmeier, Robert C. 1999. "The Risk of Negligence Liability for Trade Associations Engaged in Standards Setting or Product Certification," *Tort & Insurance Law Journal* 34(3): 785–97.
Fitzgerald, Patrick. 2016. "PricewaterhouseCoopers Settles $5.5 Billion Crisis Era Lawsuit," *Wall Street Journal*, August 26.
Folsom, Ralph A. and Larry L. Teply. 1980. "Trademarked Generic Words," *Yale Law Journal*. 89: 1323.
Food Safety News. 2014. "FDA's Taylor Stresses Industry/Government Cooperation to Enforce FSMA." *Food Safety Magazine*. www.foodsafetymagazine.com/news/fdas-taylor-stresses-industry-government-cooperation-to-enforce-fsma/
Foray, Dominique and Bengt-Aake Lundvall. 1998. *The Knowledge-Based Economy: From the economics of knowledge to the learning economy*. Paris: OECD.
Frankel, Alison. 2018. "At heart of FDIC's win v. PwC, an unsettled theory." *Reuters*. January 2.
Freeman, Jody. 2000. "Private Parties, Public Functions and the New Administrative Law," *Administrative Law Review* 52: 813–58.
Fromer, Jeanne C. 2009a. "Claiming Intellectual Property," *University of Chicago Law Review* 76(2): 719–96.
Fromer, Jeanne C. 2009b. "Patent Disclosure," *Iowa Law Review* 94(2): 539–606.
Fromer, Jeanne C. 2017. "The Unregulated Certification Mark(et)," *Stanford Law Review* 69(1): 121–200.
Fuchs, Doris, Agni Kalfagianni, and Tetty Havinga. 2009. "Actors in Private Food Governance: The Legitimacy of Retail Standards and Multistakeholder Initiatives with Civil Participation," *Agriculture and Human Values* 28(3): 353–67.
Galetovic, Alexander and Stephen Haber. 2017. "The Fallacies of Patent-Holdup Theory," *Journal of Competition Law & Economics*, 13(1): 1–44.
Galland, Jean-Pierre. 2017. "Big Third-Party Certifiers and the Construction of Transnational Regulation," *The Annals of the American Academy of Political and Social Science* 670 (March): 263–79.
Galle, Brian. 2017. "Self-Regulation of Social Enterprise," in *Research Handbook on Social Enterprise Law* (forthcoming). Available at https://papers.ssrn.com/sol3/papers.cfm?abstract_id=2978023
Gamalielsson, Jonas and Björn Lundell. 2013. "Experiences from implementing PDF in Open Source: Challenges and opportunities for standardisation processes," *8th International Conference on Standardization and Innovation in Information Technology (SIIT)*.
Gasser, Urs and John Palfrey. 2007. *DRM-protected Music Interoperability and eInnovation*, Berkman Publication Series 6, http://cyber.law.harvard.edu/interop/pdfs/interop-drm-music.pdf
Ghosh, Rishab Aiyer and Philipp Schmidt. 2006. *Open Source and Open Standards: A New Frontier for Economic Development?* United Nations University.

Gilson, Ronald and Reinier H. Kraakman. 1984. "The Mechanisms of Market Efficiency," *Virginia Law Review* 70: 549–643.
Gilson, Ronald and Reinier H. Kraakman. 2003. "The Mechanisms of Market Efficiency Twenty Years Later: The Hindsight Bias," *Journal of Corporation Law* 28: 715–42.
Goldberg, Victor P. 1988. "Accountable Accountants: Is Third-Party Liability Necessary?" *Journal of Legal Studies* 17(2): 295–312.
Goldberg, Victor P. 2006. *Framing Contract Law: An Economic Perspective*. Cambridge, MA: Harvard University Press. Originally published as: "A Reexamination of *Glanzer v. Shepard*: Surveyors on the Tort-Contract Boundary," *Theoretical Inquiries in Law*. 2: 476–510.
Goldstein, Paul. 2002. *Goldstein on Copyright*, 3rd ed. (2005 & 2017-2 Supplement). New York: Aspen.
Gravani, Robert B. 2009. "The Role of Good Agricultural Practices in Produce Safety," in Xuetong Fan, Brenda A. Niemira, Christopher J. Doona, Florence E. Feeherry, and Robert B. Gravani, eds, *Microbial Safety of Fresh Produce*. Ames, IA: Wiley-Blackwell.
Graver-de-Looper, Milca. 2016. "Registering an Acronym as a Trademark," International Asset Management – International Reports, February 16, 2016.
Greve, Georg C. F. 2008a. *Analysis on Balance: Standardisation and Patents*, FSFE, https://fsfe.org/activities/os/ps.en.pdf
Greve, Georg C. F. 2008b. *Sovereign Software: Open Standards, Free Software, and the Internet*, FSFE, https://fsfe.org/activities/policy/igf/sovsoft.en.html
Griswold, Erwin N. 1934. "Government in Ignorance of the Law – A Plea for Better Publication of Executive Legislation," *Harvard Law Review* 48(2): 198–215.
Haapanen, Anna. 2015. "Free and Open Source Software and the Mystery of Software Patent Licenses Under the GPL," *International Free and Open Source Software Law Review* 7(1): 19–28.
Halabi, Sam F. and Ching-Fu Lin. 2017. "Assessing the Relative Influence and Efficacy of Public and Private Food Safety Regulation Regimes: Comparing Codex and Global G.A.P. Standards," *Food and Drug Journal* 72(2): 262–94.
Hamilton, Robert W. 1978. "The Role of Nongovernmental Standards in the Development of Mandatory Federal Standards Affecting Safety or Health," *Texas Law Review* 56(8): 1329–1484.
Hammar, Mark. 2015. "First-, Second- & Third-Party Audits, What are the Differences?," *ISO 9001 Blog*. Archived at https://perma.cc/5UPJ-2SHN
Hanns, Ullrich. 2017. "FRAND Access to open standards and the patent exclusivity: Restating the Principles," *Concurrences*, No. 2-2017.
Hansmann, Henry. 1980. "The Role of Nonprofit Enterprise," *Yale Law Journal* 89(5): 835–901.
Hansmann, Henry. 1996. *The Ownership of Enterprise*. Cambridge, MA: Harvard University Press.
Harkrider, John D. 2013. "Seeing the Forest Through the SEPS," *Antitrust* 27(3): 10.
Hass, Nancy. 2010. "Earning Her Stripes," *Wall Street Journal Magazine*, September 10, 2010.
Heidt, Robert H. 2010. "Damned for their Judgment: The Tort Liability of Standards Development Organizations," *Wake Forest Law Review* 45(5): 1227–85.
Heiner, David A. 2011. "Five Suggestions for Promoting Competition Through Standards," *Competition Law International* 7: 20.
Hettne, Jörgen. 2008. *Rättsprinciper som styrmedel – Allmänna Rättsprinciper i EU:s Domstol*, Stockholm: Nordstedts Juridik.
Hettne, Jörgen. 2017. "Standard, Barriers to Trade and EU Internal Markets Rules: Need for a Renewed Approach," *Legal Issues of Economic Integration* 44: 409–20.
Hill, Claire A. 2004. "Regulation the Rating Agencies," *Washington University Law Quarterly* 82(1): 43–94.
Hodges, Christopher. 2005. *European Regulation of Consumer Product Safety*. Oxford: Oxford University Press.
Holmes, William C. 2012. *Intellectual Property and Antitrust Law*. New York: Clark Boardman Callaghan.
Hood, Christopher, Henry Rothstein, and Robert Baldwin. 2001. *The Government of Risk: Understanding Risk Regulation Regimes*. Oxford: Oxford University Press.
Hopkins, Bruce R. 2007. *The Law of Tax-Exempt Organizations*. Hoboken, NJ: Wiley Publishing.
Horner, Johannes. 2002. "Reputation and Competition," *American Economics Review* 92(3): 644–63.
Hovenkamp, Herbert, Mark A. Lemley, and Mark D. Janis. 2012. *IP and Antitrust: An Analysis of Antitrust Principles Applied to Intellectual Property Law*. New York: Wolters Kluwer.

Howse, Robert. 2006. "A New Device for Creating International Legal Normativity: The WTO Technical Barriers to Trade Agreement and 'International Standards.'" in C. Joerges and E. Petersmann, eds., *Constitutionalism: Multilevel Trade Governance and Social Regulation*. Oxford: Hart Publishing.

Howse, Robert and J. Langille. 2012. "Permitting Pluralism: The Seal Products Dispute and Why the WTO Should Accept Trade Restrictions Justified by Non-Instrumental Moral Values," *Yale Journal of International Law* 37: 367.

Hughes, Justin. 2005. "Size Matters (Or Should) in Copyright Law," *Fordham Law Review* 74(2): 575–638.

Hughes, Justin. 2006. "Champagne, Feta, and Bourbon: The Spirited Debate About Geographical Indications," *Hastings Law Journal* 58(2): 299–386.

Intel Corp. (n.d.). "Two decades of 'plug and play' – How USB became the most successful interface in the history of computing." www.intel.com/content/www/us/en/standards/usb-two-decades-of-plug-and-play-article.html

International M&A Partners (IMAP). 2010. *Food and Beverage Industry Global Report – 2010*. www.proman.fi/sites/default/files/Food%20%26%20beverage%20global%20report%202010_0.pdf

Jahn, Gabriele, Matthias Schramm, and Achim Spiller. 2005. "The Reliability of Certification: Quality Labels as a Consumer Policy Tool," *Journal of Consumer Policy* 28: 53–73.

Jakobs, Kai. 2006. "ICT Standards Research -Quo Vadis?," *Homo Oeconomicus* 23(1): 79–107.

Jensen, Chris and Walt Scacchi. 2010. "Governance in Open Source Software Development Projects: A Comparative Multi-level Analysis," *IFIP International Conference on Open Source Systems OSS 2010: Open Source Software: New Horizons* 130–42.

Jin, Ginger Zhe and Andrew Kato. 2006. "Price, Quality and Reputation: Evidence from an Online Experiment," *RAND Journal of Economics* 37(4): 983–1004.

Johnson. 2017. "Why Companies Don't Want You to Take Their Brand Names in Vain," *Economist*, September 9, 2017.

Jorde, Thomas M. 1987. "Antitrust and the New State Action Doctrine: A Return to Deferential Economic Federalism," *California Law Review* 75: 227–56.

Kappos, David J. 2017. "Open Source Software and Standards Development Organizations: Symbiotic Functions in the Innovation Equation," *Columbia Science and Technology Law Review* 18: 259–69.

Katcher, Susan. 2006. "Legal Training in the United States: A Brief History," *Wisconsin International Law Journal* 24: 335–75.

Katyal, Sonia K. 2010. "Trademark Intersectionality," *UCLA Law Review* 57(6): 1601–99.

Keeton, W. Page, Dan B. Dobbs, Robert E. Keeton, and David G. Owen. 1984. *Prosser and Keeton on Torts*, 5th ed. St. Paul, MN: West Pub. Co.

Kelderman, Eric. 2011. "American Bar Association Takes Heat from Advisory Panel on Accreditation," *Chronicle of Higher Education*. June 9.

Kempa, Richard. 2009. "Towards Free/Libre Open Source Software ('FLOSS') Governance in the Organisation," *IFOSSLR* 1: 61–72.

Kesan, Jay. 2011. "The Fallacy of OSS Discrimination by FRAND Licensing: An Empirical Analysis," *Illinois Public Law Research Paper No. 10–14*. https://ssrn.com/abstract=1767083

King, Rachael. 2014. "Open Source 'Eating' Software World: Samsung," Blogs *Wall Street Journal*, May 5, 2014. http://blogs.wsj.com/cio/2014/05/05/open-source-eating-software-world-samsung/

Kingsbury, Benedict, Nico Krisch, and Richard B. Stewart. 2005. "The Emergence of Global Administrative Law," *Law and Contemporary Problems* 68: 15.

Klein, Benjamin and Keith B. Leffler. 1981. "The Role of Market Forces in Assuring Contractual Performance," *Journal of Political Economy* 89(4): 615–41.

Kogan, Lawrence A. 2011. "Commercial High Technology Innovations Face Uncertain Future Amid Emerging 'BRICS' Compulsory Licensing and IT Interoperability Frameworks," *San Diego International Law Journal*. 13: 201.

Kohnke, Matthew. 2007. "Reeling in a Rogue Industry: Lethal E. coli in California's Leafy Green Produce & the Regulatory Response," *Drake Journal of Agricultural Law* 12: 493–520.

Kono, D. 2006. "Optimal Obfuscation: Democracy and Trade Policy Transparency," *American Political Science Review* 100: 369.

Kozierok, Charles M. 2005. *The TCP/IP Guide: A Comprehensive Illustrated Internet Protocols Reference*, No Starch Press.

Krechmer, Ken. 2006. "Open Standards Requirements," *International Journal of Information Technology Standards Research* 4(1): 43.

Krill, Paul. 2008. "JavaScript creator ponders past, future," *Infoworld*. www.infoworld.com/article/2653798/application-development/javascript-creator-ponders-past–future.html

Kruse, Chad M. 2006. "The Not-So-Organic Dairy Regulations of the Organic Food Production Act of 1990," *Southern Illinois University Law Journal* 30(3): 501–31.

Kuhn, Bradley M. 2014. "Why Your Project Doesn't Need a Contributor Licensing Agreement." http://ebb.org/bkuhn/blog/2014/06/09/do-not-need-cla.html

Kurtz, Leslie. 1989. "Copyright: The Scenes a Faire Doctrine," *Florida Law Review* 41(1): 79–114.

Landes, William M. and Richard A. Posner. 1987. "Trademark Law: An Economic Perspective," *Journal of Law & Economics* 30(2): 265–309.

Lane, C. 1997. "The Social Regulation of Inter-Firm Relations in Britain and Germany: Market Rules, Legal Norms and Technical Standards," *Cambridge Journal of Economics* 21: 197.

Lankarani, Nazanin. 2009. "Special Report: A Swiss Debate," *New York Times*, March 26, 2009.

Larouche, Pierre and Geertrui Van Overwalle. 2015. "Interoperability standards, patents and competition policy" in P. Delimatsis, ed., *The Law, Economics and Politics of International Standardization*. Cambridge: Cambridge University Press.

Lawson, Richard. 2017. *Exclusion Clauses and Unfair Contract Terms*, 12th ed. London: Sweet & Maxwell.

Lazer, David. 2001. "Regulatory Interdependence and International Governance," *Journal of European Public Policy* 8(3): 474.

Lerner, Josh and Jean Tirole. 2015. "Standard-Essential Patents," *Journal of Political Economy* 123: 547.

Lerner, Josh and Mark Shankerman. 2010. *The Comingled Code*. Cambridge, MA: The MIT Press.

Levi-Faur, David. 2011. "Regulation and Regulatory Governance" in David Levi-Faur, ed., *Handbook on the Politics of Regulation*. Oxford: Oxford University Press.

Levine, David. 2018. "Collaboration in open source license enforcement – a community movement is happening." Redhat. www.redhat.com/en/blog/collaboration-open-source-license-enforcement-community-movement-happening

Lewis, James A. 2010. *Government Open Source Policies*, Center for Strategic and International Studies.

Li, Jingze. 2017. "Intellectual property licensing tensions in incorporating open source into formal standard setting context – The case of Apache V.2 in ETSI as a start," *ITU Kaleidoscope: Challenges for a Data-Driven Society* 2017: 1–8.

Lisovy, R., M. Sojka, and Z. Hanzalek. 2014. "IEEE 802.11p Linux Kernel Implementation. Czech Technical University in Prague." https://rtime.felk.cvut.cz/publications/public/ieee80211p_linux_2014_final_report.pdf

Lizzeri, Alessandro. 1999. "Information revelation and certifiers," *RAND Journal of Economics* 30: 214–31.

Lohr, Steve. 2005. "Plan by 13 Nations Urges Open Technology Standards," *N.Y. Times*, September 9, 2005, www.nytimes.com/2005/09/09/technology/plan-by-13-nations-urges-open-technology-standards.html

Lopez-Berzosa, David and Annabelle Gawer. 2014. "Innovation policy within private collectives: evidence on 3GPP's regulation mechanism to facilitate collective innovation," *Technovation* 34(12): 734–45.

Loren, Lydia Pallas. 2010. "Renegotiating the Copyright Deal in the Shadow of the "Inalienable" Right to Terminate," *Florida Law Review* 62: 1329.

Loren, Lydia Pallas and Joseph Scott Miller. 2017. *Intellectual Property Law: Cases and Materials*, 5th ed. Oregon City, OR: Semaphore Press.

Lundell, Björn and Jonas Gamalielsson. 2017. "On the potential for improved standardisation through use of Open Source work practices in different standardisation organisations: How can Open Source-projects contribute to development of IT-standards?," *EURAS Proceedings*, 137–55.

Lundell, Björn, Jonas Gamalielsson, Alexander Grahn, Jonas Feist, Tomas Gustavsson, and Hendrik Strindberg. 2014. "On influences between software standards and their implementations in open source projects," *Proceedings of the 10th International Symposium on Open Collaboration* 1–10.

Lundqvist, Björn. 2014. *Standardization Under EU Competition Rules and US Antitrust Laws*. Cheltenham, UK: Edward Elgar.

Lundqvist, Björn. 2017. "European Harmonized Standards as Part of EU Law: The Implications of the James Elliot Case for Copyright Protection and, Possibly, for EU Competition Law," *Journal of Economic Integration* 44: 421–36.

Lundqvist, Björn. 2018. "Competition and Data Pools," *Journal of European Consumer and Market Law* 7(4): 146–54.

Lytton, Timothy D. 2013. *Kosher: Private Regulation in the Age of Industrial Food*. Cambridge, MA: Harvard University Press.

Lytton, Timothy D. 2014. "Competitive Third-Party Regulation: How Private Certification Can Overcome Constraints That Frustrate Government Regulation," *Theoretical Inquiries in Law* 15(2): 539–71.

Lytton, Timothy D. 2019a. *Outbreak: Foodborne Illness and the Struggle for Food Safety*. Chicago: The University of Chicago Press.

Lytton, Timothy D. 2019b. "Exposing Private Third-Party Food Safety Auditors to Civil Liability for Negligence: Harnessing Private Law Norms to Regulate Private Governance," *European Review of Private Law* 27(2): 353–78.

Lytton, Timothy D. and Lesley McAllister. 2014. "Oversight in Private Food Safety Auditing: Addressing Auditor Conflict of Interest," *Wisconsin Law Review* 2014: 289–335.

Macey, Jonathan R. 2003. "Efficient Capital Markets, Corporate Disclosure, and Enron," *Cornell Law Review* 89: 394–422.

Macey, Jonathan R. 2010. "The Demise of the Reputational Model in Capital Markets: The Problem of the 'Last Period Parasites'," *Syracuse Law Review* 60: 427–48.

Mahoney, Paul. 2005. "Public and Private Rule Making in Securities," in William A. Niskanen, ed., *After Enron: Lessons for Public Policy*. Lanham, MD: Rowman & Littlefield Publishers.

Majone, Giandomenico. 2000. "International Regulatory Cooperation: A Neo-Institutionalist Approach" in George Bermann, Matthias Herdegen, and Peter L. Lindseth, eds., *Transatlantic Regulatory Cooperation: Legal Problems and Political Prospects*. Oxford: Oxford University Press.

Mann, Ronald. 2006. "Commercializing Open Source Software: Do Property Rights Still Matter?" *Harvard Journal of Law and Technology* 20(1): 1–47.

Marasco, Amy. 2005. "Standards Development: Are You at Risk?" American National Standards Inst., www.ansi.org/news_publications/other_documents/risk?menuid=7

Marceau, G. and J. Trachtman. 2002. "The Technical Barriers to Trade Agreement, the Sanitary and Phytosanitary Measures Agreement, and The General Agreement on Tariffs and Trade: A Map of the World Trade Organization Law of Domestic Regulation of Goods," *Journal of World Trade* 36(5): 811.

Martin, Timothy W. and Andrew Grossman. 2015. "S&P To Pay $1.5 Billion to Resolve Crisis-Era Litigation," *Wall Street Journal*, February 3.

Mataija, Mislav. 2016. *Private Regulation and the Internal Market: Sports, Legal Services, and Standard Setting in EU Economic Law*. Oxford: Oxford University Press.

Maurer, Stephen M. 2017. *Self-Governance in Science: Community-Based Strategies for Managing Dangerous Knowledge*. Cambridge: Cambridge University Press.

Mavroidis, P. 2013. "Driftin' too far from shore – Why the test for compliance with the TBT Agreement developed by the WTO Appellate Body is wrong, and what should the AB have done instead," *World Trade Review* 12(3): 509.

McCarthy, J. Thomas. 2008. *McCarthy on Trademarks and Unfair Competition*, 4th ed. Eagan, MN: Clark Boardman Callaghan.

McCarthy, J. Thomas. 2017. *McCarthy on Trademarks and Unfair Competition*. Eagan, MN: Thomson West.

McGeveran, William. 2008. "Rethinking Trademark Fair Use," *Iowa Law Review* 94: 49.

McKenna, Mark P. 2007. "The Normative Foundations of Trademark Law," *Notre Dame Law Review* 82(5): 1839–916.

McKenna, Mark P. 2012. "A Consumer Decision-Making Theory of Trademark Law," *Virginia Law Review* 98(1): 67–141.

Medzmariashvili, Megi. 2013. *SRC15: The Legal Nature of Standards*, October.

Meeker, Heather. 2017. "Patrick McHardy and copyright profiteering." OpenSource.com. https://opensource.com/article/17/8/patrick-mchardy-and-copyright-profiteering

Meidinger, Errol. 2006. "The Administrative Law of Global Public-Private Regulation: The Case of Forestry," *European Journal of International Law* 17(1): 47–87.

Meidinger, Errol. 2008. "Multi-Interest Self-Governance Through Global Product Certification Programmes" in Olaf Dilling, Martin Herberg, and Gerd Winter, eds., *Responsible Business: Self-Governance and Law in Transnational Economic Transactions*. Oxford: Hart Publishing.

Melendez-Juarbe, Hiram. 2009. "DRM Interoperability," *Boston University Journal of Science and Technology law*. 15: 181.

Menchetti, Patrizio. 2000. "Legal Aspects of Standardisation in Italy" in H. Schepel and J. Falke, eds. *Legal Aspects of Standardisation in the Member States of the EC and EFTA, Volume 2: Country Reports.* Luxembourg: Office for Official Publications of the European Communities.

Mendelson, Nina A. 2014. "Private Control over Access to Public Law: The Perplexing Federal Regulatory Use of Private Standards," *Michigan Law Review* 112(5): 737–807.

Menell, Peter S. and David Nimmer. 2010. "Pooh-Poohing Copyright Law's 'Inalienable' Termination Rights," *Journal of the Copyright Society of the U.S.A.* 57: 799.

Messerlin, P. 2001. *Measuring the Costs of Protection in Europe: European Commercial Policy in the 2000s.* Washington, DC: Institute for International Economics Press.

Minder, Raphael. 2012. "In Watch Industry, a Feud over What Makes a Timepiece Swiss-Made," *New York Times*, April 27, 2012.

Mitchell, Iain and Stephen Mason. 2011. "Compatibility Of The Licensing Of Embedded Patents With Open Source Licensing Terms," *International Free and Open Source Software Law Review* 1(3): 25–58.

Molinaro, John. 2004. "Who Owns Captain America? Contested Authorship, Work-for-Hire, and Termination Rights under the Copyright Act of 1976," *Georgia State University Law Review* 21: 565.

Moodey, Glyn. 2016. "FRAND is no friend: How to make EU tech standards compatible with open source," *ArsTechnica*, September 5, 2016. https://arstechnica.com/tech-policy/2016/05/eu-tech-standards-why-frand-not-compatible-with-open-source/

Motaal, A. 2004. "The 'Multilateral Scientific Consensus' and the World Trade Organization," *Journal of World Trade* 38(5): 855.

Muller, Benoit. 2011. "Study on the Interplay between Standards and Intellectual Property Rights (IPRs): Annex V: Views and Trends with Respect to Standards and IPRs," Tender No ENTR/09/015, Final Report.

Nakagawa, J. 2011. *International Harmonization of Economic Regulation.* Oxford: Oxford University Press.

Narayanan, V.K. and Tianxu Chen. 2012. "Research on Technology Standards: Accomplishment and Challenges," *Research Policy* 41(8): 1375–406.

National Academies of Science (NAS). 2013. *Intellectual Property Challenges For Standard-Setting in the Global Economy*, Maskus, Keith and Stephen A. Merrill, eds. Washington, DC: National Academies Press.

National Academy of Sciences. 1985. *An Evaluation of the Role of Microbiological Criteria for Foods and Food Ingredients.* Washington, DC: National Academies Press.

National Research Council (NRC). 2013. *Intellectual Property Challenges For Standard-Setting in the Global Economy*, Keith Maskus and Stephen A. Merrill, eds. Washington, DC: National Academies Press.

Niazi, Eren. 2014. "5 ways open source is transforming tech in 2014," *Opensource.com*, February 18, 2014.

Nicolas, Florence. 1994. *Common Standards for Enterprises.* Luxembourg: Office for Official Publications of the European Communities.

Niemira, Brendan A, Xuetong Fan, Christopher J. Doona, Florence E. Feeherry, and Robert B. Gravani. 2009. "Research Needs and Future Directions" in Xuetong Fan, Brendan A. Niemira, Christopher J. Doona, Florence E. Feeherry, and Robert B. Gravani, eds, *Microbial Safety of Fresh Produce.* Ames, IA: Wiley-Blackwell, pp. 419–25.

Nimmer, Melville B. 1977. "Termination of Transfers under the Copyright Act of 1976," *University of Pennsylvania Law Review* 125: 947.

Nimmer, Melville B. and David Nimmer. 2013. *Nimmer on Copyright.*

Note. 1963. "Developments in the Law: Judicial Control of Actions of Private Associations," *Harvard Law Review* 76(5): 983–1100.

Note. 1966. "The Federal Register and the Code of Federal Regulations – A Reappraisal," *Harvard Law Review* 80(2): 439–51.

O'Hara, Maureen. 1981. "Property Rights and the Financial Firm," *Journal of Law & Economics* 24(2): 317–32.

Ohlhausen, Maureen K. 2006. "Enforcement Perspectives on the Noerr-Pennington Doctrine," FTC Staff Report.

Olshan, Marc A. 1993. "Standards-Making Organizations and the Rationalization of American Life," *The Sociological Quarterly* 34(2): 319–35.

Olshefsky, Jim and Joe Hugo. 2003. "How To: Getting Key Stakeholder Participation," *Standardization News.* www.astm.org/SNEWS/JUNE_2003/howto_juno3.html

Ouellette, Lisa Larrimore. 2016. "Pierson, Peer Review, and Patent Law," *Vanderbilt Law Review* 69(6): 1825.

Pacelli, Andrea. 2008. "Who Owns the Key to the Vault? Hold-up, Lock-out, and Other Copyright Strategies," 18 *Fordham Intellectual Property, Media and Entertainment Law Journal* 18: 1229.
Palmieri, Richard D. 2012. "Who's the Author? A Bright-Line Rule for Specially Commissioned Works Made for Hire," *University of Richmond Law Review* 46: 1175.
Partnoy, Frank, Richard M. Levich, Giovanni Majnoni, and Carmen Reinhart. 2002. "The Paradox of Credit Ratings" in Richard M. Levich et al. eds., *Ratings, Rating Agencies and the Global Financial System*. Norwell, MA: Kluwer Academic Publishers, 65–84.
Peer to Patent. 2018. www.peertopatent.org
Pentheroudakis, Chryssoula and Justus A. Baron. 2017. "Licensing Terms of Standard Essential Patents: A Comprehensive Analysis of Cases," JRC Science for Policy Report EUR 28302.
Perens, Bruce, Chris DiBona, Sam Ockman, and Mark Stone. 1999. "Open Source Definition" in Chris DiBona et al. eds., *Open Sources: Voices from the Open Source Revolution*. Sebastopol, CA: O'Reilly Media, pp. 171, 172.
Perens, Bruce. 2002. *Open Standards: Principles and Practice*, perens.com, https://web.archive.org/web/20020601162710/http://perens.com/OpenStandards/Definition.html
Peterson, Shane. 2007. *What Domino Effect?*, Govt. Tech., www.govtech.com/policy-management/What-Domino-Effect.html
Phelps, Jon L. 2010. "Copyleft Termination: Will the Termination Provision of the Copyright Act of 1976 Undermine the Free Software Foundation's General Public License?" *Jurimetrics Journal* 50: 261.
Pillay, Harish. 2014. "Is Open Source the Key to Innovation?," *ZDNet*, August 6, 2014.
Pohlmann, Tim. 2014. "The Evolution of ICT Standards Consortia," *Digiworld Economic Journal* 95(3): 17–40.
Pohlmann, Tim. 2017. "Empirical Study on Patenting and Standardization Activities at IEEE," http://fair-standards.org/wp-content/uploads/2017/03/IPlytics_2017_Patenting-and-standardization-activities-at-IEEE.pdf
Ramakrishnan, Shankar and Philip Scipio. 2016. "Big three in credit ratings still dominate business," *Reuters*. May 4.
Rangarajan, Anusuya, Elixabeth A. Bihn, Robert B. Gravani, Donna L. Scott, and Marvin P. Pritts. 1997. "Food Safety Begins on the Farm: Reduce Microbial Contamination with Good Agricultural Practices" (pamphlet), Good Agricultural Practices Program, Cornell University. Archived at http://perma.cc/GH48-23H3
Rapoport, Michael. 2017. "Judge Says PricewaterhouseCoopers Was Negligent in Colonial Bank Failure," *Wall Street Journal*. December 31.
Ratliff, James and Daniel L. Rubinfeld. 2013. "The Use and Threat of Injunctions in the RAND Context," *Journal of Competition Law & Economics* 9(1): 1–22.
Rees, Joseph V. 1996. *Hostages of Each Other: The Transformation of Nuclear Safety Since Three Mile Island*. Chicago: University of Chicago Press.
Reynolds, Alan. 2005. "Political Responses to the Enron Scandal" in William Niskanen, ed., *After Enron: Lessons for Public Policy*, Lanham, MD: Rowman & Littlefield Publishers, pp. 18–44.
Ribstein, Larry. 2010. *The Rise of the Uncorporation*. Oxford: Oxford University Press.
Ricknäs, Mikael. 2010. "Danish Parliament Sets Rules for Open Document Formats," *PCWorld*, www.pcworld.com/article/188153/article.html
Rockwell, Holly. 1992. "Product Liability of Endorser, Trade Association, Certifier, or Similar Party Who Expresses Approval of Product," *American Law Reports* 5: 431.
Romano, Roberta. 1998. "Empowering Investors: A Market Approach to Securities Regulation," *Yale Law Journal* 107(5): 2359–430.
Ross, Laurence H. 1980. *Settled Out of Court: The Social Process of Insurance Claims Adjustment*, 2nd ed. New York: Routledge.
Rubin, Jonathan J. 2007. "Patents, Antitrust, and Rivalry in Standard-Setting," *Rutgers Law Journal* 38: 509.
Russell, Andrew. 2006. "'Rough Consensus and Running Code' and the Internet-OSI Standards War," *Annals of the History of Computing* 28: 48.
Rysman, Marc and Timothy Simcoe. 2008. "Patents and the Performance of Voluntary Standard-Setting Organizations," *Management Science* 54(11): 1920.
Salter, Liora. 1988. *Mandated Science: Science and Scientists in the Making of Standards*. Dordrecht, Netherlands: Kluwer Academic Publishing.

Samuelson, Pamela. 1992a. "Computer Programs, User Interfaces, and Section 102(b) of the Copyright Act of 1976: A Critique of *Lotus v. Paperback*", *Law and Contemporary Problems* 55(2): 311–53. Republished in revised form. 1992. *High Technology Law Journal* 6(2): 209–70.
Samuelson, Pamela. 1992b. "Some New Kinds of Authorship Made Possible by Computers and Some Intellectual Property Questions They Raise," *University of Pittsburgh Law Review* 53(3): 685–704.
Samuelson, Pamela. 2007. "Why Copyright Excludes Systems and Processes From the Scope of Its Protection," *Texas Law Review* 85(7): 1921–78.
Samuelson, Pamela. 2016a. "Functional Compilations," *Houston Law Review* 54(2): 321–70.
Samuelson, Pamela. 2016b. "Functionality and Expression in Computer Programs: Refining the Tests for Software Copyright Infringement," *Berkeley Technology Law Journal* 31(2): 1215–300.
Samuelson, Pamela. 2016c. "Reconceptualizing Copyright's Merger Doctrine," *Journal of the Copyright Society of the USA* 63(3): 417–70.
Samuelson, Pamela and Clark D. Asay. 2018. "Saving Software's Fair Use Future," *Harvard Journal of Law & Technology*. 31: 535.
Samuelson, Pamela, Randall Davis, Mitchell D. Kapor, and J. H. Reichman. 1994. "A Manifesto Concerning the Legal Protection of Computer Programs," *Columbia Law Review* 94(8): 2308–41.
Satyanarayana, J. 2004. *e-Government: The Science of the Possible*, PHI Learning Pvt. Ltd.
Scallan, Elaine, Robert M. Hoekstra, Frederick J. Angulo, Robert V. Tauxe, Marc-Alain Widdowson, Sharon L. Roy, Jeffrey L. Jones, and Patricia M. Griffin et al. 2011. "Foodborne Illness Acquired in the United States – Unspecified Agents," *Emerging Infectious Diseases* 17(1): 16–22.
Schechter, Frank I. 1927. "The Rational Basis of Trademark Protection," *Harvard Law Review* 40(6): 813–33.
Schepel, Harm. 2005. *The Constitution of Private Governance: Product Standards in the Regulation of Integrating Markets, International Studies in the Theory of Private Law*. Oxford: Hart Publishing.
Schepel, Harm. 2011. "The Empire's Drains : Sources of Legal Recognition of Private Standardization Under the TBT Agreement" in C. Joerges and E.-U. Petersmann, eds., *Constitutionalism, Multilevel Trade Governance and International Economic Law*. Oxford: Hart Publishing.
Schepel, Harm. 2013a. "Rules of Recognition: A Legal Constructivist Approach to Transnational Private Regulation" in Paulius Jurcys, Paul F. Kjaer, and Ren Yatsunami, *Regulatory Hybridization in the Transnational Sphere*. Leiden, Netherlands: Brill Online.
Schepel, Harm. 2013b. "The New Approach to the New Approach: The Juridification of Harmonised Standards in EU Law," *Maastricht Journal of European and Comparative Law* 20(4): 521–33.
Schepel, Harm and Josef Falke. 2000. *Legal Aspects of Standardisation in the Member States of the EC and EFTA, Volume 1: Comparative Report*. Luxembourg: Office for Official Publications of the European Communities.
Schuck, Peter. 1994. "Tort Liability to Those Injured by Negligent Accreditation Decisions," *Law and Contemporary Problems* 57(4): 185–97.
Schuck, Peter. 2014. *Why Government Fails So Often: And How It Can Do Better*. Princeton, NJ: Princeton University Press.
Scott, Colin. 2010. "Standard-setting in Regulatory Regimes" in R. Baldwin, M. Cave, and M. Lodge, eds., *The Oxford Handbook of Regulation*. Oxford: Oxford University Press.
Scott, Colin. 2012. "Regulating Everything: From Mega- to Meta-Regulation," *Administration* 60: 57–85.
Seely, Oliver. 1998. "Public Domain Databases in the Sciences." www5.csudh.edu/oliver/pubdomdb.htm
Segal, David. 2011. "But Who Will Grade the Grader?" *New York Times*. February 26.
Seifter, Miriam. 2018. "Further from the People? The Puzzle of State Administration," *New York University Law Review* 93(1): 107–74.
Shah, Rajiv and Jay Kesan. 2007. *An Empirical Study of Open Standards*. Draft, on file with author.
Shah, Rajiv and Jay Kesan. 2009. "Running Code as Part of an Open Standards Policy," 14 *First Monday*.
Shah, Rajiv and Jay Kesan. 2012. "Lost in Translation: Interoperability Issues for Open Standards," *I/S: A Journal of Law and Policy for the Information Society* 8(1): 119.
Shah, Rajiv, Jay Kesan, and Andrew Kennis 2007. "Lessons for Open Standard Policies: A Case Study of the Massachusetts Experience," *International Conference on Theory and Practice of Electronic Governance*.
Shapiro, Carl and Hal Varian. 1998. *Information Rules: A Strategic Guide to the Network Economy*. Cambridge, MA: Harvard Business School Press.

Shapiro, Carl. 1983. "Premiums for High Quality Products as Returns to Reputation," *Quarterly Journal of Economics* 98(4): 659–79.
Shekhar, Varun. 2010. "Produce Exceptionalism: Examining the Leafy Greens Marketing Agreement and Its Ability to Improve Food Safety," *Journal of Food Law & Policy* 6: 267–309.
Simcoe, Timothy. 2012. "Standard Setting Committees : Consensus Governance for Shared Technology Platforms," *American Economic Review* 102(1): 305.
Soon, Adi. 2013. "'Swiss Made' Now Means More Swiss Made," *Blog to Watch*, May 15, 2013.
Spence, Michael. 1973. "Job Market Signaling," *The Quarterly Journal of Economics* 87(3): 355–74.
Spindler, Gerald. 1998. "Market Processes, Standardisation and Tort Law," *European Law Journal* 4(3): 316–36.
Staiger, R. and A. Sykes. 2011. "International Trade, National Treatment and Domestic Regulation," *Journal of Legal Studies* 40: 149.
Stango, Victor. 2004. "The Economics of Standards Wars," *Review of Network Econ.* 3: 1.
Stoll, Thimo Pascal. 2014. "Are You Still in? – The Impact of Licensing Requirements on the Composition of Standards Setting Organizations," *Max Planck Institute for Innovation & Competition Research Paper* No. 14–18. https://ssrn.com/abstract=2535735
Strauss, Peter L. 2013. "Private Standards Organizations and Public Law," *William & Mary Bill of Rights Journal* 22(2): 497–561.
Stuart, Diana. 2010. "Science, Standards, and Power: New Food Safety Governance in California," *Journal of Rural Social Sciences* 25(3): 111–40.
Stuurman, Cees and H.S.A. Wijnands. 2000. "Legal Aspects of Standardisation in the Netherlands" in H. Schepel and J. Falke, eds., *Legal Aspects of Standardisation in the Member States of the EC and EFTA*, Volume 2: Country Reports. Luxembourg: Office for Official Publications of the European Communities.
Suchman, Marc C. 1995. "Managing Legitimacy: Strategic and Institutional Approaches," *The Academy of Management Review* 20(3): 571–610.
Swann, G.M. Peter. 2000. *The Economics of Standardization: Final Report for Standards and Technical Regulations Directorate Department of Trade and Industry*. Manchester Business School, University of Manchester.
Swann, Cavin, Paul Temple, and Mark Shrumer. 1996. "Standards and Trade Performance: the UK Experience," *Economic Journal* 106(438): 1297–313.
Sykes, Alan O. 1999. "The (Limited) Role of Regulatory Harmonization in International Goods and Services Markets," *Journal of International Economic Law* 1: 49.
Tanner, Bob. 2000. "Independent Assessment by Third-party Certification Bodies," *Food Control* 11: 415–17.
Taulli, Tom. 2015. "Why All the 'Open Source' Innovation?," *Forbes*, December 23, 2015.
Taylor, Michael. 2014. "We're Reinventing Ourselves to Keep Your Food Safe, *FDA Voice*." https://blogs.fda.gov/fdavoice/index.php/2014/05/were-reinventing-ourselves-to-keep-your-food-safe/
Thompson, Richard. 2011. "Nooks and Crannies," *The Guardian*. www.theguardian.com/notesandqueries/query/0,5753,-18959,00.html
Tiller, Rob. 2008. *A Reader's Guide to the Firestar Settlement*. Red Hat Blog. www.redhat.com/en/blog/a-readers-guide-to-the-firestar-settlement
Tsilas, Nicos L. 2005. "The Threat to Innovation, Interoperability, and Government Procurement Options From Recently Proposed Definitions of 'Open Standards'," *International Journal of Communications Law and Policy* 10: 8.
Van Dam, Cees. 2013. *European Tort Law*, 2nd ed. Oxford: Oxford University Press.
Van den Bossche, P. 2008. *The Law and Policy of the World Trade Organization – Text, Cases and Materials*, 2nd ed. Cambridge: Cambridge University Press.
Van Gestel, Rob and Hans-W. Micklitz. 2013. "European Integration through Standardization: How judicial review is breaking down the club house of private standardization bodies," *Common Market Law Review*, 50(1): 145–81.
Van Harten, Herman and Thomas Nauta. 2013. "Towards Horizontal Direct Effect for the Free Movement Of Goods? – Comment on Fra.bo," *European Law Review* 38(5): 677–94.
Van Leeuwen, B.J. 2013. "From Status to Impact, and the Role of National Legislation: The Application of Article 34 TFEU to a Private Certification Organisation in Fra.bo," *European Journal of Risk Regulation* 4(3): 405–08.

Veillard, Daniel. 2012. *Standards, the Kernel and Open Source*. http://veillard.com/Talks/CLKBeijing2012.pdf

Verbruggen, Paul and Tetty Havinga, eds. 2017. *Hybridization of Food Governance: Trends, Types and Results*. Cheltenham, UK: Edward Elgar Publishing.

Verbruggen, Paul. 2017a. "Private Regulatory Standards in Commercial Contracts: Questions of Compliance. In Contract and Regulation" in R. Brownsword, R. van Gestel, and H.W. Micklitz., eds., *A Handbook on New Methods of Law Making in Private Law*. Cheltenham, UK: Edward Elgar.

Verbruggen, Paul. 2017b. "The Impact of Free Movement of Goods and Services on Private Law Rights and Remedies" in H.W. Micklitz, and C. Sieburgh, eds., *Primary EU Law and Private Law Concepts*. Cambridge, UK: Intersentia.

Verbruggen, Paul. 2019. "Good Governance of Private Standardization and the Role of Tort Law," *European Review of Private Law* 27(2): 319–52.

Verbruggen, Paul and Barend Van Leeuwen. 2018. "The Liability of Notified Bodies under the EU's New Approach: The Implications of the PIP Breast Impants Case (C-219/15)," *European Law Review* 43(3): 394–409.

Volokh, Alexander. 2014. "The New Private-Regulation Skepticism: Due Process, Non-Delegation, and Antitrust Challenges," *Harvard Journal of Law and Public Policy* 37: 931–1007.

Volpato, Annalisa. 2017. "A Court of Justice The harmonized standards before the ECJ: James Elliott Construction," *Common Market Law Review* 54(2): 591–603.

Von Bogdandy, A. 2012. "The European Lesson for International Democracy: The Significance of Articles 9–12 EU Treaty for International Organizations," *European Journal of International Law* 23(2): 315.

Weatherill, Stephen. 2013. *EU Consumer Law and Policy*, 2nd ed. Cheltenham, UK: Edward Elgar.

Webster, Nadaline. 2017. "8 Things to Know About the New EU Certification Marks," *TrademarkNow*, October 12, 2017. www.trademarknow.com/blog/8-things-to-know-about-the-new-eu-certification-marks

Weil, Nancy. 2005. *Group Urges IT Open Standards in Report*, CIO, September 12, 2005, www.cio.com.au/article/139358/group_urges_it_open_standards_report/

Werbach, Kevin. 2009. "Higher Standards Regulation in the Network Age," *Harvard Journal of Law and Technology* 23: 179.

West, Joel. 2004. "What are Open Standards? Implications for Adoption, Competition and Policy." Standards and Public Policy conference, Federal Reserve Bank of Chicago, Chicago, Illinois. http://citeseerx.ist.psu.edu/viewdoc/download?doi=10.1.1.98.786&rep=rep1&type=pdf

West, Joel. 2005. "The Economic Realities of Open Standards: Black, White and Many Shades of Gray" in Shane Greenstein and Victor Stango, eds., *Standards and Public Policy*. Cambridge: Cambridge University Press.

Wilson, J. 2002. "Standards, Regulation and Trade : WTO Rules and Developing Country Concerns" in B. Hoekman, A. Mattoo, and R. English, eds., *Development, Trade and the WTO: A Handbook*. The World Bank.

Wolff, Adam. 2017. "Relicensing React, Jest, Flow, and Immutable.js." Facebook Code. https://code.facebook.com/posts/300798627056246/relicensing-react-jest-flow-and-immutable-js/

Wood, G.B. 1961. "Marketing Agreements and Orders – Without Production Controls," in *Increasing Understanding of Public Problems and Policies*. Chicago: Farm Foundation.

Xiao, Mo. 2010. "Is quality accreditation effective? Evidence from the childcare market," *International Journal of Industrial Organization* 28(6): 708–21.

Yue, Lori Qingyan and Paul Ingram. 2012. "Industry Self-Regulation as a Solution to the Reputation Commons Problem: The Case of the New York Clearing House Association" in Timothy G. Pollock and Michael L. Barnett, eds., *The Oxford Handbook of Corporate Reputation*. Oxford: Oxford University Press.

Zhe, Jin, Ginger Zhe, and Andrew Kato. 2006. "Price, Quality and Reputation: Evidence from an Online Experiment," *RAND Journal of Economics* 37(4): 983–1004.

Zipursky, Benjamin C. 2009. "Foreseeability in Breach, Duty, and Proximate Cause," *Wake Forest Law Review* 44(5): 1247–75.

Index

Note: Page numbers for tables appear in *italics*; those for figures appear in **bold**.

2G/3G/4G/5G standards, xvii, 198–230, 220n104
3-A Sanitary Standards, Inc. (3-A SSI), 59
3GPP (Third Generation Platform Partnership), 179

Abercrombie and Fitch v. Hunting World (U.S.), 206–7, 219, 221, 222
access to standards, *see* standards, access to
Acoustical Society of America, 122
Administrative Conference of the United States (ACUS), 111n19
    recommendations on IBR, 119–20
Administrative Procedure Act (APA) (U.S.), 34, 109, 110
Adobe, 187
    Portable Document Format (PDF), 168, 206, 220
Advanced Audio Coding (AAC) standard, 221
ALLSeen Alliance, 193
American Association of Blood Banks (AABB), 66–68, 83n144, 85
American Bar Association (ABA)
    Resolution 112 on IBR, 121
American Dental Association (ADA) case (U.S.), 92–95, 99, 107
    Code on Dental Procedures and Nomenclatures, 92–95
American Medical Association (AMA), 92–94, 99, 107, 117–18
    Current Procedural Terminology (CPT), 92–94
American National Standards, 33
American National Standards Institute (ANSI), 29, 30, 59
    Essential Requirements, 33, 41, 59
    IBR Standards Portal, 122
    trademark guidelines, 214–15, 224
American Petroleum Institute (API), 29, 33, 115, 122, 210n34
American Society of Mechanical Engineers (ASME), 29, 33
American Welding Society, 122
Apple, 187, 224
    Lightning connector, 205, 221
    trademarks, 217
Association Française de Normalisation (AFNOR), 77–78, 85
ASTM International, 29, 31, 33, 218, 219n100
    access to standards, 122

ASTM v. PublicResource.org (U.S.), 104–6, 118–19, 120, 216
ATC Distribution, Inc. v. Whatever It Takes Transmissions & Parts (U.S.), 95–97, 99

Baker v. Selden (U.S.), 97–98
Banks v. Manchester (U.S.), 116
Blu-ray standard, 221
Bluetooth Special Interest Group (SIG), 224
    trademarks and certification, 211–12, 218, 221, **222**, 223, 226–27
    standard, 205, 217
Board-Tech v. Eaton (U.S.), 209, *see also* Underwriters Laboratories
British Standards Institute (BSI), 35–36, 78–79

California Department of Food and Agriculture (CDFA), 51
California Leafy Green Products Handler Marketing Agreement (LGMA), 50–53, 55–59
CE marking, 130, 162
CEN/CENELEC, 18, 37, 40, 76, 126, 134, 136, 138, 140
Certain Country of Origin Labeling (COOL) Requirements, 17
certification, product
    antitrust scrutiny, 250–51
    categories of (first, second, third party), xvii, 210, 226, 227–28, 254–55
    cost, 160–61, 239
    entry barriers, 262–63
    financial services, 256, 261–66
    flexibility of standards, 240–43
    Forest Stewardship Council, xvi, 257
    governmental involvement in, 237, 239, 245–46
    green building, 208–9, 258–59, 260, 264
    kosher foods, 232, 246, 264
    intermediaries, 252–67
    liability for, 261–66
    market power, 243, 257–58, 259–60
    non-profit status, 239–40, 264–65
    organic foods, 245–46
    partnership form, 261–66
    SSOs, by, 64, 139, 227–28

299

certification, product (cont.)
  transparency, 210, 247–48, 249–50, 260
  see also certification marks; Underwriters Laboratories
certification marks
  consumer perceptions, 235–36
  defined, 208–11, 232–35, 262–63
  ecolabels, 208–9, 258–59
  geographical indications, 236–38
  generally accepted accounting principles (GAAP), 252
  Good Housekeeping seal of approval, 232, 235
  Grown in Idaho, 209, 227n133, 232
  International Information Systems Security Certification Consortium (IISSCC) v. Security University, 215–16
  liability for use of, 77–78
  NF mark, 77–78
  non-discrimination requirement, 209, 226, 234
  Swiss Made, 236–38, 240–41, 243
  trademarks, distinguished from, 223–24, 233–35
Cisco v. Arista (U.S.), 101–2
Code Division Multiplex Access (CDMA) standard, 220
Code of Federal Regulations (CFR) (U.S.), 109
Codex Alimentarius, xvi, 13, 21, 24–25
  Codes Alimentarius Commission, 22, 27
  in *Sardines* (EC) case, see *Sardines*
competition
  between open source and standardization, see open source code software/projects
  among SSOs, 11
  standards as facilitating, 129
competition law and standardization, 11, 133, 134, 250–51
consensus decision making, see standard setting processes
copyright law
  collective works, 147–48
  Copyright Act (U.S.)
    Sec 102(b), 92–100
    Sec. 203, 143
    Sec. 314, 143
  derivative works, 153–54
  fair use doctrine, 103, 119
  hold-up, 146
  infringement, see piracy of standards
  joint works, 147–50
  merger doctrine, see copyright law, scenes a faire
  scenes a faire, 100–4
  standards, copyright in, see copyright in standards
  termination of transfers, 143
  works made for hire, 150–53
  works of the United States government, 118
copyright in standards, xvi, 179–80
  in the EU, 131
  in Germany, 132
  in the Netherlands, 132
  in the U.S., 91–107, 108, 114, 115–19, 144–45

Department of Energy (U.S.), 30
Deutsche Vereinigung des Gas- und Wasserfaches eV (DVGW), 80–82
Deutsches Institut für Normung (DIN), 78–79
Digital Video Disc (DVD) standard, 217, 223
DVB Project, 227

ECMA International
  ECMAScript, 187
economic impacts of standardization
  economic growth, 10
  innovation, 129, 177, 179, 195, 198–99
  network effects, 9
EMC case (EU), 134, 138, 140, 142
Energy Star program, 34
Environmental Protection Agency (EPA) (U.S.), 52
Ericsson, 222
Eurocontrol, see *SELEX* case
European Commission, 35, 37–38
European Environmental Citizens Organization for Standardization (ECOS), 126
European Telecommunications Standards Institute (ETSI), 18, 37, 76–77, 128, 140, 180, 188, 199, 210n34, 223, 226, 227
European Union framework for standardization
  European Commission and, 37–38, 41
  European Common Assessment Method for Standards and Specifications, 176
  European standards, 37, 41
    see also CEN/CENELEC and ETSI
  funding of standardization activity, 38, 42–52
  harmonised standards, 125, 127–28, 129–31
  International standards, 37, 41
  National standards organizations, 37, 126, 138
  New Approach, 75–79, 87, 125, 126–29, 139
  small and medium enterprises (SMEs), 37, 38, 140
  standstill principle, 39–40
  see also Treaty on the Functioning of the European Union (TFEU)

Federal Emergency Management Agency (FEMA), 30
Federal Register (U.S.), 34, 109, 110–11
  see also Office of the Federal Register (OFR)
Feist Publications v. Rural Telephone (U.S.), 99, 106
Financial Accounting Standards Board (FASB), 94
FireWire standard (IEEE 1394), 221
Fra.bo v. DVGW (Germany), 80–82, 83, 85, 87, 125, 136–37, 138, 139, 140, 142
Food and Drug Administration (FDA) (U.S.), 41, 49, 50, 53–54
  Produce Safety Rule, 53, 54
Food Safety Initiative (U.S.), 42–48
Food Safety Modernization Act of 2011 (FSMA), 53–54
Forest Stewardship Council, see certification, product
free access to standards, see standards, access to
Freedom of Information Act (FOIA) (U.S.), 33, 109, 110–12, 118

General Agreement on Tariffs and Trade (GATT)
  standards and, 13
Global Navigation Satellite Systems, xvii
GNU General Public License, see open source code software
Good Agricultural Practices (GAPs), 41, 48–49, 54–57
Google, 187
Gopher standard, 221, 222
GSM Association, 226
  GSM standard, 220n104, 223

Index

Hardwood Plywood & Veneer Association (HPVA), 70
Health Care Financing Administration (HCFA),
    Common Procedure Coding System, 117–18
    see also PMIC case
High Definition Multimedia Interface (HDMI) standard,
    218, 220, 223
Hormones (EC), 24–25
Hypertext Markup Language (HTML), 186–87
Hypertext Transport Protocol (HTTP), 224

i.Link standard (IEEE 1394), *221*
IBM, 168, 195, 220
IETF Trust, 224–25
incorporation of standards by reference into law (IBR),
    32, 34, 104–6, 107, 108–23
    dynamic incorporation, 113
    Regulations of the Office of the Federal Register, *see*
        Office of the Federal Register (OFR)
Institute of Electrical and Electronics Engineers (IEEE),
    xvi, 140, 143–55, 219, 224
    802.11, *see* Wi-Fi standard
    access to standards, 122, 180
    patent policy, 180, 195, 202
Interchange of Data between Administrations (IDA)
    agency (EU), *see* open standards, EU
International Convention for the Protection of Industrial
    Property (Paris Convention), 208
International Electrotechnical Commission (IEC), 37,
    122, 180, 187
International Fresh-Cut Produce Association, 47–49
International Information Systems Security Certification
    Consortium (IISSCC) v. Security University case
    (U.S.), 215–16
International Office of Epizootics (OIE), 22
International Organization for Standardisation (ISO),
    xvi, 10, 12n28, 13, 14, 18–19, 22–23, 27, 36, 37, 59,
    187, 257
    Access to standards, 122, 180
    Intellectual property policy, 91–92, 180
    ISO 9001, 218, 219
    MPEG standards, 182, 220
International Plant Protection Convention, 22
International Telecommunication Union (ITU), xvi, 37,
    163, 167, 180, 199, 218, 224
International Trade Commission (U.S.), 171
Internet Assigned Number Authority (IANA), 224–25
Internet Engineering Task Force (IETF), xvi, 31, 167,
    175, 180, 181, 185, 186, 194, 218, 219, 220, 224–26,
    226n123
Internet of Things (IoT), 1, 91, 217, 222
Internet Society (ISOC), 31, 224
ISEAL Alliance, Code of Good Practice, xvi, 18

Java
    Application Program Interface (API), 102–3
    trademark and logo, *221*, **222**, 227
JavaScript, 186–87
James Elliot case (EU), 125, 129–34, 139–40, 141, 142

LEED certification, *see* U.S. Green Building Council
Leafy Greens Safety Initiative, 49

LGMA, *see* California Leafy Green Products Handler
    Marketing Agreement
Lightning connector, *see* Apple
Long Term Evolution (LTE) standard (4G), 221, 223, 226
Lotus Development Corp. v. Borland International (U.S.),
    98–99, 103
Lynx standard (IEEE 1394), 221

Microsoft Corp., 172–73, 187, 195, 227
    .doc file format, 174–75
    Office, 168–69, 174–75
    Open Office XML (OOXML), 168, 169, 174–75, 176
Mills Music v. Snyder (U.S.), 154
Mitel v. Iqtel (U.S.), 100–2, 103
Motion Picture Association of America (MPAA), 232–33
Mozilla Foundation, 187
MP3, *see* International Organisation for Standardization
    (ISO), MPEG standards

National Archives and Records Administration (NARA), 112
National Commission on New Technological Uses of
    Copyrighted Works (CONTU), 103
National Fire Protection Association (NFPA), 73–74,
    115, 83n144
National Institute of Standards and Technology (NIST), 109
National Sanitation Foundation (NSF), 59
National Spa and Pool Institute (NSPI), 71–72, 82n139
National Technology Transfer and Advancement Act
    of 1995 (NTTAA) (U.S.) 32–33, 34, 110, 112,
    114, 118–19
Nederlands Normalisatie Instituut (NEN), 78
Noerr Pennington doctrine (U.S.), 141
Novell, 168

OASIS, 180, 181, 185, 195
Office of the Federal Register (OFR), 34, 111n19
    Regulations on IBR, 112–14, 120
Office of Management and Budget (OMB) Circular
    No. A-119, 32–33, 34–35, 84n151, 110, 112, 114
OOXML, *see* Microsoft
Open Connectivity Foundation, 193
Open Document Format (ODF), 168–69, 174–75, 176
Open Innovation Network (OIN), 184, 192
open source code software/projects
    Apache Software Foundation, 182, 183
    definition, 181
    development, 185, 199
    Document Foundation, 182
    Drupal 187–88
    Eclipse Foundation, 182
    Free Software Foundation, 200
    ideology/culture, xvii, 201
    intellectual property ownership, 182–83
    LibreOffice, 182
    Linux, 182
    Linux Foundation, 182, 187
    Linux Standard Base, 187
    MANO Open Source (OSM) project, 188
    market prevalence, 181, 199
    Open Course Ware, 182
    Open Source Group OSM, 188

open source code software/projects (*cont.*)
    OpenStack, 182
    Stallman, Richard, 200
    standardization, and, 177–78
        competition with, 193
    Telecom Infra Project, 193
open source code licenses,
    Apache license, 183–84, 188, 193, 195, 201
    BSD license, 181, 183, 187, 195, 200–1
    contributory licensing agreements
        (CLAs), 183
    copyleft license, 183, 191–92, 195, 200, 201, 202
    Creative Commons CC0 license, 181–82
    Facebook React project license, 183, 192, 196
    GNU General Public License (GPL), 146, 181, 183, 184, 191, 192, 194, 195, 196, 200
    interaction with FRAND patent licensing, 188–92
    ISC license, 201
    Liberty or Death clause, 191, 192, 196
    MIT license, 181, 183, 195, 201
    MXM license, 181–82
    Open Source Initiative (OSI) approved licenses, 181–82, 190, 194, 196, 200
    patent retaliation clauses, 183–84, 192, 196
    permissive licenses, 200–1
    royalty-free licensing, and, 167, 183
    termination of licenses, 144n98, 146–47
    W3C license, 182
open standards, xvii
    access to standards, *see* standards, access to
    Berkman Center definition, 161
    Brazil e-PING program, 170
    China interoperability rules, 170–71
    definitions, 159–68, 202
    Denmark definition, 165, 166, 167, 170
    European Commission definition, 160–61
    India
        definition, 166, 167
        open standards policy, 171
    ITU definition, 163
    Kretchmer definition, 161–62
    Malaysian Government Interoperability Framework for Open Source Software (MyGIFOSS), 171
    Massachusetts,
        definition, 164–65
        open standards policy, 168–69, 172–73, 176
    Minnesota,
        definition, 165
        open standards bill, 169
    New Zealand definition, 166, 167
    One World, 161–62
    openness in standard setting, *see* standard setting processes
    public participation, *see* standard setting processes
    Russian executive order, 171
    South Africa,
        definition, 165–66, 167
        open standards program, 170
    Texas
        definition, 164–65, 166–67
        open standards bill, 169–70

United Kingdom
    definition, 166
    open standards policy, 176
    vendor lock-in, avoiding, 171, 172–73
Oracle v. Google (U.S.), 102–3
Ordem dos Técnicos Oficiais de Contas (OTOC) case (EU), 137–38

Paris Convention, *see* International Convention for the Protection of Industrial Property
patent pools, 184, 190, 196, 197
patents and standards, 11
    common patent policy (ITU/ISO/IEC), 180
    disclosure policies, 180
    hold-up, 180, 200
    licensing policies,
        fair, reasonable and nondiscriminatory (FRAND) royalties, 161, 162, 163–64, 167, 180–81, 188–92, 198–200
        royalty-free, 160, 161, 162, 163–64, 165, 166, 167, 170–71, 180, 184, 192, 194, 195, 196, 197, 198–200, 201–2
Perris v. Hexamer (U.S.), 97
Pipeline & Hazardous Materials Safety Administration (PHMSA), 115, 120
piracy of standards, 218, 220n101
Practice Management (PMIC) case (U.S.), 92–95, 99, 104, 117–18
procurement and standards,
    government use in, 34, 37
    private use in, 62
PublicResource.org, *see* ASTM v. PublicResource.org

Qualcomm, 220
QWERTY keyboard, 172

SAP, 195
Sardines (EC), 19, 21, 24–25
Scorpio Music S.A. v. Willis (U.S.), 150
Seal Products (EC), 17
SELEX case (EU), 135–36, 138, 140
service mark, *see* trademark law
software in standards, *see* open source code software
Southco v. Kanebridge (U.S.), 95, 100
Southern Building Code Congress International (SBCCI), 104, 116–17
    see also Veeck case
standard setting processes
    appeals, 33
    balance of interests, 33
    consensus decision making, 10–11, 33, 161–62, 163, 166, 185
    corruption of, 60
    deference to private sector, 8–9
    development of standards, 144–45
    dispute resolution, 11
    due process, 33, 161–62
    funding of, xvi, 31, 36, 38, 42–52, 145
    multiple implementation requirement, 175–76, 186
    openness, 12, 18, 33, 161–62, 163–64
    public participation, 163–64, 167

Index

running code requirement, 176
transparency, 12, 18
updating of standards, 29–30, 161
work programmes for European standardization organizations, 38–39
standard setting organization (SSO), 8
  bylaws and policies, 62, 145
    patent policies, 180
  consortia, 11, 179–80
  European standards bodies, see European Union framework
  geographic scope, xvii
  governance, 62, 179
  national standards bodies, Europe, 35–36, 76–77
  non-profit status, 145
  organizational structure, 63, 139, 160, 166–67, 179
  participants, nature of, 12
  small and medium enterprises (SMEs), participation by, 38, 140
  staff, 145
  tort liability of, see tort law
Standardization Administration of the People's Republic of China (SAC), 170–71
standards
  access to, 31, 107, 114–15, 119–22, 160–68
    no charge/free access, 120, 121, 124, 161, 162, 163, 165, 166
    paid/charged access, xvi, 91, 92, 107, 108, 114, 115, 117, 120, 124, 125, 131, 145, 179, 189–90, 196
  copyright in, see copyright in standards
  interoperability, 173–75
  legal character of, 9, 10
  mandatory standards, 62–63
  regulation, use in, 34, 37, 42–48
  voluntary nature, 31–32, 35, 39, 62–63
standards-development organization (SDO), see standard setting organization (SSO)
standards wars, 217
Sun Microsystems, 168, 186–87, 222, 227

Technical Barriers to Trade (TBT) Agreement, see WTO Agreement on Technical Barriers to Trade (TBT)
Tire and Rim Association (TRA), 65–66
tort law
  certification and, 77–78, 261–66
  civil law countries, 79
  control thesis, 66, 82–83
  duty of care, 65, 82–86, 263
  France, 77–78, 85
    see also AFNOR
  Germany, 78–79, 80–82, 83, 85, 87
    see also fra.bo case
  misfeasance, 68
  negligence, 64–65, 82–86
  negligent misrepresentation, 72–75
  Netherlands, 78
  nonfeasance, 68–69
  Product Liability Directive (EU), 77
  regulatory compliance defense, 62
  standard setting organizations, and, 60–88

UK, 78–79, 83–84
voluntary undertaking rule, 68–72
trademark law, xvi, 198–230, 232–33
  ANSI trademark guidelines, 214–15
  ASTM v PublicResource.org, see ASTM
  certification marks, see certification marks
  comparative advertising, 216–17
  duration, 207
  distinctiveness, 206–7
  EU trademarks, 208
  generic marks, 102, 212–13, 229–30
  goodwill, 212, 214n63, 229, 233, 260, 266n64
  house marks, 217–18, 224–25
  infringement, 211–12
  licensing, see trademark licensing
  Madrid Protocol, 206, 208
  nominative fair use, 119, 214–17, 220n102, 225–26
trademark licensing, 213–14, 225, 226, 226n123, 227
  no-challenge clauses, 227
  quality control, 213–14
trade secrets, 202n26
Transmission Control Protocol (TCP), 220, 224
  see also Internet Engineering Task Force
Treaty on the Functioning of the European Union (TFEU),
  Art. 34, 125, 134–35, 137, 138, 140, 142
  Art. 101, 125, 133, 135, 137, 138, 142
  Art. 102, 135
  Art. 106, 138
  Art. 267, 129–31, 132–33, 142
  Horizontal Guidelines, 133, 140
Tuna II (U.S.), 21, 25–26, 27

Underwriters Laboratories (UL), 59, 74–75, 263, 264n57
  access to standards, 122, 162
  Board-Tech v. Eaton, see Board-Tech v. Eaton
  certification by, 208–9, 232, 252–53, 258
Uniform Serial Bus (USB) standard, see USB Interoperability Forum
Universal Mobile Telecommunications System (UMTS) standard (3G), 221, 223, 226
U.S. Constitution,
  dormant commerce clause, 140–41
U.S. Green Building Council (USGBC),
  Leadership in Energy and Environmental Design (LEED) certification, 209
USB Interoperability Forum, 226, 229
  Uniform Serial Bus (USB) standard, 205, 217, 218, 220, 223

Veeck case (U.S.), 104, 107, 116–17
Vienna Convention on the Law of Treaties (VCLT), 18, 25
VME Bus International Trade Association (VITA), 180, 195
voluntary consensus standard, 41

Western Growers Association, 42–52
Wheaton v. Peters (U.S.), 116
Wi-Fi Alliance, 167, 193, 219n98, 227–28

Wi-Fi standard (IEEE 802.11), 143–55, 186, 205, 217, 218, 219, 220, 221, 222–23, 223, 227–28
Window Covering Manufacturers Association, 69–70
World Intellectual Property Organization (WIPO), 208
World Trade Organization (WTO), xvi
  see also WTO Agreement on Technical Barriers to Trade
World Wide Web Consortium (W3C), 29, 91–92, 144n98, 167, 180, 184, 185, 186, 187, 194, 195, 229–30
  see also open source code licenses

WTO Agreement on Technical Barriers to Trade (TBT), 8–9, 13–27
  adoption of, 13
  Code of Good Practice, 17–19
  One World proposal, 162
  TBT Committee, 8
  TBT Committee Decision of 2000, 24–26

Zigbee Alliance, 221, 222